*The Renaissance Imagination*
*Important Literary and Theatrical Texts*
*from the Late Middle Ages*
*through the Seventeenth Century*

Stephen Orgel
*Editor*

# THE *PEARL* POEMS:
## An Omnibus Edition
## VOLUME 1: *PEARL* AND *CLEANNESS*

Edited by
*William Vantuono*

The Renaissance Imagination
*Volume 5*

GARLAND PUBLISHING, INC.
NEW YORK & LONDON
1984

**Library of Congress Cataloging in Publication Data**
Main entry under title:

The Pearl poems.

(The Renaissance imagination ; v. 5–  )
Includes bibliographical references.
Contents: v. 1. Pearl and cleanness.
1. English poetry—Middle English, 1100–1500.
I. Vantuono, William, 1927–      II. Series.
PR1972.G35A126   1984      821'.1      82-21026
ISBN 0-8240-5450-4 (v. 1)

Printed on acid-free, 250-year-life paper
Manufactured in the United States of America

To ORNELLA
"When one finds a worthy wife,
her value is far beyond pearls."
*Proverbs* 31:10

# CONTENTS

# PREFACE

A BRIEF HISTORY, AND A GUIDE TO THE EDITION

I am writing this Preface in late August of 1982 to present a guide to scholars who will be using this omnibus edition of the *Pearl* poems. Critics for a long time, and especially in the last decade, have recognized the common features of *Pearl, Cleanness, Patience,* and *Sir Gawain and the Green Knight* and, thus, the importance of treating these poems as a unit. (See, for example, the section on "Common Authorship" in the Appendices of this volume.) There have been definitive editions of each poem separately, but no definitive collected edition has yet appeared. The present two-volume edition, comprising definitive texts and exhaustive variorum commentary, has been designed to fill that void. I speak here of what I have attempted to do, the fifteen-year history of which will be recounted on the following pages. I leave it to the reader to judge what has been accomplished.

In the spring of 1967, I began working on a critical edition of *Patience* for my doctoral dissertation at New York University under the supervision of Professor John Fisher, presently at the University of Tennessee. The project was completed in the fall of 1968, but Professor Fisher has remained a friend and an advisor to this day.

To establish a Middle English Text for *Patience,* I first made a transcription from enlarged photostats, supplied by the New York Public Library from *Pearl, Cleanness, Patience, and Sir Gawain: Reproduced in Facsimile from the Unique MS. Cotton Nero A.x in the British Museum, EETS* 162 (Oxford, 1923). Departures from the MS, due to obvious scribal errors, were listed in the Textual Notes. To expand these notes through compilation of variant readings with other editors, I collated my text fully with the texts of the three scholars who had previously produced complete editions of *Patience*: Morris, in *Early English Alliterative Poems* (with *Pearl* and *Cleanness*), *EETS* 1 (Oxford, 1864; 2nd ed. 1869); Bateson (Manchester, 1912; 2nd ed.

1918); and Gollancz, in Volume 1 of *Select Early English Poems* (Oxford, 1913; 2nd ed. 1924).

Next I made a literal Modern English Translation, using primarily the *MED* and the *OED*. This translation formed the basis for the Glossary, to which was added grammatical elements and etymologies for a study of the language. For the Commentary, I attempted to cover all the essential scholarship of the past in the form of articles, books, and editions. The parts that completed the project by the end of 1968 were Introduction, Appendices, and Bibliography. (Anderson's edition for Manchester University Press [1969] was incorporated into my work later.)

As 1970 approached, I began work on *Cleanness*, following the same format used for *Patience*. The three editions of *Cleanness* at that time were: Morris', in *Early English Alliterative Poems, EETS* 1 (1864; 2nd ed. 1869); Menner's (New Haven, 1920); and Gollancz', in Volume 7 of *Select Early English Poems* (Oxford, 1921), completed with Glossary and Illustrative Texts in Volume 9 (1933) by Mabel Day.

There was an interruption of about a year during the early 1970s due to my discovery of the name *J. Macy* on folio 62b of the MS. With encouragement and advice from John Fisher, I did research on the Mascies in England in an attempt to uncover the identity of the poet. It was a time when other scholars were presenting evidence for a John de Mascy as the *Pearl*-poet. My own work culminated in "A Name in the Cotton MS. Nero A.X. Article 3," *Mediaeval Studies* 37 (1975) 537–42 (to be followed much later by "John de Mascy of Sale and the *Pearl* Poems," *Manuscripta* 25 [1981] 77–88).

Although work was not yet completed on *Cleanness*, I moved ahead with plans for an omnibus edition of all four poems in the MS by transcribing *Pearl* and *Gawain* from a copy of the *EETS* facsimile, reprinted in 1971 by Oxford University Press, and for full collations, I chose four significant editions of each poem.

For *Pearl*, the editors were: Morris, in *Early English Alliterative Poems, EETS* 1 (1864; 2nd ed. 1869); Gollancz (London, 1921); Gordon (Oxford, 1953); and Hillmann (Convent Station, 1961). Gollancz, who had first edited *Pearl* in 1891 and revised it in 1897, included an unrhymed translation on facing pages. Gordon had completed his work by 1938, but after publication was delayed, his wife Ida Gordon undertook a revision in 1950 for the edition that would eventually become the standard. Hillmann, like Gollancz, offered a literal translation on facing pages.

Other editors of *Pearl*, whose work I included for important notes and comment, were: Osgood (Boston, 1906); Chase (Boston, 1932); Cawley, in a volume that also contains *Gawain*, for Everyman's Library (London, 1962); and DeFord (New York, 1967). Of these, Osgood presented the most scholarly edition. DeFord offered a verse translation on facing pages.

For *Gawain*, the texts of the following editors were chosen for full collations: Madden, for the Bannatyne Club (London, 1839); Morris, *EETS* 4 (London, 1864; 2nd ed. 1869); Gollancz, *EETS* 210 (Oxford, 1940); and Davis, revision of Tolkien & Gordon's 1925 edition (Oxford, 1967). Madden, who was the first scholar to edit *Gawain*, printed a text that features the reproducing of contracted forms as they appear in the MS. Morris' edition formed the basis for important later work; Gollancz revised his text in 1897 and 1912, and these efforts culminated in the *EETS* 1940 edition, issued with Introductory Essays by Mabel Day and Mary Serjeantson. Tolkien & Gordon's 1925 edition had been considered the standard. This 1940 work offered competition, but when Davis revised Tolkien & Gordon's work in 1967, this volume became the one most widely used for *Gawain*.

Other editors of *Gawain*, whose works I examined so that I might include their scholarship at appropriate points in my edition, were: Cawley, in the volume with *Pearl*, for Everyman's Library (London, 1962); R. T. Jones (Pietermaritzburg, 1962); Waldron, for York Medieval Texts (London, 1970); Burrow, for Penguin Books (Baltimore, 1972); and Barron (Manchester, 1974). Of these, Waldron presented the most scholarly edition. Barron offered a good prose translation on facing pages.

During the course of my work, I realized that I should examine the original MS in the British Library. The American Philosophical Society in Philadelphia, to whom I express my debt of gratitude here, offered me a $600 grant, and I was able to accomplish this phase of the project in the fall of 1977. Mr. W. H. Kelliher, Assistant Keeper of Manuscripts, granted me permission to perform the study, which was greatly aided by Mr. Victor C. Carter, Chief Conservation Officer for Manuscripts, and Mr. Tony Parker, Conservation Officer, who allowed me to use their ultraviolet lamp.

Many letters and words in the MS are illegible or partly illegible because they are faded or covered with blots, stains, or smudges; other letters are placed around defects in the MS, partly torn sections, for example, with holes in them, perhaps due to excessive stretching of the vellum. Fortunately, the MS survived the fire at Ashburnham House in 1731, but, as Mr. Carter informed me, faded words along some of the margins could be due to water seeping in when the fire was being extinguished. In some places, offsets of illegible letters are readable, with the help of a mirror, on the folio that closes against the faded part.

After examining all problem areas in the original MS, I made a list of words for viewing under the ultraviolet lamp. Several faded parts of the MS were brought to light, but in many places, where the ink is irretrievably lost, viewing the illegible letters under the lamp did not solve the problem. I was able, however, to clarify any remaining difficulties relating to the Middle English Text to the degree that they could be clarified.

In the latter part of the 1970s, there were four new editions to consider, three of which included all four poems in the MS: Cawley & Anderson's *Pearl, Cleanness, Patience, Sir Gawain and the Green Knight*, for Everyman's Library (London, 1976); Anderson's *Cleanness* (Manchester, 1977); Moorman's *The Works of the Gawain-Poet* (Jackson, Mississippi, 1977); and Andrew & Waldron's *The Poems of the Pearl Manuscript*, for York Medieval Texts (London, 1978).

In the first of these, Cawley's *Pearl* and *Gawain* are virtually unchanged from his 1962 book, and Anderson's contributions of *Cleanness* and *Patience* are related to his work for Manchester University Press. Thus there was no need to incorporate this volume into my project. Anderson's scholarly single edition of *Cleanness* was, of course, examined carefully for inclusion, as were the editions of Moorman and Andrew & Waldron.

The appearance of three collected editions, coming one after the other in 1976, 1977, and 1978, signalled clearly that students were more interested than ever in studying the four poems together; yet, a definitive omnibus edition was still needed. Cawley and Anderson did not design their volume for the specialist. Moorman himself stated, "I am not attempting a variorum edition" (p. 7). Andrew and Waldron also made no claim to be composing the standard work. As one reviewer wrote in regard to the last two books, they "seem designed for use by graduate students; their teachers (who will continue to rely on the standard editions of the poems) will probably find Andrew & Waldron's edition the preferable one" (Christian K. Zacher, *Speculum* 56 [1981] 341). Knowing that the standard editions of *Pearl* and *Gawain*, the major poems in this group, were outdated, I decided to bring my project to completion, realizing fully that such a goal could be attained only because all the editors and all the other *Pearl*-poet scholars of the past had accomplished their goals, making it possible for me to benefit from their research.

I had originally planned a one-volume edition, but, because it was running to such great length, I organized the work into two volumes, undertaking a complete revision and updating of scholarship to 1980. Another new book that aided me greatly was Malcolm Andrew's *The Gawain-Poet: An Annotated Bibliography, 1839–1977*, Garland Reference Library of the Humanities, Volume 129 (New York, 1979).

In comparing Moorman's book to Andrew & Waldron's, I noticed that either one or the other is superior, depending on the parts examined. Moorman has a fuller Introduction; Andrew & Waldron's Introduction is like a critical essay with sparse documentation. Moorman has no Appendices; Andrew and Waldron have one Appendix dealing with sources. None of these editors delved deeply into matters of verse and language.

The Introduction to this omnibus edition has five divisions: "History of the Manuscript," "Possible Dates and Order of Poems," "The Poet and His Audience," "Thematic Unity of *Patience, Cleanness, Gawain,* and *Pearl,*" and "Structure of *Pearl* and *Cleanness,*" all in Volume 1, with only the "Structure of *Patience* and *Gawain*" in Volume 2. The Appendices are "Miscellaneous Information about the Manuscript," "Common Authorship," "Verse of *Patience, Cleanness, Gawain,* and *Pearl,*" "Dialect and Language," and "Sources and Analogues of *Pearl* and *Cleanness,*" all in Volume 1, with only the "Sources and Analogues of *Patience* and *Gawain*" in Volume 2.

The weight of the Introduction and Appendices is in Volume 1; only those parts that are essential to a study of *Patience* and *Gawain* are in 2. Each volume is an entity in itself so that each may be used separately, as well as with its companion. Economy was the determining factor here: a student may start by purchasing only one volume, depending upon which poetry he wishes to concentrate on first.

Most of the sections in Volume 1, especially those dealing with theme, verse, dialect and language, focus on the common features to be found among the four poems.

Moorman and Andrew & Waldron often adopted emendations of the Middle English Text made by previous editors, and, in listing variant readings, they usually limited themselves to the most widely used editions of the poems. The approach in this omnibus edition is conservative, with MS readings retained wherever possible, and the Textual Notes include variant readings from 34 previous editions: *Pearl* 10, *Cleanness* 6, *Patience* 6, and *Gawain* 12. (See the lists at the end of the Preface to Text in each volume.)

The works of Moorman and Andrew & Waldron do not include complete translations. The ones accompanying each poem in this edition provide the reader with quick keys to meaning. (That is why it is possible for a student to work with *Pearl* and *Cleanness* in Volume 1 without having to refer to the composite Glossary at the end of Volume 2.)

Neither Moorman nor Andrew & Waldron aimed for comprehensive coverage of scholarship on these poems. I have examined close to 1000 works in an attempt to include all that is essential in the Commentary. A Bibliography appears in each volume. Some repetition was unavoidable, but with this arrangement scholars working with Volume 1 need not refer to 2 for bibliographical references, and those working with Volume 2 need not refer to 1.

To divide the Glossary would have destroyed the arrangement that enables scholars to study the language of this poetry as a unit. Therefore, the composite Glossary appears at the end of Volume 2. Moorman's edition contains only an eight-page word list for a Glossary. Andrew and Waldron provide a much fuller Glossary, but these editors did not always record line numbers and specific grammatical elements. Kottler & Markman's *A Concordance to Five Middle English Poems: Cleanness, St. Erkenwald, Sir Gawain and the Green Knight, Patience, Pearl* (Pittsburgh, 1966), while proving helpful to recheck the accuracy of entries by line after my Glossary was completed, was not employed in the making of the Glossary itself, since such a computer concordance does not give Modern English meanings, specific grammatical information, or dictionary headwords.

The Glossary in this edition, whose entries were drawn from my Middle English Text and Modern English Translation, and arranged in a card catalogue, not only complements the translation but also offers to those scholars especially interested in language all that is needed for detailed study. Except for common words listed in the Preface to Glossary, information is provided for every form of every word, with specific grammatical elements noted in every instance. At the end of each entry, in lieu of etymologies, the *MED* or *OED* headword is bracketed. As I explain in the Preface to Glossary, it is hoped that this feature will provide students with a useful guide to relevant information in the major dictionaries, not only about the etymologies of words but also about variant spellings, shades of meaning, and citations in other works.

I express my gratitude here to the two scholars who have been of such great help to me. As I mentioned at the start of this Preface, Professor John Fisher first advised me in 1967 to begin the work on a small scale with *Patience,* and all through these years he encouraged me to continue the project. Finally, Professor Stephen Orgel enthusiastically approved of this edition and afterwards provided precise and expert editorial comments and advice.

I wish to thank the Council of the Early English Text Society for use of the facsimile, and the British Library for giving me access to the original MS and allowing Garland to reproduce photographs of folios in the MS.

Deserving of most special mention here is the one person who has done the most to make this work possible, my wife Ornella Vaccaro Vantuono. Only her spiritual inspiration proved more valuable than the tangible help she gave with constant typing, retyping after revisions, and long hours of proofreading.

*William Vantuono*
*August 31, 1982*

# INTRODUCTION

## HISTORY OF THE MANUSCRIPT

That the unique Cotton MS. Nero A.x. Article 3 was written in the Northwest Midlands is generally accepted, but a more specific part of that area has not been determined. McIntosh believed *Gawain*, as it stands in the manuscript, "can only *fit* with reasonable propriety in a very small area either in SE Cheshire or just over the border in NE Staffordshire,"[1] but, as Davis stated, "Acceptance of so precise a location must await publication of the supporting documents."[2] *Pearl*, *Cleanness*, and *Patience* precede *Gawain* in the quarto volume of vellum measuring about $7 \times 5$ inches. The writing is by one hand—small, sharp, and irregular—resembling printing rather than penmanship. Wright dated it not later than A.D. 1400;[3] Mathew would date it early fifteenth century.[4]

Accurate information concerning the transmission of the poems from author to scribe is not available. Oakden theorized that there were seven or possibly eight scribes involved,[5] but he based his study on editions that contain a great number of emendations to the manuscript. Since later scholarship has shown that many of these emendations were unnecessary, Oakden's theory is doubtful because he accounted for many scribal errors that evidently were never made.

There are twelve illustrations in the manuscript, four for *Pearl*, two each for *Cleanness* and *Patience*, and four for *Gawain*. Gollancz, in describing them, noted their "crude workmanship."[6] Greg, who gave evidence that they were an afterthought of later date, corrected Gollancz on some particulars and maintained that only one artist was involved. "It would have been a malicious fate that should have delivered this otherwise pleasing manuscript into the hands of two such very incompetent amateurs."[7]

Lee, however, noting that Cotton Nero A.x. is one of the earliest literary manuscripts to be illustrated, gave more credit to the artist by suggesting that the painting was done by a second hand, that of an amateur who spoiled the draftsman's work. She maintained that the illustrator, in depicting main characters in situations showing their spiritual progress, "represented well the primary 'instruction' of each poem." Though not exceptionally skilled as an illuminator or literary critic, he, nevertheless, offers the modern scholar the "rare opportunity of seeing the first critical judgment of these poems, a medieval mind reacting to a medieval work." [8]

There is no record of the manuscript for a long time after 1400, but *Gawain* must have been known in the fifteenth century, for, as Newstead observed, *The Grene Knight*, composed in the South Midland dialect about 1500, "appears to be a condensed version of *Sir Gawain and the Green Knight* with none of the literary distinction that marks its model." [9] Robbins showed that gentleman author Humfrey Newton (1466–1536), who lived in the Hundred of Macclesfield in Cheshire, may well have had an intimate acquaintance with *Gawain*. [10] Wrenn suggested that "Spenser may have known something of the work of the *Gawain*-poet." [11]

The earliest record of the manuscript is in an entry in the catalogue, now MS. Harley 1879 in the British Museum, of the library of Henry Savile of Banke in Yorkshire. Gilson noted this information, but he erred in printing *Paper* instead of *pay*, and this prompted him to say that he had not been able to track down this "copy of the *Pearl*, described as written on paper." [12] Gollancz pointed out the error, recalling there is only one known manuscript, and it is on vellum. [13]

Savile (1568–1617) collected manuscripts from the Northern monasteries; his cataloguer described the one containing the *Pearl* poems as "an owld boke in English verse beginning 'Perle pleasants to princes pay' in 4° limned." [14] The noted bibliophile Sir Robert Cotton (1571–1631) probably acquired the manuscript from Savile. Richard James, Cotton's librarian, described it as "Vetus Poema Anglicanum, in quo, sub insomnii figmento, multa ad religionem et mores spectantia explicantur." James apparently read only the opening lines and did not distinguish *Pearl* from the other poems. He bound the manuscript between two unrelated Latin works. [15]

Sister Williams noted that Cotton's collection, enlarged by his son Thomas, was given to the British nation in 1700. The 958 volumes were transferred to Ashburnham House. A fire there in 1731 destroyed 114 books and damaged 98, but fortunately the *Pearl* group was not ruined.[16] In 1753 the Cotton collection was taken to the British Museum. That Warton had access to it is known by his citation of lines from *Pearl* and *Cleanness*.[17] Madden thought it singular that Warton should not have noticed *Gawain*, "which he seems to have confounded with a preceding one, on a totally different subject."[18] With his edition of *Syr Gawayne* (1839), Madden preceded the long line of scholars who have brought the four poems of the manuscript into deserved prominence.

## POSSIBLE DATES AND ORDER OF POEMS

Scholars generally agree that the poems were not written in their order of appearance in the manuscript: *Pearl, Cleanness, Patience,* and *Gawain*. A more likely order of composition is *Patience, Cleanness, Gawain,* and *Pearl*—probably between 1370 and 1400.[19] Bateson suggested for *Patience* a date between the composition of the A-text and the B-text of *Piers Plowman*, basing his theory on a comparison of *Patience* with passages added to the B-text, such as in Passus X where it is said patriarchs, prophets, and poets "Wryten to wissen vs . to wilne no ricchesse,/And preyseden pouerte with pacience" (341–42).[20] Anderson, though inclined to accept Bateson's theory, did point out that in the C-text, Passus XIII, lines 173–76, "Porphyrius, Plato, Artistotle, Ovid, Cicero, and Ptolemy are all named as 'poetes' who have recommended patient poverty."[21] Thus, with all the authorities who have praised the two virtues together, Langland need not have had *Patience* in mind.

However, there is another guide for dating *Patience* after 1370, and that is its affinity to *Cleanness*, for which there is surer evidence. Both poems are close in tone, prosody, purpose, and subject matter, and were probably completed within a short time of each other. Gollancz favored 1373 as the earliest possible year for the composition of *Cleanness* by drawing parallels between it and the French *Book of the Knight of La Tour Landry*, which was written in 1371–1372.[22] Though his theory was opposed by Luttrell,[23] one may consider Gollancz' date for *Cleanness* a likely one by referring to *Mandeville's Travels*.

Brown proved the dependence of *Cleanness* on the French text of *Mandeville's Travels* by citing passages from the two works that are definitely analogous.[24] After mentioning that the earliest known manuscript is dated 1371, he stated, "It is scarcely possible that the *Mandeville* was known in England before this latter date" (p. 153). Letts, who believed that *Mandeville's Travels* was "probably composed shortly after 1360,"[25] also pointed out that the "earliest MS. at present known is dated 1371."[26]

Though it is possible that the poet was familiar with some earlier text that has since been lost, it is more likely that he worked from one of the French versions available to him in England after 1371. Most of the French manuscripts located in the British Museum have been dated late fourteenth century and fifteenth century.[27] Since *Mandeville's Travels* was written after 1360, the first manuscript known in France is dated 1371, and French versions known in England are dated late fourteenth century, one may plausibly conclude that *Cleanness* was not written much earlier than c. 1375. *Patience*, which probably preceded, may be placed in that same period.

*Gawain* and *Pearl*, most recent critics agree, were written during the reign of Richard II, 1377–1399.[28] Tolkien and Gordon, after noting details of costume, armor, and architecture described in *Gawain*, wrote, "The criteria, such as they are, point to a date in the last quarter of the fourteenth century, the latest possible date being determined by that of the manuscript, c. 1400."[29] Davis more cautiously pointed out that the richness of costume and furnishings, and the style of armor, would not in themselves exclude an earlier date, but, "Perhaps the repeated emphasis on complex design and lavish display is enough to imply a date towards the end of the century."[30] Gordon, who set the limits for the whole group of poems as c. 1360–1395, believed the "maturity of *Pearl* would put it late rather than early in this period."[31]

There has been disagreement over the exact order of composition of the poems. Brink placed *Gawain* before *Pearl* with *Cleanness* and *Patience* following. He called *Patience* "perhaps the writer's masterpiece."[32] Gollancz, who agreed with Brink, wrote, "Through his practice in *Cleanness* the poet seems to have attained to the finished workmanship of *Patience*."[33] The views of both Brink and Gollancz were influenced by their thinking the poet had married and had then been grieved by the death of a daughter, this being the occasion for the writing of *Pearl*. Brink wrote of *Patience*: "The prelude discloses the aging poet, who has felt the pains of poverty and privation, as well as loneliness."[34]

Most scholars, however, agree that *Patience* and *Cleanness* were composed before *Gawain* and *Pearl*. Osgood proposed the order of *Cleanness, Patience, Pearl,* and *Gawain* on artistic grounds;[35] Bateson suggested *Patience, Cleanness, Gawain, Pearl;*[36] and Menner gave the following chronology: *Patience, Purity, (The Pearl?), Gawain.*[37] Menner's study contains several noteworthy points. For example, *Cleanness* followed *Patience* because there are looser paraphrases of Biblical passages in *Cleanness* in comparison to the same passages found in *Patience,*[38] and *Gawain* was composed later than *Cleanness* because the phrase *pared out of paper* (1408) is used in *Cleanness* to describe a paper subtlety and the same phrase *pared out of papure* (802) appears in *Gawain* as a simile to describe Bercilak's castle.[39] It does seem more likely that the poet would have employed the phrase first in *Cleanness* for what it was, a paper subtlety, and then would have applied it to the description of the castle in *Gawain*.

Though Menner would definitely place *Gawain* later than *Cleanness*, he leaned toward setting *Pearl* in between, seeing the "artistic superiority of *Gawain*" as a strong argument for its being the last of the poems."[40] It is possible, however, to turn this argument the opposite way. The first point to be considered is prosodic technique. *Patience* and *Cleanness* were composed in the unrhymed long alliterative line. *Gawain* also contains this line, with the addition of the "bob and wheel," five short rhyming lines, at the end of each stanza. In *Pearl,* however, alliteration and rhyme are combined throughout in a design "unmatched in English poetry before or since."[41]

The five twelve-line stanzas in the groups are linked by a refrain, the stanza groups themselves are joined by concatenatio, and *paye,* the last word of the opening line, becomes the link-word in the last stanza-group, thus completing the circle. Even exceptions to the scheme are apparently by design. The extra stanza (lines 901–12) of Group XV makes *Pearl* end with 1212 lines; $12 \times 12$, which equals 144, relates to the architecture of the New Jerusalem (1029–32), and there are 144,000 virgins in the heavenly procession (869–70).[42] Among the twenty stanza-groups, the only point at which the linking fails is from XII to XIII, but, as Røstvig noted, the poet may have deliberately omitted the link-word to show a division of twelve and eight. The last eight stanza-groups in *Pearl* are especially concerned with heavenly bliss, and the eighth day, according to Biblical numerical symbolism, represents eternity.[43]

Structurally, the increasing complexity in the patterns of *Patience*, *Cleanness*, and *Gawain* perhaps establishes that order for these poems, and the nearly perfect symmetry in the form of *Pearl* may signify a final step toward mastery.

Thematically, *Patience* is simplest in comparison to the other three poems. Disloyal Jonas, having prayed in the impure belly of the whale (269–336), is released and swept to shore, and the poet comments, "Hit may wel be þat mester were his mantyle to wasche" (342); but the interweaving of *trawþe* and *clannesse* is not developed on a wide scale or with the degree of intricacy apparent in *Cleanness* and *Gawain*, where the interlocking of loyalty and purity forms the basis for theme. *Pearl*, in combining all the essential virtues in the person of the maiden who teaches the dreamer reconciliation to God's will, circles back to *Patience*, which points to humility as necessary for the attaining of salvation.

Pearl symbolism enters into all the poems except *Patience*. In *Cleanness*, who will see the Sovereign must be "Wythouten maskle oþer mote, as margerye-perle" (556), and even if man sins, "he may polyce hym at þe prest, by penaunce taken/Wel bryȝter þen þe beryl oþer browden perles" (1131–32). In *Gawain*, Bercilak says, " 'As perle bi þe quite pese is of prys more,/So is Gawayn, in god fayth, bi oþer gay knyȝteȝ' " (2364–65). In *Pearl*, the maiden instructs the dreamer: " 'I rede þe forsake þe worlde wode/And porchace þy perle maskelles' " (743–44).

If one were to see progression in the poet's thought from futile struggling against God's will to complete acceptance, *Patience* at one pole and *Pearl* at the other stand out prominently. *Patience* ends with no comment from the rebellious prophet Jonas. It is as if the dreamer made it for him in *Pearl*: "Lorde, mad hit arn þat agayn þe stryuen,/Oþer proferen þe oȝt agayn þy paye" (1199–1200).

## THE POET AND HIS AUDIENCE

Concerning the identity of the poet, conjectures span almost a century and a half. Guest and Madden first pointed to the Scottish poet Huchown; McNeil, Neilson, and Mackenzie supported their attribution.[44] However, Morris and MacCracken presented strong arguments against the Huchown theory.[45] Gollancz believed *Pearl* may have been written by Ralph Strode,[46] but Brown dispelled his arguments.[47] Cargill and Schlauch, viewing *Pearl* as an elegy written in 1369 on the death of Margaret, granddaughter of Edward III, and daughter of John Hastings, Earl of Pembroke, suggested John Donne or John Prat, two of Hastings' clerks, but their findings have not been generally accepted.[48] Chapman suggested John de Erghome, an Augustinian friar of York;[49] Everett counteracted his supposition.[50] Savage, surmising *Gawain* was written either for the marriage of Enguerrand de Coucy and Isabella, eldest daughter of Edward III, in 1365 or around the time of Coucy's return to France in 1376, mentioned the possibility of the poet's being a Hornby, member of a Lancashire family connected with John of Gaunt and Coucy,[51] but Savage's identification has always been considered unlikely.

Instead, attention has turned to the name Mascy. Greenwood argued for a Hugh Mascy, noting the "Hugo de" written in a fifteenth-century hand atop fol. 95 of *Gawain*, the name "Thomas Masse" found in the *St. Erkenwald* MS,[52] numerology in *Pearl*, and play on the word *mascelleȝ* in Stanza-Group XIII.[53] Nolan, supporting Greenwood's thesis on numerology, identified John de Massey, rector of Stockport in Cheshire, who died in 1376.[54] Farley-Hills pointed to the "Maister Massy" Hoccleve praises in a short poem written between 1411–1414,[55] and Peterson, after noting what he considered to be an anagram in *St. Erkenwald* for *I. d. Masse*, associated "Maister Massy" with a John Massey of Cotton in Cheshire.[56] However, Turville-Petre argued that Hoccleve's "Maister Massy" was a William Massy, John of Lancaster's General Attorney.[57]

My discovery of the name *J. Macy* among the ornamental designs beneath the illuminated *N* on fol. 62b of *Cleanness* led to research culminating in the possible identification of John de Mascy of Sale, who was rector of Ashton-on-Mersey in Cheshire between 1364 and 1401.[58] Adam, after a close study of the anomalous stanza 76 of *Pearl* (lines 901–12), found an acrostic signature of *John (de) Massi*.[59]

The fact that several John de Mascies lived in England in the late fourteenth century has intensified the research. A John de Mascy of Podington fought for Henry IV against a John de Mascy of Tatton, who sided with Henry Percy, and both were slain in 1403 at the battle of Shrewsbury when the king's forces put down the rebellion of the Earl of Northumberland.[60] Savage revealed that the Mascy of Podington was one of two commissioners appointed in 1392 to arrest disturbers in the Wirral,[61] the region of *wyldrenesse* (701) in Cheshire through which Gawain passes on his way to meet the Green Knight. "Wonde þer bot lyte/Þat auþer God oþer gome wyth goud hert louied" (701–2). Thus five John de Mascies in Cheshire alone come into immediate view.

Additional support for John de Mascy of Sale derives from Greenwood, who, though he named a Hugh, not a John, bolstered his theory about a pun on *mascelleȝ* in *Pearl* by relating it to the coat of arms of the family of Sale: "ARGENT A CHEVRON BETWEEN THREE MASCLES SABLE (to be seen in the Derby Chapel of Manchester Cathedral, and the Brereton Chapel, Cheadle)."[62] The opening of Stanza-Group XIII is about the innocent child who enters heaven and the jeweler who sold all his wealth, " 'To bye hym a perle watȝ mascelleȝ' " (732). The pun, if it is one, develops in a twofold manner. A *Mascé* is *leȝ* his pearl, and the pearl is separated from *Mascé*. It may be coincidence, but *mascelleȝ* (732) is the only *c* spelling for that word in Stanza-Group XIII; all the others are spelled with *k* that could not be pronounced as a sibilant.

Attempting to narrow down the field of John de Mascies in fourteenth-century England leads one back to the old controversy of whether the poet was a clergyman or a layman. Verses in *Cleanness* that might have settled the question unfortunately are veiled in ambiguity: "Bot, I haue herkned and herde of mony hyȝe clerkeȝ,/And als in resouneȝ of ryȝt red hit myseluen" (193–94). In the first line, the poet is referring to his having heard clerics speak out against evil, and in the second line he seems to be saying that he, too, has *red* 'declared' against evil, implying he was a cleric himself; however, *red* may also be translated 'read' and the argument remains open.

From his survey of Biblical material in *Patience*, *Cleanness*, and *Pearl*, Brown found it difficult to understand on what ground Gollancz denied the author's ecclesiastical character and concluded that it seems "moderately clear" that the poet was an ecclesiastic.[63] Osgood saw the poet as a layman, giving, among other reasons, "the decidedly unecclesiastical tone of his glorification of marriage"[64] in *Cleanness* (697–704), but his statement prompted Schofield to compare a similar passage on love in marriage by a monk, Robert Mannyng of Brunne.[65]

The question of audience hinges to some degree on the career of the poet. Hill suggested that *Patience* was addressed to "a select group whose principal concern was preaching,"[66] and that the admonishing of unclean priests in *Cleanness* (7–16) indicates a clerical audience for that poem.[67] That the poet was a devotee, if not a practitioner, of the *artes praedicandi*[68] is quite certain, for even the dream-vision *Pearl* provides evidence. Bishop, for example, in discussing lines 793–960 as a passage that affords "indisputable evidence that the author was familiar with the 'method of the theologians,' " showed how the *sensus litteralis* of the Old Testament passes through the *sensus allegoricus*, fulfilled in the Gospel, in order to reach the *sensus anagogicus* revealed in the Apocalypse.[69]

Greene, who interpreted *Pearl* as a "literary fiction" with a purpose "probably no less homiletic than *Cleanness* and *Patience*,"[70] observed that the placement of these poems before *Gawain* and *Pearl* in order of composition "suggests that the poet was an orthodox ecclesiastic in his earlier years,"[71] but Gordon evidently favored the old concept of layman father writing from grief over the death of his daughter. "He may have been a chaplain in an aristocratic household: that he once had a daughter is no decisive argument against this, for he may, for instance, have been ordained later in life. But his interest in theology might just as naturally be the interest of a pious layman who has found ecclesiastical guidance."[72]

Gerould, seeing the influence of Dante, maintained that the poet was a learned man who wrote in his own Northwest Midlands dialect to do for it what Dante had done for Tuscan in *Il Convivio*, defend his native speech.[73] With reference to the "alliterative school," Gerould asked, "Is it not probable that he and the vastly different and even more enigmatic author of *Piers Plowman*, between them, brought back into effective use what had been a medium for rural versifiers?"[74]

The tone and matter of *Gawain* leave little doubt about its aristocratic audience, but since one may still speculate on the purpose and occasion for the writing of that romance, Gerould's conjecture leads to further consideration of Hulbert's hypothesis concerning the alliterative revival.[75] Did alliterative poets in the West and North write in native dialects as a sign of opposition to the royal court? Salter called it a "pity that Hulbert's article finally rested its case upon the special issue of 'baronial opposition,' . . . the most easily refutable of its points. . . . For the facts seem to be clear: the new flowering of alliterative poetry in the west and north midlands coincides almost exactly with a period of remarkable accord between crown and baronage."[76]

However, Salter refers to Hulbert's dwelling on the middle years of the fourteenth century when Humphrey Bohun, duke of Hereford, patronized *William of Palerne*, c. 1351. During the period in which *Gawain* was most likely written, a different historical climate prevailed. Muscatine, in discussing the poet as a man who seems to be detached from the troubles of his times, wrote, "*Sir Gawain*, which is about *trawpe* and faithfulness in men, may be implying more about treachery and churlishness in its own culture than *Pearl* suggests about religious skepticism and the capitulation to grief." Crisis touches the poet, "no doubt profoundly," but *Gawain* and *Pearl* "suggest a man for whom the perfection of his art has become a kind of defense against crisis." [77]

Most modern critics lean toward dating *Gawain* after 1377. [78] Richard II, the boy king, born in 1367, came to the throne in 1377 and reigned until 1399 when he was deposed by Henry IV of the House of Lancaster. Schnyder argued that the poet's depiction of King Arthur in *Gawain* (85–99) leaves one with the "impression of an immature ruler." [79] John Fisher, referring to Schnyder's comment, suggested application of it to the contemporary English court by comparing the description of Arthur as *childgered* 'boyish' (86) to the way Gower scolds Richard II in *Vox Clamantis* VI:555. [80]

Is the poet's characterization of Arthur with his "zonge blod and his brayn wylde"(89) veiled criticism of Richard? As Fisher noted, an affirmative answer to this question does not contradict the poet's belief in the aristocratic system as it relates to the hierarchical system of heaven, for the latter "is mystically resolved into equality," [81] and while that ideal of equality is impossible of attainment on earth, kingship, in the poet's opinion, may still have offered the best form of government if a just ruler, mirroring the relationship of God the Father to his children, showed concern for his subjects. Could a boy king like Richard have filled such a role?

The theory of implied criticism in *Gawain* against the contemporary royal court may be applied on a comprehensive scale. The Green Knight, who later is revealed as Bercilak de Hautdesert, taunts Arthur and his noblemen. He sees about him only *berdlez chylder* (280), and when silence greets his challenge for the beheading game, he asks, " 'Where is now your sourquydrye and your conquestes,/Your gryndellayk, and your greme, and your grete wordes' " (311–12)? Arthur accepts the challenge, but it is Gawain who carries it out, and the innocent, gullible hero then goes in search of the Green Knight only to arrive first at Bercilak's castle where he learns how one can be so easily deceived and led into traps of falsehood if he does not recognize and accept his human failings with complete humility.

Gawain learns this lesson in places far removed from Camelot, after traveling through the northwestern regions of the *Wyrale* (701) in Cheshire, from a noble group with wisdom and maturity, powered by *Morgne þe goddes* (2452) who had sent the Green Knight "to assay þe surquidré" (2457) of the Round Table. When Gawain brings his message back to Camelot, the reception of Arthur and his court reveals the poet's characteristic ambiguity. They "laȝen loude þerat" (2514) and wear a green sash as a badge of honor in contrast to Gawain who wears the green girdle as a *token of vntrawþe* (2509). How should one interpret this laughter? [82] Is it the poet's final comment on the inability of Richard and his court to follow the moral currents that bear on the creating of a better society? A glance back at *childgered* Arthur with his "ȝonge blod and his brayn wylde" (86–89) perhaps indicates an affirmative answer.

What kind of man, in the minds of Richard's opponents, should have been king? The grandfather of Henry IV, who would claim the throne in 1399, was Henry, Duke of Lancaster, a mature, powerful nobleman who commanded respect. [83] Thiébaux argued for the influence on *Gawain* of Henry's *Le Livre de Seyntz Medicines*, written in 1354, in which there is the allegory of the fox hunt, and, in noting that one of Henry's titles was *Seigneur de Bruggerak*, suggested that the duke may have been a model for Bercilak. [84] The fact that Henry died in 1361 does not preclude a date after 1377 for the composition of *Gawain*, for the poet may have been reflecting the tendency to look back to days of glory that were no more. One line in *Gawain* seems to point in this direction: "Dubbed wyth ful dere stoneȝ, as þe dok lasted" (193). The description is of the Green Knight's horse, precious stones on a "bande of a bryȝt grene" (192) bound *as þe dok lasted* 'where the trimmed hair extended,' but *dok* to denote 'hair' is rare in Middle English; it is found only in *Gawain*, [85] and one may speculate that the poet's second meaning is that such ornamental beauty was customary *as þe dok lasted* 'while the duke lived.'

The pun, if it is one, may apply to some other duke, but if it were written with Henry in mind, there is a lead back to Dunham-Massy, for that estate was once one of Henry's holdings. [86] His connection with the Barony of Dunham, however brief it apparently was, suggests that the estate was a center for cultural activity in the fourteenth century, just as it was in the fifteenth century under the Booths.[87]

The circumstances surrounding the composition of *Pearl* have always been a subject for debate. Richardson stated that the theme of the poem is salvation, and because "a subject so large has more than academic interest. . . . there is no need to suppose a limited audience: a lay or mixed one is equally possible." The poet may have been a monk or a priest, addressing his audience "not merely as a writer with an experience to share, not merely as a teacher with a doctrine to impart, but also as a pastor with a message for them to put into practice."[88] Yet, the dilemma persists. Is *Pearl* an elegy, allegory, theological treatise, *consolatio*, or all of these genres combined?[89]

Schofield, who maintained the poem is pure allegory, nevertheless suggested an approach for those who pursue the elegiac theory. Referring to lines with personal touches, such as: "Ho watȝ me nerre þen aunte or nece" (233); " 'We meten so selden by stok oþer ston' " (380); and " 'Þou lyfed not two ȝer in oure þede' " and could never pray, " 'Ne neuer nawþer Pater ne Crede' " (483–85), he wrote, " 'Perhaps' we have here the secret of the whole story: it was not the loss of his own child that the poet had in mind, but only that of a little girl whom he had been accustomed to meet 'by stock or stone' (i.e., by the wayside), and had become devotedly attached to." Schofield concluded with the picture of a lonely priest who had taught the Pater Noster and the Creed to "this little child who had become nearer and dearer to him than aunt or niece."[90]

Developing this view further by including the likelihood that the poet knew the girl's father leads to the *consolatio*,[91] and if one believes the main purpose of *Pearl* was to console, it is plausible to assume that the poet wrote to console someone else more than himself. Bishop, though he seemed inclined toward the father-daughter theory,[92] noted as a possible source for *Pearl* the *consolatio mortis, Carmen* xxxi of Paulinus of Nola, in which Paulinus consoles Pneumatius and his wife Fidelis after the death of their son Celsus.[93]

Milroy, in presenting a theory that reconciles various arguments, believed the author could have been "an unmarried cleric writing the poem as a *consolatio* for a friend, a brother or a local dignitary, for whose bereavement he felt deeply, and assuming for that purpose a first person point-of-view."[94] His statement does not negate Richardson's suggestion that the audience of *Pearl* was a mixed one, for the poet may have written primarily for the bereaved father but also addressed his poem to others for general instruction.

It is conceivable, then, that *Pearl* was written for a nobleman who had lost a young daughter, a man who was perhaps the poet's patron. The father, in grieving over the death of his daughter, questions the ways of God, and this prompts the poet to put himself in the father's place to console him and to attempt to bring him to an understanding of the Lord's ways. In doing this, he becomes so involved in his verse, his own emotions enter in, and he thinks of the girl as someone he loved too, as perhaps he did in real life.

However, *Pearl* is more than mere *consolatio*, and its audience has grown in 600 years from the limits of England to other parts of the world. As an elegy, it praises a loved one who had died; as a dream-vision allegory, the pearl in the opening stanzas symbolizes the dead maiden who later represents purity, innocence, grace, and humility; as a theological treatise, it defends the teaching of the Church in fourteenth-century England, emphasizing the importance of divine grace and revealing how all are equally happy in God's kingdom though their positions vary within the hierarchical system; and finally, as a *consolatio*, *Pearl* lifts the spirits of those who have lost loved ones, for, above all, this sublime masterpiece, filled with beauty and mystery, makes lucid the unknown and the unreachable.


## THEMATIC UNITY OF *PATIENCE, CLEANNESS, GAWAIN,* AND *PEARL*

The thematic unity of *Patience, Cleanness, Gawain,* and *Pearl* centers around the interlocking virtues of *trawþe, humilitas,* and *clannesse* (in the double sense of integrity and chastity).[95] The humble man who is loyal to God accepts his will even in the face of adversity, and therefore remains pure. *Patience* and *Pearl* are closely paired, *Cleanness* and *Gawain* interweave thematically, and all four stand together as the poet's expression of salvation beyond this world.

Pride and rebellion of the prophet Jonas in *Patience* and the dreamer in *Pearl* block their paths to the peace that comes in accepting God's will. Both men, finding themselves in dire circumstances, complain and lament. Jonas complains about his mission to Ninive (75–96), expresses disappointment over the conversion of the Ninivites (409–28), and finally moans because of the destruction of his woodbine (479–88). " 'I keuered me a cumfort þat now is caȝt fro me,/My wodbynde so wlonk þat wered my heued' " (485–86). The dreamer laments the loss of his pearl (1–60), continues in sorrow after he has seen her in the earthly paradise (241–52), and fails to become consoled even after her opening speeches. " 'When I am partleȝ of perle myne,/Bot durande doel what may men deme' " (335–36)? Neither man is impure in the physical sense, but both, lacking the integrity that keeps one close to God, must be taught the lesson of acceptance. "And quo, for þro, may noȝt þole, þe þikker he sufferes" (6), says the poet in *Patience;* " 'Who nedeȝ schal þole. Be not so þro' " (344), says the maiden to the dreamer in *Pearl.*[96]

The thematic threads in *Cleanness* and *Gawain* evolve from the virtues of *trawþe* and *clannesse*, with *humilitas* interlaced. In *Cleanness*, sinners lacking integrity commit abhorrent deeds, defiling their souls as well as their bodies. Their acts of impurity result from the fall of rebel Lucifer and disloyal Adam. It is only after the *falce fende* (205) is cast out of heaven and "Hurled into helle-hole as þe hyue swarmeȝ" (223), and Adam *inobedyent* fails in *trawþe* (236–37), that people descend to lechery and sodomy.

In the romance, the poet combines *trawþe* and *clannesse* in a different manner. Gawain remains pure under the assault of a beautiful lady's lures, but in the struggle becomes so weakened that he falls into the trap of *vntrawþe.*[97] In the third temptation scene, when Bercilak's wife is especially provocative, he cares about his courtesy, "And more for his meschef ȝif he schulde make synne,/And be traytor to þat tolke þat þat telde aȝt" (1774–75). Loyalty and purity intertwine in a complicated knot, for Gawain's refusal to copulate with the wife stems from his desire to be true to her husband. Ironically, then, when he accepts the green girdle from the lady, thinking it may preserve his life (1856–58), and conceals it from his host, he breaks faith not only with him, but also with his earthly master Arthur, who had sent him on the mission, and his heavenly Master to whose will he had bound himself. " 'I am boun to þe bur barely tomorne,/To sech þe gome of þe grene, as God wyl me wysse' " (548–49).[98]

Cleanness represents a vast picture of *fylþe of þe flesch* following the breaking of *trawþe*. *Gawain* presents an individual portrait of a man hovering on the brink of carnal corruption before descending into *vntrawþe.* In both poems, though the process is different, the entanglement of loyalty and purity and their corresponding vices is the same.[99]

Humility's battle to subdue pride is dominant in all four poems. In *Patience,* the virtue of *pacience* is associated with *humilitas* through an equation of the first and last Beatitudes. "Thay arn happen þat han in hert pouerte,/For hores is þe heuenryche to holde foreuer" (13–14).[100] "Pay ar happen also þat con her hert stere,/ffor hores is þe heuenryche, as I er sayde" (27–28).[101] The poet then clearly shows that the two virtues go hand in hand. "Thus pouerte and pacyence arn nedes playferes" (45). *In hert pouerte* signifies 'poverty of spirit,' which is 'humility.' "Quapropter recto hic intelliguntur 'pauperes spiritu,' humiles et timentes Deum, id est, non habentes inflantem spiritum."[102] Throughout most of the poem, Jonas is neither humble nor patient. Rather than heed the words of the last Beatitude, he thinks God would care very little if he be " 'nummen in Nunniue and naked dispoyled,/On rode rwly torent wyth rybaudes mony' " (95–96). Pride remains within him even after his experience in the belly of the whale, for instead of rejoicing over the conversion of the Ninivites, he is concerned about his reputation. " 'For me were swetter to swelt asswyþe, as me þynk,/Þen lede lenger þi lore þat þus me les makeʒ' " (427–28). He must learn that to be humble, one must be patient, and to be patient, one must be humble. "Nullus profecto spiritu pauper, nisi humilis; quis enim humilis, nisi patiens? quia nemo subjicere sese potest, sine prima patientia subjectionis ipsius."[103]

In *Pearl,* the dreamer's excessive mourning amounts to a form of rebellion. "Paʒ kynde of Kryst me comfort kenned,/My wreched wylle in wo ay wraʒte" (55–56). The pearl-maiden, after speaking of the Lord's promise of resurrection, reprimands him for his *sorquydryʒe* (309), but it is difficult for the dreamer to lose sight of himself. " 'ʒe take þeron ful lyttel tente,/Paʒ I hente ofte harmeʒ hate' " (387–88). When he begins to acquiesce, the maiden welcomes him pleasingly because he is devoiding himself of " 'Maysterful mod and hyʒe pryde' " (401). Yet, he stumbles again when he cannot understand the Parable of the Vineyard (589–600), and even after he is granted the vision of heaven itself, precisely because he has seen the ultimate, he again attempts to assert his own will. "My maneʒ mynde to maddyng malte./Quen I seʒ my frely, I wolde be þere" (1154–55). In his mad desire, he attempts to cross the stream, but he is restrained, for he must learn, "Lorde, mad hit arn þat agayn þe stryuen,/Oþer proferen þe oȝt agayn þy paye" (1199–1200).

Although most of *Cleanness* juxtaposes proud villains and humble heroes, Nabuchodonosor emerges as the poet's portrait of man in conflict. No longer content with earthy dominion, he blasphemes. " 'I am god of þe grounde to gye as me lykes,/As he þat hyȝe is in heuen, his aungeles þat weldes' " (1663–64). The haughty king, at this point, resembles the rebel Lucifer, who, before being cast out of heaven, had said: " 'I schal telde vp my trone in þe tramountayne,/And by lyke to þat Lorde þat þe lyft made' " (211–12). Because of his blasphemy, Nabucho is sent by God into exile. " 'Inmydde þe poynt of his pryde, departed he þere' " (1677). Like prophet and dreamer, he must learn that being perverse induces suffering of greater intensity.

In *Gawain*, the knight is never a rebel against God's will in the way that prophet, dreamer, and king are, nor is his pride shown as a dominant trait in him, but his striving for perfection falls short because of dissimulation within himself. In breaking *trawþe* with Bercilak, he breaks *trawþe* with God, not aware, in the innocence of his muddled thinking, that he is ejaculating empty words when he says: " 'Ful wel con Dryȝtyn schape/His seruanteȝ for to saue' " (2138–39).———— " 'To Goddeȝ wylle I am ful bayn,/And to hym I haf me tone' " (2158–59).————" 'Let God worche! We loo!' " (2208). Gawain's triple pronouncement of accepting God's will, even unto death under the blade of the Green Knight's axe, is meaningless, since he wears the green girdle, which, he supposes, has the magic power to save his life. Motivated by pride of life, he must learn "that because of human frailty *no* knight can be perfect, and that in striving for perfection one must therefore learn humility."[104]

In all four poems, the central portion of the web, to which all the threads lead, is spiritual salvation, and the obstacle is the difficulty the earth-bound human has in realizing that reconciliation is the key. Jonas' last words, " 'I wolde I were of þis worlde, wrapped in moldeȝ' " (494), may be interpreted as yearning to have that promised peace of another world, but even the critic who sees despair in them may believe that the once proud prophet, after listening to God's final admonition, is ready to echo the poet's Epilogue. "Forþy, when pouerte me enpreceȝ, and payneȝ innoȝe,/ffful softly, wyth suffraunce, saȝttel me bihoueȝ" (528–29), for patience is a noble virtue, even if it displease often.

At the end of *Pearl*, the dreamer is ready to accept the pearl-maiden's admonition to " 'loue ay God, and wele and wo' " (342), knowing that, "To pay þe Prince oþer sete saȝte,/Hit is ful eþe to þe god Krystyin" (1201–2).

In *Cleanness*, Nabucho awakes, before it is too late, to the acknowledgment of God's supreme mastery. Unlike Lucifer and the hard-hearted Baltassar, he repents after a seven-year exile on the moor, for " 'he wyst ful wel who wroȝt alle myȝtes' " (1699), and because " 'he loued þat Lorde and leued in trawþe' " (1703), his kingdom is restored to him.

The knight in *Gawain* who cared for his life[105] is like Jonas. Both protagonists, at points of self-realization, rebuke themselves in similar terms. " 'Paȝ I be fol and fykel, and falce of my hert,/Dewoyde now þy vengaunce þurȝ vertu of rauthe' " (*Patience* 283–84); " 'Now am I fawty and falce, and ferde haf ben euer/Of trecherye and vntrawþe; boþe bityde sorȝe/and care' " (*Gawain* 2382–84).[106] But whereas the elderly prophet had opposed God openly, the youthful knight was never aware, until the end, that his instinct for self-preservation had prevailed over his desire to submit to God's will. After his initial mood of despair upon learning that he had been tricked, the reconciled hero wills to wear the green girdle as a *syngne* of his *surfet* (2433) to remind himself of " 'þe faut and þe fayntyse of þe flesche crabbed,/How tender hit is to entyse teches of fylþe' " (2435–36).[107]

*Trawþe, pouerte in hert*, and *clannesse* are the intertwined virtues that lead to salvation for prophet, king,[108] knight, and dreamer, for in *Patience, Cleanness, Gawain*, and *Pearl*, these four men, who were once in darkness, eventually see the light that promises the Beatific Vision.

*Patience* sets the tone. "Pay ar happen also þat arn of hert clene,/For þay her Sauyour in sete schal se wyth her yȝen" (23–24).[109] In *Cleanness*, the maxim, as it applies to those who follow righteous men like Noah, Abraham, Lot, and Daniel, appears at beginning and end. " 'þe haþel clene of his hert hapeneȝ ful fayre,/For he schal loke on oure Lorde wyth a louf-chere' " (27–28).———"Ande, clannes is his comfort, and coyntyse he louyes,/And þose þat seme arn and swete schyn se his face" (1809–10). In *Gawain*, the genre of romance does not conceal the theme of salvation, for the poet portrays the knight's spiritual progression toward humility. " 'And þus quen pryde schal me pryk for prowes of armes,/þe loke to þis luf-lace schal leþe my hert' "

(2437–38). In *Pearl*, the spotless maiden, who symbolizes union with God, reveals to the dreamer the answer to the question, " 'Lorde, quo schal klymbe þy hyȝ hylle,/Oþer rest wythinne þy holy place' " (678–79)?

> Hondelyngeȝ harme þat dyt not ille,
> Þat is of hert boþe clene and lyȝt,
> Þer schal hys step stable stylle. (681–83)[110]

In *Patience, Cleanness, Gawain,* and *Pearl*, thematic unity unfolds from tapestries woven around loyalty, humility, and purity's twofold virtue, chastity and integrity. The vision of peace in contemplation of salvation beyond this world culminates in *Pearl*, "For wern neuer webbeȝ þat wyȝeȝ weuen/Of half so dere adubmente" (71–72).

## STRUCTURE OF PEARL AND CLEANNESS

### *PEARL*

*Pearl* begins, "Perle plesaunte to prynces paye" (1); it concludes, "Ande precious perleȝ vnto his pay. Amen. Amen" (1212). In the Prologue, the dreamer in an *erber grene* (38) falls into a "slepyng-slaȝte/On þat precos perle wythouten spot" (59–60); in the Epilogue, he awakens in *þat erber wlonk* (1171). At start and finish, he is in the waking world of reality; in between, he moves toward the Beatific Vision, and that *saȝt* 'peaceful' state (52), which formerly he could not attain, is eventually realized. It is easy for the good Christian to *sete saȝte* (1201).

Illuminated letters mark the beginning of each of the twenty stanza-groups, and an additional letter *M* of *Moteleȝ* (961) starts the last stanza of Group XVI.[111] Each group has five twelve-line stanzas, except for Group XV, which has six. The extra stanza brings the total to 101, matching the number in *Gawain*. Below are the twenty-one illuminated letters with accompanying words and placement:[112]

| | | | |
|---|---|---|---|
| *Perle* (I–1) | *I* (VI–301) | *Of* (XI–601) | *Neuerþelese* (XVI–913) |
| *Fro* (II–61) | *Thenne* (VII–361) | *Grace* (XII–661) | *Moteleȝ* (961) |
| *The* (III–121) | *Blysful* (VIII–421) | *Ihecu* (XIII–721) | *If* (XVII–973) |
| *More* (IV–181) | *That* (IX–481) | *Maskelles* (XIV–781) | *As* (XVIII–1033) |
| *O* (V–241) | *The* (X–541) | *Thys* (XV–841) | *Ryȝt* (XIX–1093) |
| | | | *Delyt* (XX–1153) |

Since it is clear that the illuminator placed letters to mark divisions of twenty stanza-groups, that particular arrangement presents no problem. However, one is left to determine the structure within by a study of the poetry. The following chart, which emphasizes tripartite divisions in *Pearl*, makes no claim to read the poet's plan exactly, but the parts, after accounting for some overlapping, fall appropriately into place.

PROLOGUE (Group I)
The Garden Setting
BODY (Groups II–XIX, plus lines 1153–70)
The Vision—Part One: The Terrestrial Paradise and the Pearl-Maiden
(Groups II–IV)
The Vision—Part Two: The Homiletic Center (Groups V–XVI)
(1) Debate (V—VIII)
(2) Parable of the Vineyard, with Explanation (IX—XII)
(3) The Perle Mascelleʒ, the Lamb, and the 144,000 Virgins (XIII—XVI)
The Vision—Part Three: The New Jerusalem and the Procession
(Groups XVII–XIX, plus lines 1153–70)
EPILOGUE (lines 1171–1212 of Group XX)
Return to the Garden

Various scholars have noted tripartite divisions in *Pearl*. Everett, for example, stated: "Of the twenty equal sections of the poem the first four are mainly devoted to presenting the dreamer's state of mind and to description of the dream-country and of Pearl herself; argument and exposition occupy the central twelve sections, and the last four again contain description, this time of the New Jerusalem, and end with the poet's reflections."[113] Bishop refined Everett's summary by setting off the first stanza-group and the last, noting the balancing descriptions at beginning (Groups II–IV) and end (XVII–XIX), and dividing the central portion of twelve groups into eight (V–XII), "concerned with the maiden's claim to be a queen in heaven," and four (XIII–XVI), "her assertion that she is a bride of the Lamb."[114] Blenkner classified the first and last stanza-groups as the 'erber' frame and the dream-vision of eighteen groups in three parts: earthly paradise (II–IV), theological dialogue (V–XVI), and heavenly city (XVII–XIX). "The triple division of the dream corresponds to the theologian's traditional division of the soul's ascent to God into three stages (from *without* to *within* to *above*), which may be roughly equated to man's three sources of knowledge (sense, intellect, and inspiration)."[115]

By examining the preceding chart, one will see that the Prologue and Epilogue are clearly set apart from the Body—the Vision, which is also easily divisible into three parts. However, no one, to my knowledge, has noted that the twelve stanza-groups in the center of the Vision—Part Two (V–XVI)—may also be apportioned triadically: (1) Groups V–VIII, (2) Groups IX–XII, and (3) Groups XIII–XVI.

In Part Two (1)—V–VIII (lines 241–480)—the maiden, in the manner of debate, reprimands the dreamer for his excessive mourning and lack of faith in the mysteries of salvation, and then she tells him of her marriage to the Lamb and her position as a queen in heaven. " 'He toke myself to hys maryage,/Corounde me quene in blysse to brede' " (414–15). The dreamer, after being corrected in his mistaken notion that the maiden has likened herself to Mary, the *Quen of Cortaysye* (432), nevertheless questions her claim to being a queen, since she was so young, for what more honor might a man achieve, " 'Þat hade endured in worlde stronge,/And lyued in penaunce hys lyueʒ longe' " (476–77)?

This questioning carries over into the opening stanza of Group IX; yet, Part Two (2)—IX–XII (lines 481–720)—may be marked as another division, since the poet soon begins his paraphrase of the Parable of the Vineyard (501–72), an exemplum which reconciles the equality of the reward of salvation with the doctrine of hierarchy in heaven. When the dreamer states that he thinks her story *vnresounable* (590), the maiden continues with a long monologue justifying her position, " 'For þe grace of God is gret inoghe' " (612), and " 'Þe innocent is ay saf by ryʒt' " (720).

Verses dealing with Jesus' favoring of innocent children (711–28) span the end of Group XII and the beginning of XIII. Part Two (3)— XIII–XVI (lines 721–972)—develops pearl symbolism to its ultimate point with reference to the *perle . . . mascelleʒ* (732), representing salvation in heaven, and comparable to the penny in the Parable of the Vineyard as a symbol of divine reward. The maiden, who wears that pearl upon her breast (740, 854), continues to speak in answer to the dreamer's inquiries, revealing her knowledge of Christ the Lamb and her position as his bride among the 144,000 virgins. This section ends with the dreamer's request to enter the New Jerusalem. The maiden tells him God will prevent that, but the Lamb has granted the favor of *a syʒt þerof* (968). Thus the final Vision in Part Three is anticipated.

What may be considered the poet's greatest achievement from a structural standpoint is the nearly perfect symmetry of the divisions in *Pearl*. Within the twenty stanza-groups, not only is the Body (II–XIX) centered according to the proportions of the poem, and not only is the large middle of the Body (Part Two—V–XVI) centered in relation to passages that precede and follow, but the middle of the third triad (IX–XII) forms a neat center too. This structural heart, which presents the Parable of the Vineyard, is also the thematic heart of *Pearl*, a poem in which the perfect roundness of the three in one form corresponds to the pearl itself, the symbol of salvation in heaven with the Holy Trinity.[116]

## CLEANNESS

*Cleanness* does not have the last line echo the first, as in *Pearl*, but almost every verse in the Epilogue contains a thematic link to the Prologue. Lines 5–6, telling of God's anger with sinners, are recalled at the end when the poet says he has revealed in three ways how uncleanness strikes at the heart of the Lord and provokes him to punish (1805–8). Lines 27–28, stating that the pure man shall see God, are also recalled at the end in 1809–10. Finally, the poet's use of *gere* 'attire' (1811) recalls his opening paraphrase of the Parable of the Wedding Feast, in which clean and fitting garments symbolize virtues, and good people who are *bryȝtest atyred* (114) hold a high place in heaven.

The thirteen illuminated letters in *Cleanness* begin the following words: *Clannesse* 1, *Now* 125, *Bot* 193, *Bot* 249, *Now* 345, *On* 485, *Sypen* 557, *Olde* 601, *The* 689, *His* 781, *Ruddon* 893, *Danyel* 1157, and *Thenne* 1357.[117]

The structural plan below does not follow a thirteen-part division.

PROLOGUE (1–204)
The Parable of the Wedding Feast (51–160)
[Transition *a* (161–176), *b* (177–192), *c* (193–204)]
BODY (205–1804)
Part One: Lucifer, Adam, and Noah (205–600)
  (1) The Fall of Lucifer (205–234)     (Minor Exemplum)
  (2) The Fall of Adam and Eve (235–248)     (Minor Exemplum)
  (3) Noah and the Flood (249–544)     (Major Exemplum)
  [Transition *a* (545–556), *b* (557–570), *c* (571–600)]
Part Two: Abraham and Sara, the Sodomites, and Lot's Wife (601–1156)
  (1) Abraham and Sara (601–780)     (Minor Exemplum)

(2) The Destruction of Sodom and Gomorrah (781–1014)          (Major Exemplum)

(3) Lot's Wife (821–828 and 979–1000)          (Minor Exemplum within Major)

[Transition *a* (1015–1051), *b* (1052–1144), *c* (1145–1156)]

Part Three: Sedecias, Baltassar, and Nabuchodonosor (1157–1804)

(1) The Fall of Sedecias and the Israelites (1157–1308)          (Minor Exemplum)

[Transition *a* (1309–1320), *b* (1321–1332), *c* (1333–1356)]

(2) The Sacrilegious Feast of Baltassar (1357–1804)          (Major Exemplum)

(3) The Fall of Nabuchodonosor and His Repentance (1641–1708)   (Minor Exemplum within Major)

EPILOGUE (1805–1812)

This chart, based on a study of the poetry, is presented as a guide, without claiming to capture the poet's plan precisely. It seems, however, that one cannot justify a structural plan by adhering to the placement of the thirteen illuminated letters at every point. Among the editors, Morris, for example, presented a thirteen-part division,[118] but Menner, expressing doubt, added XIa at line 1049, XIIa at 1261, and XIIIa, b, c at 1529, 1641, and 1741.[119] Gollancz divided into thirteen sections, since he considered the placement of the letters to be in accord with the poet's plan,[120] but on an overall scale he arranged: Prologue (1–192), Part I (193–556), Part II (557–1156), Part III (1157–1804), Epilogue (1805–1812). Anderson indicated the placement of all thirteen letters in his text but divided the poem into only three sections: I (1–556), II (557–1156), III (1157–1812). Moorman, by placing a XII above line 1049, ended with fourteen sections. Andrew and Waldron made no divisions in their text.[121]

Critics have offered varying opinions also. Emerson, for example, criticized Menner for keeping the manuscript divisions at lines 345 and 689;[122] Hill agreed with Gollancz that the thirteen divisions are those of the poet.[123] In view of such lack of agreement, it seems that the best way to approach the subject of the illuminated letters is to admit that while they are, for the most part, placed judiciously, they do not always harmonize with what appears to be the poet's plan.[124]

The illuminated letter at line 193 is apparently misplaced, since the story of Lucifer's rebellion begins at 205, where there is no illumination. Some scholars have considered the letters at lines 557 and 1157 especially significant because they are four-line capitals,[125] whereas all the others, with the exception of the first eight-liner, run three lines in length. (In addition, the one at 1157 comes after a single-line space.) However, it does not seem that the four-line *S* of *Sypen* (557) should be considered more important than the three-line *O* of *Olde* (601) when the former begins a transitional passage and the latter marks the second major division of the Body. The open space above line 1157 is the only one in the *Cleanness* part of the manuscript, but if that open space is supposed to be significant, the poem would have to be considered bipartite, not tripartite.[126]

Few scholars have questioned the three-part division of the Body of *Cleanness*,[127] since the poet himself concludes: "Þus, vpon þrynne wyses, I haf yow þro schewed/Þat vnclannes tocleues in corage dere" (1805–6). Spearing observed it is a division "in accordance with the methods of medieval preachers, who normally divided the theme of a sermon into three parts, so as to treat it more amply."[128]

A study of *Cleanness* in conjunction with the preceding chart reveals how the poet balanced structure in relation to theme, for the antithetical subjects of salvation and damnation, concisely set down in lines 27–30, thread through the poem in alternate fashion from beginning to end.

The Parable of the Wedding Feast in the Prologue describes saved souls sitting at the Lord's table in contrast to the *gome vngoderly* (145) in the foul garment who is shut in a "doungoun þer doel euer dwelleȝ" (158).

The three major divisions of the Body are, in turn, divided three times, with two minor exempla accompanying a major exemplum in each part.[129] In Part One (1), Lucifer, after being cast out of heaven, is irreconcilable, "so proud watȝ his wylle" (232), and his fate is final damnation in hell, but in (2), though Adam "fayled in trawþe" (236) and received the sentence of "deþe þat drepeȝ vus alle" (246), salvation through Christ's passion is foreshadowed for mankind in the following lines: "Al in mesure and meþe watȝ mad þe vengiaunce,/And efte amended wyth a mayden þat make had neuer" (247–48). Finally, in the major exemplum (3), the destruction of mankind for *fylþe vpon folde* (251) is tempered by the preservation of Noah and his family in the ark of salvation.

In Part Two (1), salvation is signalled immediately when the Lord, in the form of three angels representing the Holy Trinity,[130] visits

Abraham and Sara who laughs when she is told she will bear a son, and then denies that she had doubted the word (649–68). However, the Lord forgives these minor offences, for Sara will conceive Isaac in the direct line of descent to Mary, the bearer of Christ, Saviour of mankind. In the major exemplum (2), the escape to safety of Lot and his daughters offsets not only the violent deaths that befall the Sodomites but also the horrible punishment given to Lot's wife in a two-part minor exemplum (3), set within the main narrative. For first flavoring the food of the angels with salt (821–28) and then looking back over her left shoulder when fleeing from Sodom (979–82), the wife is turned into a "stiffe ston, a stalworth image,/Also salt as ani se" (983–84). Such is her fate, "For two fautes þat þe fol watȝ founde in mistrauþe" (996).

In Part Three (1), Sedecias and the Israelites are condemned because they "forloyne her fayth, and folȝed oþer goddes" (1165), but in the other minor exemplum (3), set within the major narrative, Nabuchodonosor, though a sinner, is saved because, after being cast out on a moor to endure a seven-year exile, he repents, " 'loued þat Lorde and leued in trawþe' " (1703), and has his kingdom restored to him. However, in the last major exemplum, Part Three (2), misfortune prevails, for the hard-hearted Baltassar continues feasting and desecrating the holy vessels. His fate, like Lucifer's, is damnation that same night when Darius and his legions gain entry into Babylon, and the king is beaten to death in his bed (1787). "He watȝ corsed for his vnclannes, and cached þerinne" (1800).

In the Epilogue, the contrasts are culminated, and the poem ends on the note of salvation. *Vnclannes* provokes God's punishment, but *clannes* leads to the Beatific Vision.

As in any long poem, transitional passages play an important role in unifying the structure and developing the theme. At the end of the Prologue, after paraphrasing the Parable of the Wedding Feast, the poet explains its meaning (161–176), notes the many faults through which man may forfeit bliss (177–192), and names *fylþe of þe flesch* as a grievous sin (193–204).

At the end of Part One of the Body, he urges man to keep himself as clean as a pearl (545–556), tells of God's covenant with mankind (557–570), and foreshadows the destruction of the Sodomites (571–600).

At the end of Part Two, he describes the Dead Sea (1015–1051), between verses referring to the *Roman de la Rose* and others developing more pearl symbolism, praises Mary as the vessel bearing Christ and Christ as the Saviour of mankind (1052–1144), and anticipates the Baltassar exemplum (1145–56).

Finally, at the end of Part Three (1) dealing with the downfall of Sedecias and the Israelites, the poet tells how Nabuchodonosor reveres the holy vessels pillaged from the temple of Jerusalem (1309–1320), how that king believed in Daniel's God (1321–1332), and, in contrast, how Baltassar followed false gods (1333–1356).

In *Cleanness*, the interlocking of theme and structure reveals itself most clearly when a triple-three apportionment is applied, a three in one concept, symbolic of salvation in the Holy Trinity which prevails firstly, in the totality of Prologue, Body, and Epilogue; secondly, in the overall tripartite division of the Body; and, thirdly, in the triadic construction of each of the three parts of the Body.

NOTES

1. Angus McIntosh (1963) 5. In this Introduction, the notes are abbreviated. See the Bibliography at the end of this book for full references.

2. Norman Davis (1967) xiv. On p. xxvii, Davis observed that the language "is not a simple and self-consistent local dialect." It "is to some extent eclectic; yet the basis of it is no doubt, as most scholars have long believed, a dialect of the north-west midlands."

3. Cyril E. Wright (1960) 15.

4. Gervase Mathew (1968) 117.

5. James P. Oakden I (1930–35) 261–63. For refutation, see W. W. Greg (1932a). Oakden (1933b), in defense of his theory, answered Greg.

6. Sir Israel Gollancz (1923) 9.

7. W. W. Greg (1924) 227. For other negative comments on the quality of the illustrations, see R. S. Loomis and L. H. Loomis (1938) 138 and Thorlac Turville-Petre (1977) 45.

8. Jennifer A. Lee (1977) 18–19 and 43–44.

9. Helaine Newstead (1967) 57.

10. Rossell Hope Robbins (1943). See also Robbins (1950) and John L. Cutler (1952).

11. C. L. Wrenn (1943) 48.

12. Julius P. Gilson (1908) 135 and 209.

13. Sir Israel Gollancz, 2nd ed. of *Patience* (1924), pp. 3–4.

14. See E. V. Gordon (1953) ix.

15. See Sir Frederic Madden (1839) xlvii–l. Madden noted that the preceding portion of thirty-six folios consisted of a panegyrical oration by Justus de Justis, on John Chedworth, archdeacon of Lincoln, dated at Verona, 16 July 1468; the concluding portion, extending from fol. 127 to fol. 140b, consisted of theological excerpts written in a hand at the end of the thirteenth century, and at the end is added *Epitaphium de Ranulfo, abbate Ramesiensi,* who was abbot from 1231 to 1253. In 1964 the manuscript with the *Pearl* poems was rebound separately in the British Museum.

16. Margaret Williams (1967) 6. Sister Williams also noted, "In Cotton's library, books were catalogued according to their places in one or other of fourteen presses, surmounted by busts of Cleopatra, Faustina, and twelve Roman Emperors. The Pearl-Poet's book became Cotton Nero A.X."

17. Thomas Warton (1774–1790), Vol. 3, pp. 107–8.

18. Madden (1839) 299.

19. The latter date is determined by the composition of the manuscript, c. 1400. See Cyril E. Wright (1960) 15.

20. Hartley Bateson, 2nd ed. of *Patience* (1918), pp. xxv–xxviii. Elizabeth Salter (1963) 106 noted that the A-text was written about 1370 and the B-text between 1377 and 1379. Elizabeth D. Kirk (1978), after stating that both *Patience* and the B-text of *Piers Plowman* were written early in the last quarter of the fourteenth century, commented, "Most probably *Patience* influenced Langland" (88–89).

21. J. J. Anderson (1969) 21. For further study dealing with the possible influence of both *Patience* and *Cleanness* on *Piers Plowman*, see Robert J. Menner (1920) xxviii–xxx. Menner refuted Martha C. Thomas (1883) 27–32 who argued that parts of *Patience* and *Cleanness* were influenced by the B-text of *Piers Plowman*.

22. Gollancz, *Cleanness* (1921) xiii–xv.

23. C. A. Luttrell (1960).

24. Carleton F. Brown (1904) 149–53.

25. Malcolm Letts (1953) xxvii. This Volume I of *Mandeville's Travels* contains a modernized version of the Egerton text.

26. Letts (1953) xxviii. This is the Paris text, Bibliothèque Nationale, Nouv. Acq. Franç. 4515, printed for the first time by Letts in Volume II of The Hakluyt Society Series.

27. See Letts (1949) 172–74.

28. See, for example, John A. Burrow (1971) 143.

29. J. R. R. Tolkien and E. V. Gordon (1925) xxi.

30. Norman Davis (1967) xxv.

31. E. V. Gordon (1953) xliv.

32. Bernhard ten Brink (1889) 351.

33. Gollancz, 2nd ed. of *Patience* (1924), p. 5.

34. Bernhard ten Brink (1889) 351.

35. Charles G. Osgood (1906) xlix–l.

36. Hartley Bateson, 2nd ed. of *Patience* (1918) xi–xxiii.

37. Robert J. Menner (1920) xxx–xxxviii.

38. Menner (1920) xxxvi–xxxvii. Cf., for example, *Patience* 23–24 and *Cleanness* 27–28 alongside Matt. 5.8, and *Patience* 121–24 and *Cleanness* 581–86 in relation to Ps. 93.8–9.

39. Menner (1920) xxxiv.

40. Menner (1920) xxxiii.

41. Marie Borroff (1977) xvi. See pp. xvi–xix for a study of "Design and Its Significance" in *Pearl,* and pp. 32–35 on "The Metrical Form."

42. See Patricia M. Kean (1965).

43. See Maren-Sofie Røstvig (1967).

44. See Edwin Guest (1838) 459–62; Sir Frederic Madden (1839) 302–4; George P. McNeil (1888); George Neilson (1900–01) and (1902b); and Agnes Mure Mackenzie (1933) 29–38. Mackenzie argued that the *Pearl*-poet was "far more than Chaucer, the forerunner of the fifteenth century Scots poets" (30).

45. Richard Morris, 2nd ed. of *Early English Alliterative Poems* (1869), pp. v–ix; Henry N. MacCracken (1910).

46. See Gollancz' Introduction to his ed. of *Pearl* (1891c).

47. Carleton F. Brown (1904) 146–48. Gollancz, in his Introduction to his ed. of *Pearl* (1921), pp. xlvi–l, after discussing the *philosophical Strode* mentioned by Chaucer in the next to last stanza of *Troylus and Criseyde,* added: "But so far as the identity of Strode with the author of *Pearl* is concerned, all is mere conjecture; no definite piece of evidence tending to confirm it is adducible" (p. xlix). Edmund Gosse (1923) 182 called Gollancz' Strode theory "pleasing" but "pure guesswork." Nevertheless, Stephen Medcalf (1973) 673–74 advocated the theory.

48. Oscar Cargill and Margaret Schlauch (1928). Thomas A. Reisner (1973), noting that *powdered* in line 44 of *Pearl* was also a heraldic term and that families named Prat "had arms with fields either powdered or charged with a variety of floral devices," revived the claim of John Prat.

49. Coolidge Otis Chapman (1932).

50. Dorothy Everett (1932) 104–5.

51. Henry L. Savage (1938). See Savage's book, *The Gawain-Poet: Studies in His Personality and Background* (1956a).

52. For information about this manuscript, BM Harleian 2250, copied c. 1477, see Ruth Morse's ed. of *St. Erkenwald* (1975), pp. 8–12. Morse, pp. 45–48, spoke against the supposition that *Erk.* was written by the *Gawain*-poet. In contrast, Clifford J. Peterson, in his ed. of *Saint Erkenwald* (1977b), pp. 15–23, argued in favor of the theory of common authorship for *Erk.* and the *Pearl* poems.

53. Ormerod Greenwood (1956) 3–16.

54. Barbara Nolan s.v. Nolan & Farley-Hills (1971) 297–300.

55. David Farley-Hills s.v. Nolan & Farley-Hills (1971) 301–2.

56. Clifford J. Peterson (1974a) and (1974b). See also Peterson (1977a) and (1977b) 15–23.

57. Thorlac Turville-Petre (1975) 129–33. Edward Wilson (1975) 133–43 argued against the studies of Nolan and Peterson. See also Wilson's note, pp. 55–56, added to Peterson's 1977 article in *RES*. Farley-Hills (1975) answered Turville-Petre's argument against the identification of John Massy as the author of *Pearl*.

58. William Vantuono (1975). See also Vantuono (1981).

59. Katherine L. Adam (1976). Although there is, as yet, no conclusive proof, John Gardner calls the *Pearl*-poet John Massey in several places in *The Life and Times of Chaucer* (1977). Note especially the comments in Gardner's Introduction, pp. 14–15.

60. Ormerod Greenwood (1956) 15. For information about Mascy families in Cheshire, see George Ormerod (1819), 2nd ed. revised and enlarged by Thomas Helsby (1882).

61. Henry L. Savage (1931).

62. Greenwood (1956) 11. The *MED* s.v. *maskellẽs* adj. cites only *Pearl* for the use of this word.

63. Carleton F. Brown (1904) 126–27 disagreed with statements Gollancz had made in his ed. of *Pearl* (1891c), p. xlvii. Gollancz maintained that the "author of *Pearl* was certainly no priest" in his 1921 ed., pp. xl–xlvi.

64. Osgood (1906) li.

65. William Henry Schofield (1909) 673.

66. Ordelle G. Hill (1968) 103.

67. O. Hill (1965) 180–82.

68. See William Vantuono (1972b); Michael H. Means (1975); and Doris E. Kittendorf (1979).

69. Ian Bishop (1968) 55–58. See also Bishop, p. 35, on the *artes praedicandi* in *Pearl*.

70. Walter Kirkland Greene (1925) 815.

71. Greene (1925) 820.

72. Gordon (1953) xlii.

73. Gordon Hall Gerould (1936).

74. Gerould (1936) 32–33.

75. James R. Hulbert (1931).

76. Elizabeth Salter (1966) 146. Salter stated, p. 148, "But the general directions given by Hulbert in his article were sound. Aristocratic patronage is a known feature of the beginning and the end of alliterative verse writing in the Middle English period." See also Salter (1967) and C. A. Luttrell (1958).

77. Charles Muscatine (1972) 68–69.

78. See the preceding section on "Possible Dates and Order of Poems." The *MED* conjecturally dates *Gawain* c. 1390; see the "Plan and Bibliography," p. 42.

79. Hans Schnyder (1959) 19.

80. John H. Fisher (1961) 151.

81. Fisher (1961) 151–52.

82. Note the following different viewpoints: Larry D. Benson (1965a) 241 wrote, "The laughter is good-humored, for in laughing at Gawain, their representative, they are laughing at themselves." Douglas R. Butturff (1972) 147 wrote, "If we laugh at him, we are associating with a society which has proven itself incapable of taking anything seriously."

83. Henry IV was the son of John of Gaunt, fourth son of Edward III, and the duchess Blanche, daughter of Henry, Duke of Lancaster. Richard II was the son of Edward the Black Prince, eldest son of Edward III.

84. Marcelle Thiébaux (1970).

85. The *MED* s.v. *dok* n., 'trimmed hair (of tail and forelock),' cites only *Gawain*.

86. Around mid-fourteenth century the line of barons of Dunham-Massy came to an end, and, in the midst of the disputes that ensued, Henry took possession. For an account of how Dunham-Massy passed to the Booths, see pp. 526–30 in Vol. 1 of Thomas Helsby's revision of Ormerod (1819).

87. See Rossell H. Robbins (1950) 252.

88. F. E. Richardson (1962) 315.

89. Thomas C. Niemann (1974), after comparing *Pearl* to the Middle English *Vision of Tundale* (12th century) and Dante's *Divine Comedy*, concluded that viewing *Pearl* as a Vision of the Other World "offers several distinct advantages over each of the previous approaches to the poem" (225). On pp. 225–27, Niemann reconciles the various genres.

90. Schofield (1909) 664.

91. See Conley-C (1955).

92. Bishop (1968) 8–9.

93. Bishop (1968) 16–17. Bishop added evidence to the study of V. E. Watts (1963). See also Michael H. Means (1972).

94. James Milroy (1971) 208. A similar view is expressed by David Williams (1970a) 155.

95. See senses 2a and 2b of *MED clẽnnesse*.

96. Analogue noted by Osgood (1906) 69.

97. On Gawain's weakening through physical temptation, see Robert C. Pierle (1968) 209–11.

98. See Patricia M. Kean (1967) 241.

99. Discussion of the theme of *Gawain* in this study focuses on the ethical and religious interpretation to show the relationship of the romance to *Patience, Cleanness,* and *Pearl.* For a survey of other thematic approaches, as well as the ethical and religious one, see Bloomfield-HZ (1961) 38–46 and Donald R. Howard (1971) 34–36, 43–44. For a study of the game element, see John Leyerle (1975) and Robert J. Blanch (1976). (Blanch, pp. 64–66, also reviews the mythic approaches.) For an interpretation of all of *Gawain* as dream psychology in the hero's mind, see Anne Wilson (1976).

100. Paraphrase of Matt. 5.3: "Beati pauperes spiritu, quoniam ipsorum est regnum caelorum."

101. Paraphrse of Matt. 5.10: "Beati qui persecutionem patiuntur propter iustitiam, quoniam ipsorum est regnum caelorum."

102. Saint Augustine, Bishop of Hippo, Commentary on "De Sermone Domini in Monte," *PL* 34.1232.

103. Tertullian, *Liber de Patientia, PL* 1.1267. The relationship of *Patience* to this source was noted by Oliver F. Emerson (1895) 246–47.

104. See Donald R. Howard (1966) 219.

105. See Kiteley-HZ (1962).

106. Analogue noted by Kean (1967) 241.

107. Cf. Matt. 26.41: "Vigilate et orate, ut non intretis in tentationem; spiritus quidem promptus est, caro autem infirma."

108. In the Douay Bible, the note to Dan. 4.34 reads: "From this place some commentators infer that this king [Nabucho] became a true convert, and dying not long after, was probably saved."

109. Paraphrase of Matt. 5.8: "Beati mundo corde, quoniam ipsi Deum videbunt."

110. Cf. *Pearl* 678–88 to Ps. 23.3–4: "Quis ascendet in montem Domini? aut quis stabit in loco sancto eius?/Innocens manibus et mundo corde, qui non accepit in vano animam suam nec iuravit in dolo proximo suo."

111. Andrew & Waldron (1978) 100 commented, "Presumably a scribe mistook this for the beginning of a new section as a result of the extra stanza in section XV." However, since the *M* of Moteleȝ (961) is followed by the *I* of *If* (973), it may be that the illuminator deliberately set down the

initials for *Mascy Iohan*. (See the section on "The Poet and His Audience" for possible identification of a John de Mascy as the *Pearl*-poet.)

112. The *P* of *Perle* (1) is the largest in the manuscript. It extends 14 lines down. All the others in *Pearl* extend 3 lines down, except for the *F* of *Fro* (61), which extends 4. In the margin under the *T* of *The* (121), a head is sketched with what looks like a hood on it. There are faces sketched in the middle of the *G* of *Grace* (661) and the *T* of *Thys* (841).

113. Dorothy Everett (1955) 87.

114. Ian Bishop (1968) 32–34.

115. Blenkner-C (1968) 266–67.

116. For an excellent study of circular aspects in *Pearl*, see Cary Nelson (1973) 25–49. "The circular structure of *Pearl* is integral to our most vital experience of the poem and its vision. . . . Form and content in *Pearl* are not simply parallel or complementary—they are the same" (26).

117. The *C* of *Clannesse* extends 8 lines down; all the others extend 3 lines down, except for the *S* of *Sypen* (557) and the *D* of *Danyel* (1157), which extend 4. The latter comes after an open space.

118. Richard Morris (1864), 2nd ed. of *Early English Alliterative Poems* (1869).

119. Robert J. Menner (1920), p. xlv, commented, "There is no apparent reason why there should be a division at 345, 485, or 689."

120. See Gollancz' ed. of *Cleanness* (1921), pp. x–xi.

121. See, however, Andrew & Waldron (1978) 24–27 for a structural analysis that is similar to the one presented in this edition.

122. Oliver F. Emerson (1921b) 230.

123. Laurita L. Hill (1946) 69–70.

124. See A. C. Spearing (1970) 43. After referring to Spearing, R. J. Spendal (1976) argued that the capitals are regular when viewed as thematic rather than narrative guides.

125. See, for example, Anderson (1977) 1–2.

126. Laurita Hill (1946) 69 makes this point.

127. However, Michael H. Means (1975) 168 divides the theme in the following way: (1) lines 193–1048 on *fylþe of þe flesch*; (2) 1049–1148 as an exhortation to purity; (3) 1149–1804 dealing with God's vengeance for sacrilege. A different apportionment is also presented by Charlotte C. Morse (1978) 129–99, who considers the Wedding Feast "Prologue to the Poem and Epilogue to History," the three major exempla as "The

Evidence of History," and "The Christ-event" (lines 1065–1108) as "The Center of History," one part of eight in her chart, p. 132, listing the "poet's disposition of biblical stories."

128. Spearing (1970) 42–43. For two full studies that relate the methods of the poet to those of medieval preachers, see Means (1975) and Doris E. Kittendorf (1979).

129. Edwin D. Cuffe (1951) 114 observed: "The stories of Lucifer and Adam introduce the history of the Flood. The stories of Sara and of Lot's wife are told in conjunction with the destruction of Sodom, and the stories of Sedecias and Nabuchodonosor in conjunction with that of Baltasar."

130. When he sees the three angels, Abraham hurries quickly, "And, as to God, þe good mon gos hem agayne3,/And haylsed hem in on hede, and sayde: 'Hende Lorde' " (611–12). Menner (1920) 91 compared *Cursor Mundi*: "Toward him com childir thre/Liknes o god in trinité" (2707–8).

# PREFACE TO TEXT

The MS begins with a fold of two leaves containing four illustrations to *Pearl*, continues with seven gatherings of twelve leaves each, and ends with one of four leaves. Catchwords appear at the end of all the twelve-leaf gatherings, on the verso of the following folios: 54 (*Pe.*), 66, 78 (*Cl.*), 90 (*Pa.*), and 102, 114, 126 (*Ga.*). For example, "leste les þow leue my tale farand" is at the bottom of f. 54b; the first line of f. 55 is, "lestles þou leue my talle farande." In this edition, the folios are numbered according to the new foliation; therefore, the text of *Pearl* starts with f. 43, but one may note 39, the old number in ink, crossed out and 43 written below it in pencil.

## STANZAIC ARRANGEMENTS

A stanzaic arrangement is easily determined for *Pearl*, because of its twelve-line groupings in rhyme, but the long alliterative lines of *Cleanness* (and *Patience*) run continuously in the MS. Gollancz printed these poems in quatrains, attaching significance to the marks that appear quite regularly along the left-hand side of the folios every four lines. Menner (1922a) 356–57 argued against the quatrain arrangement for *Cleanness*. The scribe might have put these marks in the MS because he had a mistaken conception of what the poet intended, or perhaps because he found it a convenient device to keep a tally of the number of lines he had written. In this volume, the division of the text of *Cleanness* into verse paragraphs is for the convenience of the modern reader. (For a fuller discussion, see Appendix 3 on Verse.)

## ILLUMINATED LETTERS AND MAJUSCULES

There are 48 illuminated letters in the MS, but they do not always designate structural divisions. (For a detailed study relating to *Pearl* and *Cleanness,* see the preceding section on Structure.) As Greg (1924) 226 noted, the four biggest illuminated letters starting the poems are blue and red, with red flourishes; the others are blue, flourished with red.

Besides these illuminated letters, the MS contains many majuscules. Most of these are made differently from the corresponding miniscule, larger and fancier, but *I, 3, P,* and *W* appear in the same shape, and it is not always possible to determine if one made larger than another is supposed to indicate a majuscule. The scribe did not use capitalization according to a consistent practice; he did not always capitalize proper nouns, and sometimes he capitalized words within a line that need not have been so designated. For example, within lines of *Pearl, Emerad* (118) has a capital *E,* but *emerade* (1005) has a small *e;* in *Cleanness, mambre* (674) is not capitalized, but the adj. *Colde* inside line 1231 is. The scribe began many lines with majuscules, but the majority of lines have an initial miniscule; in *Pearl* (and *Gawain*), where the beginnings of stanzas are determinable, most, but not all of them, begin with a majuscule. It seems, therefore, that much of what the scribe did in such matters must be considered decorative. In this edition, I have used capitalization according to Modern English practices.

## PUNCTUATION AND SPELLING

Punctuation, lacking in the MS, has been supplied. The spellings have been retained, except for *i–I* to *j–J* when the latter sound is intended. The scribe's long *I* does not always represent either the pronoun "I" or the sound of *j.* For example, *I wysse* within a line is spelled *iwysse* in this edition. (See *Pe.* 151, and note also MS *Ichose* spelled *ichose* in *Pe.* 904.) There is some difficulty, due in part to the faded condition of many of the letters, in telling if the scribe always intended to make distinctions in regard to the vertical strokes that are printed *i–I* and *j–J* in this edition. The size of the strokes varies, and in some instances an unusually long one obviously represents *i,* as in *is* of *Cl.* 76.

## ABBREVIATIONS AND OTHER SCRIBAL DEVICES

Contracted forms in the MS have been expanded without indication by italic print found in some editions; see Morris', for example. In this text, the form *w*ᵗ is written *wyth* since that spelling seems to appear most often, *&* is written *and*, the crossed *q* is written *quoþ* rather than *quod* since *coþe* appears in *Ga.* 776, and the sign 9 is expanded to -*us*, though some editors have expanded it only to -*s* in some instances. The scribe used many abbreviations. (Madden's text of *Gawain* has these forms printed as they appear in the MS.) Oddities in the spelling of many proper nouns are often due to the contracted forms. Note, for example, the different marks that appear in the spelling of *Jerusalem* in *Pearl* and *Cleanness.* In the former, the mark is a long one over letters; in the latter, it is a flourish off the *l.* (See the textual notes to *Pe.* 792 and *Cl.* 1159.)

In this edition, the acute accent to mark a final weakly stressed *e* is added to words like *countré* (*Pe.* 297) and *þrefté* (*Cl.* 819). The scribe did not use that diacritic in such positions. He did, however, use certain graphemic devices, occasionally, that are not reproduced in this edition. A mark sometimes appears over an *i* as in *spuníande* (*Cl.* 1038), or *i = j* as in *íuele = juele* (*Pe.* 23), evidently to distinguish these letters from minims that precede or follow. A dot sometimes appears over a *y: compaynÿe* (*Cl.* 119), *ilÿche* (*Cl.* 228). A dot or a hyphen sometimes appears between syllables: *vnresoun·able* (*Pe.* 590), *enpryson-ment* (*Cl.* 46). The hyphen in the MS is slanted. A peculiar mannerism of the scribe shows in the occasional placement of a flourish off the top of the long stroke of *b, h, k,* or *l: ƀe* (*Cl.* 123), *ƙabbeȝ* (*Cl.* 95), *stoƙeȝ* (*Cl.* 157), *stylle* (*Pe.* 20).

## WORD CONNECTION

In the MS, numerous compounds are not joined, syllables of words are separated, and words frequently run together. For example, the scribe often placed the indefinite article *a* with the following noun or modifier, and he occasionally separated *a* from a syllable to which it belonged. At times, because he brought words so close together that they appear almost connected, it is difficult to determine if the forms are attached. The following survey, based only on the first 100 lines of *Pearl* and *Cleanness,* is intended to give the reader a sampling of the type of detailed information discussed above. Noteworthy examples after line 100 are often listed in the Textual Notes or discussed in the Commentary, especially if they relate to variant readings with previous editors.

*Pearl*

*Disconnected elements that were joined in the text of this edition:*
quere so euer 7, for dolked 11, luf daungere 11, for soþe 21, by gonne
33, by twene 44, wyth outen 48, my seluen 52, slepyng sla3te 59, to
warde 67, holte wode3 75, sunne beme3 83, for 3ete 86, þer of 99.

*Connected elements that were separated in the text of this edition:*
amyry 23, sprygande 35, ahy3 39, tomy 58, onbalke 62, þerbod 62,
inþis 65, atynde 78, aswete 94.

## Cleanness

*Disconnected elements that were joined in the text of this edition:*
who so 1, hous holde 18, wyth inne 20, wyth outen 20, hym self 23,
þer as 24, louf chere 28, for þy 33, to torne 41, halle dore 44, þer oute
44, penne fed 57, ex cused 62, by holde 64, an oþer 65, a dre3 71, for
saken 75, I wysse 84, þer after 93, what kyn 100.

*Connected elements that were separated in the text of this edition:*
inþe 4, &3if 21, ameruayl 22, acarp 23, aful 26, alouf 28, aladde 36,
asete 37, intuch 48, aworþlych 49, inhis 51, comschulde 61,
mebyhoue3 68, þeþryd 69, vchone 71, asyde 78, forto 91, þelorde 97,
feche3hem 100.

## EMENDATIONS

In keeping with a conservative approach, I have emended the MS
only in the following 34 places for *Pearl* and *Cleanness*; these emenda-
tions are also listed in the Textual Notes at the appropriate points.
(Changes dealing with capitalization and word connection are not con-
sidered emendations.) There may be readers who will disagree with
my justification of some MS readings, but since I established this text,
hoping to retain the MS forms wherever possible, I thought it proper
to proceed in that direction to the utmost degree. Readers interested
in an editorial approach that goes in the opposite direction, attributing
excessive errors to the scribe, may view Gollancz' Introduction to the
Facsimile Reproduction (*EETS* 162, 1923), pp. 12–39, where about
500 emendations are listed for all four poems. It has been my policy in
this edition to retain corrections that were apparently made by a second
hand in darker brown ink. Since these corrections fit the Middle En-
glish context, it may be that they were made by an authoritative figure.

## Pearl

| Line Number | MS Reading | Reading in This Edition | Line Number | MS Reading | Reading in This Edition |
|---|---|---|---|---|---|
| 309 | īs | is | 700 | sor | For |
| 335 | perleȝ | perle | 861 | lonbe | Lombe |
| 436 | bȳgyner | Bygynner | 997 | As þise | As Johan þise |
| 558 | wanig | waning | 1111 | glode | golde |
| 649 | out out | out | 1179 | quykeȝ | quyke |
| 678 | hylleȝ | hylle | 1185 | if | If |

## Cleanness

| Line Number | MS Reading | Reading in This Edition | Line Number | MS Reading | Reading in This Edition |
|---|---|---|---|---|---|
| 108 | þaȝ þaȝ | þaȝ | 1295 | fynde | fyndeȝ |
| 233 | lyttlel | lyttel | 1329 | vpn ende | vpon ende |
| 312 | wᵗīme | wythinne | 1405 | þe þe | þe |
| 395 | þe masse þe mase | þe mase | 1408 | glolde | golde |
| 586 | he he | he | 1506 | bryȝtȝ | bryȝte |
| 692 | if | If | 1516 | sauay | Sauteray |
| 777 | wendeȝ wendeȝ | wendeȝ | 1524 | īs | is |
| 783 | meuand meuande | Meuande | 1619 | as as swyþe | as-swyþe |
| 1178 | wyth with | wyth | 1711 | dryȝtn | Dryȝtyn |
| 1225 | souay | Souerayn | 1722 | hatȝ sende | |
| | | | | hatȝ sende | Hatȝ sende |
| 1274 | þsancta | þe Sancta | 1744 | cloler | coler |

## TEXTUAL NOTES

In the compilation of the textual notes, distinction is usually not made in regard to matters of varying editorial practices such as modernized spellings, use of brackets and hyphens, italics to indicate contracted forms in the MS, and capitalization. The variant form is usually listed only once according to the way the first editor printed it. For example, all editors read *bonkes* instead of *bukes* for *Pe.* 106; *b[o]nkes* is listed in the textual note because that is the form in Morris' edition, but not all editors who followed Morris bracketed the [*o*]. Morris placed notes in the margins of his text and after his text. When these are listed, they usually appear in parentheses. See, for example, the textual note to *Pe.* 115.

Textual notes are not listed in relation to articles on the texts of these poems (though different readings worth mentioning are discussed in the Commentary), selections appearing in anthologies, and continental editions such as *La Perla* by Federico Olivero (1936), who used Osgood's text. Notes from the collected edition of Cawley & Anderson (1976) are not listed because material in that book is in the other editions of these scholars.

ABBREVIATIONS FOR TEXTUAL NOTES

See Bibliography I at the end of this book for full references. When the same editor revised his first edition, textual notes only to his second edition are listed.

*MS* ----- *Manuscript*

*Facs.* --- *Facsimile* (See the entry for Gollancz [1923] in Bibliography I.)

*Orig.* --- The *original manuscript* was examined for all problem readings; this abbreviation appears when it may be useful for the reader to have a precise indication of this fact.

*UVR* --- *Ultra-Violet Reading*—This abbreviation is used to indicate when a word was viewed under the ultra-violet lamp in the British Library.

*Pearl*

| | |
|---|---|
| M ------- Morris (1864; 2nd ed. 1869) | H ------- Hillmann (1961) |
| | C ------- Cawley (1962) |
| O ------- Osgood (1906) | De ------ DeFord (1967) |
| G ------- Gollancz (1921) | Mo ----- Moorman (1977) |
| Ch ------ Chase (1932) | AW ----- Andrew & Waldron (1978) |
| Go ------ Gordon (1953) | eds. ---- (all noted in this list) |

*Cleanness*

| | |
|---|---|
| M ------- Morris (1864; 2nd ed. 1869) | A ------- Anderson (1977) |
| | Mo ----- Moorman (1977) |
| Me ----- Menner (1920) | AW ----- Andrew & Waldron (1978) |
| G ------- Gollancz (1921) | eds. ---- (all noted in this list) |

TRANSLATION

The translation is literal. In endeavoring to transfer meaning from Middle English to Modern English, one must account for much ellipsis; this is indicated by the use of brackets in the translation.

# PEARL

*Folio 41, the first of four illustrations of Pearl, reproduced by permission of the British Library*: The dreamer sleeps near what looks like mounds on either side of him, with plants and trees springing from them and around them. Gollancz (1923) 9 noted that the scallop-shaped streamer in blue extending upward from his head may represent the departing of his spirit into space, lines 61–64. (The illustrations in the MS are colored green, red, blue, yellow, brown, and white. For further discussion, see the sections on "History of the Manuscript" in the Introduction and "Miscellaneous Information about the Manuscript" in the Appendices.)

*Folio 41b, reproduced by permission of the British Library*: The dreamer stands by the stream separating him from the New Jerusalem. The artist could not capture the beauty of the description in lines 107–20. A large fish is drawn out of proportion to the size of the stream, even though the poet did not describe any fish.

*Folio 42, reproduced by permission of the British Library*: The dreamer is shown conversing with the pearl-maiden across the stream. Gordon (1953) x noted that her white dress, high at the neck and with long hanging sleeves, is in the fashion of the end of the fourteenth, or beginning of the fifteenth, century. The maiden's gesture, as Gordon also noted, seems to express disapproval of the dreamer's words. See especially Stanza-Group V (lines 241–300).

*Folio 42b, reproduced by permission of the British Library:* The dreamer is looking upward across the stream at the maiden behind the wall of the New Jerusalem. The wall is circular, whereas the city is described as square in the poem (lines 1023–32) in keeping with the Biblical source. Gordon (1953) xi noted that in the picture the city resembles a feudal manor, with a tower and a hall depicted behind the wall. The artist medievalized the New Jerusalem even more than the poet did. Lines 1027–28 of the poem describe *woneʒ*, but no mention is made of 'abodes' in Chapter 21 of Revelation. (See the note to lines 917–18.)

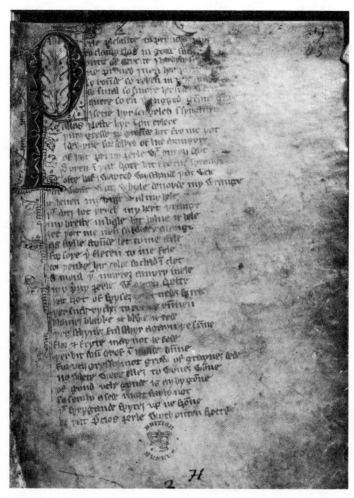

*Folio 43, the first 36 lines of Pearl, reproduced by permission of the British Library.*

I

f. 43      Perle plesaunte to prynces paye,
        To clanly clos in golde so clere,
        Oute of Oryent, I hardyly saye,
4        Ne proued I neuer her precios pere.
        So rounde, so reken in vche araye,
        So smal, so smoþe her sydeȝ were.
        Queresoeuer I jugged gemmeȝ gaye,
8        I sette hyr sengeley in synglure.
        Allas, I leste hyr in on erbere;
        Þurȝ gresse to grounde hit fro me yot.
        I dewyne, fordolked of luf-daungere,
12      Of þat pryuy perle wythouten spot.

        Syþen in þat spote hit fro me sprange,
        Ofte haf I wayted, wyschande þat wele
        Þat wont watȝ whyle deuoyde my wrange,
16      And heuen my happe and al my hele.
        Þat dotȝ bot þrych my hert þrange,
        My breste in bale bot bolne and bele.
        Ȝet, þoȝt me neuer so swete a sange
20      As stylle stounde let to me stele.
        Forsoþe, þer fleten to me fele
        To þenke hir color so clad in clot.

---

1   All illuminated letters are printed in this edition like
      the *P* of *Perle*. However, they are of different sizes
      in the MS and do not always indicate structural divi-
      sions. (See the "Structure of *Pearl* and *Cleanness*"
      in the Introduction.) Gordon, p. ix, considered it
      noteworthy that the "large Þ is avoided; in the col-
      oured letters *th* is always substituted."

## PROLOGUE: THE GARDEN SETTING

### I

f. 43    Pleasing pearl for [a] prince's pleasure,
        For [a] splendid setting in gold so bright,
        Out of [the] Orient, I certainly say,
4        I never discovered her precious equal.
        So round, so elegant in each array,
        So small, so smooth her sides were.
        Wherever I judged magnificent gems,
8        I set her apart as unique.
        Alas, I lost her in a garden;
        It slipped from me through grass into earth.
        I lament, grief-stricken by frustrated love,
12       For that special pearl without spot.

        Since it sprang from me in that spot,
        I have often pondered, desiring that splendid pearl
        That previously was accustomed to dispel my distress,
16       And increase my joy and all my well-being.
        It does yet oppress my heart grievously,
        Yet swell and burn my breast with anguish.
        Nevertheless, I never was aware of so lovely a melody
20       As [the] silent hour let slip to me.
        Truly, there floated to me many
        To remind [me] of her complexion so covered with clay.

---

  2   clere] UVR shows part of -e under brown ink smudge.
  3   saye] UVR shows -e under brown ink smudge.
  5   araye] UVR shows -e under brown ink smudge.
  8   synglure] syng[u]l[e]re: O, G, Ch.   synglere: Go, C, Mo.
11   fordolked] for-do[k]ked: G.
17   hert] hert[e]: G, Ch.

                O moul, þou marreȝ a myry juele,
24              My priuy perle wythouten spotte.

                Þat spot of spyseȝ mot nedeȝ sprede,
                Þer such rycheȝ to rot is runnen.
                Blomeȝ, blayke and blwe and rede,
28              Þer schyneȝ ful schyr agayn þe sunne.
                Flor and fryte may not be fede
                Þer hit doun drof in moldeȝ dunne,
                For vch gresse mot grow of grayneȝ dede;
32              No whete were elleȝ to woneȝ wonne.
                Of goud vche goude is ay bygonne;
                So semly a sede moȝt fayly not,
                Þat spryg ande spyceȝ vp ne sponne
36              Of þat precios perle wythouten spotte.

f. 43b          To þat spot þat I in speche expoun
                I entred, in þat erber grene,
                In Auguste, in a hyȝ seysoun,
40              Quen corne is coruen wyth crokeȝ kene.
                On huyle þer perle hit trendeled doun,
                Schadowed þis worteȝ, ful schyre and schene,
                Gilofre, gyngure, and gromylyoun,
44              And pyonys powdered ay bytwene.
                Ȝif hit watȝ semly on to sene,
                A fayr reflayr ȝet fro hit flot.
                Þer wonys þat worþyly, I wot and wene,
48              My precious perle wythouten spot.

                Bifore þat spot my honde I spenud,
                For care ful colde þat to me caȝt.
                A deuely dele in my hert denned,
52              Þaȝ resoun sette myseluen saȝt.
                I playned my perle þat þer watȝ spenned,
                Wyth fyrte skylleȝ þat faste faȝt.
                Þaȝ kynde of Kryst me comfort kenned,
56              My wreched wylle in wo ay wraȝte.

---

23    juele] mele: M, G.
24    spotte] spot: Ch.
25    mot] myȝt: M.   UVR shows *mo* of *mot* under blot.
26    runnen] runne: all eds. except M.
28    schyneȝ] schyne: AW.
34    fayly] fayle: Ch.
35    spryg ande] sprygande: MS.   spryngande: M, O, G, Ch, Go,
          C, Mo, AW.
36    spotte] spot: Ch.

10

O earth, you mar a beautiful jewel,
24      My special pearl without spot.

        That spot must necessarily be spread with spices,
        Where such wealth has sunk into decay.
        Blossoms, pale and blue and red,
28      Shine there very brilliantly against the sun.
        Flower and fruit can not be wasted
        Where it drove down into dark molds,
        For every plant must grow from dead grains;
32      Otherwise, no wheat would be taken to barns.
        From goodness each good thing is always begun;
        So excellent a seed could not fail to produce,
        So that shrubs and spices would not spring up
36      From that precious pearl without spot.

f. 43b  At that spot which I describe in speech
        I entered, within that green garden,
        In August, on a holy occasion,
40      When corn is cut with sharp sickles.
        On [the] mound where [the] pearl rolled down,
        These plants, very bright and shiny, provided shade,
        Gillyflower, ginger, and gromwell,
44      And peonies always scattered in between.
        If it was beautiful to look upon,
        A pleasant fragrance also wafted from it.
        There lies that worthy gem, I realize, indeed,
48      My precious pearl without spot.

        I clasped my hands before that spot,
        With care full cold that came upon me.
        A dismal grief dwelled in my heart,
52      Though reason would have made me peaceful.
        I mourned for my pearl that was enclosed there,
        With appalling assertions that conflicted severely.
        Though [the] character of Christ would have shown
             me solace,
56      My wretched will always moved in misery.

---

46  fayr reflayr] fayrre flayr: AW.
49  spenud] spenn[e]d: all eds. except AW.   spennd: AW.
50  caȝt] caȝt[e]: M.
51  deuely] denely: M.   de[r]uely: O.      hert] hert[e]: G, Ch.
52  saȝt] saȝt[e]: M.
53  spenned] penned: G, Ch, AW.
54  fyrte] fyr[c]e: G, Go, C, Mo, AW.   faȝt] faȝt[e]: M.
55  Kryst] Bottom of y is illegible in Orig. and in Facs.

11

<pre>
            I felle vpon þat floury flaȝt;
            Suche odour to my herneȝ schot.
            I slode vpon a slepyng-slaȝte
60          On þat precos perle wythouten spot.
</pre>

## THE VISION--PART ONE:
## THE TERRESTRIAL PARADISE AND THE PEARL-MAIDEN

### II

<pre>
            Fro spot my spyryt þer sprang in space;
            My body on balke þer bod in sweuen.
            My goste is gon in Godeȝ grace
64          In auenture þer meruayleȝ meuen.
            I ne wyste in þis worlde quere þat hit wace,
            Bot I knew me keste þer klyfeȝ cleuen.
            Towarde a foreste I bere þe face,
68          Where rych rokkeȝ wer to dyscreuen.
            Þe lyȝt of hem myȝt no mon leuen,
            Þe glemande glory þat of hem glent,
            For wern neuer webbeȝ þat wyȝeȝ weuen
72          Of half so dere adubmente.
</pre>

<pre>
f. 44       Dubbed wern alle þo downeȝ sydeȝ
            Wyth crystal klyffeȝ so cler of kynde.
            Holtewodeȝ bryȝt aboute hem bydeȝ,
76          Of bolleȝ as blwe as ble of ynde.
            As bornyst syluer þe lef onslydeȝ,
            Þat þike con trylle on vch a tynde.
            Quen glem of glodeȝ agaynȝ hem glydeȝ,
80          Wyth schymeryng schene ful schrylle þay schynde.
            Þe grauayl þat on grounde con grynde
            Wern precious perleȝ of Oryente,
            Þe sunnebemeȝ bot blo and blynde
84          In respecte of þat adubbement.
</pre>

<pre>
            The adubbemente of þo downeȝ dere
            Garten my goste al greffe forȝete.
            So frech flauoreȝ of fryteȝ were,
88          As fode, hit con me fayre refete.
</pre>

<pre>
────────────
57    flaȝt] flaȝt[e]: M.
60    precos] prec[i]os: eds.
64    meruayleȝ] meruayles: H, De.
68    rych] rych[e]: G, Ch.
</pre>

I fell upon that blossoming turf;
Such fragrance rose to my brains.
I slid into a deep slumber
60    Above that precious pearl without spot.


THE VISION--PART ONE:
THE TERRESTRIAL PARADISE AND THE PEARL-MAIDEN


II

From [that] spot my spirit then sprang into space;
My body remained there in sleep on [the] mound.
My soul has proceeded in God's grace
64    To [an] adventure where miracles transpire.
I knew not where in this world it was,
But I discovered myself cast where cliffs were cleft.
Toward a forest I turned my face,
68    Where rich rocks were to be seen.
No man could believe the light of them,
The gleaming glory that shone from them,
For [there] were never tapestries that men wove
72    Of half so lovely [an] adornment.

f. 44    Adorned were all those hills' sides
With crystal cliffs so clear in substance.
Bright woods lie around them,
76    With boles as blue as hue of indigo.
Like burnished silver hang the leaves,
Which thickly do trail upon every branch.
When light from bright openings strikes against them,
80    With shiny shimmering they shone very clearly.
The pebbles that did mingle on [the] ground
Were precious pearls from [the] Orient,
The sunbeams but dark and lusterless
84    In comparison to that adornment.

The adornments of those delightful hills
Made my soul forget all grief.
So fresh were [the] fragrances from fruits,
88    Like food, they sweetly did refresh me.


---

72    adubmente] adub[be]mente: O, G, Ch, Go, C, Mo, AW.
77    onslyde3] on slyde3: Go, AW.
81    þat on] þat [I] on: G.
82    Oryente] Oryent: Ch.


13

|        | Fowleʒ þer flowen in fryth in fere,           |
|        | Of flaumbande hweʒ, boþe smale and grete.     |
|        | Bot, sytole-stryng and gyternere              |
| 92     | Her reken myrþe moʒt not retrete,             |
|        | For quen þose bryddeʒ her wyngeʒ bete,        |
|        | Þay songen wyth a swete asent.                |
|        | So gracos gle couþe no mon gete               |
| 96     | As here and se her adubbement.                |

|        | So al watʒ dubbet on dere asyse               |
|        | Þat fryth þer fortwne forth me fereʒ.         |
|        | Þe derþe þerof for to deuyse                  |
| 100    | Nis no wyʒ worþé þat tonge bereʒ.             |
|        | I welke ay forth in wely wyse,                |
|        | No bonk so byg þat did me dereʒ.              |
|        | Þe fyrre in þe fryth þe feier con ryse        |
| 104    | Þe playn, þe plontteʒ, þe spyse, þe pereʒ,    |
|        | And raweʒ, and randeʒ, and rych reuereʒ;      |
|        | As fyldor fyn her bukes brent.                |
|        | I wan to a water by schore þat schereʒ;       |
| 108    | Lorde, dere watʒ hit adubbement.              |

| f. 44b | The dubbemente of þo derworth depe            |
|        | Wern bonkeʒ bene of beryl bryʒt.              |
|        | Swangeande swete, þe water con swepe          |
| 112    | Wyth a rownande rourde, raykande aryʒt.       |
|        | In þe founce þer stonden stoneʒ stepe,        |
|        | As glente þurʒ glas þat glowed and glyʒt,     |
|        | A stremande sterneʒ, quen stroþe-men slepe,   |
| 116    | Staren in welkyn in wynter nyʒt;              |
|        | For vche a pobbel in pole þer pyʒt            |
|        | Watʒ emerad, saffer, oþer gemme gente,        |
|        | Þat alle þe loʒe lemed of lyʒt,               |
| 120    | So dere watʒ hit adubbement.                  |

### III

|        | The dubbement dere of doun and daleʒ,         |
|        | Of wod and water and wlonk playneʒ,           |
|        | Bylde in me blys, abated my baleʒ,            |
| 124    | Fordidden my stresse, dystryed my payneʒ.     |

---

89  flowen] Orig. shows w, in darker brown ink, apparently
    altered from yʒ.
95  gracos] grac[i]os: eds.
103  feier] fei[r]er: O, G, Ch, H, De.
106  bukes] b[o]nkes: eds. Orig. has b followed by two minims.
111  Swangeande] Orig. and Facs. show s altered from w.

|      | Fowls flew there in [the] forest in flocks, |
|      | Of glowing colors, both small and huge. |
|      | Moreover, citole-string and gittern-player |
| 92   | Could not imitate their beautiful melody, |
|      | For when those birds beat their wings, |
|      | They sang in a sweet harmony. |
|      | Glee so gracious could no man obtain |
| 96   | As to hear [their song] and to see their adornment. |

|      | Thus entirely arrayed in royal style was |
|      | That forest where fortune carries me forth. |
|      | No man who has tongue is capable |
| 100  | Of depicting the glory of it. |
|      | I wandered ever onward in joyful fashion, |
|      | No hill so great that made obstacles for me. |
|      | The farther into the forest the fairer did rise |
| 104  | The plains, the saplings, the spices, the pear trees, |
|      | And hedgerows, and strands, and splendid rivers; |
|      | Like fine gold filament their currents sparkled. |
|      | I strolled to a stream that flows by [a] shore; |
| 108  | Lord, lovely was its adornment. |

| f. 44b | The adornments of those splendid depths |
|        | Revealed fair banks of bright beryl. |
|        | Swirling pleasantly, the water did sweep |
| 112    | With a whispering sound, flowing swiftly. |
|        | At the bottom there shone bright stones, |
|        | That glowed and glinted like flashes through glass, |
|        | Like streaming stars, when woodsmen sleep, |
| 116    | Gleaming in [the] sky on [a] winter's night; |
|        | For every pebble placed there in [the] stream |
|        | Was [an] emerald, sapphire, or excellent gem, |
|        | So that all the water gleamed with light, |
| 120    | So splendid was its adornment. |

### III

|      | The splendid adornments of hills and valleys, |
|      | Of wood and water and beautiful plains, |
|      | Produced happiness in me, subdued my sorrows, |
| 124  | Abolished my distress, dispelled my pains. |

---

113  stonden] stoden: AW.
115  A] A (? As.): M.  A[s]: other eds.
119  alle] all: H, Dc.
122  wlonk] wlonk[e]: G, Ch.
124  stresse] [dis]tresse: M.

Doun after a strem þat dryȝly haleȝ,
I bowed in blys, bredful my brayneȝ.
Þe fyrre I folȝed þose floty valeȝ,
128 Þe more strenghþe of joye myn herte strayneȝ.
As fortune fares þeras ho frayneȝ,
Wheþer solace ho sende oþer elleȝ sore,
Þe wyȝ to wham her wylle ho wayneȝ
132 Hytteȝ to haue ay more and more.

More of wele watȝ in þat wyse
Þen I cowþe telle, þaȝ I tom hade,
For vrþely herte myȝt not suffyse
136 To þe tenþe dole of þo gladneȝ glade.
Forþy, I þoȝt þat Paradyse
Watȝ þer oþer gayn þo bonkeȝ brade.
I hoped þe water were a deuyse
140 Bytwene myrþeȝ by mereȝ made.
Byȝonde þe broke, by slente oþer slade,
I hope þat mote merked wore,
Bot þe water watȝ depe; I dorst not wade,
144 And euer me longed a more and more.

f. 45 More and more, and ȝet wel mare
Me lyste to se þe broke byȝonde,
For if hit watȝ fayr þer I con fare,
148 Wel loueloker watȝ þe fyrre londe.
Abowte me con I stote and stare;
To fynde a forþe faste con I fonde,
Bot woþeȝ mo, iwysse, þer ware
152 Þe fyrre I stalked by þe stronde;
And euer me þoȝt I schulde not wonde
For wo þer weleȝ so wynne wore.
Þenne nwe note me com on honde,
156 Þat meued my mynde ay more and more.

More meruayle con my dom adaunt.
I seȝ byȝonde þat myry mere
A crystal clyffe ful relusaunt.
160 Mony ryal ray con fro hit rere.
At þe fote þerof þer sete a faunt,
A mayden of menske, ful debonere.

---

131 her] his: AW.
134 I tom] [tom I]: G.
136 gladneȝ] Gladneȝ: G.
138 oþer] o[v]er: O, G, Ch, Go, C, Mo, AW.

Down along a stream that incessantly flows,
I stepped with joy, my brains brimful.
The further I followed those watery vales,
128    The more [the] ardor of joy stirs my heart.
As fortune directs wherever she desires,
Whether she send solace or sorrow instead,
The man upon whom she urges her will
132    Happens to have always more and more.

More of splendor was in that array
Than I could tell, even if I had time,
For mortal imagination could not suffice
136    For the tenth part of those rich delights.
Consequently, I thought that Paradise
Was there or beyond those broad shores.
I supposed the water were a division
140    Between delights created alongside streams.
Beyond the brook, by hillside or valley,
I assumed that [a] castle would be situated,
But the water was deep; I dared not wade,
144    And always I yearned more and more.

f. 45    More and more, and yet much more
I wished to see beyond the brook,
For if it was fair where I did wander,
148    Much fairer was the more distant land.
I did stop and stare around me;
Eagerly did I endeavor to find a ford,
But, indeed, there were more perils
152    The farther I stepped along the shore;
And yet [it] always seemed to me I should not shrink
From adversity where riches so precious were.
Then [a] new marvel appeared to me close by,
156    That stirred my thoughts still more and more.

More wonders did overwhelm my mind.
I saw beyond that pleasant brook
A crystal cliff fully radiant.
160    Many royal rays did rise from it.
At the foot thereof there sat a child,
A maiden of dignity, very gentle.

---

140  myrþeȝ by mereȝ] [mereȝ] by [Myrþe]: G.
142  hope] hope[de]: M.  hope[d]: G, Ch, Go, C, AW.
144  a] a[y]: G, Go, C, AW.
154  wo] wo[þe]: G.

17

Blysnande whyt watʒ hyr bleaunt.
164    I knew hyr wel; I hade sen hyr ere.
As glysnande golde þat man con schere,
So schon þat schene anvnder schore.
On lenghe I loked to hyr þere;
168    Þe lenger, I knew hyr more and more.

The more I frayste hyr fayre face,
Her fygure fyn quen I had fonte,
Suche gladande glory con to me glace,
172    As lyttel byfore þerto watʒ wonte.
To calle hyr lyste con me enchace,
Bot baysment gef myn hert a brunt.
I seʒ hyr in so strange a place,
176    Such a burre myʒt make myn herte blunt.
Þenne vereʒ ho vp her fayre frount,
Hyr vysayge whyt as playn yuore.
Þat stonge myn hert, ful stray atount,
180    And euer þe lenger, þe more and more.

IV

f. 45b   **M**ore þen me lyste my drede aros;
      I stod ful stylle and dorste not calle.
Wyth yʒen open and mouth ful clos,
184    I stod as hende as hawk in halle.
I hope þat gostly watʒ þat porpose;
I dred onende quat schulde byfalle,
Lest ho me eschaped, þat I þer chos,
188    Er I at steuen hir moʒt stalle.
Þat gracios gay wythouten galle,
So smoþe, so smal, so seme slyʒt,
Ryseʒ vp in hir araye ryalle,
192    A precos pyece, in perleʒ pyʒt.

Perleʒ pyʒte of ryal prys
Þere moʒt mon, by grace, haf sene
Quen þat frech, as flor-de-lys,
196    Doun þe bonke con boʒe bydene.
Al blysnande whyt watʒ hir beau mys,
Vpon at sydeʒ and bounden bene

---

166    schore] shore: Go, C.
179    atount] a[s]tount: G, Ch, AW.
185    hope] hope[d]: G, Ch, Go, C, AW.
192    precos] prec[i]os: eds.

Gleaming white was her silk attire.
164 I knew her well; I had seen her before.
Like glistening gold that one does shear,
So sparkled that bright child below [the] cliff.
At length I looked at her there;
168 The longer [I looked], I knew her more and more.

The more I scrutinized her fair face,
After I had perceived her excellent form,
Such gladdening glory did glide to me,
172 As shortly before [it] was also accustomed [to do].
[The] desire to call her did impel me,
But bewilderment struck my heart a blow.
I saw her in so strange a place;
176 Such a shock could render my mind senseless.
Then she lifts up her lovely face,
Her visage white as smooth ivory.
That stung my mind, dazed quite uncontrollably,
180 And ever the longer, the more and more.


IV


f. 45b More than I desired my uneasiness increased;
I stood very still and dared not call.
With eyes open and mouth fully closed,
184 I remained as reserved as [a] hawk in [a] hall.
I imagined that the meaning was spiritual;
I feared concerning what would happen,
Afraid that she whom I found there might escape from me,
188 Before I could delay her with speech.
That beautiful, bright maiden without blemish,
So smooth, so small, so suitably slender,
Rises up in her royal array,
192 A precious damsel, adorned with pearls.

Adorned pearls of royal value
There could one, through good fortune, have seen
When that delightful damsel, like [the color of]
    fleur-de-lis,
196 Down the slope did stroll forthwith.
All shining white was her excellent cloak,
Open at [the] sides and bound beautifully

---

197 beau mys] Orig. shows five minims between a and y.
    beau uiys: M. b[leaunt of biys]: O. beau biys:
    Go, C, Mo, AW. beaumys: MS, H, De.


19

Wyth þe myryeste margarys, at my deuyse,
200   Þat euer I seȝ ȝet with myn yȝen,
Wyth lappeȝ large, I wot and I wene,
Dubbed with double perle and dyȝte.
Her cortel of self sute schene
204   Wyth precios perleȝ al vmbepyȝte.

A pyȝt coroune ȝet wer þat gyrle,
Of marjorys, and non oþer ston,
Hiȝe pynakled of cler quyt perle,
208   Wyth flurted flowreȝ, perfet vpon.
To hed hade ho non oþer werle.
Her lere-leke al hyr vmbegon,
Her semblaunt sade for doc oþer erle;
212   Her ble more blaȝt þen whalleȝ bon.
As schorne golde schyr her fax þenne schon,
On schyldereȝ þat leghe vnlapped lyȝte.
Her depe colour, ȝet, wonted non
216   Of precios perle in porfyl pyȝte.

f. 46   Pyȝt watȝ poyned and vche a hemme,
At honde, at sydeȝ, at ouerture,
Wyth whyte perle, and non oþer gemme;
220   And bornyste quyte watȝ hyr uesture.
Bot, a wonder perle wythouten wemme
Inmyddeȝ hyr breste watȝ sette so sure,
A manneȝ dom moȝt dryȝly demme
224   Er mynde moȝt malte in hit mesure.
I hope no tong moȝt endure
No sauerly saghe say of þat syȝt,
So watȝ hit clene, and cler and pure,
228   Þat precios perle, þer hit watȝ pyȝt.

Pyȝt in perle, þat precios pyse
On wyþer half water com doun þe schore.
No gladder gome, heþen into Grece,
232   Þen I quen ho on brymme wore.
Ho watȝ me nerre þen aunte or nece;
My joy, forþy, watȝ much þe more.
Ho profered me speche, þat special spyce,
236   Enclynande lowe, in wommon lore,

---

200   yȝen] [ene]: G, Ch, Go.  yzen: Mo.
208   flowreȝ] flowereȝ: H, De.
209   werle] [h]erle: O.
210   lere-leke] here heke: M, G.  [h]ere-leke: O, Ch.
         here leke: Go, Mo.  lere leke: MS, H, C, De.
215   colour] color: Ch.

|       | With the finest pearls, in my opinion, |
| 200   | That I ever yet saw with my eyes, |
|       | With large, loose sleeves, I know, indeed, |
|       | Adorned and set with paired pearls. |
|       | Her kirtle of [the] same gleaming pattern |
| 204   | Was completely surrounded with precious pearls. |

|       | That girl also wore a decorated crown |
|       | Of margarites, and no other gem, |
|       | Pinnacled high with clear white pearls, |
| 208   | With ornamented flowers, perfectly spread. |
|       | On [her] head she had no other circlet. |
|       | Her face cambric encompassing her [cheeks] completely, |
|       | Her appearance was fit for [a] duke or [an] earl; |
| 212   | Her complexion [was] more white than ivory. |
|       | Like pure, shorn gold then shone her hair, |
|       | Which lay lightly unclasped on [her] shoulders. |
|       | Her wide collar, moreover, was not void |
| 216   | Of precious pearls arrayed on [the] borders. |

| f. 46 | Adorned was [each] wristlet and every hem, |
|       | At hands, at sides, at openings, |
|       | With white pearls, and no other gem; |
| 220   | And shining white was her vesture. |
|       | Moreover, a marvelous pearl without flaw |
|       | Was set so securely amid her breast, |
|       | A man's mind might incessantly be frustrated |
| 224   | Before [his] reason could conceive of its value. |
|       | I imagine no tongue could suffice |
|       | To say any enthusiastic word of that sight, |
|       | So elegant it was, and bright and pure, |
| 228   | That precious pearl, where it was adorned. |

|       | Adorned in pearls, that precious damsel |
|       | Came down the shore on [the] opposite side of the |
|       |     stream. |
|       | No happier man [there was], from here into Greece, |
| 232   | Than I when she was at [the] edge. |
|       | She was nearer to me than aunt or niece; |
|       | My joy, therefore, was much the more. |
|       | She proffered me speech, that special damsel, |
| 236   | Bowing low, according to [a] woman's way, |

---

217 Pyȝt watȝ poyned and] Pyȝt & poyned watȝ: O, Ch.
225 tong] tong[e]: G, Ch.
229 pyse] p[r]yse: M.  py[ec]e: O, G, Ch, Go, Mo.  p[ec]e: H.
    pyce: De.
235 spyce: sp[e]ce: O, G, Ch, Go, H, De, Mo.    profered]
    O, G, H, De, and Mo read MS pfered, but the abbr.
    mark for ro is visible to the left of the p.

21

Ca3te of her coroun of grete tresore,
And haylsed me wyth a lote ly3te.
Wel wat3 me þat euer I wat3 bore,
240    To sware þat swete in perle3 py3te.


THE VISION--PART TWO: THE HOMILETIC CENTER


V

"**O**perle," quoþ I, "in perle3 py3t,
Art þou my perle þat I haf playned,
Regretted by myn one on ny3te?
244    Much longeyng haf I for þe layned,
Syþen into gresse þou me agly3te.
Pensyf, payred, I am forpayned,
And þou in a lyf of lykyng ly3te,
248    In Paradys erde, of stryf vnstrayned.
What wyrde hat3 hyder my juel vayned
And don me in þys del and gret daunger?
Fro we in twynne wern towen and twayned,
252    I haf ben a joyle3 juelere."


f. 46b   That juel, þenne, in gemme3 gente,
Vered vp her vyse wyth y3en graye,
Set on hyr coroun of perle orient,
256    And soberly after þenne con ho say:
"Sir, 3e haf your tale mysetente,
To say your perle is al awaye,
Þat is in cofer so comly clente,
260    As in þis gardyn, gracios gaye,
Hereinne to lenge foreuer and play,
Þer mys nee mornyng com neuer here.
Her were a forser for þe, in faye,
264    If þou were a gentyl jueler.

"Bot, jueler gente, if þou schal lose
Þy joy for a gemme þat þe wat3 lef,
Me þynk þe put in a mad porpose,
268    And busye3 þe aboute a raysoun bref,

---

241  quoþ] quod: M, O, Go, H, C, De. (also in 279, 325, 421,
       469, 569, 746, 758, 781, 902, and 1182)
253  gemme3] gemmy3: M. Second e is not clearly made; it may
       have been altered from y.

Took off her crown of great value,
And hailed me with a cheerful voice.
Well was [it] for me that ever I was born,
240    To answer that sweet girl in pearls adorned.


THE VISION--PART TWO: THE HOMILETIC CENTER


V

"O pearl," said I, "in pearls adorned,
Are you my pearl for whom I have lamented,
Grieving by myself alone at night?
244    Much longing have I concealed for you,
Since you slipped away from me into [the] grass.
Pensive, afflicted, I am tormented,
While you are settled in a life of delight,
248    In [this] land of Paradise, freed from strife.
What fate has sent my jewel here
And forced me into this sadness and severe frustration?
Since we were pulled apart and separated,
252    I have been a joyless jeweler."

f. 46b    That jewel, then, in splendid gems,
Lifted up her face with gray eyes,
Put on her crown of oriental pearl,
256    And afterwards she did seriously say:
"Sir, you have misdirected your speech,
To say your pearl is entirely absent,
That is so fittingly enclosed in [a] coffer,
260    As in this garden, beautifully bright,
Herein to linger forever and exult,
Here where loss nor lamentation never enter.
Here would be a coffer for you, in truth,
264    If you were a noble jeweler.

"Moreover, noble jeweler, if you shall lose
Your joy for a gem that was dear to you,
[It] seems to me you apply [yourself] to a foolish
      purpose,
268    And concern yourself about a transient matter,

---

262  nee] ne: G.  Neither e is clearly made.    here] [n]ere:
     O, G, Go, C, Mo, AW.  ner: Ch.
268  busyeȝ] Bottom of the b is open.  M noted, "Looks like
     husyeȝ in MS."

For þat þou lesteȝ watȝ bot a rose
Þat flowred and fayled as kynde hyt gef.
Now þurȝ kynde of þe kyste þat hyt con close,
272    To a perle of prys hit is put in pref;
And þou hatȝ called þy wyrde a þef,
Þat oȝt of noȝt hatȝ mad þe cler.
Þou blameȝ þe bote of þy meschef;
276    Þou art no kynde jueler."


A juel to me, þen, watȝ þys geste,
And jueleȝ wern hyr gentyl saweȝ.
"Iwyse," quoþ I, "my blysfol beste,
280    My grete dystresse þou al todraweȝ.
To be excused I make requeste;
I trawed my perle don out of daweȝ.
Now haf I fonde hyt, I schal ma feste,
284    And wony wyth hyt in schyr wodschaweȝ,
And loue my Lorde and al his laweȝ,
Þat hatȝ me broȝ þys blys ner.
Now were I at yow byȝonde þise waweȝ,
288    I were a joyfol jueler."


f. 47    "Jueler," sayde þat gemme clene,
"Wy borde ȝe men? So madde ȝe be!
Þre wordeȝ hatȝ þou spoken at ene;
292    Vnavysed, forsoþe, wern alle þre.
Þou ne woste in worlde quat on dotȝ mene;
Þy worde byfore þy wytte con fle.
Þou says þou traweȝ me in þis dene
296    Bycawse þou may wyth yȝen me se.
Anoþer, þou says in þys countré
Þyself schal won wyth me ryȝt here.
Þe þrydde, to passe þys water fre--
300    Þat may no joyfol jueler.


VI


"I halde þat jueler lyttel to prayse,
Þat loueȝ wel þat he seȝ wyth yȝe,
And much to blame and vncortoyse,
304    Þat leueȝ oure Lorde wolde make a lyȝe,

---

286  broȝ] broȝ[t]: M, O, G, Ch, Go, C, AW.    blys] blys[se]:
    G, Ch.
288  joyfol] ioyful: Go. joyful: C.
293-94] A hole in the vellum separates *quat* from *on* (293)
    and *wytte* from *con* (294).
302  loueȝ] l[e]ueȝ: G, Ch, Go, H, C, Mo, AW.

24

For what you lost was but a rose
That flowered and faded as nature directed it.
Now through [the] nature of the coffer that does
    enclose it,
272      It is established with certainty as a pearl of price;
And you have called your fate a thief,
That has clearly made for you something from nothing.
You censure the remedy of your misfortune;
276      You are no gracious jeweler."

A jewel to·me, then, was this child,
And her gentle words were jewels.
"Indeed," said I, "my beautiful, most noble maiden,
280      You completely dispel my great distress.
I make entreaty to be excused;
I believed my pearl was deprived of life.
Since I have found it, I shall rejoice,
284      And dwell with it in bright groves,
And honor my Lord and all his laws,
Who has brought me near this bliss.
Now were I with you beyond these waves,
288      I would be a joyful jeweler."

f. 47    "Jeweler," said that pure gem,
"Why do you men speak lightly? You are so foolish!
You have uttered three statements simultaneously;
292      Unwise, indeed, were all three.
You know not what in [the] world one does mean;
Your speech does run before your reason.
You say you believe me [to be] in this valley
296      Because you can see me with [your] eyes.
A second [thing], you say in this region
[You] yourself shall dwell with me right here.
The third, to cross this splendid stream—
300      That may no joyful jeweler [do].


VI


"I consider that jeweler little to be praised,
Who honors fully what he sees with eye,
And much to be blamed and discourteous,
304      Who believes our Lord would create a lie,

---

303   vncortoyse] vncort[a]yse: O, G, Ch, Go, C, Mo.
304   leue3] loue3 (Looks at first sight like *lyue3*--MS.
      rubbed, but read *leue3*.): M. Go noted, "lyue3
      *altered to* leue3 *in* MS." UVR does not clarify.
      There is either a badly made *e* after *l* or an altera-
      tion.

Þat lelly hyȝte your lyf to rayse,
Þaȝ fortune dyd your flesch to dyȝe.
Ȝe setten hys wordeȝ ful west ernays,
308 Þat loueȝ noþynk bot ȝe hit syȝe;
And þat is a poynt o sorquydryȝe,
Þat vche god mon may euel byseme,
To leue no tale be true to tryȝe,
312 Bot þat hys one skyl may dem.

"Deme now þyself if þou con dayly,
As man to God wordeȝ schulde heue.
Þou saytȝ þou schal won in þis bayly;
316 Me þynk þe burde fyrst aske leue,
And ȝet of graunt þou myȝteȝ fayle.
Þou wylneȝ ouer þys water to weue;
Er moste þou ceuer to oþer counsayl.
320 Þy corse in clot mot calder keue,
For hit watȝ forgarte at Paradys greue.
Oure ȝorefader hit con mysseȝeme.
Þurȝ drwry deth boȝ vch ma dreue
324 Er ouer þys dam hym Dryȝtyn deme."

f. 47b "Demeȝ þou me," quoþ I, "my swete.
To dol agayn þenne I dowyne.
Now haf I fonte þat I forlete,
328 Schal I efte forgo hit er euer I fyne?
Why schal I hit boþe mysse and mete?
My precios perle dotȝ me gret pyne.
What serueȝ tresor bot gareȝ men grete
332 When he hit schal efte wyth teneȝ tyne?
Now rech I neuer for to declyne,
Ne how fer of folde þat man me fleme.
When I am partleȝ of perle myne,
336 Bot durande doel what may men deme?"

"Thow demeȝ noȝt bot doel-dystresse,"
Þenne sayde þat wyȝt. "Why dotȝ þou so?
For dyne of doel of lureȝ lesse,
340 Ofte mony mon forgos þe mo.

---

307 west ernays] westernays: MS, M, G, Go, C, De, Mo, AW.
[b]esternays: O. bestornays: Ch.
308 loueȝ] loueȝ (Read leueȝ.): M. l[e]ueȝ: other eds.
309 is] Īs: MS.
312 dem] dem[e]: M, G, Ch.
313 dayly] dayle: Ch.
315 bayly] bayle: Ch.

26

Who faithfully promised to raise your spirit,
Though fortune condemned your body to die.
You who honor nothing unless you see it
308 Make his words indeed [an] idle pledge;
And that is a point of pride,
Which may ill befit every good man,
To believe no story is to be considered trustworthy,
312 Except that which his reason alone can judge.

"Judge now yourself if you did speak courteously,
As one should present words to God.
You say you shall dwell in this domain;
316 [It] seems to me you ought to ask permission first,
And you might still fail to obtain consent.
You desire to cross over this stream;
First you must submit to another plan.
320 Your body must sink more coldly into clay,
For it was condemned in [the] grove of Paradise.
Our old father did forfeit it.
Through mournful death must each man pass
324 Before God will direct him across this stream."

f. 47b "You censure me," said I, "my sweet maiden.
Then I must languish again in sorrow.
Since I have found what I had lost,
328 Must I again surrender it before I die?
Why must I both lose and find it?
My precious pearl causes me great anxiety.
What does treasure avail if [it] makes men lament
332 When they must afterwards surrender it with sufferings?
I could never care now about falling from fortune,
Nor how far from land that man may banish me.
When I am deprived of my pearl,
336 What can men expect but enduring distress?"

"You describe nothing but distress of sorrow,"
Then said that damsel. "Why do you [behave] so?
For cries of mourning concerning insignificant losses,
340 Many men often forsake the greater happiness.

---

319  counsayl] counsayl[e]: G, Ch, Go.
323  ma] man: Go, C, Mo, AW.
329-30] A hole in the vellum separates m from ete of mete
        (329) and q from ret of gret (330).
331  gareʒ] gare: G.
335  perle] perleʒ: MS, M, H, De.

Þe oȝte better þyseluen blesse,
And loue ay God, and wele and wo,
For anger gayneȝ þe not a cresse,
344   Who nedeȝ schal þole. Be not so þro,
For þoȝ þou daunce as any do,
Braundysch and bray þy braþeȝ breme,
When þou no fyrre may, to ne fro,
348   Þou moste abyde þat he schal deme.


"Deme Dryȝtyn; euer hym adyte.
Of þe way a fote ne wyl he wryþe.
Þy mendeȝ mounteȝ not a myte,
352   Þaȝ þou, for sorȝe, be neuer blyþe.
Stynst of þy strot and fyne to flyte,
And sech hys blyþe ful swefte and swyþe.
Þy prayer may hys pyté byte,
356   Þat mercy schal hyr crafteȝ kyþe.
Hys comforte may þy langour lyþe,
And þy lureȝ of lyȝtly leme;
For marre oþer madde, morne and myþe,
360   Al lys in hym to dyȝt and deme."


                    VII

f. 48   Thenne demed I to þat damyselle:
        "Ne worþe no wrathþe vnto my Lorde,
        If rapely raue, spornande in spelle.
364   My herte watȝ al wyth mysse remorde,
As wallande water gotȝ out of welle.
I do me ay in hys myserecorde.
Rebuke me neuer wyth wordeȝ felle,
368   Þaȝ I forloyne, my dere endorde,
Bot lyþeȝ me kyndely your coumforde,
Pytosly þenkande vpon þysse:
Of care and me ȝe made acorde,
372   Þat er watȝ grounde of alle my blysse.


"My blysse, my bale, ȝe han ben boþe,
Bot much þe bygger ȝet watȝ my mon.
Fro þou watȝ wroken fro vch a woþe,
376   I wyste neuer quere my perle watȝ gon.

---

342   and wele] & wele (*in* or *an*?): M.   [in] wele: G, Ch, Go,
        C, AW.
353   Stynst] Sty*n*t: G, Ch, Go, C, AW.
358   And þy] [Þat alle] þy: G.      lcme] fleme: Go, C, Mo, AW.
359   marre] marre[d]: O, G, Ch.

You ought rather to bless yourself,
And to love God always, both in prosperity and in
    misfortune,
For anguish gains you, who must necessarily suffer,
344    Nothing at all. Be not so perverse,
For though you may writhe like any doe,
Toss about and vociferate your fierce agonies,
When you can [go] no further, to nor fro,
348    You must endure what he shall ordain.

"Blame God; accuse him continually.
He will not turn a foot from the path.
Your consolations increase not a bit,
352    If you, because of grief, be never glad.
Cease from your strife and stop disputing,
And seek his mercy very swiftly and sincerely.
Your prayer may arouse his pity,
356    So that mercy shall reveal her virtues.
His solace may soften your misery,
And shine gently among your misfortunes;
For fret or fume, mourn and mutter,
360    All lies in him to determine and to ordain."

VII

f. 48    Then said I to that damsel:
"Let [there] be no offense against my Lord,
If hastily [I] rave, stumbling in speech.
364    My heart was entirely afflicted with loss,
Like pouring water [that] goes out of [a] well.
I place myself always at his mercy.
Rebuke me never with austere words,
368    Though I go astray, my precious, golden maiden,
But soothe me gently with your solace,
Compassionately being mindful of this:
You established harmony between care and me,
372    You who before were [the] basis of all my bliss.

"My bliss, my grief, you have been both,
But much the greater yet was my lamentation.
After you had been delivered from every tribulation,
376    I never knew where my pearl had gone.

---

362  wrathþe] wrath þe: MS, M.
363  rapely raue] rapely raue (rane?): M.  rapely [I] raue:
      other eds.
369  lyþeʒ] [k]yþeʒ: G, Ch, Go, C, AW.    your coumforde]
      [wyth] your coumforde: O.

Now I hit se; now leþeȝ my loþe.
And, quen we departed, we wern at on,
God forbede we be now wroþe.
380 We meten so selden by stok oþer ston.
Þaȝ cortaysly ȝe carp con,
I am bot mol and marereȝ mysse;
Bot Crystes mersy, and Mary and Jon--
384 Þise arn þe grounde of alle my blysse.

"In blysse I se þe blyþely blent,
And I a man al mornyf mate.
ȝe take þeron ful lyttel tente,
388 Þaȝ I hente ofte harmeȝ hate;
Bot now I am here in your presente,
I wolde bysech, wythouten debate,
ȝe wolde me say, in sobre asente,
392 What lyf ȝe lede erly and late,
For I am ful fayn þat your astate
Is worþen to worschyp and wele, iwysse.
Of alle my joy, þe hyȝe gate,
396 Hit is in grounde of alle my blysse."

f. 48b   "Now blysse, burne, mot þe bytyde,"
Þen sayde þat lufsoum of lyth and lere,
"And welcum here to walk and vyde,
400 For now þy speche is to me dere.
Maysterful mod and hyȝe pryde,
I hete þe, arn heterly hated here.
My Lorde ne loueȝ not for to chyde,
404 For meke arn alle þat woneȝ hym nere;
And when in hys place þou schal apere,
Be dep deuote, in hol mekenesse.
My Lorde þe Lamb loueȝ ay such chere,
408 Þat is þe grounde of alle my blysse.

"A blysful lyf þou says I lede;
Þou woldeȝ knaw þerof þe stage.
Þow wost wel when þy perle con schede,
412 I watȝ ful ȝong and tender of age,
Bot my Lorde þe Lombe, þurȝ hys Godhede,
He toke myself to hys maryage,

---

381  carp] carp[e]: G, Ch.
382  marereȝ] ma[n]ereȝ: G, Ch, Go, C, AW.   mare reȝ: H, De.
         mariereȝ: Mo.
396  in] and: C.

Now I see it; now my sorrow is soothed.
If, when we were parted, we were in harmony,
God forbid we be angry now.
380 We meet so seldom by stock or stone.
Though you can speak courteously,
I am but dust and lack vitality;
But Christ's mercy, and Mary and John--
384 These are the basis of all my bliss.

"I see you are eagerly engulfed in bliss,
And I [am] a man all mournfully subdued.
You pay very little attention to it,
388 Though I am often caught by cruel misfortunes;
But since I am here in your presence,
I would urge, without debate,
[That] you would tell me, with serious intention,
392 What life you lead all the time,
For I am extremely happy that your condition
Has come, indeed, to honor and well-being.
Of all my joy, the special kind,
396 It is at [the] basis of all my bliss."

f. 48b "Now may bliss befall you, sir,"
Then said that lovely one of figure and face,
"And [you are] welcome to walk and wade here,
400 For now your speech is pleasing to me.
Masterful mood and arrogant pride,
I assure you, are intensely despised here.
My Lord does not like to dispute,
404 For all who dwell near him are gentle;
And when you shall appear in his abode,
Be deeply devout, with complete meekness.
My Lord the Lamb always loves such behavior,
408 He who is the basis of all my bliss.

"A blissful life you say I lead;
You would know thereof the stage.
You know well when your pearl slipped away,
412 I was very young and tender of age,
But my Lord the Lamb, through his Godhead,
Accepted me for his marriage,

---

399 vyde] byde: eds. UVR does not clarify the first letter,
which is spread on the bottom, but as a *v* it may be
compared to the *v* of *vnto* 772.
406 mekenesse] mekenysse: Ch.

31

Corounde me quene in blysse to brede
416 In lenghe of daye3 þat euer schal wage;
And sesed in alle hys herytage
Hys lef is. I am holy hysse,
Hys pyese, hys prys; and hys parage
420 Is rote and grounde of alle my blysse."


## VIII

"**B**lysful," quoþ I, "may þys be trwe?
Dysplese3 not if I speke errour.
Art þou þe quene of heuene3 blwe,
424 Þat al þys worlde schal do honour?
We leuen on Marye, þat Grace of grewe,
Þat ber a Barne, of Vyrgyn Flour.
Þe croune fro hyr quo mo3t remwe,
428 Bot ho hir passed in sum fauour?
Now, for synglerty o hyr dousour,
We calle hyr Fenyx of Arraby,
Þat, freles, fle3e of hyr Fasor,
432 Lyk to þe Quen of Cortaysye."


f. 49 "Cortayse Quen," þenne syde þat gaye,
Knelande to grounde, folde vp hyr face,
"Makele3 Moder and myryest May,
436 Blessed Bygynner of vch a grace!"
Þenne ros ho vp and con restay,
And speke me towarde in þat space.
"Sir, fele here porchase3 and fonge3 pray,
440 Bot supplantore3 none wythinne þys place.
Þat Emperise al heuen3 hat3,
And vrþe and helle in her bayly.
Of erytage, 3et, non wyl ho chace,
444 For ho is Quen of Cortaysye.

"The court of þe kyndom of God alyue
Hat3 a property in hyt self beyng.
Alle þat may þerinne aryue
448 Of alle þe reme is quen oþer kyng,
And neuer oþer 3et schal depryue;
Bot, vch on fayn of oþere3 hafyng,

---

419 pyese] prese: eds. UVR does not clarify the second lette
completely, but it does resemble the top of a y with
its bottom illegible.
426 Vyrgyn Flour] vyrgyn flour: MS, M, G, Go, C, Mo, AW.
vyrgynflour: O, Ch. vyrgynflor: H, De.
430 Arraby] Arrabye: Ch.

Crowned me queen to dwell in bliss
416 In length of days that shall always endure;
And endowed with all his heritage
Is his beloved. I am entirely his,
His maiden, his honored one; and his lineage
420 Is [the] root and basis of all my bliss."

VIII

"Blissful one," said I, "can this be true?
Be not displeased if I speak with ignorance.
Are you the queen of [the] blue heavens,
424 To whom all this world must extend honor?
We accept only Mary, from whom Grace came,
Who bore a Child, Flower of [the] Virgin.
Who could remove the crown from her,
428 Unless she surpassed her in some virtue?
Now, because of [the] singularity of her sweetness,
We call her Phoenix of Araby,
Who, without fault, flew from her Creator,
432 Similar to the Queen of Courtesy."

f. 49 "Courteous Queen," then said that fair maiden,
Kneeling to [the] ground, covering up her face,
"Matchless Mother and brightest Virgin,
436 Blessed Beginner of every grace!"
Then she rose up and did delay,
And spoke to me after that interval.
"Sir, many strive for here and receive [the] reward,
440 But no usurpers [are] within this abode.
That Empress possesses all [the] heavens,
And earth and hell in her jurisdiction.
Yet, she will deprive no one of [his] heritage,
444 For she is [the] Queen of Courtesy.

"The court of the kingdom of [the] living God
Has an attribute in its very being.
Everybody who may arrive in that place
448 Is queen or king of all the realm,
And yet shall never deprive [the] others;
Moreover, each one [is] happy because of [the]
        others' having,

---

431 freles] ferles: Mo.   fereles: AW.      fleʒe] fleze: Mo.
        Fasor] fasour: Ch.
433 syde] s[a]yde: eds.
436 Bygynner] bȳgyner: MS.   bygyner: De, Mo.
441 heuenʒ] heuen[e]ʒ: O, Ch, H, De.
442 bayly] baylye: Ch.

33

And wolde her corouneȝ wern worþe þo fyue,
452   If possyble were her mendyng;
Bot my Lady, of quom Jesu con spryng,
Ho haldeȝ þe empyre ouer vus ful hyȝe,
And þat dyspleseȝ non of oure gyng,
456   For ho is Quene of Cortaysye.

"Of courtaysye, as saytȝ Saynt Poule,
Al arn we membreȝ of Jhesu Kryst.
As heued and arme and legg and naule
460   Temen to hys body, ful trwe and tyste,
Ryȝt so is vch a Krysten sawle
A longande lym to þe Mayster of Myste.
Þenne loke what hate oþer any gawle
464   Is tached oþer tyȝed þy lymmeȝ bytwyste.
Þy heued hatȝ nauþer greme ne gryste
On arme oþer fynger, þaȝ þou ber byȝe.
So fare we alle wyth luf and lyste
468   To kyng and quene by cortaysye."

f. 49b   "Cortaysé," quoþ I, "I leue,
And charyté grete be yow among,
Bot my speche þat yow ne greue--
472   . . . . . . . . . . . . . . . . . . . .
Þyself in heuen ouer hyȝ þou heue,
To make þe quen, þat watȝ so ȝonge.
What more honour moȝte he acheue,
476   Þat hade endured in worlde stronge,
And lyued in penaunce hys lyueȝ longe,
Wyth bodyly bale hym blysse to byye?
What more worschyp moȝt ho fonge
480   Þen corounde be kyng by cortaysé?

IX

"That cortaysé is to fre of dede,
ȝyf hyt be soth þat þou coneȝ saye.
Þou lyfed not two ȝer in oure þede.
484   Þou cowþeȝ neuer God nauþer plese ne pray,

---

457   Poule] P[a]ule: O, G, Ch.
458   Jhesu] ihū: MS. ihesu: M. Jesu: other eds. (See also
        the textual note to 711.)
460   tyste] t[r]yste: all eds. except O.
461   sawle] G, Go, Mo, and AW read MS sawhe, but in the Orig.
        the darker brown ink on the e indicates a correction
        may heve been made to sawle.

34

|       | And would wish their crowns were then worth five, |
| 452   | If their improvement were possible; |
|       | But my Lady, from whom Jesus did spring, |
|       | Holds the empire full high over us, |
|       | And that displeases no one in our assemblage, |
| 456   | For she is [the] Queen of Courtesy. |

|       | "Due to courtesy, as says Saint Paul, |
|       | We are all members of Jesus Christ. |
|       | As head and arm and leg and navel |
| 460   | Belong to his body, fully secure and joined, |
|       | Just so is every Christian soul |
|       | A member belonging to the Master of Spiritual Mysteries. |
|       | Then observe to what degree hate or any envy |
| 464   | Is rooted or fastened among your limbs. |
|       | Your head has neither anger nor resentment |
|       | Against arm or finger, though you wear jewelry. |
|       | Thus we all exist in love and happiness |
| 468   | As kings and queens with courtesy." |

| f. 49b | "I believe," said I, "courtesy |
|        | And great charity are among you, |
|        | But since my conversation does not offend you-- |
| 472    | . . . . . . . . . . . . . . . . . . . . . . |
|        | You raise yourself too high in heaven, |
|        | To make yourself queen, who had been so young. |
|        | What more honor might he achieve, |
| 476    | Who had endured steadfastly in [the] world, |
|        | And lived in penance throughout the length of his life, |
|        | To secure happiness for himself through human suffering? |
|        | What greater honor might he obtain |
| 480    | Than to be crowned king through courtesy? |

IX

|       | "That courtesy is too liberal in action, |
|       | If it be true what you do say. |
|       | You lived not two years in our land. |
| 484   | You could never either please God or pray, |

---

469  Cortaysé] Cortays[y]e: G, Ch.
473] Marks at end of line 473 indicate someone noticed that
        line 472 is missing.
475  more honour] more-hond: M.
479  ho] h[e]: all eds. except M.
480  cortaysé] cortays[y]e: O, G, Ch.
481  cortaysé] cortays[y]e: G, Ch.

Ne neuer nawþer Pater ne Crede,
And quen mad on þe fyrst day!
I may not traw, so God me spede,
488   Þat God wolde wryþe so wrange away.
Of countes, damysel, par ma fay,
Wer fayr in heuen to halde asstate,
Oþer elleȝ a lady of lasse aray;
492   Bot a quene--hit is to dere a date!"

"Þer is no date of hys godnesse,"
Þen sayde to me þat worþy wyȝte,
"For al is trawþe þat he con dresse,
496   And he may do noþynk bot ryȝt.
As Mathew meleȝ in your messe
In sothfol Gospel of God Almyȝt,
Insample he can ful grayþely gesse,
500   And lykneȝ hit to heuen lyȝte.
'My regne,' he saytȝ, 'is lyk on hyȝt
To a lorde þat hade a uyne I wate.
Of tyme of ȝere þe terme watȝ tyȝt,
504   To labor vyne watȝ dere þe date.

f. 50   "'Þat date of ȝere wel knawe þys hyne.
Þe lorde ful erly vp he ros
To hyre werkmen to hys vyne,
508   And fyndeȝ þer summe to hys porpos.
Into accorde þay con declyne
For a pené on a day, and forth þay gotȝ,
Wryþen, and worchen, and don gret pyne,
512   Keruen, and caggen, and man hit clos.
Aboute vnder þe lorde to marked totȝ,
And ydel men stande he fyndeȝ þerate.
"Why stande ȝe ydel?" he sayde to þos.
516   "Ne knawe ȝe of þis day no date?"

"'"Er date of daye hider arn we wonne."
So watȝ al samen her answar soȝt.
"We haf standen her syn ros þe sunne,
520   And no mon byddeȝ vus do ryȝt noȝt."
"Gos into my vyne; dotȝ þat ȝe conne."
So sayde þe lorde and made hit toȝt.
"What resonabele hyre be naȝt be runne
524   I yow pray, in dede and þoȝte."

---

486   fyrst] fyrst[e]: G, Ch.
491   Oþer] Aþer: M, O, Ch. Oþen: De.
499   Insample] in sample: MS. In sample: M, O, Go, C, H, De,
          Mo, AW.

Not ever either Pater or Creed,
And on the first day [you were] made [a] queen!
I can not believe, so may God bless me,
488 That God would turn so wrongly away [from right].
As [a] countess, damsel, by my faith,
[It] would be proper to hold rank in heaven,
Or else a lady of lower position;
492 But a queen--that is too glorious a beginning!"

"There is no end to his goodness,"
That worthy maiden then said to me,
"For everything that he does ordain is truth,
496 And he can do nothing but right.
As Matthew tells in your mass
In [the] truthful Gospel of Almighty God,
He does very fittingly devise [a] parable,
500 And compares it to radiant heaven.
'My realm,' he says, 'on high is similar
To a lord who had a vineyard I know.
At [the] time of year the period was appointed,
504 The season was excellent to cultivate [the] vineyard.

f. 50 "'These households know well that season of [the] year.
The lord rose up very early
To hire workmen for his vineyard,
508 And finds there some for his purpose.
They do submit to [an] agreement
For a penny a day, and they go forth,
Twist about, and toil, and exert great effort,
512 Cut, and bind, and make them (the vines) secure.
About the third hour the lord to [the] market goes,
And he finds idle men standing in that place.
"Why do you stand idle?" he said to them.
516 "Do you not know [the] hour of this day?"

"'"We have come here before [the] dawning of day."
Thus was their answer given all together.
"We have stood here since the sun rose,
520 And no man has asked us to do anything at all."
"Go into my vineyard; do what you can."
Thus said the lord and made it binding.
"I ask of you, in action and intention,
524 What reasonable service may be discharged by night."

---

505  þys] [h]ys: G.
510  on] omitted by G.
523  resonabele] resnabele: G.
524  pray] pay: M, O, G, Ch, Go, C, Mo, AW.

Þay wente into þe vyne and wroȝte,
And al day þe lorde þus ȝede his gate,
And nw men to hys vyne he broȝte
528    Welneȝ wyl day watȝ passed date.

"'At þe day, of date of euensonge,
On oure byfore þe sonne go doun,
He seȝ þer ydel men, ful stronge,
532    And sade to hen wyth sobre soun,
"Wy stonde ȝe ydel þise dayeȝ longe?"
Þay sayden her hyre watȝ nawhere boun.
"Gotȝ to my vyne, ȝe men ȝonge,
536    And wyrkeȝ and dotȝ þat at ȝe moun."
Sone þe worlde bycom wel broun;
Þe sunne watȝ doun, and and hit wex late,
To take her hyre he mad sumoun.
540    Þe day watȝ al apassed date.

X

"'The date of þe daye þe lorde con knaw;
Called to þe reue: "Lede, pay þe meyny.
Gyf hem þe hyre þat I hem owe,
544    And, fyrre, þat non me may reprené,
Set hem alle vpon a rawe,
And gyf vch on inlyche a peny.
Bygyn at þe laste þat standeȝ lowe,
548    Tyl to þe fyrste þat þou atteny."
And þenne þe fyrst bygonne to pleny,
And sayden þat þay hade trauayled sore.
"Þese bot on oure hem con streny.
552    Vus þynk vus oȝe to take more.

"'"More haf we serued, vus þynk so,
Þat suffred han þe dayeȝ hete,
Þenn þyse þat wroȝt not houreȝ two;
556    And þou dotȝ hem vus to counterfete!"

---

527   nw] nw[e]: G, Ch.
529   day, of date] date of day: O, G, Ch, Go, C, Mo, AW.
532   sade] Thin line under d, like bottom stroke of y, indi-
       cates d may have been corrected from y. sa[y]de: M,
       O, Ch.   hen] hem: eds.
535   ȝe men] ȝemen: MS, eds.
538   and and] and: M, O, G, Ch, Go, C, Mo, AW.
542   meyny] meny: G.  meyne: Ch.
543   owe] [a]we: G, Ch.

They went into the vineyard and worked,
And all day the lord thus went his way,
And he brought new men to his vineyard
528  Almost until [the] day had passed [its] end.

"'During the day, about [the] time of evensong,
One hour before the sun would go down,
He saw there idle men, very strong,
532  And said to [the] laborers in [a] serious voice,
"Why do you stand idle throughout the length of this day?"
They said their hiring had been nowhere arranged.
"Go to my vineyard, you young men,
536  And work and do that which you can."
Soon the earth became very dark;
The sun was down, and when it had grown late,
He gave summons [for all] to receive their payment.
540  The day had entirely passed [its] end.

X

f. 50b  "'The lord did know the time of the day;
[He] called to the reeve: "Man, pay the group.
Give them the wage that I owe them,
544  And, furthermore, so that no one may censure me,
Set them all in a row,
And give each one fully a penny.
Begin with the last who stand low,
548  Until you reach to the first."
And then the first began to complain,
And said that they had labored strenuously.
"These did strain themselves only one hour.
552  [It] seems to us we ought to receive more.

"'"We have deserved more, so [it] seems to us,
Who have endured the day's heat,
Than those who toiled not two hours;
556  And you consider them to be like us!"

---

544  reprené] repreue: M.  repren[y]: O, G, H.  reprene: MS,
          Ch, De, Mo.
546  peny] pene: Ch.
547  lowe] l[a]we: G, Ch.
548  atteny] attene: Ch.
549  pleny] plene: Ch.
550  hade] had: H, De.
551  on oure] an [h]oure: M.     streny] strene: Ch.
555  wroӡt] wroӡt[e]: M.

39

Þenne sayde þe lorde to on of þo:
"Frende, no waning I wyl þe ȝete.
Take þat is þyn owne and go.

560 And I hyred þe for a peny, agrete,
Quy bygynneȝ þou now to þrete?
Watȝ not a pené þy couenaunt þore?
Fyrre þen couenaunde is noȝt to plete.

564 Wy schalte þou, þenne, ask more?

"'"More, weþer, louyly is me my gyfte,
To do wyth myn quatso me lykeȝ,
Oþer elleȝ þyn yȝe to lyþer is lyfte

568 For I am goude and non byswykeȝ?"
'Þus schal I,' quoþ Kryste, 'hit skyfte.
Þe laste schal be þe fyrst þat strykeȝ,
And þe fyrst þe laste, be he neuer so swyft,

572 For mony ben calle, þaȝ fewe be mykeȝ.'
Þus pore men her part ay pykeȝ,
Þaȝ þay com late and lyttel wore,
And þaȝ her sweng wyth lyttel atslykeȝ,

576 Þe merci of God is much þe more.

f. 51 "More haf I of joye and blysse hereinne,
Of ladyschyp gret and lyueȝ blom,
Þen alle þe wyȝeȝ in þe worlde myȝt wynne,

580 By þe way of ryȝt to aske dome.
Wheþer welnygh now I con bygynne
In euentyde, into þe vyne I come.
Fyrst of my hyre my Lorde con mynne.

584 I watȝ payed anon, of al and sum.
Ȝet, oþer þer werne þat toke more tom,
Þat swange and swat for long ȝore,
Þat ȝet of hyre noþynk þay nom,

588 Paraunter noȝt schal to ȝere more."

Then more I meled and sayde apert:
"Me þynk þy tale vnresounable.
Goddeȝ ryȝt is redy and euermore rert,

592 Oþer Holy Wryt is bot a fable.
In Sauter is sayd a verce ouerte,
Þat spekeȝ a poynt determynable.

---

557  on] MS has *om*, with third minim crossed out.
558  waning] wanig: MS, H, De.  wrang: M.
560  agrete] a grete: M.
564  ask] ask[e]: G, Ch.
565  louyly] l[awe]ly: O, Ch.  l[e]uyly: G.

40

Then the lord said to one of them:
"Friend, I intend to do you no harm.
Take what is your own and go.
560      If I hired you for a penny, all told,
Why do you begin to wrangle now?
Was not a penny your compact then?
More than [that] payment is not to be claimed.
564      Why, then, shall you ask more?

"'"And yet, is my right to give more proper for me,
In doing with mine whatever pleases me,
Or else is your eye raised toward malice
568      Because I am generous and deprive no one?"
'Thus,' said Christ, 'shall I arrange it.
The last shall be the first who enters,
And the first the last, be he ever so swift,
572      For many are called, though few are [the] chosen ones.'
Thus humble men always obtain their share,
Though they may come late and expend little effort.
And though their labor may slip away with little result,
576      The mercy of God is much the more.

f. 51    "More have I of glory and bliss in this place,
Of great ladyship and life's supremacy,
Than all the people in the world might gain,
580      In seeking judgment through the means of justice.
Even if I did begin now almost
At eventide, into the vineyard I came.
My Lord did think of my reward first.
584      I was paid immediately, in every respect.
Yet, there were others who spent more time,
Who formerly had labored and sweat for [a] long while,
Who had yet received nothing of [their] reward,
588      [And] perhaps shall not for years more."

Then I spoke more and said openly:
"Your story seems unreasonable to me.
God's justice is prompt and forever fixed,
592      Or Holy Writ is but a fable.
In [the] Psalter a simple verse is spoken,
Which relates a definite point.

---

572    calle] calle[d]: M, O, G, Ch, Go, C, AW.
581    welnygh] wel nygh[t]: M.
586    long] long[e]: G, Ch.
588    to ȝere] toȝere: MS, O, G, Ch, Go, H, C, De, Mo, AW.
591    euermore] Final e is illegible.    rert] (ert?): M.

'Þou quyteȝ vch on as hys desserte,
596    Þou hyȝe Kyng, ay pertermynable.'
Now he þat stod þe long day stable,
And þou to payment com hym byfore,
Þenne þe lasse in werke to take more able,
600    And euer þe lenger, þe lasse, þe more."

XI

"Of more and lasse in Godeȝ ryche,"
Þat gentyl sayde, "lys no joparde,
For þer is vch mon payed inlyche,
604    Wheþer lyttel oþer much be hys rewarde;
For þe gentyl Cheuentayn is no chyche,
Queþersoeuer he dele nesch oþer harde.
He laueȝ hys gyfteȝ as water of dyche,
608    Oþer goteȝ of golf þat neuer charde.
Hys fraunchyse is large þat euer dard
To hym þat matȝ in synne rescoghe.
No blysse betȝ fro hem reparde,
612    For þe grace of God is gret inoghe.

f. 51b    "Bot, now þou moteȝ, me for to mate,
Þat I my peny haf wrang tan here.
Þou sayȝ þat I þat com to late
616    Am not worþy so gret lere.
Where wysteȝ þou euer any bourne abate,
Euer so holy in hys prayere,
Þat he ne forfeted by sumkyn gate
620    Þe mede, sumtyme, of heueneȝ clere?
And ay þe ofter þe alder þay were
Þay laften ryȝt and wroȝten woghe.
Mercy and grace moste hem þen stere,
624    For þe grace of God is gret innoȝe.

"Bot, innoghe of grace hatȝ innocent.
As sone as þay arn borne by lyne,
In þe water of babtem þay dyssente.
628    Þen arne þay boroȝt into þe vyne.
Anon, þe day, wyth derk endente,
Þe niȝt of deth dotȝ to enclyne.
Þat wroȝt neuer wrang er þenne þay wente,
632    Þe gentyle Lorde þenne payeȝ hys hyne.

_____

596    pertermynable] pretermynable: all eds. except AW.
610    rescoghe] no scoghe (In the MS. it looks like *rescoghe*.):
613    now] inow: Ch.
615    com] come: C, H, De.

42

'You reward each one according to his merit,
596 You high King, always judging perfectly.'
Now if you come for compensation before him
Who remained stable the long day,
Then those who work less are able to receive more,
600 And increasingly, the less [they do], the more [they
receive]."

## XI

"Concerning more and less in God's kingdom,"
That noble maiden said, "no confusion exists,
For each man there is fully compensated,
604 Whether little or much be his reward;
For the noble Chieftain is no miser,
Whether he act gently or firmly.
He pours forth his gifts like water from [a] drain,
608 Or currents in [a] whirlpool that never varied.
His privilege is great who always stood in awe
Of him who brings salvation from sin.
No blessing will be withheld from them,
612 For the grace of God is great enough.

f. 51b "Yet, now you claim, in order to disconcert me,
That I have obtained my penny wrongly here.
You say that I who came too late
616 Am not worthy of so excellent [an] abode.
Where did you ever know any man to bow humbly,
Always so holy in his devotion,
Who did not forfeit in some kind of way,
620 At some time, the reward of heaven's brightness?
And always the older they were the more often
They abandoned righteousness and did wrong.
Mercy and grace must guide them then,
624 For the grace of God is great enough.

"However, [the] innocent child has enough of grace.
As soon as they are born through lineal descent,
They descend into the water of baptism.
628 Then they are brought into the vineyard.
Soon, the day, adorned by dusk,
Does yield to the night of death.
Those who never did wrong before they departed,
632 The noble Lord then rewards as his servants.

---

616 lere] [h]ere: O, G, Ch.  fere: Go, C, Mo, AW.
628 boroȝt] broght: Ch.
630 niyȝt] myȝt: M, O, G, Ch, H, De.

43

Þay dyden hys heste; þay wern þereine.
Why schulde he not her labour alow--
3ys, and þay hym at þe fyrst fyne?
636 For þe grace of God is gret innoghe.

"Ino3e is knawen þat mankyn grete
Fyrste wat3 wro3t to blysse parfyt.
Oure forme-fader hit con forfete
640 Þur3 an apple þat he vpon con byte.
Al wer we dampned, for þat mete,
To dy3e in doel, out of delyt,
And syþen wende to helle hete,
644 Þerinne to won wythoute respyt;
Bot þeron com a bote as-tyt.
Ryche blod ran on rode so roghe,
And wynne water, þen, at þat plyt.
648 Þe grace of God wex gret innoghe.

f. 52 "Innoghe þer wax out of þat welle,
Blod and water of brode wounde.
Þe blod vus bo3t fro bale of helle,
652 And delyuered vus of þe deth secounde.
Þe water is baptem, þe soþe to telle,
Þat fol3ed þe glayue so grymly grounde,
Þat wasche3 away þe gylte3 felle
656 Þat Adam wyth inne deth vus drounde.
Now is þer no3t in þe worlde rounde
Bytwene vus and blysse, bot þat he wythdro3,
And þat is restored in sely stounde,
660 And þe grace of God is gret innogh.

XII

"Grace innogh þe mon may haue,
Þat synne3 þenne new, 3if hym repente,
Bot wyth sor3 and syt he mot hit craue,
664 And byde þe payne þerto is bent;
Bot resoun of ry3t þat con not raue
Saue3 euermore þe innossent.
Hit is a dom þat neuer God gaue,
668 Þat euer þe gyltle3 schulde be schente.

---

635  3ys] 3y[rd]: M.    3y...: O.    hym] hem: all eds. except
     H and AW.    fyrst] fyrst[e]: G, Ch.
645  þeron com] þer on com: MS, M.   þer oncom: O, G.
647  wynne water] wynne [&] water: M.

44

They did his bidding; they were therein.
Why should he not recognize their labor--
Yes, and recompense them with the first group completely?
636 For the grace of God is great enough.

"[It] is known well enough that proud mankind
First was created for perfect happiness.
Our first father did forfeit it
640 Through an apple that he did bite upon.
We were all damned, because of that meal,
To die in distress, away from delight,
And then to go to hell's heat,
644 Therein to remain without respite;
But after that a pardon came quickly.
Rich blood ran on [the] cross so rough,
And fine water, then, during that undertaking.
648 The grace of God flowed bountifully enough.

f. 52 "Enough there streamed out from that source,
Blood and water from [the] gaping wound.
The blood redeemed us from [the] torments of hell,
652 And delivered us from the second death.
The water is baptism, to tell the truth,
That resulted from the spear so keenly sharpened,
That washes away the bitterness of sin
656 With which Adam drowned us in death.
Now there is nothing in the round world
Between us and happiness, except what he (Adam)
    rescinded,
And that is restored in [a] blessed hour,
660 And the grace of God is great enough.

XII

"Grace enough the man may have,
Who then sins anew, if he repent,
But he must crave it with regret and grief,
664 And endure the penalty [that] is attached to it;
But [the] cause of justice which can not err
Always saves the innocent.
It is a sentence that God never imposed,
668 That the guiltless should ever be punished.

---

649  out] out out: MS.
656  inne] in: G.
660] Ch omits *And*.

45

Þe gyltyf may contryssyoun hente,
And be þurȝ mercy to grace þryȝt,
Bot he to gyle þat neuer glente
672    At inoscente is saf and ryȝte.

"Ryȝt þus, þus, I knaw wel in þis cas,
Two men to saue is God, by skylle,
Þe ryȝtwys man schal se hys face,
676    Þe harmleȝ haþel schal com hym tylle.
Þe Sauter hyt satȝ þus in a pace:
'Lorde, quo schal klymbe þy hyȝ hylle,
Oþer rest wythinne þy holy place?'
680    Hymself to onsware he is not dylle:
'Hondelyngeȝ harme þat dyt not ille,
Þat is of hert boþe clene and lyȝt,
Þer schal hys step stable stylle.'
684    Þe innosent is ay saf by ryȝt.

f. 52b   "The ryȝtwys man also sertayn
Aproche he schal þat proper pyle--
Þat takeȝ not her lyf in vayne,
688    Ne glauereȝ her nieȝbor wyth no gyle.
Of þys ryȝtwys, saȝ Salamon playn
How kyntly oure con aquyle.
By wayeȝ ful streȝt he con hym strayn,
692    And scheued hym þe rengne of God awhyle.
As quo says, 'Lo, ȝon louely yle!
Þou may hit wynne if þou be wyȝte.'
Bot, hardyly, wythoute peryle,
696    Þe innosent is ay saue by ryȝte.

"Anende ryȝtwys men, ȝet saytȝ a gome,
Dauid in Sauter, if euer ȝe seȝ hit:
'Lorde, þy seruaunt draȝ neuer to dome,
700    For non lyuyande to þe is justyfyet.'
Forþy, to corte quen þou schal com,
Þer alle oure causeȝ schal be tryed,

672   At] And: Go.   As: C, AW.       inoscente] in-oscen[c]e: G.
      and] [by]: G.
673   þus, þus] þus: M, O, G, Ch, Go, C, Mo, AW.
675   face] Looks like *fate* in MS, but scribe's *c* sometimes
      resembles *t*; cf. textual note to line 714.
678   hyȝ] hyȝ[e]: G, Ch.     hylle] hylleȝ: MS, M.
683   step] step[pe]: G, Ch.
688   nieȝbor] [n]eȝbor: O, G, Ch.
689   saȝ] saȝ (*satȝ*?): M.   sayz: AW.

The guilty may obtain contrition,
And be thrust into grace through mercy,
But he who never deviated toward deceit
672  Is redeemed and justified with [the] innocent.

"Rightly so, therefore, I know well in this matter,
[If] God, by agreement, is to redeem two men,
The righteous man shall see his face,
676  The innocent person shall go to him.
The Psalter says it thus in a passage:
'Lord, who shall climb your high hill,
Or rest within your holy place?'
680  He himself is not slow to answer:
'He who did not evilly do harm with his hands,
Who is both pure and brave of heart,
There shall his footsteps settle permanently.'
684  The innocent one is always redeemed by right.

f. 52b  "The righteous man also certainly
Shall approach that perfect dwelling--
Those who spend not their life in vanity,
688  Nor deceive their neighbor through any guile.
Concerning this righteous man, Solomon clearly reveals
How kindly mercy did prevail.
He did direct himself along very straight paths,
692  And the kingdom of God appeared to him for a time.
As one may say, 'Behold, that lovely isle!
You may reach it if you are courageous.'
However, certainly, without peril,
696  The innocent one is always redeemed by right.

"Concerning righteous men, yet says a man,
David in [the] Psalter, if ever you saw it:
'Lord, never bring your servant to judgment,
700  For no one living is justified before you.'
Therefore, when you shall come to [the] court,
Where all our causes shall be tried,

---

690  How kyntly oure con] How kyntly oure [Kyng hym] con: O, Ch.
      How kyntly oure [Koyntyse hym] con: G.  How Koyntise
      onoure con: Go, C, Mo.  How kyntly on[o]re con: H, De.
      Hym Koyntyse oure con: AW.
691  he] ho: Go, H, C, Mo.
698  seȝ] s[y]ȝ: G, Ch, Go.
700  For] sor: MS.
701  com] com[e]: G, Ch.
702  tryed] [c]ryed: G, AW.

Alegge þe ryӡt, þou may be innome
704    By þys ilke spech I haue asspyed.
Bot, he on rode þat blody dyed,
Delfully þurӡ hondeӡ þryӡt,
Gyue þe to passe, when þou arte tryed,
708    By innocens, and not by ryӡte.

"Ryӡtwysly quo con rede
He loke on bok and be awayed
How Jhecu hym welke in areþede,
712    And burneӡ her barneӡ vnto hym brayde
For happe and hele þat fro hym ӡede.
To touch her chylder þat fayr hym prayed.
His dessypeleӡ, wyth blame, let be hym bede,
716    And wyth her resouneӡ ful fele restayed.
Jhecu þenne hem swetely sayde:
'Do way! Let chylder vnto me tyӡt;
To suche is heuenryche arayed.'
720    Þe innocent is ay saf by ryӡt.

## XIII

f. 53    "Ihecu con calle to hym hys mylde,
And sayde hys ryche no wyӡ myӡt wynne,
Bot he com þyder ryӡt as a chylde;
724    Oþer elleӡ, neuermore com þerinne.
Harmleӡ, trwe, and vndefylde,
Wythouten mote oþer mascle of sulpande synne,
Quen such þer cnoken on þe bylde,
728    Tyt schal hem men þe ӡate vnpynne.
Þer is þe blys þat con not blynne,
Þat þe jueler soӡte þurӡ perré pres,
And solde alle hys goud, boþe wolen and lynne,
732    To bye hym a perle watӡ mascelleӡ.

"This makelleӡ perle þat boӡt is dere,
Þe joueler gef fore alle hys god,
Is lyke þe reme of heuenesse clere.
736    So sayde þe Fader of folde and flode;

---

709  quo con] quo [so] con: G.    con] cone: Ch.
711  Jhecu] Ihc̄: MS.  Ihesuc: M.  Jesus: other eds.  (This
      note applies also to 717, 721, and 820, except that
      the MS has illuminated 'I' at 721, and Gollancz and
      Gordon have 'Iesus' there.  The MS has 'Iesu' at 453
      and 'ihū' at 458.)
714  touch] Looks like *touth* in MS, but scribe's *c* sometimes

[If you] declare yourself just, you may be trapped
By this same statement I have noted.
However, he who died bloodily on [the] cross,
Painfully pierced through [the] hands,
May permit you to pass, when you are tried,
Through innocence, and not through justice.

"Whoever can read correctly
May look at [the] book and be informed
How Jesus himself walked among ancient folk,
And people brought their children to him
For [the] blessings and healings that flowed from him.
They courteously beseeched him to touch their children.
His disciples, with reproof, ordered to let him be,
And restrained very many with their statements.
Jesus then graciously said to them:
'Step aside! Let children come to me;
For such is [the] kingdom of heaven prepared.'
The innocent child is always redeemed by right.

## XIII

f. 53
"Jesus did call to him his humble disciples,
And said no man could attain his kingdom,
Unless he came there just as a child;
Otherwise, never again could [he] enter into that place.
Innocent, honest, and undefiled,
Without stain or spot of polluting sin,
When such there knock on the edifice,
Men shall quickly open the gate for them.
There is the bliss that can not cease,
That the jeweler sought through precious stones,
And [he] sold all his wealth, both woolen and linen,
To buy himself a pearl [that] was spotless.

"This peerless pearl that is dearly purchased,
For [which] the jeweler gave all his wealth,
Is like the realm of heaven's brightness.
So said the Father of land and water;

---

resembles *t*; cf. textual note to line 675.
715  hym] h[e]*m*: O, G, Ch, Go, C, Mo.
721  Ihecu] Ryȝt: AW.
732  perle watȝ] perle [þat] watȝ: M.
733  makelleȝ] ma[s]kelleȝ: O, G.  makeleȝ: H.
735  heuenesse clere] heuenes [sp]ere: G, Ch.

For hit is wemle3, clene, and clere,
And endele3 rounde, and blyþe of mode,
And commune to alle þat ry3tywys were.
740    Lo, euen inmydde3 my breste hit stode!
My Lorde, þe Lombe, þat schede hys blode,
He py3t hit þere in token of pes.
I rede þe forsake þe worlde wode
744    And porchace þy perle maskelles."

"O maskele3 perle in perle3 pure,
Þat bere3," quoþ I, "þe perle of prys,
Quo formed þe þy fayre fygure,
748    Þat wro3t þy wede, he wat3 ful wys.
Þy beauté com neuer of nature;
Pymalyon paynted neuer þy vys,
Ne Arystotel nawþer, by hys lettrure,
752    Of carpe þe kynde þese properté3.
Þy colour passe3 þe flour-de-lys;
Þyn angel-hauyng so clene corte3.
Breue me, bry3t, quat-kyn offys
756    Bere3 þe perle so maskelle3?"

f. 53b    "My makele3 Lambe þat al may bete,"
Quoþ scho, "my dere Destyné
Me ches to hys make, alþa3 vnmete
760    Sumtyme semed þat assemblé.
When I wente fro yor worlde wete,
He calde me to hys bonerté.
'Cum hyder to me, my lemman swete,
764    For mote ne spot is non in þe.'
He gef me my3t and als bewté.
In hys blod he wesch my wede on dese,
And coronde clene in vergynté,
768    And py3t me in perle3 maskelle3."

"Why, maskelle3 bryd, þat bry3t con flambe,
Þat reiate3 hat3 so ryche and ryf,
Quat-kyn Þyng may be þat Lambe
772    Þat þe wolde wedde vnto hys vyf?
Ouer alle oþer so hy3 þou clambe,
To lede wyth hym so ladyly lyf.
So mony a comly anvnnder cambe
776    For Kryst han lyued in much stryf;

739    ry3tywys] ry3twys: eds.
752    carpe] carpe[d]: G, Ch, Go, C, AW.    properté3]
          propert[y]3: O, G, Ch.
755    offys] of priys (The MS. has triys.): M.  of triys: G.
757    makele3] ma[s]kele3: O, G.

For it is spotless, pure, and sparkling,
And perfectly round, and fair in appearance,
And common to all who would be righteous.
740 Behold, its position [is] exactly amid my breast!
My Lord, the Lamb, who shed his blood,
Placed it there as [a] token of peace.
I advise you to abandon the mad world *Faith is a matter*
744 And purchase your spotless pearl." *of the Heart.*

"O spotless pearl in pure pearls,
Who possesses," said I, "the pearl of price,
Whoever formed your fair figure for you, *still thinking*
748 He who designed your vesture, was very wise. *physical*
Your beauty never originated from nature;
Pygmalion never delineated your visage,
Nor did Aristotle either, in his writing,
752 Speak of the character of these qualities.
Your color surpasses the fleur-de-lis;
Your angelic demeanor accords so completely.
Tell me, bright maiden, what kind of position
756 The pearl so spotless maintains?"

f. 53b "My peerless Lamb who can comfort all,
My precious Destiny," said she,
"Chose me as his spouse, although that union
760 Would have formerly seemed unsuitable.
When I went from your maddened world,
He called me to his goodness.
'Come here to me, my sweet darling,
764 For stain or spot is not in you.'
He gave me power and beauty also.
In his blood he cleansed my garment on [the] dais,
And crowned [me] splendidly in virginity,
768 And adorned me in spotless pearls."

"Why, spotless bride, who brightly does sparkle,
Who possesses royal powers so rich and abundant,
What kind of Being may that Lamb be
772 Who would wed you as his wife?
Over all others you climbed so high,
To lead with him [a] life so exalted.
So many a noble lady beneath [her] headdress
776 Has lived for Christ in much hardship;

---

768 And py3t me] [He] py3t me: G. Pyght me: Ch.
775 anvnnder] on vunder: M. onvunder: O, G, Go, Mo, AW.
    onunder: Ch, H, C, De. Orig. shows a at the beginning
    of the word more clearly.

51

And þou con alle þo dere out dryf,
And fro þat maryag al oþer depres,
Al-only þyself, so stout and styf,
780  A makeleʒ may, and maskelleʒ!"

XIV

"Maskelles," quoþ þat myry quene,
"Vnblemyst I am, wythouten blot,
And þat may I wyth mensk menteene,
784  Bot 'makeleʒ Quene' þenne sade I not.
Þe Lambes vyueʒ in blysse we bene,
A hondred and forty þowsande flot,
As in þe Apocalyppeʒ hit is sene.
788  Sant Johan hem syʒ al in a knot
On þe hyl of Syon, þat semly clot.
Þe apostel hem segh in gostly drem,
Arayed to þe weddyng in þat hyl-coppe,
792  Þe nwe cyté o Jerusalem.

f. 54  "Of Jerusalem I in speche spelle,
If þou wyl knaw what-kyn he be,
My Lombe, my Lorde, my dere Juelle,
796  My Joy, my Blys, my Lemman fre.
Þe profete Ysaye of hym con melle,
Pitously, of hys debonerté,
Þat gloryous Gyltleʒ þat mon con quelle
800  Wythouten any sake of felonye.
As a schep to þe slaʒt þer lad watʒ he;
And as lombe þat clypper in lande men,
So closed he hys mouth fro vch query
804  Quen Jueʒ hym jugged in Jherusalem.

---

778  maryag] maryag[e]: G.
784  sade] sa[y]de: O, Ch.
785  Lambes] Lambeʒ: Go.
786  forty þowsande] forty [fowre] þowsande: G, Go, C.
788  Johan] Iohan: M. John: other eds. (The MS has 'Ion'
     at 383 and 818, 'Iohn̄' at 788, 836, 867, 985 (o
     squeezed before h), 996, 1008, 1009, 1021, 1032,
     1033, and 1053, 'Ihon̄' at 984, and 'Ihn̄' at 1020.)
791  hyl-coppe] hyl-cot: Ch.
792  o] M read MS u, but Osgood noted, "imperfect o."
     Jerusalem] Ierusalem: M. Jersalem: Ch. Jerusalem:
     other eds. (The MS has 'Ilrm̄' at 792, 793, 805, 817,

And you did drive out all those noble women,
And exclude all others from that marriage,
Solely by yourself, so proud and firm,
780    A matchless maiden, and spotless!"

## XIV

"Spotless," said that fair queen,
"Unblemished I am, without stain,
And that I can maintain with honor,
784    But 'unequalled Queen' then said I not.
We are the Lamb's wives of renown,
A hundred and forty thousand in company,
As it is seen in the Apocalypse.
788    Saint John saw them all in a throng
On the hill of Sion, that beautiful knoll.
The apostle saw them in [a] spiritual dream,
Arrayed for the wedding on that hilltop,
792    The new city of Jerusalem.

f. 54    "I shall tell in [a] speech about Jerusalem,
If you wish to know what kind [of Being] he is,
My Lamb, my Lord, my precious Jewel,
796    My Joy, my Glory, my noble Spouse.
The prophet Isaias of him did speak,
Compassionately, of his meekness,
That glorious guiltless One whom men did slay
800    Without any reason associated with felony.
He was led there like a sheep to the slaughter;
And like [a] lamb that shearers in fields appraise,
So he closed his mouth after every query
804    When [the] Jews judged him in Jerusalem.

---

828, 829, 840, 841, 919, 941, 950, and 987, 'Ihēm'
at 804, and 'Irlm̄' at 816. However, the long mark is
not always directly over one letter.)
799   Gyltle3] Go noted that first *l* is "*altered faintly from
s in* MS."
800   felonye] felon[e]: G, Ch.
802   lande men] lande nem: M, O, G, Ch, H, De. hande nem:
Go, C, Mo, AW. Go (p. 74) wrote that the "second
stroke of the *h* has been joined to the first upright
stroke of the *a*," but the Orig. does show *lande* more
clearly.
803   query] quer[e]: G.

"In Jerusalem watȝ my Lemman slayn,
And rent on rode wyth boyeȝ bolde.
Al oure baleȝ to bere ful bayn,
808    He toke on hymself oure careȝ colde.
Wyth boffeteȝ watȝ hys face flayn,
Þat watȝ so fayr onto byholde.
For synne, he set hymself in vayn,
812    Þat neuer hade non hymself to wolde.
For vus he lette hym flyȝe and folde,
And brede vpon a bostwys bem.
As meke as lomp þat no playnt tolde,
816    For vus he swalt in Jerusalem.

"Jerusalem, Jordan, and Galalye--
Þeras baptysed þe goude Saynt Jon,
His wordeȝ acorded to Ysaye.
820    When Jhecu con to hym warde gon,
He sayde of hym þys professye:
'Lo, Godeȝ Lombe, as trwe as ston,
Þat dotȝ away þe synneȝ dryȝe,
824    Þat alle þys worlde hatȝ wroȝt vpon!'
Hymself ne wroȝt neuer ȝet non;
Wheþer, on hymself he con al clem.
Hys generacyoun quo recen ccn,
828    Þat dyȝed for vus in Jerusalem?

f. 54b    "In Jerusalem, þus, my Lemman swatte;
Twyeȝ for Lombe watȝ taken þare
By trw recorde of ayþer prophete,
832    For mode so meke and al hys fare.
Þe þryde tyme is, þerto, ful mete,
In Apokalypeȝ wryten ful ȝare.
Inmydeȝ þe trone þere saynteȝ sete,
836    Þe apostel Johan hym saytȝ as bare,
Lesande þe boke with leueȝ sware,
Þere seuen syngnetteȝ wern sette in seme;
And at þat syȝt vche douth con dare,
840    In helle, in erþe, and Jerusalem.

---

810    onto] on to: eds.
815    lomp] lomb: M, O, G, Ch.
817]    G, Go, C, and AW supply *In* at the beginning of the line.
825    wroȝt] wroȝt[e]: G.

"In Jerusalem was my beloved slain,
And slit open on [the] cross by bold ruffians.
Fully prepared to suffer for all our sins,
808 He took upon himself our grievous sorrows.
His face, that was so fair to behold,
Was bruised by buffets.
Because of sin, he submitted himself to contempt,
812 He who never had any [sin] himself to subdue.
For us he allowed himself to be whipped and laid low,
And stretched upon a sturdy beam.
As meek as [a] lamb who sounded no lament,
816 He died for us in Jerusalem.

"Jerusalem, Jordan, and Galilee--
Where the good Saint John baptized,
His words accorded with Isaias.
820 When Jesus did go toward him,
He said of him this prophecy:
'Behold, God's Lamb, as true as stone,
Who takes away the burdensome sins,
824 Which all this world has committed openly!'
[He] never even committed any himself;
Nevertheless, he did claim all to himself.
Who can recount his generation,
828 He who died for us in Jerusalem?

f. 54b "In Jerusalem, thus, my Beloved suffered;
[He] was revealed as [the] Lamb twice there
In [the] true account of both prophets,
832 Because of [his] mood so meek and all his ways.
The third time is, for this purpose, very suitable,
Written in [the] Apocalypse very clearly.
Amid the throne where saints sat,
836 The apostle John tells about him just as plainly,
Opening the book with square pages,
Where seven seals were set on [the] border;
And at that sight each group did bow in awe,
840 In hell, on earth, and in Jerusalem.

---

829 swatte] sw[e]te: O, G, Ch, Go, C, AW.
830 þare] þere: M, O.  Go noted a is probably altered from e.
836⹁ saytʒ] syʒ: O, Ch.  saʒ: G, Go, C, AW.
838 in seme] in-seme: M, O, G, Ch.

"Thys Jerusalem Lombe hade neuer pechche
　　Of oþer huee bot quyt jolyf,
　　Þat mot ne masklle moȝt on streche
844　For wolle quyte so ronk and ryf.
　　Forþy, vche saule þat hade neuer teche
　　Is to þat Lombe a worthyly wyf,
　　And þaȝ vch day a store he feche,
848　Among vus commeȝ no noþer strot ne stryf.
　　Bot, vch on enlé we wolde were fyf;
　　Þe mo þe myryer, so God me blesse!
　　In compayny gret, our luf con þryf
852　In honour more, and neuer þe lesse.

　　"Lasse of blysse may non vus bryng
　　Þat beren þys perle vpon oure bereste,
　　For þay of mote couþe neuer mynge,
856　Of spotleȝ perleȝ þa beren þe creste.
　　Alþaȝ oure corses in clotteȝ clynge,
　　And ȝe remen for rauþe wythouten reste,
　　We þurȝoutly hauen cnawyng.
860　Of on dethe ful oure hope is drest.
　　Þe Lombe vus gladeȝ; oure care is kest.
　　He myrþeȝ vus alle at vch a mes.
　　Vch oneȝ blysse is breme and beste,
864　And neuer oneȝ honour ȝet neuer þe les.

f. 55　"Lest les þou leue my talle farande,
　　In Appocalyppece is wryten in wro.
　　'I seghe,' says Johan, 'þe Loumbe hym stande
868　On þe mount of Syon, ful þryuen and þro,
　　And wyth hym maydenneȝ, an hundreþe þowsande,
　　And fowre and forty þowsande mo.
　　On alle her forhedeȝ wryten I fande
872　Þe Lombeȝ nome, hys Fadereȝ also.
　　A hue fro heuen I herde þoo,
　　Lyk flodeȝ fele laden runnen on resse,
　　And as þunder þroweȝ in torreȝ blo,
876　Þat lote, I leue, watȝ neuer þe les.

---

843　masklle] mask[e]lle: G.
845　teche] M saw MS *tethe*, but *c* sometimes resembles *t*; cf.
　　　textual note to line 714.
848　no noþer] nonoþer: MS, De.　non oþer: M, O, Ch, H, Mo.
　　　[n]oþer: G.　nouþer: Go, C, AW.
854　bereste] breste: Ch.
856　þa] þa[y]: M.　þa[t]: O, G, Ch, Go, C, Mo, AW.
860　on] Go noted that *o* of *on* is blotted and illegible.

*Extra Stanza?*

"This Lamb of Jerusalem never had [a] patch
Of [any] other color but beautiful white,
Upon which stain or spot might spread
844    Through [the] white wool so rich and abundant.
Therefore, each soul who never had guilt
Is a worthy wife for that Lamb,
And though every day he gathers a group,
848    Among us comes not either contention or discord.
Furthermore, we would wish each single one were five;
The more the merrier, so may God bless me!
In [a] large company, our love does flourish
852    With more honor, and never the less.

"Less of bliss may no one bring to us
Who wear this pearl upon our breast,
For they who wear the diadem of spotless pearls
856    Could never think of quarreling.
Although our corpses decay in clods,
And you lament with grief without rest,
We possess understanding completely.
860    Our hope has been fully realized through one death.
The Lamb comforts us; our care is cast away.
He gladdens us all at every festive gathering.
Each one's ecstasy is wondrous and best,
864    And never one's honor yet ever the less.

f. 55    "Lest you should believe my splendid story false,
In [the] Apocalypse [it] is written in [a] passage.
'I saw,' says John, 'the Lamb himself standing
868    On the mount of Sion, very noble and steadfast,
And with him virgins, a hundred thousand,
And four and forty thousand more.
I found written on all their foreheads
872    The Lamb's name, his Father's also.
I heard a voice from heaven then,
Like [the] voice of many waters running in [a] rush,
And as thunder peals among leaden peaks,
876    That sound, I believe, was never the less.

---

dethe] deth: H, De.
861  Lombe] lonbe: MS. lou[m]be: G. MS has two minims between
     *o* and *b*.
862  myrþeʒ] myrþes: H, De.
865  talle] tale: all eds. except AW.
867  þe] þa: H, De.
873  fro] from: Go, C, Mo.
874  laden] l[e]den: G, Ch.

"'Nauþeles, þaȝ hit schowted scharpe,
And ledden loude alþaȝ hit were,
A note ful nwe I herde hem warpe;
880     To lysten þat watȝ ful lufly dere.
As harporeȝ harpen in her harpe,
Þat nwe songe þay songen ful cler,
In sounande noteȝ, a gentyl carpe;
884     Ful fayre þe modeȝ þay fonge in fere.
Ryȝt byfore Godeȝ chayere,
And þe fowre besteȝ þat hym obes,
And þe aldermen so sadde of chere,
888     Her songe þay songen neuer þe les.

"'Nowþelese, non watȝ neuer so quoynt,
For alle þe crafteȝ þat euer þay knewe,
Þat of þat songe myȝt synge a poynt,
892     Bot þat meyny. Þe Lombe þay swe,
For þay arn boȝt fro þe vrþe aloynte
As newe fryt, to God ful due;
And to þe gentyl Lombe hit arn anjoynt,
896     As lyk to hymself of lote and hwe,
For neuer lesyng ne tale vntrwe
Ne towched her tonge for no dysstresse.'
Þat moteles meyny may neuer remwe
900     Fro þat maskeleȝ Mayster neuer þe les."

f. 55b   "Neuer þe les let be my þonc,"
Quoþ I, "my perle, þaȝ I appose.
I schulde not tempte þy wyt so wlonc;
904     To Krysteȝ chambre þat art ichose.
I am bot mokke and mul among,
And þou so ryche, a reken rose;
And bydeȝ here by þys blysful bonc,
908     Þer lyueȝ lyste may neuer lose.
Now, hynde, þat sympelnesse coneȝ enclose,
I wolde þe aske a þynge expresse,
And þaȝ I be bustwys, as a blose,
912     Let my bone vayl, neuerþelese.

---

892  þay] þa[t]: O, G, Ch, Go, C, Mo, AW.
895  anjoynt] amoynt: M.
898  dysstresse] dysstres: Ch.
905  among] amon[c]: G, Ch.

"'Nevertheless, though it sounded sharply,
And although it were [a] loud voice,
A canticle quite new I heard them sing;
880 To listen to it was indeed highly pleasing.
As harpers harp on their harps,
They sang that new song very clearly,
With melodious notes, a noble hymn;
884 They followed the modes in unison very skillfully.
Directly before God's throne,
And the four beasts that obey him,
And the ancients so dignified in mood,
888 They sang their song never the less.

"'Nevertheless, no one was ever so clever,
In spite of all the techniques that they ever knew,
Who could sing a note of that song,
892 Except that group. They follow the Lamb,
For they have been purchased from the distant earth
As first fruits, to God fully due;
And they have been joined to the gentle Lamb,
896 As similar to himself in speech and appearance,
For lying or untrue tale never
Touched their tongue under any circumstance.'
That spotless assembly can never be separated
900 From that spotless Master any the less."

f. 55b "Never the less let my thanks be,"
Said I, "my pearl, though I inquire.
I should not try your intelligence so superb;
904 You have been chosen for Christ's bridal chamber.
I am but dirt and dust together,
And you [are] so noble, a beautiful rose;
And [you] dwell here by this delightful shore,
908 Where life's pleasures can never fade.
Now, gracious damsel, in whom simplicity does reside,
I would ask you a thing directly,
And though I may be boisterous, like a blast of wind,
912 Let my plea avail, nevertheless.

---

910 expresse] expres: Ch.
911 blose] [w]ose: G. bose: AW.
912 vayl] vayl[e]: G, Ch.

"Neuerþelese, cler I yow bycalle,
   If ʒe con se hyt be todone;
As þou art gloryous, wythouten galle,
916      Wythnay þou neuer my ruful bone.
Haf ʒe no woneʒ in castel-walle,
Ne maner þer ʒe may mete and won?
Þou telleʒ me of Jerusalem, þe ryche ryalle,
920      Þer Dauid dere watʒ dyʒt on trone,
Bot by þyse holteʒ hit con not hone;
Bot in Judee hit is, þat noble note.
As ʒe ar maskeleʒ vnder mone,
924      Your woneʒ schulde be wythouten mote.

"Þys moteleʒ meyny þou coneʒ of mele,
Of þousandeʒ þryʒt, so gret a route,
A gret ceté, for ʒe arn fele,
928      Yow byhod haue, wythouten doute.
So cumly a pakke of joly juele
Wer euel don schulde lyʒ þeroute;
And by þyse bonkeʒ þer I con gele,
932      And I se no bygyng nawhere aboute,
I trowe alone ʒe lenge and loute,
To loke on þe glory of þys gracous gote.
If þou hatʒ oþer bygyngeʒ stoute,
936      Now tech me to þat myry mote."


f. 56    "That mote þou meneʒ in Judy londe,"
Þat specyal spyce þen to me spakk,
"Þat is þe cyté þat þe Lombe con fonde
940      To soffer inne sor for maneʒ sake,
Þe olde Jerusalem to vnderstonde,
For þere þe olde gulte watʒ don to slake;
Bot þe Nwe þat lyʒt of Godeʒ sonde,
944      Þe apostel in Apocalyppce in theme con take.
Þe Lompe þer wythouten spotteʒ blake
Hatʒ feryed þyder hys fayre flote,
And as hys flok is wythouten flake,
948      So is hys mote wythouten moote.

---

914  todone] to done: MS, eds.
918  won] won[e]: G.
919  þe] the: H, De.
932] G, Ch, Go, C, Mo, AW delete MS & at start of line.
934  gracous] grac[i]ous: eds.

"Nevertheless, I call upon you clearly,
If you can see it be revealed;
Since you are glorious, without rancor,
916    You would never refuse my compassionate request.
Have you no houses inside [the] walls of the castle,
Nor manors where you may meet and linger?
You tell me of Jerusalem, the royal realm,
920    Where noble David was established on [the] throne,
But it can not be situated in these woods;
That splendid city is only in Judea.
Since you are spotless beneath [the] moon,
924    Your abodes should be without spot.

"This spotless company you do speak of,
Gathered into thousands, so huge a crowd,
Would oblige you to have, without doubt,
928    A great city, for you are many.
So comely a group of elegant jewels
Would be unfavorably affected should [they] lie in the
    open;
And by these shores where I do linger,
932    If I see no buildings anywhere about,
I would imagine you stay and stroll alone,
To look upon the splendor of this delightful stream.
If you have other stately buildings,
936    Lead me now to that excellent city."

f. 56    "That city you mention in [the] land of Judea,"
That special damsel then said to me,
"Is the city that the Lamb did seek
940    To suffer in sorrow for man's sake,
To be understood as the old Jerusalem,
For there the old guilt was made to abate;
But the New Jerusalem that descended through God's
    dispensation,
944    The apostle in [the] Apocalypse did take as [his] theme.
The Lamb there without black spots
Has led his lovely company to that place,
And just as his flock is without blemish,
948    So is his city without spot.

---

935   bygynge3] lygynge3: O, G, Ch, H, De.  UVR does not clarify
      first letter.
938   spakk] spake: Ch.
944   Apocalyppce] Apocallypce: H, De.  Ch omits second *in*.
945   Lompe] lombe: M, O, G, Ch.

"Of moteȝ two to carpe clene,
And Jerusalem hyȝt boþe, nawþeles,
Þat nys to yow no more to mene
952   Bot 'Ceté of God' oþer 'Syȝt of Pes'.
In þat on, oure pes watȝ mad at ene;
Wyth payne to suffer þe Lombe hit chese.
In þat oþer is noȝt bot pes to glene,
956   Þat ay schal laste, wythouten reles.
Þat is þe borȝ þat we to pres,
Fro þat oure fresch be layd to rote,
Þer glory and blysse schal euer encres
960   To þe meyny þat is wythouten mote."

"Moteleȝ may, so meke and mylde,"
      Þen sayde I to þat lufly flor,
"Bryng me to þat bygly bylde,
964   And let me se þy blysful bor."
Þat schene sayde: "Þat God wyl schylde.
Þou may not enter wythinne hys tor.
Bot, of þe Lombe I haue þe aquylde
968   For a syȝt þerof, þurȝ gret fauor.
Vtwyth to se þat clene cloystor
Þou may, bot inwyth, not a fote.
To strech in þe strete þou hatȝ no vygour,
972   Bot þou wer clene wythouten mote.


THE VISION--PART THREE:
THE NEW JERUSALEM AND THE PROCESSION


XVII

f. 56b   "If I þis mote þe schal vnhyde,
           Bow vp towarde þys borneȝ heued,
And I, anendeȝ þe on þis syde,
976   Schal sve tyl þou to a hil be veued."
Þen wolde no lenger byde,
Bot lurked by launceȝ so lufly leued,
Tyl on a hyl þat I asspyed,
980   And blusched on þe burghe, as I forth dreued,

---

949   moteȝ] motes: all eds., except AW.   motez: AW.
958   Fro] Fre: Mo.   fresch] flesch: eds.   Looks like *fresth*
      in MS, but see textual notes to lines 675, 714, and 84

"To speak clearly of two cities,
And both called Jerusalem, nevertheless,
Is to mean to you no more
952    Than 'City of God' or 'Vision of Peace'.
In that one, our salvation was settled immediately;
The Lamb chose it in order to suffer in pain.
[There] is nothing but peace to obtain in that other,
956    That shall last forever, without cessation.
That is the city to which we advance,
After our young bodies are laid away to decay,
Where glory and bliss shall always increase
960    For that assembly that is without spot."

"Spotless maiden, so meek and mild,"
Then said I to that lovely flower,
"Bring me to that stately city,
964    And let me see your blessed abode."
That bright damsel said: "God will prevent that.
You may not enter within his kingdom.
However, I have prevailed upon the Lamb for you
968    For a sight of it, through great favor.
To see that splendid city from without
You may, but from within, not a foot.
You have no strength to stride in the street,
972    Unless you were completely without spot.


               THE VISION--PART THREE:
            THE NEW JERUSALEM AND THE PROCESSION


                        XVII

f. 56b   "If I shall reveal this city to you,
Go up toward [the] head of this stream,
And I, across from you on this side,
976    Shall follow until you are directed to a hill."
Then [I] wished to linger no longer,
But slipped through branches so beautifully in leaf,
Until I, on a hill, discovered [it],
980    And gazed upon the city, as I strode onward,


_____

977  wolde no] wolde [I þer] no: G.   wolde [I] no: other eds.

By3onde þe brok fro me warde keued;
Þat schyrrer þen sunne wyth schafte3 schon.
In þe Apokalypce is þe fasoun preued,
984    As deuyse3 hit, þe apostel Jhoan.

As Johan þe apostel hit sy3 wyth sy3t,
I sy3e þat cyty of gret renoun,
Jerusalem, so nwe and ryally dy3t,
988    As hit wat3 ly3t fro þe heuen adoun.
Þe bor3 wat3 al of brende golde bry3t,
As glemande glas burnist broun,
Wyth gentyl gemme3 anvnder py3t
992    Wyth bantele3 twelue on basyng boun.
Þe foundemente3 twelue of riche tenoun;
Vch tabelment wat3 a serlype3 ston,
As derely deuyse3 þis ilk toun
996    In Apocalyppe3, þe apostel Johan.

As Johan þise stone3 in Writ con nemme,
I knew þe name after his tale.
Jasper hy3t þe fyrst gemme,
1000    Þat I on þe fyrst basse con wale;
He glente grene in þe lowest hemme.
Saffer helde þe secounde stale.
Þe calsydoyne, þenne, wythouten wemme,
1004    In þe þryd table con purly pale.
Þe emerade, þe furþe, so grene of scale,
Þe sardonyse, þe fyfþe ston,
Þe sexte, þe rybé--he con hit wale
1008    In þe Apocalyppce, þe apostel Johan.

f. 57    3et joyned Johan þe crysolyt,
Þe seuenþe gemme in fundament,
Þe a3tþe, þe beryl, cler and quyt,
1012    Þe topasye twynne-how, þe nente endent;
Þe crysopase, þe tenþe, is ty3t,
Þe jacyngh, þe enleuenþe gent,
Þe twelfþe, þe gentyleste in vch a plyt,
1016    Þe amatyst purpre, wyth ynde blente.

---

981    keued] [br]eued: O.
988    wat3] was: Go.
995    ilk] ilke: Ch.
997    As Johan þise] As þise: MS, M.
998    name] name[3]: G.
999    fyrst] fyrst[e]: G, Ch.

Set down opposite me beyond the brook;
It sparkled with rays more radiant than [the] sun.
In the Apocalypse is its appearance shown,
984 As John the apostle portrays it.

As John the apostle saw it in [a] vision,
I saw that city of great renown,
Jerusalem, so new and royally embellished,
988 As it had come down from the heavens.
The city was entirely of pure, glistening gold,
Like gleaming glass burnished brightly,
With precious stones adorned beneath
992 In twelve tiers built at [the] base.
The twelve foundations [were] with rich jointings;
Each tier was a separate stone,
As the apostle John, in [the] Apocalypse,
996 Skillfully portrays this same town.

Since John did designate these stones in Scripture,
I knew the names after his account.
The first gem was called jasper,
1000 Which I did perceive on the first foundation;
It glistened greenly on the lowest fringe.
Sapphire occupied the second position.
The chalcedony, then, without stain,
1004 Did truly glow dimly on the third tier.
The emerald, the fourth, so green on [the] surface,
The sardonyx, the fifth stone,
The sixth, the ruby--he did perceive them
1008 In the Apocalypse, the apostle John.

f. 57 John also enumerated the chrysolite,
The seventh gem in [the] foundation,
The eighth, the beryl, clear and white,
1012 The double-colored topaz, the ninth adorned;
The chrysoprase, the tenth, is fastened,
The jacinth, the splendid eleventh,
The twelfth, the gentlest in every setting,
1016 The purple amethyst, blended with indigo.

---

1000 fyrst] fyrst[e]: G, Ch.
1004 þryd] þryd[de]: G, Ch.
1007 rybé] [sarde]: G.
1012 twynne-how] twynne how: MS, M.   twynne-hew: Go, C, Mo, AW.
1014 jacyngh] jacyngh[t]: G, Go, C, AW.
1015 gentyleste] [try]este: G, AW.

Þe wal abof þe bantels bent,
Of jasporye, as glas þat glysnande schon.
I knew hit by his deuysement

1020     In þe Apocalyppeȝ, þe apostel Jhan.

As Johan deuysed, ȝet saȝ I þare
Þise twelue degrés wern brode and stayre.
Þe cyté stod abof, ful sware,

1024     As longe, as brode, as hyȝe, ful fayre.
Þe streteȝ of golde, as glasse, al bare;
Þe wal of jasper, þat glent as glayre.
Þe woneȝ wythinne enurned ware

1028     Wyth alle-kynneȝ perré þat moȝt repayre.
Þenne helde vch sware of þis manayre
Twelue forlonge space er euer hit fon
Of heȝt, of brede, of lenþe to cayre,

1032     For meten hit syȝ, þe apostel Johan.

## XVIII

As Johan hym wryteȝ, ȝet more I syȝe.
Vch pane of þat place had þre ȝateȝ;
So twelue in poursent I con asspye.

1036     Þe portaleȝ pyked of rych plateȝ,
And vch ȝate of a margyrye,
A parfyt perle þat neuer fateȝ.
Vch on in Scrypture a name con plye

1040     Of Israel barneȝ, folewande her dateȝ,
Þat is to say, as her byrþ-whateȝ;
Þe aldest ay fyrst þeron watȝ done.
Such lyȝt þer lemed in alle þe strateȝ,

1044     Hem nedde nawþer sunne ne mone.

f. 57b     Of sunne ne mone had þay no nede.
Þe self God watȝ her lambe-lyȝt,
Þe Lombe her lantyrne, wythouten drede.

1048     Þurȝ hym blysned þe borȝ al bryȝt.
Þurȝ woȝe and won my lokyng ȝede;
For sotyle cler, noȝt lette no lyȝt.

---

1017  bent] b[r]ent: G, Ch.
1018  Of jasporye] Masporye: M. O jasporye: other eds. The
      tiny *f* inserted above the line between *o* and *j* is
      in the same brown ink. Osgood believed *f* is in
      *later hand.*
1030  Twelue forlonge space er] Twelue [þowsande] forlonge er:
1035  poursent] pourseut: O, Ch, H, De, Mo.

66

                The wall of jasper, that glisteningly shone
                Like glass, rose above the tiers.
                I recognized it by his description
1020            In the Apocalypse, the apostle John.

                As John described, there I also saw
                These twelve steps were broad and steep.    Square = perfect
                The city stood above, completely square,
1024            Very equally as long, as wide, [and] as high.
                The streets [were] of gold, like glass, all clear;
                The wall of jasper glistened like glair.
                The abodes within were embellished
1028            With every kind of jewelry that could be gathered.
                Then each square of this habitation contained
                Twelve furlongs' space before it ever ceased
                To extend in height, in breadth, [and] in length,
1032            As the apostle John saw it measured.


                                    XVIII

                As John himself writes, I saw still more.
                Each side of that city had three gates;
                Thus I did observe twelve in compass.
1036            The gates were adorned with splendid plates,
                And each gate [was] of a pearl,
                A perfect pearl that never fades.
                Each one did yield a name from Scripture
1040            Of Israel's children, following their dates,
                That is to say, according to their dates of birth;
                The oldest was forever engraved first thereon.
                Such light shone there in all the streets,
1044            They needed neither sun nor moon.

f. 57b          They had no need of sun or moon.
                The very God was their lamplight,
                The Lamb their lantern, without doubt.
1048            Because of him the city sparkled very brilliantly.
                Through wall and city my vision passed;
                Because of [the] tenuous transparency, nothing
                    obstructed any light.

---

1036    rych] rych[e]: G, Ch.
1041    byrþ-whate3] byrþ whate3: MS, M, O, Ch, H, De.
            byrþ[e]-whate3: G.
1046    self] self[e]: G, Ch.    lambe-ly3t] lompe ly3t (MS. lombe):
            M. lompely3t: O, G, Ch.    lombe-ly3t: Go, Mo, AW.
            lombe ly3t: H, De.    Orig. shows a of lambe more clearly.
1050    no3t] mo3t: M.    ly3t] [s]y3t: G, AW.

                                    67

Þe hyȝe trone þer moȝt ȝe hede,
1052 Wyth alle þe apparaylmente vmbepyȝte,
As Johan þe appostel in termeȝ tyȝte.
Þe hyȝe Godeȝ self hit set vpone.
A reuer of þe trone þer ran outryȝte;
1056 Watȝ bryȝter þen boþe þe sunne and mone.

Sunne ne mone schon neuer so swete
A þat foysoun flode out of þat flet.
Swyþe hit swange þurȝ vch a strete,
1060 Wythouten fylþe oþer galle oþer glet.
Kyrk þerinne watȝ non ȝete,
Chapel ne temple þat euer watȝ set.
Þe Almyȝty watȝ her mynyster mete,
1064 Þe Lombe, þe Sakerfyse, þer to reget.
Þe ȝateȝ stoken watȝ neuer ȝet,
Bot euermore vpen at vche a lone.
Þer entreȝ non to take reset,
1068 Þat bereȝ any spot anvndeȝ mone.

The mone may þerof acroche no myȝte.
To spotty ho is, of body to grym;
And also, þer ne is neuer nyȝt,
1072 What schulde þe mone þer compas clym
And to euen wyth þat worþly lyȝt
Þat schyneȝ vpon þe brokeȝ brym?
Þe planeteȝ arn in to pouer a plyȝt,
1076 And þe self sunne ful fer to dym.
Aboute þat water arn tres ful schym,
Þat twelue fryteȝ of lyf con bere ful sone.
Twelue syþeȝ on ȝer þay beren ful frym,
1080 And renowleȝ nwe in vche a mone.

f. 58 Anvnder mone so gret merwayle
No fleschly hert ne myȝt endeure,
As quen I blusched vpon þat baly,
1084 So ferly þerof watȝ þe fasure.
I stod as stylle as dased quayle,
For ferly of þat freuch fygure,

---

1058 A] A[s]: O, G, Ch, Go, C, Mo, AW.
1063 mynyster] mynster: Go, H, C, De, Mo, AW.
1064 reget] refet: Go, C, Mo, AW.
1068 anvndeȝ] an-vnder: eds.
1073 to euen] to-euen: O.
1076 self] self[e]: G, Ch.

You could see the high throne there,
1052  With all the heavenly retinue arrayed round about,
      Just as John the apostle set [it] down in words.
      The great God himself sat upon it.
      A river ran straight out from the throne there;
1056  [It] was brighter than both the sun and moon.

      Sun or moon never shone as pleasantly
      As that blessed stream from that source.
      Swiftly it sped through every street,
1060  Without filth or scum or slime.
      Moreover, therein was not [any] church,
      Chapel or temple that ever was built.
      The Almighty was their proper cathedral,
1064  The Lamb, the Sacrifice, there to be received again.
      The gates were never locked yet,
      But [were] open always at every byway.
      No one enters there to receive refuge,
1068  Who bears any spot comparable to [the] moon.

      The moon can gain no power in that place.
      She is too spotty, too dull in body;
      And besides, where night is never,
1072  Why should the moon rise there in an arc
      And compete with that glorious light
      That shines upon the water of the brook?
      The planets are in too poor a condition,
1076  And the very sun full far too dark.
      Around that water are very bright trees,
      Which do produce twelve fruits of life very quickly.
      Twelve times a year they bloom very abundantly,
1080  And renew again at every moon.

f. 58  Beneath [the] moon no human heart
      Could endure so great [a] miracle,
      As when I gazed upon that city,
1084  So marvelous was the appearance of that place.
      I stood as still as [a] dazed quail,
      Due to [the] wonder of that brilliant vision,

*[Handwritten margin note: heavens are a perfect body, the stars do not move, no Johannes Kepler.]*

---

1081  gret] great: Go, C.
1082  endeure] endure: Ch.
1083  baly] ba[y]ly: O.  ba[y]l[e]: G, Ch, Go, H, C, Mo.
1084  fasure] falure: M.
1086  freuch] french (*fresch*?): M.  frelich: Go, Mo.
      frech: AW.

Þat felde I nawþer reste ne trauayle,
1088   So watʒ I rauyste wyth glymme pure.
For, I dar say wyth conciens sure,
Hade bodyly burne abiden þat bone,
Þaʒ alle clerkeʒ hym hade in cure,
1092   His lyf wer loste anvnder mone.


XIX

Ryʒt as þe maynful mone con rys,
  Er þenne þe day-glem dryue al doun,
So sodanly, on a wonder wyse,
1096   I watʒ war of a prosessyoun.
Þis noble cité of ryche enpresse
Watʒ sodanly ful, wythouten sommoun,
Of such vergyneʒ, in þe same gyse,
1100   Þat watʒ my blysful anvnder croun;
And coronde wern alle of þe same fasoun,
Depaynt in perleʒ and wedeʒ qwyte.
In vch oneʒ breste watʒ bounden boun
1104   Þe blysful perle wythouten delyt.

Wyth gret delyt, þay glod in fere
On golden gateʒ þat glent as glasse.
Hundreth þowsandeʒ I wot þer were,
1108   And alle in sute her liuréʒ wasse.
Tor to knaw þe gladdest chere.
Þe Lombe byfore con proudly passe,
Wyth horneʒ seuen of red golde cler.
1112   As praysed perleʒ his wedeʒ wasse.
Towarde þe throne þay trone a tras;
Þaʒ þay wern fele, no pres in plyt,
Bot mylde as maydeneʒ seme at mas,
1116   So droʒ þay forth wyth gret delyt.


f. 58b   Delyt þat hys come encroched
To much hit were of for to melle.
Þise aldermen, quen he aproched,
1120   Grouelyng to his fete þay felle.

---

1092  wer] were: Go, C.
1093  rys] ryse: Ch.
1097  enpresse] enpr[y]se: O, G, Ch, Go, H, C, Mo.
1104  wythouten] with gret: M, O, G, Ch, Go, C, Mo, AW.

|       | So that I experienced neither rest nor anxiety,
| 1088  | I was so entranced by [that] pure spiritual light.
|       | Therefore, I dare say with positive conviction,
|       | Had [a] mortal man experienced that revelation,
|       | Though all [the] clerks took him for treatment,
| 1092  | His life would be lost beneath [the] moon.


XIX

|       | Just as the great moon does rise,
|       | Before the sun sinks completely down,
|       | Thus suddenly, in a wonderful way,
| 1096  | I was aware of a procession.
|       | This noble city of magnificent glory
|       | Was suddenly full, without summons,
|       | Of such virgins, in the same dress,
| 1100  | As was my beautiful maiden beneath [the] crown;
|       | And all were crowned in the same fashion,
|       | Adorned with pearls and white robes.
|       | On each one's breast was firmly fastened
| 1104  | The splendid pearl beyond delight.
|       | With great delight, they proceeded in company
|       | Over golden roads that gleamed like glass.
|       | Hundreds of thousands I know there were,
| 1108  | And their clothes were all alike.
|       | [It was] difficult to discover the happiest expression.
|       | The Lamb did pass proudly in front,
|       | With seven horns of clear red gold.
| 1112  | His garments were like prized pearls.
|       | They stepped in line toward the throne;
|       | Though they were many, [there was] no crowding in
|       |     [their] arrangement,
|       | But mild as sweet maidens at mass,
| 1116  | Thus they went forth with great delight.

| f. 58b | [The] delight that his approach aroused
|        | Would be too much to tell about.
|        | These ancients, when he drew near,
| 1120   | Fell prostrate at his feet.

1108  liureȝ] liure: G.
1111  golde] glode: MS.
1112  wedeȝ] wede: G.
1117  þat hys] þat [þer] hys: O, G, Ch.

Legyounes of aungeleȝ, togeder uoched,
Þer kesten ensens of swete smelle.
Þen glory and gle watȝ nwe abroched;
1124    Al songe to loue þat gay Juelle.
Þe steuen moȝt stryke þurȝ þe vrþe to helle,
Þat þe Vertues of heuen of joye endyte,
To loue þe Lombe his meyny in-melle.
1128    Iwysse, I laȝt a gret delyt.

Delit, þe Lombe for to deuise,
Wyth much meruayle, in mynde went.
Best watȝ he, blyþest, and moste to pryse,
1132    Þat euer I herde of speche spent.
So worþly whyt wern wedeȝ hys,
His lokeȝ symple, hymself so gent,
Bot a wounde, ful wyde and weete, con wyse
1136    Anende hys hert, þurȝ hyde torente.
Of his quyte syde his blod out sprent.
Alas, þoȝt I, who did þat spyt?
Ani breste for bale aȝt haf forbrent
1140    Er he þerto hade had delyt.

The Lombe delyt non lyste to wene.
Þaȝ he were hurt and wounde hade,
In his sembelaunt watȝ neuer sene,
1144    So wern his glenteȝ gloryous glade.
I loked among his meyny schene
How þay wyth lyf wern laste and lade.
Þen saȝ I þer my lyttel quene
1148    Þat, I wende, had standen by me in sclade.
Lorde, much of mirþe watȝ þat ho made
Among her fereȝ, þat watȝ so quyt.
Þat syȝt me gart to þenk to wade,
1152    For luf-longyng in gret delyt.

## XX

  Delyt me drof in yȝe and ere;
    My maneȝ mynde to maddyng malte.
Quen I seȝ my frely, I wolde be þere
1156    Byȝonde þe water, þaȝ ho were walte.
I þoȝt þat noþyng myȝt me dere,
To fech me bur and take me halte,

1125  þurȝ þe vrþe] þurȝ vrþe: H, De.
1133  hys] hys[e]: G, Ch.

Legions of angels, called together,
There scattered incense of [a] sweet smell.   *Smell, sight,*
Then glory and bliss were proclaimed anew;   *Sound*
1124   All sang to honor that noble Jewel.
The sound could strike through the earth to hell,
When the Virtues of heaven chant with joy,
To praise the Lamb in the midst of his company.
1128   Indeed, I experienced a great delight.

Delight, in observing the Lamb,
With much amazement, passed into [my] mind.
He was [the] best, most gracious, and [the] greatest
      to esteem,
1132   That I ever heard described in speech.
His garments were so becomingly white,
His looks humble, himself so noble,
But a wound, very wide and wet, did show
1136   Near his heart, torn through [the] skin.
His blood spurted out from his white side.
Alas, thought I, who committed that outrage?
Any breast ought to have burned with misery
1140   Before it had taken delight in that.

No one would wish to doubt the Lamb's delight.
Though he were injured and had [a] wound,
[It] was never noticed in his expression,
1144   So cheerful were his glorious glances.
I observed among his bright company
How filled and charged with life they were.
Then I saw there my little queen
1148   Who, I believed, had stood by me in [the] valley.
Lord, much of merriment was what she made
Among her companions, she who was so white.
That vision caused me to intend to wade,
1152   Due to [the] loving desire for great delight.


XX

f. 59   Delight entered into me through eye and ear;
My mortal mind was reduced to madness.
When I saw my lovely maiden, I desired to be there
1156   Beyond the water, though she would be upset.
I thought that nothing could thwart me,
To bring me grief and cause me to waver,

---

1143  sembelaunt] semblaunt: Ch.

73

```
              And to start in þe strem schulde non me stere,
1160          To swymme þe remnaunt, þaʒ I þer swalte.
              Bot, of þat munt I watʒ bitalt.
              When I schulde start in þe strem astraye,
              Out of þat caste I watʒ bycalt.
1164          Hit watʒ not at my Prynceʒ paye.


              Hit payed hym not þat I so flonc
              Ouer meruelous mereʒ, so mad arayde.
              Of raas, þaʒ I were rasch and ronk,
1168          Ʒet, rapely þerinne I watʒ restayed,
              For ryʒt as I sparred vnto þe bonc,
              Þat brathe out of my drem me brayde.
              Þen wakned I in þat erber wlonk.          EPILOGUE:
1172          My hede vpon þat hylle watʒ layde,         RETURN TO
              Þeras my perle to grounde strayd.          THE GARDEN
              I raxled and fel in gret affray,
              And, sykyng, to myself I sayd,
1176          "Now al be to þat Prynceʒ paye."


              Me payed ful ille to be out fleme
              So sodenly of þat fayre regioun,
              Fro alle þo syʒteʒ so quyke and queme.
1180          A longeyng heuy me strok in swone,
              And, rewfully þenne, I con toreme.
              "O perle," quoþ I, "of rych renoun,
              So watʒ hit me dere þat þou con deme
1184          In þys veray avysyoun.
              If hit be ueray and soth sermoun
              Þat þou so stykeʒ in garlande gay,
              So wel is me in þys doel-doungoun,
1188          Þat þou art to þat Prynseʒ paye."

f. 59b        To þat Prynceʒ paye hade I ay bente,
              And ʒerned no more þen watʒ me geuen,
              And halden me þer in trwe entent,
1192          As þe perle me prayed, þat watʒ so þryuen,
              As helde drawen to Goddeʒ present,
              To mo of his mysterys I hade ben dryuen;
```

---

1168   restayed] restayd: O, Ch.
1170   brathe] brat[h]þe: O, Go, C, Mo, AW. O believed þ is
       *"apparently superimposed"* on *h*, but the letter be-
       tween *t* and *e* looks more like an *h* in the Orig.
1177   out fleme] out-fleme: eds.
1179   quyke] quykeʒ: MS, M.

And no one would restrain me from starting into the
　　　stream,
1160　To swim the remainder, even if I would perish there.
However, I was startled from that intention.
When I was supposed to spring impetuously into the
　　　stream,
I was called back from that purpose.
1164　It was not to my Prince's liking.

It pleased him not that I thus would rush
Over marvelous streams, so madly resolved.
Though I would be swift and strong in racing,
1168　Yet, I was immediately restrained in that matter,
For just as I sprang to the shore,
That violent movement drew me out of my dream.
Then I awoke in that beautiful garden.　　　*EPILOGUE:*
1172　My head was laid upon that mound,　　　*RETURN TO*
Where my pearl had strayed into [the] earth.　*THE GARDEN*
I started up and dropped down in great dismay,
And, sighing, to myself I said,
1176　"Now all may be to that Prince's liking."

[It] pleased me very poorly to be driven out
So suddenly from that splendid region,
From all those sights so vivid and pleasing.
1180　A heavy yearning sent me into [a] swoon,
And, sorrowfully then, I did lament.
"O pearl," said I, "of rich renown,
So dear was it to me what you did declare
1184　In this truthful vision.
If it be reliable and true speech
That you thus are set within [the] noble garland,
Then [it] is well with me in this miserable prison,
1188　Since you are to that Prince's liking."

f. 59b　Had I always aimed for that Prince's liking,
And desired no more than was given to me,
And maintained myself in that way with true intent,
1192　As the pearl, who was so beautiful, implored me,
When certainly drawing toward God's presence,
I would have been led to more of his mysteries;

---

1180　swone] swoune: Ch.
1181　toreme] to reme: MS, eds.
1185　If] īf: MS.
1186　styke3] st[r]yke3: O, G, Ch, AW.
1190　geuen] g[y]uen: G, Ch, Go, C.
1193　helde] helde[r]: O.

|      | Bot ay wolde man of happe more hente |
| 1196 | Þen moȝten by ryȝt vpon hem clyuen. |
|      | Þerfore, my joye watȝ sone toriuen, |
|      | And I kaste of kytheȝ þat lasteȝ aye. |
|      | Lorde, mad hit arn þat agayn þe stryuen, |
| 1200 | Oþer proferen þe oȝt agayn þy paye. |

|      | To pay þe Prince oþer sete saȝte, |
|      | Hit is ful eþe to þe god Krystyin, |
|      | For I haf founden hym, boþe day and naȝte, |
| 1204 | A God, a Lorde, a Frende ful fyin. |
|      | Ouer þis hyul þis lote I laȝte, |
|      | For þyty of my perle enclyin, |
|      | And syþen to God I hit bytaȝte, |
| 1208 | In Krysteȝ dere blessyng, and myn, |
|      | Þat, in þe forme of bred and wyn, |
|      | Þe preste vus scheweȝ vch a daye. |
|      | He gef vus to be his homly hyne, |
| 1212 | Ande precious perleȝ vnto his pay.   Amen.   Amen. |

1196   moȝten] moȝte: G, Go, C, AW.
1198   kytheȝ] kyþeȝ: H, De.
1201   sete saȝte] sete [hym] saȝte: O.
1202   Krystyin] Krystyn: Ch.
1204   fyin] fyn: Ch.

|      | But man always would wish to seize more of happiness |
| 1196 | Than could be allotted to him with justice. |
|      | Therefore, my joy was soon shattered, |
|      | And I was cast from lands that endure forever. |
|      | Lord, mad are they who strive against you, |
| 1200 | Or present to you anything against your liking. |

|      | To please the Prince or to be made peaceful, |
|      | It is very easy for the good Christian, |
|      | For I have found him, both day and night, |
| 1204 | A God, a Lord, a very excellent Friend. |
|      | I experienced this adventure upon this mound, |
|      | Through pity for my humble pearl, |
|      | And then I entrusted it to God, |
| 1208 | With Christ's glorious blessing, and mine, |
|      | [Christ] whom, in the form of bread and wine, |
|      | The priest shows to us every day. |
|      | May he allow us to be his gracious servants, |
| 1212 | And precious pearls to his liking. Amen. Amen. |

---

1205   hyul] hyl (MS. *hyiil*.): M.  hyiil: O.  Dot over first
       minim of *u* is apparently one of several insignificant
       marks on this folio.
1206   enclyin] enclyn: Ch.
1211   gef] gyve: Ch.

# CLEANNESS

*Folio 60, reproduced by permission of the British Library:* Noah, his wife, and their three sons with two of the wives are in an open boat that is different from the ark described in lines 309–20. There is space for the head of the third wife to the right, but no figure appears there. The boat is similar to the one Jonas sailed in, pictured on folio 86. A hand propeller is being employed, despite the fact that the poet stated in line 419 that the craft was without such an instrument. Noah does not look much different from the sailor throwing Jonas overboard on folio 86.

*Folio 60b, reproduced by permission of the Bristish Library:* There are only three people drawn. Daniel, Baltassar, and the queen. (See lines 1619–41.) Various minor details are delineated such as the writing on the wall, the hand with the stylus, and a wide-mouthed goblet. Daniel does not look much different from the prophet Jonas shown preaching to the Ninivites on folio 86b.

PROLOGUE: THE PARABLE OF THE WEDDING FEAST

f. 61   Clannesse whoso kyndly cowþe comende,
      And rekken vp alle þe resounȝ þat ho by riȝt askeȝ,
      Fayre formeȝ myȝt he fynde in forering his speche,
      And in þe contrare kark and combraunce huge,
5     For wonder wroth is þe Wyȝ þat wroȝt alle þinges
      Wyth þe freke þat, in fylþe, folȝes hym after,
      As renkeȝ of relygioun þat reden and syngen,
      And aþrochen to hys presens, and presteȝ arn called,
      Thay teen vnto his temmple and temen to hym seluen;
10    Reken, wyth reuerence, þay rechen his auter.
      Þay hondel þer his aune body and vsen hit boþe.
      If þay in clannes be clos, þay cleche gret mede,
      Bot if þay conterfete crafte, and cortaysye wont,
      As be honest vtwyth, and inwith alle fylþeȝ,
15    Þen ar þay synful hemself, and sulped altogeder,
      Loþe God and his gere, and hym to greme cachen.


      He is so clene in his courte, þe Kyng þat al weldeȝ,
      And honeste in his housholde, and hagherlych serued
      With angeleȝ enourled in alle þat is clene,
20    Boþe wythinne and wythouten, in wedeȝ ful bryȝt;
      And ȝif he nere scoymus and skyg, and non scaþe louied,
      Hit were a meruayl to much; hit moȝt not falle.


      Kryst kydde hit hymself in a carp oneȝ,
      Þeras he heuened aȝt happeȝ and hyȝt hem her medeȝ.


---

3  forering] (*forering = for-bering*?): M.  for[þ]ering: other
     eds.
5  wonder] First minim of *n* resembles *r*.
10  Reken] Reken[ly]: G.    rechen] first *e* illegible.
     rychen: A, AW.

PROLOGUE: THE PARABLE OF THE WEDDING FEAST

f. 61      Whoever could commend cleanness properly,
           And count up all the narratives that she requires by right,
           Splendid themes could he find for fashioning his speech,
           But in the contrasting themes [about uncleanness] great
                distress and disaster,
5          For exceedingly angry is the God who created all things
           With the man who, in filth, follows after him,
           Such as men of religion who preach and sing,
           And come into his presence, and are called priests.
           They go to his temple and join themselves to him;
10         Promptly, with reverence, they approach his altar.
           They handle there his own body and receive it as well.
           If they be contained in cleanness, they obtain great
                reward,
           But if they simulate virtue, and lack courtesy,
           So as to be honest on the outside, but [have] all
                impurities within,
15         Then they are sinful themselves, and stained altogether,
           Scorn God and his gear, and raise him to wrath.

           He is so clean in his court, the King who controls
                everything,
           And noble in his household, and appropriately served
           By angels enveloped in all that is pure,
20         Both within and without, in garments very bright;
           And if he were not disdainful and fastidious, and [if
                he] loved evil,
           It would be too great a marvel; it could not happen.

           Christ made it known himself in a speech once,
           In which he praised eight blessings and promised the
                rewards for them.

---

15   sulped] sulpe[n]: G, AW.
16   Loþe] Boþe: M, G, A, AW.  UVR does not clarify, but *lo*
        close together looks like *bo*; cf. textual note to line 187.
21   And ȝif] &ȝif: MS. Nif: eds.

83

25      Me myneȝ on one amonge oþer, as Maþew recordeȝ,
        Þat þus of clannesse vncloseȝ a ful cler speche:
        "Þe haþel clene of his hert hapeneȝ ful fayre,
        For he schal loke on oure Lorde wyth a louf-chere."
        As so saytȝ: To þat syȝt seche schal he neuer,
30      Þat any vnclannesse hatȝ on auwhere abowte;
        For he þat flemus vch fylþe fer fro his hert
        May not byde þat burye þat hit his body neȝen.


        Forþy, hyȝ not to heuen in hatereȝ totorne,
        Ne in þe harlateȝ hod, and handeȝ vnwaschen,
35      For what vrþly haþel þat hyȝ honour haldeȝ
        Wolde lyke if a ladde com lyþerly attyred,
f. 61b  When he were sette solempnely in a sete ryche,
        Abof dukeȝ on dece, wyth dayntys serued?
        Þen þe harlot wyth haste helded to þe table,
40      Wyth rent cokreȝ at þe kne, and his clutte trascheȝ,
        And his tabarde totorne, and his toteȝ oute,
        Oþer ani on of alle þyse, he schulde be halden vtter,
        With mony blame ful bygge, a boffet paraunter,
        Hurled to þe halle-dore, and harde þeroute schowued,
45      And be forboden þat borȝe to bowe þider neuer,
        On payne of enprysonment and puttyng in stokkeȝ;
        And thus schal he be schent for his schrowde feble,
        Þaȝ neuer in talle ne in tuch he trespas more.


        And, if vnwelcum he were to a worþlych prynce,
50      Ȝet hym is þe hyȝe Kyng harder in her euen,
        As Maþew meleȝ in his masse of þat man ryche,
        Þat made þe mukel mangerye to marie his here dere,

---

26  clannesse] Me noted first s corrected from ȝ by scribe.
28  louf-chere] bone chere: M, Me, Mo. [le]ue chere: G, AW.
        loue chere: A.   Orig. shows f more clearly.
30  auwhere] anwhere (aywhere?): M.
32  burye] burne (Looks like burre in MS.): M.   bur[n]e: Me,
        Mo.   burre: G, A, AW.      neȝen] neȝe: G, A, AW.
34  harlateȝ] harloteȝ: M.

25 [This] reminds me of one among others, such as Matthew
    mentions,
 Which presents a very clear message about cleanness
    in this way:
 "The man pure in his heart is blessed very abundantly,
 For he shall look upon our Lord with the countenance
    of love."
 Then [it] also signifies: He shall never come to that
    sight,
30 Who has any uncleanness on him anywhere about;
 For he who banishes every filth far from his heart
 Can not endure that it should draw near his body in
    that city.

  Therefore, hasten not to heaven in torn garments,
 Nor in the beggar's hood, and with unwashed hands,
35 For what earthly man who holds high honor
 Would be pleased if a fellow came poorly attired,
f. 61b When he were placed solemnly on a splendid throne,
 Above dukes on dais, served with dainties?
 Then [if] the knave would proceed with haste to the
    table,
40 With leggings ripped at the knee, and his trousers
    patched,
 And his upper garment torn, and his hairs [sticking]
    out,
 Or any one of all these, he would be thrown outside,
 With very many strong rebukes, a blow perhaps,
 Hurled to the hall-door, and shoved firmly thereout,
45 And [he] would be forbidden to ever go there into
    that city,
 Under pain of imprisonment and placing in stocks;
 And thus he shall be ruined because of his inferior
    clothing,
 Though he may never trespass again in word or in deed.

  And so, if he would be unwelcome to a noble prince,
50 The high King is yet more firm with him in this
    situation indeed,
 As Matthew tells in his mass-gospel about that wealthy
    man,
 Who arranged the great banquet to marry his beloved
    heir,

---

38 duke3] dukes: M.
40 clutte] clutte[3]: G.  trasche3] trasches: M. trasche[d]: G.
43 paraunter] peraunter: eds.
49 worþlych] (?*worldlych*, worldly): M. wor[d]lych: Me, Mo, AW.
  w[e]r[d]lych: G.
50 in her euen] (*in her* [?*herin*]): M. in [heven]: Me.
  *in* heuen: G, A, Mo, AW.

And sende his sonde þen to say þat þay samne schulde,
And in comly quoyntis to com to his feste;
55  "For my boles and my boreȝ arn bayted and slayne,
And my fedde fouleȝ fatted wyth sclaȝt,
My polyle, þat is penne-fed, and partrykeȝ boþe,
Wyth scheldeȝ of wylde swyn, swaneȝ, and croneȝ.
Al is roþeled and rosted ryȝt to þe sete.
60  Comeȝ cof to my corte er hit colde worþe."


When þay knewen his cal, þat þider com schulde,
Alle excused hem by þe skyly he scape by moȝt.
On hade boȝt hym a borȝ, he sayde, by hys trawþe.
"Now tue I þeder als-tyd þe toun to byholde."
65  Anoþer nayed also and nurned þis cawse:
"I haf ȝerned and ȝat ȝokkeȝ of oxen,
And for my byȝeȝ hem boȝt. To bowe haf I mester
To see hem pulle in þe plow. Aproche me byhoueȝ."
"And I haf wedded a wyf," sower hym þe þryd.
70  "Excuse me at þe court. I may not com þere."
Þus þay droȝ hem adreȝ, wyth daunger, vch one,
Þat non passed to þe plate, þaȝ he prayed were.


f. 62  Thenne þe ludych lorde lyked ful ille,
And hade dedayn of þat dede; ful dryȝly he carpeȝ.
75  He saytȝ: "Now for her owne sorȝe þay forsaken habbeȝ.
More to wyte is her wrange þen any wylle gentyl.
Þenne gotȝ forth, my gomeȝ, to þe grete streeteȝ,
And forsetteȝ, on vche a syde þe ceté aboute,
Þe wayferande frekeȝ on fote and on hors,
80  Boþe burneȝ and burdeȝ, þe better and þe wers.
Laþeȝ hem alle luflyly to lenge at my fest,

---

57  partrykeȝ] partrykes: M.
64  tue] t[ur]ne: eds.
67  byȝeȝ] hyȝeȝ: eds.  UVR does not clarify, but when bottom

And then sent his messenger to say that they should
     gather,
And in fitting finery come to his feast;
55     "For my bulls and my boars have been baited and slain,
And my well-fed fowls fattened for [the] slaughter,
My poultry, which is fed in the pen, and partridges too,
With slices of wild swine, swans, and cranes.
Everything has been brought together and roasted right
     to the proper point.
60     Come quickly to my court before it becomes cold."

When they learned of his invitation, those who
     should go there,
All excused themselves with the reason they could
     escape by.
One had bought himself a property, he said, on his
     honor.
"Now I must journey there immediately to see the
     dwelling."
65     Another refused also and gave this reason:
"I have longed for and obtained yokes of oxen,
And bought them for my harnesses. I have [a] duty to go
To see them pull at the plow. I am obliged to be
     close by."
"And I have wedded a wife," swore the third to him.
70     "Excuse me at the court. I can not go there."
Thus they drew themselves away, with opposition,
     each one,
So that none passed to the area, though he had been
     invited.

f. 62     Then the lord of the people was very poorly
     pleased,
And showed disdain for that deed; he speaks very
     seriously.
75     He says: "Now they have refused through their own fault.
Their wrong-doing is to be denounced more than any
     pagan's lust.
Then go forth, my servants, into the wide streets,
And stop, on every side around the city,
The wayfaring people on foot and on horse,
80     Both men and women, the better and the worse.
Graciously invite them all to linger at my feast,

---

     of *b* is open, letter resembles *h*; cf. textual note to
     *Pe.* 268.
69   sower] (*swer*?): M.  so wer: Me, G, A, Mo, AW.
72   plate] place: eds.

And brynge3 hem blyþly to bor3e as baroune3 þay were,
So þat my palays plat ful be py3t al aboute.
Þise oþer wreche3, iwysse, worþy no3t wern."


85      Þen þay cayred and com, þat þe cost waked,
        Bro3ten bachlere3 hem wyth, þat þay by bonke3 metten,
        Swyere3 þat swyftly swyed on blonke3,
        And also fele vpon fote, of fre and of bonde.
        When þay com to þe courte, keppte wern þay fayre,
90      Sty3tled wyth þe stewarde, stad in þe halle,
        Ful manerly, wyth marchal, mad for to sitte.
        As he wat3 dere of degré, dressed his seete.


        Þenne segge3 to þe souerayn sayden þerafter:
        "Lo, lorde, wyth your leue, at your lege heste,
95      And at þi banne, we haf bro3t, as þou beden habbe3,
        Mony renischche renke3, and 3et is roum more."
        Sayde þe lorde to þo lede3: "Layte3 3et ferre,
        Ferre out in þe felde, and feche3 mo geste3.
        Wayte3 gorste3 and greue3, if ani gome3 lygge3.
100     What-kyn folk so þer fare, feche3 hem hider.
        Be þay fers, be þay feble, forlote3 none,
        Be þay hol, be þay halt, be þay on-y3ed,
        And þa3 þay ben boþe blynde and balterande cruppele3,
        Þat my hous may holly by halke3 by fylled,
105     For, certe3, þyse ilk renke3 þat me renayed habbe,
        And denounced me no3t, now, at þis tyme,
        Schul neuer sitte in my sale my soper to fele,
        Ne suppe on sope of my seue, þa3 þay swelt schulde."


f. 62b   Thenne þe sergaunte3, at þat sawe, swengen þeroute,
110      And diden þe dede þat demed, as he deuised hade,

---

83  plat ful] plat-ful: M.  platful: G, A.  Words seem
        separated in MS.
86  metten] Me noted n corrected from 3 by scribe.
98  Ferre] Fer[k]e[3]: G, AW.
101 forlote3] for-lete3: G.

And bring them merrily to [this] dwelling as if they
    were barons,
So that my palace may be made absolutely full all
    around.
These other wretches, indeed, were not worthy."

85      Then they went out and returned, those who searched
    the area,
Brought young men with them, whom they met by hill-
    sides,
Squires who swiftly followed on steeds,
And also many people on foot, among nobles and among
    serfs.
When they arrived at the court, they were treated well,
90    Directed by the steward, standing in the hall,
[And] very politely, by [the] marshal, made to sit.
As he was noble in rank, his seat was arranged.

      Then [the] servants said to the lord after that:
"Behold, lord, by your leave, at your sovereign behest,
95    And according to your edict, we have brought, as you
    have ordered,
Many lowborn men, and still [there] is more room."
The lord said to these men: "Seek still further,
Far out on the land, and bring more guests.
Search furze fields and groves, in case any men
    linger [there].
100    Whatever kind of folk go there, bring them here.
Be they strong, be they weak, overlook none,
Be they healthy, be they lame, be they one-eyed,
And even if they may be both blind and hobbling
    cripples,
So that my house may be completely filled to [the]
    corners,
105    For, certainly, these same men who have refused me,
And proclaimed me insignificant, now, at this time,
Shall never sit in my hall to taste my supper,
Nor swallow one sop of my stew, even if they should
    perish."

f. 62b    Then the servants, with that report, rush out of
    there,
110    And did the deed that was decreed, as he had related,

---

104   may] Me noted *m* apparently corrected from *ia* by scribe.
      halkeȝ] halkes: M.
108   þaȝ] þaȝ þaȝ: MS.    swelt] The *w*, with two flourishes off
      the top, may be by a second hand. Orig. shows brown
      ink much darker than that used in the MS.
110   þat demed] þat [is] demed: M, Me, Mo. þat [watȝ] demed:
      G, AW.

And wyth peple of alle plyte₃ þe palays þay fyllen.
Hit weren not alle on wyue₃ sune₃, wonen wyth on fader.
Wheþer þay wern worþy oþer wers, wel wern þay stowed,
Ay þe best byfore and bry₃test atyred,

115  Þe derrest at þe hy₃e dese, þat dubbed wer fayrest,
And syþen on lenþe bilooghe, lede₃ inogh,
And ay asegge soerly, semed by her wede₃.
So with marschal at her mete mensked þay were.
Clene men in compaynye forknowen wern lyte,

120  And ₃et, þe symplest in þat sale wat₃ serued to þe fulle
Boþe with menske and wyth mete, and mynstrasy noble,
And alle þe layke₃ þat a lorde a₃t in londe schewe;
And þay bigonne to be glad, þat god drink haden,
And vch mon wyth his mach made hym at ese.


125  Now, inmydde₃ þe mete, þe mayster hym biþo₃t
       Þat he wolde se þe semblé þat samned was þere,
And rehayte rekenly þe riche and þe poueuer,
And cherisch hem alle wyth his cher, and chaufen her
       joye.
Þen he bowe₃ fro his bour into þe brode halle,

130  And to þe best on þe bench, and bede hym be myry,
Solased hem wyth semblaunt, and syled fyrre,
Tron fro table to table, and talkede ay myrþe;
Bot as he ferked ouer þe flor, he fande wyth his y₃e
Hit wat₃ not for a halyday honestly arayed,

135  A þral þry₃t in þe þrong, vnþryuandely cloþed,
Ne no festiual frok, bot fyled with werkke₃.

116  bilooghe] biloogh: A.  Anderson treats mark off h as
       flourish instead of abbr. for e.
117  asegge] a segge: M, Me, A, Mo.  a[s] segge[s]: G, AW.
       soerly] (soberly?): M.  s[e]erly: G.  soberly: A.
       serly: AW.
122  layke₃] Darker a indicates alteration over some other
       letters.

And they fill the palace with people of all ranks.
They were not all one [kind of] wife's sons, conceived
    by one [kind of] father.
Whether they were noble or less fortunate, they were
    placed well,
The best and most brilliantly attired always in front,
115     The noblest, who were arrayed most adequately, on the
    high dais,
And then many men at length, below,
And always delineated individually, seen by their
    garments.
Thus they were treated courteously at their meal by
    [the] marshal.
Elegant men in [the] company were recognized quickly,
120     And yet, the plainest man in that hall was served to
    the limit,
Both with honor and with equity, and splendid
    minstrelsy,
And all the entertainments that a lord ought to show
    on land;
And they who had good drink began to be glad,
And each man made himself at ease with his mate.

125     Now, in the middle of the meal, the master decided
That he would see the company which was gathered there,
And courteously encourage the rich and the poor,
And comfort them all with his kindness, and increase
    their joy.
Then he goes from his place into the wide hall,
130     And to the best on the bench, and bade them to be merry,
Cheered them with [his] hospitality, and passed on
    further,
Stepped from table to table, and always talked with
    delight;
But as he moved across the floor, he perceived with
    his eye
[That] someone was not decently dressed for a festival,
135     A thrall thrust in the throng, improperly clothed,
Not with any festive frock, but [with one] defiled
    by [dirty] deeds.

---

123  bigonne] bignne: A.    haden] Looks like *laden* because
    smaller stroke of *h* is barely visible; *ha* and *la* re-
    semble each other when smaller stroke of *h* merges
    with *a*.
127  poueuer] (MS. poueu*e*r): M.  poueren: M, Me, G, Mo, AW.
    pouer: A.
136  Ne no] Ne [i*n*] no: G.

Þe gome watȝ vngarnyst wyth god men to dele,
And gremed þerwyth þe grete lorde, and greue hym he
    þoȝt.

"Say me, frende!" quoþ þe freke wyth a felle chere.

140     "Hov wan þou into þis won in wedeȝ so fowle?
Þe abyt þat þou hatȝ vpon, no halyday hit menskeȝ.
Þou, burne, for no brydale art busked in wedeȝ.
How watȝ þou hardy þis hous for þyn vnhap neȝe,
In on so ratted a robe and rent at þe sydeȝ?

f. 63    Þou art a gome vngoderly in þat goun febele.
146     Þou praysed me and my place ful pouer and ful nedé,
Þat watȝ so prest to aproche my presens hereinne.
Hopeȝ þou I be a harlot þi erigaut to prayse?"


Þat oþer burne watȝ abayst of his broþe wordeȝ,

150     And hurkeleȝ doun with his hede. Þe vrþe he biholdeȝ.
He watȝ so scoumfit of his scylle, lest he skaþe hent,
Þat he ne wyst on worde what he warp schulde.


Þen þe lorde wonder loude laled and cryed,
And talkeȝ to his tormenttoureȝ: "Takeȝ hym!" he biddeȝ

155     "Byndeȝ byhynde at his bak boþe two his handeȝ,
And felle fettereȝ to his fete festeneȝ bylyue.
Stik hym stifly in stokeȝ, and stekeȝ hym þerafter
Depe in my doungoun þer doel euer dwelleȝ,
Greuing, and gretyng, and gryspyng harde

160     Of teþe tenfully togeder, to teche hym be quoynt."


Thus comparisuneȝ Kryst þe kyndom of heuenn
To þis frelych feste þat fele arn to called,
For alle arn laþed luflyly, þe luþer and þe better
Þat euer wern fulȝed in font, þat fest to haue.

165     Bot, war þe wel if þou wylt. Þy wedeȝ ben clene

---

138   lorde] lord: M, Me, Mo.  (G, p. 71, noted "e blotted.")
139   quoþ] quod: M, Me.  (also in 345, 349, 621, 729, 733, 739
       757, 761, 765, 925, 929 & 1593).
143   vnhap neȝe] vnhap [to] neȝe: all eds. except A.

The man was unprepared to associate with good men,
And the great lord became angry with him, and he
　　　intended to reprimand him.

"Tell me, friend!" said the lord in a fierce mood.
140　"How did you come into this place in garments so
　　　unbecoming?
The clothing that you have on honors no festival.
You, man, are not dressed in garments for [a]
　　　wedding feast.
How could you be [so] presumptuous to approach this
　　　house in your miserable condition,
In a robe so ragged and ripped at the sides?
f. 63　You are a wretched man in that worn-out gown.
146　You honored me and my position very poorly and very
　　　inadequately,
You who had been so quick to approach my presence in
　　　this place.
Do you think I would be a trifler to praise your garment?"

That other man was dismayed by his angry words,
150　And lowers his head. He beholds the ground.
He was so embarrassed by the argument, afraid that he
　　　would receive harm,
That he knew not one word that he should utter.

Then the lord very loudly cursed and cried out,
And [he] talks to his torturers: "Take him!" he orders.
155　"Bind both his hands behind his back,
And quickly fasten cruel fetters to his feet.
Set him firmly in stocks, and shut him after that
Deep in my dungeon where sorrow continually dwells,
In grieving, and weeping, and bitter gnashing
160　Of teeth painfully together, to teach him to be
　　　courteous."

Thus Christ compares the kingdom of heaven
To this courtly feast to which many are called,
For all are graciously invited, the bad and the
　　　better people
Who ever were baptized in [a] font, to attend that
　　　feast.
165　However, guard yourself well if you desire [to attend].
　　　Your garments must be clean

---

146　nedé] [g]nede: all eds. except A.
148　erigaut] erigant: M.
159　gryspyng] grysp[yt]yng: G.
161　heuenn] heueñ: MS, M.　heven: Me.　heuen: G, A, Mo, AW.

And honest for þe halyday, lest þou harme lache,
For aproch þou to þat Prynce of parage noble.
He hates helle no more þen hem pat ar sowle.


Wich arn, þenne, þy wedeȝ þou wrappeȝ þe inne,
170    Þat schal schewe hem so schene schrowde of þe best?
Hit arn þy werkeȝ, wyterly, þat þou wroȝt haueȝ
And lyued, wyth þe lykyng þat lyȝe in þyn hert.
Þat þo be frely and fresch fonde in þy lyue,
And fetyse of a fayr forme, to fote and to honde,
175    And syþen alle þyn oþer lymeȝ lapped ful clene;
Þenne may þou se þy Sauior and his sete ryche.


For fele fauteȝ may a freke forfete his blysse,
Þat he þe Souerayn ne se þen--for slauþe one,
As for bobaunce, and bost, and bolnande priyde.
180    Þroly into þe deueleȝ þrote man þryngeȝ bylyue
f. 63b  ffor couetyse, and colwarde, and croked dedeȝ,
ffor monsworne, and mensclaȝt, and to much drynk,
For þefte, and for þrepyng. Vnþonk may mon haue
For roborrye, and riboudrye, and resouneȝ vntrwe,
185    And dysheriete and depryue dowrie of wydoeȝ,
ffor marryng of maryageȝ, and mayntnaunce of schreweȝ,
For traysoun, and trichcherye, and tyrauntyré boþe,
And for fals famacions, and fayned laweȝ.
Man may mysse þe myrþe þat much is to prayse
190    For such vnþeweȝ as þise, and þole much payne,
And in þe Creatores cort com neuermore,
Ne neuer see hym with syȝt for such sour tourneȝ.


Bot, I haue herkned and herde of mony hyȝe clerkeȝ,

---

172    lyued] lyned: A.
177    fele] fele[r]: G, AW.
179    priyde] pryde: Me, Mo.

And fitting for the festival, lest you experience
    misfortune,
Because you must draw near to that Prince of noble
    lineage.
He hates hell no more than [he hates] them who are
    impure.

What are, then, your clothes [that] you wrap
    yourself in,
170     That must show themselves as bright garments of the
    best quality?
They are your actions, certainly, that you have
    established
And lived by, with the desires that lie in your heart.
Take care in your lifetime that those may be noble
    and clean,
And fashioned in a fair form, at feet and at hands,
175     And then all your other limbs very neatly clothed;
Then may you see your Saviour and his royal throne.

A man may forfeit his happiness through many faults,
So that he may not see the Sovereign then--through
    sloth for one,
As through pomp, and presumption, and puffed up pride.
180     Man steadfastly makes [his] way promptly into the
    devil's throat
f. 63b   For covetousness, and villainy, and wrong deeds,
For perjury, and murder, and too much drink,
For larceny, and for quarreling.  Man may receive
    censure
For robbery, and ribaldry, and false statements,
185     And disinheriting and depriving widows of dowers,
For marring of marriages, and maintenance of
    mistresses,
For treason, and treachery, and tyranny too,
And for false rumors, and feigned laws.
Man may miss the mirth that is to be praised
    abundantly
190     For such sins as these, and suffer great hardship,
And come nevermore into the Creator's court,
Nor ever see him with sight because of such immoral
    actions.

Furthermore, I have listened and heard from many
    important clerics,

---

187  boþe] (loþe?): M.  When written close together, *bo* and
    *lo* look alike; cf. textual note to line 16.

And als in resoune3 of ry3t red hit myseluen,
195 Þat þat ilk proper Prynce þat Paradys welde3
Is displesed at vch a poynt þat plyes to scaþe,
Bot neuer 3et in no boke breued I herde
Þat euer he wrek so wyþerly on werk þat he made,
Ne venged for no vilté of vice ne synne,
200 Ne so hastyfly wat3 hot for hatel of his wylle,
Ne neuer so sodenly so3t vnsoundely to weng,
As for fylþe of þe flesch þat foles han vsed;
For, as I fynde, þer he for3et alle his fre þewe3,
And wex wod to þe wrache for wrath at his hert.


## PART ONE: LUCIFER, ADAM, AND NOAH


205 ffor þe fyrste, felonye þe falce fende wro3t
Whyl he wat3 hy3e in þe heuen, houen vpon lofte,
Of alle þyse aþel aungele3 attled þe fayrest.
And, he vnkyndely, as a karle, kydde are Ward.
He se3 no3t bot hymself, how semly he were.
210 Bot, his Souerayn he forsoke, and sade þyse worde3:
"I schal telde vp my trone in þe tramountayne,
And by lyke to þat Lorde þat þe lyft made."
With þis worde þat he warp, þe wrake on hym ly3t.
Dry3tyn, wyth his dere dom, hym drof to þe abyme,
215 In þe mesure of his mode, his met3 neuer þe lasse;
Bot, þer he tynt þe tyþe dool of his tour ryche.


f. 64 Þa3 þe feloun were so fers, for his fayre wede3,
And his glorious glem þat glent so bry3t,
As sone as Dry3tyne3 dome drof to hymseluen,
220 Þikke þowsande3, þro þrwen þeroute,
Fellen fro þe fyrmament, fende3 ful blake,

---

201 weng] weng[e]: Me.
203 þewe3] þewes: M.

And also declared it myself with statements of truth,
195 That that same proper Prince who rules Paradise
Is displeased with every condition which yields to evil,
But never yet from any book have I heard declared
That he ever punished so perversely one work that he
made,
Nor sought vengeance for any meanness of vice or sin,
200 Nor was angry so hastily because of opposition to his
will,
Nor ever sought so suddenly to exact penalties
adversely,
As for filth of the flesh which sinners have practiced;
For, as I notice, then he forgot all his noble virtues,
And became fierce with the punishment because of
wrath in his heart.


PART ONE: LUCIFER, ADAM, AND NOAH


205 At the start, the false fiend committed treachery
While he was high in the heaven, raised aloft,
Designated the noblest of all these glorious angels.
And yet, he behaved unnaturally before [his] Guardian,
like a churl.
He saw nothing but himself, how fair he was.
210 Moreover, he forsook his Sovereign, and said these
words:
"I shall set up my throne by the north pole-star,
And be similar to that Lord who made the heavens."
With this statement that he delivered, the disaster
fell upon him.
God, with his severe judgment, drove him into the abyss,
215 According to the measure of his [rebellious] mood,
his capacities none the less;
Furthermore, there he lost the tenth part of his
splendid paradise.


f. 64 Though the wretch had been so proud, with his
beautiful garments,
And his glorious beam that shone so brightly,
As soon as God's decree was passed upon him,
220 Numerous thousands, violently thrown out of there,
Fell from the firmament, very black fiends,

---

208 are Ward] areward: MS, M.  a reward: Me, G, A, Mo, AW.
211 tramountayne] tra mountayne: M.

97

Sweued at þe fyrst swap as þe snaw þikke,
Hurled into helle-hole as þe hyue swarmeȝ;
Fylter fenden folk forty dayeȝ lencþe

225   Er þat styngande storme stynt ne myȝt;
Bot, as smylt mele vnder smal siue smokeȝ for þikke,
So fro heuen to helle þat hatel schor laste,
On vche syde of þe worlde, aywhere ilyche.


3is, hit watȝ a brem brest and a byge wrache,
230   And ȝet, wrathed not þe wyȝ, ne þe wrech saȝtled,
Ne neuer wolde, for wylnesful, his worþy God knawe,
Ne þray hym for no pité, so proud watȝ his wylle.
Forþy, þaȝ þe rape were rank, þe rawþe watȝ lyttel.
Þaȝ he be kest into kare, he kepes no better.


235   Bot, þat oþer wrake þat wex on wyȝeȝ, hit lyȝt
Þurȝ þe faut of a freke þat fayled in trawþe,
Adam inobedyent, ordaynt to blysse.
Þer pryuély in Paradys his place watȝ devised.
To lyue þer in lykyng þe lenþe of a terme,
240   And þenne enherite þat home þat aungeleȝ forgart,
Bot þurȝ þe eggyng of Eue, he ete of an apple
Þat enpoysened alle pepleȝ þat parted fro hem boþe,
For a defence þat watȝ dyȝt of Dryȝtyn seluen,
And a payne þeron put and pertly halden.
245   Þe defence watȝ þe fryt þat þe freke towched,
And þe dom is þe deþe þat drepeȝ vus alle.
Al in mesure and meþe watȝ mad þe vengiaunce,
And efte amended wyth a Mayden þat make had neuer.

---

222  Sweued] Weued (wened?): M.  UVR does not clàrify, but
     offset on my enlarged photostat shows what resembles
     initial s, like the others in the line.
224  Fylter] Fyltyr: M, G.  Offset on my enlargement shows
     -ter; initial letters are not clear.
225  Er þat] Confirmed by offset in my enlargement.
226  Bot] Confirmed by offset.      smokeȝ] smokes: M.
     for þikke] for-þikke: M, Me, Mo, AW.
229  3is, hit] Þis hit (3is?): M.  Þis hit: Me, A, Mo.
     3isse, hit: G.  Neither UVR nor enlargement clarifies

Swirling at the first stroke like the thick snow,
Whirling into hell's hole like swarms of bees into
    the hive;
Fiendish folk pressed together forty days in length
225 Before that stinging storm could end;
Yet, as [a] sardine dinner under [a] fine broth smokes
    with thickness,
Thus from heaven to hell did that deadly shower extend,
On every side of the world, everywhere in the same way.

Yes, it was a grave misfortune and a powerful
    punishment,
230 And still, the devil did not grieve, nor did the wretch
    become reconciled,
Nor would [he] ever, because of obstinacy, acknowledge
    his noble God,
Nor pray to him for any pity, so proud was his will.
Therefore, though the treachery were terrible, the
    grief was little.
Though he be plunged into misfortune, he desires no
    better.

235 Yet, that other disaster that came upon people
    developed
Through the fault of a man who failed in loyalty,
Disobedient Adam, ordained for bliss.
Privately there in Paradise his dwelling was designed.
[He was] to live there in happiness the length of a
    term,
240 And then to inherit that home which [the] angels had
    forfeited,
But through the urging of Eve, he ate of an apple
That poisoned all peoples who descended from both of
    them,
Because of a prohibition that had been determined by
    God himself,
And a punishment placed thereon and plainly revealed.
245 The prohibited thing was the fruit that the man tasted,
And the sentence is the death which strikes us all.
The punishment was carried out completely, with reason
    and justice,
And afterwards amended through a Maiden who never had
    [a] mate.

---

first letter in line.
231 wylnesful] wyl[fulnes]: Me, Mo, AW.
233 lyttel] lyttel: MS.
237 inobedyent] in obedyent: MS, M. (obedience?): M.
245 towched] w made like that of swelt--see textual note to
    line 108. Darker brown ink in Orig. of words on bottom
    right of this folio indicates retracing.
247 vengiaunce] veng[a]unce: Me.
248 had] hade: M.

99

250 $\mathbf{B}$ot, in þe þryd, watʒ forþrast al þat þryue schuld.
Þer watʒ malys mercyles and mawgré much scheued,
Þat watʒ for fylþe vpon folde þat þe folk vsed,
Þat þen wonyed in þe worlde wythouten any maysterʒ.

f. 64b   Hit wern þe fayrest of forme and of face als,
Þe most and þe myriest þat maked wern euer,
255  Þe styfest, þe stalworþest, þat stod euer on fete,
And lengest lyf in hem lent, of ledeʒ alle oþer,
ffor hit was þe forme foster þat þe folde bred,
Þe aþel auncetereʒ suneʒ þat Addam watʒ called,
To wham God hade geuen alle þat gayn were,
260  Alle þe blysse boute blame þat bodi myʒt haue,
And þose lykkest to þe lede þat lyued next after.
Forþy, so semly to see syþen wern none.



Þer watʒ no law to hem layd, bot loke to kynde,
And kepe to hit and alle hit cors clanly fulfylle;
265  And þenne founden þay fylþe in fleschlych dedeʒ,
And controeued agayn kynde contrare werkeʒ,
And vsed hem vnþryftyly, vch on on oþer,
And als with oþer, wylsfully, vpon a wrange wyse.
So ferly fowled her flesch þat þe fende loked
270  How þe deʒter of þe douþe wern derelych fayre,
And fallen in felaʒschyp wyth hem on folken wyse,
And engendered on hem jeaunteʒ wyth her japeʒ ille.
Þose wern men meþeleʒ, and maʒty on vrþe,
Þat for her lodlych laykeʒ alosed þay were.
275  He watʒ famed for fre þat feʒt loued best,
And ay þe bigest in bale þe best watʒ halden;

---

257  ffor] A mark off bottom left of *r*, perhaps a slip of the
pen, makes letter resemble a modern *x*.      forme foster
forme-foster (*forme-fostereʒ*): M.   forme-foster: Me,
G, Mo.

Yet, with the third disaster, everything that should
    flourish was crushed.
250  There was merciless severity and much displeasure
    shown,
That was due to impurity on earth which the people
    practiced,
Who lived then in the world without any masters.
f. 64b  They were the fairest in form and in face also,
The greatest and the most handsome who were ever
    created,
255  The strongest, the bravest, who ever stood on feet,
And longest life remained in them, of all other men,
For this was the first offspring that the earth
    produced,
The noble sons of the ancestor who was called Adam,
To whom God had given all that could be profitable,
260  All the happiness without imperfection that [a]
    person could have,
And afterwards [he gave] those most similar joys to
    the people who lived next.
Therefore, none were so fair to be seen then.

There was no law set upon them, except [that] locked
    in nature,
And [the stipulation] to keep to it and to fulfill
    fittingly all its regulations;
265  But then they discovered impurity in carnal deeds,
And contrived contrary works against nature,
And practiced them dissolutely, each one on [the]
    other,
And also against others, wilfully, in a wrong manner.
[They] defiled their flesh so horribly that the fiends
    observed
270  How the daughters in the group were extremely beauti-
    ful,
And engage in sexual intercourse with them according
    to [the] custom of people,
And engendered giants on them through their evil
    deceptions.
Those were ruthless men, and mighty upon earth,
Who were known through their loathsome pastimes.
275  He was reputed as [a] noble man who loved to fight best,
And always the most eminent in evil-doing was con-
    sidered the noblest;

258  Addam] adam: M.  Adam: Me, A, Mo, AW.  Adam: G.
261  lede] (For *lede* read *lede3*?): M.

101

And þenne eueleȝ on erþe ernestly grewen,
And multyplyed monyfolde inmongeȝ mankynde,
For þat þe maȝty on molde so marre þise oþer,
280    Þat þe Wyȝe þat al wroȝt ful wroþly bygynneȝ.

When he knew vche contré coruppte in hitseluen,
And vch freke forloyned fro þe ryȝt wayeȝ,
Felle temptande tene towched his hert,
As Wyȝe, wo hym withinne, werp to hymseluen:
285    "Me forþynkeȝ ful much þat euer I mon made,
Bot I schal delyuer and do away þat doten on þis molde,
And fleme out of þe folde al þat flesch wereȝ,
Fro þe burne to þe best, fro bryddeȝ to fyscheȝ.
f. 65    Al schal doun and be ded, and dryuen out of erþe,
290    Þat euer I sette saule inne; and sore hit me rweȝ
Þat euer I made hem myself. Bot, if I may herafter,
I schal wayte to be war her wrencheȝ to kepe."

Þenne in worlde watȝ a wyȝe wonyande on lyue,
Ful redy and ful ryȝtwys, and rewled hym fayre.
295    In þe drede of Dryȝtyn his dayeȝ he vseȝ,
And, ay glydande wyth his God, his grace watȝ þe more.
Hym watȝ þe nome Noe, as is innoghe knawen.
He had þre þryuen suneȝ, and þay þre wyueȝ.
Sem soþly þat on; þat oþer hyȝt Cam,
300    And þe jolef Japheth watȝ gendered þe þryd.

Now God in nwy to Noe con speke.
Wylde, wrakful wordeȝ, in his wylle, greued:
"Þe ende of alle-kyneȝ flesch þat on vrþe meueȝ
Is fallen forþ-wyth my face, and forþer hit I þenk.
305    Wyth her vnworþelych werk, me wlateȝ wythinne;
Þe gore þerof me hatȝ greued, and þe glette nwyed.
I schal strenkle my distresse and strye al togeder,
Boþe ledeȝ and londe, and alle þat lyf habbeȝ.

---

279  marre] marre[d]: G.
281  coruppte] corupte: M.

And then evils on earth increased intensely,
And multiplied many times among mankind,
Because the powerful ones on earth harmed these others
    so much,
280    So that the God who created everything begins [to
    complain] very grievously.

When he recognized every region corrupt in itself,
And every man separated from the true paths,
[A] grievously distressing bitterness touched his
    heart,
So that God, with sorrow within him, said to himself:
285    "[It] displeases me very much that I ever made man,
But I shall destroy and put away those who behave
    irrationally on this earth,
And drive out of the land all who have flesh,
From the man to the beast, from birds to fishes.
f. 65    All shall [fall] down and be dead, and driven from earth,
290    In whom I ever placed [a] soul; and it grieves me deeply
That I ever made them myself. However, that I may
    [look] to the future,
I shall take precautions to be careful to preserve
    their means of existence."

A man with vitality was then dwelling in [the] world,
Very able and very righteous, and [he] maintained
    himself well.
295    He passes his days in the fear of God,
And, always living with his God, his grace was the
    greater.
The name Noah was [given] to him, as [it] is widely
    known.
He had three handsome sons, and they [had] three wives.
Sem [was] truly the first; the other was named Cham,
300    And the gallant Japhet was engendered the third.

Now God did speak to Noah with bitterness.
Wild, angry words, according to his mood, seethed:
"The end of every kind of creature who moves on earth
Has come before my sight, and I intend to speed it.
305    Because of their unworthy conduct, I am disgusted within;
The filth of it has offended me, and the corruption has
    annoyed [me].
I shall send down my punishment and destroy all together,
Both men and land, and all that have life.

---

297  innoghe] innogh: A.
304  forþ-wyth] forþ wyth: MS, M, Me, Mo.

"Bot, make to þe a mancioun--and þat is my wylle--
310 A cofer closed of tres, clanlych planed.
Wyrk woneʒ þerinne for wylde and for tame,
And þenne cleme hit wyth clay comly wythinne,
And, alle þe endentur dryuen, daube wythouten;
And þus of lenþe and of large þat lome þou make.
315 Þre hundred of cupydeʒ þou holde to þe lenþe,
Of fyfty fayre ouerþwert forme þe brede,
And loke euen þat þyn ark haue of heʒþe þretté,
And a wyndow wyd vpon, wroʒt vpon lofte,
In þe compas of a cubit, kyndely sware,
320 A wel dutande dor, don on þe syde.
Haf halleʒ þerinne, and halkeʒ ful mony,
Boþe boskeʒ and boureʒ, and wel bounden peneʒ,
For I schal waken vp a water to wasch alle þe worlde,
And quelle alle þat is quik wyth quauende flodeʒ,
f. 65b Alle þat glydeʒ and gotʒ and gost of lyf habbeʒ.
326 I schal wast, with my wrath, þat wons vpon vrþe,
Bot my forwarde wyth þe I festen on þis wyse,
For þou in reysoun hatʒ rengned and ryʒtwys ben euer.


"Þou schal enter þis ark wyth þyn aþel barneʒ,
330 And þy wedded wyf. With þe þou take
Þe makeʒ of þy myry suneʒ. Þis meyny of aʒte
I schal saue of monneʒ sauleʒ, and swelt þose oþer.
Of vche best þat bereʒ lyf, busk þe a cupple.
Of vche clene, comly kynde, enclose seuen makeʒ.
335 Of vche horwed, in ark halde bot a payre,
For to saue me þe sede of alle ser kyndeʒ;
And ay þou meng wyth þe maleʒ þe mete ho-besteʒ,
Vche payre by payre, to plese ayþer oþer.
Wyth alle þe fode þat may be founde frette þy cofer,
340 For sustnaunce to yowself and also þose oþer."


---

312 wythinne] wythinme: MS.
318 wyd vpon] wyd vpon[ande]: G, A, AW.    lofte] Looks like
     loste in MS, but scribe may have missed joining top of
     t to f.

"However, make for yourself a structure--and that
          is my will--
310   A vessel enclosed with planks, smoothed perfectly.
      Design dwellings therein for wild creatures and for tame,
      And then plaster it with clay appropriately within,
      And, with all the seals fastened, daub [it] on the
          outside;
      And thus in length and in width you must make that
          vessel.
315   You must measure about three hundred cubits for the
          length,
      Form the width about fifty cubits right across,
      And certainly see that your ark has thirty cubits in
          height,
      And a wide window to be opened, made on top,
      In the measurement of a cubit, appropriately square,
320   [And] a door closing well, constructed on the side.
      Have halls therein, and very many nooks,
      Both shrubs and shelters, and pens fastened well,
      For I shall stir up a rainstorm to wash all the world,
      And kill all that is alive with throbbing floods,
f. 65b  All that comes and goes and has spirit of life.
326   I shall ruin, in my wrath, what dwells upon earth,
      But my covenant with you I seal in this manner,
      Because you have reigned with reason and have always
          been righteous.

      "You shall enter this ark with your noble children,
330   And your wedded wife.  You shall take with you
      The spouses of your pleasant sons.  This company of
          eight
      I shall save among [the] souls of mankind, but [I]
          shall destroy those others.
      From every beast that bears life, obtain for yourself
          a couple.
      From every clean, fair kind, enclose seven pairs.
335   From every unclean kind, keep only one pair in [the]
          ark,
      In order to save the seed for me of all [the] various
          species;
      And always you must mingle with the males the appro-
          priate females,
      Each pair by pair, to please each other.
      Fill your vessel with all the food that can be found,
340   For sustenance for yourself and also those others."

---

322  Boþe] Me noted e perhaps corrected from o, and what looks
     like retraced words in bottom lines of f. 65.
     boske3] boske[n]3: G, AW.
324  þat] MS has þat þat, with second one crossed out.

105

Ful grayþely gotʒ þis god man and dos Godeʒ hestes,
In dryʒ dred and daunger, þat durst do non oþer.
Wen hit watʒ fettled and forged, and to þe fulle grayþed
Þenn con Dryʒttyn hym dele dryʒly þyse wordeʒ:

345 "Now, Noe," quoþ oure Lorde, "art þou al redy?
      Hatʒ þou closed þy kyst wyth clay alle aboute?"
    "ʒe, Lorde, wyth þy leue," sayde þe lede þenne.
    "Al is wroʒt, at þi worde, as þou me wyt lanteʒ."
    "Enter in þenn," quoþ he, "and haf þi wyf wyth þe,
350 Þy þre suneʒ, wythouten þrep, and her þre wyueʒ.
    Besteʒ, as I bedene haue, bosk þerinne als,
    And when ʒe arn staued styfly, stekeʒ yow þerinne.
    Fro seuen dayeʒ ben seyed, I sende out bylyue
    Such a rowtande ryge þat rayne schal swyþe,
355 Þat schal wasch alle þe worlde of werkeʒ of fylþe.
    Schal no flesch vpon folde by fonden on lyue,
    Outtaken yow aʒt in þis ark staued,
    And sed þat I wyl saue of þyse ser besteʒ."

      Now Noe neuer systeʒ þat niyʒ he bygynneʒ
360   Er al wer stawed and stoken, as þe steuen wolde.
f. 66 Thenne sone com þe seuenþe day, when samned wern alle,
      And alle woned in þe whichche, þe wylde and þe tame.


      Þen bolned þe abyme and bonkeʒ con ryse;
      Waltes out vch walle-heued in ful wode stremeʒ.
365   Watʒ no brymme þat abod vnbrosten. Bylyue,
      Þe mukel, lauande loghe to þe lyfte rered.
      Mony clustered clowde clef alle in clowteʒ.
      Torent vch a rayn-ryfte and rusched to þe vrþe,
      ffon neuer in forty dayeʒ, and þen þe flod ryses,
370   Ouerwalteʒ vche a wod and þe wyde feldeʒ.


_____

341  god man] godman: A.
359  Now] No partly faded.      systeʒ] (stynteʒ?): M.
     sty[n]tez: Me, G, A, Mo, AW.      niyʒ] niyʒ[t]: M, A,
     AW.  [n]yʒ[t]: Me, G, Mo.

106

This good man goes very agreeably and carries out
     God's commands,
With enduring awe and submission, he who dared do
     nothing else.
When it was fashioned and constructed, and fitted to
     the limit,
Then did God seriously speak these words to him:

345      "Now, Noah," said our Lord, "are you all ready?
Have you covered your ark with clay all around?"
"Yes, Lord, by your leave," the man said then.
"Everything is done, according to your word, because
     you gave me wisdom."
"Enter in then," said he, "and take your wife with you,
350     Your three sons, without debate, and their three wives.
Bring beasts therein also, as I have bidden,
And when you are firmly situated, shut yourselves
     therein.
After seven days have passed, I shall send out quickly
Such a roaring tempest that shall shed rain intensely,
355     That shall wash all the world of deeds of filth.
No flesh on earth shall be found with life,
Excepting you eight in this enclosed ark,
And seed that I wish to save from these various beasts."

Now Noah never stops that arduous activity he must
     undertake
360     Until all were placed and locked in, as the voice [of
     God] decreed.
f. 66   Then soon came the seventh day, when all were gathered,
And all were situated in the ark, the wild creatures
     and the tame.

Then the sea depths swelled and did rise over
     embankments;
[Water] springs out from every source in very wild
     streams.
365     [There] was no river that remained unleashed. Quickly,
The powerful, pouring water mounted toward the heavens.
Many clustered clouds cracked completely into pieces.
Every curtain of rain tore out and rushed to the earth,
Never ceased for forty days, and then the flood rises,
370     Overflows every wood and the wide fields.

---

360   Er] Partly faded.
364   walle-heued] w[e]lle-heved: Me, Mo.
366   loghe] logh: A.

For when þe water of þe welkyn wyth þe worlde mette,
Alle þat deth moȝt dryȝe drowned þerinne.
Þer watȝ moon for to make when meschef was cnowen
Þat noȝt dowed, bot þe deth, in þe depe stremeȝ.
375 Water wylger ay wax, woneȝ þat stryede,
Hurled into vch hous, hent þat þer dowelled.


ffyrst, feng to þe flyȝt alle þat fle myȝt.
Vuche burde wyth her barne þe byggyng þay leueȝ,
And bowed to þe hyȝ bonk þer brentest hit wern,
380 And, heterly, to þe hyȝe hylleȝ þay aled on faste;
Bot al watȝ nedleȝ her note, for neuer cowþe stynt
Þe roȝe raynande ryg, þe raykande waweȝ,
Er vch boþom watȝ brurdful to þe bonkeȝ eggeȝ,
And vche a dale so depe þat demmed at þe brynkeȝ.
385 Þe moste mountayneȝ on mor, þenne, watȝ no more dryȝe,
And, þeron flokked þe folke, forferde of þe wrake.


Syþen þe wylde of þe wode on þe water flette.
Summe swymmed þeron, þat saue hemself trawed.
Summe styȝe to a stud and stared to þe heuen,
390 Rwly, wyth a loud rurd, rored for drede.
Hareȝ, hertteȝ also, to þe hyȝe runnen.
Bukkeȝ, bauseneȝ, and buleȝ to þe bonkkeȝ hyȝed;
And alle cryed for care to þe Kyng of heuen.
Recouerer of þe Creator þay cryed, vch one.
395 Þat amounted þe mase; his mercy watȝ passed,
And alle his pyté departed fro peple þat he hated.


f. 66b    Bi þat þe flod to her fete floȝed and waxed,
Þen vche a segge seȝ wel þat synk hym byhoued.
Frendeȝ fellen in fere and faþmed togeder
400 To dryȝ her delful deystyné and dyȝen alle samen.

---

379  wern] wer[e]: Me.
380  aled] [h]aled: M, G, AW.
382  ryg, þe] ryg [&] þe: M.    ryg [ne] þe: G.
385  þenne, watȝ no more] þenne [on] more: G.    watȝ] were: A.

108

When the water from the heavens met with the earth,
All who could suffer death drowned therein.
There was moaning to be done when [the] misfortune
    was known
That nothing would avail, except death, in the deep
    streams.
375    [The] water that destroyed dwellings always grew
    more powerful,
Swept into each house, [and] seized what existed there.

First, all who could flee took to flight.
Each woman leaves the home with her children,
And [all] hurried to the high hills where it would
    be steepest,
380    And, intensely, upon the high hills they grieved in
    hardship;
But all their effort was useless because the tempest,
    shedding rain turbulently,
[And] the rolling waves never could stop
Until every river bed was brimful to the shores' edges,
And every dale in such deep water that overflowed at
    the borders.
385    The tallest mountains on [the] moor, then, had no
    more dry land,
And yet, the people assembled on them, terrified by
    the disaster.

Then the wild creatures of the wood floated on
    the water.
Some who hoped to save themselves swam in it.
Some leaped upon a pillar and stared at the heavens,
390    Piteously, in a loud voice, roaring with fear.
Hares, [and] harts also, ran to the high hills.
Bucks, badgers, and bulls hurried to the slopes;
And all cried out in distress to the King of heaven.
They cried for aid from the Creator, each one.
395    He increased the confusion; his mercy had passed,
And all his pity had departed from people whom he
    despised.

f. 66b    When the flood flowed to their feet and increased,
Then every person saw clearly that he must sink.
Friends joined in companionship and clung together
400    To endure their terrible destiny and to die all
    the same.

---

386  forferde] for ferde: M, Me, A, Mo, AW.
395  þe mase] þe masse þe mase: MS. þe masse, þe mase (Read
    þe mase.): M.
400  deystyné] destyne: G. destyné: AW.

Luf loke₃ to luf and his leue take₃,
For to ende alle at one₃ and foreuer twynne.
By forty daye₃ wern faren, on folde no flesch styryed,
Þat þe flod nade al freten wyth fe₃tande wa₃e₃,
405   For hit clam vche a clyffe cubites fyftene
Ouer þe hy₃est hylle þat hurkled on erþe.


Þenne mourkne in þe mudde most, ful nede,
Alle þat spyrakle inspranc.  No sprawlyng awayled,
Saue þe haþel vnder hach and his here straunge,
410   Noe, þat ofte neuened þe name of oure Lorde,
Hym, a₃tsum in þat ark, as aþel God lyked.
Þer alle lede₃ in lome lenged druye.


Þe arc houen wat₃ on hy₃e wyth hurlande gote₃,
Kest to kythe₃ vncouþe, þe clowde₃ ful nere.
415   Hit waltered on þe wylde flod, went as hit lyste,
Drof vpon þe depe dam; in daunger hit semed
Withouten mast, oþer myke, oþer myry bawelyne,
Kable, oþer capstan to clyppe to her ankre₃,
Hurrok, oþer hande-helme hasped on roþer,
420   Oþer any sweande sayl to seche after hauen.
Bot flote forthe wyth þe flyt of þe felle wynde₃.
Whederwarde-so þe water wafte, hit rebounde.
Ofte hit roled on rounde and rered on ende.
Nyf oure Lorde hade ben her Lode₃mon, hem had lumpen
harde.


425   Of þe lenþe of Noe lyf, to lay a lel date,
Þe sex hundreth of his age--and none odde ₃ere₃--
Of secounde monyth, þe seuenþe day ry₃te₃,
Towalten alle þyse welle-hede₃, and þe water flowed;
And þrye₃ fyfty þe flod of folwande daye₃.
430   Vche hille wat₃ þer hidde wyth yre₃ ful graye.


---

401  to] Curved stroke from bottom of *t* circles around into
an *o*.


110

[The] lover looks at [his] beloved and takes his leave,
To die all at once and to part forever.
When forty days had passed, no creature stirred on
    earth,
Whom the flood had not completely destroyed with
    clashing waves,
405    As it climbed each cliff fifteen cubits
Above the highest hill that lay on earth.

Then, necessarily indeed, all in whom life
    dwelled
Must rot in the mire. No striving availed,
Except for the man under [the] hatch and his unusual
    company,
410    Noah, who often mentioned the name of our Lord,
Him, as one of eight in that ark, as [the] noble
    God desired.
All [the] people there in [that] vessel remained dry.

The ark was raised on high by whirling currents,
Flung toward strange lands, very near the clouds.
415    It tossed about on the wild flood, went as it wished,
Drove upon the deep water; it seemed in danger
Without mast, or boom support, or favorable bowline,
Cable, or capstan to clip to her anchors,
Bilge, or hand helm fastened on [the] rudder,
420    Or any billowing sail to seek after [a] harbor.
[It] only floated forth in the tumult of the fierce
    winds.
Wherever the water rose, it rebounded.
It often rolled around and towered on end.
If our Lord had not been their Guide, misfortune would
    have befallen them.

425    To set a correct date concerning the length of
    Noah's life,
In the six hundredth year of his age--and with no
    odd years--
In [the] second month, the seventh day comes to pass,
    [and]
All these fountainheads broke open, and the water
    flowed;
And the flood [prevailed] three times fifty of [the]
    following days.
430    Each hill was hid there by very gray vapors.

---

427  seuenþe] seuen[te]þe: G, A, Mo. seuentenþe: AW.
430  yreʒ] (yþeʒ?): M. y[þ]ez: Me, G, A, Mo, AW.

Al wat₃ wasted þat þer wonyed þe worlde wythinne,
Þer euer flote, oþer flwe, oþer on fote ₃ede.

That ro₃ly wat₃ þe remnaunt, þat þe rac dryue₃,
Þat alle gendre₃ so joyst wern joyned wythinne.


435      Bot, quen þe Lorde of þe lyfte lyked hymseluen
         For to mynne on his mon his meth þat abyde₃,
         Þen he wakened a wynde on wattere₃ to blowe,
         Þenne lasned þe llak þat large wat₃ are.
         Þen he stac vp þe stange₃, stoped þe welle₃,
440      Bed blynne of þe rayn; hit batede as fast.
         Þenne lasned þe lo₃ lowkande togeder.


         After harde daye₃ wern out, an hundreth and fyfté,
         As þat lyftande lome luged aboute,
         Where þe wynde and þe weder warpen hit wolde,
445      Hit sa₃tled on a softe day, synkande to grounde.
         On a rasse of a rok, hit rest at þe laste,
         On þe mounte of Mararach of Armené hilles,
         Þat oþerwaye₃ on Ebrv hit hat þe Thanes.
         Bot þa₃, þe kyste in þe crage₃ wern closed to byde.
450      ₃et fyned not þe flod, ne fel to þe boþeme₃.
         Bot þe hy₃est of þe egge₃ vnhuled wern a lyttel,
         Þat þe burne bynne borde byhelde þe bare erþe.


         Þenne wafte he vpon his wyndowe and wysed þeroute
         A message fro þat meyny hem molde₃ to seche.
455      Þat wat₃ þe rauen so ronk þat rebel wat₃ euer.
         He wat₃ colored as þe cole corby, al vntrwe;
         And he fonge₃ to þe fly₃t and fanne₃ on þe wynde₃,
         Hale₃ hy₃e vpon hy₃t to herken tyþynge₃.
         He crouke₃ for comfort when carayne he fynde₃
460      Kast vp on a clyffe þer costese lay drye.


---

431  þat þer wonyed] þat wonyed: G, AW.
432  Þer euer] Þ[at] euer: G, AW.     on] Inserted above line.
441  lasned] la[u]sned: G.
442  an hundreth] on hundreth: Me, Mo.
447  Mararach] Ararach: G, A, AW.
449  wern] (were?): M.  wer[e]: Me, G, A, Mo, AW.


112

All who dwelled there within the world had been
                destroyed,
        Where ever [they] floated, or flew, or went on foot.
f. 67   That tottering ark, which the storm drives, was the
                remainder,
        Within which all classes of creatures so snugly were
                joined.

435     However, when the Lord of the heavens wished
        To think of the man who awaits his moderation,
        Then he wakened a wind to blow on [the] waters,
        Then lessened the lake which was large before.
        Then he compressed the whirlpools, plugged the springs,
440     [And] ordered ceasing of the rain; it abated just as
                quickly.
        Then the streams closing together subsided.

        After a hundred and fifty difficult days had
                passed,
        As that tossing vessel was dragged about,
        Where the wind and the weather wished to fling it,
445     It settled on a calm day, sinking to [the] ground.
        On a ridge of a rock, it rested at last,
        On the mount of Ararat in [the] hills of Armenia,
        Which is otherwise called the Thanes in Hebrew.
        Yet, the ark on the crags had to remain closed.
450     The flood still did not cease, nor did [it] sink to
                the foundations.
        Only the highest of the crests were uncovered a little,
        So that the man on board could behold the bare earth.

        Then he flung open his window and sent out there
        A messenger from that menagerie to seek soil for them.
455     That was the raven so rash who was always rebellious.
        He was perverted just like the heartless raven, com-
                pletely untrue;
        And he takes to flight and flutters in the winds,
        Soars high with strength to seek tidings.
        He croaks with comfort when he finds carrion
460     Cast up on a cliff where coasts lay dry.

---

456   cole corby, al] cole, corbyal: M, Me, A, AW.   cole,
        corby al: G.   cole corbyal: Mo.
458   Hale3] Houe3: M, Me, Mo.   UVR shows hale3 more clearly.
        tyþynge3] typþynges: M.
460   costese] costes: A.

113

He hade þe smelle of þe smach and smoltes þeder sone,
Falleȝ on þe foule flesch and fylleȝ his wombe,
And sone ȝederly forȝete ȝisterday steuen,
How þe cheuetayn hym charged, þat þe kyst ȝemed.
465 Þe rauen raykeȝ hym forth, þat reches ful lyttel
How alle fodeȝ þer fare, elleȝ he fynde mete.


Bot, þe burne bynne borde, þat bod to hys come,
Banned hym ful bytterly wyth bestes alle samen.
f. 67b He secheȝ anoþer sondeȝmon and setteȝ on þe doune,
470 Bryngeȝ þat bryȝt vpon borde, blessed and sayde:
"Wende, worþelych wyȝt, vus woneȝ to seche.
Dryf ouer þis dymme water. If þou druye fyndeȝ,
Bryng bodworde to bot, blysse to vus alle.
Þaȝ þat fowle be false, fre be þou euer."


475 Ho wyrle out on þe weder on wyngeȝ ful scharpe.
Dreȝly, alle a longe day, þat dorst neuer lyȝt,
And when ho fyndeȝ no folde her fote on to pyche,
Ho vmbekesteȝ þe coste and þe kyst secheȝ.
Ho hitteȝ on þe euentyde and on þe ark sitteȝ.
480 Noe nymmes hir anon and naytly hir staueȝ.


Noe on anoþer day nymmeȝ efte þe dovene,
And byddeȝ hir bowe ouer þe borne efte bonkeȝ to seche;
And ho skyrmeȝ vnder skwe and skowteȝ aboute,
Tyl hit watȝ nyȝe at þe naȝt, and Noe þen secheȝ.


485 On ark, on an euentyde, houeȝ þe dowue.
On stamyn ho stod and stylle hym abydeȝ.
What! Ho broȝt in hir beke a bronch of olyue,
Gracyously vmbegrouen, al wyth grene leueȝ.
Þat watȝ þe syngne of sauyté þat sende hem oure Lorde,
490 And þe saȝtlyng of hymself wyth þo sely besteȝ.
Þen watȝ þer joy in þat gyn where jumpred er dryȝed,
And much comfort in þat cofer þat watȝ clay-daubed.


Myryly on a fayr morn, monyth þe fyrst
Þat falleȝ formast in þe ȝer, and þe fyrst day,

---

464 kyst] [ch]yst: G, AW.
469 doune] (*douue* or *douene*?): M. dou[v]e: Me. dou[u]e: G,
Mo, AW. doue: A.
475 wyrle] wyrle[d]: G, AW. wyrles: A.

114

He caught the stench from the scent and goes there
     immediately,
Falls on the foul flesh and fills his paunch,
And soon promptly forgot yesterday's command,
How the leader who attended the ark had instructed him.
465     The raven hastens forth, he who cares very little
How all creatures fare there, provided that he find food.

However, the man on board, who waited for his return,
Cursed him very bitterly with beasts all the same.
f. 67b  He seeks another messenger and calls on the dove,
470     Brings that fair bird on board, blessed [it] and said:
"Go, worthy creature, to seek abodes for us.
Pass over this dark water. If you find dry land,
Bring news to [the] boat, bliss to us all.
Though that fowl may be false, you are always honor-
     able."

475     She whirled out in the air on very sharp wings.
Incessantly, all through a long day, it dared never
     come down,
And when she finds no land to set her foot on,
She soars around the area and seeks the ark.
She descends in the evening and sits on the ark.
480     Noah takes her at once and encloses her properly.

Noah again seizes the dove on another day,
And orders her to go over the water then to seek shores;
And she glides beneath [the] sky and scouts around,
Until it was near to the night, and Noah then searches.

485     The dove hovers above [the] ark in the evening.
She perched on [the] prow and quietly awaits him.
What! She brought in her beak a branch of olive,
Beautifully flourishing, all with green leaves.
That was the sign of salvation which our Lord sent them,
490     And the reconciling of himself with those blessed beasts.
Then there was joy in that ark where [they] chattered
     until [they] were parched,
And much comfort [was] in that vessel that was daubed
     with clay.

Merrily on a fair morning of the first month
Which falls earliest in the year, and the first day,

---

476   a longe] alonge: MS, Me, A, Mo, AW.  a-longe: G.
481   dovene] do[wv]e: Me, Mo.  doveue: G.  dove: A.  dowue: AW.
485   dowue] downe (*downe* = *dovene* [see lines 469, 481]): M.
491   where jumpred] where [watȝ] jumpred: G.   dryȝed] dryȝe: G.

495   Lede₃ lo₃en in þat lome and loked þeroute
     How þat wattere₃ wern woned and þe worlde dryed.
     Vch on loued oure Lorde bot lenged ay stylle,
     Tyl þay had typyng fro þe Tolke þat tyned hem þerinne.
     Þen Gode₃ glam to hem glod, þat gladed hem alle,
500   Bede hem drawe to þe dor; delyuer hem he wolde.


     Þen went þay to þe wykket, hit walt vpon sone,
     Boþe þe burne and his barne₃ bowed þeroute.
     Her wyue₃ walke₃ hem wyth, and þe wylde after,
     Þroly þrublande in þronge, þrowen ful þykke.
f. 68   Bot, Noe of vche honest kynde nem out an odde,
506   And heuened vp an auter, and hal₃ed hit fayre,
     And sette a sakerfyse þeron of vch a ser kynde
     Þat wat₃ comly and clene; God kepe₃ non oþer.


     When bremly breṇed þose beste₃, and þe breþe rysed,
510   Þe sauour of his sacrafyse so₃t to hym euen
     Þat al spede₃, and spylle₃. He spekes wyth þat ilke
     In comly comfort, ful clos, and cortays worde₃:
     "Now, Noe, no more nel I neuer wary
     Alle þe mukel mayny molde for no manne₃ synne₃,
515   For I se wel þat hit is sothe þat alle manne₃ wytte₃
     To vnþryfte arn alle þrawen wyth þo₃t of her hertte₃,
     And ay hat₃ ben and wyl be ₃et. Fro her barnage,
     Al is þe mynde of þe man to malyce enclyned.
     Forþy, schal I neuer schende so schortly at ones,
520   As dysstrye al, for mane₃ synne, daye₃ of þis erþe.
     Bot, waxe₃ now, and wende₃ forth, and worþe₃ to monye;
     Multyplye₃ on þis molde, and menske yow bytyde.
     Sesoune₃ schal yow neuer sese, of sede ne of heruest,
     Ne hete ne no harde forst, vmbre ne dro₃þe,

---

514 mayny molde] mayny [on] molde: M, Me, Mo, AW. mayny-molde:
   G, A.
515 manne₃] [segg]e₃: G, A, AW.

495 People smiled in that vessel and observed out there
How the waters had diminished and the earth had dried.
Each one praised our Lord but remained always still,
Until they had word from the Creator who had enclosed
    them therein.
Then God's powerful call, that gladdened them all,
    glided to them,
500 [And] ordered them to draw towards the door; he would
    deliver them.

Then they went to the door, [and] flung it open
    quickly.
Both the man and his children stepped out there.
Their wives walk with them, and the wild creatures
    behind,
Firmly clashing in [a] throng, set together very closely.
f. 68 However, Noah took out an odd one from each clean kind,
506 And raised up an altar, and hallowed it properly,
And set a sacrifice thereon of each distinct species
That was fair and clean; God desires nothing else.

When those beasts burned vigorously, and the vapor
    rose,
510 The scent of the sacrifice ascended straight to him
Who blesses all, and yet can destroy. He speaks to
    that same man
With appropriate consolation, very privately, and with
    courteous words:
"Now, Noah, no more will I ever condemn
All the huge household of earth for any man's sins,
515 Because I see clearly that it is true that all man's
    faculties
Are completely drawn to destruction by [the] determina-
    tion of their minds,
And [this] always has been and will be yet. From their
    childhood,
The mind of man is entirely inclined to malice.
Therefore, I shall never punish so abruptly at the
    same time,
520 So as to destroy all, because of man's sin, during ages
    of this earth.
However, increase now, and go forth, and grow into many;
Multiply on this earth, and honor shall come to you.
Seasons shall never cease for you, of seed or of harvest,
Or heat or any hard frost, shade or drought,

---

520 for manez synne] *sȳne* inserted above line in same brown ink.
    for manez [dedes]: Me, AW.  for [þe douþe]: G.    dayeʒ]
    [in] dayeʒ: M.

525      Ne þe swetnesse of somer, ne þe sadde wynter,
       Ne þe ny3t ne þe day, ne þe newe 3ere3,
       Bot euer renne restle3. Rengne3 3e þerinne. "


          Þerwyth, he blesse3 vch a best and byta3t hem þis erþe
       Þen wat3 a skylly skyu alde, quen scaped alle þe wylde,
530      Vche fowle to þe fly3t, þat fyþere3 my3t serue,
       Vche fysch to þe flod, þat fynne couþe nayte,
       Vche beste to þe bent, þat þat bytes on erbe3;
       Wylde worme3 to her won wryþe3 in þe erþe.
       Þe foxe and þe folmarde to þe fryth wynde3,
535      Herttes to hy3e heþe, hare3 to gorste3,
       And lyoune3 and lebarde3 to þe lake-ryftes.
       Herne3 and haueke3 to þe hy3e roche3,
       Þe hole-foted fowle to þe flod hy3e3,
       And vche best at a brayde þer hym best lyke3.
540      Þe fowre freke3 of þe folde fonge3 þe empyre.


f. 68b     Lo, suche a wrakful wo for wlatsum dede3
       Parformed þe hy3e Fader on folke þat he made.
       Þat he chysly hade cherisched he chastysed ful hardee
       In devoydynge þe vylanye þat venquyst his þewe3.


545          fforþy, war þe now, wy3e þat worschyp desyres,
       In his comlych courte, þat Kyng is of blysse,
       In þe fylþe of þe flesch þat þou be founden neuer,
       Tyl any water in þe worlde to wasche þe fayly,
       ffor is no segge vnder sunne so seme of his crafte3.
550      If he be sulped in synne, þat sytte3 vnclene.
       On spec of a spote may spede to mysse
       Of þe sy3te of þe Souerayn þat sytte3 so hy3e;
       ffor þat schewe me schale in þo schyre howse3,
       As þe beryl bornyst, byhoue3 be clene,
555      Þat is sounde on vche a syde, and no sem habes,
       Wythouten maskle oþer mote, as margerye-perle.


---

529   skyu alde] skyualde: MS, M, Me, A, Mo, AW.  sky[l]nade: G.
532   þat þat] þat: eds.
534   foxe] fox: eds.  Orig. shows abbr. for *e* after *x*.

525      Or the sweetness of summer, or the sombre winter,
Or the night or the day, or the new years,
But always shall flow continuously. You shall prevail
     therein."

Forthwith, he blesses every beast and allotted this
     earth to them.
Then [there] was the old capacity to proceed, when all
     the wild creatures escaped,
530      Each fowl to flight, whom feathers could serve,
Each fish to the water, who could flap fins,
Each beast to the field, that which bites on herbs;
Wild reptiles twist into the earth to their dwellings.
The fox and the polecat leap to the woodland,
535      Harts to high heaths, hares to furze fields,
And lions and leopards to the ravines.
Eagles and hawks [soar] to the high rocks,
The web-footed fowl hastens to the stream,
And each beast in a moment [goes] where [it] pleases
     him best.
540      The four men of the land inherit the empire.

f. 68b     Behold, such a vengeful misfortune for detestable
     deeds
The high Father enacted upon people that he created.
Those whom he fondly had cherished he chastised very
     severely
By voiding the villainy that had vanquished his ordi-
     nances.

545      Therefore, beware yourself now, [the] man who desires
     to worship,
In his noble court, him who is King of glory,
That you never be found in the filth of the flesh,
To the degree that any water in the world may fail to
     purify you,
Because [there] is no person under [the] sun so proper
     in his pursuits.
550      If he be stained by sin, he lives impurely.
One speck of a spot may speed [him] toward [the] loss
Of the sight of the Sovereign who sits so high;
For he who shall appear among those bright dwellings
Must be pure like the polished beryl,
555      Which is sound on every side, and has no flaw,
Without spot or stain, like [the] precious pearl.

---

543  hardee] hard[e]: Me, Mo.
550  þat sytteȝ] þat [ne] sytteȝ: M.

Syþen þe Souerayn in sete so sore forþoȝt
Þat euer he man vpon molde merked to lyuy,
For he in fylþe watȝ fallen, felly he uenged.
560 Quen fourferde alle þe flesch þat he formed hade,
Hym rwed þat he hem vp rerde, and raȝt hem lyflode,
And efte þat he hem vndyd; hard hit hym þoȝt,
For quen þe swemande sorȝe soȝt to his hert,
He knyt a couenaunde cortaysly wyth monkynde þere,
565 In þe mesure of his mode and meþe of his wylle,
Þat he schulde neuer, for no syt, smyte al at oneȝ,
As to quelle alle quykeȝ for qued þat myȝt falle,
Whyl of þe lenþe of þe londe lasteȝ þe terme.
Þat ilke skyl, for no scaþe, ascaped hym neuer,
570 Wheder wonderly he wrak on wykked men after.


    Ful felly, for þat ilk faute, forferde a kyth ryche
In þe anger of his ire þat arȝed mony,
And al watȝ for þis ilk euel, þat vnhappen glette,
Þe venym, and þe vylanye, and þe vycios fylþe,
575 Þat bysulpeȝ manneȝ saule in vnsounde hert,
Þat he his Saueour ne see wyth syȝt of his yȝen,
f. 69 Þat alle illeȝ he hates as helle þat stynkkeȝ;
Bot, non nuyeȝ hym on naȝt ne neuer vpon dayeȝ
As harlottrye vnhonest, heþyng of seluen.
580 Þat schameȝ for no schrewedschyp schent mot he worþe.


    Bot sauyour, mon, in þyself, þaȝ þou a sotte lyuie,
Þaȝ þou bere þyself babel, byþenk þe sumtyme
Wheþer he þat stykked vche a stare in vche steppe yȝe,
ȝif hymself be bore blynde. Hit is a brod wonder.
585 And he þat fetly in face fettled alle eres--


577  Þat alle] Alle: G, Mo, AW. Þus alle: A.
581  sauyour] sa[v]or: Me. sauour: A. sauor: Mo.

120

Since the Sovereign on [his] throne was so deeply
          displeased
That he had ever established man to live on earth,
Because he had fallen into filth, he punished fiercely.
560   When all the creatures that he had formed were killed,
      [It] grieved him that he had raised them up, and had
          given them life,
And then that he had destroyed them; it seemed severe
          to him,
For when the distressing sorrow struck at his heart,
He knit a covenant courteously with mankind there,
565   In the measure of his mood and moderation of his will,
That he would never, in any situation, smite all at once,
So as to kill all living things because of evil which
          might occur,
As long as the time endures for the duration of the
          earth.
That same agreement, throughout any evil, never escaped
          him,
570   Wherever he wreaked vengeance excessively on wicked men
          afterwards.

      Very violently, for that same sin, a splendid land
          was destroyed
In the rage of his wrath which terrified many,
And [it] was all because of this same evil, that cursed
          corruption,
The venom, and the villainy, and the vicious filth,
575   Which pollutes man's soul with impure thoughts,
So that he can not see, with [the] sight of his eyes,
          his Saviour,
f. 69  Who hates all evils like hell that stinks;
However, nothing annoys him at night or ever during days
Like ignoble immorality, abusing of oneself.
580   He who is not ashamed of [such] wickedness must be
          destroyed.

      Only realize, man, within yourself, though you live
          like a wretch,
Though you bear yourself like a babbler, consider
          sometime
Whether he who established each sense of sight in every
          bright eye
Could be born blind himself.  That would be a great
          wonder.
585   And he who neatly fixed all ears on [the] face--

_____

584  hymself] Looks like *hymsele* in MS, but when horizontal bar
     of *f* swings upward, *f* resembles *e*.

If he hatӡ losed þe lysten, hit lyfteӡ meruayle.
Trave þou neuer þat tale vnntrwe þou hit fyndeӡ.
Þer is no dede so derne þat ditteӡ his yӡen.
Þer is no wyӡe in his werk, so war ne so stylle,

590 Þat hit ne þraweӡ to hym þro er he hit poӡt haue;
For he is þe gropande God, þe Grounde of alle dedeӡ,
Rypande of vche a ring þe reynyeӡ and hert,
And þere he fyndeӡ al fayre a freke wythinne,
Þat hert honest and hol, þat haþel he honoureӡ,

595 Sendeӡ hym a sad syӡt to se his auen face;
And harde honyseӡ þise oþer, and of his erde flemeӡ.


Bot, of þe dome of þe douþe for dedeӡ of schame,
He is so skoymos of þat skaþe, he scarreӡ bylyue.
He may not dryӡe to draw allyt, bot drepeӡ in hast;

600 And þat watӡ schewed schortly by a scaþe oneӡ.


## PART TWO: ABRAHAM AND SARA,
## THE SODOMITES, AND LOT'S WIFE


Olde Abraham in erde oneӡ he sytteӡ,
Euen byfore his hous-dore vnder an oke grene.
Bryӡt blykked þe bem of þe brode heuen.
In þe hyӡe hete þerof Abraham bideӡ.

605 He watӡ schunt to þe schadow vnder schyre leueӡ.


Þenne watӡ he war on þe waye of wlonk wyӡeӡ þrynne.
If þay wer farande, and fre, and fayre to beholde,
Hit is eþe to leue by þe last ende,
For þe lede þat þer laye þe leueӡ anvnder,

610 When he hade of hem syӡt, he hyӡeӡ bylyue;
And, as to God, þe good mon gos hem agayneӡ,
And haylsed hem in on hede, and sayde: "Hende Lorde,

f. 69b Ӡif euer þy mon vpon molde merit disserued,
Lenge a lyttel with þy lede, I loӡly biseche.

---

586 he] he he: MS.
587 vnntrwe] vn-trwe: eds.  Orig. shows bar over *v* as abbr.
     for additional *n*.
590 þro] þre (þer?): M.  Line through *o* of þro perhaps indi-
     cates *e* was corrected to *o*.

If he has lost the sense of hearing, it would create
    [a] miracle.
You never should believe that false story [if] you
    should discover it.
There is no deed so hidden that escapes his eyes.
There is no man in his conduct, so cautious nor so
    secretive,
590    That it (evil) does not draw misfortune upon him before
    he could have realized it;
For he is the scrutinizing God, the Originator of all
    deeds,
Examining the emotions and thoughts in every man,
And when he finds everything good within a man,
That heart pure and sound, he blesses that being,
595    Sends him a divine vision to see his own face;
But [he] severely denounces these others, and banishes
    [them] from his abode.

Furthermore, in the sentencing of the people for
    deeds of shame,
He is so disdainful of that evil, he threatens quickly.
He can not endure to delay, but strikes in haste;
600    And that was revealed abruptly by a disaster once.

PART TWO: ABRAHAM AND SARA,
THE SODOMITES, AND LOT'S WIFE

Old Abraham sits once on land,
Directly before his house door under a green oak.
The sun shone brightly from the wide heavens.
Abraham lingers in the intense heat of it.
605    He was slanted toward the shade under glistening leaves.

Then he became aware of three handsome men on the path.
That they were splendid, and noble, and fair to behold,
Would be easy to believe by the final outcome,
For the man who lingered there beneath the leaves,
610    When he caught sight of them, hurries quickly;
And, as if to God, the good man goes towards them,
And greeted them as one individual, and said: "Noble Lord,
f. 69b   If ever your man deserved merit on earth,
Linger a little while with your host, I humbly implore.

594  Þat hert] [Wyth] hert: G, AW.
600  scape] sc[h]aþe: G, AW.
611  good mon] goodmon: A, AW.
612  on hede] onhede: eds.

615 Passe neuer fro þi pouere, ȝif I hit pray durst,
Er þou haf biden with þi burne and vnder boȝe restted;
And I schal wynne yow wyȝt of water a lyttel,
And fast aboute schal I fare; your fette wer waschene.
Restteȝ here on þis rote, and I schal rachche after
620 And brynge a morsel of bred to baune your hertte."

"ffare forthe," quoþ þe frekeȝ, "and fech as þou
seggeȝ.
By bole of þis brode tre we byde þe here."

Þenne orppedly into his hous he hyȝed to Sare,
Comaunded hir to be cof and quyk at þis oneȝ.
625 "Þre metteȝ of mele menge and ma kakeȝ.
Vnder askeȝ ful hote happe hem byliue.
Quyl I fete sumquat fat, þou þe fyr bete,
Prestly, at þis ilke poynte, sum polment to make."

He cached to his covhous and a calf bryngeȝ,
630 Þat watȝ tender and not toȝe, bed tyrue of þe hyde,
And sayde to his seruaunt þat he hit seþe faste;
And he, deruely, at his dome, dyȝt hit bylyue.

Þe burne to be bareheued buskeȝ hym þenne,
Clecheȝ to a clene cloþe and kesteȝ on þe grene,
635 Þrwe þryftyly þeron þo þre þerue kakeȝ,
And bryngeȝ butter wythal and by þe bred setteȝ.
Mete messeȝ of mylke he merkkeȝ bytwene,
Syþen potage and polment in plater honest.
As sewer, in a god assyse, he serued hem fayre,
640 Wyth sadde semblaunt and swete, of such as he hade,
And God, as a glad gest, mad god chere,
Þat watȝ fayn of his frende and his fest praysed.
Abraham, al hodleȝ, wyth armeȝ vp folden,
Mynystred mete byfore þo men þat myȝtes al weldeȝ.

645 Þenne þay sayden as þay sete samen, alle þrynne,
When þe mete watȝ remued, and þay of mensk speken:
"I schal efte here-away, Abram," þay sayden,
"Ȝet er þy lyueȝ lyȝt leþe vpon erþe,

---

620 baune] banne: M, Me. bau[m]e: G, A, Mo, AW.
629 covhous] cobhous (*cov-hous* = cow-house?): M.
630 tyrue] tyrne: M.

124

615  Never depart from your humble servant, if I might dare
                request it,
      Until you have remained with your man and rested under
                [the] tree;
      And I shall bring you quickly a little bit of water,
      And I shall move about swiftly; your feet should be washed.
      Rest here by this tree trunk, and I shall go after
620  And bring a bite of bread to strengthen your hearts."

          "Go forth," said the men, "and do as you say.
      We shall wait for you here by [the] trunk of this broad
                tree."

          Then he hurried resolutely into his house to Sara,
      Commanded her to be swift and agile at this moment.
625  "Mix three measures of meal and make cakes.
      Enclose them quickly under very hot ashes.
      While I obtain some kind of vessel, you kindle the fire,
      Promptly, at this same point, to make some pottage."

          He hastened to his cow shed and brings a calf,
630  Which was tender and not tough, commanded the skin to
                be stripped off,
      And said to his servant that he should boil it immedi-
                ately;
      And he, boldly, at the command, prepared it quickly.

          The man then fixes himself to be bareheaded,
      Snatches up a clean cloth and casts [it] on the green,
635  Laid those three unleavened cakes properly upon it,
      And brings butter also and places [it] by the bread.
      He sets appropriate portions of milk in between,
      Then vegetable soup and pottage in suitable plates.
      Like a steward, in a good fashion, he served them well,
640  In [a] dignified and pleasant manner, with such as he had,
      And God, like a glad guest, made good cheer,
      He who was pleased with his friend and praised his feast.
      Abraham, completely hoodless, with arms folded up,
      Supervised [the] meal before those men who possess all
                powers.

645      Then they said as they sat together, all three,
      When the food was removed, and they spoke with courtesy:
      "I shall [come] here again, Abram," they said,
      "Even before your life's light is subdued upon earth,

---

639  god] gvd: A. What looks like a *v* may have been changed to *o*.
643  vp folden] vp-folden: eds.

f. 70 And þenne schal Sare consayue and a sun bere,
650 Þat schal be Abrahameȝ ayre, and after hym wynne,
 Wyth wele and wyth worschyp, þe worþely peple,
 Þat schal halde in heritage þat I haf men ȝark."

 Þenne þe burde byhynde þe dor for busmar laȝed,
 And sayde sothly to hirself, Sare þe madde:
655 "May þou traw for tykle þat þou tonne moȝteȝ
 And I so hyȝe out of age, and also my lorde?"
 ffor soþely, as says þe Wryt, he wern of sadde elde,
 Boþe þe wyȝe and his wyf. Such werk watȝ hem fayled
 Fro mony a brod day byfore. Ho barayn ay byene,
660 Þat selue Sare wythouten sede, into þat same tyme.

 Þenne sayde oure Syre þer he sete: "Se! So Sare
  laȝes,
 Not trawande þe tale þat I þe to schewed.
 Hopeȝ ho oȝt may be harde my hondeȝ to work?
 And ȝet, I avow verayly þe avaunt þat I made.
665 I schal ȝeply aȝayn and ȝelde þat I hyȝt,
 And sothely sende to Sare a sonn and an hayre."
 Þenne swenged forth Sare and swer by hir trawþe
 Þat for lot þat þay laused ho laȝed neuer.
 "Now, innoghe! Hit is not so," þenne nurned þe Dryȝtyn
670 "For þou laȝed aloȝ; bot let we hit one."

 With þat, þay ros vp radly, as þay rayke schulde,
 And setten toward Sodamas her syȝt alle at oneȝ,
 ffor þat cité þerbysyde watȝ, sette in a vale
 No myleȝ fro Mambre mo þen tweyne,
675 Where so wonyed þis ilke wyȝ þat wendeȝ wyth oure Lorde
 For to tent hym wyth tale and teche hym þe gate.
 Þen glydeȝ forth God. Þe god mon hym folȝeȝ.
 Abraham heldeȝ hem wyth, hem to conueye
 In towarde þe cety of Sodamas, þat synned had þenne.

652 men ȝark] men ȝark[ed]: Me, A, Mo, AW. [h]e[m] ȝark[ed]:
  G.
654 sothly] (? *softly* or *sotly* = foolishly): M. sot[y]ly:
  G, A, Mo.
655 tonne] t[em]e: Me, Mo, AW. terme: A.
657 he] hit: A.
659 byene] by ene: MS. (? *bycame*): M. b[e]ne: Me. by[d]ene
  G, Mo, AW. had bene: A.

And then shall Sara conceive and bear a son,
650       Who shall be Abraham's heir, and after him shall beget,
          In virtue and in honor, the worthy offspring,
          Who shall hold in heritage what I have ordained for men."

          Then the woman behind the door laughed with disdain,
          And the foolish Sara indeed said to herself:
655       "Can you believe that you could conceive with excitement
          When I [am] so advanced in age, and my lord also?"
          For truly, as the Scripture says, they were of advanced
               age,
          Both the man and his wife.  Such activity had failed them
          From many a long day before.  She had been always barren,
660       That same Sara without offspring, up to that same time.

          Then, from where he sat, our Lord said: "Look!  Sara
               thus laughs,
          Not believing the story that I revealed to you.
          Does she think anything can be hard for my hands to
               accomplish?
          And yet, I verily avow the promise that I made.
665       I shall promptly [come] again and bring about what I
               promised,
          And truly send to Sara a son and an heir."
          Then Sara hastened forth and swore on her honor
          That throughout [the] talk that they uttered she had
               never laughed.
          "Now, [say] no more!  It is not so," the Lord then said,
670       "For you laughed softly; but we shall let it alone."

          With that, they rose up quickly, since they should
               depart,
          And set their sight toward Sodom all at the same time,
          For that city was nearby, situated in a vale
          No more than two miles from Mambre,
675       Where then dwelled this same man who goes with our Lord
          To inform him by word and to show him the way.
          Then God goes forth.  The good man follows him.
          Abraham goes with them to escort them
          On toward the city of Sodom, which had sinned then.

---

666   sonn] soñ: MS, M.   soun: Me, G, A, Mo, AW.
668   laused] lansed (*laused*?): M.   lansed: Me, Mo.
669   innoghe] innogh: A.
675   Where so] Where-so: M, G, A, Mo, AW.
677   god mon] godmon: M, G, A, AW.
679   In towarde] Towarde: AW.

680         In þe faute of þis fylþe, þe Fader hem þretes;
           And sayde þus to þe segg þat sued hym after;
           "How myȝt I hyde myn hert fro Habraham þe trwe,
           Þat I ne dyscouered to his corse my counsayl so dere,
           Syþen he is chosen to be chef chyldryn fader,
f. 70b     Þat so folk schal falle fro to flete alle þe worlde?
686        And vche blod in þat burne blessed schal worþe,
           Me bos telle to þat tolk þe tene of my wylle,
           And alle myn atlyng to Abraham vnhaspe bilyue.


           "The grete soun of Sodamas synkkeȝ in myn ereȝ,
690         And þe gult of Gomorre gareȝ me to wrath.
           I schal lyȝt into þat led and loke myseluen
           If þay haf don as þe dyne dryueȝ on lofte.
           Þay han lerned a lyst þat lykeȝ me ille,
           Þat þay han founden in her flesch, of fauteȝ þe werst.
695        Vch male matȝ his mach a man as hymseluen,
           And fylter folyly in fere, on femmaleȝ wyse.
           I compast hem a kynde crafte, and kende hit hem derne,
           And amed hit in myn ordenaunce oddely dere,
           And dyȝt drwry þerinne doole alþerswettest;
700        And þe play of paramoreȝ I portrayed myseluen,
           And made þerto a maner myriest of oþer.
           When two true togeder had tyȝed hemseluen,
           Bytwene a male and his make such merþe schulde conne,
           Wel nyȝe pure paradys moȝt preue no better,
705        Elleȝ þay moȝt honestly ayþer oþer welde.
           At a stylle, stollen steuen, vnstered wyth syȝt,
           Luf-lowe hem bytwene lasched so hote,
           Þat alle þe meschefeȝ on mold moȝt hit not sheke.
           Now haf þay skyfted my skyl and scorned natwre,
710        And hentteȝ hem in heþyng an vsage vnclene.
           Hem to smyte for þat smod smartly I þenk,
           Þat wyȝeȝ schal be, by hem, war worlde wythouten ende.

---

685   so folk] so [fele] folk: G.
692   If] Íf: MS.
703   conne] (come?): M.  co[m]e: other eds.

680   Because of the guilt of this impurity, the Father
              threatens them;
      And [he] said thus to the man who followed after him:
      "How could I hide my thoughts from the loyal Abraham,
      So that I would not reveal to his person my plan so noble,
      Since he is chosen to be [the] chief father of children,
f. 70b   From whom then people shall descend to populate all the
              world?
686   If each descendant of that person shall be blessed,
      [It] behooves me to tell to that man the fierceness of
              my temper,
      And to unfold all my intentions to Abraham promptly.

      "The loud sound in Sodom sinks into my ears,
690   And the guilt of Gomorrah moves me to wrath.
      I shall go down into that group and see myself
      If they have acted according to the way the noise
              rises on high.
      They have learned a lust which pleases me poorly,
      Which they have found in their flesh, the worst of faults.
695   Every male makes his mate a man like himself,
      And [they] join sinfully in companionship, one in the
              manner of a female.
      I devised a natural way for them, and entrusted it to
              them privately,
      And deemed it in my ordinance singularly precious,
      And established love therein as the sweetest part of all;
700   And I myself conceived the pleasure of lovers,
      And created for this purpose a manner [the] most enjoy-
              able among others.
      When two truly had joined themselves together,
      Between a male and his spouse such joy would be
              experienced,
      Well near pure paradise could prove no better,
705   Provided that they could honestly possess each other.
      At a silent, secret hour, hidden from sight,
      Love's flame could glow between them so warmly,
      That all the misfortunes on earth could not disturb it.
      Now they have altered my arrangement and scorned nature,
710   And [they] handle themselves with abuse in an impure way.
      I intend to smite them swiftly for that filth,
      So that men shall be, because of them, careful without
              end in the world."

---

708   sheke] sleke: eds.   Orig. shows smaller stroke of *h* off
      bottom of *e*.

129

Þenne arȝed Abraham, and alle his mod chaunge
For hope of þe harde hate þat hyȝt hatȝ oure Lorde.
715   Al sykande, he sayde: "Sir, wyth yor leue,
Schal synful and sakleȝ suffer al on payne?
Weþer euer hit lyke my Lorde to lyfte such domeȝ,
Þat þe wykked and þe worþy schal on wrake suffer,
And weye vpon þe worre half þat wrathed þe neuer?
720   Þat watȝ neuer þy won, þat wroȝteȝ vus alle.
f. 71  Now, fyfty fyn frendeȝ wer founde in ȝonde toune,
In þe cety of Sodamas, and also Gomorre,
Þat neuer lakked þy laue, bot loued ay trauþe,
And reȝtful wern and resounable, and redy þe to serue,
725   Schal þay falle in þe faute þat oþer frekeȝ wroȝt,
And joyne to her juggement her juise to haue?
Þat nas neuer þyn note; vnneuened hit worþe
Þat art so gaynly a God and of goste mylde."


"Nay, for fyfty," quoþ þe Fader, "and þy fayre spech
730   And þay be founden in þat folk of her fylþe clene,
I schal forgyue alle þe gylt þurȝ my grace one,
And let hem smolt, al unsmyten, smoþely at oneȝ."


"Aa!  Blessed be þow," quoþ þe burne, "so boner and
     þewed,
And al haldeȝ in þy honde, þe heuen and þe erþe.
735   Bot, for I haf þis talke, tatȝ to non ille
ȝif I mele a lyttel more, þat mul am and askeȝ.
What if fyue faylen of fyfty þe noumbre,
And þe remnaunt be reken, how restes þy wylle?"
"And fyue wont of fyfty," quoþ God, "I schal forȝete a
740   And wythhalde my honde for hortyng on lede."


---

713  chaunge] chaunge[d]: eds.
732  unsmyten] A noted: "y of *unsmyten* first formed erroneousl
     on last stroke of *m*."

Then Abraham was terrified, and his mood changed completely
    In expectation of the painful punishment which our Lord has promised.
715    Utterly sighing, he said: "Lord, by your leave,
    Shall [the] sinful and [the] innocent all suffer one punishment?
    And yet would it ever please my Lord to lift such judgments,
    That the wicked and the worthy must suffer one penalty,
    And come upon you to protect [the] group who never grieved you?
720    That was never your way, you who created all of us.
f. 71   Now, [if] fifty fine friends were found in yonder dwelling,
    In the city of Sodom, and also Gomorrah,
    Who never failed your law, but always loved truth,
    And were honorable and reasonable, and ready to serve you,
725    Shall they fall because of the fault which other men committed,
    And share in their punishment to receive their doom?
    That was never your purpose; it would be unmentionable
    For you who are so gracious a God and of gentle spirit."

    "Nay, for fifty," said the Father, "and your noble speech,
730    If they be found within that group clean from their filth,
    I shall forgive all the guilt through my grace alone,
    And let them go, completely unsmitten, peacefully together."

    "Ah! Blessed are you," said the man, "so gracious and good,
    And all is maintained by your hand, the heaven and the earth.
735    However, as I have this talk, take to none [of it] displeasingly
    If I, who am dust and ashes, speak a little more.
    What if five fail the number of fifty,
    And the remainder be worthy, how would your will lean?"
    "Even if five are lacking from fifty," said God, "I shall forget all
740    And withhold my hand from hurting one person."

---

735  I haf] I towched haf: AW.
739  wont] Inserted above line in same brown ink.

131

"And quat if faurty be fre, and fauty þyse oþer?
Schalt þow schortly al schende, and schape non oþer?"
"Nay, þaӡ faurty forfete, ӡet fryst I a whyle,
And voyde away my vengaunce, þaӡ me vyl þynk."

745   Þen Abraham obeched hym, and loӡly him þonkkeӡ.
"Now, sayned be þou, Sauiour, so symple in þy wrath.
I am bot erþe ful euel, and vsle so blake,
For to mele wyth such a Mayster as myӡteӡ hatӡ alle.
Bot, I haue bygonnen wyth my God, and he hit gayn þynke⸲
750  ӡif I forloyne, as a fol, þy fraunchyse may serue.
What if þretty þryuande be þrad in ӡon touneӡ?
What! Schal I leue if my Lorde, if he hem leþe wolde?"

   Þenne þe godlych God gef hym onsware.
"ӡet for þretty in þrong I schal my þro steke,
755  And spare spakly of spyt in space of my þeweӡ,
And my rankor refrayne four þy reken wordeӡ."

f. 71b  "What for twenty?" quoþ þe tolke. "Vntwyneӡ þou hem
    þenne?"
"Nay, ӡif þou ӡerneӡ hit, ӡet ӡark I hem grace.
If þat twenty be trwe, I tene hem no more,
760  Bot relece alle þat regioun of her ronk werkkeӡ."

   "Now, aþel Lorde," quoþ Abraham, "oneӡ a speche,
And I schal schape no more þo schalkkeӡ to helpe.
If ten trysty in toune be tan, in þi werkkeӡ,
Wylt þou mese þy mode and menddyng abyde?"
765  "I graunt," quoþ þe grete God. "Graunt mercy," þat oþe⸲

   And þenne arest þe renk and raӡt no fyrre,
And Godde glydeӡ his gate by þose grene wayeӡ;
And he conueyen hym con wyth cast of his yӡe,
And als he loked along þere as oure Lorde passed,
770  ӡet he cryed hym after wyth careful steuen:

---

745 Abraham] [þe burne]: G.  loӡly] [hy]ӡly: Me.
  [b]oӡ[som]ly: G.

"And what if forty be honorable, and these others
    faulty?
Shall you abruptly destroy all, and arrange nothing else?"
"Nay, if forty would be wronged, I would still delay a
    while,
And put aside my punishment, though [this] appears
    inadequate to me."

745      Then Abraham bowed to him, and thanks him humbly.
"Now, blessed are you, Saviour, so easy in your anger.
I am only very inferior dust, and ashes so black,
To speak with such a Master as [he who] has all powers.
However, I have begun with my God, and he considers it
    appropriate.
750    If I go astray, like a fool, your generosity may avail.
What if thirty worthy persons would be punished in
    those cities?
What!  Must I believe that my Lord would vanquish them?"

Then the courteous God gave [an] answer to him.
"Even for thirty in [that] throng I shall subdue my wrath,
755    And spare [them] promptly from harm straightway with my
    ordinances,
And restrain my rancor because of your fine words."

f. 71b    "What about twenty?" said the man.  "Would you
    destroy them then?"
"Nay, if you desire it, I shall yet ordain grace for them.
If that twenty be true, I shall punish them no more,
760    But shall pardon all in that region of their rash deeds."

"Now, noble Lord," said Abraham, "a speech once more,
And I shall contrive no more to help those men.
If ten be found trustworthy in [the] cities, according
    to your designs,
Will you moderate your mood and permit absolution?"
765    "I agree," said the great God.  "Many thanks," [said]
    that other.

And then the man ceased and went no further,
And God goes his way along those green paths;
But he (Abraham) did follow him with [a] glance from
    his eyes,
And as he looked along there where our Lord passed,
770    Again he cried after him in [a] sorrowful voice:

---

752  if my Lorde, if] [o]f my Lorde, if: Me, A, Mo, AW.  [o]f my
    Lorde, [n]if: G.
769  als] *ls* squeezed together.  as: Me, Mo.

"Meke Mayster, on þy mon to mynne if þe lyked,
Loth lengeȝ in ȝon leede, þat is my lef broþer.
He sytteȝ þer in Sodomis, þy seruaunt so pouere,
Among þo mansed men þat han þe much greued.
775    Ȝif þou tyneȝ þat toun, tempre þyn yre,
As þy mersy may malte, þy meke to spare."

        Þen he wendeȝ his way, wepande for care,
Towarde þe mere of Mambre, wepande for sorewe,
And þere in longyng al nyȝt he lengeȝ in wones,
780    Whyl þe Souerayn to Sodamas sende to spye.

His sondes into Sodamas watȝ sende in þat tyme,
In þat ilk euentyde, by aungels tweyne,
Meuande mekely togeder as myry men ȝonge,
As Loot, in a loge-dor, lened hym alone,
785    In a porche of þat place, pyȝt to þe ȝates,
Þat watȝ ryal and ryche, so watȝ þe renkes seluen.

        As he stared into þe strete þer stout men played,
He syȝe þer swey in asent swete men tweyne.
Bolde burneȝ wer þay boþe, wyth berdles chynneȝ,
790    Royl, rollande fax, to raw sylk lyke,
Of ble as þe brere-flour whereso þe bare scheweed.
Ful clene watȝ þe countenaunce of her cler yȝen.
f. 72   Wlonk whit watȝ her wede, and wel hit hem semed,
Of alle featureȝ ful fyn, and fautleȝ boþe.
795    Watȝ non autly in ouþer, for aungels hit wern.


        And þat þe ȝep vnderȝede, þat in þe ȝate sytteȝ,
He ros vp ful radly and ran hem to mete;
And loȝe he louteȝ hem to, Loth, to þe grounde,
And syþen soberly: "Syreȝ, I yow byseche
800    Þat ȝe wolde lyȝt at my loge and lenge þerinne.
Comeȝ to your knaueȝ kote, I craue, at þis oneȝ.

---

777   wendeȝ] wendeȝ wendeȝ: MS. wendeȝ, wendeȝ: M.
778   wepande] [morn]ande: Me, A, AW. [murn]ande: G.
        sorewe] In darker brown ink in Orig., apparently by a
        second hand. Cf. textual notes to 108 and 245 for
        references to darker ink and same flourished w in
        *swelt* and *towched*. so[rȝe]: M, Me, Mo.
781   sondes] sonde: G, AW.
783   Meuande] meuand meuande: MS. Meuand meuande: M. Meuand:
        AW.

134

"Gentle Master, if [it] should please you to think of
        your man,
Lot, who is my dear brother, lives within that group.
He dwells there in Sodom, your servant so humble,
Among those accursed men who have grieved you greatly.
775     If you should destroy that town, temper your ire,
Since your mercy can temper [it], to spare your meek man."

        Then he goes his way, weeping with worry,
Toward the boundary of Mambre, weeping with sorrow,
And he lingers there in grief all night in [his] chambers,
780     While the Sovereign sent [messengers] to Sodom to observe.

        His messengers had been sent into Sodom at that time,
On that same evening, by means of two angels,
Moving calmly together like fine young men,
While Lot, by a lodge-door, sat by himself,
785     On a porch situated at the gates of that city
That was royal and rich, as was the man himself.

        As he stared into the street where bold men frolicked,
He saw there striding in harmony two handsome men.
They were both noble men, with beardless chins,
790     Splendid, flowing hair, similar to raw silk,
[And] with complexion like the brier flower wherever
        the bare skin showed.
The expression in their clear eyes was very bright.
f. 72   Beautifully white was their clothing, and it suited
        them well,
With all fashionings very fine, and flawless too.
795     [There] was nothing lacking in either, for they were
        angels.

        When he who sits by the gates caught sight of the
        agile angels,
He rose up very quickly and ran to meet them;
And Lot humbly bows towards them to the ground,
And then earnestly [says]: "Sires, I beseech you
800     So that you would come to my dwelling and remain therein.
Come to your servant's house, I beg, at this moment.

---

785     place] Me noted second stroke of *p* covers extra *l*.
789     wer] were: Me.
790     Royl] R[yo]l: G, AW.
791     scheweed] schew[e]d: Me, Mo.
795     autly] au[c]ly: Me, G, A, Mo, AW.
799     soberly] soberly [sat3]: M.
801     knaue3] knaues: M, G, A, AW.

135

I schal fette yow a fatte your fette for to wasche.
I norne yow bot for on ny3t ne3e me to lenge,
And in þe myry mornyng 3e may your waye take."
805       And þay nay þat þay nolde ne3 no howse3,
Bot stylly þer in þe strete, as þay stadde wern,
Þay wolde lenge þe long na3t, and logge þeroute.
Hit wat3 hous inno3e to hem, þe heuen vpon lofte.
Loth laþed so longe, wyth luflych worde3,
810       Þat þay hym graunted to go, and gru3t no lenger.


Þe bolde to his byggyng brynge3 hem bylyue,
Þat ryally arayed, for he wat3 ryche euer.
Þe wy3e3 wern welcom as þe wyf couþe.
His two dere do3tere3 deuoutly hem haylsed,
815       Þat wer maydene3 ful meke, maryed not 3et;
And þay wer semly, and swete, and swyþe wel arayed.


Loth þenne ful ly3tly loke3 hym aboute,
And his men amonestes mete for to dy3t.
"Bot þenkke3 on hit be þrefté, what þynk so 3e make,
820       For wyth no sour ne no salt serue3 hym neuer."


Bot 3et, I wene þat þe wyf hit wroth to dyspyt,
And sayde softely to hirself, þis vnfauere hyne:
"Loue3 no salt in her sauce.  3et, hit no skyl were
Þat oþer burne be boute, þa3 boþe be nyse."
825       Þenne ho sauere3 wyth salt her seue3, vch one,
Agayne þe bone of þe burne þat hit forboden hade,
And als ho scelt hem in scorne, þat wel her skyl knewen
Why, wat3 ho wrech so wod, ho wrathed oure Lorde.


f. 72b    Þenne seten þay at þe soper.  Wern serued bylyue
830       Þe gestes gay, and ful glad, of glam debonere,
Wela wynnely wlonk, tyl þay waschen hade.
Þe trestes tylt to þe wo3e, and þe table boþe.


---

802  to] Line through o may indicate correction from e; cf.
     textual note to line 590.
812  ryally arayed] ryally [wat3] arayed: M.  [wat3] ryally
     arayed: Me, G, A, AW.

I shall fetch you a vat to wash your feet.
I urge you to remain near me only for one night,
And in the merry morning you may go your way."
805     But they refused because they wished not to enter any
          houses,
But quietly there in the street, where they were standing,
They would linger the long night, and lodge out there.
The heaven on high was house enough for them.
Lot pleaded so long, with pleasing words,
810     That they agreed to go with him, and resisted no longer.

The noble man brings them promptly to his dwelling,
Which was arrayed royally, for he had always been wealthy.
The angels were welcomed according to the way the wife
          knew.
His two dear daughters, who were very meek maidens,
815     Not married yet, greeted them devoutly;
And they were fair, and sweet, and very well dressed.

Lot then very quickly looks around himself,
And exhorts his servants to prepare dinner.
"Only remember to be proper with it, whatever thing
          you make,
820     For never serve them with any leavened bread or any salt."

However, I believe that the wife sprinkled it for
          spite,
When this ill-disposed servant said softly to herself:
"[They] allow no salt in their sauce. Yet, that would
          be no reason
For that other man to be without [it], even if both be
          foolish."
825     Then she flavors their stews with salt, each one,
Against the order of the man who had forbidden it,
And she also scattered it with scorn, she who clearly
          knew the agreement.
Why, she was so spiteful [a] wretch, she angered our Lord.

f. 72b     Then they sat at the supper. The noble guests
830     Were served quickly, and very cheerfully, with gracious
          conversation,
Very delightfully splendid, until they had washed.
The trestles were tilted towards the wall, and the
          table too.

---

822   vnfauere] vn-sauere: eds.    hyne] G noted: "h altered
      from þ."
831   Wela wynnely] welawynnely: MS.  Welawynnely: all eds.
      except A.

ffro þe seggeʒ haden souped and seten bot a whyle,
Er euer þay bosked to bedde, þe borʒ watʒ al vp,

835  Alle þat weppen myʒt welde, þe wakker and þe stronger,
To vmbelyʒe Lotheʒ hous, þe ledeʒ to take.
In grete flokkeʒ of folk, þay fallen to his ʒateʒ,
As a scowte-wach scarred; so þe asscry rysed.
Wyth kene clobbeʒ of þat clos þay clatʒ on þe woweʒ,

840  And wyth a schrylle, scharp schout, þay schewe þyse word
"If þou loujeʒ þy lyf, Loth, in þyse wones,
ʒete vus out þose ʒong men þat ʒorewhyle here entred,
Þat we may lere hym of lof, as oure lyst biddeʒ,
As is þe asyse of Sodomas to seggeʒ þat passen."

845  Whatt! Þay sputen and speken of so spitous fylþe.
What! Þay ʒeʒed and ʒolped of ʒestande sorʒe,
Þat ʒet þe wynd, and þe weder, and þe worlde stynkes
Of þe brych þat vp braydeʒ þose broþelych wordeʒ.


Þe god man glyfte wyth þat glam and gloped for noyse.

850  So scharpe schame to hym schot, he schrank at þe hert,
For he knew þe costoum þat kyþed þose wrecheʒ.
He doted neuer for no doel so depe in his mynde.
"Allas!" sayd hym þenne Loth, and lyʒtly he ryseʒ,
And boweʒ forth fro þe bench into þe brode ʒates.

855  What! He wonded no woþe of wekked knaueʒ
Þat he ne passed þe port þe pil to abide.
He went forthe at þe wyket and waft hit hym after,
Þat a clyket hit cleʒt clos hym byhynde.


Þenne he meled to þo men mesurable wordeʒ,

860  For harloteʒ, wyth his hendelayk, he hoped to chast:
"Oo, my frendeʒ so fre, your fare is to strange.
Dotʒ away your derf dyn, and dereʒ neuer my gestes.
Avoy! Hit is your vylaynye ʒe vylen yourseluen.
And ʒe ar jolyf gentylmen, your japeʒ ar ille.

f. 73  Bot, I schal kenne yow by kynde a crafte þat is better.
866  I haf a tresor in my telde of tow my fayre deʒter,
Þat ar maydeneʒ vnmard for alle men ʒette.

---

839  clatʒ] clat[er]ʒ: G.  clater: A.  clatrez: AW.
840  þyse] þys: A.    worde] worde[ʒ]: G, AW.
841  wones] woneʒ: M.
849  god man] godman: A, AW.

After the men had supped and sat only a while,
Before they ever could prepare for bed, the city was
completely aroused,
835 All who could wield weapons, the weaker and the stronger,
To surround Lot's house, to seize the angels.
In great flocks of people, they rush towards his gates,
Like a group of guards alerted; thus the clamor rose.
With sturdy clubs they beat on the walls of that enclosure,
840 And with a shrill, sharp shout, they utter these words:
"If you love your life, Lot, among these dwellings,
Bring out to us those young men who entered here before,
So that we can teach them of love, as our lust demands,
Since [this] is the custom in Sodom with men who pass by."
845 What! They spewed out and spoke of such vicious filth.
What! They shouted and threatened with mounting disgust,
So that still the wind, and the weather, and the world
stink
From the sin that those terrible words raise up.

The good man shuddered because of that shouting and
was distressed with [the] noise.
850 Such sharp shame sprang upon him, he shrank at the heart,
For he knew the custom that those wretches practiced.
He had never been stunned by any misfortune so deeply
in his mind.
"Alas!" Lot said to himself then, and he rises quickly,
And goes forth from the bench toward the wide gates.
855 What! He feared no harm from [the] wicked rogues
When he passed the door of the dwelling to confront
[them].
He went forth to the gate and flung it after him,
So that a latch locked it securely behind him.

Then he spoke reasonable words to those men,
860 For he hoped to restrain [the] scoundrels with his
courtesy:
"O, my friends so noble, your behavior is too strange.
Set aside your bold clamoring, and never bother my guests.
Shame! It is through your villainy [that] you defile
yourselves.
Even if you are gallant gentlemen, your schemes are evil.
f. 73 However, I shall teach you a practice that is better
by nature.
866 I have a treasure in my house in my two fair daughters,
Who are maidens still unmarred for all men.

---

855 no woþe] [for] no woþe: G.
856 pil] peril: eds.
864 jape₃] iapes: M.

139

In Sodamas, þaȝ I hit say, non semloker burdes.
Hit arn ronk, hit arn rype, and redy to manne.
870 To samen wyth þo semly, þe solace is better.
I schal biteche yow þo two þat tayt arn and quoynt,
And laykeȝ wyth hem as yow lyst, and leteȝ my gestes one.


Þenne þe rebaudeȝ so ronk rerd such a noyse,
Þat aȝly hurled in his ereȝ her harloteȝ speche.
875 "Wost þou not wel þat þou woneȝ here a wyȝe strange,
An outcomlyng, a carle? We kylle of þyn heued.
Who joyned þe be jostyse oure japeȝ to blame,
Þat com a boy to þis borȝ, þaȝ þou be burne ryche?"
Þus þay probled, and þrong, and þrwe vnbe his ereȝ,
880 And distressed hym wonder strayt wyth strenkþe in þe
prece.


Bot, þat, þe ȝonge men so ȝepe ȝornen þeroute,
Wapped vpon þe wyket, and wonnen hem tylle,
And by þe hondeȝ hym hent, and horyed hym wythinne,
And steken þe ȝates ston-harde wyth stalworth barreȝ.


885 Þay blwe a boffet in-blande, þat banned peple,
Þat þay blustered as blynde as Bayard watȝ euer.
Þay lest of Loteȝ logging any lysoun to fynde,
Bot nyteled þer alle þe nyȝt for noȝt at þe last.
Þenne vch tolke tyȝt hem þat hade of tayt fayled,
890 And vch on roþeled to þe rest, þat he reche moȝt.
Bot, þay wern wakned, al wrank, þat þer in won lenged,
Of on þe vglokest vnhap þat euer on erd suffred.


Ruddon of þe day-rawe ros vpon vȝten,
When merk of þe mydnyȝt moȝt no more last.
895 Ful erly þose aungeleȝ þis haþel þay ruþen,
And glopnedly, on Godeȝ halue, gart hym vp ryse.
Fast þe freke ferkeȝ vp, ful ferd at his hert.

---

871-76] Scribe wrote around tear in vellum on f. 73, but all
readings are legible.

In Sodom, if I may say it, [there are] no fairer ladies.
They are impetuous, they are mature, and ready for man.
870 To join with those fair ones, the satisfaction would
        be better.
I shall give you those two who are vigorous and graceful,
And [you] may make merry with them as you wish, but let
        my guests alone."

Then the villains so vile raised such a racket,
Those who horribly hurled into his ears their scoundrels'
        speech.
875 "Do you not fully realize that you live here as a strange
        man,
An outsider, a churl? We could chop off your head.
Who appointed you to be judge to blame our actions,
You who came as a commoner to this city, even if you
        are [a] rich man?"
Thus they pushed, and squeezed, and uttered [threats]
        around his ears,
880 And pressed upon him very closely with strength in the
        pressing.

However, at that, the young men so nimble ran out
        there,
Swung open the gate, and reached toward him,
And seized him by the hands, and drew him inside,
And closed the gates firmly with stalwart bars.

885 The cursed people struck a blow together,
At which they blundered as blindly as Bayard ever had.
They wished to find by Lot's dwelling any entertainment,
But fretted there all the night for nothing in the end.
Then each man attracted them who had failed to obtain
        satisfaction,
890 And each one mingled with the rest, those whom he could
        reach.
Yet, they would be shocked, all sinners, who remained
        there in [the] city,
By the most horrible misfortune that ever was suffered
        on earth.

Reddish coloring of the rays of dawn rose at daybreak,
When [the] darkness of the midnight could last no more.
895 Those angels arouse this man very early,
And urgently, on God's behalf, made him rise up.
The man gets up quickly, fully afraid in his heart.

_____

891  al wrank] (wrang?): M.  awrank: A.
892  vnhap þat euer] vnhap euer: G, A, AW.

141

Þay comaunded hym cof to cach þat he hade,
"Wyth þy wyf, and þy wyȝeȝ, and þy wlonk deȝtters,
900    For we laþe þe, Sir Loth, þat þou þy lyf haue.
f. 73b  Cayre tid of þis kythe, er combred þou worþe,
With alle þi here, vpon haste, tyl þou a hil fynde.
Foundeȝ faste on your fete; bifore your face lokes,
Bot bes neuer so bolde to blusch yow bihynde,
905    And loke ȝe stemme no stepe, bot strecheȝ on faste.
Til ȝe reche to a reset, rest ȝe neuer,
For we schal tyne þis toun and trayþely disstrye.
Wyth alle þise wyȝeȝ so wykke, wyȝtly devoyde,
And alle þe londe wyth þise ledeȝ we losen at oneȝ.
910    Sodomas schal ful sodenly synk into grounde,
And þe grounde of Gomorre gorde into helle,
And vche a koste of þis kyth clater vpon hepes."


     Þen laled Loth: "Lorde, what is best?
If I me fele vpon fote þat I fle moȝt,
915    Hov schulde I huyde me fro hem þat hatȝ his hate kynned
In þe brath of his breth þat brenneȝ alle þinkeȝ,
To crepe fro my Creatour and know not wheder,
Ne wheþer his fooschip me folȝeȝ bifore oþer bihynde?"


     Þe freke sayde: "No foschip oure Fader hatȝ þe schewe
920    Bot hiȝly heuened þi hele fro hem þat arn combred.
Nov walle þe a wonnyng þat þe warisch myȝt,
And he schal saue hit for þy sake, þat hatȝ vus sende
        hider,
For þou art oddely þyn one out of þis fylþe,
And als, Abraham, þy broþer, hit at himself asked."

---

906-912] Same tear noted above in 871-76 note comes through on
     f. 73b; scribe wrote around it.
912   kyth] kythe: M, G, AW. Scribal mark off first stroke of
     h need not be taken as abbr. for -e; cf. similar mark
     in same place in *hyne* 822.
915   hem] h[y]m: G, A, AW.
917   and know] [I] know: G, AW.

They commanded him promptly to take what he had,
"With your wife, and your intended sons-in-law, and
your lovely daughters,
900 For we urge you, Sir Lot, that you save your life.
f. 73b Go quickly from this land, before you are crushed,
With all your family, in haste, until you find a hill.
Travel swiftly on your feet; look before your face,
But be never so bold to look behind you,
905 And make sure you stop no footstep, but stride away
speedily.
Until you arrive at a refuge, you must never rest,
For we shall overturn this town and painfully demolish [it].
Because of all these people so wicked, [we] shall rapidly
destroy,
And all the land with these beings we shall void at once.
910 Sodom shall very suddenly sink into [the] ground,
And the ground of Gomorrah shall rush into hell,
And every region of this land shall crumble in heaps."

Then Lot lamented: "Lord, what is best?
If I advance myself on foot so that I might flee,
915 How would I hide myself from him who has prepared his
punishment
In the fire of his wrath that burns all things,
Go from my Creator and know not where,
Nor whether his enmity will strike me in front or in
back?"

The angel said: "Our Father has declared no enmity
toward you,
920 But has highly praised your goodness apart from them
who are condemned.
Now choose for yourself a dwelling that could protect you,
And he who has sent us here shall save it for your sake,
For you are singularly by yourself out of this filth,
And also, Abraham, your brother, has asked it for him-
self."

---

920 hi3ly] hil3y: A.
921 walle] wale: all eds. except M. Orig. shows *le* squeezed
together; cf. textual note to line 769.
924 þy broþer] þyn em: M, Me, Mo. þy[n eme]: G, A, AW.
Orig. shows Broþer, in much darker brown ink, apparently
by a second hand. UVR does not clarify what is beneath.

925        "Lorde, loued he worþe," quoþ Loth, "vpon erþe!
            Þen is a cité herbisyde þat Segor hit hatte.
            Here vtter on a rounde hil hit houeȝ, hit one.
            I wolde, if his wylle wore, to þat won scape."

            "Þenn fare forth," quoþ þat fre, "and fyne þou neuer,
930        Wyth þose ilk þat þow wylt, þat þrenge þe after,
            And ay goande on your gate, wythouten agayn-tote,
            For alle þis londe schal be lorne longe er þe sonne
                rise."


            Þe wyȝe wakened his wyf and his wlonk deȝteres,
            And oþer two myri men þo maydeneȝ schulde wedde,
935        And þay token hit as-tyt and tented hit lyttel.
            Þaȝ fast laþed hem Loth, þay leȝen ful stylle.
f. 74      Þe aungeleȝ hasted þise oþer and aȝly hem þratten,
            And enforsed alle fawre forth at þe ȝateȝ.
            Þo wern Loth, and his lef, his luflyche deȝter.
940        Þer soȝt no mo to sauement of cities aþel fyue.


            Þise aungeleȝ hade hem by hande out at þe ȝateȝ,
            Prechande hem þe perile, and beden hem passe fast.
            "Lest ȝe be taken in þe teche of tyraunteȝ here,
            Loke ȝe bowe now bi bot; boweȝ fast hence."
945        And þay kayre ne con and kenely flowen.


            Erly, er any heuen-glem, þay to a hil comen.
            Þe grete God, in his greme, bygynneȝ on lofte
            To wakan wedereȝ so wylde. Þe wyndeȝ he calleȝ,
            And þay wroþely vp wafte and wrastled togeder,
950        Fro fawre half of þe folde, flytande loude.
            Clowdeȝ, clustered bytwene, kesten vp torres,
            Þat þe þik þunder-þrast þirled hem ofte.
            Þe rayn rueled adoun, ridlande þikke,
            Of felle flaunkes of fyr and flakes of soufre,
955        Al in smolderande smoke, smachande ful ille;
            Swe aboute Sodamas and hit sydeȝ alle,
            Gorde to Gomorra þat þe grounde laused.

---

926  Þen] Þe[r]: all eds. except M.
935  as-tyt] as tyt: MS, M, G.  as t[a]yt: Me, A, Mo, AW.
944  boweȝ] bo[sk]eȝ: G.

925      "Lord, may he be praised on earth!" said Lot.
"Then [there] is a city nearby that is called Segor.
It rises by itself here out on a round hill.
I would, if [it] were his will, escape to that city."

      "Then go forth," said that noble angel, "and you
          must never stop,
930    With those same people whom you will [guide], who will
          press after you,
And continually moving on your way, without looking
          backwards,
For all this land shall be destroyed long before the
          sun rises."

      The man wakened his wife and his lovely daughters,
And [the] other two handsome men those maidens were
          supposed to wed,
935    But they considered it quickly and heeded it little.
Though Lot urged them firmly, they lay very still.

f. 74   The angels hastened these others and urged them awfully,
And drove all four forth to the gates.
Those were Lot, and his wife, [and] his lovely daughters.
940    There went no more to safety from [those] five splendid
          cities.

      These angels took them by [the] hand out through the
          gates,
Preaching to them of the peril, and advised them to pass
          quickly.
"Lest you be included in the guilt of tyrants here,
Make sure you go now to salvation; go away fast."
945    And they did not turn back and escaped daringly.

      Early, before any daylight, they came to a hill.
The great God, in his anger, begins on high
To arouse tempests so wild. He calls the winds,
And they violently sprang up and wrestled together,
950    From [the] four sides of the earth, roaring loudly.
Clouds, clustered at intervals, rose up like peaks,
Which the abundant thrusts of thunder often pierced.
The rain fell down, flowing thickly,
With destructive sparks of fire and flakes of sulphur,
955    All in smothering smoke, smelling very badly;
[It] curled about Sodom and struck all sides,
Rushed into Gomorrah so that the ground opened.

---

945   kayre ne con] kayre-ne con: M.
948   wakan] wak[e]n: G, AW.
957   laused] lansed: M.

Abdama and Syboym, þise ceteis, alle faure,
Al birolled wyth þe rayn, rostted and brenned,
960 And ferly flayed þat folk þat in þose fees lenged;
For when þat þe helle herde þe houndeȝ of heuen,
He watȝ ferlyly fayn, vnfolded bylyue
Þe grete barreȝ of þe abyme; he barst vp at oneȝ,
Þat alle þe regioun torof in riftes ful grete,
965 And clouen alle in lyttel cloutes, þe clyffeȝ aywhere,
As lauce leueȝ of þe boke þat lepes in twynne.
Þe brethe of þe brynston bi þat hit blende were.
Al þo citees and her sydes sunkken to helle.
Rydelles wern þo grete rowtes of renkkes wythinne.
970 When þay wern war of þe wrake þat no wyȝe achaped,
Such a ȝomerly ȝarm of ȝellyng þer rysed,
Þerof clatered þe cloudes; þat, Kryst myȝt haf rawþe.


f. 74b     Þe segge herde þat soun, to Segor þat ȝede,
And þe wenches hym wyth, þat by þe way folȝed.
975 Ferly ferde watȝ her flesch, þat flowen ay ilyche,
Trynande ay a hyȝe trot, þat torne neuer dorsten.
Loth and þo luly-whit, his lefly two deȝter,
Ay folȝed here face, bifore her boþe yȝen.


       Bot, þe balleful burde þat neuer bode keped
980 Blusched byhynden her bak þat bale for to herkken.
Hit watȝ lusty Lothes wyf þat ouer he lyfte schulder
Ones ho bluschet to þe burȝe, bot bod ho no lenger
Þat ho nas stadde a stiffe ston, a stalworth image,
Also salt as ani se, and so ho ȝet standeȝ.
985 Þay slypped bi and syȝe hir not, þat wern hir
               samen-feres,
Tyl þay in Segor wern sette and sayned our Lorde.
Wyth lyȝt loueȝ vp lyfte, þay loued hym swyþe
Þat so his seruauntes wolde see and saue of such woþe.


---

966   lauce] lance: M, Me, Mo.


146

Adama and Seboim, these cities, all four,
Were completely scorched by the rain, roasted and burned,
960    And the people who remained in those places were
            extremely terrified;
For when the hellish fiend heard the hounds of heaven,
He was exceedingly joyful [and] opened quickly
The great barriers of the abyss; he broke [them] open
            at once,
So that all the region ripped apart in very great clefts,
965    And the cliffs crumbled everywhere, all in little
            fragments,
Like loose leaves of the book which springs into two
            parts.
The smoke of the brimstone had streamed together by
            that time.
All those cities and their surroundings had sunk into hell.
Those great crowds of people within were helpless.
970    When they were aware of the disaster that no man could
            escape,
Such a painful outcry of yelling rose there,
The clouds were shattered by it; at that, Christ might
            have pity.

f. 74b    The man who went to Segor heard that sound,
And the women who followed along the way with him.
975    Extraordinary fear possessed their beings, those who
            fled constantly,
Maintaining always a fast trot, those who never dared
            turn.
Lot and those lily-white ladies, his two lovely daughters,
Always moved directly ahead, both their eyes in front.

However, the wretched woman who never kept [a] command
980    Looked behind her back to observe that destruction.
It was admirable Lot's wife who glanced once at the city
Over her left shoulder, but she lived no longer
Because she was standing like a solid stone, a stalwart
            image,
Like [the] salt in any sea, and thus she still stands.
985    They slipped by and did not see her, those who had
            been her companions,
Until they were situated in Segor and were blessing
            our Lord.
With joyous praises lifted up, they greatly honored him
Who thus would see and save his servants from such harm.

---

981  he] he[r]: eds.

147

Al wat₃ dampped, and don, and drowned by þenne.
990 Þe lede₃ of þat lyttel toun wern lopen out for drede,
Into þat malscrande mere, marred bylyue,
Þat no₃t saued wat₃ bot Segor, þat sat on a lawe,
Þe þre lede₃ þerin, Loth and his de₃ter;
For his make wat₃ myst, þat on þe mount lenged
995 In a stonen statue þat salt sauor habbes,
For two fautes þat þe fol wat₃ founde in mistrauþe.
On, ho serued at þe soper salt bifore Dry₃tyn,
And syþen, ho blusched hir bihynde, þa₃ hir forboden were
For on ho standes a ston, and salt for þat oþer,
1000 And lalle lyst on hir lik, þat arn on launde bestes.


Abraham ful erly wat₃ vp on þe morne
Þat alle na₃t much niye hade no mon in his hert.
Al in longing for Loth, leyen in a wache,
Þer he lafte hade oure Lorde, he is on lofte wonnen.
1005 He sende toward Sodomas þe sy₃t of his y₃en,
Þat euer hade ben an erde of erþe þe swettest.
As aparaunt to Paradis þat plantted þe Dry₃tyn.
Nov is hit plunged in a pit like of pich fylled.
f. 75 Suche a roþun of a reche ros fro þe blake.
1010 Aske₃ vpe in þe ayre and vselle₃ þer flowen
As a fornes ful of flot þat vpon fyr boyles
When bry₃t, brennande bronde₃ ar bet þer anvnder.
Þis wat₃ a uengaunce violent þat voyded þise places,
Þat foundered hat₃ so fayr a folk and þe folde sonkken.


1015 Þer faure citees wern set nov is a see called,
Þat ay is drouy, and dym, and ded in hit kynde,
Blo, blubrande, and blak, vnblyþe to ne₃e,
As a stynkande stanc þat stryed synne,
Þat euer of synne and of smach smart is to fele.

---

993 lede₃ þerin] lede₃ [lent] þer-in: G. ledez þerin lent:
AW.
1000 lalle] alle: eds. Orig. shows la squeezed together; cf.
textual notes to 769 and 921.
1002 much] [so] much: M. no mon] nom[e]n: Me, G, A, Mo, AW.
1009 roþun] roþum: A.

Everybody was doomed, and dead, and drowned by then.
990  The people of that little town had run out in fear,
Into that confusing sea, [and] had perished quickly,
Since nothing was saved except Segor, which was set on
a hill,
[And] the three people therein, Lot and his daughters;
For his spouse was missing, she who had remained on
the hill
995  As a stone statue which has [a] savor of salt,
Because of two faults of unfaithfulness in which the
fool was found.
First, she served salt before God at the supper,
And then, she looked behind her, though [it] were for-
bidden for her.
For one she stands like a stone, and like salt for that
other,
1000  And loyal creatures, who are beasts on land, like to
lick on her.

Abraham was up very early in the morning
Because all night no man had [that] much worry in his
heart.
All in longing for Lot, placed as a lookout,
Where he had left our Lord, he is situated on high.
1005  He directed the sight of his eyes toward Sodom,
Which always had been the most beautiful region on earth.
The Lord had created it as heir apparent to Paradise.
Now it is plunged in a suitable pit filled with pitch.
f. 75  Such a stench from the smoke rose from the black pit.
1010  Ashes and embers flew up in the air there
As from a cauldron full of fat that boils upon fire
When bright, burning brands are kindled beneath there.
This was a violent punishment that voided these places,
That has struck down such comely people and submerged
the land.

1015  A sea is now named where [the] four cities had been
situated,
Which is always murky, and dim, and dead because of its
nature,
Dark, seething, and black, unpleasant to approach,
Like a stinking pool that overwhelmed sin,
That is always to smell of sin and of bitter scent.

---

1015  Þer faure] Þ[er þe] f[y]u[e]: G, AW. Þere fyue: A.
Þer fyue: Mo. Orig. shows all letters, except þ and
f, in darker brown ink, apparently by second hand; cf.
textual note to 924.  is] Inserted above line in
darker brown ink.
1019  synne] s[mell]e: Me, G, Mo, AW.

149

1020     Forþy, þe derk Dede See hit is demed euermore,
          For hit dedeȝ of deþe duren þere ȝet;
          For hit is brod, and boþemleȝ, and bitter as þe galle,
          And noȝt may lenge in þat lake, þat any lyf bereȝ,
          And alle þe costeȝ of kynde hit combreȝ, vch one,
1025     For lay þeron a lump of led, and hit on loft fleteȝ,
          And folde þeron a lyȝt fyþer, and hit to founs synkkeȝ,
          And þer water may walter to wete any erþe,
          Schal neuer grene þeron growe, gresse ne wod nawþer.
          If any schalke to be schent wer schowued þerinne,
1030     Þaȝ he bode in þat boþem broþely a monyth,
          He most ay lyue in þat loȝe in losyng euermore,
          And neuer dryȝe no dethe to dayes of ende;
          And as hit is corsed of kynde, and hit coosteȝ als,
          Þe clay þat clenges þerby arn corsyes strong,
1035     As alum and alkaran, þat angré arn boþe,
          Soufre sour, and saundyuer, and oþer such mony;
          And þer walteȝ of þat water in waxlokes grete
          Þe spuniande aspaltoun þat spysereȝ sellen;
          And suche is alle þe soyle by þat se halues,
1040     Þat fel fretes þe flesch and festred bones.
          And þer ar tres by þat terne of traytoures,
          And þay borgouneȝ and beres blomeȝ ful fayre,
          And þe fayrest fryt þat may on folde growe,
          As orenge, and oþer fryt, and apple-garnade,
f. 75b   Also red, and so ripe, and rychely hwed
1046     As any dom myȝt deuice of dayntyeȝ--oute;
          Bot quen hit is brused, oþer broken, oþer byten in twynn
          No worldeȝ goud hit wythinne--bot wyndowande askes.
          Alle þyse ar teches and tokenes to trow vpon ȝet,
1050     And wittnesse of þat wykked werk and þe wrake after
          Þat oure Fader forferde for fylþe of þose ledes.


        Þenne vch wyȝe may wel wyt þat he þe wlonk louies,
        And if he louyes clene layk, þat is oure Lorde ryche,
         And to be couþe in his courte þou coueytes þenne,

---

1038   spuniande] (*spinnande*?): M.  spu[m]ande: Me, G, A, Mo, AW.
1040   fretes þe flesch] fretes [&] flesch: G.    festred]
       (*festres*?): M.  festre[s]: Me, A, Mo, AW.

| | |
|---|---|
| 1020 | Therefore, it has been named the dark Dead Sea forever, |
| | Because its deeds of death endure there yet; |
| | For it is broad, and bottomless, and bitter like the bile, |
| | And nothing that bears any life can linger in that water, |
| | And it perverts all the elements of nature, each one, |
| 1025 | For lay thereon a lump of lead, and it floats on top, |
| | And lay thereon a light feather, and it sinks to [the] bottom, |
| | And where [its] water may overflow to wet any earth, |
| | Green herbage shall never grow thereon, grass nor shrubbery either. |
| | If any man were cast therein to be killed, |
| 1030 | Though he remained in that terrible pit a month, |
| | He must continually live in that sea with decay always increasing, |
| | And never suffer any death for days on end; |
| | And since it is cursed by nature, and its coasts also, |
| | The clays that cling thereby are strong substances, |
| 1035 | Such as alum and bitumen, that are both pungent, |
| | Bitter sulphur, and sandever, and many others of the same kind; |
| | And there emerges from that water in the shape of great curls of wax |
| | The thriving asphalt that apothecaries sell; |
| | And such is all the soil along [the] sides of that sea, |
| 1040 | Which fiercely consumes the flesh and decayed bones. |
| | And there are trees by that sea of traitors, |
| | And they sprout and bear very beautiful blossoms, |
| | And the fairest fruit that can grow on land, |
| | Such as oranges, and other fruit, and pomegranates, |
| f. 75b | As red, and as ripe, and royally colored |
| 1046 | As any imagination could conceive concerning delicacies --on the outside; |
| | But when it is bruised, or broken, or bitten in two, |
| | No earth's goodness [is] inside it--only winnowing ashes. |
| | All these are symbols and signs to believe in yet, |
| 1050 | And testimony to that wicked conduct and the punishment afterwards |
| | When our Father destroyed [the cities] because of [the] filth of those people. |

Then every man can well understand that he loves
the pure person,
And if he who is our noble Lord loves clean conduct,
And [if] you desire to be known in his court then,

---

1041  traytoures] traytoures [kynde]: G.
1048  wyndowande] wydowande: M.
1051  forferde] for[þ]erde: G.  forþered: A.  forþrede: AW.

1055 To se þat Semly in sete, and his swete face,
Clerrer counseyl counsayl con I non, bot þat þou clene
worþe.

For, Clopyngnel, in þe compas of his clene *Rose*,
Þer he expouneȝ a speche to hym þat spede wolde
Of a lady to be loued: "Loke to hir sone,
1060 Of wich beryng þat ho be, and wych ho best louyes,
And be ryȝt such in vch a borȝe, of body and of dedes,
And folȝ þe fet of þat fere þat þou fre haldes,
And if þou wyrkkes on þis wyse, þaȝ ho wyk were,
Hir schal lyke þat layk þat lyknes hir tylle."

1065 If þou wyl dele drwrye wyth Dryȝtyn þenne,
And lelly louy þy Lorde, and his leef worþe,
Þenne confourme þe to Kryst and þe clene make.
Þat euer is polyced als playn as þe perle seluen;
For loke fro fyrst þat he lyȝt wythinne þe lel Mayden,
1070 By how comly a kest he watȝ clos þere,
When venkkyst watȝ no vergynyté, ne vyolence maked.
Bot, much clener watȝ hir corse; God kynned þerinne.
And efte, when he borne watȝ in Beþelen þe ryche,
In wych puryté þay departed. Þaȝ þay pouer were,
1075 Watȝ neuer so blysful a bour as watȝ a bos þenne,
Ne no schroude-hous so schene as a schepon þare,
Ne non so glad vnder God as ho þat grone schulde;
For þer watȝ seknesse al sounde, þat sarrest is halden,
And þer watȝ rose reflayr where rote hatȝ ben euer,
1080 And þer watȝ solace and songe wher sorȝ hatȝ ay cryed;
f. 76 For aungelles wyth instrumentes of organes and pypes,
And rial, ryngande rotes, and þe reken fyþel,
And alle hende þat honestly moȝt an hert glade
Aboutte my Lady watȝ lent quen ho delyuer were.

---

1056 counseyl counsayl] counseyl: Me, Mo, AW.   counsayl: G, A.
1057 For Clopyngnel] For [so] Clopyngnel: G.
1071] MS has *he* before *venkkyst* crossed out.

1055      To see that fair Lord on [his] throne, and his glorious
             face,
        I can not advise clearer counsel, but that you become pure.

        Therefore, Clopinel, within the scope of his fine
             *Rose,*
        Expounds there a speech for him who would wish to prosper
        With a lady to be loved: "Be certain about her at once,
1060      Concerning which manner that she maintains, and what
             she loves best,
        And be just the same in every place, in appearance and
             in actions,
        And follow the example of that loved one whom you con-
             sider noble,
        And if you move in this manner, though she could be stern,
        That behavior which harmonizes with hers shall please her."

1065      If you wish to receive love from God then,
        And to love your Lord truly, and to become his friend,
        Then conform yourself to Christ and make yourself clean.
        He is always purified as perfectly as the pearl itself;
        For observe from [the] start when he entered within the
             loyal Maiden,
1070      By how beautiful a miracle he was enclosed there,
        When no virginity was vanquished, nor physical violation
             committed.
        Furthermore, her body was much purer; God was conceived
             therein.
        And afterwards, when he was born in the splendid Bethle-
             hem,
        In what purity they were parted. Though they were poor,
1075      [There] was never so blissful a bower as a manger was
             then,
        Nor any sacristy as bright as the stable there,
        Nor anyone under God so glad as she who should groan;
        For there was sickness, that is considered most painful,
             completely cured,
        And there was [a] fragrance of roses where stench has
             always been,
1080      And there was solace and song where sorrow has always
             sounded;
f. 76     For angels with instruments of organs and pipes,
        And royal, ringing rotes, and the fine fiddle,
        And all courteous people who could honestly gladden a
             heart
        Had lingered around my Lady when she had been delivered.

---

1075  a bos] abos: MS, M.  (*abof?*): M.
1076  schroude-hous] schroude ho*us*: MS, M, G, AW.

1085       Þenne watȝ her blyþe Barne burnyst so clene
      Þat boþe þe ox and þe asse hym hered at ones.
      Þay knewe hym by his clannes for Kyng of nature,
      For non so clene of such a clos com neuer er þenne;
      And ȝif clanly he þenne com, ful cortays þerafter,
1090       Þat alle þat longed to luþer, ful lodly, he hated.
      By nobleye of his norture, he nolde neuer towche
      Oȝt þat watȝ vngoderly oþer ordure watȝ inne.
      Ȝet, comen lodly to þat Lede, as laȝares monye,
      Summe lepre, summe lome, and lomerande blynde,
1095       Poysened, and parlatyk, and pyned in fyres,
      Drye folk, and ydropike, and dede at þe laste.
      Alle called on þat cortaysé and claymed his grace.
      He heled hem wyth hynde speche of þat þay ask after,
      For whatso he towched also-tyd tourned to hele,
1100       Wel clanner þen any crafte cowþe devyse.
      So clene watȝ his hondelyng, vche ordure hit schouied;
      And þe gropyng so goud, of God and Man boþe,
      Þat, for fetys of his fyngeres, fonded he neuer
      Nauþer to cout ne to kerue wyth knyf ne wyth egge.
1105       Forþy, brek he þe bred blades wythouten,
      For hit ferde freloker, in fete, in his fayre honde,
      Displayed more pryuyly when he hit part schulde,
      Þenne alle þe toles of Tolowse moȝt tyȝt hit to kerue.

      Þus is he kyryous and clene, þat þou his cort askes.
1110       Hov schulde þou com to his kyth bot if þou clene were?
      Nov ar we sore, and synful, and sovly, vch one.
      How schulde we se þen, may we say, þat Syre vpon throne
      Ȝis, þat Mayster is mercyable. Þaȝ þou be man fenny,
      And al tomarred in myre whyl þou on molde lyuyes,

---

1101   clene] [h]en[d]e: G, AW.     schouied] schonied: eds.
1107   pryuyly] pry[st]yly: G.
1111   Nov] Now: Mo.     sovly] sov[er]ly: M.
1112   vpon] upon: Me, A.   Menner normalized MS *v* to *u*.

1085       Then her gracious Child was shining so brightly
      That both the ox and the ass honored him at once.
      They recognized him by his purity as King of nature,
      For no one so clean had ever come before then from such
          an enclosure;
      And if he came chastely then, [he was] very refined
          thereafter,
1090       So that he scorned, indeed contemptuously, everything
          that pertained to evil.
      Because of [the] nobility of his background, he would
          never touch
      Anything that was squalid or had filth within.
      Yet, repulsive beings came to that Man, such as many
          sick persons,
      Some leprous, some lame, and blundering blind,
1095       Poisoned, and palsied, and tormented by inflammatory
          diseases,
      Choleric people, and dropsical, and [the] dead at last.
      All called on that courtesy and claimed his grace.
      He healed them of what they asked for with divine words,
      For whatever he touched turned immediately to well-being,
1100       Certainly cleaner than any skill could devise.
      So perfect was his handling, it cast out every unclean
          thing;
      And the touching [was] so effective, of God and Man both,
      That, because of [the] skills in his fingers, he never
          tried
      Either to cut or to carve with knife or with sharp
          instrument.
1105       Therefore, he broke the bread without blades,
      For it parted more perfectly, in fact, in his deft hands,
      [And] spread more carefully when he would divide it,
      Than [if] all the tools of Toulouse might contrive to
          cut it.

      Thus he is perfect and pure, that one whose court
          you seek.
1110       How should you enter into his kingdom unless you be pure?
      Now we are afflicted, and sinful, and soiled, each one.
      How should we see then, may we say, that Lord upon [his]
          throne?
      Yes, that Master is merciful.  Though you may be [a]
          sinful man,
      And completely marred with mire while you live on earth,

---

1114   whyl] whyle: G, AW.  Scribal mark off *l*, the same as the
      one off the *h* of kyth 912, is apparently not abbr. for
      *-e*; cf. textual note to line 912.

1115    Þou may schyne þur3 schryfte, þa3 þou haf schome serued  
       And pure þe with penaunce tyl þou a perle worþe.

f. 76b    Perle praysed is prys þer perré is schewed,  
       Þa3 hym not derrest be demed to dele for penies.  
       Quat may þe cause be called? Bot for hir clene hwes  
1120    Þat wynnes worschyp abof alle whyte stones,  
       For ho schynes so schyr, þat is of schap rounde,  
       Wythouten faut oþer fylþe, 3if ho fyn were,  
       And wax euer in þe worlde. In weryng so olde,  
       3et þe perle payres not, whyle ho in pyese lasttes;  
1125    And if hit cheue þe chaunce vncheryst ho worþe,  
       Þat ho blyndes of ble in bour þer ho lygges,  
       Nobot wasch hit wyth wourchyp, in wyn, as ho askes.  
       Ho, by kynde, schal becom clerer þen are.  
       So if folk be defowled by vnfre chaunce,  
1130    Þat he be sulped in sawle, seche to schryfte,  
       And he may polyce hym at þe prest, by penaunce taken,  
       Wel bry3ter þen þe beryl oþer browden perles.

       Bot, war þe wel! If þou be waschen wyth water of  
          schryfte,  
       And polysed als playn as parchmen schauen,  
1135    Sulp no more þenne in synne þy saule þerafter,  
       For þenne þou Dry3tyn dyspleses wyth dedes ful sore,  
       And entyses hym to tene more trayþly þen euer,  
       And wel hatter to hate þen hade þou not waschen,  
       For when a sawele is sa3tled and sakred to Dry3tyn,  
1140    He holly haldes hit his, and haue hit he wolde.  
       Þenne efte lastes hit likkes, he loses hit ille,  
       As hit were rafte wyth vnry3t and robbed wyth þewes.  
       War þe, þenne, for þe wrake! His wrath is achaufed,  
       For þat þat ones wat3 his schulde efte be vnclene.

---

1118  hym] h[it]: G.  ho: A.  hyt: AW.  
1123  wax euer] (sense seems to require ... *wax ho euer*): M.  
        wax [ho] euer: G, A.

1115        You may shine through shrift, even if you have deserved
               shame,
        And purify yourself with penance until you become a pearl.

f. 76b    [The] prized pearl is eminent where jewelry is shown,
        Though it is not considered most costly to exchange for
               pennies.
        What may the reason be attributed to?  Only because of
               her pure colors
1120        That one gains esteem above all white stones,
        For she shines so brightly, she that is of round shape,
        Without flaw or filth, if she be perfect,
        And always flourishes in the world.  With such long
               wearing,
        Yet the pearl is not impaired, as long as she stays in
               one piece;
1125        And if it occurs by chance [that] she may be neglected,
        So that she darkens in hue in [the] place where she lies,
        Only wash her with care, in wine, as she requires.
        She, because of [her] nature, shall become clearer than
               before.
        So if mankind be marred by ignoble events,
1130        So that he be stained in [his] soul, [he] should seek
               for shrift,
        And he can purify himself with the priest, by accepting
               penance,
        Much more brightly than the beryl or embroidered pearls.

        However, guard yourself well!  If you be cleansed
               by [the] water of confession,
        And polished as plainly as smoothed parchment,
1135        Then stain your soul with sin no more after that,
        For then you displease God with very grievous deeds,
        And provoke him to punish more painfully than ever,
        And certainly to despise [you] more severely than had
               you not been purified,
        For when a soul is reconciled and consecrated to God,
1140        He considers it completely his, and he would wish to
               keep it.
        Then, [if] it favors sins again, he banishes it with
               displeasure,
        Since it would be defiled by wrong-doing and robbed of
               virtues.
        Guard yourself, then, from the punishment!  His wrath
               would be aroused,
        Because that which was once his should be impure again.

---

1124    pyese] pryse: AW.
1143    is achaufed] [hat3] achaufed: G.

1145        Þaȝ hit be bot a bassyn, a bolle, oþer a scole,
           A dysche, oþer a dobler þat Dryȝtyn oneȝ serued,
           To defowle hit euer vpon folde fast he forbedes.
           So is he scoymus of scaþe, þat scylful is euer.
           And þat watȝ bared in Babyloyn in Baltaȝar tyme,
1150        Hov harde vnhap þer hym hent, and hastyly sone,
           For he þe vesselles avyled þat vayled in þe temple,
           In seruyse of þe Souerayn sumtyme byfore.
f. 77       3if ȝe wolde tyȝt me a tom, telle hit I wolde,
           Hov charged more watȝ his chaunce, þat hem cherych nold
1155        Þen his fader forloyne þat feched hem wyth strenþe,
           And robbed þe relygioun of relykes alle.


PART THREE: SEDECIAS, BALTASSAR,
AND NABUCHODONOSOR


          D anyel, in his Dialokeȝ, devysed sumtyme,
             As ȝet is proued expresse, in his Profecies,
           Hov þe gentryse of Juise and Jherusalem þe ryche
1160        Watȝ disstryed wyth distres and drawen to þe erþe,
           ffor þat folke, in her fayth, watȝ founden vntrwe,
           Þat haden hyȝt þe hyȝe God to halde of hym euer;
           And he hem halȝed for his, and help at her nede,
           In mukel meschefes mony þat meruayl to here.
1165        And, þay forloyne her fayth, and folȝed oþer goddes,
           And þat wakned his wrath, and wrast hit so hyȝe
           Þat he fylsened þe faythful in þe falce lawe
           To forfare þe falce in þe faythe trwe.


           Hit watȝ sen in þat syþe þat 3edechyas rengned
1170        In Juda, þat justised þe Juyne kynges.
           He sete on Salamones solie on solemne wyse,
           Bot of leauté he watȝ lat to his Lorde hende.

---

1159  Jherusalem] Iherusalem: M.  (The MS has *Ihrlm* (1159), *Ir*
        (1180, 1235), *irlm* (1432), and *isrlm* (1441); in each
        instance, there is a flourish off the *l*. This abbrev
        tion mark is different from the one in *Pearl*. See th
        textual note to *Pearl* 792.)

1145    Even if it be only a basin, a bowl, or a cup,
        A dish, or a platter that once served God,
        He firmly forbids to ever defile it on earth.
        Thus he who is always just is disdainful of evil.
        And that was revealed in Babylon in Baltassar's time,
1150    How terrible misfortune seized him there, and very
                quickly,
        Because he desecrated the vessels that had prevailed
                in the temple,
        In [the] service of the Sovereign sometime before.
f. 77   If you would set the time for me, I would tell it,
        How more burdened was his fate, he who would not
                cherish them,
1155    Than [that] of his sinful father who had seized them
                by force,
        And had robbed the religious house of all [its] relics.


        PART THREE: SEDECIAS, BALTASSAR,
            AND NABUCHODONOSOR


        Daniel, in his Dialogues, formerly described,
        As [it] is still plainly proved, according to his
                Prophecies,
        How the gentry of Jewish people and the splendid
                Jerusalem
1160    Were destroyed with violence and drawn to the earth,
        Because that race, who had promised the great God
        To honor him always, had been found false in their faith;
        And he had consecrated them as his, and had aided [them]
                in their needs,
        In many great misfortunes that [are] amazing to hear of.
1165    And yet, they forsook their faith, and followed other
                gods,
        And that aroused his wrath, and incited it so intensely
        That he helped the faithful of the false law
        To destroy the false people of the true faith.


        This was seen in that time when Sedecias reigned
1170    In Juda, he who governed the kings of the Jews.
        He sat on Solomon's throne in [a] solemn manner,
        But he was lacking in loyalty to his noble Lord.

---

1164  meruayl to] meruayl [is] to: M, Me, Mo, AW.   [is] meruayl
          to: G.  meruayl were to: A.
1169  3edechyas] 3edethyas: A.  Looks like 3edethyas in MS, but
          c and t sometimes resemble each other; cf. textual
          note to Pe. 845.

He vsed abominaciones of idolatrye,
And lette ly3t bi þe lawe þat he wat3 lege tylle.

1175      Forþi, oure Fader vpon folde a foman hym wakned.
          Nabigodeno3ar nuyed hym swyþe.
          He pursued into Palastyn wyth proude men mony,
          And þer he wast wyth werre þe wones of þorpes.
          He her3ed vp alle Israel and hent of þe beste
1180      And þe gentylest of Judee in Jerusalem biseged,
          Vnbewalt alle þe walles wyth wy3es ful stronge,
          At vche a dor a do3ty duk, and dutte hem wythinne,
          For þe bor3 wat3 so bygge baytayled alofte,
          And stoffed wythinne wyth stout men to stalle hem þerou

1185      Þenne wat3 þe sege sette þe ceté aboute.
          Skete skarmoch skelt.   Much skaþe lached.
          At vch brugge a berfray on basteles wyse,
f. 77b    Þat seuen syþe vch a day asayled þe 3ates.
          Trwe tulkkes in toures teueled wythinne,
1190      In bigge brutage of borde, bulde on þe walles.
          Þay fe3t, and þay fende of, and fylter togeder,
          Til two 3er ouertorned.   3et, tok þay hit neuer.

          At þe laste, vpon longe, þo ledes wythinne,
          Faste fayled hem þe fode.   Enfaminied monie.
1195      Þe hote hunger wythinne hert hem wel sarre
          Þen any dunt of þat douthe þat dowelled þeroute.
          Þenne wern þo rowtes redles in þo ryche wones.
          Fro þat mete wat3 myst, megre þay wexen,
          And þay stoken so strayt þat þay ne stray my3t
1200      A fote fro þat forselet to forray no gouerdes.

          Þenne þe kyng of þe kyth a counsayl hym takes,
          Wyth þe best of his burnes, a blench for to make.

─────────────

1178   wyth] wyth with: MS.
1179   Israel] israel: M.  (The MS has isrl, with a flourish o
          the l.  In lines 1294 and 1314, the word is written v
          no abbreviation mark.)

He practiced abominations of idolatry,
And behaved negligently in the law to which he was
    pledged.

1175        Therefore, our Father aroused against him an enemy
    upon earth.
Nabuchodonosor afflicted him greatly.
He advanced into Palestine with many proud men,
And there he ruined in battle the abodes of [the]
    villages.
He stirred up all Israel and seized the best
1180    And the noblest people of Judea in [the] besieged
    Jerusalem,
Surrounded all the walls with very strong men,
[Placed] at every gateway a doughty duke, and trapped
    them inside,
Since the city was so strongly embattled above,
And fortified within with valiant men to stop them out
    there.

1185        Then the siege was set around the city.
Skirmishes spread quickly. Much harm followed.
At every drawbridge [was] a battering ram in [the] form
    of [a] tower on wheels,
f. 77b   Which assailed the gates seven times every day.
Loyal warriors on towers battled on the inside,
1190    Behind [a] strong rampart of wood, built on the walls.
They fight, and they hold [them] off, and mingle together,
Until two years passed. Yet, they (the Chaldeans)
    never took it.

        At last, at length, for those people within,
The food was failing them fast. Many starved.
1195    The sharp hunger within hurt them much more deeply
Than any blow from that army which dwelled out there.
Then those crowds were helpless in those splendid
    habitations.
After the food was missed, they became emaciated,
And they were pinned in so tightly that they could
    not stray
1200    A foot from that fortification to gather any gourds.

        Then the king of the land calls a meeting himself,
With the best of his warriors, to devise a stratagem.

---

1183  baytayled] b[a]tayled: Me, G, Mo, AW.
1194  Enfaminied] enfa[m]ined: G, AW.
1200  gouerdes] goudes: eds. Orig. shows abbr. for *er* over
      first minim of *u*.

Þay stel out on a stylle ny3t er any steuen rysed,
And harde hurles þur3 þe oste er enmies hit wyste,
1205    Bot er þay atwappe ne mo3t þe wach wythoute,
Hi3e skelt wat3 þe askry þe skewes anvnder.
Loude alarom vpon launde lulted wat3 þenne.
Ryche, ruþed of her rest, ran to here wedes.
Hard hattes þay hent and on hors lepes.
1210    Cler claryoun crak cryed on lofte.


By þat, wat3 alle on a hepe, hurlande swyþee,
Fol3ande þat oþer flote, and fonde hem bilyue,
Ouertok hem as-tyd, tult hem of sadeles,
Tyl vche prynce hade his per put to þe grounde;
1215    And þer wat3 þe kyng ka3t wyth Caldé prynces,
And alle hise gentyle forjusted on Jerico playnes,
And presented wern as presoneres to þe prynce rychest,
Nabigodeno3ar noble in his chayer;
And he þe faynest freke þat he his fo hade,
1220    And speke spitously hem to, and spylt þerafter
Þe kynges sunnes in his sy3t. He slow euervchone,
And holkked out his auen y3en heterly boþe,
And bede þe burne to be bro3t to Babyloyn þe ryche,
f. 78    And þere in dongoun be don to dre3e þer his wyrdes.


1225    Now se! So þe Souerayn set hat3 his wrake.
Nas hit not for Nabugo ne his noble nauþer
Þat oþer depryued wat3 of pryde with paynes stronge,
Bot for his beryng so badde agayn his blyþe Lorde;
ffor hade þe Fader ben his frende, þat hym bifore kepe
1230    Ne neuer trespast to him in teche of mysseleue,
To colde wer alle Caldé and kythes of Ynde.
3et take Torkye hem wyth, her tene hade ben little.

---

1211   swyþee] swyþ[e]: Me, Mo.
1220   spylt] spylt [hem]: G.
1224   dongoun] doungoun: Me, G, Mo.

They slipped out on a still night before any sound rose,
And [they] sneak quickly through the army before [their]
     enemies knew it,
1205     But before they could escape the guard out there,
The clamor was noisily spread beneath the clouds.
[A] loud call to arms was sounded upon land then.
Noble warriors, aroused from their rest, ran for their
     clothes.
They seize hard hats and leap on horses.
1210     [A] clear call of a clarion sounded on high.

By that time, everybody was in a group, rushing
     swiftly,
Following that other company, and [they] found them
     promptly,
Overtook them swiftly, [and] knocked them off saddles,
Until each prince had his peer placed on the ground;
1215     And there was the king captured by Chaldean princes,
And all his nobles were defeated on Jericho's plains,
And were presented as prisoners to the most royal prince,
Noble Nabuchodonosor on his throne;
And he [was] the happiest man because he had his enemies,
1220     And [he] spoke cruelly to them, and after that killed
The king's sons in his sight. He slew one and all,
And viciously gouged out both his (Sedecias') own eyes,
And ordered the man to be brought to the splendid Babylon,
f. 78     And then to be placed in [a] dungeon to endure there
     his fate.

1225     Observe now! Thus the Sovereign has imposed his
     penalty.
It was not because of Nabucho or his noble warriors
     either
That [the] other was deprived of [his] high position
     with harsh punishments,
But because of his behavior so bad against his gracious
     Lord;
For had the Father, who had protected him before, re-
     mained his friend,
1230     Or [had Sedecias] never trespassed against him with [the]
     sin of disloyalty,
All Chaldea and [the] lands of India would have been too
     powerless [against him].
Even take Turkey with them, their fierceness would have
     been slight.

---

1225  Souerayn] soueray: MS.
1231  To colde wer alle Caldé] to Colde wer alle Calde: MS.
     To C[a]lde wer alle calde: Me.

3et, nolde neuer Nabugo þis ilke note leue
Er he hade tuyred þis toun and torne hit to grounde.
1235    He joyned vnto Jerusalem a gentyle duc þenne,
His name watȝ Nabuȝardan, to noye þe Jues.
He watȝ mayster of his men and myȝty himseluen,
Þe chef of his cheualrye, his chekkes to make.
He brek þe bareres as bylyue, and þe burȝ after,
1240    And enteres in ful ernestly in yre of his hert.

What! Þe maysterry watȝ mene. Þe men wern away,
Þe best boȝed wyth þe burne þat þe borȝ ȝemed,
And þo þat byden wer fo biten with þe bale hunger,
Þat on wyf hade ben worþe þe welgest fourre.
1245    Nabiȝardan noȝt, forþy, nolde not spare;
Bot, bede al to þe bronde vnder bare egge.

Þay slowen of swettest, semlych burdes,
Baþed barnes in blod, and her brayn spylled.
Prestes and prelates, þay presed to deþe,
1250    Wyues and wenches, her wombes tocoruen,
Þat her boweles out borst aboute þe diches;
And al watȝ carfully kylde, þat þay cach myȝt,
And alle swypped vnswolȝed of þe sworde kene,
Þay wer cagged and kaȝt on capeles, al bare,
1255    Festned fettres to her fete vnder fole wombes,
And broþely broȝt to Babyloyn þer bale to suffer,
To sytte in seruage and syte. Þat sumtyme wer gentyle
Now ar chaunged to chorles and charged wyth werkkes,
1259    Boþe to cayre at þe kart and þe kuy mylke,
f. 78b  Þat sumtyme sete in her sale, syres and burdes.

And ȝet, Nabuȝardan nyl neuer stynt
Er he to þe tempple tee wyth his tulkkes alle.
Betes on þe barers, brestes vp þe ȝates,
Slouen alle at a slyp þat serued þerinne,
1265    Pulden prestes bi þe polle and plat of her hedes,
Diȝten dekenes to deþe, dungen doun clerkkes,

---

1234  tuyred] t[yrv]ed: Me, G, A, Mo, AW.
1243  fo] so: eds.
1253  alle swypped] alle [þat] swypped: all eds. except A.

Yet, Nabucho would never dismiss this same matter
Until he had stripped this city and smashed it to [the]
    ground.
1235  He assigned to Jerusalem a noble duke then,
Whose name was Nabuzardan, to harass the Jews.
He was master of his men and mighty himself,
The leader of his army in making his attacks.
He broke down the barriers immediately, and the bulwark
    beyond,
1240  And enters in very eagerly with anger in his heart.

What! The mastery was weakened. The men were away,
The best overcome by the man who had conquered the city,
And those that remained were terribly bitten by the
    painful hunger,
So that one woman would have been worth the healthiest
    four.
1245  Consequently, Nabuzardan would spare nothing;
Moreover, [he] subjected everybody to the sword under
    [its] exposed edge.

They killed off [the] loveliest, fair ladies,
Bathed children in blood, and spilled their brains.
They pressed priests and prelates to death,
1250  Cut out the wombs of wives and maidens,
So that their bowels burst out around the ditches;
And everybody whom they could capture was cruelly killed,
And all [who] escaped unharmed from the sharp sword
Were bound and placed on horses, completely naked,
1255  Fastened with fetters upon their feet under [the]
    horses' bellies,
And quickly brought to Babylon to suffer hardship there,
To be situated in servitude and sorrow. Those who were
    formerly nobles
Now are changed to churls and burdened with labors,
1259  Both to pull at the cart and to milk the cows,
f. 78b  Those who formerly sat in their hall, lords and ladies.

And yet, Nabuzardan will never cease
Until he goes to the temple with all his warriors.
[They] beat on the barriers, break open the gates,
Slew all with a stroke who served therein,
1265  Pulled priests by the crown and chopped off their heads,
Doomed deacons to death, knocked down clerks,

---

1255  Festned] UVR shows what looks like hyphen between MS
    *fest* and *ned,* as G noted.
1257  To sytte] So sytte: Me, Mo.  UVR shows *to* more clearly.

And alle þe maydenes of þe munster maȝtyly ho kyllen
Wyth þe swayf of þe sworde þat swolȝed hem alle.

Þenne ran þay to þe relykes as robbors wylde,
1270    And pyled alle þe apparement þat pented to þe kyrke,
Þe pure pyleres of bras pourtrayd in golde,
And þe chef chaundeler charged with þe lyȝt,
Þat ber þe lamp vpon lofte þat lemed euermore
Bifore þe Sancta Sanctorum þer selcouth watȝ ofte.
1275    Þay caȝt away þat condelstick, and þe crowne als
Þat þe auter hade vpon, of aþel golde ryche,
Þe gredirne and þe goblotes garnyst of syluer,
Þe bases of þe bryȝt postes, and bassynes so schyre,
Dere disches of golde, and dubleres fayre,
1280    Þe vyoles and þe vesselment of vertuous stones.
Now hatȝ Nabuȝardan nomen alle þyse noble þynges,
And pyled þat precious place, and pakked þose godes.
Þe golde of þe gaȝafylace to, swyþe gret noumbre,
Wyth alle þe vrnmentes of þat hous, he hamppred togeder
1285    Alle he spoyled spitously in a sped whyle
Þat Salomon so mony a sadde ȝer soȝt to make.
Wyth alle þe coyntyse þat he cowþe clene to wyrke,
Deuised he þe vesselment, þe vestures clene.
Wyth slyȝt of his ciences, his Souerayn to loue,
1290    Þe hous and þe anournementes he hyȝtled togedere.
Now hatȝ Nabuȝardan nimmend hit al samen,
And syþen bet doun þe burȝ and brend hit in askes.


Þenne, wyth legiounes of ledes, ouer londes he rydes
Herȝeȝ of Israel þe hyrne aboute.
1295    Wyth charged chariotes, þe cheftayn he fyndeȝ,
f. 79    Bikennes þe catel to þe kyng þat he caȝt hade,
Presented him þe presoneres in pray þat þay token,
Moni a worþly wyȝe whil her worlde laste,
Moni semly syre sonn, and swyþe rych maydenes,
1300    Þe pruddest of þe prouince, and prophetes childer
As Ananie, and Aȝarie, and als Miȝael,

---

1267  ho kyllen] hokyllen: MS, M, G, A, Mo, AW. h[e] kyllen:
     Me.
1271  of] o illegible because of blot.
1273] A noted: "b of ber badly formed, perhaps altered from
     w."
1274  þe Sancta Sanctorum] (The MS has þsancta scor, with an
     abbreviation mark after the r. Cf. the textual note
     to 1491.)

And all the maidens in the temple they violently kill
With the swipe of the sword that destroyed them all.

Then they ran to the relics like wild robbers,
1270    And seized all the furnishings that belonged to the
        temple,
The pure pillars of brass painted with gold,
And the main candlestick laden with the light,
Which bore the lamp on high that shone constantly
Before the Holy of Holies where miracles often occurred.
1275    They took away the candelabrum, and also the band
That the altar had around it, of splendid, royal gold,
The grating and the goblets adorned with silver,
The bases of the bright pillars, and basins so shiny,
Precious plates of gold, and beautiful platters,
1280    The cups and the vessels with valuable stones.
Now has Nabuzardan seized all these splendid things,
And pillaged that precious place, and packed those goods.
The gold of the treasury also, [a] very great amount,
He stored together with all the ornaments of that temple.
1285    In a short while, he spitefully despoiled everything
That Solomon so many a continuous year had labored to
        accomplish.
With all the ability that he possessed to work perfectly,
He had fashioned the vessels [and] the elegant vestures.
By means of his skills, to honor his Sovereign,
1290    He had embellished the temple and the furnishings together.
Now has Nabuzardan seized them all together,
And afterwards destroyed the city and burned it to ashes.

Then, with legions of men, he rides across lands,
[And] plunders round about the corners of Israel.
1295    With loaded chariots, he finds the chieftain,
f. 79  Gives to the king the treasure that he had taken,
[And] presented to him the prisoners that they had cap-
        tured as prey,
Many a worthy man while their kingdom lasted,
Many handsome sons of lords, and very noble maidens,
1300    The proudest in the province, and prophets' disciples
Such as Ananias, and Azarias, and also Misael,

---

1281  Nabuȝardan] Nebuȝardan: A.
1291  nimmend] numnend (nummen?): M.  num[men]: Me.  num[m]en:
      G.  nummen: A, Mo, AW.
1294  hyrne] hyrne[ȝ]: G, AW.
1295  fyndeȝ] fynde: MS.
1297  presoneres] prisoneres: M, AW.
1299  sonn] sone: M.  soun: Me, G, A, Mo, AW.

And dere Daniel also, þat watȝ deuine noble,
With moni a modey moder-chylde, mo þen innoghee.

And, Nabugodenoȝar makes much joye.
1305 Nov he þe kyng hatȝ conquest and þe kyth wunnen,
And dreped alle þe doȝtyest and derrest in armes,
And þe lederes of her lawe layd to þe grounde,
And þe pryce of þe profecie presoners maked.

Bot þe joy of þe juelrye, so gentyle and ryche--
1310 When hit watȝ schewed hym so schene, scharp watȝ his
wonder.
Of such vessel auayed þat vayled so huge
Neuer ȝet nas Nabugodenoȝar er þenne.
He sesed hem wyth solemneté. Þe Souerayn he praysed,
Þat watȝ Aþel ouer alle, Israel Dryȝtyn.
1315 Such god, such gomes, such gay vesselles
Comen neuer out of kyth to Caldee reames.
He trussed hem in his tresorye in a tryed place,
Rekenly, wyth reuerens, as he ryȝt hade,
And þer he wroȝt as þe wyse, as ȝe may wyt hereafter,
1320 For hade he let of hem lyȝt, hym moȝt haf lumpen worse.


Þat ryche in gret rialté rengned his lyue.
As conquerour of vche a cost, he cayser watȝ hatte,
Emperour of alle þe erþe, and also þe saudan,
And als þe god of þe grounde watȝ grauen his name;
1325 And al þurȝ dome of Daniel, fro he deuised hade
Þat alle goudes com of God, and gef hit hym bi samples,
Þat he ful clanly bicnv his carp bi þe laste,
And ofte hit mekned his mynde, his maysterful werkkes.
Bot, al drawes to dyȝe wyth doel vpon ende.
1330 Bi a haþel neuer so hyȝe, he heldes to grounde,
And so Nabugodenoȝar, as he nedes moste.
f. 79b For alle his empire so hiȝe, in erþe is he grauen.

---

1303 innoghee] in-noghe: eds.  MS has abbr. for additional
e after h.
1308 profecie] profetie: A.    presoners] prisoners: M, AW.

And honorable Daniel as well, who was [a] noble prophet,
With many a haughty person, more than enough.

And so, Nabuchodonosor shows great joy.
1305    Now he has conquered the king and gained the land,
And slain all the bravest and noblest in arms,
And driven into the ground the leaders of their law,
And made the honored men of the prophecies prisoners.

But the beauty of the precious ornaments, so excellent
    and rich--
1310    When this was revealed to him gleaming so greatly, his
    wonder was keen.
Never yet before then had Nabuchodonosor been
Told of such vessels that prevailed so abundantly.
He received them with solemnity. He praised the Sovereign
Who was King over all, Israel's God.
1315    Such possessions, such prizes, such magnificent vessels
Never came out of [a] land into [the] realms of Chaldea.
He stored them in his treasury in a secure place,
Fittingly, with reverence, as he properly should have,
And in this matter he acted like a wise man, as you may
    learn hereafter,
1320    For had he behaved negligently toward them, worse fortune
    might have befallen him.

That rich king reigned in great royalty during his
    lifetime.
As conqueror of every coast, he was called kaiser,
Emperor of all the earth, and also the sultan,
And his name was engraved as the god of the ground;
1325    And all [came about] through [the] counsel of Daniel,
    after he had taught
That all goods come from God, and had shown it to him
    through parables,
So that he quite perfectly recognized the message in
    the end,
And it often humbled his mind [and] his arrogant actions.
However, all live to die with suffering in [the] end.
1330    Be a man ever so great, he sinks into [the] ground,
And so too Nabuchodonosor, as he necessarily had to.
f. 79b    In spite of all his empire so vast, he is buried in
    [the] earth.

---

1315   god] god[es]: G.     gomes] go[un]es: G, A, AW.
1329   vpon ende] vpn ende: MS.

Bot þenn þe bolde Baltaȝar, þat watȝ his barn aldest,
He watȝ stalled in his stud and stabled þe rengne
1335 In þe burȝ of Babiloyne, þe biggest, he trawed,
Þat nauþer in heuen ne no erþe hade no pere;
For he bigan in alle þe glori þat hym þe gome lafte,
Nabugodenoȝar, þat watȝ his noble fader.

So kene a kyng in Caldee com neuer er þenne,
1340 Bot honoured he not hym þat in heuen wonies.
Bot fals fantummes of fendes, formed with handes,
Wyth tool out of harde tre, and telded on lofte,
And of stokkes and stones. He stoute goddes callȝ,
When þay ar gilde al with golde and gered wyth syluer,
1345 And þere he kneles, and calleȝ, and clepes after help;
And þay reden him ryȝt, rewarde he hem hetes,
And if þay gruchen him his grace, to gremen his hert,
He cleches to a gret klubbe and knokkes hem to peces.
Þus in pryde and olipraunce his empyre he haldes,
1350 In lust, and in lecherye, and loþelych werkkes;
And hade a wyf for to welde, a worþelych quene,
And mony a lemman, neuer þe later, þat ladis wer called
In þe clernes of his concubines and curious wedeȝ,
In notyng of nwe metes and of nice gettes,
1355 Al watȝ þe mynde of þat man on misschapen þinges,
Til þe Lorde of þe lyfte liste hit abate.


Thenne þis bolde Baltaȝar biþenkkes hym ones
To vouche on avayment of his vayne gorie.
Hit is not innoghe to þe nice al noȝty þink vse,
1360 Bot if alle þe worlde wyt his wykked dedes.


Baltaȝar þurȝ Babiloyn his banne gart crye,
And þurȝ þe cuntré of Caldee his callyng con spryng,
Þat alle þe grete vpon grounde schulde geder hem samen

---

1336 ne no erþe] (on?): M. ne [on] erþe: Me, G, A, Mo, AW.
    hade no] hade [he] no: G.
1339 neuer] Abbr. mark over u denoting er extends horizon-
    tally to the left, making it resemble a bar.

But then the bold Baltassar, who was his oldest child,
Was enthroned in his place and established the kingdom
1335    In the city of Babylon, the mightiest, he believed,
That neither in heaven nor any land had any equal;
For he began in all the glory that the man had left him,
Nabuchodonosor, who had been his noble father.

So powerful a king had never come into Chaldea before
    then,
1340    But he did not honor him who dwells in heaven.
[He honored] only false figures of fiends, formed by
    hands,
With tools out of hard wood, and set on high,
And of stocks and stones. He calls upon [the] terrible
    gods,
When they are gilded completely with gold and adorned
    with silver,
1345    And there he kneels, and cries out, and calls after help;
And [if] they counsel him correctly, he promises them
    [a] reward,
But if they refuse him his favor, for offending his
    feelings,
He snatches up a great club and knocks them to pieces.
Thus he maintains his empire in pride and vanity,
1350    In lust, and in lechery, and loathsome actions;
And [he] had a wife to possess, a worthy queen,
And many a mistress, none the less, who were called
    ladies.
On the beauty of his concubines and fancy garments,
On noting of new delicacies and of foolish acquisitions,
1355    Entirely on distorted things was the mind of that man,
Until the Lord of the heavens desired it to stop.

Then this bold Baltassar decides one time
To give an exhibition of his foolish filth.
It is not enough for the wanton man to practice all
    immoral actions,
1360    Unless all the kingdom know his wicked deeds.

Baltassar made his proclamation be uttered throughout
    Babylon,
And through the country of Chaldea his summons did spread,
That all the great people upon land should gather them-
    selves together,

---

1344   ar] are: Me, Mo.
1347   him his grace] him grace: G.
1358   vayne gorie] vayne g[l]orie: M.  vayneg[l]orie: other eds.
1359   innoghe] innogh: A.

And assemble at a set day at þe saudans fest.
1365    Such a mangerie to make þe man watʒ auised,
        Þat vche a kythyn kyng schuld com þider.
        Vche duk, wyth his duthe, and oþer dere lordes
f. 80   Schulde com to his court to kyþe hym for lege,
        And to reche hym reuerens, and his reuel herkken,
1370    To loke on his lemanes, and ladis hem calle.


        To rose hym in his rialty, rych men soʒtten,
        And mony a baroun ful bolde, to Babyloyn þe noble.
        Þer bowed toward Babiloyn burnes so mony.
        Kynges, cayseres ful kene, to þe court wonnen,
1375    Mony ludisch lordes þat ladies broʒten,
        Þat to neuen þe noumbre to much nye were;
        For þe bourʒ watʒ so brod, and so bigge alce,
        Stalled in þe fayrest stud þe sterreʒ anvnder,
        Prudly, on a plat playn, plek alþerfayrest,
1380    Vmbesweyed on vch a syde wyth seuen grete wateres,
        Wyth a wonder wroʒt walle, wruxeled ful hiʒe,
        Wyth koynt carneles aboue, coruen ful clene,
        Troched toures bitwene, twenty spere lenþe,
        And þiker þrowen vmbe þour wyth ouerþwert palle.
1385    Þe place þat plyed þe pursaunt wythinne
        Watʒ longe, and ful large, and euer ilych sware,
        And vch a syde vpon soyle helde seuen myle,
        And þe saudans sete sette in þe myddes.
        Þat watʒ a palayce of pryde, passande alle oþer,
1390    Boþe of werk and of wunder, and walle al aboute,
        Heʒe houses wythinne, þe halle to hit med,
        So brod bilde in a bay þat blonkkes myʒt renne.



        When þe terme of þe tyde watʒ towched of þe feste,
        Dere droʒen þerto and vpon des metten;
1395    And Baltaʒar vpon bench was busked to sete,
        Stepe, stayred stones of his stoute throne.
        Þenne watʒ alle þe halle-flor hiled wyth knyʒtes,
        And barounes at þe side-bordes bounet aywhere,
        For non watʒ dressed vpon dece bot þe dere seluen,
1400    And his clere concubynes in cloþes ful bryʒt.

---

1390    walle] walle[d]: G, A, AW.
1391    med] m[a]d: Me.


172

|       | And assemble on a set day for the sultan's feast. |
| 1365 | The chief servant was ordered to prepare a banquet so great, |
|       | Since each native king would come there. |
|       | Each duke, with his company, and other noble lords |
| f. 80 | Would come to his court to proclaim him as monarch, |
|       | And to pay homage to him, and hearken to his revelry, |
| 1370 | To look upon his mistresses, and call them ladies. |

|       | To honor him according to his royalty, rich men and |
|       | Many a very brave baron went to the splendid Babylon. |
|       | There moved toward Babylon so many men. |
|       | Very great kings [and] kaisers arrived at the court, |
| 1375 | [And] many lords of the people who brought ladies, |
|       | That to name the number would be too much trouble; |
|       | For the city was so broad, and so big also, |
|       | Situated in the most beautiful place beneath the stars, |
|       | Proudly, on a flat plain, the fairest of all spots, |
| 1380 | Surrounded on every side by seven large streams, |
|       | By a marvelously made wall, designed very majestically, |
|       | With elegant embrasures above, carved quite perfectly, |
|       | Pinnacled towers at intervals, [the] length of twenty spears, |
|       | And with paling placed crosswise, more closely set around there. |
| 1385 | The area that extended within the boundary |
|       | Was long, and very wide, and unchangingly square, |
|       | And each side with soil contained seven miles, |
|       | And the sultan's residence was situated in the center. |
|       | That was a dwelling-place of splendor, surpassing all others, |
| 1390 | Both in actuality and in imagination, and walled all around, |
|       | High houses within, the palace connected to them, |
|       | Constructed so spaciously in a section in which steeds could gallop. |

|       | When the time of the season had arrived for the feast, |
|       | Noble guests traveled to that place and met at [the] dais; |
| 1395 | And Baltassar was prepared to sit on [the] royal seat, |
|       | Above [the] shiny, raised stones of his stately throne. |
|       | Then all the hall-floor was occupied by knights, |
|       | And barons everywhere proceeded to the side tables, |
|       | For no one was arrayed upon [the] dais except the honored host himself, |
| 1400 | And his comely concubines in very bright garments. |

---

1393 towched] Part of *w* stained. to vsched: M. þe feste]
    Orig. shows þe on same line 1393 and *feste* written
    above defect in vellum on f. 80.

173

When alle segges were þer set, þen seruyse bygynnes.
Sturnen trumpen strake steuen in halle,
Aywhere by þe wowes wrasten krakkes,
f. 80b  And brode baneres þerbi, blusnande of gold.


1405    Burnes berande þe bredes vpon brode skeles
        Þat were of sylueren syȝt, and seerved þer wyth
        Lyfte logges þerouer, and on lofte coruen,
        Pared out of paper, and poynted of golde,
        Broþe baboynes abof, besttes anvnder,
1410    Foles in foler, flakerande bitwene,
        And al in asure and ynde, enaumayld ryche,
        And al on blonkken bak, bere hit on honde.


        And ay þe nakeryn noyse, notes of pipes,
        Tymbres and tabornes tulket among;
1415    Symbales and soneteȝ sware þe noyse,
        And bougounȝ busch, batered so þikke.


        So watȝ serued fele syþe þe sale alle aboute,
        Wyth solace, at þe sere course, bifore þe self lorde.
        Þer þe lede and alle his loue lenged at þe table.
1420    So faste þay weȝed to him wyne, hit warmed his hert,
        And breyþed vppe into his brayn, and blemyst his mynde,
        And al waykned his wyt, and wel neȝe he foles;
        For he wayteȝ on wyde, his wenches he byholdes
        And his bolde baronage aboute bi þe woȝes.


1425    Þenne a dotage ful depe drof to his hert,
        And a caytif counsayl he caȝt bi hymseluen.
        Maynly his marschal þe mayster vpon calles,
        And comaundes hym cofly coferes to lauce,


---

1402  Sturnen] Sturne: G, A, AW.
1405  þe] þe þe: MS.
1406  sylueren syȝt] syluer i[n] s[u]yt: G.      seerved]
      s[e]rved: Me, Mo, AW.  seve[s]: G, A.      þer wyth]
      þer-wyth: eds.

When all [the] people were placed there, then service
    begins.
Powerful trumpets blow [the] call in [the] hall,
Everywhere along the walls echoes sound,
f. 80b  And broad banners [hang] from them (the trumpets),
    gleaming with gold.

1405       Servants [are] carrying the roasted meats on broad
    platters
That were of silvern appearance, and were served there
    with
Raised arbors over them, and curved on top,
Cut out of paper, and trimmed with gold,
Grotesque gargoyles above, beasts beneath,
1410      Birds in foliage, fluttering in between,
And all in azure and indigo, enamelled richly,
And all on horses' backs, to hold them up handily.

And continually the noise of kettledrums, notes of
    pipes,
Echoed among timbrels and tabors;
1415      Cymbals and bells answer the sound,
And drumsticks thump, reverberating so continuously.

Thus [much] was served many times all around the hall,
With pleasure, at the various courses, before the same
    lord.
The man and all his mistresses lingered there at the
    table.
1420      They served wine to him so swiftly, it warmed his heart,
And rose up into his brain, and impaired his mind,
And completely weakened his understanding, and he becomes
    well near stupefied;
As he looks about blankly, he beholds his wenches
And his noble company around by the walls.

1425      Then a very grievous folly came into his mind,
And he devised a wicked plan by himself.
The master loudly calls upon his marshal,
And commands him to open coffers quickly,

---

1408   golde] glolde: MS.
1414   tulket] tu[k]ket: G.
1419   loue] l[e]ue: G.
1423   wenches he byholdes] wenches by-holdes: G.
1428   lauce] lance: M, Me, Mo.·

175

And fech forþe vessel þat his fader broȝt,
1430   Nabugodenoȝar, noble in his strenþe,
Conquerd with his knyȝtes, and of kyrk rafte,
In Judé, in Jerusalem, in gentyle wyse.
"Bryng hem now to my borde; of beuerage hem fylles.
Let þise ladyes of hem lape; I luf hem in hert.
1435   Þat schal I cortaysly kyþe, and þay schin knawe sone
Þer is no bounté in burne lyk Baltaȝar þewes."

    Þenne towched to þe tresour þis tale watȝ sone,
And he wyth keyes vncloses kystes ful mony.
1439   Mony burþen ful bryȝt watȝ broȝt into halle,
f. 81   And couered mony a cupborde with cloþes ful quite.
Þe jueles out of Jerusalem, wyth gemmes ful bryȝt,
Bi þe syde of þe sale were semely arayed.
Þe aþel auter of brasse watȝ hade into place,
Þe gay coroun of golde gered on lofte.
1445   Þat hade ben blessed bifore wyth bischopes hondes,
And wyth besten blod busily anoynted,
In þe solempne sacrefyce þat goud sauor hade,
Bifore þe Lorde of þe lyfte, in louyng hymseluen,
Now is sette for to serue Satanas þe blake,
1450   Bifore þe bolde Baltaȝar, wyth bost and wyth pryde.

    Houen vpon þis auter watȝ aþel vessel,
Þat wyth so curious a crafte coruen watȝ wyly.
Salamon sete him seuen ȝere and a syþe more,
Wyth alle þe syence þat hym sende þe souerayn Lorde,
1455   For to compas and kest, to haf hem clene wroȝt;
For þer wer bassynes ful bryȝt of brende golde clere,
Enaumaylde wyth aȝer, and eweres of sute,
Couered cowpes foul clene, as casteles arayed,
Enbaned vnder batelment wyth bantelles quoynt,
1460   And fyled out of fygures of ferlylé schappes.
Þe coperounes of þe cauacles, þat on þe cuppe reres,

---

1429  forþe vessel] forþ [þ]e vessel: G, A, AW.
1429-30] Because of defect in vellum, noted in 1393 above, lines
     begin in from margin on f. 80b.
1437  towched] towchede: Me, Mo.
1441  Jerusalem] (The MS has *isrlm*, with a flourish off the *l*.
     See the textual note to 1159.)

And to fetch forth [the] vessels that his father had
    brought,
1430    Nabuchodonosor, noble in his strength,
Secured through his knights, and taken from [the] temple,
In Judea, in Jerusalem, in the manner of pagans.
"Bring them now to my table; fill them with beverage.
Let these ladies drink from them; I love them at heart.
1435    This shall I graciously show, and they shall soon know
There is no virtue in man like Baltassar's virtues."

    Then this command was conveyed at once to the
    treasurer,
And he with keys unlocks very many chests.
1439    Many very bright burdens were brought into [the] hall,
f. 81    And many a sideboard was covered with very white cloths.
The treasures from Jerusalem, with very bright gems,
Were suitably arranged along the side of the hall.
The excellent altar of brass was put into place,
The elegant band of gold adorned on high.
1445    What had been blessed before by bishops' hands,
And sacredly consecrated with blood of beasts,
In the solemn sacrifice that had [a] pleasant savor,
Before the Lord of the heavens, for praising him,
Now is set to serve the black Satan,
1450    Before the bold Baltassar, with pomp and with pride.

    Splendid vessels had been raised upon this altar,
That had been cleverly shaped with so elaborate a skill.
Solomon had given himself seven years and a bit more,
With all the knowledge that the sovereign Lord had sent
    to him,
1455    In order to plan and to create, to have them perfectly
    made;
For there were very bright basins of clear, refined gold,
Enamelled with azure, and ewers to match,
Very elegant lidded goblets, constructed like castles,
Fortified beneath [the] battlements with elaborate tiers,
1460    And filed out in figures of marvelous forms.
The ornamental tops of the lids, which rise on the
    goblets,

---

1452  so] Looks like *fo* in MS, but letters are squeezed together,
    and it may be an *s* attached to the *o*.
1453  seuen] *eue* stained.
1460  out of] out on: A.    ferlylé] (*ferlyke*?): M.
    ferly[ch]e: Me.
1461  cauacles] canacles: M.  c[ov]acles: Me, G, A, Mo, AW.
    cuppe reres] cuppe[s] rere: G.

Wer fetysely formed out in fylyoles longe,
Pinacles pyȝt þer apert, þat profert bitwene,
And al bolled abof wyth braunches and leues,
1465    Pyes and papejayes purtrayed withinne,
As þay prudly hade piked of pomgarnades,
For alle þe blomes of þe boȝes wer blyknande perles,
And alle þe fruyt in þo formes of flaumbeande gemmes;
Ande safyres, and sardiners, and semely topace,
1470    Alabaundarynes, and amaraunȝ, and amattised stones,
Casydoynes, and crysolytes, and clere rubies,
Penitotes, and pynkardines, ay perles bitwene,
So trayled and tryfled a-trauerce wer alle.
Bi vche bekyr ande þe bolde, þe brurdes al vmbe,
1475    Þe gobelotes of golde grauen aboute;
f. 81b   And fyoles fretted wyth flores and fleeȝ of golde.
Vpon þat avter watȝ al aliche dresset.


Þe candelstik bi a cost watȝ cayred þider sone,
Vpon þe pyleres apyked, þat praysed hit mony,
1480    Vpon hit baseȝ of brasse, þat ber vp þe werkes,
Þe boȝes bryȝt þerabof, brayden of golde,
Braunches bredande þeron, and bryddes þer seten,
Of mony kyndes, of fele kyn hues,
As þay, wyth wynge vpon wynde, hade waged her fyþeres;
1485    Inmong þe leues of þe lampes wer grayþed.
And oþer louflych lyȝt þat lemed ful fayre,
As mony morteres of wax, merkked wythoute
Wyth mony a borlych best, al of brende golde.
Hit watȝ not wonte in þat wone to wast no serges,
1490    Bot in temple of þe trauþe trwly to stonde,

---

1470  Alabaundarynes] Alabaunderynes: M. Alabaundeirynes: A.
      amattised] amaffised: all eds. except A. amastised:
      A.
1474  bekyr ande þe bolde] bekyrande þe bolde: MS, M.
      bekyr ande bol[l]e: Me, G, A, Mo, AW.
1478  bi a cost] bi acost: A.
1479  Vpon] V illegible. A noted: "Vpon from u.-v. [ultra-
      violet photograph]."

Were artfully shaped out in long pinnacles,
Pinnacles set there skillfully, which projected at
        intervals,
And were completely embossed above with branches and
        leaves,
1465    [And] magpies and parrots fashioned within,
As if they proudly had pecked on pomegranates,
For all the blossoms among the boughs were gleaming
        pearls,
And all the fruit [was] in the forms of glowing gems;
And sapphires, and sardian stones, and excellent topaz,
1470    Almandines, and emeralds, and amethystine stones,
Chalcedonies, and chrysolites, and clear rubies,
Peridots, and carnelian stones, with pearls always in
        between,
Were all so neatly traced and trefoiled across.
On every beaker and the edifice, all around the rims,
1475    The goblets of gold were engraved round about;
f. 81b   And [the] cups were adorned with flowers and butterflies
        of gold.
Everything was arrayed alike upon that altar.

        Soon carried there by a conveyance was the candela-
        brum,
Upon the polished pillars, so that many praised it,
1480    Upon its bases of brass, that bolstered up the parts,
The bright boughs above there, embellished with gold,
Branches spreading thereon, and birds perched there,
Of many species, of various kinds of hues,
As if they, with wings in [the] wind, had fluttered
        their feathers;
1485    Among the leaves on the lamps [they] were arrayed.
And other lovely lights that shone very beautifully,
Such as many mortars of wax, were designed on the outside
With many a massive beast, all of refined gold.
It had not been accustomed to waste any candles in that
        place,
1490    But truly to stand in [the] temple of the truth,

---

1482    seten] soten: A.
1483    kyndes] [curious] kyndes: Me, Mo.    [cler] kyndes: G.
        koynt kyndes: AW.
1485    lampes] [launces] lampes: Me, A, Mo.    [lefsel] lampes:
        G. lyndes lampes: AW.
1486    louflych] louelych: M, G.    (Looks like *louflych*.): M.
        Orig. shows *fl* in darker brown ink, as if alteration
        were made.

179

Bifore þe Sancta Sanctorum, soþefast Dryȝtyn
Expouned his speche spun ally to special prophetes.


    Leue þou wel þat þe Lorde þat þe lyfte ȝemes
Displesed much at þat play in þat plyt stronge,
1495    Þat his jueles so gent wyth jaueles wer fouled,
Þat presyous in his presens wer proued sumwhyle.
Soberly in his sacrafyce summe wer anoynted,
Þurȝ þe somones of himselfe þat syttes so hyȝe.
Now a boster on benche bibbes þerof,
1500    Tyl he be dronkken as þe deuel and dotes þer he syttes.


    So þe Worcher of þis worlde wlates þerwyth,
Þat in þe poynt of her play he poruayes a mynde,
Bot er harme hem he wolde in haste of his yre,
He wayned hem a warnyng þat wonder hem þoȝt.


1505    Nov is alle þis guere geten glotounes to serue,
Stad in a ryche stal, and stared ful bryȝte.
Baltaȝar, in a brayd, bede vus þerof.
"Weȝe wyn in þis won. Wassayl!" he cryes.
Swyfte swaynes ful swyþe swepen þertylle,
1510    Kyppe kowpes in honde kyngeȝ to serue,
In bryȝt bolleȝ ful bayn birlen þise oþer,
f. 82   And vche mon for his mayster machches alone.
Þer watȝ rynging, on ryȝt, of ryche metalles
Quen renkkes in þat ryche rok rennen hit to cache,
1515    Clatering of couacleȝ þat kesten þo burdes,
As sonet out of sauteray, songe als myry.


    Þen þe dotel on dece drank þat he myȝt;
And þenne arn dressed dukeȝ and prynces.
Concubines and knyȝtes, bicause of þat merthe.
1520    As vch on hade hym in helde, he haled of þe cuppe.


---

1491  Sancta Sanctorum] (The MS has *scā scor,* with an abbrevia-
      tion mark after the *r* and a line under the *r.* Cf. the
      textual note to 1274.)    soþefast] [þer] soþefast:
      Me, G, A, Mo, AW.
1492  spun ally] spunally: MS.  sp*iri*tually: M, G, A, AW.
      spyrytually: Me, Mo.
1494  stronge] str[a]nge: G.
1506  bryȝte] bryȝtȝ: MS, M.  (?*bryȝte.*): M.
1507  vus] [b]us: Me, Mo.

Before the Holy of Holies, [where the] true God
Expounded his flourishing messages to unite [himself]
    with special prophets.

You may well believe that the Lord who controls the
    heavens
Was greatly displeased with that festivity in that
    strange situation,
1495    When his treasures so excellent, which had formerly
Proved precious in his presence, were defiled by rogues.
Some had been soberly consecrated in his sacrifice,
Through the summons of himself who sits so high.
Now a braggart on [a] bench imbibes from them,
1500    Until he be drunk as the devil and raves where he sits.

The Creator of this world is so greatly disgusted
    with it,
That he prepares a plan at the height of their amusement,
But before he would harm them in [the] haste of his anger,
He would send them a warning which would seem [a] wonder
    to them.

1505    Now all this gear is fetched to serve gluttons,
Set in a splendid position, and shining very brilliantly.
Baltassar, with a rash outburst, exhorted [everyone] to
    make use of it.
"Serve wine in this place. Drink heartily!" he shouts.
Swift servants very quickly rush to it,
1510    Seize cups close by to serve kings,
Serve these others very eagerly in bright bowls,
f. 82    And each man matches [himself] only with his master.
In truth, there was ringing of rich metals
When servants in that splendid palace scurry to obtain it,
1515    Clattering of lids which those lords lifted,
Like music from [a] psaltery, [a] song just as merry.

Then the fool on [the] dais drank what he could;
And then dukes and princes are toasted,
Concubines and knights, as a result of that revelry.
1520    As each one held himself in allegiance, he drank from
    the goblet.

---

1515  Clatering] Abbr. for *n* is more over the *g* than the *i*,
    probably to avoid merging with abbr. for *er* above
    *t* and *i*.    couacleȝ] conacleȝ: M.
1516  sauteray] saueray: MS.
1518  þenne arn dressed dukeȝ] þenne [drinkez] arn dressed
    [to] dukez: Me. þenne [þat derrest] arn dressed,
    dukeȝ: G. þenne derfly arn dressed dukez: AW.
1520  in helde] inhelde: Me, Mo, AW.

So long likked þise lordes þise lykores swete,
And gloryed on her falce goddes, and her grace calles,
Þat were of stokkes and stones, stille euermore.
Neuer steuen hem astel, so stoken is hor tonge.
1525 Alle þe goudee, golden goddes þe gauleȝ ȝet neuenen,
Belfagor, and Belyal, and Balssabub als,
Heyred hem as hyȝly as heuen wer þayres,
Bot hym þat alle goudes giues, þat God þay forȝeten.

For, þer a ferly bifel, þat fele folk seȝen.
1530 Fyrst knew hit þe kyng, and alle þe cort after.
In þe palays pryncipale, vpon þe playn wowe,
In contrary of þe candelstik, þat clerest hit schyned,
Þer apered a paume, wyth poyntel in fyngres,
Þat watȝ grysly and gret, and grymly he wrytes.
1535 Non oþer forme bot a fust, faylande þe wryste,
Pared on þe parget, purtrayed lettres.

When þat bolde Baltaȝar blusched to þat neue,
Such a dasande drede dusched to his hert
Þat al falewed his face and fayled þe chere.
1540 Þe stronge strok of þe stonde strayned his joyntes.
His cnes cachches to close, and cluchches his hommes,
And he, wyth plattyng his paumes, displayes his lerms,
And romyes as a rad ryth þat roreȝ for drede,
Ay biholdand þe honde, til hit hade al grauen,
1545 And rasped on þe roȝ woȝe runisch saueȝ.
When hit þe scrypture hade scraped wyth a scrof penne,
As a coltour in clay cerues þo forȝes,

---

1524 is] ís: MS.
1525 goudee] goude: eds.
1527 Heyred] He[ry]ed: G.
1529 For, þer] For-þ[y]: G, AW.
1532 þat clerest] þ[er] clerest: G, AW.
1541 and cluchches] & [he] cluchches: G.

Thus these lords tasted these pleasant liquors [a] long
while,
And honored only their false gods, and call for their aid,
Those that were of stocks and stones, motionless all the
time.
Never [a] word could be pledged by them, so fastened is
their tongue.
1525 The wretches still call upon all the yellowish, golden
gods,
Beelphegor, and Belial, and Beelzebub also,
Honoring them as highly as if heaven were theirs,
But they forget that God who gives all good things.

Therefore, a miracle occurred there, which many
people saw.
1530 The king recognized it first, and all the court after-
wards.
In the principal palace, upon the bare wall,
Next to the candelabrum, which illuminated it most
clearly,
There appeared a hand, with [a] stylus in [its] fingers,
Which was horrible and huge, and hideously it writes.
1535 No other figure but a fist, lacking the wrist,
Cut into the plaster, fashioning letters.

When that bold Baltassar looked upon that fist,
Such a stunning fright rushed to his heart
That his face turned completely pale and lost its
composure.
1540 The severe impact of the shock strained his joints.
His knees double up tightly, and his hamstring muscles
bend,
And he, by smacking together his palms, displays his
anxieties,
And moans like a scared steer that bellows in fear,
Always beholding the hand, until it had completely
engraved,
1545 And scraped on the rough wall strange sayings.
When it had scratched out the scripture with a cutting
pen,
As a plowshare in soil carves the furrows,

---

1542 And he, wyth] & wyth: G.      displayes] dispyses: AW.
       lerms] lers: M, Me, Mo.    ler[u]s: G.  leres: A, AW.
1545 rasped] rasked: Mo.
1546 scrof] Looks like strof in MS, but c and t sometimes
       look alike; cf. textual note to line 1169.
1547 þo] þ[e]: G, AW.

Þenne hit vanist verayly and voyded of syȝt;
Bot þe lettres bileued ful large vpon plaster.


1550      Sone, so, þe kynge, for his care, carping myȝt wynne.
He bede his burnes boȝ to, þat were bok-lered,
To wayte þe wryt, þat hit wolde, and wyter hym to say;
"For al hit frayes my flesche, þe fyngres so grymme."
Scoleres skelten þeratte þe skyl for to fynde,
1555      Bot þer watȝ neuer on so wyse couþe on worde rede,
Ne what ledisch lore, ne langage nauþer,
What typyng ne tale tokened þo draȝtes.


         Þenne þe bolde Baltaȝar bred ner wode,
And ede þe ceté to seche segges þurȝout,
1560      Þat wer wyse of wychecrafte, and warlaȝes oþer
Þat con dele wyth demerlayk and deuine lettres.
"Calle hem alle to my cort, þo Caldé clerkkes,
Vnfolde hem alle þis ferly þat is bifallen here,
And calle wyth a hiȝe cry he þat þe kyng wysses
1565      In expounyng of speche þat spredes in þise lettres,
And make þe mater to malt my mynde wythinne,
Þat I may wyterly wyt what þat wryt menes,
He schal be gered ful gaye in gounes of porpre,
And a coler of cler golde clos vmbe his þrote.
1570      He schal be prymate and prynce of pure clergye,
And of my þreuenest lordeȝ þe þrydde he schal,
And of my reme þe rychest to ryde wyth myseluen,
Outtaken bare two--and þenne he þe þrydde."


         Þis cry watȝ vp caste, and þer comen mony,
1575      Clerkes out of Caldye þat kennest wer knauen,
As þe sage sathrapas þat sorsory couþe.
Wycheȝ and walkyries wonnen to þat sale,
Deuinores of demorlaykes þat dremes cowþe rede,
Sorsers, and exorsismus, and fele such clerkes,

1551   were] MS has abbr. for e after r. wer: Me, A, Mo.
1559   ede] (bede?): M. [b]ede: Me, A, Mo, AW. [eþ]ede: G.
1566   make] make[s]: G, A, AW.


184

f. 82b   Then it vanished verily and withdrew from sight;
        But the letters remained very prominently upon [the]
           plaster.

1550      Soon, then, the king, in his anxiety, was able to
           regain [his] speech.
        He requested his people who were book-learned to come,
        To look upon the scripture, those who would [try] it,
           and to interpret for him plainly;
        "For the fingers so grim terrify my flesh completely."
        Scholars hurried to that place to discover the meaning,
1555      But there was never one so wise [who] could decipher
           one word,
        Nor what land's learning [it was], nor [the] language
           either,
        [Nor] what news or story those lines signified.

        Then the bold Baltassar became nearly mad,
        And proceeded to seek throughout the city men
1560      Who were wise in witchcraft, and other wizards
        Who did deal with magic art and supernatural writings.
        "Call them all to my court, those Chaldean clerks,
        Reveal to them completely this miracle that has occurred
           here,
        And call out with a loud shout [that] he who guides the
           king
1565      In [the] interpreting of [this] message that spreads
           with these letters,
        And causes the matter to penetrate inside my mind,
        So that I can clearly understand what that scripture
           means,
        Shall be arrayed very elegantly in gowns of purple,
        And a collar of clear gold encircled around his throat.
1570      He shall be [the] leader and prince of true learning,
        And he shall [be] the third among my most prosperous
           lords,
        And the richest to ride with me in my realm,
        Excepting only two--and then he [shall be] the third."

        This cry was cast up, and many came there,
1575      Clerks from Chaldea who were known as [the] wisest,
        Such as the governors' sages who practiced sorcery.
        Witches and sorceresses arrived at that hall,
        Diviners of magical arts who could interpret dreams,
        Magicians, and conjurers, and many such clerks,

---

1571   schal] schal [be]: G.
1579   and exorsismus] [of] exorsismus: G, A, AW.

1580      And, alle þat loked on þat letter as lewed þay were  
As þay had loked in þe leþer of my lyft bote.

Þenne cryes þe kyng and kerues his wedes.  
What! He corsed his clerkes and calde hem chorles.  
f. 83    To henge þe harlotes he heʒed ful ofte.  
1585     So watʒ þe wyʒe wytles he wed wel ner.

Ho herde hym chyde, to þe chambre, þat watʒ þe chef  
    quene.  
When ho watʒ wytered bi wyʒes what watʒ þe cause  
Suche a chaungande chaunce in þe chef halle,  
Þe lady, to lauce þat los þat þe lorde hade,  
1590     Glydes doun by þe grece and gos to þe kyng.  
Ho kneles on þe colde erþe and carpes to hymseluen  
Wordes of worchyp wyth a wys speche:

"Kene kyng," quoþ þe quene, "kayser of vrþe,  
Euer laste þy lyf in lenþe of dayes.  
1595     Why hatʒ þou rended þy robe for redles hereinne,  
Þaʒ þose ledes ben lewed lettres to rede,  
And hatʒ a haþel in þy holde, as I haf herde ofte,  
Þat hatʒ þe gostes of God þat gyes alle soþes?  
His sawle is ful of syence, saʒes to schawe,  
1600     To open vch a hide þyng of aunteres vncowþe.  
Þat is he þat ful ofte hatʒ heuened þy fader  
Of mony anger ful hote wyth his holy speche.  
When Nabugodenoʒar watʒ nyed in stoundes,  
He devysed his dremes to þe dere trawþe.  
1605     He keuered hym wyth his counsayl of caytyf wyrdes.  
Alle þat he spured hym in space he expowned clene,  
Þurʒ þe sped of þe Spyryt þat sprad hym wythinne,  
Of þe godelest goddeʒ þat gaynes aywhere.  
ffor his depe diuinité, and his dere sawes,  
1610     Þy bolde fader Baltaʒar bede by his name.  
Þat now is demed Danyel of derne coninges,  
Þat caʒt watʒ in þe captyuidé in cuntré of Jues.

---

1589   lauce] (*lance*?): M.  
1593   kayser] A noted: "a of *kayser* apparently altered from *y*."  
1595   for redles] forredles: Me, Mo.

1580　　And yet, all who looked upon that writing were as ignorant
　　　　As if they had looked at the leather of my left boot.

　　　　Then the king laments and tears his garments.
　　　　What! He cursed his clerks and called them churls.
f. 83　Very often he wanted to hang the knaves.
1585　　The man was so much without reason he very nearly went mad.

　　　　She, in the chamber, who was the chief queen, heard
　　　　　　him raving.
　　　　When she was informed by people what the reason was
　　　　For such a turning fortune in the main hall,
　　　　The lady, to relieve that distress which the lord had,
1590　　Glides down along the steps and goes to the king.
　　　　She kneels on the cold ground and says to him
　　　　Words of honor in a wise speech:

　　　　"Great king," said the queen, "kaiser of earth,
　　　　May your life endure eternally with length of days.
1595　　Why have you ripped your robe because of unwise ones
　　　　　　in this place,
　　　　Even if those persons have been [too] ignorant to inter-
　　　　　　pret [the] letters,
　　　　When [you] have a man in your domain, as I have heard
　　　　　　often,
　　　　Who receives the revelations from God who maintains
　　　　　　all truths?
　　　　His soul is full of knowledge to decipher messages,
1600　　To uncover each hidden thing concerning strange events.
　　　　That one is he who very often has uplifted your father
　　　　In many very severe tribulations with his holy speech.
　　　　When Nabuchodonosor was troubled at times,
　　　　He interpreted his dreams according to the precious truth.
1605　　He delivered him with his counsel from evil fate.
　　　　All that he (the king) asked him he (Daniel) soon after
　　　　　　explained perfectly,
　　　　Through the power of the Holy Spirit that spread within
　　　　　　him,
　　　　From the greatest of gods who prevails everywhere.
　　　　Because of his profound knowledge, and his priceless
　　　　　　words,
1610　　Your noble father bade Baltassar to be his name.
　　　　That one now is called Daniel of secret skills,
　　　　Who was seized in the captivity in [the] country of
　　　　　　[the] Jews.

---

1598　gostes] gost: G, AW.
1608　godelest] godel[i]est: G, AW.

Nabuȝardan hym nome, and now is he here,
A prophete of þat prouince, and pryce of þe worlde.
1615 Sende into þe ceté to seche hym bylyue,
And wynne hym wyth þe worchyp to wayue þe bote,
And þaȝ þe mater be merk þat merked is ȝender,
He schal declar hit also as hit on clay stande."


1619    Þat gode counseyl at þe quene watȝ cached as-swyþe.
f. 83b   Þe burne byfore Baltaȝar watȝ broȝt in a whyle.
When he com bifore þe kyng and clanly had halsed,
Baltaȝar vmbebrayde hym, and: "Leue sir," he sayde,
"Hit is tolde me bi tulkes þat þou trwe were
Profete of þat prouynce þat prayed my fader,
1625 Ande þat þou hatȝ in þy hert holy connyng,
Of sapyence þi sawle, ful soþes to schawe.
Goddes gost is þe geuen, þat gyes alle þynges,
And þou vnhyles vch hidde þat HeuenKyng myntes;
And here is a ferly byfallen, and I fayn wolde
1630 Wyt þe wytte of þe wryt þat on þe wowe clyues,
For alle Caldé clerkes han cowwardely fayled.
If þou wyth quayntyse conquere hit, I quyte þe þy mede.
For, if þou redes hit by ryȝt, and hit to resoun brynge
Fyrst telle me þe tyxte of þe tede lettres,
1635 And syþen þe mater of þe mode mene me þerafter,
And I schal halde þe þe hest þat I þe hyȝt haue,
Apyke þe in porpre cloþe, palle alþerfynest.
And þe byȝe of bryȝt golde abowte þyn nekke,
And þe þryd þryuenest þat þrynges me after
1640 Þou schal be, baroun vpon benche; bede I þe no lasse."


Derfly, þenne, Danyel deles þyse wordes:
"Ryche kyng of þis rengne, rede þe oure Lorde.
Hit is surely soth þe Souerayn of heuen
Fylsened euer þy fader and vpon folde cheryched,

---

1616  þe worchyþ] þ[i] worchyp: G.    wayue] wayne: eds.
1618  also as] also [cler], as: G, AW.    stande] standeȝ: G.
       standes: A.  UVR does not show -ȝ.
1619  as-swyþe] as as swyþe: MS.

Nabuzardan captured him, and now he is here,
A prophet from that province, and [an] honored man in
    the world.
1615    Send into the city to seek him quickly,
And persuade him with honor to offer you [the] remedy,
And though the matter may be murky that is marked in
    that place,
He shall pronounce it just as it stands on [the]
    plaster."

1619      That good counsel from the queen was followed at once.
f. 83b  The man was brought before Baltassar in a while.
When he had come before the king and had greeted [him]
    politely,
Baltassar embraced him, and: "Dear sir," he said,
"It has been told to me by people that you were truly [a]
Prophet of that province that my father plundered,
1625    And that you have in your mind divine understanding,
With wisdom in your soul, to declare truths fully.
God's spirit that guides all things is instilled in you,
And you can uncover each hidden thing that [the] King
    of Heaven destines;
And a miracle has occurred here, and I eagerly would wish
1630    To understand the meaning of the scripture that cleaves
    to the wall,
For all Chaldean clerks have failed disgracefully.
If you can conquer it with cunning, I shall give you
    your reward.
Therefore, if you can read it with correctness, and can
    bring it to understanding,
First tell me the text of the linked letters,
1635    And then reveal to me thereafter the substance of the
    thought,
And I shall fulfill for you the promise that I have
    pledged to you,
Adorn you with purple cloth, garments the finest of all,
And the ring of bright gold around your neck,
And you shall be the third most prosperous person who
    follows after me,
1640    [A] baron in [the] royal council; I offer you no less."

Promptly, then, Daniel delivers these words:
"Royal king of this realm, may our Lord guide you.
It is certainly true the Sovereign of heaven
Always aided your father and esteemed [him] on earth,

---

1621] A noted: "s of *halsed* altered from some other letter,
    perhaps ʒ."
1622  Leue] [B]eue: G, AW.
1632  conquere] con quere: G, AW.

1645      Gart hym grattest to be of gouernores alle,
            And alle þe worlde in his wylle welde, as hym lykes.
            Whoso wolde wel do, wel hym bityde;
            And quos deth so he deȝyre, he dreped als fast.
            Whoso hym lyked to lyft, on lofte watȝ he sone;
1650      And quoso hym lyked to lay, watȝ loȝed bylyue.


         "So watȝ noted þe note of Nabugodenoȝar,
            Styfly stabled þe rengne bi þe stronge Dryȝtyn;
            ffor, of þe Hyȝest, he hade a hope in his hert
            Þat vche pouer past out of þat Prynce euen,
1655      And whyle þat watȝ cleȝt clos in his hert,
            Þere watȝ no mon vpon molde of myȝt as hymseluen,
f. 84     Til hit bitide on a tyme towched hym pryde
            For his lordeschyp so large and his lyf ryche.
            He hade so huge an insyȝt to his aune dedes
1660      Þat þe power of þe hyȝe Prynce he purely forȝetes.


         "Þenne blynnes he not of blasfemy, onto blame þe
            Dryȝtyn.
            His myȝt mete to Goddes he made wyth his wordes:
            'I am god of þe grounde to gye as me lykes,
            As he þat hyȝe is in heuen, his aungeles þat weldes.
1665      If he hatȝ formed þe folde and folk þervpone,
            I haf bigged Babiloyne, burȝ alþerrychest,
            Stabled þerinne vche a ston in strenkþe, of myn armes,
            Moȝt neuer myȝt, bot myn, make such anoþer.'


         "Watȝ not þis ilke worde wonnen of his mowþe one
1670      Er þenne þe Souerayn saȝe souned in his eres:
            'Now Nabugodenoȝar innoȝe hatȝ spoken.
            Now is alle þy pryncipalté past at ones,

---

1646  lykes] lyke[d]: G, AW.
1648  deȝyre] deȝyre[d]: G.
1655  þat watȝ] þat [coyntise] watȝ: G.  þat counsayl watz: AW
1661  blasfemy, onto] blasfemyon to: MS, M.  blasfemy on to:
       Me, G, A, Mo, AW.

1645       Caused him to be [the] greatest of all rulers,
           And to control all the kingdom according to his will,
                as [it] would please him.
           To whomever [he] would wish to do well, prosperity
                would come to him;
           And whose death he might thus desire, he would kill just
                as quickly.
           Whomever [it] pleased him to extoll, at [the] top he
                soon would be;
1650       And whomever [it] pleased him to put down, [he] would
                be put down quickly.

          "Thus was famous the rule of Nabuchodonosor,
          [Who] firmly established the kingdom through the great
                God;
          For, concerning the highest Lord, he had a belief in
                his heart
          That every power proceeded directly from that Prince,
1655       And while that [belief] was locked firmly in his heart,
          There was no man upon earth with power like him,
f. 84     Until it happened at one time pride touched him
          Because of his lordship so vast and his luxurious life.
          He had so great an opinion of his own deeds
1660       That he forgets completely the power of the high Prince.

          "Then he ceases not from blasphemy, in censuring the
                Lord.
          He made his might equal to God's with his words:
          'I am god of the ground to rule as [it] pleases me,
          As he [does] who is high in heaven, who governs his
                angels.
1665       If he has created the earth and people upon it,
          I have built Babylon, the wealthiest of all cities,
          Establishing therein, by my powers, each stone with
                strength.
          Never [any] might, except mine, could construct another
                so great.'

          "Scarcely had this same statement issued from his
                mouth
1670       Before the Sovereign's speech sounded in his ears:
          'Now Nabuchodonosor has spoken enough.
          Now has all your sovereignty passed away at once,

---

1664   þat weldes] Orig. shows darker brown ink; apparently
          second hand wrote over other letters.
1669   worde wonnen] worde one wonnen: G.       mowþe one] mowþe:
          Me, G, A, Mo, AW.  Orig. shows *one* written smaller at
          end of line; it may be by another hand.

And þou, remued fro monnes sunes, on mor most abide,
And in wasturne walk, and wyth þe wylde dowelle,
1675  As best, byte on þe bent of braken and erbes,
Wyth wroþe wolfes to won, and wyth wylde asses.'

"Inmydde þe poynt of his pryde, departed he þere.
Fro þe soly of his solempneté, his solace he leues,
And carfully is out kast to contré vnknawen,
1680  Fer into a fyr-fryth þere frekes neuer comen.
His hert heldet vnhole. He hoped non oþer,
Bot a best þat he be, a bol oþer an oxe.
He fares forth on alle faure. Fogge watჳ his mete,
And ete ay as a horce when erbes were fallen.
1685  Þus he countes hym a kow, þat watჳ a kyng ryche,
Quyle seuen syþeჳ were ouerseyed someres, I trawe.
By þat, mony þik thyჳe þryჳt vmbe his lyre,
Þat alle watჳ dubbed and dyჳt in þe dew of heuen.

"ffaxe, fyltered and felt, flosed hym vmbe;
1690  Þat schad fro his schulderes to his schyre-wykes,
And twentyfolde twynande, hit to his tos raჳt,
Þer mony clyuy as clyde hit clyჳt togeder.
His berde ibrad alle his brest to þe bare vrþe,
f. 84b  His browes bresed as breres aboute his brode chekes,
1695  Holჳe were his yჳen, and vnder campe hores,
And al watჳ gray, as þe glede, wyth ful grymme clawres
Þat were croked and kene, as þe kyte pauue.
Erne-hwed he watჳ, and al ouer brawden,
Til he wyst ful wel who wroჳt alle myჳtes,
1700  And cowþe vche kyndam tokerue and keuer when hym lyked

"Þenne he wayned hym his wyt, þat hade wo soffered,
Þat he com to knawlach and kenned hymseluen.
Þenne he loued þat Lorde and leued in trawþe
Hit watჳ non oþer þen he þat hade al in honde.

---

1687  thyჳe] th[e]ჳe: G.  fytherez: AW.
1689  flosed] floჳed: AW.
1690  schyre-wykes] sch[e]re-wykes: Me, G, Mo, AW.
1696  clawres] clawes: A.

192

And you, removed from [the] sons of man, must endure
    on [a] moor,
And walk in wilderness, and dwell with the wild animals,
1675    Like [a] beast, to feed in the fields from fern and herbs,
To live with fierce wolves, and with wild asses.'

"In the middle of the height of his pride, he departed
    to that place.
From the seat of his solemnity, his solace he leaves,
And is cast out miserably into [an] unknown country,
1680    Far into a woodland of firs where people never came.
His mind became unsound. He imagined nothing else,
But that he be a beast, a bull or an ox.
He goes forth on all fours. Overgrown grass was his food,
And [he] ate hay like a horse when herbs had withered.
1685    Thus he who had been a noble king considers himself a cow,
While summers were passing by seven times, I believe.
By then, many thick plant stems pressed around his lair,
Which was entirely adorned and dressed with the dew of
    heaven.

"Hair, joined and matted, circled around him;
1690    It spread from his shoulders to his groin,
And twenty times entwining, it extended to his toes,
Where many interlocked as if poultice had stuck them
    together.
His beard covered all his breast to the bare earth,
f. 84b    His eyebrows bristled like briers around his broad cheeks,
1695    His eyes were hollow, and under shaggy hairs,
And [he] was completely gray, like the kite, with very
    ugly claws
That were crooked and keen, just like the kite's feet.
He was colored like an eagle, and completely bent over,
Until he knew very well who had established all powers,
1700    And could cut off and recover each kingdom when [it]
    pleased him.

"Then he (God) sent him who had suffered misfortune
    his reason,
So that he returned to understanding and recognized
    himself.
Then he honored that Lord and believed in truth [that]
It was none other than he who held all in hand.

---

1697  pauue] paune (?*panne*): M.  paune: Me, Mo, AW.  paume: A.
1703  loued] laued (*loued*?): M.  *o* may have been corrected
    from *a* or *e*, but the letter is closed on the bottom
    like an *o*.

1705    Þenne sone watȝ he sende agayn, his sete restored.
           His barounes boȝed hym to blyþe of his come.
           Haȝerly, in his aune hwe, his heued watȝ couered,
           And so ȝeply watȝ ȝarked and ȝolden his state.

           "Bot þou, Baltaȝar, his barne and his bolde ayre,
1710    Seȝ þese syngnes wyth syȝt and set hem at lyttel.
           Bot ay hatȝ hofen þy hert agaynes þe hyȝe Dryȝtyn,
           Wyth bobaunce and wyth blasfamye bost at hym kest,
           And now his vessayles avyled in vanyté vnclene,
           Þat in his hows hym to honour were heuened of fyrst.
1715    Bifore þe barounȝ hatȝ hom broȝt and byrled þerinne
           Wale wyne to þy wenches in waryed stoundes.
           Bifore þy borde hatȝ þou broȝt beuerage in þ'edé
           Þat blyþely were fyrst blest wyth bischopes hondes,
           Louande þeron lese goddeȝ þat lyf haden neuer,
1720    Made of stokkes and stoneȝ þat neuer styry moȝt;
           And for þat froþande fylþe, þe Fader of heuen
           Hatȝ sende into þis sale þise syȝtes vncowþe,
           Þe fyste wyth þe fyngeres þat flayed þi hert,
           Þat rasped renyschly þe woȝe wyth þe roȝ penne.

1725    "Þise ar þe wordes here wryten, wythoute werk more,
           By vch fygure, as I fynde, as oure Fader lykes:
           MANE, TECHAL, PHARES, merked in þrynne,
           Þat þretes þe of þyn vnþryfte vpon þre wyse.
1729    Now expowne þe þis speche spedly I þenk.
f. 85    MANE menes als much as: 'Maynful Gode
           Hatȝ counted þy kyndam bi a clene noumbre,
           And fulfylled hit in fayth to þe fyrre ende.'
           To teche þe of TECHAL, þat terme þus menes:
           'Þy wale rengne is walt in weȝtes to heng,
1735    And is funde ful fewe of hit fayth-dedes.'
           And PHARES folȝes, for þose fawtes, to frayst þe trawþ
           In PHARES fynde I forsoþe þise felle saȝes:
           'Departed is þy pryncipalté. Depryued þou worþes.

---

1707  hwe] hwef: AW.
1711  Dryȝtyn] dryȝtn: MS.
1715  hom] hem: G.

1705    Then he was soon sent back, his throne restored.
        His barons bowed to him gladly on his return.
        Appropriately, with his own crown, his head was covered,
        And thus his kingdom was quickly established and given
            back [to him].

        "But you, Baltassar, his son and his noble heir,
1710    Saw these signs with sight and considered them of little
            value.
        [You] have only exalted your self continually against
            the high God,
        Flung boasts at him with vanity and with blasphemy,
        And now defiled his vessels in filthy foolishness,
        Those that were uplifted at first to honor him in his
            temple.
1715    [You] have brought them before the barons and served
            therein
        Choice wine to your wenches during cursed hours.
        Before your table you have brought beverage in the
            splendid treasures
        Which were first blessed ceremoniously by bishops' hands,
        Honoring with them false gods who never had life,
1720    Made of stocks and stones that could never move;
        And because of that disgusting filth, the Father of heaven
        Has sent into this hall these strange sights,
        The fist with the fingers which terrified your heart,
        That scraped the wall fiercely with the rough pen.

1725    "These are the words written here, without further ado,
        According to each letter, as I perceive, as [it] pleases
            our Father:
        MANE, THECEL, PHARES, marked in three parts,
        Which warn you of your ruin in three ways.
1729    Now I intend to interpret this message for you speedily.
f. 85   MANE means just so much as [this]: 'Almighty God
        Has measured your kingdom according to a perfect number,
        And finished it in truth to the farther end.'
        To tell you of THECEL, that term thus means:
        'Your noble reign has been compelled to hang in [the]
            balance,
1735    And is found fully lacking in its deeds of honor.'
        And PHARES follows, because of those faults, to test
            the truth.
        In PHARES I truly find these dire sayings:
        'Your sovereignty shall be terminated. You shall be
            deprived.

---

1717   þ'edé] þede: MS, M, Me, A, Mo.  þ['ydres]: G.
1722   Hat₃ sende] hat₃ sende hat₃ sende: MS.
1735   fayth-dedes] fayth dedes: MS, M, A.

Þy rengne rafte is þe fro and raȝt is þe Perses.

1740 Þe Medes schal be maysteres here, and þou of menske
schowued.'"


Þe kyng comaunded anon to clepe þat wyse
In frokkes of fyn cloþ, as forward hit asked.
Þenne sone watȝ Danyel dubbed in ful dere porpor,
And a coler of cler golde kest vmbe his swyre.
1745 Þen watȝ demed a decré bi þe duk seluen.
Bolde Baltaȝa bed þat hym bowe schulde
Þe comynes al of Caldé, þat to þe kyng longed,
As to þe prynce pryuyest, preued þe þrydde,
Heȝest of alle oþer, saf onelych tweyne,
1750 To boȝ after Baltaȝar in borȝe and in felde.
Þys watȝ cryed and knawen in cort als fast,
And alle þe folk þerof fayn, þat folȝed hym tylle.


Bot, howso Danyel watȝ dyȝt, þat day ouerȝede.
Nyȝt neȝed ryȝt now wyth nyes fol mony,
1755 For daȝed neuer anoþer day þat ilk derk after
Er dalt were þat ilk dome þat Danyel deuysed.


Þe solace of þe solempneté in þat sale dured,
Of þat farand fest, tyl fayled þe sunne.
Þenne blykned þe ble of þe bryȝt skwes.
1760 Mourkenes þe mery weder, and þe myst dryues,
Þorȝ þe lyst of þe lyfte, bi þe loȝ medoes.
Vche haþel to his home hyȝes ful fast.
Seten at her soper, and songen þerafter.
Þen foundeȝ vch a felaȝschyp fyrre at forþ-naȝtes.


1765 Baltaȝar to his bedd with blysse watȝ caryed,
f. 85b Reche þe rest, as hym lyst. He ros neuer þerafter,
For his foes in þe felde in flokkes ful grete,


---

1739  raȝt is þe] raȝt þe is: A.
1744  coler] cloler: MS.
1746  Baltaȝa] baltaȝa[r]: eds.

196

Your kingdom shall be taken from you and shall be given
    to the Persians.
1740    The Medes shall be masters here, and you shall be cast
    from [your] honorable position.'"

The king immediately commanded that wise man to be
    clothed
In garments of fine cloth, since [the] agreement re-
    quired it.
Then Daniel was soon adorned in very precious purple,
And a collar of clear gold was placed around his neck.
1745    Then a decree was ordained by the king himself.
Bold Baltassar commanded that all the commoners of Chaldea,
Who belonged to the king, should bow to him,
As to the most special prince, established as the third
    [in rank],
Highest of all others, except only two,
1750    To follow after Baltassar in town and in country.
This was proclaimed and recognized at court just as
    quickly,
And all the people in that place, who submitted to him,
    rejoiced.

Yet, no matter how Daniel was adorned, that day
    passed by.
Night drew near directly now with very many misfortunes,
1755    For another day would never dawn after that same night
Until that same doom which Daniel had described would
    be delivered.

The pleasure of the ceremonial observance of that
    excellent feast
Endured in that hall until the sun failed.
Then the color of the bright clouds faded.
1760    The fair weather becomes murky, and the mist drifts,
At the will of the wind, along the low meadows.
Each man hurries very hastily to his home.
[They] sat at their supper, and sang after that.
Then each forms a companionship further into the late
    part of the night.

1765    Baltassar was carried to his bed in bliss,
f. 85b  To gain rest, as [it] pleased him. He never rose
    after that,
For his foes in the field in very large flocks,

---

1747  al of] alof: MS. a lof: M.    Caldé] calde: MS, M.
1756  Danyel] The *el* is inserted above the line in tiny print.
1766  þe] þe[r]: G.

Þat longe hade layted þat lede his londes to strye,
Now ar þay sodenly assembled at þe self tyme.
1770    Of hem wyst no wyȝe þat in þat won dowelled.
Hit watȝ þe dere Daryus, þe duk of þise Medes,
Þe prowde prynce of Perce, and Porros of Ynde,
Wyth mony a legioun ful large wyth ledes of armes,
Þat now hatȝ spyed a space to spoyle Caldeeȝ.


1775    Þay þrongen þeder in þe þester on þrawen hepes,
Asscaped ouer þe skyre watteres and scaþed þe walles,
Lyfte laddres ful longe and vpon lofte wonen,
Stelen stylly þe toun er any steuen rysed.
Wythinne anoure, of þe niyȝt, an entré þay hade.
1780    3et, afrayed þay no freke.  Fyrre þay passen,
And to þe palays pryncipal þay aproched ful stylle.


Þenne ran þay in, on a res, on rowtes ful grete.
Blastes out of bryȝt brasse brestes so hyȝe.
Ascry scarred on þe scue, þat scomfyted mony.
1785    Segges slepande were slayne er þay slyppe myȝt.
Vche hous heyred watȝ wythinne a honde-whyle.
Baltaȝar in his bed watȝ beten to deþe,
Þat boþe his blod and his brayn blende on þe cloþes.
The kyng in his cortyn watȝ kaȝt bi þe heles,
1790    Feryed out bi þe fete, and fowle dispysed,
Þat watȝ so doȝty þat day and drank of þe vessayl.
Now is a dogge also dere þat in a dych lygges.


For, þe mayster of þyse Medes on þe morne ryses.
Dere Daryous, þat day dyȝt vpon trone,
1795    Þat ceté seses ful sounde and saȝtlyng makes
Wyth alle þe barounȝ þeraboute þat bowed hym after.


And þus watȝ þat londe lost for þe lordes synne,
And þe fylþe of þe freke þat defowled hade
Þe ornementes of Goddeȝ hous, þat holy were maked.
1800    He watȝ corsed for his vnclannes, and cached þerinne,
Done doun of his dyngneté for dedeȝ vnfayre,

1776  scaþed] sca[l]ed: Me, A, Mo.  sca[yl]ed: G, AW.
1779  anoure] an oure: eds.    niyȝt] nyȝt: M, Me, G, Mo.
1786  heyred] he[ry]ed: G.

Who long had sought to destroy that man's lands,
Now are suddenly assembled at the same time.
1770 No man who dwelled in that city knew about them.
It was the noble Darius, the duke of these Medes,
The proud prince of Persia, and Porus of India,
With many a very large legion of men of arms,
Who now have observed an opportunity to despoil [the]
Chaldeans.

1775 They assembled there in the darkness in compact
companies,
Sneaked across the clear waters and breached the walls,
Lifted very long ladders and arrived at [the] top,
[And] stole silently into the city before any sound rose.
They had an entry, in the night, within [the] domain.
1780 Still, they aroused no man. They pass farther,
And they approached very quietly towards the principal
palace.

Then they ran inside, in a rush, in very large crowds.
Blasts from bright trumpets burst out so intensely.
Shouting, which shocked many, sprang to the sky.
1785 Sleeping men were slain before they could escape.
Each house was plundered within a short space of time.
Baltassar was beaten to death in his bed,
So that both his blood and his brains blended on the
sheets.
The king inside his curtain was caught by the heels,
1790 Dragged out by the feet, and humiliated disgracefully,
He who was so bold that day and drank from the vessels.
Now a dog that lies in a ditch is just as dear.

Therefore, the master of these Medes rises in the
morning.
Noble Darius, adorned that day upon [the] throne,
1795 Controls that city very securely and makes peace
With all the barons around there who followed after him.

And thus was that land lost because of the lord's sin,
And the filth of the man who had defiled
The ornaments of God's temple, which had been made
sacred.
1800 He was condemned because of his uncleanness, and caught
therein,
Knocked down from his dignified position because of
foul deeds,

---

1799-1801] These last three lines of f. 85b start in from the
margin because of defect in vellum.

And of þyse worldes worchyp wrast out foreuer;
And ȝet, uf lykynges on lofte letted, I trowe
To loke on oure lofly Lorde late bitydes.


## EPILOGUE


1805        Þus, vpon þrynne wyses, I haf yow þro schewed
Þat vnclannes tocleues in corage dere
Of þat wynnelych Lorde þat wonyes in heuen,
Entyses hym to be tene, telled vp his wrake.
Ande, clannes is his comfort, and coyntyse he louyes,
1810    And þose þat seme arn and swete schyn se his face.
Þat we gon gay in oure gere, þat grace he vus sende,
Þat we may serue in his syȝt, þer solace neuer blynneȝ.
        Amen.

---

1803   uf] of: eds.
1804   bitydes] betydes: G.
1805   wyses] weyss: A.

f. 86    And turned out forever from this world's honor;
        And moreover, if joys on high were considered, I believe
        [It] would be late [for him] to look upon our beloved
           Lord.


## EPILOGUE


1805      Thus, in three ways, I have earnestly revealed to you
        That uncleanness penetrates within [the] precious heart
        Of that dear Lord who dwells in heaven,
        [And] provokes him to be bitter, calling forth his
           punishment.
        On the other hand, cleanness is his comfort, and he
           loves wisdom,
1810    And those who are proper and pure shall see his face.
        That we may proceed gallantly in our attire, may he
           send us that grace,
        So that we may serve in his sight, where solace never
           ceases. Amen.

---

1808   telled] (*telles*?): M.  tel[des]: Me, Mo, AW.
1811   þat grace] [his] grace: G.

# ABBREVIATIONS

# ABBREVIATIONS FOR GRAMMATICAL TERMS
## AND OTHER TERMS

| | |
|---|---|
| a. | adjective |
| abbr. | abbreviation |
| absol. | absolute |
| acc. | accusative |
| adj. | adjective, adjectival |
| adv. | adverb, adverbial |
| advb. | adverbial |
| art. | article |
| assoc. | associated |
| attrib. | attributive, attributively |
| auxil. | auxiliary |
| c. | *circa* 'about' |
| card. | cardinal |
| cf. | *confer* 'compare' |
| cl. | clause |
| coll. | collective, collectively |
| comp. | comparative |
| compar. | comparative |
| condit. | conditional |
| conj. | conjunction |
| corresp. | corresponding |
| dat. | dative |
| def. | definite |
| demons. | demonstrative |
| dial. | dialect |
| emph. | emphatic |
| fem. | feminine |
| f. or fol. | folio |
| f., ff. | and the following |
| fig. | figurative, figuratively |
| fut. | future |
| gen. | genitive |
| ger. | gerund |
| imper. | imperative |
| impers. | impersonal |
| ind. | indicative |
| indef. | indefinite |

| | |
|---|---|
| inf. | infinitive |
| infin. | infinitive |
| infin. tr. prog. | infinitive translated progressively |
| infl. | influenced |
| infl. dat. | inflected dative |
| infl. infin. | inflected infinitive |
| int. | interjection |
| interj. | interjection |
| interrog. | interrogative |
| intr. | intransitive |
| masc. | masculine |
| n (after a line number) | note in Commentary |
| n. | noun |
| neg. | negative |
| neut. | neuter |
| nom. | nominative |
| num. | number, numeral |
| obj. | object |
| pa. | past |
| pa. pple | past participle |
| part. adj. | participial adjective |
| pass. | passive |
| perf. | perfect |
| perf. p. | perfect participle |
| phr. | phrase |
| pl. | plural |
| poss. | possessive |
| post. c. | postponed construction |
| pp. | past participle |
| pp. tr. prog. | past participle translated progressively |
| ppl. | past participle |
| ppl. a. | participial adjective |
| ppl. adj. | participial adjective |
| pr. | present |
| prec. | preceding |
| pred. | predicate |
| predic. | predicate |
| pref. | prefix |
| prep. | preposition |
| prob. | probably |
| prog. | progressive, progressively |
| pron. | pronoun |
| pr. p. | present participle |
| pt. | preterite (past tense) |
| refl. | reflexive |
| rel. | relative, related |
| sb. | somebody |
| sb. | substance, substantive |
| sb. adj. | substantival adjective |

| | |
|---|---|
| sg. | singular |
| sth. | something |
| str. | strong |
| subj. | subjunctive |
| suf. | suffix |
| suff. | suffix |
| sup. | superlative |
| superl. | superlative |
| s.v. | under the word or heading (L *sub verbo* or *voce*) |
| t. | tense |
| tr. or trans. | translate, translated, translates, translating, translation, translator |
| trans. | transitive |
| ult. | ultimately |
| v. | verb, verbal |
| v., vv. | verse, verses |
| var. | variant |
| vb. | verbal |
| vbl. | verbal |
| voc. | vocative |
| wk. | weak |

## ABBREVIATIONS FOR LANGUAGES AND DIALECTS

| | | | |
|---|---|---|---|
| AF | Anglo-French | Mod. E. | Modern English |
| Dan. | Danish | Norw. | Norwegian |
| Du. | Dutch | OE | Old English |
| EFris. | East Frisian | OF | Old French |
| G | German | OHG | Old High German |
| Icel. | Icelandic | OI | Old Icelandic |
| L | Latin | ON | Old Norse |
| LG | Low German | ONF | Old Northern French |
| MDu. | Middle Dutch | Scand. | Scandinavian |
| ME | Middle English | Swed. | Swedish |
| ML | Medieval Latin | WFris. | West Frisian |
| MLG | Middle Low German | | |

## ABBREVIATIONS FOR TITLES OF POEMS
## IN THE MANUSCRIPT

*Cl.*   *Cleanness*                          *Pa.*   *Patience*
*Ga.*   *Sir Gawain and the*                 *Pe.*   *Pearl*
        *Green Knight*


## ABBREVIATIONS FOR TITLES OF OTHER WORKS
## OF LITERATURE

| | |
|---|---|
| *Awntyrs* | *The Awntyrs off Arthure at the Terne Wathelyn* |
| Chaucerian *Romaunt* | (The Middle English translation in John Fisher's *The Complete Poetry and Prose of Geoffrey Chaucer,* 1977) |
| *Destr. Troy* | *The Gest Hystoriale of the Destruction of Troy* |
| *E.E. Psalter* | *An Early English Psalter* |
| *Erk.* | *St. Erkenwald* |
| *Owl & N* | *The Owl and the Nightingale* |
| *P. Pl.* | *Piers Plowman* |
| *Parl. Thre Ages* | *The Parlement of the Thre Ages* |
| *Peterb. Chron.* | *The Peterborough Chronicle* |
| *Roman* | *Le Roman de la Rose* |
| *RR* | *Le Roman de la Rose* |
| *Sir Ferumb.* | *Sir Ferumbras* |
| *Wars Alex.* | *The Wars of Alexander* |


## ABBREVIATIONS FOR PARTS
## OF THE BIBLE

| | | | |
|---|---|---|---|
| Acts | The Acts of the Apostles | Lam. | Lamentations |
| Cor. | Corinthians | Matt. | Matthew |
| Dan. | Daniel | Para. | Paralipomenon |
| Deut. | Deuteronomy | Ps. | Psalm(s) |
| Ezec. | Ezechiel | Rev. | Revelation (Apocalyps |
| Gal. | Galatians | Rom. | Romans |
| Gen. | Genesis | Song | Song of Songs (Can- |
| Heb. | Hebrews | | ticle of Canticles) |
| Jer. | Jeremias | Vulg. | Vulgate Bible |

COMMENTARY

PREFACE TO COMMENTARY

For the dates of editions of editors whose names appear in this Commentary, see the end of the Preface to Text. References to other works have the name of the author, the date in parentheses, and page number(s), when needed. An *a, b,* or *c* after a date indicates more than one work in the same year by the same author. For complete information, see the Bibliography at the end of this book.

There are references in this Commentary which direct the reader to notes on *Patience* and *Gawain* in Volume 2. The designation 'TG-Davis' refers to Tolkien & Gordon's edition of *Gawain* and Davis' revised second edition; it is often used when the information provided is the same in both editions.

The *MED* uses a single parenthesis to indicate an inflected form, as in *gladnes(se.* In this Commentary, wherever such a citation appears within parentheses, the single parenthesis is closed to avoid confusion. See, for example, *Pearl* 136n.

*PEARL* COMMENTARY

*1-60* Elliott (1961) 70 referred to this opening stanza-
group to show how the poet, in keeping with two rhetorical
aspects stressed by Matthew of Vendôme in his *Ars Versifica-*
*toria* (c. 1175), linked his descriptions to the mood of the
story and enhanced the beauty of the poem. "Sixty lines suf-
fice to create not merely an apt setting heavy with melan-
choly, but to introduce the theme of life and death and re-
birth which is at the heart of *Pearl*." See also Elliott (1961)
71-75 and (1974) for a study of northern landscape features in
*Ga.*, along with his "Hills and Valleys" (1978) and "Woods and
Forests" (1979) in the *Gawain* country.

Luttrell (1978), in "The Introduction to the Dream in
*Pearl*," traced in lines 1-60 the courtly love elements turning
to the Christian concept of *Consolatio Mortis* in the Death and
Resurrection theme.

*1* As Gordon noted, the first two lines are probably not
an apostrophe to the pearl. Schofield (1909) 600 stated,
"Like the lapidaries in general, our poem opens with the name
of the gem to be described." Marbodus' *De Gemmis* was the basis
for all medieval lapidaries. For pearl symbolism, cf. *Cl.*
553-56, 1067-68, 1116-32, and *Ga.* 2364-65.

Osgood, pp. xxxii-xxxiii, suggested the poet was familiar
with the prologue to the life of Saint Margaret of Antioch in
Jacobus de Voragine's *Legenda Aurea*. Like Gollancz, he argued
that the pearl-maiden was perhaps the poet's daughter, named
Margaret or Margery. See Earl (1972) for a study of the pos-
sible relationship between "Saint Margaret and the Pearl
Maiden."

Hoffman-C (1960) 91, refuting Hillmann's interpretation of
the pearl in the opening stanza as a real, material gem lost
by a jeweler, pointed out that the first meaning of the pearl
is carried throughout the poem in stanzas comprising lines
277-88, 325-36, 373-84, 901-12, and 1165-1212. "It is the
pearl lost in human terms, in worldly and fleshly terms."

Osgood and Gollancz believed *prynces* refers to Christ.
Gordon noted here it means literally a prince of this world

and symbolically Christ. Line 1 anticipates the last stanza-group where the reference to Christ the Prince is direct in 1164, 1176, 1188, 1189, and 1201. *Paye,* the link-word in the last stanza-group, ends the first and last lines of the poem, lines that contain similar vocabulary and phrasing. See Ebbs (1958) 523 and Vantuono (1971) 67-68 for discussion of this rhetorical device in *Cl., Pa.,* and *Ga.*

   2 Osgood and Gollancz glossed *to* 'too'. Gordon and sub-sequent editors considered *to clanly clos* a split infin. Wright (1939) 2-3 suggested the reading given here: *To clanly clos* 'For (a) splendid setting' parallels *to prynces paye.* See *MED clēnlī* adj. and *clōs* n. Sense 3a of the latter defines 'the mansion of heaven, (Christ's) abode', with citation from *Glade us maiden* 12: "Crist up stey. . He bar him seluen into is clos." As Wright observed, the first two lines foreshadow the pearl-maiden's appearance on the golden roads of heaven (1105-6).
   Osgood, relating *golde* to the "coffer, i.e. Paradise" (259-72), believed line 2 may contain an allusion to the maiden's tomb. He cited *Destr. Troy* 13791-94 to prove that golden tombs and reliquaries were common in Northern alliterative poems. Blanch-B (1965) 87 noted that gold, the usual setting for gems described in the medieval lapidaries, symbolizes the divine kingdom. Bishop (1968) 83-84 traced this setting image through *Pe.* to the *garlande gay* of 1186, believing there may be an allusion there to a golden *corona,* which, "in the ecclesiastical art of the time, symbolized the New Jerusalem." (See also 1186n.)

   3 Origen, in his Commentary on Matt. 13.45-46, a passage paraphrased by the poet in 730-35, contrasted the less perfect British pearl with the Indian pearl, "rounded off on the outer surface, very white in colour, very translucent, and very large in size" (*The Ante-Nicene Fathers,* tr. of The Writings of the Fathers down to A.D. 325, ed. Allan Menzies, Vol. 9 [New York, 1912], p. 417). Stern-C (1955) 75 pointed out the Orient is the "eastern direction literally representative of the most priceless gems and anagogically representative of sun, light, Christ, and Jerusalem."

   4 Hillmann read *proued ... her* 'tested its' to support her view that a real jeweler and gem are designated here. For *proued* 'discovered', cf. *OED prove* v., sense 3, 'to find out'. Gordon compared the fem. pronouns denoting 'pearl' in *Cl.* 1119-28.

   6 Gordon, comparing 190, showed such descriptions may apply to female figures. Hillmann considered them applicable only to a jewel. Kean (1967) 157, after referring to Lydgate's

*Life of St. Margaret*: "And smal she was by humylite," related
this virtue to 722-23 to show that the pearl is a proper sym-
bol for children entering heaven.

    *8* Cf. *synglerty* 429, referring to the unique sweetness
of Blessed Mary. Fick (1885), in his prefatory notes, first
proposed emending *synglure* to *synglere*. Hillmann noted that
emendation is unnecessary since *-ure* varies with *-ere* in words
of French origin, as in *gyngure* 43. The *OED* cited only *Pe*.
s.v. *singlure* 'uniqueness', but the line may be placed with
those s.v. *singler* a. Variant spellings in the MS do not nec-
essarily mean that the pronunciations were different.

    *9* *Erber*(e) appears again in 38 and 1171. The *MED* cites
*Pe*. s.v. *hĕrbĕr* n.1, sense a, 'pleasure garden'. Gordon
glossed 'grassy place in a garden, often among trees', a meaning
comparable to *MED*, sense f, 'a grassy plot, a patch of green-
sward'. More than one sense fits *Pe*. Note b, 'herb garden',
in relation to the *erber* of lines 35-44.
    Wellek-B (1933) 22 believed the poet fell asleep on a
grave, "clearly pictured in the illustration to lines 57-64"
on f. 41. Hamilton-B (1955) 39, comparing the Garden of Eden,
"where the maiden soul of man fell to earth and was lost," saw
the dreamer asleep on the sloping crest of a hill, shadowed by
trees and flowers, not "on or beside a grave or clump of plants"
(48). The illustration is not precise in its details, but what
looks like mounds may be represented on either side of the pros-
trate form of the dreamer.
    Hillmann supposed the poet was talking about an expert
jeweler who lost his gem while examining it in the outdoor
light. Luttrell-B (1965) 82-83, in discussing the *erber grene*
38 and the *huyle* 41 where the pearl rolled down, stated that
the *erber* remains both a grass-plot and a garden so that the
poet could apply allegory and give scope to garden imagery.
"The garden and the turfed mound, in the context of the loss,
*could* be a graveyard and a grave" (84).
    Kean (1967) 16 associated the *erber* with the *hortus con-
clusus* of Song of Songs 4.12, the 'enclosed garden' that figu-
ratively represents Christ's church containing faithful souls.

    *10* The usual reading of *yot* as a variant of *ȝode,* pt. of
*gon,* seems adequate, since unvoicing of *-d* to *-t* suits the rhyme
scheme. For other examples of unvoicing, see the notes to 460,
754, and 761. Greene (1925) 821-22, comparing line 245 and the
tone of lament in that stanza, believed the figure of a child
lost in infancy was employed "as a literary device to impart
the spiritual lesson of divine grace" (826). Hamilton (1958)
179-80, thinking of how the pouring out of one's soul suited
her allegorical interpretation, derived *yot* from *OED yet* 'pour,
gush forth'. Andrew & Waldron's *yot* 'fell (like a tear)'
accords with Hamilton's etymology.

*11* Hillmann and Moorman took *dewyne* as a weak pt. without *-d,* since the narrator is here recalling the time when his pearl was lost, but 'lament' is fitting either as a switch to the historic pr. t. or to give the impression that, although he has already had the reconciliatory dream he is about to relate, he may still miss his pearl. (Cf. 17-18.)

Gollancz emended to *for-do*[*k*]*ked* and tr. 11-12: "I pine, robbed by Love's severing power/Of that privy pearl without a spot." Luttrell (1978) 275-77 supported Gollancz' emendation, but with a different interpretation: the narrator laments because he is deprived of the pearl's *luf-daungere,* her sweet thraldom.

Gordon and Moorman accord with the citation of *Pe.* by the *MED* s.v. *lŏve* n.1, 4b, *luf-daungere* 'the power of love', but senses 4 and 5 of *MED daunğēr* substantiate 'frustrated love'. Cf. *daunger* 'frustration' 250, and see Barron (1965) 13-15. Andrew & Waldron defined 'aloofness, distance of the beloved'.

Schofield (1904) 182-83 believed line 11 echoes *RR* 2968ff., where Danger drives the Lover away from the Rose. Hillmann thought *luf-daungere* denotes the dominion the pearl exercises over the affections of the jeweler--"in other words, his inordinate love for his earthly treasure," but Pilch-C (1964) 168 stated, "Here it becomes apparent for the first time that the pearl has a symbolic meaning and represents a beloved human being."

Kean (1967) 16 compared Song of Songs 2.5, *quia amore langueo* 'because I languish with love', and 5.7-8, where the Bride and Bridegroom are separated, pointing out that the mingling of Biblical allusion with the diction of secular love poetry was not unusual for a medieval poet. Note, for example, Christ's words to the pearl-maiden: "Cum hyder to me, my lemman swete" (763).

*12* Macrae-Gibson-C (1968) 205, discussing link-words in the thematic structure, noted that because the pearl without *spot* 'blemish' could not be found in a particular *spot* 'place' on earth, the dreamer must leave the *erber* in the second stanza-group to rediscover his spiritual pearl in heaven. "Thus the refrain- and echo-words of the first stanza-group lay the foundation for much of the later development of the poem."

McGalliard (1969) 279-90 showed how the link-words and thought are "wedded in an unusually ordered but harmonious partnership.... Instead of announcing the content of the poem, [the links] organize it, focus it, concentrate it around a series of nuclei of attitude and emotion" (290).

*14* 'Pondered' seems more suitable than the usual *wayted* 'watched'. Cf. *OED wait* v.1, 3b, 'to watch mentally, consider attentively'. For *wele* 'splendid pearl', cf. *weal* sb.1, 2d, applying to a person. Gordon, Moorman, and Andrew & Waldron tr. 'precious thing', Hillmann 'wealth'.

*15* Hillmann surmised the jeweler's absorption in his trea-
sure caused him to overlook his *wrange* 'sin' of covetousness,
but Gordon's *wrange* 'sorrow' accords with the tone of lament in
this stanza. 'Distress' also suits the context.

*17* As Gordon noted, Þat refers to the mental action of
line 14, the dreamer's saddened state due to the loss of his
pearl. Gollancz and Chase added *-e* to *hert*. Emerson (1921a)
134, also seeking to make the line regular, imputed carelessness
to the scribe. Savage (1956b) 127 refuted this viewpoint, not-
ing that the poet apparently had a choice of pronunciation
with or without *-e*.

*17-24* Cf. the dreamer's conflict described in 51-56.

*18* The usual reading *bele* 'burn' (ON *bæla*) seems fitting
here. Cawley tr. 'festers', apparently following Luttrell (1955)
207-9 who argued for 'to suppurate', possibly from Old Swedish
*bulin, bolin* 'swollen' (presuming a lost Scandinavian verb
*\*bela*).

*19-22* Gollancz compared *euensonge* (vespers) 529. Osgood
and Gordon suggested the poet was describing the genesis of *Pe*.
Hamilton (1958) 182, in agreement with Wright (1940) 315-16,
refuted their explanation, seeing in these lines the first sense
of peace, developed more fully in the next stanza.
     Kean (1967) 42 related the theme to the *erber* in associa-
tion with the Garden of Eden where Adam and Eve heard the voice
of God, and the *hortus conclusus* of the Song of Songs, espe-
cially 2.14: "sonet vox tua in auribus meis: vox enim tua
dulcis, et facies tua decora." ("let thy voice sound in my
ears: for thy voice is sweet, and thy face comely.") Blenk-
ner-C (1968) 237-39, believing the *sange* must come from within
or above, noted that it presages the song of the birds (91-94),
the 144,000 virgins (877-88), and the angels (1124-27).
     Andrew & Waldron followed the reading of Davenport (1974)
who contrasted the dreamer's past consolation and present des-
olation: "Never yet did a song seem to me to have such sweet-
ness as a moment of peace let steal over me. In truth there
used to come fleetingly to me many (such moments). To think
of her colour clad, as now, in mud!"
     However, Gollancz' suggestion illumines the dreamer's
reflections on his loss, for, in the chanting of vespers,
whose liturgy deals with the promise of the Lord, v. 36 of
the opening Ps. 104 touches upon death: "Et percussit omne
primogenitum in terra eorum, primitias omnis laboris eorum."
("And he slew all the firstborn in their land: the firstfruits
of all their labour.") In line 894 the maiden is among the
144,000 virgins, "As newe fryt, to God ful due." It is only
after his vision that the dreamer is able to accept fully the
Lord's promise of resurrection. (See also 529n.)

*21*  Donaldson (1972) 80-82 suggested emending *Forsoþe* 'Truly' to *Forþoȝtes* 'Regrets', so that *fele* 'many' may refer to a specific n., but relating *fele* to the 'many (melodies)' heard at the silent hour makes good sense.

*22*  Osgood compared images of the grave in 320 and 857. Kean (1967) 23 added line 958 in discussing the relationship of these images to the *memento mori* poems of the fourteenth century.

*23*  See Chapman (1945) 17-18 for other examples of personification in the *Pearl* poems. Morris read *mele* 'discourse'; Gollancz considered it an emendation: *myry mele* 'joyous thing'. However, the mark over the first minim denotes *i* equalling *j* in *juele*.

*25*  Osgood and Pilch-C (1964) 172-74 compared Thomas de Hale's "Love Ron" in which the unsullied maiden is called "swetture þan eny spis" (line 168). The pearl-maiden is called *special spyce* in 235 and 938. Pilch, while noting representation of the bride as a *hortus conclusus* with spices springing forth in Song of Songs 4.12-16, pointed out that the details of the garden of spices in *Pe.* 43-46 remind one more of the orchard of *Deduiz* 'Pleasure' in *RR* 1341-44.

*26*  Dunlap (1977) 183-84 pointed to the double-entendre of *rot--rote*. The maiden's body, having sunk into *rot* 'decay', has run to Christ, the *rote* 'root' (420) of all her bliss, for only after the body is *layd to rote* (958) can the soul enter heaven. In discussing vegetation puns in *Pe.*, Dunlap noted that the "growth of the human soul, like that of plants, is based on regeneration, in kind, through death, and is cultivated by God" (181).

Northup (1897) 334 called *runnen* an example of apocope. While -*e* was often not pronounced, one cannot be sure if the same principle was applied to -*n*. *Runnen* may be a scribal error, but I am retaining it, since the policy in this edition is to make no emendations in matters dealing with rhyme, rhythm or alliteration. See the notes to *Pe.* 791 and 802 for examples of imperfect rhyme.

*27-28*  Gollancz compared the Chaucerian *Romaunt*: "Agayne the sonne an hundred hewes,/Blewe, yelowe, and reed, that fressh and newe is" (1577-78). Hillmann tr. *schyneȝ* 'will shine'. Andrew & Waldron followed Luttrell-B (1965) 71 who suggested emending to *schyne* to make the v. an infin. dependent on *mot* 25 so that the whole stanza would be an argument, "the narrator saying that spices, flowers, and fruit *ought* to spring from the pearl," but, as Bishop (1968) 141 noted, one may assume that the spices have already sprung from the pearl. Lines 41-44 of the next stanza support Bishop's view.

*29* The flower later symbolizes both mortality and immortality. In 269-70 the maiden is compared to a rose that *flowred and fayled*; in 906 she is called a *reken rose,* in 962 a *lufly flor.* The symbols of pearl and flower come together in 269-72 in a context that deals with death and resurrection. *Fryte* 29 anticipates the reference to the maiden among the 144,000 virgins purchased from the distant earth, "As newe fryt, to God ful due" (894).

Gordon, Moorman, and Andrew & Waldron tr. *fede* 'faded', Hillmann 'withered' (OF *fade).* The *MED,* following Gollancz, cited *Pe.* s.v. *fēde* ppl. (OI *feyja* 'to rot, decay'), but sense 2 s.v. *fāde* adj. 'wasted' is suitable, if one considers that the poet switched the vowel from *a* to *e* for rhyme. (Cf. *ware* in rhyme position instead of *were* in 151 and 1027.) Vasta-C (1967) 191-93, questioning such a vowel shift and noting the narrator's "interior disharmony," suggested *feden* 'to feed': the narrator wishes that "flower and fruit may not be permitted to feed on his Pearl.... Thus he desires that the natural process of corruption-generation should suspend itself."

However, this stanza focuses more on the idea of life coming from death. Kean (1967) 68-70 discussed the concept of blossoms of immortality springing from mortality, citing St. Bonaventura's *Vitis Mystica* which relates the flowers to virtues, the white lily to chastity, the blue violet to humility, and the red rose to patience and love. (Cf. *Pe.* 27.)

*31-32* Gordon noted these lines are closely paralleled in *P. Pl.* C-text, XIII, 179-81, but direct relationship is uncertain since both passages are based on John 12.24-25 in which Christ speaks figuratively of his approaching death and resurrection. Cf. also 1 Cor. 15.36-37. Johnson-C (1953) 34 associated *grayneȝ* with pearls. See *MED grain,* 3b, 'precious stone'. Richardson (1962) 312-13 related the harvest theme to the wine-harvest in the Parable of the Vineyard (501-72), and considered it fitting that *Pe.* should conclude with a reference to the bread and wine of the Eucharist (1209). *Woneȝ* 'barns' anticipates symbolically the *woneȝ* 'abodes' (1027) of the New Jerusalem.

*35* Hillmann separated MS *sprygande,* making emendation unnecessary. The scribe often ran words together. Cf. *Ga.* 46n on *glaumande.*

*37-48* Wrenn (1943) 31-32, noting that the flowers are symbols of powers of spiritual healing, discussed this stanza in relation to the April Eclogue of Spenser's *Shepheardes Calender,* lines 136-44. On p. 48, he compared Spenser's *madding mynd* 25 to *Pe.* 1154. Cf. also *garres ... greete* in the opening line of the April Eclogue to *Pe.* 331.

*39-40* Osgood, p. xvi, Schofield (1909) 616, and Hillmann identified the *hyʒ seysoun* as the Assumption of the Virgin, August 15, because it relates to the comparison the poet makes later (421-56) between the pearl-maiden and Blessed Mary. Gollancz favored Lammastide, August 1, because of the cutting of corn. Gordon agreed, noting the poet may have been suggesting the "gathering of the Lord's harvest, with the pearl as one of the 'first-fruits'; cf. 894."

Knightley (1961) 97, following the suggestion of Madeleva (1925), supposed the poet was referring to the feast of the Transfiguration, the 8th day, "which in biblical exegesis signifies the last day and therefore eternity." Bishop (1968) 86, feeling the whole month of August provides the cue for mentioning the action of reaping, stated, "The poet is alluding to the traditional 'occupations of the months'--an iconographical commonplace in medieval miniatures, sculptures and stained glass." Moorman surmised that *hyʒ* may be a variant (or possibly scribal error) for *híʒ* or *héʒ* 'hay', and tr. "hay season when the grain is cut with sharp sickles."

If one were to make a choice, Gollancz' identification of Lammastide, given further support by Andrew & Waldron, appears fitting due to the many vegetation symbols in *Pe.* associating the maiden with spice, flower, fruit, and seed.

*41* The *huyle* is evidently the particular spot to be associated with *floury flaʒt* 57 and *balke* 62. Gordon, who defined 'grave-mound', recalling Gollancz' association of the word with modern dialect *hile*, current in south-east Lancashire (Rochdale), glossed *huyle* 41, *hyul* 1205, and *hylle* 1172 separately from *hil*, *hyl(le)* 'hill' 678, 789, 976, 979. Hillmann, with one glossary entry for all, tr. *huyle* 'hillock' (OE *hyll*), a likely place to lose a pearl, but hardly suggesting the "appearance of a well-kept grave-mound." However, if one recalls the image of the dead grain in the ground bringing forth growth (29-36), figuratively depicting Christ's death and resurrection, 'mound' with the connotation 'grave-mound' suits the context of 41, 1172, and 1205. With all the variant spellings in this MS, one glossary entry for all forms seems sufficient, involving two separate senses of *MED hil(le* n. [OE *hyl*]: 1a, 'a natural elevation, hill, mountain', and 2a, 'a man-made hill or mound'. The *MED* cites *Pe.* 41 and 1205 separately s.v. *hīl* n. [Prob. OE *\*hygel* hillock; akin to OI *hugl* & G *hügel*.].

*43* Gollancz compared the Chaucerian *Romaunt* 1367-72. Stern-C (1955) 76 interpreted these spices as earthly manifestations of heaven's beneficence: gilliflower, an aromatic and *healing* clove; ginger, an aromatic and *energizing* anti-irritant; gromwell, bearing "polished white, stony nutlets very much like *pearls*." Gollancz (1891c) 109 noted that

medieval man compared gromwell seeds to pearls. Wintermute
(1949) suggested the poet placed the word in climactic position
because of the resemblance. Bishop (1968) 87-88 cited *MED*
*grŏmil* n., sense a, *Agnus Castus*: "It haȝt qwyt seed lyk a
perle ston." Wilson (1971a) pointed out that though *pearl-
plant* as a synonym for *gromwell* is not found in English until
the late sixteenth century, a Latin term for *gromwell* current
in the poet's time was *margarita rusticorum*.

*44* Cf. *powdered* to *poudred* (*Ga.* 800) describing the dis-
persal of pinnacles on Bercilak's castle. Reisner (1973) noted
the word was employed in the technical language of heraldry.
See, for example, *OED powder* v.1, sense 4, 'to ornament with
spots or small devices scattered over the surface'. Recalling
Cargill and Schlauch (1928), Reisner suggested identification
of the *Pearl*-poet with John Prat, a clerk attached to the house-
hold of John, Duke of Lancaster, since families that bore the
name of Prat in fourteenth-century Europe "had arms with fields
either powdered or charged with a variety of floral devices."

*46* Andrew & Waldron, following Gollancz (1891c), assumed
the word division of the MS may be wrong and changed *fayr
reflayr* to *fayrre flayr*, tr. 45-46: "If it was lovely to look
at, still fairer was the scent that floated from it." However,
as Gordon noted, the sense is satisfactory as the text stands.

*47* Cf. the verse tag *wot and wene* in 201. To avoid repe-
tition, a loose tr. has been employed.

*49* 'Spenud', with a bar over the e denoting a following
*n,* may be the MS form, rhyming vocally with *denned* 51. Cf.
suffixes with other than e vowel in *coruon* (*Ga.* 797) and
*flemus* (*Cl.* 31). The scribe's two minims for both *n* and *u*
do not allow for differentiation of these letters. (Note
Morris' *denely* 'loud' instead of *deuely* 51 and Madden's *anne*
for *aune* in *Ga.* 10.)

*51* Hillmann tr. *deuely* 'wicked', feeling the grief of
the "jeweler" should be defined as such, but Gordon's 'dreary'
accords better with *care ful colde* 50 and *playned* 53. One may
consider word-play, since medieval man considered it sinful to
mourn excessively over the death of a person.

*52* Bishop (1968) 73-74, disagreeing with Gordon's conten-
tion that *resoun* does not echo *RR* 2997f., compared the *Roman's*
Lady Reason, who has much in common with Boethius' Lady Philos-
ophy. *Sette ... saȝt* occurs again in 1201 after the dreamer
has been made peaceful by the maiden's teaching and the vision
that was granted to him.

*53* Andrew & Waldron, believing the poet usually avoided identical rhyme, adopted Gollancz' emendation of *spenned* to *penned*. (They also followed Gollancz in emending *tryed* 702 to *cryed* because *tryed* appears in line 707.) However, *spenned*, the same v. as *spenud* 49 (ON *spenna*) but with slightly different connotation, seems suitable.

Hamilton (1958) 183 suggested *OED spend* v.1 (OE *spendan*) 'lost' to accord better with her "lost pearl equals lost grace" interpretation. One may consider word-play: the dreamer has 'lost' grace because of too much mourning over his pearl 'enclosed' there.

Fletcher (1921) long ago demonstrated a multi-level approach to *Pe.* and the possibility of reconciling the elegiac and allegorical theories. Allen (1971) 137-39, with reference to Fletcher and Wellek-B (1933), noted that the letter and the spiritual allegory need not be in opposition, since "biblical and historical people may be understood as figures without denying their existence."

*54* Hillmann, rejecting emendation to *fyrce*, tr. *fyrte* 'violence' (OF firté). The *MED* cited *Pe.* s.v. *frighten* v., sense c. However, *MED fēren* v.1 lists a pp. *fērt*. For *fyrte* 'appalling' as a pp. tr. prog., cf. *vmbegon* 210 and *folde* 434, and see Mustanoja (1960) 549-51.

*55-56* Johnson-C (1953) 34 noted word-play on *kynde,* "both nature and kindness." As Hillmann observed, the 'character of Christ' implies Christ's virtues, including his humble suffering on earth, which should teach the dreamer acceptance of God's will.

*57* Luttrell-B (1965) 70 defined *floury flaȝt* 'flowery slab of turf', rejecting the 'flowery mead' identification of Elliott (1951). Citations s.v. *MED flaught* n. point toward Luttrell's view.

*58-59* Kean (1967) 18 compared Song of Songs 5.1-2, which describes aromatical spices in the *hortus conclusus,* sleep, and the voice of the beloved beckoning. Blanch (1973) 61, pointing ahead to *ensens of swete smelle* (1122) scattered by angels in the New Jerusalem, noted that sweet-smelling spices and flowers "are conventionally emblematic of heaven and God's grace."

*60* For retention of *precos,* cf. omission of *i* in *graco*(u): 95, 934 and *precos* 192. Four occurrences may indicate a varia spelling. (*MED grāciŏus* lists a form without *i*.)

*61* Osgood's 'space', adopted by deFord, was supported by Bloomfield (1969) 302: "In the fourteenth century it was be-

lieved that one's spirit did travel in space in a vision or
even in sleep." Hillmann tr. *in space* 'at once'; Gordon
glossed 'after a time', with Cawley, Moorman, and Andrew &
Waldron in agreement.

62 Gordon's *sweuen* 'sleep (or dream)' represents the
readings of editors. Spearing (1970) 111, following Kean,
suggested placing a semicolon after *bod* and tr. *sweuen* 'vision',
but *auenture* 64 may be associated with the vision; Andrew &
Waldron placed a period after *bod* but still tr. *sweuen* 'sleep'.

65 Gordon, comparing 293, tr., "I had no idea at all where
it was," but Hillmann's literal reading seems fitting here.
Andrew & Waldron, crediting Pearsall & Salter (1973) 56, cited
Honorius of Autun's reference to paradise as a delightful place
in the Orient (*PL* 172.1117).

66 Gordon's *cleuen* 'clove the air' (OE *clēofan*) is pref-
erable to Osgood's 'abide' (OE *clifian*). However, tr. 'were
cleft', pt. pl. pass., pictures jagged cliffs in the air, like
steeples. Cf. the similar alliteration of *clouen* ... *clyffeʒ*
(*Cl*. 965) and *clyff* ... *cleue* (*Ga*. 2201).

67 The superb imagery of the terrestrial paradise prevails
to line 120. Schofield (1904) 189-90 compared Ch. 33 of
*Mandeville's Travels*. Osgood, pp. 57-58, compared similar
imagery in the *Troy* and *Alexander* romances. M. Williams (1970)
discussed "Oriental Backgrounds & the *Pearl*-Poet." See also
Curtius (1948) 195-200 for discussion of descriptions of the
*locus amoenus* in Latin poetry of the Middle Ages, Patch (1950)
190 for a comparison of *Pe.* to "other world" descriptions,
Blanch-B (1965) 87 for reminiscences of the Garden of Love in
*RR,* and Finlayson (1974) for a study of how the three *loci* in
*Pe.*, garden, earthly paradise, and heaven, relate to the devel-
opment of the dreamer's soul from darkness to illumination.

73-77 Blanch-B (1965) 87, noting that crystal and silver
in the medieval lapidaries were considered inferior reflec-
tions of gold, hence appropriate for a terrestrial paradise
setting, showed how the poet underscored the difference be-
tween this region and the New Jerusalem described in lines
980-1092.

77 The *OED* cited *Pe.* s.v. *onslide* 'to unfold'; Hillmann
glossed *onslydeʒ* 'glide on, slip away', comparing OE *aslidan*.
Since the leaves can only seem to slip away from the branches,
tr. 'hang' seems suitable. Gordon, who did not recognize a
compound here, took *on* as an adv. and glossed *on slydeʒ* 'slides
on (the trees)'. Andrew & Waldron tr. 'slid over each other'.

*78* Gordon and Hillmann glossed *trylle* 'quiver', but *OED trill* v.2, sense 3, 'trail' is fitting here. Moorman tr. 'quivers', Andrew & Waldron 'quivered'. The auxiliary v. *con* may be either pr. t. 'do' or pa. t. 'did', but the former seems more suitable, since *onslyde3* is pr. t. Tajima (1975), examining "The *Gawain*-Poet's Use of *Con* as a Periphrastic Auxiliary," concluded that it is almost always used to place the infin. in rhyming position. Note, for example, the usage in line 81.

*79* Hillmann tr. *glode3* 'glades'; Moorman and Andrew & Waldron adopted Gordon's 'clear patches of sky' (*MED glāde* n.1, sense b). However, the description seems to be of sunlight coming through 'bright openings' in trees (*MED,* sense a). In *Ga.* the word denotes 'patches (of grass)' 2181 and a 'snowy surface' 2266.

*81* Eds. gave the sense of sound for *grynde* 'grind, crunch' but tr. 'mingle' as an extension of *MED grīnden* v.1, 1d, gives a wider view of the dreamer's seeing the landscape around him.

*82* See 3n on the dreamer's Oriental pearl. Tristman-C (1970) 279 saw the image of pearls here anticipating the dreamer's view of the 144,000 virgins in procession (1096-1104)

*83* Cf. 1076. Neither sun nor moon is needed in the New Jerusalem.

*87-88* Blenkner (1971) 38-42 discussed vegetation imagery in *Pe.* These lines recall 29, 46, and 58, and foreshadow the description of the fruit-bearing trees of life in 1077-80, based on Rev. 22.2.

*95* See 60n.

*98* See Patch (1950) 222-29 for discussion of the allegorical tradition of the Goddess Fortuna, and Kean (1967) 237-39 and Bishop (1968) 74-76 for the poet's use of *fortune* in *Pe.* in lines 98, 129, 306, as it differs in meaning from *wyrde* 249, 273 and *Destyné* 758, The pearl-maiden utters *Destyné* as a synonym for Christ, *wyrde* is a power God exerts, but, as Kean noted, *fortune* is used "for the particular turn which events take in the world."

*102* Hieatt (1965) 141 noted the dream psychology, doing easily what is impossible or painful in the real world.

*104-5* Added to the vegetation imagery recalling 25-36 are the rivers of spiritual life, to be followed by *fyldor* (106) anticipating heaven. *Reuere3,* placed so close to *water* (107), the main stream, has caused some difficulty. Gollancz

'river-meads' was favored by Gordon, Moorman, and Andrew &
Waldron, but Hillmann's 'rivers' seems suitable, for the poet
may have had in mind Genesis 2.10-14, where the river that
waters Eden divides into four branches.

*106*  Eds. read *b[o]nkes* instead of *bukes*, as if an *o* or
part of it were missing, but the MS reading may be retained
as a *b* followed by two minims representing *u*. See 49n on *n-u*
confusion, and cf. *bukes* as a variant spelling of *MED bek* n.1
'small stream' to the *u-e* variants of *lude-lede-leude* (*Ga.*
133, 126, 675).

*107*  Gordon, after identifying *water* as the river of life
(Rev. 22.1), flowing from heaven into the terrestrial paradise
(see 974, 1055-60), defined *schereʒ* 'meanders along', stating,
"The identity and sense of this word are uncertain." The v.
may be a form of *MED chāren* 'move'. Cf. in *Ga. schere* 334 for
the n. *chere,* and see *Ga.* 161ln for similar variants.

*113*  Schofield (1904) 190 compared a description in *Mande-
ville's Travels* of pearls at the bottom of a lake in Ceylon.
Osgood doubted the dependence of these verses on *Mandeville,*
but *gemme gente* 118 may imply noble pearls. (See 118n.)
Gollancz compared the Chaucerian *Romaunt* 125-27. French
*fo(u)ns* occurs in both *Mandeville* and *RR. Cl.* 1026 has *founs*
in a passage which C. Brown (1904) 149 showed is dependent on
the French *Mandeville.*
     Gollancz tr. *stonden* 'shone'. Revard (1962) supported this
reading with reference to *OED stand* v., sense 33, observing
that 'shone' rather than 'stood' is in "accord with the poet's
heightened language." Gordon glossed 'stand' pr. t. Andrew
& Waldron emended to *stoden* 'shone' because "this portion of
the narrative is consistently in the pa. t.," but *stonden* may
be taken as a pa. t. form by analogy with the pp. *standen* in
*Pe.* 519, 1148. Besides, *-en* does occur in pt. pl. strong
verbs as in *weuen* (*Pe.* 71).

*115*  MS *a,* gliding to the *s* of *stremande,* may be a short-
ened form of *as.* Note the omission of the final letter of
monosyllabic words in 144, 309, 429, 792, and 1058.
     *Strothe* 'wooded' is used attrib. in *Ga.* 1710. The *OED*
suggested it may be metathetically adapted from ON *storð* 'small
wood'. Gordon gave to *stroþe-men* the generalized poetic sense
'men of this world'. The literal 'woodsmen' is also suitable
here. Elliott (1979) 61-62, after noting the cognate OE *strōd*
'marshy land overgrown with brushwood' and the emphasis on
water in this passage, stated that *stroþe-men,* while it may
literally mean 'dwellers in a marshy woodland', is singularly
fitting in this stanza as a "symbol of country people, like
Hardy's Woodlanders."

*116* For pr. p. *staren,* a form different from the usual
*-ande* in this MS, cf. *runnen* 874, *drawen* 1193, and see Mustanoja
(1960) 569-70 for similar examples in ME.

*118* The phrase *gemme gente* perhaps denotes pearls, as it
does in 253. Blanch-B (1965) 88-89 noted that *beryl* (line 110)
signifies rebirth into a new and purer life, *emerad* signifies
good faith and suggests chastity, and *saffer* denotes hope,
truth, and wisdom. All three jewels "point to the prerequisite
for heavenly existence." For cleansing symbols involving blood
and water in relation to Christ's death on the cross and the
sacrament of baptism, see 649-56 and 766.

*127* Osgood's *floty* 'watery' (OE *flot, flotian* + *y*) was
adopted by most editors and the *MED.* Moorman favored Hillmann'
'undulating'.

*129-32* Gordon, Hillmann, and Moorman rendered *frayneȝ*
'makes trial'. The *MED* cited *Pe.* s.v. *frainen* v., sense 5,
'to choose or desire', a suitable meaning given by Morris,
Osgood, Gollancz, and Andrew & Waldron. See 98n on the allu-
sion to the Goddess Fortuna. Osgood compared 1195 in a stanza
that deals with the conflict between man's desire and God's
will.
   Macrae-Gibson-C (1968) 206 noted the development of the
dreamer's conflict with the use of the link-word *more* in
Stanza-Group III. In X, the link-word is again *more;* the
laborers in the vineyard think they deserve *more* 552-53. In
contrast, the souls in heaven, instead of envying one another,
wish their crowns were worth five (451) and that every soul
were five--*þe mo þe myryer* 850. (See also 1195n.)

*131* Andrew & Waldron emended *her* to *his* and tr. 131-32:
"the man to whom she sends his desire seeks to have more and
more (of it) all the time." However, MS *her* may stand, for
the poet is evidently saying that fortune may send more and
more of either solace or sorrow, as she wills. At this point,
the dreamer is receiving her benefits, but he has also experi-
enced her sting.

*136* Gollancz capitalized *Gladneȝ,* believing the poet was
thinking of Dame Gladness in *RR.* Gordon, Hillmann, and Andrew
& Waldron glossed 'joys, gladness' (*MED gladnes(se),* 1c, 'sour
of joy'). Rendering *gladneȝ* 'delights' is fitting here. Moor
man referred to Emerson (1927) 813 who took the word as the pl
of *MED glāden* n., 'cleared space in a wood'.

*137* Gollancz compared *paradys erthly* in the Chaucerian
*Romaunt* 648. The garden of the *Roman,* that of Eden in Genesis
and the *hortus conclusus* of Solomon's Song of Songs all share

common features of the *locus amoenus*. (See 67n.) Here and in 248 *Paradys(e)* may denote the divine kingdom, since the dreamer, though his conception is earth-bound, apparently feels he is approaching heaven. (Cf. 295-300n.)

138 Fowler (1960) 29 and Hillmann showed that MS *oþer* may be retained. The dreamer thinks that Paradise must be either on his side of the stream or on the opposite side.

139-40 Morris (1891a) 603 suggested emending *myrþeʒ* to *myrcheʒ* 'boundaries'. Osgood glossed *myrþeʒ* 'pleasance, pleasure garden' and *mereʒ* 'boundary-lines'. Gollancz' emendation to [*mereʒ*] *by* [*Myrþe*], based on the Chaucerian *Romaunt* 1409-16, where *Déduit*, the Lord of the Garden, is called *Mirthe*, was supported by Day (1934). Bone (1937) refuted Gordon and Onions (1932) 131 who rendered *myrþeʒ* 'pleasure-gardens'. Moorman followed Gordon who, in his edition, suggested: "I thought the stream was a division made by pools, separating the delights." Andrew & Waldron, except for their rendering of *myrþeʒ* as 'pleasure-gardens', agreed.

Fowler (1960) tr., "I thought that the water was a deception/Made by meres among the delights," feeling the dreamer may have thought that although the water seemed continuous and impassable, if he walked along the shore, he would eventually find an opening. Hillmann tr., "I supposed the water was a division/Between joyances with boundaries made," arguing that the dreamer here pictured Paradise as a "hierarchy of states of beatitude with boundaries fixed between them."

Gordon's reading seems best, except that *mereʒ* 'streams' is used in this edition, instead of 'pools', to depict the rushing currents of the water. (Cf. the images in 111-12.) The dreamer sees the water as a division between the delights on his side and on the opposite side. (Note 137-38, 141-42, and 147-48.) *Mere(ʒ)* denotes water in lines 158 and 1166; *by mereʒ made* 'created alongside streams' modifies *myrþeʒ*.

142 *Hope* is a pt. with loss of -*d* before þ. Cf. 185, 286, 572, 752, and see Day (1919) and Gordon and Onions (1932) 132-36 for discussion in relation to the other poems in the MS.

144 *Euer* ... *a* may be a variant of *euer* ... *ay* 'always'. See 115n.

151 The context of 151-54 favors *woþeʒ* 'perils' (ON *vaði*), given by Osgood, Gollancz, Gordon, Moorman, and Andrew & Waldron. The dreamer is looking for a way to cross the stream, perilous because of its depth (143) and its swirling (111). Hillmann tr. *woþeʒ* 'searchings' from OE *wāþ*. (See also 375n on *woþe*.)

227

*161-68* The figure of the maiden is central to the debate over elegy or allegory in *Pe.*, a debate tempered by the recognition of both genres in the poem. For a survey of scholarship on the subject from Wellek-B (1933) to the beginning of the 1970s, see Eldredge (1975) 172-78. Piehler (1971), relating *Pe.* to Jungian dream psychology, viewed the maiden as a symbolic manifestation of the dreamer's lost innocence, but still concluded that the "text allows us little alternative to interpreting the maiden as primarily the poet's daughter; the symbolic roles we have distinguished are no more than aspects of her manifestation which enable us to see her as more than herself in a state of glory" (162). For negative criticism of Piehler's psychological interpretation, see Levine (1977).

*161-62* Hillmann tr. *faunt* 'youthful being', believing, p. xx, that the jeweler's material pearl has now been transformed into his soul, symbolized by the maiden. Gollancz, Gordon, Moorman, and Andrew & Waldron tr. 'child'. *MED faunt* shows the word may mean 'young child' or 'infant', without specification of age. *Mayden of menske* qualifies the meaning in this context, and if one is to judge by the illustrations on folios 42 and 42b, she may be called a young child of advanced stature. Osgood, p. xxv, referred to St. Augustine's *The City of God* 22.14: "Quid ergo de infantibus dicturi sumus, nisi quia non in ea resurrecturi sunt corporis exiguitate, qua mortui; sed quod eis tardius accessurum erat tempore, hoc sunt illo Dei opere miro atque celerrimo recepturi" (*PL* 41.776). ("Now as touching infants, I say they shall not rise again with that littleness of body in which they died, but that the sudden and strange power of God shall give them a stature of full growth" [tr. John Healey, Vol. 2, p. 380].)

*163* Cf. 197. *MED blēaunt* defines 'silk fabric' for the garments worn in *Pe.* and *Ga.* 879 and 1928. Rev. 19.8 describes *byssino* 'fine linen' for the garment the bride of Christ wears, but the poet sometimes altered Biblical details without changing the essential meaning. (Cf. 785-86n.)

*165* OED *sheer* v.1, 'to make bright or pure', following Morris and Gollancz, cited *Pe.*, but Osgood, comparing 106 and 213, favored the image of shorn gold (OE *sceran*), adopted by subsequent editors.

*166* *Schore* evidently denotes the 'cliff' of 159. Gordon, in his glossary, compared *schore* 'ridge' (*Ga.* 2161).

*171-72* Cf. 15-16.

*175-76* Hillmann, following Madeleva (1925) 131, believed these lines undermine the theory that *Pe.* is a lament for a

dead child because the dreamer "could not reasonably, as a
Christian, be surprised at seeing his little dead daughter
there." Spearing (1970) 132 pointed out that one need not
suppose the dreamer will always think and feel with reason.
He failed to do so in the garden (51-56).

*179* OED *sting* v.1, sense 5, fig., defines 'to affect with
a sudden sharp mental pain or an access of painful emotion'.
The poet effectively demonstrates in lines 173-88 dream psy-
chology in the mind of his persona, who is speechless and yet
afraid the maiden might leave if he does not speak to her.
See 102n for reference to an opposite psychological effect.
    Andrew & Waldron followed Gollancz in emending *atount* to
*astount,* arguing that the "alliteration would appear to sup-
port the emendation," but the poet did not use alliteration
regularly in *Pe.,* and *atount* 'dazed', which Gordon derived
from OF *ato(u)ner,* is suitable.

*184* Hammerle (1936) compared *The Castle of Perseverance,*
c. 1425: "As a hawke, I hoppe in my hende halle" (406). Chap-
man (1945) 20, viewing the parallelism to 1085 as a Virgilian
mannerism, listed sixty-two examples among the four poems in
the MS.

*185* See 142n on retention of *hope.* Most editors adopted
Osgood's *porpose* 'intended meaning', a sense different from
'purpose' (267, 508). The poet presents his persona as one
who is predisposed to receive spiritual instruction and in-
sights, like St. John who had seen the heavenly procession
*in gostly drem* 790. P.G. Thomas (1938) 222, following Gollancz,
tr. 'vision', but OED *purpose* sb. does not substantiate this
reading. Andrew & Waldron tr., "I thought that the quarry was
spiritual," rendering *porpose* 'quarry' from OED, sense 1, but
the hunting image, while suitable elsewhere in the stanza,
seems a bit strained here.

*188* In view of 173-74 and 182-83, *steuen* 'speech' (Morris,
Osgood, Hillmann) seems preferable to 'meeting' (Gollancz,
Gordon, Andrew & Waldron).

*190* Cf. the description of the pearl in 6.

*192* See 60n.

*193* See 745-46n for discussion of *perle3 ... prys.*

*194* As line 63 indicates, the dreamer has received this
'good fortune' through the *grace* of God.

*195* Osgood compared 753. Hoffman-C (1960) 99, tracing the flower imagery through 207-8, 269-70, 753, 906-8, and 961-62, noted the constant identification of flower, fruit, and jewel with the maiden, related to the "death-and-resurrection motif, which has a further presentation in the two Jerusalems and the figure of Christ." (See also 29n.)

*197-220* Schotter (1979), after discussing "The Poetic Function of Alliterative Formulas of Clothing in the Portrait of the *Pearl* Maiden," concluded that while the poet depicts her with the language associated with romance heroines, he carefully omits the most gaudy formulas so that the "maiden's portrait can be seen, once the dreamer's focus on outward and visible signs has been overcome, to be perfectly appropriate to her role as one of the Brides of the Lamb" (195).

*197* Cf. 163. *Mys* denotes the loose outer garment the maiden wears over her *cortel* (203). As Gollancz noted, line 197 is not an exact repetition of 163, the reference there being to the maiden's general attire. In 197-220 the poet depicts the details of her dress. Osgood's emendation to *bleaunt of biys* is more radical than Gordon's *beau biys* 'fair fine linen', based on Rev. 19.8. MS *beaumys* seems better disconnected. (Cf. 35n.) Gollancz (1891c) first read *beau mys*. Hillmann's *beaumys* is derived from *be* 'around' + *aumys*. *Mys* is a shortening of *MED amit* n., (variant *amis*). See 802n for other examples of aphetic forms of OF words.

*199* Cf. *marjorys* 206, *margyrye* 1037, and *margerye-perle* symbolizing the pure soul in *Cl*. 556. M. Williams (1970) 104, referring to the Vulgate's *margarita,* commented that the triple meaning of jewel, flower, and a girl's name is played upon in *Pe.*

*201* See 47n on the verse tag. Gollancz correctly observed that *lappe3 large* are depicted in the MS illustrations on folios 42 and 42b. However, as Gordon pointed out in his 228n, the pictured details do not always agree with the poetic descriptions. For example, pearls are not clearly visible in the illustrations, and the maiden's hair is not hanging loose. Gordon noted that in the poet's eyes, "Her costume is a simple form of the aristocratic dress of the second half of the fourteenth century.... Her golden hair flowed loose over her neck and shoulders, as befitted a maiden and a bride." (See also 213-14n.)

*205* Gollancz commented on the crown as a symbol of virginity. Cf. 767: "coronde clene in vergynté." It is also a symbol of salvation in heaven. See 253-55n and 451n. Fletcher (1921) 11, citing 205-6 and 217-19 to compare the

maiden's adornment in pearls to the description of Mary in
Albertus Magnus' *De Laudibus Beatae Mariae Virginis,* wrote,
"The 'faithful soul' in the poem, the little child, is bedecked
with but one gem, one virtue, the pearl of innocence." How-
ever, it may be that the many pearls described on the maiden's
dress and crown (199-219) symbolize her virtues in general,
such as innocence, purity, humility, and grace, all subordinate
to the *wonder perle* (221) on her breast, Matthew's *perle of
prys* (746), symbol of the heavenly kingdom.

206  By taking *gyrle* (205) in conjunction with *of marjorys,*
one may consider word-play on the name of the maiden.  (Cf.
199n.)

208  Eds. rendered *vpon* as the adv. 'on it', but the adj.
'spread' fits the context too. Cf. *vpon* 'open' in 198.

209  Osgood emended to *herle* 'imbraided fillet', but Gordon
explained *werle* as a synonym for crown, deriving it from *OED
whirl (whorl)* sb., the idea being that the maiden wore no other
'circlet' to confine her hair. The *OED* cited only *Pe.* s.v.
*werle* 'covering, attire', with derivation from *wear* v. + *-le*.

210  Morris and Gollancz emended to *here heke,* taking *heke*
as a variant of *eke* 'also'. Osgood rendered *here-leke* 'locks
of hair'. Moorman followed Gordon who also emended to *here*
'hair' and glossed *leke* as the pt. 'enclosed', with *semblaunt*
(211) as its object: "'Her hair, lying all about her, enclosed
her countenance." However, since the maiden's hair is de-
scribed in 213-14, it may be the poet described another feature
here. Hillmann tr. *lere leke* 'face radiance', kept *vmbe gon*
separate, and glossed *gon* 'beamed'. Andrew & Waldron agreed
with Cawley who retained the MS forms with a reading that seems
preferable: "Her face was enclosed all around (i.e. with a
wimple)." The *MED* also suggested this reading s.v. ? *lēre
leke* n., '? face linen, wimple'. Cambric is a fine white
linen used for the wimple worn by women in the late medieval
period.

212  Osgood noted, "Though from the walrus, ivory was
generally called whale's bone." Gollancz compared the de-
scription of a banner in *Wynnere and Wastoure:* "Whitte als
the whalles bone" (181).

213-14  Lucas (1977), after noting that in the second half
of the fourteenth century it was customary for ladies to wear
their hair bound and/or covered, stated: "Free-flowing hair
is appropriate to the pearl-maiden firstly as an unmarried
girl (the Dreamer's child), and also subsequently as a bride
(of the Lamb) and as a queen (of the heavenly kingdom)."

*215* Chase and Hillmann, following Cook (1908) 199, tr.
*colour* 'collar'. See also Schofield (1909) 658-60, Hulbert
(1927) 119, and Emerson (1927) 816. Chase adopted Cook's sug-
gestion to expand the MS abbr. to *r* rather than *ur,* but *colour*
may stand as a variant spelling. Gordon, with most editors
in agreement, glossed *colour* '(white) complexion', but the
poet described the maiden's *ble* 'complexion' in 212. Cf. the
description of pearls on material in 197-204 and 217-19. For
*depe* 'wide', see *MED dēp* adj., 1c and 1d.

*217* Morris and Osgood interpreted *poyned* as pp., 'trimmed,
pierced', but Gollancz observed that the 'wristlet' was part
of the long, narrow sleeve of the kirtle, worn beneath the
cloak. (See 197-204.)

*218* Cf. *Cl*: "And fetyse of a fayr forme, to fote and to
honde" (174). The poet there explains the allegory of the
Parable of the Wedding Feast in which clothes represent deeds
and thoughts. In *Pe.*, too, the outer attire symbolizes the
inner soul.

*219* Cf. 206.

*220* As Gollancz noted, *uesture* denotes the maiden's
entire array. Cf. 163.

*221-28* The *wonder perle* is the *perle of prys* (Matt.
13.45-46), mentioned first here, then a bit past the middle
of the poem (732-46), and finally toward the end (854, 1103-4).
(See 730-35n.)

*229* Emendations here and in 235 seem unnecessary, since
*e* sometimes varies with *i(y)*. Note *enpresse* 1097 instead of
*enpryse, geuen* 1190 instead of *gyuen,* and *hym* 'them' for *hem*
635.

*231* Cf. *Ga.* 2023 where *Grece* is also in rhyme position.

*233* *Nerre* is ambiguous. Osgood, Gollancz, and Gordon
believed the poet was probably referring to his daughter.
Hillmann glossed *nerre* adv. comp. 'nearer', stating, "not in
relationship but in position, locality." Since the word may
express the idea of one's being simply more dear to another
than any other person, it is possible the poet had in mind a
little girl who was not related to him by blood, but to whom
he had formed a close attachment. Those who support only the
allegorical theory discount any autobiographical element.
See, for example, Schofield (1909) 657. On the other hand,
the seemingly personal references in the poem are many. Green
(1925) 816-17 cited forty-one lines with personal touches,

among them 161-62, 164, 167-68, 233, 241-45, 378-80, and 483-
85. Bishop (1968) 8, who favored Gordon's view, noted, never-
theless, that the maiden may have been a god-child, grandchild,
or even a younger sister of the poet. Milroy (1971) 208 sug-
gested the poet may have been an "unmarried cleric writing
the poem as a *consolatio* for a friend, a brother or a local
dignitary, for whose bereavement he felt deeply, and assuming
for that purpose a first person point-of-view."

235 See 229n for retention of MS *spyce*. The spice image
is carried throughout *Pe*. The spot where the pearl was lost
is spread with spices (25, 35), the dreamer sees spices in the
terrestrial paradise (104), and the maiden is again called
*specyal spyce* (938). At the basis of this image is the sym-
bolic death-and-resurrection seed that fell into the ground.
See 31-32n. Osgood compared the reference to the Virgin, "Heil
spice swettist of sauour," line 29 of "Hail, Blessed Mary!"
in *Hymns to the Virgin & Christ, The Parliament of Devils,
and other Religious Poems*, ed. F.J. Furnivall, *EETS, OS* 24
(London, 1868).

245 Cf. similar images in 10, 30, and 41 to denote the
loss of the pearl.

249-50 Cf. *luf-daungere* 11. As Bishop (1968) 75-76 noted,
the dreamer eventually becomes content even though he considers
himself in a *doel-doungoun* 1187. (See 1182-88n.) Higgs (1974)
studied the personal progress of the dreamer who learns "to
see in present evil the prospects of eventual good through the
power of God" (388).

252 Cf. the implied reference to a *juelere* in lines 1-8.
Hillmann supposed the dreamer is represented as an actual
'jeweler', but the link-word in this stanza-group is apparently
used metaphorically. (See 730n.)

253-55 The pearl in pearls puts on her crown of pearls;
the pure soul clothed in virtues puts on her crown of vir-
ginity and salvation. (See 205n and 451n.) In 745-46 the
dreamer addresses the maiden as a spotless pearl in pure
pearls, possessing the *perle of prys* (heaven). Hoffman-C
(1960) 90-91 discussed the multiple meanings of the pearl
figure. Gordon viewed the pearl-maiden as a lost child's
soul. Hillmann supposed the dreamer, at this point, is view-
ing his own soul safely enclosed in heaven, "were he a noble
jeweler (264)." Mahl (1966) equated the maiden with the
"concept of the pure Church which, when it became corrupted
in the world, [the dreamer] had lost" (28).

254 Emerson (1927) 817 compared Guenevere's *yȝen gray*

in *Ga.* 82, also rhyming with *say*. *Graye,* a favorite color of women's eyes in ME poetry, may denote a bluish gray.

*259* Gollancz compared the *cofer* in *Cl.,* denoting the ark of salvation in 310, 339, and 492. It may also mean 'treasure chest' (*coferes, Cl.* 1428, for the vessels in the temple of Jerusalem), 'casket', and 'treasure house'. The maiden describes herself as being in this *cofer,* the treasure chest of heaven. See 2n for a possible allusion to her tomb. Andrew & Waldron referred to Piehler (1971) 145 who discussed the ambiguity between the senses 'treasure chest' and 'coffin'.

*260 Gardyn* occurs only here in *Pe.,* recalling the *erber(e)* of lines 9 and 38, but the latter is the garden of loss whereas this garden represents heaven. The poet anticipates the theme of death for the body in the earthly garden and resurrection for the soul in the heavenly garden (265-76).

*262* Hillmann retained MS *here* by tr. þer 'since' at the start of the line. I have transposed 'here' to the beginning of the line in the Mod. E. tr.

*263 Forser* as a metaphor for heaven relates to *cofer* 259 and *gardyn* 260. *Cofer* and the *forser* doubly enforce the concept of the pure soul like a jewel, safely encased in Christ's strongbox of heaven. The *gardyn* suggests a vegetation image with God as the Gardener who cares for one's soul. See *MED gardiner* n., sense b.

*269-72* Flower and jewel imagery again merge in the death-and-resurrection theme. (See 29n.) *Rose* (269), the material pearl—the maiden's body, blossomed and decayed as nature directed, but from this decay rose the *perle of prys,* her soul. Lines 29-30 describe flower and fruit that cannot be wasted where the pearl drove down into dark molds, for from this loss comes the *reken rose* (906), the immortal maiden.

Cf. *kynde of the kyste* to *kynde of Kryst* (55). *Kyste,* the treasure chest of heaven, echoes *Kryst,* who cares for souls, and recalls *cofer* (259) and *forser* (263). The symbolic significance of *perle of prys* is different in 746. Here it signifies the maiden's soul; there the *perle of prys,* which the maiden wears on her breast, represents heaven. (See 745-46n.)

Hillmann, interpreting this stanza as an attack upon covetousness, tr. *put in pref* 'put to the test'. Gordon's 'has proved in fact to be', the sense given by other editors, receives support s.v. *OED proof* sb., I. 1, 'evidence sufficient (or contributing) to establish a fact or produce belief in the certainty of something'.

*273-76* Gordon's paraphrase of 274 clarifies the connota-
tion: "has made an eternal pearl out of a short-lived rose."
Kellogg-C (1956), seeing in this passage an allusion to the
Augustinian doctrine of *creatio ex nihilo,* concluded that the
"Pearl-maiden would not be saying that God has favored the
dreamer by making his mortal rose into an immortal pearl, but
rather that the Dreamer, instead of complaining against God
for a presumed injustice, should be praising God for his very
existence." The context of this stanza, however, indicates
that the Augustinian doctrine of *creatio ex nihilo* prevails
here firstly in relation to the maiden who, like all mankind,
was created by God from nothing, had to die and decay physically
(269-70) because of Adam's sin, but then was spiritually re-
vived (271-72) due to Christ's death on the cross. (See 637-
60.) The dreamer should be thankful for the maiden's glorified
state and accordingly for the opportunity he has of achieving
it in the future.
      Bishop (1968) 19 compared the 'life is a loan' consolatory
topic quoted by Sister Mary Beyenka (*Consolation in St. Augus-
tine* [Washington, D.C., 1950], pp. 102-4) from a Letter of
Augustine to Probus: "God has taken nothing of yours, when He
took His own possession; He is like a creditor to whom only
thanks are now due." As Bishop noted, the dreamer will be con-
soled in the end, knowing the maiden is in the possession of
her rightful owner.

*277-78* Most editors rendered *geste* 'guest'. Hulbert
(1927) 119 believed the alliteration suggests Morris' old read-
ing, 'tale, saying' (*MED ğĕst(e)* n.1). Word-play may be in-
volved, but the primary sense seems to relate to the maiden.
The *MED* cited *Pe.* s.v. *gest* n., 3a, 'one newly arrived in a
place', but 'newborn child', sense 1c, may apply in the fig.
sense, newly born into Paradise. The maiden is called *faunt*
'child' in 161.
      Rupp (1955) saw word-play in both lines: "A jewel (pearl)
to me then was this guest (the Pearl-maiden) or tale (pearl),
and jewels (pearls) were her gentle words (pearls)." Citing
Matt. 7.6: "neque mittatis margaritas vestras ante porcos"
("neither cast ye your pearls before swine"), Rupp believed
the dreamer, not aware of the irony in his words, may be
classified as 'porcos', at this point, in need of the maiden's
instruction, but the poet, "with his authorial foreknowledge,"
sees the complete relationship between dreamer and maiden.

*279-88* Rupp's observation that a distinction must be made
between the poet and his persona is supported by these lines,
for the dreamer fails to understand the spiritual import of
what the maiden has said. The poet creates such situations to
lead to debate and homily, techniques which dominate the cen-
tral portion of *Pe.*

*282* Hoffman-C (1960) 96-98 compared 23-24, 305-6, 319-22, 857-60, 957-58, and 1206 for images which emphasize a physical, literal death, not a figurative loss associated with symbolic interpretations.

*286* For loss of -*t* in *bro3*, due to following þ, cf. 142n.

*287* *Wawe3* denotes the tossing currents of the rapidly flowing stream. See 111-12.

*290* Osgood, noting the foolishness of opposing God's will is an important theme in *Pe.*, compared 55-56, 267, 1166, and 1199. Cf. also 338-48 and 359-60.

*294* In 363 the dreamer shows he is aware of his stumbling speech.

*295-300* Spearing (1970) 151-52, refuting Kean's contention that the dreamer believed the maiden was on earth, defined *dene* as a sector of heaven and commented that the dreamer should have believed the maiden was there without having seen her. The next stanza recalls Christ's words in John 20.29: "quia vidisti me, Thoma, credidisti; beati qui non viderunt et crediderunt." ("Because thou hast seen me, Thomas, thou hast believed: blessed are they that have not seen, and have believed.") The dreamer, besides believing only what he sees, also thought he could dwell in that region and cross the stream. These are the three errors he uttered in 282-88; the maiden will refute all three in the next two stanzas (301-24).

*302* Here and in 308 *loue3,* recalling 285, heightens the word-play contrast with *leue3* 304 and *leue* 311. Hamilton-B (1955) 42 favored retention of the MS form in 302.

*307* Osgood emended *westernays* to *besternays* 'reversed' (OF *bestorneis*). Most editors, following Henry Bradley (revision of *A Middle English Dictionary*, ed. F.H. Stratmann [Oxford, 1891], p. 708), retained *westernays* 'reversed, awry' as an altered form of *besternays,* "the alteration being due to the influence of *west,* since the word was applied to a church which faced west instead of east as was then usual" (Gordon). The *OED* cited only *Pe.* s.v. *westernais* adv.

Hillmann's division to *west ernays* 'empty pledge' seems suitable. (See 35n for similar examples of disjoining.) *OED weste* a. 'desolate' relates to *waste* a., sense 4, 'idle, vain' in relation to speech. *MED ērnes* n., sense 2, defines 'pledge'. Hillmann compared Ps. 88.35: "neque profanabo testamentum meum et quae procedunt de labiis meis non faciam irrita." ("Neither will I profane my covenant: and the words that proceed from my mouth I will not make void.") See also Hillmann (1943).

*309* In 401-2 the maiden tells the dreamer arrogant pride
has no place in Paradise. See Blenkner-C (1968) 230 for dis-
cussion of three deadly sins noted in *Pe.*, pride (301-10),
anger (341-60), and envy (613-16). Concerning envy, cf. also
445-68 and 845-52.

*313* Gordon glossed *dayly* 'contend' (ON *deila*), Hillmann
'speak lightly' (OF *dalien*), Andrew & Waldron 'speak'. Lutt-
rell (1962a) 447-48 and Moorman favored 'to talk courteously',
a suitable sense, since the maiden had referred to the dreamer
as being *vncortoyse* (303). *MED dālien* v. lists 'to converse
politely', sense 1a, and 'to speak in a solemn manner', 1b,
citing *Pe.* s.v. the latter, but the former seems better.

*315* *Bayly* (*MED baillī(e)* n., 3b) is the same n. that
appears in 442. However, in 442 *-ly* must be sounded to rhyme
with *Cortaysye* 444. The rhymes between 313-19 indicate that
*-y* is sounded like *-e*.

*321* *Paradys greue* is synonymous with the Garden of Eden.
*Greue* evidently alludes to that specific part of the garden
in which the apple tree grew. *Paradys(e)* in 137 and 248
apparently denotes the divine kingdom. (See 137n.)

*322* In 639-60 the maiden tells of the *ȝorefader*'s (Adam's)
sin and man's salvation through Christ's crucifixion.

*323* Emendation of *ma* to *man* seems unnecessary. Cf. s.v.
*OED me* indef. pron. (with *ma* listed as a variant) *Sir Ferumb.*
2828: "Ma calþ me Gyoun of Borgoygne." *Boȝ* 'must' is a vari-
ant spelling of *bos* (*Cl.* 687).

*326* Andrew & Waldron compared line 11.

*331-32* For *he* 'they', cf. the forms *he* (*ho*) for the nom.
pl. in *Cl.* 62, 657, and 1267 (OE *heo*), and see *Cl.* 62n. Gor-
don's interpretation of *men* as a sg. indef. pron. was adopted
by subsequent editors.

*334* Andrew & Waldron noted an "allusion to the theme of
exile, common in OE poetry." See, for example, *The Wanderer*
and *The Seafarer* in *Seven Old English Poems,* ed. John C. Pope
(Indianapolis, 1966).

*335* Hillmann retained *perleȝ*, tr. 'peerless one', but,
as Gordon noted, the scribe probably repeated ȝ from *partleȝ*.
Cf. similar repetitions in 678 and 1179.

*336* Through the dreamer's lack of understanding, the
poet advances the dramatic dialogue. Spearing (1970) 152

compared Chaucer's dreamer in *The Book of the Duchess*. (See
also 279-88n.)

*342* For *and* ... *and* 'both ... and', see *MED and* conj.
(& adv.), 1c. (a). For *wele* and *wo* as synthetic datives, cf.
*perle* 53, *coumforde* 369, and *harmeȝ* 388.

*343* The idiom *not a cresse* 'nothing at all' (*MED cresse*
n., sense 2) is transposed to the next line in the Mod. E. tr.

*344-48* Cf. *Pa*. 1-8, 524-31 and *Pe*. 349-60, 1199-1200.
Osgood and Gordon observed that the call for patience and
obedience to God's will is similar in both poems.

*349* Gordon's *adyte* 'accuse' (OF *aditer*), previously noted
by Emerson (1922) 67-68 and adopted by subsequent editors,
seems preferable to 'arrange, dispose' (OE *adihtan*), given by
Osgood and Gollancz. Gordon compared Ps. 50.6 for the sense
of the whole stanza.

*351* DeFord and Moorman agreed with Hillmann who tr.,
"Thy opinions amount to not a mite." Taking *mendeȝ* as a vari-
ant for *mynde,* she rejected the sense 'recompense', given by
other editors, because to say amends are valueless before God
would be un-Christian. However, *mendeȝ* 'consolations' (*OED
mend* sb., sense 2, 'remedy'), also suits this context: man
gains no comfort by opposing God's will.

*353* Savage (1956b) 127 noted that *stynst* is a correct
form for the imper. sg. and may be retained. Cf. 3rd person
sg. *stysteȝ* in *Cl*. 359 from ON *stytta*.

*356* Andrew & Waldron, comparing *Pa*. 31-33, commented:
"*Mercy* is a quasi-personification."

*358* Emerson (1927) 819, refuting Osgood's "and lightly
drive thy frowns away" (with *leme* from ON *lemja* 'beat'), and
Gollancz' emendation of & to *þat alle* (with tr. *of lyȝtly
leme* 'glance lightly off'), interpreted *of* 'among' as a prep.
in post. c. governing *lureȝ*, and *leme* as the v. 'shine'. (Cf.
the sense in 119 and 1043.) The *MED* cited *Pe*. s.v. *lēmen* v.1,
sense b, 'drive away', and accounted for Gordon's emendation
by adding [? read: *fleme*], but *lēmen* v.2, 1b, 'shine, radiate'
substantiates Emerson's reading, followed by Hillmann and
deFord. Cawley, Moorman, and Andrew & Waldron adopted Gordon's
*fleme* 'banish'.

*359* Gordon corrected earlier editors' emendation--*marred
oþer madde* 'marred or made'. His *myþe* 'conceal (one's feel-
ings)'--OE *mīþan*--was adopted by subsequent editors, but the

v. may be from *OED mouth* (*muth*) with *y* for *u* needed for rhyme.
For other *i*(*y*)-*u* variants, cf. *huyle* 41--*hylle* 1172, *gylte₃*
655--*gulte* 942, and *rybé* 1007 alongside *rubies* in *Cl.* 1471.
The idea of concealment does not seem to be involved in the
thought of this passage, whereas *myþe* 'mutter' is appropriate
to the sense.

*363* Most editors inserted [*I*] into the ME text, but there
is much ellipsis in the poems of this MS. Note, for example,
*Pe.* 96, 331, 362, 365, and 977.

*364-65* Gollancz, comparing Lamentations 2.19 and Ps. 61.8
construed 365-66 together: "Like water pouring from a well, I
readily resign myself to God's gracious will." Gordon's read-
ing, adopted by subsequent editors, seems preferable. Cf. Ps.
21.15: "Sicut aqua effusus sum." ("I am poured out like
water."), and 362-63 to verse 14: "aperuerunt super me os suum,
sicut leo rapiens et rugiens." ("They have opened their mouths
against me, as a lion ravening and roaring.")

*368* Andrew & Waldron followed Rønberg (1976) who, reject-
ing the usual reading *endorde* 'adored (one)'--OF *adorer*, with
altered prefix--defined 'gold-adorned' (OF *endorer*). The mai-
den is compared to *glysnande golde* (165), and there are refer-
ences to gold in lines 2 and 213. The *MED* s.v. *endōren* v.
records the word only in the restricted sense, 'to cover or
coat (a roast or other dish) with a glaze (usually made from
the yolks of eggs)', but Rønberg noted that in Godefroy's
*Dictionnaire de l'Ancienne Langue Française,* there are several
examples of *endorer* with the non-culinary meaning.

*369* Osgood, who retained *lyþe₃* 'soothe', inserted [*wyth*]
into the text, but *coumforde* 'with (your) solace' may be inter-
preted as a synthetic dat. (See 342n for other examples.)
Emendation of *lyþe₃* to *kyþe₃* 'show' seems unnecessary. Hillmann
rendered *lyþe₃* 'yield'.

*375* Cf. 151n on *woþe₃* 'perils'. The *OED* s.v. *wothe* sb.
and a., 'the condition of being exposed to or liable to injury
or harm', cited *Pe.* Morris and Gollancz read 'path', Hillmann
and deFord 'search'. Wright (1939) 11-12 felt it would be con-
tradictory for the dreamer to think the maiden had been deliv-
ered from peril and yet say he never knew where she had gone,
but one must take into account the confused state of the dream-
er. (See Hieatt [1965] 140.) Besides, lines 248, 478, and
1187 show the dreamer was aware of earthly tribulations, and
line 376 may simply mean that though he knew the maiden had
died, he was uncertain of her place in eternal life. His en-
suing debate with her substantiates this view.

*378-80*  See 233n on personal touches in *Pe*.

*382*  Gollancz (1891c), following Morris, emended and tr.
*marreʒ mysse* 'grief woundeth me'.  Osgood retained *marereʒ*
'botcher's', tr., "I am worth no more than a botcher's blunder,
good for nothing."  (The *MED* s.v. *marrer* n. evidently followed
Osgood.)  An anonymous reviewer of Gollancz' edition (*Athenæum*
[1891] 185) and Holthausen (1893) 146 proposed emending to
*manereʒ* 'manners'; Gollancz (1921) was the first editor to
adopt this emendation.
     Schofield (1909) 663 suggested *mariereʒ* or *margereʒ*: "I am
but dust and lack margeries (pearls)," a reading accepted by
Hamilton (1958) 185 and Moorman.  Smithers (1948-49) 60-62
argued to retain the MS form by tr. *marereʒ mysse* 'dung-raker's
muck', deriving *marereʒ* from OF *marrier* 'a labourer who uses
a *marre*' (tool employed for gardening), and *mysse* from MDu.
*misse* (*messe*) 'manure, dung, dirt'.  Holman (1951), attempting
to authenticate Osgood's reading by citing Jeremias 18.1-6,
where the reference is to the potter making vessels of clay,
paraphrased, "I am only clay and a botcher's mistake; for I
was marred in the potter's hands."  Hillmann divided the word
into *mare reʒ* 'great eloquence (onrush of speech)'--ME *resse*
(*Pe*. 874), OE *ræs*--believing the dreamer was referring to his
lack of power of speech.
     However, *marereʒ* may be interpreted as a n. sg. variant
spelling of *OED marrow* sb.1, for which sense 2 lists various
fig. applications relating to spiritual 'vitality'.  (See also
*MED marwe* n.1, sense 3.)  There are spellings with -ʒ and -*w*,
and in this MS ʒ sometimes equals *w*: *folʒed* 127--*folewande*
1040.  A similar variant involving -*gh* occurs in *rescoghe*
(*Pe*. 610)--*rescowe* (*Ga*. 2308).  Cf. also the same sound in
three different spellings of the following three link-words
in *Pe*.: *inoghe* 612, *now* 613, and *innoʒe* 624.  The medial *e* of
*marereʒ* is simply an intervening vowel.  (Cf. *boroʒt* 628 and
*bereste* 854.)  There may be word-play involving *OED marrow*
sb.2 'companion', for the dreamer is lacking his pearl as a
companion.  Finally, one may compare 971 for the fig. applica-
tion.  There, when the maiden tells the dreamer he has no
*vygour* 'strength' to stride in the street of the New Jerusa-
lem, she is referring to his lack of spiritual vitality.

*383*  Gordon, who noted that the 'mercy' is Christ's, not
Mary's and John's, believed the poet had in mind the three
figures in the crucifixion scene.  Savage (1956b) 128 pointed
to the "rood on its screen in the parish church, with the
figures of Mary and [the apostle] John on either side of it."
Hamilton (1958) 185-86 thought it more likely that the line
refers to Mary and the apostle as they are portrayed in
scenes of the Last Judgment, praying for sinners.  (See also
*Ga*. 1788n.)

*386* For *mornyf* 'mournfully' as an adv. without *-ly*, cf.
*gracios* 'beautifully' 260 and *Cl*. 146n.

*388* Gordon glossed *harme₃ hate* 'hot grief', noting that
sorrows were traditionally hot in OE poetry, as in *The Sea-
farer*. Moorman noted Hillmann's 'burning wrongs'; Andrew &
Waldron tr. 'burning sorrows'. 'Cruel misfortunes' also suits
the context. For *hate* 'cruel', see *MED hōt* adj., sense 4b,
where *Pe*. is cited.

*393-96* Hamilton (1958) 186 felt that in the context of
this stanza-group (361-420), 'bliss' can only mean eternal
blessedness: "It goes without saying that a medieval Catholic
would have been liable to ecclesiastical censure for asserting
that the blessed condition of his child in heaven, or of any
other creature, was the foundation of all his bliss, the high-
way to his own beatitude." Because the maiden expresses un-
qualified approval in the next stanza, Hamilton believed the
dreamer must have been addressing his own soul. Her interpre-
tation, however, limits the sense of 'bliss', which can mean
mortal joy as well as beatitude. The former sense apparently
prevails in 372-73 and 396, the latter in 384-85, 397, 408,
and 420. There does not seem to be anything erroneous in the
dreamer's saying his greatest earthly happiness is knowing she
is eternally blessed. This attitude shows his spiritual prog-
ress, foreshadowing the end when he again expresses satisfac-
tion because of the maiden's blessed state (1185-88).

*399* Eds. read *byde* 'stay', but the first letter resembles
a spread *v* or *b*, or even a badly made *w*. *Vyde* may be a variant
of *wade* 143, 1151. The *OED* lists *wide* as a Scand. variant.
The *v* of *vyde*, pronounced *w*, is comparable to *vyf* 'wife' 772;
alliteration on *w* is retained in both lines. In 143 the
dreamer said he dared not 'wade' because the water was deep,
but he was thinking of crossing over then. In this passage,
the maiden's welcoming him to 'wade' on his side of the stream
may relate to a symbolic act of cleansing in preparation for
the time when he would be able to cross over. (Note line
405.)

*401-2* Cf. 309n. 'Pride', the first of the seven deadly
sins, contrasts with humility. In *Cl*. 205-34, Lucifer's pride
is the origin of sin. The maiden's approval of the dreamer
in this stanza stems from the spiritual progress he has made.
As Blenkner-C (1968) 267 stated, "The narrator's experience is
presented in terms which reveal a markedly consistent progres-
sion from the worldly to the religious point of view." (See
also 393-96n.)

*407* Reference to Christ as the sacrificial Lamb occurs

here for the first time. The qualities of the Lamb such as
innocence, spotlessness, meekness, and radiance are those quali-
ties which the pearl-maiden possesses. In 795-96 the Lord is
Lamb, Jewel, Joy, Glory, and Spouse.

*410 OED stage* sb., sense 3, defines 'degree or step in the
ladder of virtue or honor'. The poet here anticipates the
fuller view the dreamer will have of other blessed souls in
heaven, according to a hierarchical system. Note, for example,
453-66 and 1096-1128, and see 445-48n for further discussion.

*411-12* Lines 10 and 245 present images of the pearl's
slipping into grass. *OED shed* v.1 lists a variety of other
meanings: 'depart', relating to death; 'come apart', to a
decaying body; 'pour out' to loss of grace. (See Hamilton
[1958] 180 on the last sense.) Supporters of the elegiacal
theory see a personal reference in these lines. (Cf. 233 and
483-85.) The allegorists maintain that the pearl is here being
identified with the dreamer's soul, "spiritually immature," as
Hillmann says, when it fell to the ground.

*413-14* Madeleva (1925) 152-54 applied these lines only
to the religious, but, as Hillmann noted, it is the "teaching
of Catholic mysticism that Christ is the destined spiritual
Bridegroom of all souls of good will." (See lines 845-46.)
In 785-87 the maiden refers to herself as one of the Lamb's
wives of renown.

*415* Osgood's *brede* 'dwell' (OE *brēdan*) seems preferable
to Gordon's 'flourish' (OE *brǣdan*). *MED brēden* v.3, 3c, 'live,
dwell', cites *Pe.* One may consider double-entendre: *in blysse
to brede* 'to dwell in (heavenly) bliss' is 'to flourish in
spiritual blessedness'.

*417* See 703n for other examples of the poet's use of legal
terminology. Gordon compared *erytage* 443 and Rom. 8.16-17:
"Ipse enim Spiritus testimonium reddit spiritui nostro, quod
sumus filii Dei. Si autem filii, et heredes: heredes quidem
Dei, coheredes autem Christi; si tamen compatimur, ut et
conglorificemur." ("For the Spirit himself giveth testimony
to our spirit, that we are the sons of God. And if sons, heirs
also; heirs indeed of God, and joint-heirs with Christ: yet
so, if we suffer with him, that we may be also glorified with
him.") Reisner (1975) discussed this passage and what follows
in Stanza-Group VIII in relation to legal procedures in four-
teenth-century England.

*419* Eds. used stop punctuation at the end of 418 and read
*prese* 'great worth' (Gordon) instead of *pyese,* but what they
took for an *r* in the MS looks more like the top of a *y.* For

other examples of *y* with its bottom illegible, see the textual
note to *Kryst* 55, *Cl.* 32n, and Anderson's note on *spynde* in
*Pa.* 104, read as *sprude* by previous editors. Cf. *pyese* 'maiden'
to *pyece* in 192. *Prys* 'honored one' is a sb. adj.; cf. *prys*
(*Ga.* 1247) and *pryce* (*Cl.* 1308, 1614).

*422* Cf. 381-82 on the dreamer's awareness of his short-
comings.

*423* Neilson (1902a) 72-74, in an article associating *Pe.*,
*Awntyrs*, and *Erk.* as works of Huchown of the Awle Ryale, com-
pared Gregory's mistaking his mother for the queen of heaven
in the *Trentalle Sancti Gregorii*. Matthews (1960) 208-9,
noting similarities between *Ga.* and the *Awntyrs*, suggested
they may be due to the influence of *Ga.* on the latter poem.
See also Hanna (1974) 14-16 for discussion of similar verse
techniques in *Pe.*, *Ga.*, and the *Awntyrs*. (On pp. 44-46, he
noted parallels in the descriptions of the deer hunts in the
two romances.)

*425* *Grace* here refers to Christ. Hillmann, correcting
Osgood's note, pointed out that, according to Catholic doc-
trine, Mary is sometimes called the "Channel of Grace," but
the "Source of Grace" is God alone.

*426* Whiteley (1931) asked if *of Vyrgin Flour* meant "out
of a spotless virginity" or "a child of purest excellence"?
Fairchild (1931) supported the second meaning, favored only
by Moorman among previous editors. See the citations s.v.
*MED flóur* n.1, fig., sense 1c (c), 'with reference to the
Christ child'. *Flour*, in post. c. for rhyme, parallels *Grace*
425. Christ's qualities on a grand scale relate to those of
the pearl-maiden on a smaller scale. She is both flower and
gem, just as Jesus is called *Flour* here and *Juelle* in 795 and
1124. (Cf. 269-72n and 407n.)

*429-30* Osgood, p. xxi, noted that Blanche is called
Phoenix of Araby in Chaucer's *Book of the Duchess* (982).
The phoenix, a bird of Egyptian legend, which burned itself
and rose from its own ashes, is a medieval symbol usually
representing Christ. However, as Fletcher (1921) 15-16 ob-
served, Albertus Magnus compared Mary to the phoenix in *De
Laudibus Beatae Mariae Virginis* VII, iii, 1: "Maria una sola
est mater et virgo. Unde et comparatur phoenici, quae est
unica avis sine patre."

*431* Gordon corrected previous editors who had equated
*Fasor* with *fasure* 'appearance' (1084). Hillmann (1943) 43
first noted the analogy between Mary and the phoenix is that
Mary, born free from original sin by divine grace, was imma-

culate at conception. Hillmann tr. *hyr* 'its', but the phoenix
symbol was used in the medieval period for both Christ's death
and resurrection and Mary's purity and virginity, and the con-
text of 429-32 favors fem. usage.

   *Freles* 'without fault' (*MED frēlēs* adj.), given by most
editors, is fitting. Hamilton (1958) 187 suggested emending
to *fer(e)les* 'without equal'; Luttrell (1962a) 448, Moorman,
and Andrew & Waldron supported this reading. However, the
sense 'faultless' applies well to the Immaculate Conception
of Mary. Emerson (1927) 820-21 suggested derivation from OF
*frele*, with addition of *-les* and coalescing of the *l*'s. Gor-
don, p. 100, favored derivation from ON *frẏjulaust*.

   *432* The form of *Cortaysye,* the link-word in this stanza-
group, varies. Note *cortayse* adj. (433). In 445 *court* is the
link-word. As Gordon noted, the primary meaning of *Cortaysye*
is divine grace. Mary, "from whom Grace came" (425), "Blessed
Beginner of every grace" (436), may aptly be called "Queen of
Courtesy." The pearl-maiden, too, possesses divine grace as
one of the queens in heaven (468). *Cortaysye* also connotes
charity and pity, and Mary is the mediatrix between God and
men who seek his mercy. In lines 467-68 souls in heaven live
*wyth luf ... by cortaysye*; lines 469-70 refer to *cortaysé* and
*charyté*.

   Milroy (1971) 203 noted the significance of the *caritas*
expounded by St. Paul in 1 Cor. 13, closely related to 1 Cor.
12.12-27, upon which *Pe.* 457-66 is based. The absence of *gawle*
'envy' 463 in the heavenly souls points up their great
*cortaysye*. As Paul says in 1 Cor. 13.4, "caritas non aemula-
tur" ("charity envieth not"). For further discussion of the
poet's use of *cortaysye*, see also Brewer (1966), Evans (1967),
and Matsui (1971).

   *433* The *OED* lists *sede* as a pt. form of *say*, and in this
MS *y* sometimes varies with *e*. (Cf. 229n.)

   *434* For *folde* 'covering' as a pp. tr. prog., see 54n.
Gollancz thought the maiden was covering her face in the hang-
ing folds of her garment. Andrew & Waldron followed Gordon
who rendered *folde vp hyr face* 'with her face upturned'.
Moorman agreed with Hillmann who suggested the maiden was
"covering her face with her hands," in "horror at the jeweler's
ignorant but blasphemous question" (423). Hillmann's gloss
is fitting, but the maiden's movement may be taken as a ges-
ture of humble adoration for Mary, not horror over the dream-
er's question.

   *435* The pearl-maiden is called *may* in 780 and 961. In
*Ga.* 1795 *may* refers to Bercilak's wife. (See *Ga.* 1795n.)

*436*  Mary is the 'Beginner' of every grace in that she gave birth to Jesus.  (See 425n.)

*439*  Gordon compared the metaphor of the race in St. Paul's 1 Cor. 9.24-25.  Oakden (1968) 345-46, discussing liturgical influence of the Septuagesima cycle, noted that the maiden has on the incorruptible crown of salvation mentioned by Paul. (See 451n.)  Andrew & Waldron's tr. (like Gordon's and Hillmann's), "Sir, here many strive for and win a prize," makes it seem as if those in heaven have need to strive for a reward.  Rendering *here* as dat. 'for here' (heaven) in relation to *porchase₃* 'strive' makes it clear that the striving is done before one enters heaven, which is the reward.

*444*  The dreamer first called Mary *Quen of Cortaysye* (432), showing he was not ignorant of basic Christian doctrines.  The poet presents his persona as one who needs to accept much of what he knows, but his emotions stand in the way.  See 51-56. In the end he does accept.  See 1199-1200.

*445-48*  Fisher (1961) 151-52 cited these lines to point out in *Pe*. the recognition of grades in the hierarchy of heaven, a hierarchy "mystically resolved into equality."  This stanza and the next anticipate the Parable of the Vineyard (501-72), dealing with the concept that all receive the same reward regardless of how much work they do, a concept that is complicated by the difficulty of reconciling this "same reward" with the hierarchical doctrine.  All attain salvation and are happy to the fullness of their capacity to be happy.  In this sense, all are equally content.  Yet, there are ranks in heaven, as lines 453-66 and 1096-1128 show.  (See also 603-4n.)
  The maiden herself holds a special position as a young virgin.  One may compare glasses of different sizes filled to the brim.  The glasses are souls, and the liquid inside represents happiness.  Though all are filled to capacity, the larger ones contain more than the smaller.  For a similar comparison using the 'pint-pot and the quart-pot' metaphor, Moorman (1968) 48 cited Dorothy L. Sayers, *Introductory Papers on Dante* (New York, 1954), p. 57.  See also Gordon, pp. xxiv-xxv, for refutation of the view that *Pe*. contains heresy because it asserts that the heavenly reward is the same for all.

*445-52*  Blanch (1973) 74 compared "The London Lapidary of King Philip" in *English Mediaeval Lapidaries,* ed. Joan Evans and Mary S. Serjeantson, *EETS, OS* 190 (1933), pp. 19-20: "nyne ordres of angeles þat lyven in þat joye þat noon hath enuye of othre, þat is þe life corouned, in þe which shal noon entre but he be kyng corouned or quene, for all be corouned be name."

*451*  Osgood compared 849, where the concept and choice of

the number five are similar. The crown, which represents the maiden's virginity in 767, here typifies the incorruptible crown of salvation. (See 205n, 253-55n, and 439n.)

*457-66* Pilch-C (1964) 177 observed that in this passage, based on 1 Cor. 12.12-27, the body of Christ, considered by its members, symbolizes the hierarchy of the heavenly society. The poet's method here is abbreviatio. He ordinarily employed amplificatio, as in lines 501-72 paraphrasing Matt. 20.1-16. See Parr (1970) for a full discussion of "Rhetoric and Symbol in the *Pearl*."

*459* Only Morris and Osgood among the editors glossed *naule* 'nail'. Osgood believed 'navel' offended poetic delicacy, but medieval writers did not regard the image in this way. As Fletcher (1921) 2 noted, Albertus Magnus compared the Virgin Mary's navel to a wine-cup in the hand of the Holy Ghost in *De Laudibus Beatae Mariae Virginis* V, ii, 68.

*460* Osgood's retention of *tyste* as a variant of *ty3te* 'tight' has not been accepted. Gordon, who emended to *tryste* 'faithfully', noted that there is no instance in the MS of *st* for *3t*. For *tyste* 'joined', cf. *OED tissed* ppl. a. (OF *tistre*), used in association with weaving. The citation in the *OED* is 1585, but *tissed* stems from *tissue* sb. and v., for which there are ME quotations. For other examples of unvoicing of *-d* to *-t*, see 10n. The poet may have related the sense 'joined' (or 'woven together') to parts of the body, as in 1 Cor. 12.24: "Deus temperavit corpus ei." ("God hath tempered the body together.")

*462* Morris suggested *myste* 'mysteries', and the *OED* cited *Pe.* s.v. *mist* sb.2, comparing *misty* a.2, 'characteristic of spiritual mysteries'. Osgood, Gollancz, and Hillmann took *myste* as a variant of *my3te* 'might', but Gordon, who again noted the unlikelihood of *st* being used for *3t*, glossed 'spiritual mysteries', comparing *spiritualibus* in 1 Cor. 12.1. Moorman and Andrew & Waldron adopted this reading. Wright (1939) 12, following Emerson (1922) 70, interpreted *myste* (OF *miste* adj.) as a sb. adj. and tr. *Mayster of myste* 'Master of gentility'. Murtaugh (1971), citing *OED mist* sb.3, a shortened form of *mister* sb.1, 'occupation, service', proposed 'Master of ministries'. The poet may have been employing his characteristic word-play on more than one meaning, but there is sufficient evidence to support Morris' original suggestion as the primary sense.

*463* *Gawle,* agreeing with *sawle* 461, is apparently a variant spelling of *galle* 'rancor' 915 (*MED galle* n.1, sense 3a), where the context again favors the meaning related to the vice. *Galle* 189, 1060 (*MED galle* n.2, sense 2a) denotes physical impurity. (The *MED* cited *Pe.* 189 under n.1 and 463 under n.2, but these placements should apparently be reversed.)

*464* Cf. the fig. use of *tachched* 'rooted' in *Ga.* 2512 and see the note.

*472* Gollancz supplied: [Me þynk þou speke₃ now ful wronge.] Consider also: *To speke of a nwe note I long.* "I desire to speak of a new matter." However, as Crawford (1967) 118 noted, the missing line is perhaps prescribal. "The poet may have avoided formal perfection for fear of excessive vanity offending God." Nelson (1973) 33 added: "*Pearl*'s partial roundness, aching for completion, is the emblem of a flawed circle. It is an appropriate vehicle for our fallen perception--for the poet's expression of his vision and our experience of it."

*479* For *ho* 'he', see *MED hē* pron. 1, where *ho* is listed as a variant spelling, and cf. *ho* 'he' in *Ga.* 1389. Morris tr. *ho* 'she', paraphrasing, "He desires to know what greater honour she can have."

*481* Andrew & Waldron, following Hillmann, rendered *Cortayse* as a sb. adj. 'Courteous One' (God), but one may place an accent over *-é* in *cortaysé*, as Gordon did, and consider the n. 'courtesy' as a personification in this line.

*483-85* Morris, Osgood, Gollancz, and Gordon believed these lines refer to a child who died before the age of two. Osgood noted that clergymen were instructed to teach people, especially children, the Pater Noster and the Creed. Madeleva (1925) 160-64 argued that a novice in the religious life could be considered a child since she would know no more than the rudiments, after two years, in a series of spiritual meditations that needed to be learned along with the Pater and the Creed.

Hillmann maintained that the dreamer, in his confused state, thought he was addressing his lost material pearl imported from the Orient only two years before and personified in the maiden, who really represents his soul. Carson (1965), noting that the learning of prayers would be required for a newly baptized adult who had come to England from another land, interpreted "*Pearl* as an elegy in which the poet laments not the loss of a two-year old daughter but that of a girl with whom his relationship is romantic rather than paternal" (17).

However, the statement in 483 that the maiden lived not two years in the land, taken with 412: "I was very young and tender of age," does not seem to fit an adult. Madeleva and Hillmann showed that simple vocal prayers were recommended for the early stages of conversion, but lines 484-85 say that the maiden could not pray, "Not ever either Pater or Creed," and one might expect that after almost two years a novice or a convert would have learned something.

*488* Gollancz compared 350. The poet continues to show the dreamer's obtuseness.

*489* Spearing-B (1962) 113 compared line 211, noting that a countess is the wife of an earl: the dreamer "is unable to conceive of a hierarchy in any other than these familiar terms."

*492* Gollancz, Gordon, and Moorman rendered *date* 'goal', Hillmann 'term', Andrew & Waldron 'rank'. Cf. the sense 'beginning' to *date* 'dawning' 517. In 486 the dreamer doubted that the maiden could be made a queen on the first day.

*497-98* The reference is to the Gospel for Septuagesima Sunday. Oakden (1968) 343-45 and Bishop (1968) 124-25 discussed liturgical influence in *Pe*. As Oakden noted, since Septuagesima forms the beginning of the second part of the ecclesiastical year comprising the seasons of Lent, Passiontide, and Easter, it fit the poet's theme of mortality, death, and resurrection. See also Gatta (1974) on "Transformation Symbolism and the Liturgy of the Mass in *Pearl*."

*499* Joining MS *in sample* (*MED ensaumple* n., 3a, 'parable') clarifies *he* as a reference to Christ.

*501-72* Placed near the center of the poem, the Parable of the Vineyard (Matt. 20.1-16) illustrates why the pearl-maiden, who lived such a short time on earth (the vineyard), received the same reward (the penny representing the Beatific Vision) as those who endured a lifetime of struggle. In fact, due to her innocence and God's grace, her rank in heaven is higher than many.

*503-4* Osgood rendered *terme* 'end', believing the reference is to the grape-harvest in mid-autumn. Gordon's *terme* 'appointed period' and *date* 'season' appear to be the proper meanings. Kean (1967) 52, citing the description of the work being done in line 512, noted that the season is March, as shown in *Très Riches Heures du Duc de Berry*. *MED lāb̆ouren* v., 1b, 'to cultivate (vines)', substantiates this interpretation.

*505* As Gordon noted, þys may be rendered 'these'. (Cf. þis worteȝ 'these plants' 42.) *Hyne* is then n. coll. Gollancz *hyne* 'household' may be the correct sense, but the poet's general meaning apparently includes all members of households. Cf. *MED hīne* n., 1b, 'a religious familia, monastic community' in

place names. The *patrifamilias* of Matt. 20.1 means "house-
holder', the sense given by Hillmann, but the poet sometimes
altered Biblical details. (Cf. 163n.) Osgood, Gordon, Moor-
man, and Andrew & Waldron rendered *hyne* 'laborers' in agree-
ment with *MED* 2b.

512  Hillmann tr. *man hit clos* 'gather the harvest', but
this is not the grape-harvest season. (See 503-4n.) *Keruen*
denotes the pruning of the vines, which are also being bound
and made secure. For coll. *hit* 'them', see *MED hit* pron.,
2f.

513  *Vnder* 'the third hour' is about nine o'clock in the
morning.

518  Gollancz' *soჳt* 'given' (OE *sōhte*, pa. t. of *sēcan*),
followed by Gordon, Moorman, and Andrew & Waldron, seems ap-
propriate. Osgood and Hillmann glossed 'sighed, murmured'
(OE *swōgan*).

523-24  Eds. rendered *hyre* 'wage, reward', but *MED hīr(e*
n., 2d, 'service', is fitting, and MS *pray* 'ask' may be re-
tained. Hillmann construed 522-23 together as part of the
narrative, retained *pray,* and tr. 524: "I call on you through
bond and intent."

529  As Savage (1956b) 128 noted, this line may stand
without emendation. For *at* 'during', see *MED at* prep., 4a.
'Evensong' is the *undeciman* 'eleventh hour' (about 5 P.M.) of
Matt. 20.6, the sixth in a system of seven canonical hours
and the time for celebrating vespers. See 19-22n for dis-
cussion of the possibility that *sange* denotes the chanting
of vespers. The poet may have foreshadowed there the maid-
en's entrance into the vineyard (earth) about the eleventh
hour (581-82) and her immediate reward (583-84).

532  MS *hen* may be retained as coll. usage of *MED hīne*
n., 2b, 'a farm laborer'. The *MED* lists *hen(e* as a variant
spelling.

535  The words *ჳe* and *men* run together in the MS, but so
do they in 290 where they obviously had to be separated.
Editors tr. *ჳemen* 'hired laborers, yeomen'.

536  Gollancz defined *at* 'which' as a Northern rel. pron.
from ON *at.* Gordon interpreted þ*at at* as a development of
þ*at þat* because *at* "does not occur as a relative elsewhere
in this group of poems." However, cf. *at* 'which' in *Ga.*
2205.

*538* Hillmann retained *and and*, tr. 'and when'. Cf. *Ga.* 2137n.

*546* Most editors tr. *inlyche* 'alike, equally'. Hillmann followed Hamilton (1958) 188-89 who noted that *inlyche* occurs only in *Pe.* and is better rendered 'fully' here and in line 603. This reading suits the interpretation of the Parable of the Vineyard more exactly, since each soul receives 'fully' the reward of salvation, even though there are ranks in the hierarchical system of heaven. (See 603-4n for further discussion.) The *MED* cited *Pe.* s.v. *inlīche* adv., 'alike, equally', but lines 546 and 603 would be better listed s.v. *inlī* adv., 1c, 'wholly'. The variant spelling *inliche* appears there.

*552* Macrae-Gibson-C (1968) 210 noted the significance of the link-word *more* in this stanza-group in relation to its use as the link in Group III. The dreamer then yearned for more and more (144-45). In 599-600 he will take up the complaint of the laborers who thought they should have received more, but by the end of the poem (1189-1200) he will accept God's will concerning *more and lasse* (601).

*555* Matt. 20.12 reads: "Hi novissimi una hora fecerunt." ("These last have worked *but* one hour.") The poet paraphrases this verse in 551 but adds 555 to remind us that the maiden "lyfed not two ȝer in oure þede" (483).

*558* Morris emended *wanig* to *wrang*, which accords with Matt. 20.13: "Amice, non facio tibi iniuriam." ("Friend, I do thee no wrong.") Most editors emended to *waning* 'diminution, loss'. Hillmann tr., "Friend, I will not concede thee lacking," but her derivation of *wanig* from OE *wan* plus *-ig* is doubtful. Emerson (1927) 822, crediting Fick, noted that *OED waning* vbl. sb. (OE *wanung*) could render the Vulgate's *iniuriam*. See sense 1b, 'damage inflicted by a person'. Emerson also suggested that *ȝete* is the v. represented by *MED gēten* v.1, for which the variant spelling *ȝeten* is listed. Cf. in *Cl.* *ȝat* 66 and *ȝete* 842. Moorman followed Fowler (1959) 582 who took *waning* from OE *wānung* and tr., "Friend, I will allow thee no lamentation," but Emerson's interpretation seems preferable.

*565* Emerson (1927) 822-23 noted that the emendations made by Osgood and Gollancz were unnecessary. *Louyly* 'proper' (*MED lŏvelī* adj., 2c) renders closely enough *licet* 'lawful' (Matt. 20.15). Gordon, Hillmann, Moorman, and Andrew & Waldron considered *louyly* a variant spelling of *laȝely* 'lawful'. Gollancz, Gordon, and Hillmann rendered *more* 'moreover', but it may be tr. 'more' as a modifier of *louyly*, with *weþer* 'and yet' (*OED whether* adv.) intervening. For *gyfte* 'right to give', see *OED gift* sb., I.1.

*568* *Byswyke3* is the Northern form of the pr. 1 sg. in this syntax. Gordon noted that when a pron. was the subject of more than one v., the second v. ended in -(e)*s,* no matter what the person of the pron. was. This point was also made by both Gollancz and an anonymous reviewer of his editions of *Pearl* and *Cleanness* in *TLS* (1922): 18 May, p. 319; 25 May, p. 343; and 1 June, p. 364.

*570-72* Cf. Matt. 20.16: "Sic erunt novissimi primi, et primi novissimi; multi enim sunt vocati, pauci vero electi." ("So shall the last be first, and the first last. For many are called, but few chosen.") The second part of the Vulgate's verse also appears in Matt. 22.14 at the end of the Parable of the Wedding Feast, paraphrased in *Cl.* 51-160. (In *Cl.* 162 the poet includes only that many are called to that feast.)

A key to the interpretation of *Pe.* may be in Augustine's "Sermo LXXXVII," *PL* 38.533, tr. by Robertson-C (1950a) 295: "We shall all be equal in that reward, the last like the first, and the first like the last. For that penny is eternal life, and all will be equal in eternal life. Although they will be radiant with a diversity of merits, one more, one less, that which pertains to eternal life will be equal to all." Augustine's writing, as Robertson noted, explains the doctrine of hierarchy in heaven: all receive salvation, but there are different degrees of glory in God's kingdom. (Cf. also 1 Cor. 15.41.)

*Myke3,* which renders the Vulgate's *electi,* may have special significance for the pearl-maiden whose place in heaven is higher than many. See, for example, 577-80. Hamilton (1958) 187-88 supported Gordon's interpretation of *myke3* as an aphetic form of *amike* 'friend' (L *amicus*), with the extended sense 'chosen companions of the Lord'. Hillmann tr. *myke3* 'chosen ones', but suggested derivation from OE *mæcca* 'companion'.

*574* Eds. took *wore* as a variant of *were* and rendered *lyttel* 'lowly, unimportant', but *were* is pt., and this tense does not accord well with the tenses of the other verbs in 573-76. *Wore* 'expend' may be a variant of *OED ware* v.2, found in *Ga.* 402, 1235.

*581-82* The pearl-maiden is one who toiled the least in the vineyard, one who came at the eleventh hour, almost at the time of evening. (See 529n.) Osgood considered Augustine's interpretation in *PL* 38.533 an inversion of these lines because Augustine says the ones called at the eleventh hour are those who became Christians when they were decrepit. However,

Robertson-C (1950a) 293-94, noting that later commentators
frequently changed details without changing the basic meaning
or *sentence,* cited and tr. Bruno Astensis, twelfth century,
for an interpretation that fits *Pearl*: "But the eleventh hour
is the hour at which one of whatever age begins to serve when
he approaches his end and is near death. Not only the youth-
ful and the aged, but also even children have this hour" (*PL*
165.237). As Robertson noted, the pearl-maiden is, therefore,
simply stressing the fact that she was baptized only shortly
before death. See also Bishop (1968) 122-25, who cited the
interpretation of the Parable of the Vineyard by Honorius 'of
Autun' in *PL* 172.858. Honorius specifically included those
who die as infants in the same category as those who are con-
verted "in decrepita aetate."

   *588* In contrast to the maiden who went to heaven immedi-
ately (584), those who lived longer and committed sin had a
debt to pay. (See 617-22.) As Hillmann noted, the reference
is apparently to purgatory where souls not entirely cleansed
of sin must endure a fixed term. Most editors tr. *toȝere*
'this year', but *to ȝere more* 'for years more' seems prefer-
able. (See 35n for examples of connected words in the MS that
need to be separated.)

   *591* Emerson (1922) 74 suggested *rert* 'fixed, established'
(Hillmann). Moorman and Andrew & Waldron favored 'upraised,
supreme' (Gollancz and Gordon).

   *595-96* Cf. Ps. 61.12-13: "Semel locutus est Deus; duo
haec audivi: quia potestas Dei est,/et tibi, Domine, miseri-
cordia; quia tu reddes unicuique iuxta opera sua." ("God hath
spoken once, these two things have I heard, that power belong-
eth to God,/and mercy to thee, O Lord; for thou wilt render
to every man according to his works.") The line under *p* of
*pertermynable* is the abbr. for *er.* Though Gordon, following
earlier editors and the *OED*, read *pretermynable* 'foreordain-
ing', he suggested *pertermynable* from ME *termyne* v., with
*per* as an intensive prefix, to express the concept *quia potes-
tas Dei est.* The sense '(power of) judging perfectly' relates
to God's justice being 'forever fixed' (591). The reference
is only to the *poynt* (594) concerned with God's power, not to
the second point in Ps. 61.13 concerned with the Lord's mercy,
for the dreamer must still learn, in the next stanza-group
(601-660), that the grace of God is great enough for the inno-
cent child.
   *Pertermynable* 'judging perfectly' is derived from the *OED*
prefix 1 *per-,* I.2, 'thoroughly' plus *terminable* a. from
*termine* v., sense 1, 'to determine'. Kaske (1959) 418-21,
supporting Gordon's suggestion, tr. 'speaking or declaring
enduringly'. Hillmann read *Pretermynable* 'Infinite (Before

the terminable)', comparing, among other Biblical verses, Ps.
73.12. Andrew & Waldron, crediting Kean (1967) 191, glossed
*pertermynable* 'supreme in judgment'.

*603-4* All editors, except Hillmann and Moorman, tr.
*inlyche* 'alike, equally'. For tr. 'fully', see 546n. All are
'fully' compensated in having gained heaven, but 'little or
much' may be the reward because various individuals have dif-
ferent ranks. For discussion of the system of hierarchy in
heaven, see also the notes to 410, 445-48, 546, and 570-72.
   C. Brown (1904) 133-37 believed the poet was following the
fourth-century heretic Jovinian, who asserted that the heavenly
rewards are equal. Osgood, pp. xxxix-xl, though he accepted
Brown's interpretation, felt it was "at variance with the
poet's social ideas," especially since the orthodox view is
clearly implied in *Cl.* 113-24. Fletcher (1921) 17-19 refuted
Brown, noting passages in *Pe.* that prove the poet was in accord
with the prevalent Christian doctrine of graded heavenly re-
wards. See, for example, 577-80, where the pearl-maiden speaks
of having more *blysse* than others, and 887, which indicates the
*aldermen* are closer to God's throne than she is. For further
discussion refuting Brown, see also Sledd (1940) 381, Hamilton
(1943) 372, and Hillmann's 603-6n. For an attempt to revive
Brown's argument, see Oiji (1961) 46-57.

*606 Nesch oþer harde*, as Gordon observed in his 603-4n,
probably refers to God's way of meting out rewards and punish-
ments. However, it does not seem that the distinction here is
between salvation and eternal damnation. *Harde* may imply
punishment for sinners who must endure the penalty of atone-
ment. See 661-64. Wellek-B (1933) 25-26 discussed *gratia
prima*, free grace given by God in baptism to remit original
sin, and *gratia secunda*, additional grace given in proportion
to one's merits. The grown-up person may lose his title to
free grace by sinning or add to his title by performing good
works. The maiden speaks of those who forfeit their title in
617-22.

*607-8* Cf. the water symbolism here to the stream flowing
from God's throne (107, 934, 974, 1055-60) and the baptismal
water (627) springing from Christ's wound (647-55). In con-
trast, the simile involving water in 364-65 perhaps represents
the dreamer's loss of grace, due to despair. Gordon's "streams
from a deep source that has never ceased to flow" (608) is
fitting, but *goteȝ* may denote 'currents', as in *Cl.* 413, *MED
gŏulf*, sense b, defines 'whirlpool', and *chāren* v.1, 3a, lists
'to change or vary in character, condition, or attitude'. Cf.
this simile depicting God's grace going around in a circle to
pure souls with the description of the *garlande gay* (1186).

*609-10*  Cf. the sense given here to Gordon's: "That man's
privilege is great who ever stood in awe of Him who rescues
sinners." Mitchell (1964) supported this reading, pointing to
*MED fraunchīs(e* n., 1c, 'spiritual freedom; esp., the privi-
leged state of Adam and Eve before the fall'. *Dard* is the pt.
of *dare* 839. *Hym* refers to the *gentyl Cheuentayn* (605),
Christ who died on the cross to save mankind after the sin of
Adam. (See 637-60.)

Visser-C (1958), by comparing other ME auxil. verbs used
to connote motion, defined *dard* 'dared to go' and tr., "That
man's privilege is great who (at a certain moment in his life)
had the courage to go or turn to Him [God] who rescues sin-
ners." Kaske (1959) 422-25, basing his interpretation on
John 1.14, 16-18, the concept of the Word made flesh, pro-
posed the following sense: The liberality of Him Who was ever
hidden (God the Father) is abundant to Him Who makes rescue
in sin (God the Son).

Andrew & Waldron, attempting to avoid a "clash between
sing. *Hys* and pl. *hem* (611)," tr. 609-12: "His (God's) gene-
rosity is great (*or* abundant): those who at any time in their
lives submitted to Him who rescues sinners--from them no bliss
will be withheld, for the grace of God is great enough." How-
ever, the poet sometimes switched from sg. to pl. (see 687-
88n), and Gordon's reading seems suitable here.

*612*  The emphasis on God's grace in this Stanza-Group XI
anticipates Group XII, especially the climactic concept, ex-
tending into XIII, of one's not being able to enter heaven
unless he come there as a child (709-28). C. Brown (1904)
129-30 noted that the poet, in stressing God's grace for sal-
vation, sided with the English theologian Thomas Bradwardine
(died 1349), whose *De Causa Dei contra Pelagium* opposed Semi-
Pelagianism. The followers of Pelagianism held that merit
acquired by right conduct was more important than divine grace
to obtain salvation.

*613-16*  Wood (1973), regarding these lines as a paraphrase
of 551-56, in which the early-comers to the vineyard complain,
associated the dreamer with the early-comers and argued that
critics, while overstressing his sorrow at losing his pearl,
have "given too little attention to the resentment and envy
with which he regards her present good fortune" (9). Wood
compared the dreamer to Old Man (Adam) in relation to Old
Law (Old Testament) concepts, until he learns the lesson of
grace taught by the maiden.

*613*  Chase accepted the emendation of *now* to *inow* by
Emerson (1927) 824, and Macrae-Gibson-C (1968) 210 supported
it, but Gordon pointed out that the link is not broken, since
*now* echoes *inoghe* 612 in sound. Cf. the echoing of sound,

not a repetition of the same word, in *court* 445, following
*Cortaysye* 444.

*616* Osgood and Gollancz, following Morris' suggestion,
emended *lere* to *here* (variant of *hyre* 'wage'). Gordon, fol-
lowed by Cawley, Moorman, and Andrew & Waldron, emended to
*fere* 'fortune, rank, dignity' (OF *afeire*). Hillmann tr. MS
*lere* 'recompense', considering it a variant of *MED lūre* n.1.
For *lere* 'abode', see *MED leir* n.1, sense e, 'a place where
someone dwells'. The poet perhaps anticipates here *heuene3*
*clere* (620), the maiden's abode.

*617* Most editors considered *abate* a variant of *abyde*
'endure' (OE *ābīdan*), but derivation from OF *abatre* seems
preferable. Emerson (1922) 75, though he took *abate* as a pp.
rather than an infin., suggested sense 1b, 'to bow humbly',
s.v. *MED abāten, -i(en*, where *Pe.* is cited. Hillmann tr. 'to
lose zeal' (*MED* 4b), thinking it would be contrary to Christ-
ián teaching for the maiden to say that "no matter how prayer-
ful a man's life may be, he will at some time fall into sin."
However, the maiden is apparently merely asking the dreamer
if he ever knew any man who did not sin during his lifetime,
even though he prayed often, for men ordinarily lose their
innocence as they grow older (621-22), whereas the maiden,
having died soon after being baptized, never lost her inno-
cence. (See 625-32.) As Fletcher (1921) 4 observed, the
grown person can humble himself like a child through contri-
tion, but "he is not *by nature* one with the perfect exemplar
of Innocence, Christ, as is the little child."

*625* The reference to baptism in 627 favors reading 'inno-
cent child' here, just as the context of 711-28 favors that
reading in 720. See *MED innocent* n., sense e.

*626* Emerson (1927) 824 supported Morris' *lyne* 'lineage',
which seems fitting here. Most editors placed a comma after
*borne* and rendered *lyne* 'regular order' (Osgood) or 'order of
birth' (Hillmann).

*630* *To,* governing *niy3t,* is in post. c. Gordon noted
that the spelling *niy3t* occurs in *Ga.* 929 and *Cl.* 1779.

*632* Cf. coll. *hyne* 'servants' 1211, and the idea at the
end of the poem that God's 'servants' are 'precious pearls'
*vnto his pay.*

*635* Concerning the first word in this line, Osgood, who
edited from photographs, wrote, "I am at a loss for the in-
tended reading." Examination of the original MS under the
ultra-violet lamp substantiates Gollancz' *3ys* in his 1921

edition.  (He read ʒy[ld] in his 1891 edition.)

Gordon, Moorman, and Andrew & Waldron, following Wright
(1939) 16, took *at þe fyrst* as an adv. phr., *fyne* as an adv.,
and tr. 'pay them first in full'.  Hillmann adopted Gollancz'
'at the first day's close'.  Revard (1964) interpreted *fyne*
as a n. and tr. 'according to the original contract'.  How-
ever, *fyne* 'completely' may be rendered adverbially, and *fyrst*
as a n. refers to the 'first group' who came into the vine-
yard, *þe fyrst* (549) who began to complain when they learned
that the others were going to receive a penny also.

Davis (1954) 98 noted that emendation of *hym* to *hem* is
unnecessary, since *hym* is occasionally used as a pl. form in
this MS.  (See 229n.)

*639*  The *forme-fader* Adam is named specifically in 656.
Osgood compared 639-45 to *St. Erkenwald* 294-98.  Cf. also
*Cl.* 235-48.

*648*  God's grace to cleanse and save mankind flowed in
both the blood Christ shed at his crucifixion and the water
mingled with blood spurting from his side (646-47).  The mai-
den explains this symbolism in the next stanza, a symbolism
that recalls the stream (107), separating the terrestrial
paradise from the heavenly, and anticipates the Lamb's shed-
ding of blood (741) and the pearl-maiden's garment being
cleansed by this blood (766).  See Rev. 7.14-17 and 22.14-17
for the basis of this blood and water symbolism, and Johnson-C
(1953) 41 for discussion of the imagery.

*652*  The *deth secounde,* as Hillmann noted, refers to the
condemnation of souls at the Last Judgment.  See Rev. 2.11,
20.6, 20.14, and 21.8.

*654*  As Gollancz observed, this incident in John 19.34 is
amplified in the apocryphal gospel of Nicodemus.  Longinus,
whose name corresponds to the Greek term for 'lance', was the
soldier who pierced Christ's side.

*655*  Eds. rendered *gylteʒ* as a pl. n., but Otten (1971)
suggested reading *gylteʒ* 'of sin' as a gen. and *felle* as a
n. (Latin *fel* 'gall, bitterness'--*MED fel(le)* n.).  Noting
that the reference is to Adam's singular original sin, Otten
compared *þe olde gulte* (942) and cited patristic and liturgi-
cal sources, among them Tertullian's *De Baptismo* in which
baptismal water is mentioned in conjunction with the spear
that pierced Christ's side.

*656  Wyth,* governing *þat* 'which', is a prep. in post c.

*658*  Most editors took *he* as a reference to God, but

Hillmann, with deFord and Moorman in agreement, pointed out
that the logical and grammatical antecedent of *he* is *Adam*
(656).

*659* As Hillmann noted, *sely stounde* refers to the time
when baptism is received.

*661-64* See Osgood's note (660ff.) for discussion of the
doctrine. The person who, living in this world, sins after
being baptized, commits what is called 'actual sin', different
from the 'original sin' cleansed by baptism. 'Actual sin' is
forgiven by the sacrament of penance, if the guilty one is
contrite (669-70). The baptized innocent child is saved with-
out need of penance, in contrast to the person who is always
in danger of sinning the older he becomes (617-22).

*665* Osgood glossed *resoun* 'fair consideration', noting
that the personified *Resoun* in *P. Pl.*, Passus IV, is distin-
guished for his justice. (See the A-text, lines 117-45.)
Gordon followed Gollancz' tr., "but Reason, straying not from
right." Hillmann tr. 'sentence of justice'. Andrew & Waldron
capitalized *Resoun* and commented, "God is here portrayed as a
quasi-personification of reason." However, rendering *resoun
of ry3t* 'cause of justice' also suits the context.

*672* Hillmann noted that MS *at* may be retained by tr. *at
inoscente* 'with (the) innocent'. Gordon's *ry3te* 'justified,
sanctified by divine grace' reveals the double-entendre of
this link-word, involving two senses of *OED right* sb.1: (I)
'just or equitable treatment' (strict justice); and (II)
'justifiable claim, on legal or moral grounds, to have or
obtain something' (one's privilege). In 684, 696, and 720,
when the pearl-maiden says, "The innocent one (child) is
always redeemed by right," she evidently means the privilege
the innocent have through justification by divine grace. This
privilege applies with certainty to the child who dies soon
after baptism. In 708 *ry3te* 'justice' concludes a stanza that
shows the ordinary man, so liable to sin on earth, should not
presume to enter heaven on the grounds of strict justice, but
must first become like the innocent child (717-28).

*673-76* The poet apparently distinguishes between the
righteous man who enters heaven through penance (661-64) and
the innocent one who joins God immediately. The doctrine of
hierarchy may be implied. The innocent one, like the pearl-
maiden, has a higher rank in heaven. See Fletcher (1921)
17-18 on this point.

*674* Cf. elliptical [if] in 703. Early editors rendered
*god* 'good', but Hillmann's 'God', followed by deFord, Moorman,

and Andrew & Waldron, seems preferable.

*675-76*  Cf. the reference to the Beatific Vision in *Pa*.
23-24 and *Cl*. 27-28.

*678-83*  Cf. Ps. 23.3-4 and Ps. 14.1-2, 5.  It seems that
*he* (680) refers to the Lord, as Hillmann interpreted it.
Andrew & Waldron tr. 680: "He (the Psalmist) is not slow to
answer himself."

*681  Hondelynge₃* 'with his hands' tr. in part *innocens
manibus* 'the innocent in hands' of Ps. 23.4.  The *MED* s.v.
*hŏndlinges* adv. cites *Pe*. and *Cursor Mundi* 3933.

*687-88*  The maiden again takes up Ps. 23.4.  Cf. the
switch from sg. *man* ... *he* (685-86) to pl. *her* 'their' to the
syntax of 609-11 and 617-23.

*689*  Osgood, Gollancz, Hillmann, and Moorman defined *sa₃*
'saw', but Gordon's 'says' seems preferable, since the refer-
ence is to the Biblical writing attributed to Solomon.  The
'righteous man' is Jacob.  Andrew & Waldron emended *sa₃* to
*sayz*, but, as Gordon noted, comparing *sade* 532 instead of
*sayde* as an example of an *a-ay* spelling variant, the MS form
may be retained here.

*690-92*  Bradley (1890b) 201 compared Wisdom 10.10: "Haec
profugam irae fratris iustum deduxit per vias rectas et
ostendit illi regnum Dei et dedit illi scientam sanctorum,
honestavit illum in laboribus et complevit labores illius."
("She conducted the just, when he fled from his brother's
wrath, through the right ways, and shewed him the kingdom of
God, and gave him the knowledge of the holy things, made him
honourable in his labours, and accomplished his labours.")
    Emendation of line 690 may be avoided by scanning with
four stresses--"Hŏw kýnt/lў oúr/ĕ cón / ăquýle."--and con-
sidering the following readings: *kyntly* 'kindly' as a variant
of *MED kīndelī* adj. (cf. *dyt* 681 instead of *dyd*); *oure* 'mercy'
from *OED ore*[1], sense 2 (Morris glossed 'prayer'); and *aquyle*
'prevail' (cf. the sense of *aquylde* 967).  Granting that the
poet altered the Biblical verse (cf. 163n), one need not
emend *he* to *ho* 'she' to agree with fem. Wisdom.  Mercy did
prevail for Jacob, for he was not only given a vision of
heaven (Gen. 28.11-17), but he was also permitted to escape
the wrath of his brother Esau, who sought to murder him (Gen.
27.41-45).
    See Rathborne (1963) for a summary of emendations.  Gor-
don, Cawley, and Moorman followed Bradley (1890b) 201 who
changed *he* to *ho* and suggested, "How [koyntyse on]oure con
aquyle." ("How wisdom obtained honor.")  Osgood followed

Gollancz (1890) 223: "How kyntly oure [kyng him] con aquyle."
("How kindly our King welcomed him.")  In his 1921 edition,
Gollancz substituted *Koyntyse* for *kyng*.  Hillmann, reading
*onre* instead of *oure*, and emending to *on[o]re*, tr. 690: "How
fittingly honor (he) did receive."  Andrew & Waldron emended
*How kyntly* to *Hym Koyntyse*: "(that) our Wisdom received him,"
and read *He* (Wisdom) in 691, believing the poet changed the
gender of the personification, "possibly to conform to the
common medieval identification of Wisdom with Christ."
    Rathborne, noting liturgical influence in *Pe.* and the fact
that *Dominus* occurs in liturgical texts dealing with Wisdom
10.10, favored the reading which appeared in Gollancz' 1891
edition: "How kyntly oure [lord hym] con aquyle."

    *702*  Gollancz' emendation of *tryed* to [*c*]*ryed*, adopted by
Andrew & Waldron because of alliteration and the recurrence
of *tryed* 707, seems unnecessary.  (Cf. 53n.)  Apparently the
poet did not always avoid identical rhyme.  *Clere* is repeated
(735, 737), and Andrew & Waldron did not follow Gollancz'
emendation there.

    *703*  Interpreting *Alegge* as imper., Osgood tr. 'urge your
privilege', Gollancz 'renounce thy right'; both rendered
*innome* 'received'.  Everett & Hurnard (1947), noting legal
phraseology in this passage, argued for the reading adopted
by Gordon and subsequent editors: *Alegge* 'declare' is sub-
junctive; *innome* 'trapped' is pp. (*MED inimen* v., 2c).  Cf.
legal terminology in 417, 563, 580, 594, and 613.

    *707-8*  These lines anticipate 709-28.  Even the righteous
man must become like the innocent child through God's grace
before he may enter heaven.  The aspect of humility is im-
plied here.  (See 401-8.)

    *715*  Emendation of *hym* to *hem* 'them' is unnecessary.
Moorman, for example, rendered *let be hem bede* 'bade them
cease', as if *hem* referred to the *burneȝ* 'people' (712).
Andrew & Waldron tr. MS *hym* 'them' and placed *Let be* in quota-
tion marks: "His disciples commanded them with reproof 'Leave
off!'"

    *721*  The link-word *ryȝt* of the preceding stanza-group
does not appear here, the only place in the poem lacking con-
catenation.  Macrae-Gibson-C (1968) 213, following Gordon's
discussion (pp. 88-89), felt the missing link is due to
textual corruption.  McGalliard (1969) 288, citing Medary
(1916) 265 and noting that according to the conventions of
"linking" poems, a link might be omitted if the line con-
tained a proper name or if the link-word appeared in an ad-
jacent verse, believed the poet may have availed himself of

the latter privilege, since *ryȝt* does appear in line 723.
Andrew & Waldron considered "unacceptable both syntactically
and metrically" the suggestion of Emerson (1927) 825 to add
*Ryȝt* 'Straightway' at the beginning of the line, but they did
substitute *Ryȝt* 'Justice' for *Ihecu*, believing the poet in-
tended to personify "Jesus as 'Justice', and that MS *Jesus*
is a scribal substitution for the sake of greater explicit-
ness."

However, the omission may be prescribal. Røstvig (1967)
326-32 argued that the poet, working with numerical symbolism,
deliberately made a break here to divide *Pearl* into twelve
stanza-groups, followed by eight, thereby making more promi-
nent the fact that the last eight deal with the eternal bliss
of those who are saved by the Lamb. The eighth day, according
to Biblical numerical symbolism, signifies eternity. See also
Casling & Scattergood (1974) 87-89 for an argument favoring
the view that the break in stanza-linking at this point was
deliberately made by the poet.

*Mylde* is a sb. adj., evidently referring to Christ's
'humble disciples' (Gollancz, Gordon, Cawley, and Andrew &
Waldron). Osgood suggested 'little child' (Matt. 18.2) but
also noted the reference may be to the disciples (Mark 9.34).
Hillmann and Moorman favored 'tender ones (children)', but
the doctrinal pronouncement of 721-28 would be more appro-
priately directed to the disciples rather than to the children.

*730* Spearing (1970) 160 noted pearl symbolism is resumed
in this stanza-group from Group V. The jeweler (dreamer) of
V is reintroduced here, as the poet, to retain the identifi-
cation, alters Matt. 13.45 by calling the 'merchant' a 'jew-
eler'. (See 252n.)

*730-35* See 221-28n. Matt. 13.45-46 reads: "Iterum simile
est regnum caelorum homini negotiatori quaerenti bonas mar-
garitas;/inventa autem una pretiosa margarita, abiit et ven-
didit omnia quae habuit et emit eam." ("Again the kingdom of
heaven is like to a merchant seeking good pearls./Who when
he had found one pearl of great price, went his way, and sold
all that he had, and bought it.") Osgood (735-43n) gave the
various patristic viewpoints concerning pearl symbolism.
(See also Schofield [1909] 634-37.) The poet followed the
Vulgate closely in making Matthew's 'pearl of price' (746)
symbolize heaven itself, but, as Schofield observed, much of
the thought of the Church Fathers comes into the entire struc-
ture of *Pearl*, for this gem, according to the Fathers, may
also represent Christ, the Virgin, gospel teaching, purity,
grace, and truth.

Osgood cited Ephrem's hymn on the death of children
(*Select Hymns and Homilies,* tr. H. Burgess, p. 14): "Like
pearls in diadems children are inserted in the kingdom."

Hillmann rightly refuted Osgood's comment that the poet's
interpretation of the pearl of great price "is somewhat con-
fused." Representing *heuenesse clere* (735), this pearl is
worn by the maiden on her breast in 222 and 740, and the image
is extended to other souls in heaven in 854 and 1103. When
the dreamer first saw it (221-28), he did not fully understand
its significance. Now he is advised to abandon the mad world
and purchase it (743-44).

732 See Macrae-Gibson-C (1968) 214 for discussion of word-
play on the link-words in this stanza-group. *Makelle3* replaces
*mascelle3* in 733 and 757; in 780 the two come together. The
dreamer is corrected (781-84), as he had been before (421-56),
when the maiden says she is *maskelles* 'spotless' (781) but not
*makele3* 'unequalled' (784), for that title belongs only to
the Virgin Mary. The pearl of price is both spotless and
peerless (732-33). See Gordon's 733n and Baird (1973) for
arguments favoring retention of MS *makelle3* (733) and *makele3*
(757).

735 Cf. *heuene3 clere* 'heaven's brightness' in line 620.
Hillmann translates in this way as opposed to 'bright heavens',
given by most editors.

737-38 Cf. 5-6 and 221. Editors rendered *mode* 'temper'
(Osgood), 'lustre' (Gollancz), 'character' (Gordon), 'tone'
(Hillmann), 'spirit' (Moorman); for the meaning 'appearance',
which seems more suitable, see MED *mǫd* n., 4a, where *Pe.* is
cited.

739 Cf. 675 and 685-88 on salvation for the righteous.
For the intervening vowel in *ry3tywys,* cf. *boro3t* 628, *bereste*
854, and *mynyster* 1063.

740 Osgood and Gordon read *stode* 'stood' as a v., but
the pa. t. does not suit the context well. Gollancz and Hill-
mann interpreted *hit* as gen. 'its' and *stode* as a n. 'setting,
position'. Moorman and Andrew & Waldron, following Hamilton
(1958) 190, tr. 'shone'.

745-46 The spotless pearl (pure soul) adorned with pearls
(virtues) possesses the pearl of price (heaven). See 253-55n
and 855-56n for a similar fusing of pearl symbols, and 269-72n
for discussion of the phrase *perle of prys* in that context.
The phrasing of another occurrence differs slightly: "Perle3
py3te of ryal prys" (193). The poet, therefore, employs
*perle(3)... prys* alliteration three times, first to denote
the pearls (virtues) the maiden wears (193), secondly to
represent the maiden's soul (272), and thirdly to denote the
large pearl (heaven) she wears on her breast (746). All these

symbols come together in 745-46.

*749-52*  Gordon thought it "highly probable" that the poet
echoed the *Roman* (ed. Langlois 16013f.) where it is argued
that neither philosophers like Plato and Aristotle "nor the
artist, not even Pygmalion, can imitate successfully the works
of Nature."  Pilch-C (1964) 165-67 opposed Gordon, noting that
"Jean de Meun speaks of the superiority of nature to art, i.e.,
to man's creation," but the poet's point is not to contrast
nature with art but to show "the inferiority of both to God."

*751*  *Lettrure* 'writing' (Osgood and Hillmann) seems pref-
erable to 'learning, science' (Gollancz, Gordon, Moorman, and
Andrew & Waldron).

*752*  See 142n on omission of *-d* in *carpe,* rendered emphat-
ically 'did speak' with the auxil. tr. in 751.  *Of carpe* is
an inversion, and *properté3* is gen. 'of (these) qualities'.

*753*  Osgood compared the description of the maiden in 195.

*754*  Editors rendered *corte3* as an adj. corresponding to
*cortayse,* but the word may be from *MED cŏrden* v.1, an aphetic
form of *accorden.*  For unvoicing of *d* to *t,* cf. *dyt* 681,
*kyntly* 690, and *wete* 761.

*755*  Morris thought he was emending 'oftriys' to *of priys*
'of value'.  Gollancz rendered *triys* as a form of 'truce'--
"What kind of peace bears as its symbol the spotless pearl"
(755-56)?  However, Gordon & Onions (1933) 180-81, citing a
reviewer of Gollancz' 1921 edition of *Pearl* in *TLS* (May 18,
1922), noted that *triys* 'truce' is "phonologically inadmis-
sible," and then sparked the controversy over *ostriys* 'oysters'
by pointing to Henry Bradley's notation on the margin of the
staff copy of Morris' *Early English Alliterative Poems* in the
Oxford Dictionary room.  Osgood had read MS *offys* 'position',
noting that the second *f* is spread on top, but Gordon accepted
Osgood's reading only as a "happy emendation."
    Davis (1954) 98-99, in his review of Gordon's edition,
pointed out that after examining the MS anew, he saw *offys*
as the true form, for the disputed mark read as the abbrevia-
tion for *ri* is a "plain tick, at the same angle as the off-
stroke of *f.*"  My own viewing of the word under the ultra-
violet lamp in the British Library supports Davis' observa-
tion.  The tops of *f*'s are not always securely joined in the
MS.  Note, for example, the *f* of *of* 752.
    Hillmann and subsequent editors accepted *offys* as the MS
reading, but Donaldson (1972) 75-79 argued again for *ostriys*
not only as the MS reading--"What kind of oysters produce a
pearl like you?"--but also as a type of allegory the poet

might have used. As Davis, to whom Donaldson does not refer, commented, if only *offys* "can be accepted as the scribe's intention we may be spared long notes about truce and oysters."

*761* Moorman followed Hillmann who, disagreeing with *wete* 'wet' given by previous editors, derived the word from OE *wite* and tr. *worlde wete* 'world's woe'. However, *wete* may be the pp. of *OED wede* v. (Cf. pt. *wed* 'went mad' in *Cl*. 1585.) For other examples of unvoicing of *d* to *t*, see 754n. *Worlde wete* corresponds in meaning, then, to *worlde wode* 743. Andrew & Waldron supported *wete* 'wet'.

*763-64* See 11n on phrasing associated with secular love poetry. Christ is called *Lemman* 'Spouse, Beloved' in 796, 805, and 829. Cf. Song of Songs 4.7-8 and the application of these verses, with the refrain *Veni, coronaberis,* in "A Song of Great Sweetness to His Daintiest Dam," *Hymns to the Virgin and Christ,* ed. F.J. Furnivall, *EETS, OS,* 24 (1868), pp. 1-3.

*765* This line helps to explain the matured state of the child's soul in heaven. See 161-62n.

*766* Cf. Rev. 7.14 and 22.14. Lines 646, 705, and 801-16 refer to Christ's shedding his blood for man's salvation. See 218n on the garment metaphor.

*767* The crown symbolizes both virginity and salvation. See 205n, 253-55n, and 451n. Luttrell (1962b) discussed the pearl as a symbol of virginity in other medieval works, among them those of the Knight of La Tour Landry and Gower.

*768* *Pyȝt* echoes the link-word of Stanza-Group IV, and this line recalls the dominant image in that group of the maiden adorned with pearls representing virtues, such as power, beauty, purity, and virginity (765-67).

*769* Osgood compared *bryd ... flambe* to *flaumbande ... brydde*ȝ 90-93. In the latter context the word denotes 'birds'. The pearl-maiden, bride of Christ, possesses qualities of the Virgin Mary, who was compared to the Phoenix of Araby in line 430. In 94 the birds sing; in 882 the brides of the Lamb sing.

*775* As Hillmann noted, *anvnnder cambe* is a conventional phrase, complimentary to ladies. Since the next line speaks of living for Christ in hardship, there may be an allusion to the religious life here. Bloomfield (1969) 302 supposed the reference was to the female martyrs whom the pearl-maiden surpassed in heaven's hierarchy.

*777-80*  The poet again presents the dreamer as confused
and incredulous in order that the maiden may continue to re-
veal spiritual mysteries.  She had already explained (433-56)
she is not equal to Mary.  Cf. *Makele₃ Moder* 435 to *makele₃
Quene* 784, and see 279-88n and 444n on the distinction to be
made between the poet and his persona.

*785-86*  Gordon and Cawley followed Gollancz in emending
line 786 so that 144,000 would be named, the number given in
Rev. 14.1,3 and in lines 869-70.  (On the poet's altering of
Biblical details, see 163n.)  Hulbert (1927) 118, feeling the
insertion of [*fowre*] into 786 made the metre clumsy, asked,
"Could not the poet use a 'round number'?"  Robertson-C (1950b)
19 also supported the MS reading as a sort of poetic license,
noting it was a familiar technique in sermons to suggest a
familiar Biblical passage by merely hinting at it, or by quot-
ing it incompletely.  (See 869-70n for a discussion of the
144,000 virgins in *Pe.* and in Rev.)

*789*  As Clark & Wasserman (1979) 4 pointed out, the dreamer
has recognized *clot* only as 'clay' (22), but the enlightened
maiden, besides considering this meaning (320, 857), also
refers to the New Jerusalem as *clot*.  Thus, death in the
earthly *clot* leads to resurrection in the heavenly *clot*.  See
Clark & Wasserman's "The Spatial Argument of *Pearl*: Perspec-
tives on a Venerable Bead" for a study of how the poet, in
having the maiden guide the dreamer from views of earthly
appearance toward an understanding of spiritual truths,
"grounds abstract principles in concrete physical circum-
stances, ... creating a graphic doubleness, whereby moral
stance is reflected and expressed by physical position and
surroundings" (1).

*790*  E. Wilson (1968) discussed "The 'Gostly Drem' in
*Pearl*."  Of the three kinds of mystical visions--corporeal,
spiritual, and intellectual--the dreamer's, like the Apocal-
yptic vision of St. John, is classified formally as spiritual.
Wilson, arguing that the dreamer was unready for a spiritual
vision but in need of one, concluded: "Only after the maiden's
instruction is his dream spiritual in terms of his interior
disposition," and "only then does he have the ghostly vision
of Jerusalem" (101).  On this point, see also pp. 15-19 of
Wilson's book, *The Gawain-Poet* (1976).

*791*  Only Chase adopted the emendation to *hyl-cot* of
Emerson (1922) 77 for the sake of perfect rhyme, but Hillmann
noted that *cot* in OE and ME generally referred to lowly
dwellings.  (On the poet's occasional use of imperfect rhymes,
see 26n and 802n.)

*797-804*  Cf. the prophecy of the passion of Christ in
Isaias 53, especially v. 7: "Oblatus est quia ipse voluit et
non aperuit os suum, sicut ovis ad occisionem ducetur, et quasi
agnus coram tondente se obmutescet et non aperiet os suum."
("He was offered because it was his own will, and he opened
not his mouth: he shall be led as a sheep to the slaughter,
and shall be dumb as a lamb before his shearer, and he shall
not open his mouth.")  Osgood, Gollancz, Gordon, Hillmann, and
Andrew & Waldron punctuated 799-804 as a quotation within a
quotation, but since not all the words of these six lines are
in Isaias, the passage may be taken as a continuation of the
maiden's speech.  Cf. her free paraphrase of Matthew in 730-35.
See also Bishop (1968) 126-27 on the punctuation of this pas-
sage, and cf. 825-28n.

*800*  Moorman adopted Gordon's loose tr., "No criminal
charge being proved against him."  Andrew & Waldron glossed
*sake of felonye* 'criminal charge'; Hillmann tr., 'cause of
felony'.  *Sake of felonye* 'reason associated with felony' fol-
lows Hillmann.  For *of* 'associated with', cf. *Ga.* 2506.  The
*OED,* in accordance with Morris' old reading, cited *Pe.* s.v.
*sake* sb., sense 3, 'guilt, fault', but sense 2 gives: *"Without
sake,* without good reason (= L. *sine causa*)."

*802*  The MS reading is apparently *lande,* not *hande.*  Edi-
tors' emendation of *men* to *nem* (OE *niman* 'seize') seems unnec-
essary.  (See 26n and 791n on imperfect rhymes.)  The detail
of 'seizing' a lamb is not in Isaias 53.7, and *men* may be taken
as an aphetic form of *MED āmen* v., sense 2, 'appraise' (OF
*aesmer*).  This Lamb was one to be appraised.  For other exam-
ples of aphetic forms of OF words, cf. *mys* 197, *myke₃* 572, and
*corte₃* 754.  There may also be word-play on senses 4 and 5 of
*MED āmen,* 'intend (an injury), aim (a blow)', relating to
Christ's crucifixion.

*803*  *Query* 'query' (medieval Latin *querere* 'to ask'),
given by Gollancz and Hillmann, seems preferable to 'complaint'
(*OED query* sb.2), given by Osgood, Gordon, and Andrew & Wal-
dron.  Gollancz emended to *quere,* but *i(y)-e* are interchange-
able in this MS, and, if the poet's pronunciation were not in
harmony, there are examples in *Pe.* of imperfect rhymes, as
802n shows.

*806*  Moorman favored Hillmann's belief that the *boye₃*
'ruffians' refer to the two men who were hanged with Christ,
but the sense of Gollancz' translation, followed by Gordon and
Andrew & Waldron, seems preferable: "and rent on rood by bois'-
rous churls."  (Andrew & Waldron compared *Pa.* 95-96.)  *Rent*
'slit open' reminds one not only of the nails that were driven
into Christ's hands and feet by the soldiers but also of the

sword that pierced his side (654).

*810* *Onto* 'to' may be taken as a variant spelling of *vnto* 'to' 712, 718.

*811* Eds. rendered *set hymself in vayn* 'set himself at nought'. For the reading given here, cf. *OED vain* a. and sb., II. 6a, in the phr. *to take ... in vain* 'to treat with contempt'.

*812* Hillmann's *wolde* 'subdue' (OE *wealdan*) seems preferable to Gordon's 'possess, be responsible for'. Andrew & Waldron's *to wolde* 'in (His) possession' follows the reading of Wright (1939) 17.

*815* Cf. Lompe 'Lamb' 945 and contrast *lambe-lyȝt* 'lamplight' 1046. As Gordon noted, such reverse spellings are characteristically Western. There may be word-play on the idea of Christ the Lamb, shedding his light as Lamp of the world.

*817-18* The reference is to John the Baptist, to be distinguished from the apostle John, mentioned in 834-36 as the writer of the Apocalypse. Osgood, saying there is no "account of John's having preached or baptized elsewhere than in the region of Jordan," believed þeras must refer to Jordan, but the poet may have interpreted history loosely here for the sake of his verse. (Cf. 163n, 785-86n, and 837n on altering Biblical details.)

*822* Johnson-C (1953) 44 noted how the phr. *trwe as ston* "recalls the symbolic overtones of jewel-stone imagery" in *Pe*. Christ is called *Juelle* in 795 and 1124, the maiden is named 'jewel' in 23, 249, 253, 277, and in 929 souls in heaven are called 'jewels'. Gordon pointed out that *trewe as ston* is part of the couplet written above the illustration of Bercilak' wife visiting Gawain on f. 129 in the MS.

*823* Osgood and Gordon glossed *dryȝe* as an adj. 'heavy' (ON *drjúgr*), which seems preferable to Hillmann's v. 'dry, blot' (OE *dryg(e)an*).

*824* Eds. did not regard *vpon* as an adv., but cf. the adjectives *vpon* 198, 208, and *vpen* 1066, and see *OED open* adv., III. B, where *Cursor Mundi* 26215 is cited: "His penance open must be schaun."

*825-28* Cf. 797-804n on punctuation. Osgood, Gollancz, Gordon, Hillmann, and Andrew & Waldron included these lines in the quotation beginning at line 822, but, as both Emerson

(1927) 826 and Bishop (1968) 126 noted, John does not speak these words.

826 Most editors tr. *clem* 'claim' (OF *clamer*), which suits the context well. (*MED claimen* v. lists *clemen* as a variant spelling.) Morris (1891a) 603, Hillmann, and Moorman favored 'smear' (OE *clǣman*). Hillmann felt this word expresses the "loathsomeness of sin," but the metaphorical image of Christ's smearing sins on himself seems a bit strained.

829 Since the previous three stanzas refer to Christ's passion, MS *swatte* suits the context well as the pt. of *OED sweat* v., II. 8, 'to suffer severely'. As Savage (1956b) 127 noted, emendation to the adj. *swete* 'sweet' for rhyme seems unnecessary. The pronunciation may have been different, but imperfect rhymes occur elsewhere. See 802n and 803n.

830-34 The first two places in which Christ is spoken of as the Lamb are Isaias 53.7 and John 1.29. (See 797-804 and 821-24.) The third place is the Apocalypse. As Gollancz observed, "From here to l. 1128 the Apocalypse is the main source of the poet's inspiration." Gordon noted that *aȝer prophete* (831) refers to Isaias and John the Baptist, but the Baptist's words quoted in lines 822-24 come down through the Gospel of the apostle John (1.29), who also wrote the Apocalypse. (See line 836.)

836 Emendation of MS *sayt3* 'tells' to *sy3* or *sa3* 'saw' seems unnecessary. The apostle John did tell about his vision of the Lamb in the Apocalypse. *Hym* 'about him' in in the dative case.

837 As Gordon, p. xxx, noted, the book of Revelation was a scroll, but the poet describes it as a medieval book with square pages. See 817-18n for reference to other instances of the poet's altering Biblical details.

838 The earlier reading *in-seme* 'together' is not as suitable as Gordon's *in seme* 'to (the) border', adopted here.

839 *Dard* 'stood in awe' suits the context of 609; here *dare* 'bow in awe' accords better with Rev. 5.8, which describes the four living creatures and the twenty-four ancients falling down before the Lamb.

840 The Jerusalem mentioned here is the New Jerusalem, the heaven of the Apocalypse, to be distinguished from the Old Jerusalem on earth. See 937-60. The first time the link-word was used in line 792 of this stanza-group it referred to the New Jerusalem. Thus Stanza-Group XIV begins and ends with

descriptions of the heavenly Jerusalem, and in between Christ's
suffering in the earthly Jerusalem is depicted. The poet's
circular structure is evident even in smaller passages.

*841* Gordon followed earlier editors in rendering *pechche*
'sin, impurity' (OF *peché*). Hillmann followed Emerson (1922)
81-82 who argued for 'patch' (AN *peche*), which seems prefer-
able. (Cf. *OED patch* sb.1.) Moorman tr. 'shred', Andrew &
Waldron 'fault'.

*848* MS *nonoþer* needs to be separated; the double negative
*no noþer* may be rendered 'not either', with *noþer* taken as a
variant spelling of *nouþer*.

*852* Reading *neuer þe lesse* as three separate elements is
appropriate here. Cf. 864, 876, 888, 900, and 901. Only in
912 and 913 does joining the elements and tr. 'nevertheless'
seem fitting. One cannot always go by MS authority because
the scribe was often inconsistent in his connecting or dis-
connecting of syllables, and letter formations and the use of
abbreviations add to the difficulty of determining word-connec-
tion with certainty. For example, *lestles*, which begins line
865, needs to be separated. Concerning the syllables in ques-
tion in the lines mentioned at the beginning of this note,
*neuer*, which has the abbr. for *er* in all instances except 901
and 913, is always separate, and *þe* is apparently attached to
the following word only in 852, 864, 876, and 900.

*854* Again the *wonder perle*, worn on the maiden's breast
(221-22), Matthew's *pretiosa margarita* (730-46), is mentioned,
as it will be in 1103-4. The theme of salvation in God's
kingdom spans the entire poem.

*855-56* For *þa* 'who', cf. *Ga.* 877 and see *OED tho* rel.
pron., III. 5. The idea of there being no quarreling among
the blessed was anticipated in 848. Cf. also 463-66. Hill-
mann tr. *crest* 'best', as if the reference were to the pearl
worn on the maiden's breast, but most editors defined 'crown',
which seems more suitable. It is noteworthy that the pearl
of price (heaven) and the crown of pearls (salvation and
virginity) are described in close proximity in the following
three passages: 205-28, 853-56, and 1100-4. In addition, the
crown of *vergynté* (767) is mentioned fairly close to the
*perle of prys* (746). The pearl-maiden, one of 144,000 *virgins*,
has obtained *salvation* in *heaven*. See also 745-46n on fusing
of pearl symbols.

*859* Gordon compared 1 Cor. 13.11-12 and pointed out that
Augustine in *De Peccatorum Meritis et Remissione* applied the
promise of complete knowledge specifically to the baptized
infant.

*860* Osgood, Gollancz, Gordon, Moorman, and Andrew & Waldron agreed that *on dethe* refers to Christ's death on the cross, through which the hope of salvation has been realized. Hillmann tr., "Our hope of one death is established fully," explaining 'hope' in relation to avoiding the *deth secounde* (652).

*862* Most editors rendered *mes* 'mass', but Hillmann's derivation from OF *mes* 'feast' seems preferable, since there is no mass in heaven, as it is known here on earth. The reference is to the symbolic heavenly banquet, the allegory of which is explained in *Cl.* 161-64 after the Parable of the Wedding Feast.

*865* *Talle* may be retained. Cf. *masklle* 843 and *talle* 'word' in *Cl.* 48. Morris and Andrew & Waldron glossed *les* 'false'. Cf. 897-98. This adj. goes well here as the primary meaning, with word-play on 'less' as a secondary meaning. Gordon suggested 'false', but he, like other editors, glossed *les* 'less'.

*865-900* Cf. Rev. 14.1-5. Oakden (1968) 348-50, stressing liturgical influence in *Pe.*, noted that this Biblical passage forms the Epistle for the Feast of Holy Innocents on December 28.

*869-70* Cf. 785-86. *Maydenne3* renders *virgines* of Rev. 14.4 and may be tr. 'virgins'. As Gordon noted, "Many theologians understood the *virgines* to be celibates of the Church irrespective of their sex on earth." Robertson-C (1950b) 19 cited Augustine *PL* 35.2437 for proof of this point. *MED maiden* n., sense 2d, gives ME citations which denote men as virgins. In 785 Lamb's 'wives' are named, but every pure soul in heaven, male or female, is considered the bride of Christ. There is no reason to assume that the poet intended to portray everyone in the group as female, like the pearl-maiden. In 448 and 468 he refers to the souls in heaven as kings and queens. In 1099 he uses *vergyne3* to describe those in the procession. In 1115 *maydene3* 'maidens', since it occurs in a simile, does not indicate that only females were among the 144,000.

Hart (1927), refuting Sister Madeleva's assertion that children had no place in the band of virgins, noted that at the time *Pe.* was written, virginity was upheld as a virtue even in a child. She cited Chaucer's "Prioress' Tale" in which the seven-year-old *clergeoun* is praised as a "gemme of chastite" (609), one who follows the Lamb as a "martir sowded to virginitee" (579).

*875* *Torre3* 'peaks' suits the context. The *OED* s.v. *tor*

sb. (Gaelic *tòrr*), sense 2, cites *Pe.* and *Cl.* 951 with the
meaning, '? a heavy mass of cloud', but adds, "the sense 'rock
mass' seems also possible." (Cf. sense 1, 'a rocky peak; a
hill'.) Moorman agreed with Gordon who tr., "as thunder rolls
among dark hills." Gordon noted, "The term *tor* is still used,
in the south Pennine region, of high, sharply rising hills."
Andrew & Waldron glossed 'towering cloud', supposing *torre₃*
is more likely "from OF *tur* 'tower', used metaphorically here."

*881-84* Chapman (1931) 179-80, pointing to *mode₃* 'modes'
(884) especially, suggested that the poet had more than a
passing knowledge of church music. Gordon glossed 'strains
of music', thinking it doubtful that the technical sense of
*mode₃* existed in English before the sixteenth century, but the
*OED* s.v. *mode* sb., I. 1a, cites Chaucer's Boethius II. pr. i.
20 with a meaning for *moedes* similar to Chapman's reading.
Hillmann tr. 'modes'; Moorman and Andrew & Waldron agreed
with Gordon.

Cohen (1976), taking up Chapman's suggestion, argued that
the allegory and the structure of *Pe.* are based upon the
musical mode system in two separate movements: the Song of
Earth (first twelve stanza-groups); and the Song of Heaven
(last eight stanza-groups).

*883* Editors believed *carpe* refers to the matter of the
song, but it may be a synonym for *songe* (882). See *MED carp*
n., sense c, 'song'.

*885-88* Rev. 14.3 says only the 144,000 sang the canticle
before the throne, the four beasts, and the ancients. (Cf.
889-92.) Hillmann noted that the *fowre beste₃* represent
animated nature: man, birds, cattle, and wild animals (Rev.
4.7). Fletcher (1921) 16-17 pointed out that medieval theolo-
gians identified the 24 *aldermen* (Rev. 4.4), who appear again
in 1119-20, as the twelve patriarchs of the Old Testament and
the twelve apostles of the New Testament.

*892* Emerson (1922) 83-84 showed that MS þay may be re-
tained by employing full-stop punctuation after *meyny*.

*893-94* Hoffman-C (1960) 99-101 discussed the fruit-
flower-jewel imagery relating to the theme of death and res-
urrection. For example, 894 recalls 29-35 and anticipates
1077-80. (See the notes to 19-22, 29, 195, 269-72, 906, 962,
and 1077-80.)

*900* *Neuer* 'any' is due to negative *neuer* 899. Cf. the
double negative constructions in *Pe.* 864 and *Ga.* 460-61.

*901* Adam (1976) 3 noted the possibility of a pun, 'never
(to) thee less'.

*901-12* These lines form a sixth stanza in this group.
All the other groups have five. Brink (1889) 349 suggested
one should be omitted. Osgood (p. xlvi) and Gollancz (853-
64n) suspected a scribe copied the second one by mistake.
Gordon (p. 88) considered lines 901-12 superfluous. However,
this sixth stanza seems authentic. Chapman (1939) 257, com-
paring numerical symbolism in Dante and *Pe.*, argued that the
poet deliberately planned 101 stanzas, dividing the first 99
into three groups of approximately equal length and adding
the last two an an epilogue. Davis (1954) 100 pointed out
that the extra stanza makes the total come to 101, the same
as in *Ga*.

Kean (1965) 50 did not find Chapman's tripartite division
of *Pe.* convincing, but she did support his contention that
the poet employed numerical symbolism. Adding the extra
stanza makes the poem contain 1212 lines instead of 1200;
12 x 12 equals 144, and there are 144,000 virgins in the
heavenly procession; 12 and 12 is also appropriate to the
ground plan of the New Jerusalem (992-1035). Cf. also the
trees that produce 12 fruits of life 12 times a year (1077-
80). Bishop (1968) 28-29 supported Kean's views with further
evidence. For additional arguments favoring the authenticity
of this stanza, see Greenwood (1956) 7-9, Røstvig (1967),
Nolan & Farley-Hills (1971) 298, Finkelstein (1973) 427-32,
Adam (1976) 2-6, and Nolan (1977) 197-98.

*905* Osgood compared 382, Gollancz *Cl.* 736; cf. also
*Cl.* 747.

*906* See 269-72n for discussion of the mortal *rose* that
fades. This *reken* rose, which the pearl-maiden has become,
is the immortal flower of heaven. (See 962n and 1176n.)

*909* *Sympelnesse* typifies the innocent maiden, as Gordon
suggested, her lack of deceit. (See 897-98.) Hillmann com-
pared 2 Cor. 8.2, 9.11, 9.13, and especially 11.3 in which
Paul commends as a virtue the "simplicitate quae est in
Christo" ("simplicity that is in Christ"). The 144,000
virgins are like the Lamb in 'speech and appearance' (896).

*911* Morris and Osgood glossed *blose* 'blaze, flame' (ON
*blossi*); Gollancz emended to [w]*ose* 'wild man' (OE -*wāsa* in
the compound *wuduwāsa*). In agreement with Gollancz (1891c),
Gordon, and Hillmann, the *MED* s.v. *blōse* '? an uncouth per-
son' (OF *blos* 'deprived, empty') cited only *Pe*. Andrew &
Waldron, following a suggestion made by Gordon, emended *blose*
to *bose* 'peasant', a form of *MED bōce* n., 3d, "a 'lump of a
man' (used disparagingly)." However, *blose* may be a variant
spelling of *MED blās* n., sense a, 'blowing (of wind), a gust'.
The vowel shift from *a* to *o* fits the rhyme scheme. (Cf.

271

*ware* 151 and *wore* 154 in rhyme position instead of *were*.)

*913* Most editors rendered *cler* as an adv. 'clearly, with a clear voice', which seems appropriate. Andrew & Waldron interpreted the word as a sb. adj. in the vocative case, 'beautiful one', referring to the pearl-maiden.

*917-18* Gordon observed how the poet's verses and the illustration on f. 42b medievalize the New Jerusalem. Cf. the use of *tor* 966, *wone3* and *manayre* in 1027-29, and calling the 'city' a *mote* in lines 936, 948, and 973.

*919-22* Here and in the next stanza, the dreamer asks foolish questions for a man who by now should know more about heavenly mysteries, but this is the technique the poet used to keep the plot moving. Hieatt (1965) 140-41, discussing how this "confusion and lack of logic, by waking standards," may be accounted for by the dream-vision psychology of medieval literature, compared the "dawsed" dreamer in Chaucer's *Book of the Duchess*. (Cf. 336n.)

*923-24* *Maskele3* recalls one of the link-words of Stanza-Group XIII. *Mone* anticipates the link for Group XVIII. In this group, the word-play on *mote* 'spot (stain)' and 'city' (New Jerusalem), merging in line 948 of the central stanza, recalls the first group in *Pe*. with its play on *spot* (pearl without 'spot') and the 'spot' where she was buried. See Macrae-Gibson-C (1968) 215-17 for further discussion.

*929-30* The poet extends his *juele* metaphor throughout the entire poem. The maiden is called a 'jewel' in line 23 and Stanza-Group V, the dreamer is called a 'jeweler' in V, Matthew's merchant becomes a 'jeweler' in lines 730 and 734, and Christ is called *Juelle* in 795 and 1124.

*932* Hillmann placed dashes at the end of lines 931 and 932; in this way she retained MS & at the beginning of 932, considering the line parenthetical. The MS reading may also be retained by tr. *And* 'If'; see *MED and* conj. (& adv.), sense 5a.

*934* See 60n on retention of MS *gracous*.

*935* Hillmann, following Osgood and Gollancz, read *lygynge3* 'lodgings'. Editors who printed *bygynge3* considered it an emendation of the MS. However, the tiny bottom loop that completes the *b* may be faded, or perhaps, being squeezed against the *y*, it was not made clearly.

*938* The pearl-maiden is called *special spyce* (235).

Just as he echoed the jewel metaphor in 929-30, the poet does
so with the spice symbol here.  (See 31-32n, 43n and 235n.)

942  *Olde gulte* denotes original sin created by the fall
of Adam and Eve.  (Cf. 655n.)

945  See 815n for discussion of *Lompe* 'Lamb'.

947  Osgood glossed *flake* 'pinfold', Gollancz 'hurdle'
(ON *flaki*).  Gordon's 'blemish' (*MED flāke* n.1, sense b) was
adopted by subsequent editors.  Hillmann suggested ON *flekkr*
for the etymology.  (Cf. *flakes of soufre* in *Cl.* 954.)

948  Osgood and Gollancz mistakenly rendered *moote* 'moat'.

952  Cf. 'City of God' to Heb. 12.22 and Rev. 3.12, and
'Vision of Peace' to Ezec. 13.16.  Both epithets denote the
heavenly Jerusalem, even though the maiden speaks of the
earthly Jerusalem in 953-54.

953  Editors rendered *pes* 'peace', but the precise denota-
tion seems to differ slightly from 'peace' 955.  For *pes* 'sal-
vation', cf. *OED peace* sb., 3b.  Hillmann tr. *at ene* 'former-
ly'; Gordon glossed *mad at ene* 'arranged, settled'.  *At ene*
'immediately' indicates the poet may have been thinking of the
exact time of Christ's death on the cross when mankind's sal-
vation was accomplished.

958  *Fresch* 'young bodies' has been read *fresth,* but the
scribe wrote *c* and *t* almost alike, and in this instance the
top bar of the *c* may have been merely extended a bit to the
left.  In view of the poet's frequent use of the sb. adj.,
the emendation to *flesch* seems unnecessary.  Cf. *frech* 'de-
lightful damsel' (195), cited by the *MED* s.v. *frēsh* adj., 7a,
and la 'new' for the meaning 'young bodies'.  *Layd to rote*
recalls *to rot is runnen* (26) in the stanza describing spices,
blossoms, and fruit which sprang from the buried pearl.

961  The *M* of *Moteleʒ* is an extra illuminated letter,
making the total 21 in *Pe.*  Morris began Stanza-Group XVII
here, but, according to the linking system, that section
should begin with the illuminated *I* of 973.  Morris numbered
XXI sections in all, since he made lines 961-72 stand as one
group.

962  The flower metaphor, relating to the death-and-
resurrection theme, began with the mention of *flor* (29); it
may be traced through 269 (mortal rose), 906 (immortal rose),
and to the end of the poem.  In 426 Jesus is the 'Flower of
(the) Virgin'; in 195 and 753 the color of the pearl-maiden

273

is compared to 'fleur-de-lis'. In 1079 the fruit trees bloom; in 1186 the maiden is set within the *garlande gay*.

*963-64* The dreamer desires that which cannot be fully realized, as in 283-88. Now, however, as the maiden explains (965-72), he will receive a vision of the New Jerusalem.

*965-72* See Blenkner-C (1968) 250-51 for a discussion of how this preface to the final *visio* contains an allusion to the Blessed Trinity: *God* (the Father) 965, *Lombe* (the Son) 967, and *fauor* (grace of the Holy Spirit) 968. All-powerful God through his Son Jesus brings grace to men. Blenkner related this concept to the distinction of the three persons "according to power, wisdom, and goodness, who operate, dispose, and will."

*967* Cf. *aquyle* 'prevail' 690. There may be word-play here, based on a hunting metaphor: *aquylde* 'pursued' the Lamb for a favor. *MED aquīlen*, sense b, defines 'to pursue (game)'. (See 1085n for reference to other hunting images in the poems of the MS.) The *MED*, adopting the usual interpretation, cited *Pe.* s.v. sense a, 'to obtain'.

*969* Morris and Gollancz tr. *cloystor* 'cloister'. Bloomfield (1969) 302 rejected 'enclosure' (Osgood, Gordon, Hillmann) because this denotation obscures the traditional image of heaven as a 'cloister'. Andrew & Waldron glossed 'city, city wall'. 'City' is fitting. Other synonyms the poet used for *cyty* are *bylde* (963), *mote*(3) (936-37, 948-49, 973), and *won* (1049).

*969-72* Johnson (1979), in discussing structural, thematic, and imagistic correspondences between *Pe.* and John 20.11-18, related the maiden's injunction to the dreamer not to cross the stream to the motif of the *Noli me tangere* "Do not touch me" (Christ's words [in John 20.17] to the grieving Mary Magdalene when he appears to her by the sepulchre after his resurrection on Easter morning). Johnson noted the pre-eminence of spiritual knowledge over corporeal knowledge. "The final poetic resurrection of spirit and growth in faith is prepared for by the resurrection of Christ in a garden and His consolation to Mary, the garden changing with the awareness of the mourner" (105-6). (See lines 289-324 for the first time the maiden tells the dreamer he cannot cross the stream.)

*973-84* Andrew & Waldron (973-1032n) credited Kean (1967) 207-9 for comparison to Matilda, on the other side of the stream, directing Dante to his vision in the opening 18 lines of *Purgatorio,* Canto XXIX.

977 Editors inserted [*I*] after *wolde,* but the subject is often understood, especially if it appears elsewhere in the passage, as it does here in 979 and 980. Cf. 168 and 363, and see 363n for other examples of ellipsis.

*979-81* Cf. *Tyl* ... *þat* 'Until' (548). Gollancz observed, "The poet does not see the city on the hill, but he, being on a hill, beholds the New Jerusalem." In Rev. 21.10, John is taken up to a high mountain to see the city coming down out of heaven from God. (Cf. 986-88.) Most editors accepted Gollancz' interpretation, but Moorman supposed the "poet, unlike the Apostle John ... sees from a river valley the Heavenly City *on* a hill."

992 The wall rises above the *bantele*₃ (*fundamenta duo-decim* 'twelve foundations' of Rev. 21.14). Cf. the *wal abof þe bantels bent* (1017). In the description of lidded goblets constructed like castles (*Cl.* 1459), *bantelles* denotes tiers of masonry projecting from the top of a wall beneath battlements, but the picture in *Pe.* is different. Synonyms for *bantele*₃ (992) are *foundemente*₃ (993) and *degrés* (1022). The qualifying adj. 'twelve' occurs in all three instances. Editors have agreed with Gordon & Onions (1933) 184-85 on this interpretation. For an argument maintaining that the *bantele*₃ in *Pe.* are the highest parts of the fortification, see Kean (1967) 214-15. Viewing the illustration on f. 42b does not settle the argument, for there neither steps nor projecting outworks are shown, and the wall is round in contrast to the foursquare described in *Pe.* 1023 and Rev. 21.16.

997 Since 'John' is the link-word in this stanza-group, emendation of the text is being made with the insertion of *Johan.*

*999-1016* On the naming of twelve stones, cf. the description of the goblets in *Cl.* 1469-72, and see the note. As Schofield (1909) 604-7 pointed out, what may seem like a mere catalogue to the modern reader held symbolic significance for the medieval man with some knowledge of the religious use to which lapidaries were put. Stern-C (1955) 82-85, Blanch-B (1965) 91-96, and Blanch (1973) 69-75 discussed the following symbols in relation to *Pearl*: 1 jasper (faith), 2 sapphire (hope), 3 chalcedony (good works), 4 emerald (chastity), 5 sardonyx (repentance), 6 ruby (Jesus), 7 chrysolite (prophecies and miracles of Jesus), 8 beryl (resurrection), 9 topaz (nine orders of angels), 10 chrysoprase (earthly travail), 11 jacinth (safety in far places), 12 amethyst (Christ's purple robe). Blanch, noting that gold symbolizes heaven, referred to *strete*₃ *of golde* (1025), *golden gate*₃ (1106), and the Lamb's seven horns of *red golde cler* (1111). Cf. the description of the pearl *in golde so clere* (2), and see the note.

*1001*   Emerson (1927) 829 compared *Mandeville's Travels,*
"where, in the description of the steps in the palace of
Prester John, we have 'another of jasper grene.'"   (See, for
example, the edition of M.C. Seymour [Oxford UP, 1968], Ch.
30, p. 213.)

*1004*   For *pale* 'glow dimly', see *OED pale* v.2, sense 1,
'grow dim'.   Gordon noted in Trevisa's tr. of Bartholomeus
Anglicus, *De Proprietatibus Rerum* (xvi, xvii), the description
of chalcedony as a pale stone of dim color.

*1007*   Since Rev. 21.20 lists the sardius as the sixth
stone, Gollancz emended *rybé* to *sarde,* but the poet sometimes
altered Biblical details.   (See, for example, 163n and 785-
86n.)   As Gordon noted, *as her byrþ-whateȝ* (1041) indicates
the poet connected the description of the New Jerusalem with
the details of Aaron's ephod and breast-plate in Exodus 28.
17-20, where the sardius is named as the first of 12 stones,
and early commentators associated the sardius with the ruby.
(See 1041n.)

*1011*   The beryl signifies resurrection.   Osgood compared
*Cl.* 554-56, where the poet speaks of souls that must be as
pure as the beryl and the pearl to enter heaven.   (Cf. also
*Cl.* 1132.)   In *Pe.* 110, the banks of the stream which separate
the terrestrial paradise from God's kingdom are of *beryl bryȝt,*
and in that stream are emeralds, sapphires, and *gemme gente*
(118), perhaps pearls.   (See 118n.)   Røstvig (1967) noted
that the eighth day signifies eternity.   (See 721n.)   The
beryl is the eighth stone in the foundation.

*1012*   MS *twynne-how* may stand.   The *MED* s.v. *heu* n. lists
*hou* and *howe* among many variant spellings.   Gollancz and Gor-
don cited Bede's Commentary on Rev. (*PL* 93.200) which de-
scribes the double-color of the topaz, probably in reference
to its yellow-green.   Topaz signifies the nine orders of
angels in the lapidaries.   Note references to angels in *Pe.*
1121 and 1126, and see Blanch-B (1965) 95.

*1014*   Emendation of MS *jacyngh* is not necessary.   Gordon
& Onions (1932) 136 explained the form as loss of -*t* before
a word beginning with þ.   (See 142n.)

*1015*   Andrew & Waldron followed Gollancz in emending
*gentyleste* to *tryeste,* but the MS reading is suitable.   Gordon
pointed out that the London Lapidary says the amethyst is
*comfortable in all sorowes,* and in the Latin Lapidary in MS.
Digby 13 the amethyst is "said to have protecting power against

a long list of dangers and misfortunes." (See P. Studer and
J. Evans, *Anglo-Norman Lapidaries* [Paris, 1924], p. 380.)

*1017* Gollancz emended to *b[r]ent* 'steep'; Gordon, Moor-
man, and Andrew & Waldron rendered *bent* as a pp. 'fixed, set';
and Hillmann tr. 'extended'. Taking *bent* as pt. 'rose' seems
like a fitting extension of meaning from *MED bĕnden* v.1, 1d,
'to pull up (a drawbridge)'.

*1025* Gordon noted that *bare* does not mean the golden
streets were transparent. As in the general idea of the
simile in Rev. 21.21, they, being free from filth, only shone
like transparent glass.

*1026* For pleonastic *þat*, cf. 939 and 951. Gollancz re-
futed Osgood's *glayre* 'amber'. In his glossary, Gordon noted
that *glayre* was used in the illumination of manuscripts. (See
*MED glaire* n., sense a, 'white of an egg, albumen'.) Gol-
lancz' observation that the description in this line indi-
cates the dreamer could see through the wall seems to be cor-
rect. (Cf. 1049-50n.)

*1027* No mention is made of 'abodes' in Ch. 21 of Rev.
The poet apparently added these to make the city conform to
a medieval stronghold. (Cf. 917-18n.)

*1029-30* Gordon, rejecting Osgood's *sware* 'side of a
square' and Gollancz' 'dimension', pointed out that since
the city is cubic in form, each side is a square. Because
Rev. 21.16 gives a measurement of twelve thousand furlongs,
Gollancz emended the MS text. Gordon thought the omission
of *þowsande* may have arisen from "the poet's use of a com-
mentary in which the verse explained was given in an abbre-
viated form." Moorman (1965) 72-73 noted that *twelue forlonge*
accords better with the dimensions of a medieval *manayre*.
See 917-18n and 1027n on the poet's altering of Biblical de-
tails to make the city conform to a medieval structure.

*1035* Hillmann and Moorman followed Osgood's *pourseut*
'succession', but *n* and *u* cannot be distinguished in this MS,
and *poursent* 'compass' is a more likely reading. See *OED
purcinct* sb., and cf. *Cl. pursaunt* 'boundary' 1385. As Gor-
don noted, 'succession' as a meaning of *pursuit* is not known
in ME.

*1041* Morris and Osgood misinterpreted *byrþ-whate3*, mak-
ing *whate3* equal *wat3* 'was'. Gollancz defined 'birth omens',
but Gordon's 'fortunes of birth, order of birth' provides
the proper sense. Exodus 28.10 describes names engraved
"iuxta ordinem nativitatis eorum" ("according to the order

of their birth") in the description of the stones of Aaron's
ephod. As Gordon noted, the passages in Exodus and Rev. 21
were "traditionally associated because of their similar lists
of precious stones." (See 1007n.)

*1046*  Only Cawley has what appears to be the MS reading.
*Lambe,* though it is faded, reveals an *a* rather than an *o.*
God in the person of Christ the Lamb (1047) sheds the light
of the Holy Ghost like a lamp. (Cf. 815n on word-play.)

*1049-50*  No verse in Rev. 21 or 22 says the apostle John
looked through the wall, but this appears to be the poet's
meaning. (Cf. 1026n.) The primary sense of *woȝe* and *won* is
'wall' and 'city', but the poet may also be implying that the
dreamer has overcome his earlier 'care' and 'anxiety' (*OED
wough* sb.2 'misfortune' and *wone* sb.3 'expectation'), as
spiritual *lyȝt* enters his soul. Cf. the sense of 1087-88.
   Gordon tr. *For sotyle cler* 'For (all) being transparent
and clear'. *MED clēr* n. '? transparentness' cites *Pe.* Gol-
lancz' emendation of *lyȝt* to *[s]yȝt* was adopted by Andrew &
Waldron because the "poet appears to avoid identical rhyme"--
*lyȝt* ends 1046--and because the "sense of 1049f requires
*syȝt.*" However, MS *lyȝt* seems suitable, and this is at least
the third time Andrew & Waldron have followed an emendation
by Gollancz because the "poet appears to avoid identical
rhyme." (See 53n and 702n.)

*1052*  Hillmann's *apparaylmente* 'hosts of Heaven', in accord
with Rev. 4.2-10 and 7.9-11, seems preferable to Gordon's
'adornment, array'. *MED appareil(le)ment* follows Gordon, but
cf. *ap(p)areil,* 2a, 'martial array, a host'.

*1055*  This river is the source of the stream to which the
dreamer strolled. (See 107n.)

*1058*  For the retention of MS *a,* see 115n. *Foysoun,* n.
used attrib., is usually tr. 'copious, abundant', but 'blessed'
may be substantiated by citations s.v. *MED foisŏun,* sense 1c.
Hillmann read *flet* as the v. 'flowed'; Gordon and Andrew & Wal-
dron glossed 'floor, ground (of city)' (*MED flet* n.), but tr.
'source' indicates the poet may have been making specialized
use of *MED flēte* n., 2a, 'tidal estuary, watercourse'. Moorman
tr. *flet* 'flood'.

*1059*  Cf. the description in 111.

*1061*  Day (1923) suggested reading *ȝete* 'granted, bestowed'
(OE *gēatan, gētan*), with omission of *-ed,* but *ȝete* 'moreover'
suits the context well here.

1063  For retention of MS *mynyster*, see 739n on words with
intervening vowels.

1064  The *OED* lists a v. *reget* 'to obtain again', with the
first citation dated 1604, and cites *Pe.* alone without etymo-
logy or meaning s.v. another *reget* obs. Osgood glossed 're-
produce'; Gordon, Cawley, Moorman, and Andrew & Waldron
adopted the emendation of Wright (1939) 20-21 to *refet* 're-
freshment'. Hillmann followed Gollancz' 'get again, redeem',
citing the reference to the slain Lamb in Rev. 5.6-9. The
*OED* s.v. *re-*, sense 3, states that words formed with this
Latin prefix began to make their appearance in English c̆.
1200. The poet apparently attached the prefix to *MED gēten*
v.1. For *reget* 'be received again' as a pass. infin., cf.
*prayse* 'be praised' 301. The reference here is to the meeting
of the soul with Christ the Lamb in heaven, not to the recep-
tion of the Eucharist, for, as Hillmann noted in refutation
of Osgood, there is no mass in heaven, as it is known on
earth. There are only festive gatherings. (See 862n.) At
these gatherings, the Lamb passes proudly in front, the visi-
ble wound in his side giving no pain but serving to recall
his sacrifice on the cross. (See 1110-1144.)

1068  For retention of *anvndeჳ* 'comparable to', cf. *MED
anent(es* prep., 5b. The moon is a defiled spot compared to
the purity needed to enter heaven. (See 1070.)

1073  Gordon noted that the *to* before *euen* is pleonastic
because *to euen* is the second of two infinitives following
the auxil. v. *schulde*. The *worþly lyჳt* is the "glory of God,"
and the "Lamb is the lamp thereof" (Rev. 21.23). Cf. 1046-47.

1076  Cf. 83 which describes the sunbeams as dark and
lusterless in comparison to the pearls on the ground of the
terrestrial paradise. In the New Jerusalem neither sun nor
moon is needed. (See 1044-45.)

1077-80  The *fryteჳ* image recalls 29, 87, and 894. In 29
fruit grows from the spot where the pearl sank into decay, in
87 the dreamer is refreshed by the fragrance of fruits grow-
ing in the terrestrial paradise, and in 894 the pearl-maiden
is described as *newe fryt* purchased from the earth, *to God
ful due*. See 938n for reference to jewel and spice metaphors
and 962n for discussion of the flower metaphor.

1081-92  In 221-28 the pearl on the maiden's breast is
beyond description. Now the dreamer says mortal man would
not be able to endure the sight of the New Jerusalem. As the
poem progresses, the imagery reaches more sublime levels.

*1083* *MED baille* n.2 cites *Pe.* s.v. sense a, 'the wall
surrounding a castle or fortified city', but sense b, 'a court
within such a wall', seems more appropriate here to describe
the *baly* 'city'. Emendation seems unnecessary, since *a* varies
with *ay* and -*y* varies with -*e*.

*1085* Osgood compared Chaucer's *Clerk's Tale*: "couche as
doth a quaille" (1206). Observing the animal similes in *Pe.*
184 and 345, he stated in his 345n, "Such allusions may arise
from the poet's interest in the hunt." Cf. also 967n, the
effective *hounde₃ of heuen* image in *Cl.* 961, and the following
passages in *Ga.*, noted by Osgood: 1126-77, 1319-71, 1412-70,
1561-1622, 1690-1732, and 1893-1921.

*1086* Moorman adopted Gordon's emendation of *freuch* to
*frelich*, suggested by Morris in his glossary. The *MED*, fol-
lowing Osgood, cited *Pe.* s.v. *frough* adj., 1b, 'delicate;
? delightful', but *freuch* may be a variant spelling of *frech*
195 and *fresch* 958, perhaps influenced by the French diphthong
*eu*. (Cf. *endeure* 1082.) For the meaning 'brilliant', see
*MED frēsh* adj., 6b (a). Andrew & Waldron thought it necessary
to emend to *frech*.

*1088* Eds. rendered *glymme* 'radiance, brightness', listing
it separately from *glem* 79, and the *MED* cited only *Pe.* s.v.
*glimme* n., but the word may be a variant of *glem*. For the
meaning 'spiritual light', see *MED glēm* n., fig., 2a, and cf.
1073n. For other examples of the *i(y)-e* variant, see 229n.

*1089-92* Higgs (1974) 400 concluded that this passage
implies the dreamer now realizes he must die before he can
enter the New Jerusalem.

*1093-96* Gordon noted that *maynful* possibly implies a
full moon. A full white moon bears resemblance to a pearl,
and all the virgins wear the great pearl on their breast
(1103-4). Cf. in Song of Songs 6.9 the second of four similes
describing the appearance of Christ's spouse: "Quae est ista,
quae progreditur quasi aurora consurgens, pulchra ut luna,
electa ut sol, terribilis ut castrorum acies ordinata?" ("Who
is she that cometh forth as the morning rising, fair as the
moon, bright as the sun, terrible as an army set in array?")

*1094* The time reference here anticipates the ending of
the dreamer's vision. On this point, see Macrae-Gibson-C
(1968) 216-17.

*1097* Savage (1956b) 127 favored retention of MS *enpresse*.
The *MED* s.v. *emprīse* lists *enprese* as a variant spelling. For
other examples of the *i(y)-e* variant, see 229n and 1088n.

*1101-4*  This quatrain condenses the description of the pearl-maiden in 197-228. The *pretiosa margarita* is described there for the first time and here for the last time. See 730-35n for further discussion.

*1104*  Hillmann showed that MS *wythouten* may be retained. See *OED without* B. prep., I. 2b, 'so as to exceed; beyond'.

*1106*  Cf. 1025, and see 2n on gold as a symbol for heaven.

*1107*  The reference is to the 144,000 virgins. Cf. 785-86 and 869-70.

*1110*  The image of the Lamb leading the procession is based on Rev. 14.1-4. There is no detailed description given there, as in *Pe*. 1096-1116, but a procession is implied in verse 4: "hi sequuntur Agnum quocumque ierit." ("These follow the Lamb whithersoever he goeth.")

*1111*  This image requires a symbolic reading. Cf. in Rev. 5.6 the "Agnum stantem tanquam occisum, habentem cornua septem et oculus septem, qui sunt septem spiritus Dei missi in omnem terram." ("Lamb standing as it were slain, having seven horns and seven eyes: which are the seven Spirits of God, sent forth into all the earth.") Blanch-B (1965) 97 noted that the number 'seven' may be "identified with the seven sacraments, the graces of which flow from the redemptive sacrifice of the Lamb as Christ." Cf. also the seven virtues and the eight Beatitudes which become seven, since the first and the last are similar. (See *Pa*. 29-40.) Gollancz observed that Christ's head is compared to gold in Song of Songs 5.11. Other examples in *Pe*. of striking images that must be viewed symbolically are the names of the Lamb and the Father written on the foreheads of the 144,000 virgins (871-72), the four beasts before God's throne (886), and the blood spurting from the wounded side of the Lamb (1135-37).

*1115-16*  This simile, which reminds one of *maydeneȝ* in an earthly church procession, does not indicate the poet believed the 144,000 were all females. (See 869-70n for a fuller discussion.)

*1119*  See 885-88n on the poet's first reference to the *aldermen*.

*1124-27*  Al 1124 apparently refers to the singing of the 144,000 virgins (1113-16), the ancients (1119-20), and the *legyounes of aungeles* (1121), though only one order of the last group is mentioned in 1126. This song is evidently not the same one the maiden describes to the dreamer in 837-92

(Rev. 14.2-3), for it is said in both the Bible and the poem that only the 144,000 virgins could sing that one. The dreamer, having heard the song of the birds in the terrestrial paradise (91-94), now hears a greater song coming from the New Jerusalem, one that was perhaps foreshadowed in lines 19-22. (See the note.)

*1126* Osgood noted the *Vertues of heuen,* one of the nine orders of angels, were first described in Ch. 8 of *De Cœlesti Hierarchia,* a treatise attributed to Dionysius. Hillmann referred to Dante's *Paradiso* XXVIII, where all nine orders are described. On the casting out of heaven of the tenth and highest order led by Lucifer, see *Cl.* 205-34.

*1135-37* See 1111n for other examples of Apocalyptic images that should be read symbolically. This one, apparently suggested by the reference to the slain Lamb in Rev. 5.6, describes the Lamb's blood spurting from his side for the salvation of mankind. Cf. 649-56 which relates Christ's shedding of blood and water to the pouring out of God's grace. Rev. 7.14, like 22.14, speaks of those who "laverunt stolas suas et dealbaverunt eas in sanguine Agni." ("have washed their robes, and have made them white in the blood of the Lamb.") Cf. the maiden's words to the dreamer: "In hys blod he wesch my wede on dese" (766).

*1141* Hillmann, following Wright (1939) 21-22, tr. *wene* 'imagine', but the meaning 'doubt', given by most editors, seems like a suitable extension of *OED ween* v., sense 1, 'to think'. Gollancz noted the phrase *but wene* 'without doubt' s.v. *OED ween* sb., 4b.

*1147* The dreamer's calling the maiden 'my little queen' indicates he has learned the lesson taught in lines 421-68.

*1151-52* While Blenkner-C (1968) 259-61 validly observed, especially in view of 1179-80, that the proper antecedent of *sy3t* is not just the sight of the pearl-maiden, but the "final *visio* in its entirety," it also seems true, in view of 1155-56, that the dreamer's seeing the maiden in the midst of all the splendor is the climactic motivating factor leading to his desire to cross the stream. *Luf-longyng* may be both compared and contrasted with *luf-daungere* (11). The dreamer is no longer frustrated in his love for his lost pearl, but he must necessarily be thwarted in his mad desire to take part in her delight.

*1153-55* Hillmann, opposing Madeleva (1925) 46-47 who saw in these lines "the desire, which all mystics share, 'to die and leave the world' in order to enjoy eternal happiness with

God," supposed line 1154 records the "folly of the jeweler's
uncontrolled passion for beauty." However, this entire stanza,
especially line 1160, may indicate a subconscious death wish
on the part of the dreamer. In *Pa.* 427, as in 488 and 494,
Jonas wants to *swelt* 'perish' in order to be relieved of the
world's ills. The dreamer has learned acceptance, but that
he was also conscious of tribulations on earth is proved by
lines 1187-88.

*1154* Hillmann tr. gen. *mane₃*, literally 'man's', as the
adj. 'mortal'.

*1156* For *walte* 'upset', see *OED walt* v. (early ME *walten*
= OHG *walzan*), fig. 3c, 'to fall (into anger)'. Hillmann's
'vexed' (OE *wælan*), accepted by Moorman, is preferable to
Gordon's 'cast, set' (OE *wæltan*), followed by Andrew & Waldron.
As Hillmann noted, the maiden had earlier (318-24) given the
dreamer reasons that prohibited his crossing the stream.

*1158* Moorman and Andrew & Waldron accepted Gordon's "by
striking me a blow or stopping my advance." Hillmann, fol-
lowing Gollancz, tr., "To work up speed for myself and to
spring high." The former interpretation seems preferable.
For the tr. given here, see *MED bir(e* n.1, sense 4, 'an out-
burst (of grief)', and *halten* v., fig. 2b, 'to waver'.

*1164* *Paye*, the link-word of this stanza-group, recalls
line 1 where the reference to Christ the Prince was antici-
pated. (See ln.)

*1166* Hillmann, following Osgood, tr. *mere₃* 'boundaries',
but most editors favored 'waters'. The poet is evidently
describing the moving 'streams' within the one body of water,
as in line 140.

*1171* The scene reverts to the beginning. Cf. *erber(e)*,
lines 9 and 38.

*1174* Moorman and Andrew & Waldron followed Gordon who
glossed *raxled* 'stretched (myself)' but Hillmann's 'started
up' seems preferable. *Fel* 'dropped down' apparently denotes
a physical movement also, as with *felle* 57. Gordon glossed
*fel in gret affray* 'became greatly agitated'; Hillmann tr.
'fell into great confusion'.

*1177* Eds. compounded *out fleme* and interpreted variously.
The *OED*, Osgood, and Gollancz defined n. 'exile'. Moorman
and Andrew & Waldron followed Gordon who glossed 'driven out',
based on OE *ūt* + *flēme* adj. Hillmann, following Morris, Day
(1919) 414-15, and Oakden I (1930-35) 82, read *outfleme* as a

pp. with omission of *-d* for rhyme. This interpretation seems acceptable, though one need not compound the words.

*1181*  Joining MS *to reme,* as Gollancz suggested, provides a suitable reading here.

*1182-88*  See Bishop (1968) 75-76 for a comparison of this passage to the first speech the dreamer addresses to the pearl-maiden (241-52). Both begin with *O perle,* and there is a correspondence between *del ... daunger* 250 and *doel-doungoun* 1187. The dreamer, who was formerly a tormented man, is now content because of the maiden's glorified state. (See also 249-50n.)

*1185*  Among the four poems in the MS, the term *sermoun* occurs only here, reminding one that the long central portion of *Pe.* (Stanza-Groups V-XVI, lines 241-972) is largely homiletic, in the tradition of *Cl.* and *Pa.* Cf. Rev. 22.6: "Haec verba fidelissima sunt et vera." ("These words are most faithful and true.")

*1186*  Morris' suggestion, made in his glossary, to emend *styke3* to *stryke3* 'walk, go', was followed by Osgood, Gollancz, Chase, and Andrew & Waldron in the belief that the *garlande* denotes the maiden's crown. However, as Gordon noted, comparing the use of *styke3* in *Cl.* 157 and 583, and crediting Hillmann-C (1945) 13-14, the *garlande* is apparently a metaphorical description of the circle of the blessed in heaven, conveying an image either of a jewelled coronet or of a flowered wreath.

Bishop (1957) and (1968) 30-31, 83-84, arguing that the *garlande* represents the final stage in the development of a lapidary metaphor begun in line 2, saw it as a golden ecclesiastical *corona* typifying the New Jerusalem, with its gems symbolizing souls. The *MED* s.v. *gerlōnd* n. lists citations for 'wreath of flowers' s.v. sense 1a and 'coronet of gold' s.v. 2a where *Pe.* is cited, but Hillmann's reference to Dante supports the 'flowered wreath' metaphor: *ghirlanda* (*Paradiso* X, 92) and *ghirlande* (XII, 20). In both passages, Dante pictures encircling souls as flowers, using *piante* 'blossoms' in the former and *sempiterne rose* 'sempiternal roses' in the latter.

Lines 1182-86 bring together the double image of the maiden as pearl and flower. She is addressed as *perle* in 1182 and then pictured within the garland, recalling that she had been described as a *reken rose* (906), a 'beautiful rose' of immortality, and a *lufly flor* (962). (See 962n for further discussion of the flower metaphor in *Pe.*)

*1190*  For retention of MS *geuen,* see 229n.

*1193* Morris glossed *helde* as an adv. 'willingly'; Osgood emended to *helder* 'rather'. Emerson (1927) 831 and Wright (1939) 22 suggested emending to *holde* 'loyally'. Gollancz, Gordon, and Andrew & Waldron rendered *as helde* 'very likely, quite probably' (ON *heldr*). Moorman agreed with Hillmann who took *helde* as the pp. of *MED hēlden* and tr. 1193: "Thus disposed, drawn to God's presence." However, *helde* 'certainly' seems fitting; see *MED helde* adv., sense a. For *as* 'when', see *MED as* conj., sense 10; for *drawen* as a pr. p., see 116n.

*1195* See 129-32n on the use of the link-word *more* in Stanza-Groups III and X. The dreamer now realizes that one must be humble to be led to *mo* 'more' (1194) of God's mysteries.

*1199-1200* See 344-48n on the call for patience and acceptance of God's will.

*1201* Cf. *sette ... sa3t* 52. The dreamer could not be made peaceful then because of the grief that dwelled in his heart. The phr. is echoed now in a contrasting situation, for the dreamer has conquered his own *wreched wylle* 56.

*1204* The concept of friendship with God is found in the Bible. Cf., for example, Song of Songs 5.16: "ipse est amicus meus" ("he is my friend"). Hamilton-B (1955) 250 noted Wisdom 7.14 and John 15.15. In *Cl.* 1229-32 the poet says had Sedecias been God's friend, misfortune would not have befallen. See also 570-72n on *myke3*.

*1205* For a discussion of *hyul* and related words, see 41n. Osgood, Gordon, and Moorman rendered *lote* 'fortune'; Hillmann tr. 'destiny' from *MED lŏt* n.1 (OE *hlot*). Gollancz defined 'vision' from *MED lōt(e* n. (ON *lāt*). Andrew & Waldron tr. 'happening, chance', noting the possibility of a pun on 'speech, word'. *MED lŏt* n.1 cited *Pe.* s.v. sense 1c, 'fortune, destiny, adventure'. The last meaning seems fitting.

It was characteristic of the poet to recall earlier parts of his poem as he drew toward the end. See, for example, the notes to 1201, 1207, and 1212. Here he may be recalling 61-64, where the dreamer's spirit leaves his body and proceeds *in auenture*. In both 64 and 1205, it is understood that the poet is denoting a spiritual adventure and that the words *auenture* and *lote* take in all that occurs from the time the dreamer falls asleep (59) to the time he awakens (1171).

*1206* Hoffman-C (1960) 96 tr., "For pity of my pearl lying prostrate." Editors who supplied translations of this line gave the following sense: "lying prostrate for sorrow for my pearl" (Andrew & Waldron). However, rendering *enclyin* 'humble' in reference to the maiden accords with the poet's emphasis on submission to God's will (1199-1200). Humility is one of the lessons the maiden taught earlier (401-8). (See also 6n.) The *MED* cited *Pe.* s.v. *enclīn* adj., sense 1, 'bowed down; submissive, humble'.

*1207 Hit* recalls *hit* (10, 13), used alongside *her* (4, 6) and *hyr* (8, 9). Hillmann, who tr. all these forms as neuter in her belief that a material pearl was lost in the garden by an actual jeweler, wrote: "The concluding stanza shows the jeweler ready, through renunciation (*byta3te*, 1207), to enter upon the mystical life." (Cf. 4n.) Bloomfield (1969) 301, in discussing the opening stanza, opposed Hillmann's interpretation, which he believed to be based on an "excessive literalism.... Rhetorical hyperboles about 'never finding (or even testing) its peer' need not be uttered by a jeweler to have validity."

*1207-8* Because this formula was often used in the fifteenth and sixteenth centuries in addresses from parent to child, Davis-C (1966) felt these lines might indicate the poet was speaking of his child. However, in an appendix, pp. 329-34, he noted the same form of blessing in passages that do not contain addresses from parent to child. Cowen (1978) revealed that the formula also appears in *Ipomedon*, lines 7095-6, at the end of a comment by the narrator on the changeability of women's affections. It must be concluded, then, that lines 1207-8 prove nothing definite about the relationship between the poet and the pearl-maiden.

*1208* Hillmann, Cawley, and deFord followed Hamilton (1955) 124 who suggested *myn* 'memory'. However, reading *myn* 'mine' seems preferable, since this meaning relates to the dreamer's entrusting his pearl to God (1207).

*1209-10* Garrett (1918) studied *Pe.* in relation to the teachings of the Eucharist, noting the symbolic connection between the gem and the Host. Ackerman-C (1964) 157-61, discussing the allusion to the Parable of the Vineyard and specifically to the penny in Friar Lorens' exposition of the fourth petition of the *Pater Noster* in *Le Somme des Vices et des Vertues,* c. 1279, observed that Lorens equated the daily bread (the consecrated Host) with the penny of the parable.

Sklute (1973) noted that the dreamer has finally realized that he does not have to leave earth to approach the godhead, for it is "present for him in the Eucharist whose essential mystery is in its offer of the bliss of heaven here on earth" (679). Eldredge (1978) compared William Woodford's images of the Eucharistic wafer in *De Sacramento Altaris* to the poet's descriptions of the pearl, notably roundness as a symbol of perfection, purity, and simplicity, and as a reflection of

the shape of the penny paid to the workers in the Parable of
the Vineyard.

*1211* Gollancz and Gordon interpreted pr. subj. *gef* 'may
allow' as a variant spelling of *gyue*. (Cf. *gef* 'may grant'
in *Ga*. 2068.) Moorman and Andrew & Waldron followed Hillmann
who glossed the v. as pt. 3 sg. 'gave, granted', rejecting
the idea that *Pe*. ends with the conventional medieval prayer.
However, this conclusion resembles those of *Cl*. and *Ga*. which
contain the conventional prayer.
The adj. *homly* 'gracious' (*MED*, sense 3a) appears only
here in the MS. The *MED*, in accordance with the reading given
by most editors, cited *Pe*. s.v. sense 1b with fig. application
for *homly hyne*, 'belonging to a household (God's servants)'.
Andrew & Waldron glossed 'humble, obedient (*perh. also of*
[God's] household)'. The word conveys multiple meanings in
this context, for souls in heaven (God's household) are gra-
cious, humble, and obedient.
F.E. Richardson (1962) 312 observed how the poet recalls
the Parable of the Vineyard, paraphrased in 501-72, and ap-
plies the lesson to his audience by using *hyne*. Cf. the use
of that word in 505 and 632, especially the latter. Good
souls, both on earth and in heaven, are frequently called
'servants' in the Bible. Hillmann compared Ephesians 2.18-19
and Rev. 19.10. See also Rev. 7.3 and 22.3, 6, 9.
Tristram (1976) viewed *Pe*.--along with *Ga*., *Piers Plowman*,
Chaucer's poetry, and Dante's *Commedia*--as an affirmation of
"the vision which lies at the end of an arduous pilgrimage"
(212). The unremitting search leads to the Triumph of Life,
associated with Christ and the Eternal Life. The poet re-
veals, in his conclusion, that servants of God on earth will
become his servants in heaven, like the precious pearl.

*1212* The end echoes the beginning. (See ln.) A similar
technique is used in the other poems of the MS. In *Pa*. the
last line echoes the first; in *Ga*. line 2525, the last before
the final bob and wheel, is like 1; and in *Cl*. the theme is
identified in beginning and end, with 1805-8 recalling 5-6
and 1809-10 recalling 27-28.

*CLEANNESS* COMMENTARY

*1* One should interpret *clannesse* widely. Cf. s.v. *MED*
*clĕnnesse* n., 2a, 'moral purity, sinlessness, innocence, up-
rightness, integrity', Trevisa's tr. of Higden's *Polychronicon*
4.221: "Cato was greet in clennes of lyf [*Higd.*
*(2)*: vertuous
lyfe; L vitae integritate]." This broad meaning includes the
specific sense s.v. *MED* 2b, 'chastity'.

*2* For *resoun3* 'narratives', see *OED reason* sb.1, sense 3.

*3* *MED fŏrme* n., 6b, 'literary device or idea', cites *Cl*.
Since the poet emphasizes the punishment of unclean people,
his *forme3* 'themes' about cleanness are used sparingly. See,
for example, lines 27-28, 553-56, 1052-1132, and 1809-10.
Emendation of *forering* to *forþering*, suggested by J.
Thomas (1908) 44 and Bateson (1918) 377, seems unnecessary,
for the poet, anticipating the allegory on clothing in his
paraphrase of the Parable of the Wedding Feast (51-160),
apparently used *forering* 'fashioning' (*MED furrūren*) figura-
tively. Cf. the similar alliteration in *Ga.* 2029: "And fayre
furred wythinne wyth fayre pelures."

*4* The *MED* cited *Cl*. s.v. *contraire* n., 2c, *in (the)*
*contraire* 'on the contrary' and *cŏmbraunce* n., 1a, 'trouble,
difficulty', but see sense 1a for 'contrasting themes' and
1b for 'disaster'. Moorman followed Menner who tr., "But in
(undertaking) the contrary (i.e. the praise of Impurity) he
would find great difficulty and trouble." Andrew & Waldron
agreed with Anderson: "and in doing the contrary [i.e.,
denigrating cleanness] great trouble and difficulty." How-
ever, in view of the three major narratives that follow, Noah
and the Flood (249-544), The Destruction of Sodom and Gomor-
rah (781-1014), and The Sacrilegious Feast of Baltassar
(1357-1804), it seems the poet means that *kark* and *combraunce*
are to be found in themes about uncleanness, not that there
would be difficulty in praising or dispraising the virtue
or the vice.

*7-16* O. Hill (1965) 180-82 felt this admonishing of un-
clean priests indicates a clerical audience for *Cl.* Stone
(1971) 77 observed it is the only attack on corrupt clergymen
in the works of the *Pearl*-poet. Clark & Wasserman (1978b)
287-90, in discussing the importance of this passage in rela-
tion to the rest of the poem, contrasted Nabucho (dove) with
Baltassar (raven--sinful priest) and noted that "essentially
all characters in the story are either doves who will return
[to God] through grace, or ravens who are doomed to feed on
their own pride until it is too late" (290). (See lines 453-
92 for the episode involving the dove and the raven.)

*10* Anderson and Andrew & Waldron read *rychen* 'prepare'
instead of *rechen* 'approach', believing the obscured second
letter is more like *y* than *e*, but one cannot be certain, and
what can be seen of it looks like the top of an *e* squeezed
against the *c*.

*11* Reception of the Holy Eucharist, the transubstantia-
tion of bread and wine into the body and blood of Christ, is
one of the seven sacraments of the Church. Since vessels con-
tain the elements, the poet anticipates the vessel metaphor
here. (See 1145-47n.) Morse (1971) and (1978) 185-207 studied
the vessel imagery in *Cl.*

*15-16* Andrew & Waldron, following Gollancz in emending
*sulped* to *sulpen* 'defile', tr., "they ... altogether defile
both God and his utensils." Anderson, in agreement with Thomas
(1922a) 64, kept *sulped* and tr., "Then they (themselves) are
sinful, and both God and His vessels are utterly defiled."
However, reading *Loþe* 'Scorn' instead of *Boþe* at the start of
16, as Menner and Moorman did, also makes it possible to re-
tain *sulped* in a suitable translation. It is difficult to
distinguish *l* from *b* when the scribe placed the letter close
to a following *o*. Cf. *louf-chere* 28, read as *bone chere* by
Morris, Menner, and Moorman.
    The *MED*, following Menner, cited *Cl.* s.v. *gēre* n., 5a,
'affairs', but in view of the implied reference to holy ves-
sels in line 11, *gere* 'gear' (Morris) seems preferable. As
Morse (1971) 204 pointed out, God's 'gear' would be any of the
altar furnishings. There is anticipation here of the use of
*guere* (1505) to denote the holy vessels from the temple of
Jerusalem.

*21* Eds. read *Nif,* but *&* is apparently joined to *ȝif* in
the MS.

*27-28* Cf. *Pa.* 23-24. The source is Matt. 5.8.

*28* Menner and Moorman followed Morris who glossed *bone*

'good'. Gollancz and Andrew & Waldron, thinking the MS has
*bone,* emended to *leue* 'glad'. Anderson read *loue* as a variant
of *loȝ(e), lowe* 'low' and tr. *loue chere* 'humble bearing'.
Bateson (1924) 98 suggested the compound *loue-chere,* but the
final letter of the first word looks more like *f* than *e.* (Cf.
the shape of *f* in *ful* 27.) The poet apparently applied *louf-
chere* 'countenance of love' to the Lord. For rendering *a* 'the',
cf. *a reche* 'the smoke' 1009 and *a schepon* 'the stable' 1076.

*29-30* Such a pronouncement does not immediately follow
Matt. 5.8, but the poet's contrasting statement here may be
based on Matt. 5.20. Morris tr. *as so saytȝ* 'as one says'.
Gollancz noted, "'as if it thus says' (impersonal)," and Men-
ner's glossary indicates a similar interpretation. Nevanlinna
(1974) 584, in line with Morris' reading, considered the clause
a corruption of *as who* to *as so,* which was "not infrequent in
those areas where *who* was dialectally pronounced without any
consonant sound." Andrew & Waldron followed Anderson who tr.
'That is to say', suggesting derivation from ON phrases of the
type *þat segir svá.* For the reading in this edition, *As* 'Then'
is based on *MED as* conj., sense 1, 'in the same way as', [it]
is elliptical, and *so* is taken as the adv. 'also'.

*32* Gollancz, Anderson, and Andrew & Waldron read *burre*
'shock'. Though Menner saw the fourth letter as the top of a
*y,* he adopted Morris' *burne* 'man'. Moorman agreed. However,
examining the word under the ultra-violet lamp does show what
looks like the top of a *y,* and *burye* 'in (that) city' may be
taken as a synthetic dat. Cf. *borȝe* 'into (that) city' 45.
*MED burgh* n.1 does not list *burye* as a variant spelling, but
*burgh* n.2, drawn from n.1, does. For other examples of *y* with
its bottom illegible, see *Pe.* 419n.
    MS *neȝen,* clearly seen under the ultra-violet lamp, may
stand as the subjunctive 'should draw near', used with *hit.*
For the combination of sg. subject and pl. form of a verb, cf.
*hit arn* in *Pe.* 895, 1199.

*40* Gollancz emended to *clutteȝ trasched* 'old clothes be-
mired', but *clutte* 'patched' (*MED clŏuten* v.1, sense b) seems
preferable. Menner, Moorman, and Andrew & Waldron followed
Skeat (1901) 305 who took *trascheȝ* as the pl. of ME *trash*
'rags' (Swed. *trasa*). Anderson defined 'old shoes', suggested
by the *OED* s.v. *trash* sb. Morris glossed 'trousers ?', which
may be the correct sense. The *OED* s.v. *trouse* sb.2, which
developed into Mod. E. *trousers,* notes that the word was ap-
parently taken in the 16th c. from Irish (and Scotch Gaelic)
*triubhas,* recorded about 1500, but consider the earlier occur-
rence of *trues* in the following citation s.v. sense 1a: "1306
*Pleas of Crown (Irel.)* 34-5 *Edw. I,* m. 10d, Vnum crannoc ..
vnus arcus cum sagittis .. vna spartha (unum par) [so app.;

MS. faint] s[o]tularium cum trues .. precii vnius denarii et oboli."

*41* Morris glossed *tote3* 'toes'; Anderson and Andrew & Waldron favored Gollancz' 'points of shoes'. Skeat (1901) 303-4, deriving *tote3* from LG *tote* 'a peak', tr., "The ends (probably of his toes) peeped out," but Menner stated, "It seems to me as probable that the 'ends' are his elbows." Moorman followed Menner. However, *tote3* may be a variant of *OED tate* sb.1, sense 1, 'a small tuft or lock of hair'. The *OED* cited Douglas' *Æneis* VI. v. 11: "Apon his chin feill cannos haris gray, lyart feltat tatis." The sense suits *Cl.*, since the hair on one's chest would show through a *tabarde totorne,* and this passage should conclude with a description of the upper part of the body. For the *o-a* spelling variant before letters that are not nasals, cf. *harlote3* 860--*harlate3* 34 and *olde* 601--*alde* 529.

*42* Anderson derived pp. *halden* from *MED hēlden* v., sense 1a. (a), 'throw out (ashes)', but *halden* 'thrown' may be taken as an extension in meaning of *MED hōlden* v.1, sense 20a, 'to perform (an action)'.

*43* Eds. expanded the abbr. mark under the *p* of *paraunter* to *er* (*peraunter*), but when the first syllable of this word is spelled out in the MS, it is always *par-*. Note, for example, *Pe.* 588 and *Ga.* 1850, 2343.

*48* Morris suggested a clothing metaphor by glossing *talle* = *tuly* (?) and *tuch* 'cloth'. Anderson tr. *talle* 'general appearance' (OF *ta(i)lle*) and *tuch* 'detail of dress', comparing the uses of *towch* for 'small part' in *Ga.* 120, 1301, and 1677. However, *talle* 'word' and *tuch* 'deed', given by Skeat (1901) 289-90, also suits the context. Skeat compared the alliteration in *Ga.* 1301: *towch ... at sum tale3 ende* 'allusion ... at some story's conclusion'. For the doubling of *l,* cf. *talle* 'story' in *Pe.* 865.

*49* All editors, except Anderson, followed Morris' suggestion to emend *worþlych* to a word meaning 'worldly', because it "restores the contrast between the earthly ruler in this line and the king of heaven in the next" (Andrew & Waldron). However, as Emerson (1921b) 233 pointed out, the contrast is sufficiently evident in the MS readings: *worþlych prynce* 'noble prince' (of earth) and *hy3e Kyng* 'high King' (of creation).

*50* Emendation of MS *in her euen* seems unnecessary. *Her* 'this situation' is ordinarily spelled *here,* but the dropping of final *e* is validated by the following *e* of *euen.* *MED hēr*

adv., 2c, substantiates this reading. For *euen* 'indeed', cf.
*Ga.* 2464 and see *MED ēven* adv., sense 9.

*51 Masse* 'mass-gospel' evidently refers to Matthew's
gospel recited at mass. Kelly & Irwin (1973) 238 observed
the poet was referring to a specific portion used on the nine-
teenth Sunday after Pentecost, the Parable of the Wedding
Feast. (The poet, in his paraphrase [51-160], draws from
Luke 14.16-24, as well as from Matt. 22.2-4 and 8-14.) Kelly
& Irwin noted that the epistle of that mass, taken from Ephe-
sians 4.23-28, suggests (along with Ephesians 4.19-22) the
garment image found in Matthew.

*54* Since *to com* is the second of two infinitives dependent
on the auxil. v. *schulde* (53), *to* is pleonastic. (Cf. *Pe.*
1073n.)

*55* Luttrell (1952) interpreted *bayted* as 'worried with
dogs', giving evidence that this activity may have occurred
with domestic animals as early as the fourteenth century.
See also Morgan (1952) and Luttrell (1956b). The n. *bate*
'baiting' appears in *Ga.* 1461. Anderson, who followed Lutt-
rell, noted that baiting was done "in order to improve the
flavour of the meat by forcing the animals to exert them-
selves." Moorman and Andrew & Waldron followed Menner and
Gollancz who glossed *bayted* 'fattened'.

*59* Morris and Moorman tr. *reþeled* 'prepared'; Menner
defined '? bring together, ? prepare'. Anderson and Andrew &
Waldron followed Gollancz who, believing the word to be dif-
ferent from *roþeled* 890 and *raþeled* in *Ga.* 2294, interpreted
it as a dialect variant of *rozzle* 'to heat' and tr. 'cooked'.
The word may be the same, however, in all three instances.
One may conclude that here the roasted meats were 'brought
together' to form a variety for serving, in line 890 the
Sodomites 'mingled' with one another for sinful pleasure,
and in *Ga.* 2294 *raþeled* describes a stump with roots 'en-
twined' in rocky ground. (See 41n on *o-a* spelling variants.)
*OED roþel* v. cited only *Cl.* with the statement: '(Of obscure
origin and doubtful meaning.)'. See, however, *OED ratheled*
(where *Ga.* is cited), related to *raddled* ppl. a. 1, 'inter-
twined'. The first citation there is 1562, but *raddle* v.1 is
from *raddle* sb.1, an adaptation of AF *reidele*. In *The Parle-
ment of the Thre Ages* (line 261 of the Thornton text), *rothe-
lede* denotes the uttering of words; thus the sense 'bringing
together' (of words) also applies.

Moorman favored Gollancz' *sete*, sb. adj., 'proper point'
and Menner's *ryȝt to þe sete* 'appetizingly'. (Cf. *Ga.* 889n.)
Andrew & Waldron agreed with Anderson's 'right to the sitting
down (at table)'. There may be word-play: the meat had to be

roasted to the *sete* 'proper point' to be served at the *sete* 'seat (at table)'.

62 For *he* 'they', cf. the pl. usage of *he* 657 and *ho* 1267. The *MED* lists many entries s.v. *hē* pron. 3, 1a, 'of persons: they'. Most of them are Midland and Southern, but cf. the use of *heo* in *Joseph of Arimathie,* a West Midland poem of the 14th century: "Þenne þei seȝen Ihesu crist in þat ilke foorme,/Þat heo seȝen him .. whon heo furst comen" (282-83). See also *Pe.* 331-32n.

64 Previous eds. read MS *tne* and emended to *t[ur]ne,* but *tue* (OE *tēon*) may be taken as the pr. sg. subjunctive of the same v. that appears in *Ga.* 1093 as the pp. *towen* 'journeyed'. (See also *Ga.* 1671n.) For confusion caused by the lack of distinguishing features between *n* and *u,* cf. Morris' reading of *anwhere* for *auwhere* 30.

65 See Davenport (1977) for discussion of *nurned,* found in ME only in *Cl., Ga.,* and *St. Erkenwald.*

67 Eds. read *hyȝeȝ* 'servants', but *byȝeȝ* 'harnesses' gives the line a strong, three-stress alliterative pattern, which the poet used most often. Considering that the bottom part of the *b* is open, the word is the same that appears as *byȝe* 1638 to describe the ring of bright gold for Daniel's neck. For the meaning 'harnesses', see *MED bei* n., 1b, 'a chain or collar about the neck of an animal'.

69 *Sower* may be taken as a variant of *swer* 667, as Emerson (1919) 496 noted. All editors, except Morris, separated to *so wer* and tr. *wer* 'defended, excused' (OE *werian*). For the intervening *o* in *sower,* cf. *dowelle* 1674. Menner believed that the alliteration on *w* is destroyed, but the *o* may have been inserted to retain that alliteration here and in line 1674. For alliteration on the second syllable of a word, cf. *excuse* of the next line.

72 Emerson (1919) 496 noted a reading for *plate.* See *OED plot* sb., sense 2, 'an area or piece of ground', and cf. Caxton's *Eneydos* xxxvi 125: "We requyre onely ... a lityll plotte of grounde where we maye dwelle in peas." (See 41n on *a-o* variants.)

73 Anderson glossed *ludych* and *ludisch* 1375 'princely, noble', comparing OE *lēod* masc. 'prince'. The usual reading is 'of the people' or 'of the land'; cf. *ledisch lore* 'land's learning' 1556 and see *MED lēdish* adj.2. The poet may have been punning again: the *ludych lorde* 'lord of the people' was *ludych* 'noble'.

*75* Cf. *sorȝe* 'disgust' 846. Previous eds. tr. 'sorrow', but fig. use of *sorȝe* 'fault' (*OED sore* sb.3--ON *saur-r* 'dirt') suits the context. There may be double-entendre: the guests who refused the invitation committed a *sorȝe* 'fault' that would lead to their *sorȝe* 'misfortune'. Cf. *Pa*. 275: Jonas is in the whale's belly in sin, sorrow, and *sorȝe* 'filth'.

*76* Menner's *wylle gentyl* 'heathen rage' (OE *willa* 'desire') seems preferable to Morris' 'forlorn gentile' and Gollancz' 'Gentile error' (ON *villr*). Tr. 'pagan's lust' (OE *willa*) is also appropriate. Cf. the negative sense in line 687: *tene of my wylle* 'fierceness of my temper'. Anderson defined 'gentile wilfulness', Andrew & Waldron 'gentile (i.e. heathen) perversity'.

*77* Eds. rendered *streeteȝ* 'roads, highways' outside the city (Matt. 22.9: *exitus viarum*) rather than 'streets' within the city (Luke 14.21: *plateas et vicos civitatis*). In lines 51-164, the poet amalgamated Matt. 22.2-4, 8-14 and Luke 14.16-24, and it is sometimes difficult to tell from whom he drew. Anderson favored the reading from Matthew because *wayferande frekeȝ* 79 and *by bonkeȝ* 86 "suggest the countryside rather than the town." However, since wayfaring people and hills can be found in a city, one may conclude that the poet intended Luke's reading here. *Cete* is mentioned in 78, and it is not until 97-99 that the lord tells the servants to seek still further, far out on the land, in furze fields and groves (Luke 14.23: *Exi in vias et saepes* "Go out into the highways and hedges").

*96* Eds. rendered *renischche* 'strange', but 'lowborn', an an extension of 'rough' to denote people not versed in the manners of the nobility (those *of bonde* 88), also suits the context. Cf. the apparent distinction between nobility and lower classes in the phr. þe *better and* þe *wers* 80. Forms of this word in ME appear only in *Cl.*, *Pa.*, *Ga.*, *Erk.*, and *Wars Alex.* Sundén (1929) 47-55 suggested derivation from OE *hrēoh* 'rough'. Hoffman (1970) argued for two derivations: (1) *run-* spellings from OE *rūn* 'secret, mystery'; (2) *ren-* spellings from OE *hrēoh*. There may be more than one derivation, but, because of the many variant spellings in this MS, it is difficult to make a distinction in sense between *run-* and *ren-* spellings.

The meanings given in this edition are based on context. *Pa. runyschly* 191 describes how Jonas is being questioned 'roughly'. *Ga. runischly* 'fiercely' 304 and *runisch* 'fierce' 457 are similar in sense to *Cl. renyschly* 'fiercely' 1724; in all three instances, violent movement is involved, with eyes (304), reins (457), and pen (1724). In *Cl.* 1545, since *runisch saueȝ* refers to the 'strange sayings' on the wall of

Baltassar's hall, the poet may have had 'runic' in mind for word-play. (Weston [1912] included 'runes' in the translation of line 1545.) Binz (1921) suggested that *runish/rennish* are both derived from OE *rūn* 'secret, runic character'. A word related in meaning is OE *(ge)rȳne* 'mystery, dark saying', that which Savage (1926) gave for the etymology of *roynyshe* in *Erk.* 52.

*98* Andrew & Waldron adopted Gollancz' emendation of *Ferre* to *Ferkeʒ* 'Go' to avoid repetition with *ferre* at the end of line 97, but the poet may have used such repetition for rhetorical emphasis. For the two translations of *ferre*, 'far' and 'further', cf. the usage in *Ga.* 1093 and 2151.

*110* Emendation by insertion of an auxil. v. before *demed* seems unnecessary, since *demed* 'was decreed' may be taken as a single v. in the pass. voice. See *Ga.* 120n for other examples. Anderson avoided emendation by considering þat *demed* a relative clause, 'those who made proclamation', qualifying *sergaunteʒ* 109.

*112* This line is not in either Matt. or Luke, the poet's sources. Andrew & Waldron commented: "those who were begotten by one father did not all have the same mother—they were not all legitimate." However, an allegorical interpretation seems fitting here, for the poet is apparently stressing that people *of alle plyteʒ* 'of all ranks' (111) are called to the heavenly banquet: sons from families that were *worþy* 'noble', as well as those from families that were *wers* 'less fortunate' (113), from both the *clene* 'elegant' and the *symplest* 'plainest' (119-20). (A deeper meaning may involve the concept that people of all religions are called to the banquet.) For *on* 'one (kind of)', see *OED one* a., sense 13.

*113* Cf. *worþy oþer wers* to *of fre and of bonde* 88 and þe *riche and þe poueuer* 127.

*113-20* Cf. *Pe.* 445-48n and 570-72n on the doctrine of hierarchy in heaven. The clothes represent one's deeds and desires (169-72), and those dressed best are closest to the front because, having lived best, they have a greater capacity for happiness. "And ʒet, þe symplest in þat sale watʒ serued to þe fulle" (120).

*117* MS *asegge* may stand as the pp. 'delineated' (OE *āsecgan*). Cf. the sense 'described' in the *Peterb. Chron.* cited by the *MED* s.v. *asecgen*: "Nis eaðe to asecgenne þises landes earmða" (1104).
    Anderson, following Morris' suggestion, emended *soerly* to *soberly* 'dignified'; Moorman agreed with Menner who glossed

*soerly* as the adj. 'filthy, base' (ON *saurligr*); and Andrew &
Waldron, following Emerson (1919) 496-97 and Gollancz, emended
to *serly* 'severally'. However, *soerly* 'individually' may be
taken as a variant of *serly*. Emerson (1921b) 235, noting
*hardee* 543 and *swyþee* 1211, stated that the scribe may have
written such a curious *oe* for *e* (*ee*). Cf. in *Ga. trowoe* 813
and *boerne* 1570.

*118* Cf. 121 for similar alliteration, word-play, and the
enforcing of the allegory. All were served at the *mete* 'meal'
(118) with *mete* 'equity' (121). For the latter interpretation,
cf. *mette₃* 'measures' or 'equal portions' (625). The pun is
missed by glossing *mete* 'food' for line 121, as Menner, Gol-
lancz, and Anderson did.

*119* Anderson and Andrew & Waldron followed Gollancz who
tr. *forknowen wern lyte* 'were by no means neglected' (*MED
forknouen* ppl., where only *Cl.* is cited), but it seems prefer-
able to tr. 'recognized' (*MED for(e)-knouen* v.), as Menner and
Moorman did. Moorman gave no meaning for *lyte*; Menner glossed
'few', thinking the poet was saying "there were few 'clene men
in compaynye'." Rendering *lyte* 'quickly' recalls the descrip-
tion of the noblest men on the high dais (115). *MED light(e*
adv. 2, 1c, defines 'quickly', and this adv. is from *light*
adj. 2, where the variant spelling *līt(e* is listed.

*127* Morris noted 'poueuer' as the reading. Emerson (1919)
497 observed that one need not emend, since there are "numerous
similar repetitions" in the MS. Note, for example, the dis-
cussion of *soerly* in 117n.

*136* The elliptical [dirty] clarifies the meaning of
*werkke₃* 'deeds'. The allegory, explained in 169-76, was anti-
cipated in 33-48.

*143* Insertion of *to* before *ne₃e* is unnecessary, since
*ne₃e* 'to approach' may be rendered as a plain infin., which
occurs frequently in ME. Cf. *greue* 'to reprimand' 138, and
see Mustanoja (1960) 514 for further discussion.

*144* Considering *on* 'one' pleonastic reveals a construc-
tion similar to that which appears at the start of line 892.

*146* Most editors emended to *gnede* 'niggardly, beggarly',
but the MS form may be retained with an accent over the final
*e* of *nedé* (*OED needy* a.). Cf. *reken* 10 and *pouer* 146 for
other examples of adverbs without *-ly*. Anderson retained
*nede* as an adj. 'meagre' and tr., "You set a very poor and
meagre value on me and my house."

*148* Gollancz, believing the *erigaut* was "by no means a shabby garment ... but something ultra-fashionable," a costume worn by a low minstrel, compared a passage in the *Book of the Kinght of La Tour Landry,* but no sound evidence is presented for equating *erigaut* with the *cote hardy* mentioned in the *Book.* There are only two other quotations in the *MED* under *herigaud,* and neither one describes the garment as being ultra-fashionable or as being worn by a minstrel. For a fuller refutation of Gollancz' theory, see Luttrell (1960).

*160* *Quoynt* 'courteous', an extension of *OED quaint* a. (adv.), sense 5, 'elegant', points up the allegory, since the man in the improper garment lacked the *cortaysye* that connotes divine grace. (See *Pe.* 432n.) Morris, Gollancz, and Andrew & Waldron tr. *quoynt* 'wise', Menner, Moorman, and Anderson 'well-dressed'.

*162* See *Pe.* 570-72n for comment on this line.

*163-64* Cf. lines 80-81.

*169-76* Cf. the poet's explanation of the clothing metaphor, especially lines 171-72, to Augustine's statement in "Sermo XC," *PL* 38.561: "Vestis quippe illa in corde, non in carne inspiciebatur; quæ si desuper fuisset induta, etiam servis non fuisset occultata." ("The garment that was looked for is in the heart, not on the body; for had it been put on externally, it could not have been concealed even from the servants.") [Trans. in *A Select Library of the Nicene and Post-Nicene Fathers of the Christian Church,* ed. Philip Schaff, Vol. 6; rpt. Grand Rapids, Michigan, 1956, p. 393.] Cf. also *PL* 38.562: "'Finis autem præcepti est,' Apostolus dicit, 'charitas de corde puro, et conscientia bona, et fide non ficta (1 Tim. I, 5).' Hæc est vestis nuptialis." ("'Now the end of the commandment,' says the Apostle, 'is charity out of a pure heart, and of a good conscience, and of faith unfeigned.' [I Tim. 1.5] This is 'the wedding garment.'") [Trans. in Schaff, p. 394.]

*172* Anderson read *lyned* 'lined' instead of *lyued* 'lived by' and tr., "and (which you have) lined with the good disposition of your heart."

*177* Andrew & Waldron followed Gollancz in emending *fele* to *feler* 'more', but *fele* 'many' seems appropriate in reference to all the faults listed in lines 178-88.

*178-88* Kittendorf (1979) 324 compared 1 Cor. 6.9-10. However, the poet's list of sins is much more extensive and includes *bobaunce, bost,* and *priyde* near the top. The fact that *slauþe* is named first is probably due only to the demands of alliteration. Cf. also Matt. 15.19 and Gal. 5.19-21.

*185* *Dysheriete* 'disinheriting' and *depryue* 'depriving', infinitives tr. prog., have the force of gerunds. Cf. this pattern to the pp. used in an active sense, as with *stad* 'standing' 90, and see Mustanoja (1960) 511-82 for discussion of the three non-finite verbal forms in ME: infinitive, gerund, and participle.

*186* Eds. defined *schreweȝ* 'wicked persons, villains, evildoers', but since the reference is apparently to females, 'mistresses' pinpoints the meaning better. Cf. *OED shrew* sb.2, sense 3, 'a woman given to railing or scolding or other perverse or malignant behavior'. Gardner (1965) 154 tr. 'whores'; M. Williams (1967) 128 tr. 'wenches'.

*192* Morris, Menner, and Gollancz glossed *sour* 'vile' (ON *saurr* 'filth'). Anderson glossed 'vile' but favored the etymology given by Luttrell (1955) 216: OE *sūr* (*OED sour* a. & sb.1, II. 4, 'extremely distasteful or disagreeable'). Luttrell tr. *sour tourneȝ* 'disgusting practices'; 'immoral actions' also suits the context. *Sour* appears again in *Cl.* as the sb. adj. 'leavened bread' 820 and the adj. 'bitter' 1036. Cf. also *soure* 'unpleasant' in *Ga.* 963.

*194* Menner, Gollancz, and Anderson glossed *red* 'read', but this interpretation does not accord with *herkned and herde* 193 and *breued I herde* 197. The poet was apparently referring to oral recitation. Cf. *reden* 'preach' 7 and *redde* 'said' in *Ga.* 443.

*197* Cf. *Ga.* 2521n on alliteration and oral delivery.

*200* Editors' glossaries indicate they believed the poet's phr. *hatel of his wylle* denotes the 'anger of his (God's) will', and *MED hãtel* adj., sense d, cites only *Cl.* with this meaning. Anderson glossed *hatel* 'hatred', but without comment. Since *hot* means 'angry', rendering *hatel of his wylle* 'opposition to his will' avoids redundancy and makes clear an important aspect of the poet's theme: disloyalty in the form of hostility toward God's will is an evil that leads to all other sins. Cf. *MED,* sense a, 'hostile'. The adj. in *Cl.* is used as a n., and 'opposition' is a Mod. E. synonym for 'hostility'. For *of* 'to', cf. *MED of* prep., 18b.

*205* *ffor þe fyrste* 'At the start' may be compared to *fro fyrst* 'from (the) start' 1069 and *of fyrst* 'at first' 1714. See also *MED for* prep., 15b, 'at (a point in time)'. The caesura does not always divide a line evenly; for another

example of unbalancing to the left, cf. 203. Morris placed a
comma after 204, a period after 205 and paraphrased: "For the
first fault the devil committed, he felt God's vengeance."
Menner and Gollancz recognized that line 205 begins a new pas-
sage, but they gave no specific entry for *ffor* in their glos-
saries. Anderson glossed the word as a conj. 'thus, now';
Andrew & Waldron, with a period after 204, tr. 205: "For the
false fiend committed the first crime."

Menner, p. 76, stated that the poet wrote about the fall
of Lucifer (205-34) and of Adam (235-48) because he wanted to
illustrate that God did not become angry in his punishment of
the disloyal angels and the first parents, but he did grow
fierce when he sent the flood because that punishment was
directed against carnal sin. This view has been generally
accepted. (See, for example, Gollancz' Preface, pp. xv-xvi;
Anderson's Introduction, p. 4; Moorman's note to 204ff.; and
Andrew & Waldron's 213-15n.) Menner's interpretation implies
that the poet, contrary to Christian doctrine, considered the
lesser sin of carnal corruption the greater, and the greater
sin of disloyalty to God the lesser, but *Cl.* is a sophisticated
homily, and the poet's audience probably understood that words
used to denote degrees of emotion in God, being anthropomor-
phic, need not imply doctrinal opinions. For a different in-
terpretation of the poet's placing of the Lucifer and Adam
exempla before his main narratives, see 247n.

*208* Eds. accepted the *OED*'s suggestion for *a reward* 'a
recompense' as an improvement over Morris' *areward* 'apostate'.
Anderson, for example, glossed *kydde a reward* 'made return,
responded'; Andrew & Waldron tr., "And he made a recompense
unnaturally, like a churl." However, by separating MS *areward*
to *are Ward* 'before (his) Guardian', one may note a connection
to Anglo-Saxon tradition. Cf. the opening of Caedmon's
'Hymn': "Nū sculon herian heofon-rīċes Weard." *Ward* was still
used to denote a 'guardian' in the ME period, as *OED ward*
sb.1 shows. Other rare synonyms for God are *Cheuentayn* in
*Pe.* 605 and *Lodeȝmon* in *Cl.* 424.

*211-12* In England, the devil was associated with the
north country. Cf. Chaucer's *The Friar's Tale* in which the
devil, disguised as a yeoman, says his dwelling is "fer in
the north contree" (1413). *Tramountayne* 'north pole star',
as the *OED* pointed out, was originally so called in Italy and
Provence because it was visible beyond the Alps. Emerson
(1919) 497-98 directed the reader to Skeat's notes on the
fall of Lucifer, pp. 24-26, in Vol. II of his edition of
*P. Pl.*

The source for Lucifer's rebellion is Isaias 14.12-14.
Cf. *Cl.* to vv. 13-14: "qui dicebas in corde tuo: In caelum
conscendam, super astra Dei exaltabo solium meum; sedebo in

monte testamenti, in lateribus aquilonis;/ascendam super alti-
tudinem nubium, similis ero Altissimo." ("And thou saidst in
thy heart: I will ascend into heaven, I will exalt my throne
above the stars of God, I will sit in the mountain of the cove-
nant, in the sides of the north./I will ascend above the height
of the clouds, I will be like the most High.") The note to
v. 12 in the Douay Bible states that what is said of the king
of Babylon in this passage, according to the letter, "may also
be applied, in a spiritual sense, to Lucifer the prince of
devils." The poet foreshadows the fall of Baltassar in the
last episode of *Cl*. (See Zavadil [1962] 171-85 for discussion
of the analogies of Babylon with hell and Baltassar with the
devil.)

*215* All editors, except Anderson, equated *metȝ* with *mess*
'pity, mildness'. Anderson, following the *OED*, glossed *metȝ*
'blow' (OF *mes*) and tr., "Nevertheless, His blow was in keep-
ing with the moderation of His nature." However, it seems
more likely that the poet was referring to Lucifer's *metȝ*
'capacities' to do evil, not to God's pity. This characteriza-
tion of Satan anticipates lines 229-34, a passage in which the
proud, stubborn fiend defies the Creator. *Metȝ* is the same n.
that occurs as *metteȝ* 'measures' 625 from OE *(ge)met*.

*216* Morris' *tour* 'tower' accords with the idea that Luci-
fer lost the tenth part of the heavenly kingdom. Cf. *Cursor
Mundi*: "And þus he lost þat heȝe tour" (487). Anderson and
Andrew & Waldron agreed with Gollancz who believed that *tour*,
referring to God's loss of his angels, was an aphetic form of
OF *atour* 'entourage', but the word here, as Menner noted in
his glossary, may be applied to heaven. Cf. *Pe*. 966: "Þou
may not enter wythinne hys tor." See also Fowler (1973) 332:
"Though he [Lucifer] lost there the tithe portion of his rich
tower."

*222-24* Eds. glossed *swarmeȝ* as a v., but it seems the
poet was describing movement of the 'swarms of bees' into the
hive. For *hyue* as a synthetic dat., cf. 32n. In *The Summoner's
Prologue*, lines 1693-98, Chaucer compares friars to bees going
out and in of "an hyve ... the develes ers."
  The poet exaggerated the number of days the angels fell.
*Forty* fits the alliteration and anticipates the number of
days the rain fell during the flood. Stone (1971) 87 observed
that Caedmon has the devils falling only three days and nights.
Menner, in citing *The Fall and Passion*, noted seven days and
snow imagery similar to *Cleanness*. "Seue daies a seue niȝt .
as ȝe seeþ þat falliþ snowe:/vte of heuen hi aliȝt . an in to
helle wer iþrow" (13-14). *P. Pl*. B-text I reads: "But fellen
out in fendes liknesse . nyne dayes togideres" (119). See
also Whiting & Whiting (1968) 527-28.

*226* Morris glossed *smylt* '? decayed', Gollancz 'fine', Menner and Moorman 'strained'. Anderson glossed 'refined', comparing MDu. and MLG *smilten*; Andrew & Waldron tr., "but as sieved meal smokes very thickly under a fine sieve." The word, however, may be from OE *smelt* 'sardine', as the poet describes devils like fish in the lake of hell. Cf. *Erk*. 302: "Quen we are dampnyd dulfully into þe depe lake." Eds. rendered *siue* 'sieve', but this word may be equated with *seueȝ* 'stews' 825. Cf. in *Ga*. 892 fish in *sewe* 'broth'.

*229* Anderson, reading Þis instead of *ȝis*, commented in his textual note: "Þ of Þis from u.-v." (ultra-violet photograph). However, my examination of that first letter under the ultra-violet lamp in the British Library did not reveal to me a clear reading, and *ȝis* suits the context well.

*230* Morris did not record *wyȝ* in his glossary. Gollancz (1919) 154 equated *wyȝ* with Satan, but in his edition he glossed 'God', as all other editors did. *Wyȝ* denotes 'God' in line 5, alliterating with *wroth*, but the meaning there is that God *does* become angry with sinners. It does not seem likely that the poet would say God *did not* become wrathful with Lucifer and the rebellious angels, especially in view of the punishment described in 219-29. For *wrathed not* 'did not grieve', cf. the connotation of *wrathed* in *Ga*. 726 and see *OED wrath* v., sense 5, 'to bring to grief'. Lines 230-34 refer to Satan, then, who shows no sorrow for his sin and continues to defy God. *Wyȝ(e)* usually denotes people, but the poet often adapted words in an alliterative pattern according to the meaning of the passage. Cf. 498n on his different uses of *Tolke*.

*231* It seems unnecessary to emend MS *wylnesful* 'obstinacy' to *wylfulnes*, as Menner, Moorman, and Andrew & Waldron did. The *OED* cited *Cl*. s.v. *wilnesful*, explaining the form as the gen. of *wilne* 'desire' sb. + *-ful*.

*231-32* Cf. *Cursor Mundi*: "For god oweþ not ȝif him mercy/ Þat þer aftir wolde not cry" (485-86).

*233* All editors, except Anderson, defined *rape* 'blow', as if the word referred to God's punishment. Gollancz compared Swed. *rappa* v. Anderson glossed 'fall, ruin' (ON *hrap*). 'Treachery' (AF *rape*) also suits the context.

*247* Menner, p. 76, believed the poet told about Lucifer and Adam to illustrate "acts of vengeance in which God did *not* become angry." (See also 205n.) However, one may interpret differently: first Lucifer sinned through pride, the worst of the deadly sins, and then he tempted the first par-

ents to commit disobedience; because of the fall of Adam and
Eve, mankind descended to lechery, which prompted God to send
the flood. Thus there is a logical explanation for the poet's
placement of the Lucifer and Adam exempla before his major
narratives. C. Brown (1904) 121 noted the poet's probable
indebtedness to 2 Peter 2.4-7 in which the punishment of
wicked angels, the flood, and the destruction of Sodom and
Gomorrah are mentioned in that order.

Eds. gave readings for *mesure* and *meþe* that make it seem
as if the poet wished to portray God's mildness towards Adam
and Eve. However, no mercy was shown when the first parents
were banished from the Garden of Eden. For *mesure* 'reason',
cf. *P. Pl.* B-text XIV: "And if men lyued as mesure wolde .
shulde neuere more be defaute" (70). For *meþe* 'justice', cf.
*OED methe* sb., sense 1, 'proportion', the citation there from
*E. E. Psalter* LXXIX. 6: "Þou salt ... gif vs drink in teres
in meth [Vulg. in mensura]," and OE *mǣð* 'what is meet, right'.

*257* Morris thought *forme foster* denoted Adam. Kock (1903)
368 corrected the reading to 'first offspring'.

*258* Eds. expanded MS *adm* (with abbr. mark over *m*) to
'Adam'. I am reading 'Addam', for in line 237 MS *am* (with
the same abbr. mark) shows that mark represents a preceding
*da*. The mark is similar to the one that denotes *ra* in 'grace'
296.

*261* *Lykkest* 'most similar joys', as a sb. adj., relates
to *hade geuen* 259. Morris suggested emending *lede* to *ledeӡ*.
Other editors believed that n. referred to Adam. For example,
Andrew & Waldron tr., "and those who lived immediately after
were most like the man (Adam)." However, *lede* may be rendered
collectively as 'people', whom God favored.

*269-72* In the Fragment of the *Book of Noah* CVI, 13-15,
placed after the *Book of Enoch* in *The Apocrypha and Pseudepi-
grapha of the Old Testament in English*, ed. R.H. Charles, Vol.
2 (Oxford UP, 1913), p. 279, Enoch speaks of angels of heaven
who "transgress the law, and have united themselves with women
and commit sin with them, and have married some of them, and
have begot children by them. And they shall produce on the
earth giants not according to the spirit, but according to the
flesh, and there shall be a great punishment on the earth, and
the earth shall be cleansed from all impurity." The poet ap-
parently used apocryphal material here to portray evil angels
turned fiends spreading more corruption among mankind after
the fall of Adam and Eve. In the Vulgate, Gen. 6.2-4 describes
*filii Dei* 'sons of God' taking to themselves *filias hominum*
'daughters of men', but since the Septuagint Bible refers to
'angels of God' instead of 'sons of God', the earliest Church

Fathers accepted the *Book of Enoch* as part of the Biblical canon. Tertullian, for example, in *Apologeticus* 22.3 tells of how "angelis quibusdam sua sponte corruptis corruptior gens daemonum evaserit" ("certain angels corrupted themselves and how from them was produced a brood of demons"). Later Church Fathers such as Augustine and Jerome discredited the *Book of Enoch,* and equated the Vulgate's *filii Dei* with the descendants of Seth and the *filias hominum* with the descendants of Cain.

279 Gollancz emended *marre* to *marred* 'afflicted', but MS *marre* may be taken as a pa. t. with omission of *-d* before the þ of þ*ise.* (See *Pe.* 142n for other examples.) Menner, Anderson, and Andrew & Waldron rendered *marre* 'corrupt', but 'harmed' seems suitable here to denote the injury done by the evil monsters to the innocent among mankind (þ*ise* oþ*er*).

284 Eds. rendered *wyȝe* 'man, one': "as one anguished inwardly He said to Himself" (Anderson). However, reading *Wyȝe* 'God' suits the context and shows how the poet drew from his source, for lines 283-84 mark a transition from verse 6 to 7 of Gen. 6, in which the reference to God is direct. The Douay Bible, in the note to verse 6, explains the anthropomorphism: "God, who is unchangeable, is not capable of repentance, grief, or any other passion. But these expressions are used to declare the enormity of the sins of men, which was so provoking as to determine their Creator to destroy these his creatures, whom before he had so much favoured."

292 The usual reading of this line, stemming apparently from the glossary of Menner s.v. *wrench* 'trick, deceitful deed', is: "I shall make sure to be careful that I take note of their deceitful deeds" (Andrew & Waldron). Morris glossed 'device', but without explanation. The *OED,* which does not cite *Cl.,* lists s.v. sense 2 of *wrench* (OE *wrenc*) sb.1 'deceit', but sense 1 has 'cunning or wily action, artifice', and one may derive 'means of existence' from this, since the poet is apparently anticipating the preservation of Noah, his family, and the animals.

307 *Strenkle* 'send down' anticipates the Lord's 'scattering' of rain to bring on the flood. For *distresse* 'punishment', cf. *MED,* sense 1d, 'damage'. Anderson rendered *strenkle my distresse* 'scatter (put forth) my power'. Moorman adopted Menner's 'dispel my grief'.

312 Kelly & Irwin (1973) 246, discussing the flood as a type of Baptism and the ark as a symbol for the vessel of the body, noted that the ark is covered with pitch in Gen. 6.14, but the poet changed the detail to 'clay' and also used *clay-daubed* in line 492. "We recall that God formed man's

body of the slime of the earth (*Gen.* 2.7), and as man's flesh
is clay so the covering of the Ark is clay."

*313* Gollancz tr., "all the jointing having been fastened
with nails," but it seems the poet was describing the tight
closures or 'seals' made by the placing of the planks. Ander-
son and Andrew & Waldron agreed with Menner who defined *endentur*
'jointing by means of notches'. Because details in the illus-
trations do not always match the poet's descriptions, the per-
forations visible in the illustration of the ark on f. 60
should not determine this textual reading. For example, the
ark in this picture has no top covering and is being operated
with a hand tiller and an oar, but the poet described the boat
*withouten ... hande-helme* (417-19).

*318* Anderson and Andrew & Waldron followed Gollancz in
emending *vpon* to *vponande* 'opening', but MS *vpon* may be re-
tained as a pass. infin. 'to be opened'. Cf. *to wyte* 'to be
denounced' 76 and *to prayse* 'to be praised' 189.

*322* Morris, Menner, and Moorman rendered *boskeȝ* 'bushes'.
Andrew & Waldron adopted Gollancz' emendation to *boskenȝ* 'divi-
sions of a cow-house'. Anderson glossed *boskeȝ* 'cow-houses',
comparing Medieval Latin *boscar*, but in lines 530-39 all types
of animals leave the ark, among them *Wylde wormeȝ* who would
have entwined themselves around *boskeȝ* 'shrubs' (Mod. E.
'woody plants').

*333-38* As Anderson noted, the poet combines two Biblical
accounts here, Gen. 6.19-20 and 7.2-3. The clean animals are
ceremonially pure. Noah sacrifices some of these when the
flood ceases. (See lines 505-10, based on Gen. 8.20-21.)

*342* Gollancz' *daunger* 'subjection' seems preferable in
this context to Menner's 'danger', adopted by Andrew & Waldron.
Anderson glossed 'awe (of God)'.

*359* Emendation of *stysteȝ* to *stynteȝ* (OE *styntan*) seems
unnecessary, since the former may be derived from ON *stytta*
(*OED stutte* v.). Cf. the medial *s* in *stysteȝ* to intervening
consonants in *hastyfly* 200, *lencþe* 224, and *strenkþe* 880.
  Since *niyȝ* 'arduous activity' (OF *anui*) suits this context,
emendation to a form for 'night' seems unnecessary. The word
looks like *myȝ* in the MS, but a mark does not always appear
over an *i* to distinguish that minim from preceding ones. Cf.
*niyȝt* 1779, read by editors as *myȝt*, and see also *Pe.* 630n.

*362* The poet's wide usage to denote the ark meets the
demands of alliteration; cf. *kyst* 346, *bot* 473, *cofer* 310,
*lome* 412, *gyn* 491, and *mancioun* 309. Morris s.v. *whichche*

cited *Promptorium Parvulorum*: '*Hutche* or *whyche,* cista, archa'.

363  *Bonkeʒ* may be interpreted as a synthetic dat., 'over embankments'. The *MED* s.v. *bank(e* n.1, 1d, following Gollancz' 'edges of the water', cited only *Cl.* with the meaning '? the crest of a wave'. Andrew & Waldron glossed 'bank of water'. Anderson rendered *abyme* 'depths of the earth' rather than 'sea depths' and tr. *bonkeʒ con ryse* 'the land rose up'.

363-72  F. Moorman (1905), in an article praising the nature descriptions of the poet, noted the "similarity of style between this passage and some of the sea-pictures in Old English poetry, especially those of the *Exodus*" (105). Jacobs (1972), after discussing these verses and 947-72 in *Cl., Pa.* 129-64, and *Ga.* 1998-2005 in relation to other ME alliterative poetry, concluded that only the *Gawain*-poet displays individual originality. It is in keeping with what we know of him that he alone should show himself as "consistently the master of the storm-topos rather than its servant" (714-15).

365  *Brymme* apparently refers to a body of water (Morris' definition), not to a 'bank', as most editors glossed it. No editor placed a period after *vnbrosten,* but, with this punctuation, *Bylyue* modifies *rered* (366). For other examples of enjambement, cf. 159-60 and 171-72, and *Pa.* 43-44 and 53-54.

375  Morris and Menner equated *wylger* 'more powerful' with ME *wilgern* 'perverse', but Gollancz showed the relationship of this word to *welgest* 'healthiest' 1244, noting OE *welig* 'rich, prosperous' and comparing ON *vælig,* derived from MLG *welich* 'strong'. Anderson interpreted *wylger* as a variant of *wylder,* comparing the v. *awilgeð* beside *awildeþ* in *Ancrene Wisse.*

380  Since the people had already hurried to the high hills (379), reading *haled* 'hastened' is redundant. (Editors who retained MS *aled* kept that meaning.) For *aled* 'grieved', see *MED eilen, -ien* v. (variant *alen*), sense 4, and cf. *ayled* 'afflicted' in *Ga.* 438. For *faste* 'hardship', see the *MED* s.v. *fast(e* n., 3b.

382  Cf. 354. Morris' insertion of *&* and Gollancz' of *ne* after *ryg* 'tempest' seem unnecessary. Olszewska (1942) 244-45 suggested that the original version of *Cl.* had *rayn and ryg* (Old West Norse *hregg ok regn*). Though Norse influence may be noted here, Olszewska's reading is based on a switching of the terms in the formula, and MS *raynande* 'shedding rain' may stand. In the translation, *þe roʒe raynande ryg* 'the tempest, shedding rain turbulently' is transposed to

the preceding line. For elliptical [And] at the start of
382, cf. *Pe.* 363n, *Ga.* 11n, and [and] in *Ga.* 845-46.

*385* Gollancz emended *wat͡ȝ no* to *on* 'alone' and tr., "The
highest mountains on the moor then alone were more dry," but,
as Moorman and Andrew & Waldron pointed out, the MS reading
may be retained, the sense being that even the tallest moun-
tains were becoming flooded but served as a temporary haven
for the people. Anderson emended *wat͡ȝ* to *were* to agree with
*mountayne͡ȝ*, but *moste mountayne͡ȝ* may be taken singularly in
reference to the group of 'tallest mountains'. (Cf. 781n.)
For *wat͡ȝ* 'had', cf. lines 886 and 1092; for *dry͡ȝe* 'dry land'
as a sb. adj., cf. *druye* 472. Anderson glossed *dry͡ȝe* 'secure'
(OI *drjúgr*).

*395* Moorman followed Menner who tr. *þat amounted þe mase*
'so that the state of confusion increased'. Anderson tr.
'that amounted to vanity', deriving *mase* from *OED maze* sb.,
sense 1. Andrew & Waldron, following Gollancz, tr. 395: "so
that the confusion signified that His mercy had passed," but
they also suggested, 'it came to damn-all', for the first half
of the line, comparing the use of *mase* in *P. Pl.* B. Prol. 196.
In this edition, Þat 'That One, He' refers to *Creator* 394.
Davenport (1978) 223 suggested: Þat *amounted þe mase* 'The one
who built up the confusion' (God).

*411* Morris glossed *a͡ȝtsum* 'sorrowful'. Bateson (1918)
380 noted that the word refers to Noah and his family. *MED*
*eighte-sum* cites only *Cl.* and *Cursor Mundi* 9672.

*418* *Capstan* is a device for hauling up the anchor. In
*Pa.* 103, it is called *wyndas* 'windlass'. See *Pa.* 101-8 for
other nautical descriptions.

*419* Cf. *Pa.* 185n on the use of *hurrok* 'bilge'. Ekwall
(1912) 169 suggested that the word is related to ME *thurrock*
'bilge', and Macdonald (1953) 277 supported this interpreta-
tion. The *MED*, following Menner, defined 'part of a vessel
next to the stern'. Morris glossed 'oar', Gollancz 'some
detachable part of the boat', Anderson and Andrew & Waldron
'rudder-band,' and Moorman 'stern'.

*427* Emendation of *seuenþe* to a word meaning 'seventeenth'
may be avoided, for the poet was apparently recapitulating
*sone com þe seuenþe day* (361), using Gen. 7.10 for part of
his source: "Cumque transissent septem dies, acquae diluvii
inundaverunt super terram." ("And after the seven days were
passed, the waters of the flood overflowed the earth.") It
was the seventeenth day of this second month, as Gen. 7.11
states, but the reference need not be to the day of the month
here.

Eds. rendered ry3te3 as the adv. 'precisely', but the v.
ry3te3 'comes to pass' (OE *rihtan*), which appears in *Ga.* 308,
is fitting here.

*430* Emending yre3 to yþe3 'waves' seems unnecessary. *Yre3*
may be a variant of *ayre* 'air' 1010. See *MED air* n.1, 4c, and
cf. the description of misty hills in *Ga.* 2081.

*433* Andrew & Waldron agreed with Morris & Skeat (1872)
and Gollancz who glossed ro3ly 'fortunate' (OE *rōw* 'mild').
Moorman, following Thomas (1922a) 65, equated ro3ly with *rwly*
'sorrowful'. Menner glossed '? rough', noting the adj.
*roghlych* in *Pa.* 64, and Anderson interpreted the word as a
sb. adj. 'troubled vessel'. 'Tottering ark' also suits the
context. Cf. the description in 421-23 and the use of ro3(e)
to denote turbulent movement in *Pa.* 144 and 147.

*439* Stange3 'whirlpools', with voicing of the consonant
before -e3, is from *OED stank* sb., sense 1 (OF *estanc*); cf.
*stanc* 'pool' 1018. Anderson glossed 'floodgates', even though
the first instance of this sense 2 in the *OED* is dated 1604,
because Gen. 8.2 reads: "Et clausi sunt fontes abyssi, et
cataractae coeli." ("The fountains also of the deep, and the
flood gates of heaven were shut up.") However, the poet some-
times altered Biblical details. See *Pe.* 163n for reference
to other examples.

*447* Gen. 8.4 mentions only *super montes Armeniae* 'upon
the mountains of Armenia'. To make the poet's addition accord
with the French source cited in 448n, Gollancz, Anderson, and
Andrew & Waldron emended to *Ararach,* but the poet perhaps wrote
*Mararach* to fit a basic AA/AX alliterative pattern on *M,* and
it may be that Mount Ararat was also referred to as *Mararach*
through association with "a roche that was wone to ben callid
Mariak, where Cristis *archa* with othere relikis where kept"
(*The Bodley Version of Mandeville's Travels,* ed. M.C. Seymour,
*EETS,* 253 [1963], p. 61). *Mariak,* the Holy Rock of Bethel,
and Ararat are allegorically associated: Christ's *archa* 'wood-
en coffer', from which he rose for the salvation of mankind,
was kept in the former, and the coming of Noah and his group
from their *archa* on *Mararach* also meant salvation for mankind.

*448* C. Brown (1904) 153 showed the dependence of *Cl.* on
the French text of *Mandeville's Travels* by citing, among other
passages, the following from p. 74 of George Warner's edition
for the Roxburghe Club (1889): "Et la delez y ad vn autre mon-
taigne qad a noun Ararach, mes ly Iuys lappelent Thanez, ou
larche Noe se arresta." Gollancz pointed out that one of the
variant spellings for *Thanes* is *Chano,* representing *Kuh-i-Nuh*
(Noah's mountain), the Persian name for Ararat.

*449* MS *wern,* a pl. variant of *were,* may be retained here as the v. relating to sg. *kyste* because *Bot þaȝ* 'Yet' places the construction in the subjunctive mood. For *wern* 'had', cf. the usage in 403 and 442.

*456* The *MED* considered *corbyal* erroneous but cited *Cl.* with that spelling s.v. *corbel* n. However, *corby* may be the MS reading, corresponding to *MED corb* n., with *-y* equalling *-e* as in *skyly* (62) and *skylly* (529). In this instance, the word division is difficult to determine; *cor by al vn* all seem to be slightly separated.

Eds. rendered *colored ... cole* (charcoal) literally, but the poet may have intended fig. meanings as the primary ones to stress the idea that the raven was *vntrwe.* For *colored* 'perverted', see *MED cŏlŏuren* v., 3b; for *cole* 'heartless', see *MED cōl* adj., sense 2.

*457* Anderson glossed *fanneȝ* 'glides (with outspread wings)', but 'flutters' is also fitting, since the image of gliding is in the poet's use of *haleȝ* 'soars' 458.

*458* The usual reading of *vpon hyȝt* 'aloft' redounds with *hyȝe* 'high'. Cf. 'with strength' to *vpon hyȝt* 'with force' (*Pa.* 219), where *hale* also alliterates. For the meaning, cf. *MED heigh* adj., 3a, 'strong, powerful'.

*459* This detail is not in Gen. 8.6-7, the poet's source, nor are the descriptions of the raven, its actions, and Noah's reaction to its disobedience (lines 453-68). Menner noted that the bird's finding of carrion as the explanation of its failure to return to the ark stemmed from Jewish and Arabic tradition, coming through the writings of the Church Fathers into Middle English.

*464* Gollancz and Andrew & Waldron followed Fischer (1900) 42 and Schumacher (1914) 169 in emending *kyst* to [*ch*]*yst* for alliteration. However, the poet sometimes used imperfect alliterative combinations, as Menner noted in his Introduction, p. lvii.

*469* The MS has *doūe,* with u representing v and the long mark over it a following n. Cf. *dovene* 481. Both occurrences show retention of the early ME *n*-declension of fem. nouns for the dat. and the acc. (See *An Elementary Middle English Grammar,* J. Wright and E.M. Wright, 2nd ed. [Oxford UP, 1928], p. 144.) The *ne* ending of *doune* is an example of metathesis. Cf. *sakerfyse* 507--*sacrafyse* 510. Knigge (1885) 54 favored Morris' suggested emendation to *douue,* and all editors adopted it.

*473* *Bot* 'boat' seems to be the primary meaning, as Thomas (1922a) 65 noted, but the poet was apparently punning again. *Bot* could also mean 'remedy', and news about dry land arriving at the 'boat' would offer the 'remedy' Noah and his group were seeking. Morris glossed 'boot', Gollancz 'help', Anderson 'boat'; Andrew & Waldron followed Menner who interpreted the word as a variant of the v. *bod* and tr., "Bring a message to announce (foretell) bliss to us all."

*475* Morris & Skeat (1872) read 'wyrle*s*', evidently designating the abbr. mark after the *l* of 'wyrle' as *es* rather than *e*, but that same mark elsewhere represents *e*. (Cf., for example, 'loghe' 366.) Andrew & Waldron adopted Gollancz' emendation to 'wyrle[d]', but *wyrle* may be taken as a pt. form without ending before a vowel. (See *Pa.* 219n for other examples.) Anderson printed *wyrles* and noted, "MS wyrl + *curved stroke*." He considered that mark here and in a word like 'loghe' a mere flourish. (See p. 11 of his edition.)

*481* See 469n on the spellings *doune* and *dovene*.

*485* Nom. case *dowue* is the proper spelling here.

*491* Moorman, following Morris and Menner, rendered *where jumpred er dry3ed* 'where confusion [had] long been endured'; Andrew & Waldron followed Anderson who, interpreting *jumpred* as a part. adj. used as a n., tr. 'where the motley company had suffered before'. Gollancz emended to *where [wat3] jumpred er dry3e* 'where was riveted before for many a long year', taking *jumpred* to be a "hitherto unidentified early use of 'Jumper,' to drill by means of a jumper."
However, one may supply elliptical [they], and define *jumpred* 'chattered' from *MED jumperen* v. 'to put (words) together in a disorderly manner', and *dry3ed* 'were parched'. (Cf. the A-text of *P. Pl.* I, line 25: "And drink whon thou drui3est . but do hit not out of resun.") Considering the use of *dryed* 'had dried' 496, there is a subtle linking device: the inhabitants of the ark were so happy in anticipating the touch of dry land they talked until they were dry.

*498* Here, *Tolke* apparently refers to God, but in line 889 it denotes a Sodomite and in 757 Abraham. Cf. the use of *Wy3* to denote 'God' in line 5, but *wy3* 'man' (Abraham) 675 and 'devil' 230.

*504* Cf. þ*robled* 'pushed' 879, with similar alliteration, and *Destr. Troy*: "A thoner and a thicke rayne þrublet in the skewes" (12496). Menner and Gollancz took þ*rublande* as a variant of *thrumble* 'crowd together', but it may be a variant of *OED trouble* v., sense 2, 'interfere, interrupt' from OF

*tru(o)bler.* For another example of development of a ME frica-
tive from a stopped consonant, cf. *roþeled* 59, 890 from AF
*reidele.*

*514* MS *mayny molde* 'household of earth' may be retained
by considering *molde* an uninflected gen. in post. c. Gollancz
and Anderson compounded *mayny-molde* 'main earth', following
Emerson (1919) 504 who took *mayny* as a variant of *maine.*

*523-27* See *Ga.* 500-35n for discussion of the longer de-
scription of the passing of the seasons.

*529* *Skyu* and *alde* run together in the MS, as do *askylly*
and *quenscaped.* Morris read *skylly* 'purpose' and *skyualde*
'ordained', comparing the latter to *skyfte* (OE *scyftan*).
Menner favored Morris' reading, but Gollancz, believing the
MS contained *skynalde,* emended to *skylnade* 'dispersal' (ON
*skilnaðr*). Other editors adopted the interpretation of Lutt-
rell (1955) 214-15. For example, Anderson rendered *skylly*
*skyualde* 'clear splitting-up', deriving *skyualde* from ON
\**skifald* n., formed on the v. *skifa* 'cut into slices'.
In reading *skylly skyu alde* 'old capacity to proceed',
*skylly* 'capacity' (*OED skill* sb.1, sense 6) has -*y* representing
-*e* (cf. *skyly* 62, alliterating with *scape*), *skyu* infin. 'to
proceed' (*OED skew* v.2, aphetic form of ONF *eskiu(w)er* 'to
slip away, move sideways') has *u* representing *w* (cf. *Trawe*
587 for *Trawe* and *covhous* 629 for *cowhous*), and *alde,* in
post. c., is a variant of *Olde* 601, 1123 (cf. *aldest* 1333).

*540* The *fowre freke3* are Noah and his three sons: Sem,
Cham, and Japheth, named in lines 297-300.

*544* Þewe3 'ordinances', the reading given by Morris,
Menner, and Moorman, is fitting here, since people at the time
of the flood had set aside God's laws when they sinned. Gol-
lancz glossed 'noble qualities'; Andrew & Waldron tr. 'vir-
tues'. Anderson gave 'good nature' as the sense in 544, 755,
and 1436. However, 'ordinances' suits the context well in
755; see 1436n for þewes 'virtues'.

*551* Eds. interpreted *mysse* as a v., but it may be read
as a n. Cf. similar usage in *Pe.* for *mys* 262 and *mysse* 364.

*553* For discussion of *me* as ethic dat., see *Ga.* 1905n.

*554-56* Cf. 1132 for mingling of beryl and pearl symbols.
In *Pe.*, banks of bright beryl are described (110), and the
eighth foundation stone of the New Jerusalem is of beryl (1011).
In the medieval lapidaries, the beryl represents Resurrection
(see *Pe.* 999-1016n) and the sacraments of Baptism and Matri-

mony. See Kelly & Irwin (1973) 251-54 for discussion of the beryl-pearl symbol in *Cl*.

*561-62* Kolve (1966) 254-55 cited these lines, as well as 203-4, 281-85, 302, and 513-20, to show how the poet sometimes imagined God in the "character of a courtly prince or king, passionate, aristocratic, authoritarian." See also 205n and 284n on the poet's use of anthropomorphism in his portrayal of the Creator.

*566* In line with editors' readings (Morris 'sin', Gollancz 'sorrow', Menner and Moorman 'vexation', Anderson 'evil'), the *OED* cites *Cl*. s.v. *site* sb.1 (ON *\*sȳt*). However, the primary meaning may be 'situation' (cf. *Pa*. 517n) from *OED site* sb.2 (AF *site*), with the possibility of word-play involving the sense 'trouble'.

*576* The poet stresses that the sinner cannot see God; cf. 29-30, 551-52, 1111-12, and 1804. He also points out, according to the sixth Beatitude (Matt. 5.8), that the reward of the good man is the sight of the Lord; see 27-28, 594-95, 1054-55, and 1810. The placing of these passages is symmetrically arranged in relation to the contrasting themes of *clannesse* and *vnclannesse*.

*577* Emendation is unnecessary if one renders Þat 'Who' in reference to *Saueour* 576 and considers *he* pleonastic. In line 168, the Lord *hates helle*; in *Pa*. 274-75, the devil and hell are related to stinking filth.

*581* *Sauyour* 'realize' may be retained as a variant of *sauour*, for there are many examples in this MS of words with intervening vowels. (Cf. *sower* 69, *vengiaunce* 247, and see *Pe*. 739n.)

*581-86* These lines paraphrase Ps. 93.8-9. Cf. *Pa*. 121-24.

*590* Anderson and Andrew & Waldron followed Menner who read Þro 'quickly', paraphrasing 589-90: "However cautiously and secretly a man may work, his thoughts fly swiftly to God even before he has conceived them." Gollancz glossed 'the whole distance' for Þro (OE Þurh), but the poet seems to be saying the Þro 'misfortune' comes down from God as punishment. Man Þraweʒ 'does draw' it upon himself when he sins.

*592* Rev. 2.23 reads: "Ego sum scrutans renes et corda." ("I am he that searcheth the reins and hearts.") Cf. also Ps. 7.10, Wisdom 1.6, and Jeremias 17.10. Most editors rendered *reynyeʒ* 'reins' (Mod. E. 'kidneys, loins; seat of feelings, affections, or passions'). The meaning 'emotions' is fitting here.

*595* Previous eds. rendered *sad* 'solemn', but 'divine' suits the context well and may be employed as another example of the poet's rare vocabulary usage.

*598* Cf. *scarreȝ* 'threatens' to *scarred* 'alerted' 838 and 'sprang' 1784. Morris and Gollancz, in line with *OED scare* v., sense 2, rendered *scarreȝ* 'is frightened', Menner tr. 'scatters', comparing Psalms 58.12 and 88.11 where the Psalmist speaks of the Lord's 'scattering' his enemies (Vulgate *dispergere*), and Luttrell (1955) 211-12, noting Nynorsk *skjerra* 'gush, fly out', and Swed. dialect *skjarra* 'to frighten', tr. 'to be provoked, react fiercely'.

*600* Andrew & Waldron adopted Gollancz' emendation of *scaþe* to *schaþe* to maintain *sch-* alliteration in the line, but the poet occasionally deviated from a precise pattern. (See 464n.) In line 58, *sch* alliterates with *sw*; in line 566, the combination is *sch--s--sm*.

*611* The *wlonk wyȝeȝ þrynne* of line 606 are three angels who represent the Lord, and are identified as God in lines 641 and 677. Note the use of sg. *I* and pl. *þay* in 647. For application to the doctrine of the Trinity, Menner compared *Cursor Mundi*: "Toward him com childir thre/Liknes o god in trinité" (2707-8).

*612* Previous eds. tr. *onhede* 'unity, as one'. It is difficult to determine the spacing in the MS, but the elements may be read separately. For other examples of *hede* 'individual', see *MED hēd* n.1, 2a. (a).

*620* Cf. Gen. 18.5: "Ponamque buccellam panis, et confortate cor vestrum." ("And I will set a morsel of bread, and strengthen ye your heart.") The *MED* s.v. *bannen* v., 5b, 'to banish (care, fear)', cited *Cl*. Morris read *banne* 'comfort, strengthen' (Old Scotch *bawne*); Menner viewed *banne* as an aphetic form of *enbaned* 'fortified' 1459. Gollancz and other editors emended to *baume* 'comfort', but the usual meaning for that v. is 'to treat with ointment, to embalm'. *Baune* may be read as a variant spelling of *MED bŏunen* v., 'prepare'; tr. 'strengthen' represents an extension of the primary meaning and accords with the sense of L *confortate*. Cf. the sense of the adv. *boun* 'firmly' in *Pe*. 1103.

*627* *Fat* 'vessel' (Morris and Gollancz) seems preferable to 'fat, fatted calf' (Menner, Anderson, and Andrew & Waldron). Cf. *fatte* 'vat' 802, where there is similar alliteration.

*643* Anderson glossed *vpfolden* 'uplifted (in prayer)', but it may be that the poet described Abraham here simply with folded arms, as he supervised the meal. Menner glossed 'folded', Gollancz 'covered', and Andrew & Waldron 'extended'.

*652* MS ʒark may stand. Occasionally *-ed* is omitted from a pt. or a pp. even though there is no following word beginning with a dental in the line. Cf. in *Cl. chaunge* 713 and *ask* 1098, in *Pe. fleme* 1177, and see *Pa.* 219n. Morris placed a comma after *heritage* and retained ʒark as the adj. 'select', modifying *men*.

*654* Anderson and Moorman followed Gollancz who emended *sothly* to *sotyly* 'privily' (OF *sotil*), pointing out that Gen. 18.12 has *occulte* 'secretly'. Andrew & Waldron retained *sothly* but tr. 'softly', comparing *Ga.* 673. However, 'truly' suits the context in *Ga.*, and in *Cl.* the poet may have departed slightly from his source to emphasize that Sara was *sothly* 'indeed' guilty of lack of faith.

*655* Andrew & Waldron followed Morris and Menner who tr. *for tykle* 'on account of the uncertainty' (*OED tickle* a. (adv.), sense 5). Emerson (1919) 505, comparing *voluptati* 'pleasure' in Gen. 18.12, defined 'pleasant, wanton' (*OED*, sense 2, 'pleasantly stirred or excited'). Gollancz, Fowler (1973) 332-33, and Anderson favored this reading. Rendering *tykle* as the sb. adj. 'excitement' also suits the context.
Morris glossed *tonne* (or *toune* ?) 'conceive', but he gave no explanatory note. The emendation of Emerson (1919) 506 to *teme* 'bring forth' was adopted by Menner, Moorman, and Andrew & Waldron. (Anderson's *terme* is apparently a misprint, for his note and glossary show that he intended to use *teme*.) Gollancz retained *tonne*, comparing OE *tunne* 'barrel', glossed 'conceive', and noted 'to be big with child'. However, *tonne* may be a variant of *take* (ON *taka*). Cf. the pp. *tone* in *Ga.* 2159. *OED take* v. lists *tan* as a variant spelling for the infin. For the meaning 'conceive', cf. sense III. 14b, 'to bring (a person) into some relation to oneself, specifically in reference to marriage or cohabitation'.

*657* Cf. *he* 62 and *ho* 1267 for 'they', and see 62n. Anderson, adopting Gollancz' suggestion to emend *he* to *hit*, interpreted *hit wern* idiomatically as 'they were'.

*659* The spelling *byene* prompted Morris to suggest '? *bycame*', Menner to emend to *bene* (Anderson *had bene*), and other editors to *bydene* 'continuously'. However, MS *by ene* joined as *byene* 'had been' may stand as a variant spelling for the v.

*668* Gollancz favored the *u* spellings for *laused* 'uttered' (ON *lauss*) in all five instances of *Cl.* (See also 957, 966,

1428, and 1589.) The phr. *loused suche wordes* in *Erk.* 178
shows that the v. was used in the context of speaking. See
Luttrell (1956a) 293-96 for a full discussion.

685  *Flete,* literally 'overflow, flood' (*MED flēten* v.1,
5a), may be tr. 'populate' here. Contrast the time of the
flood when the world was depopulated by overflowing water.

697-708  Osgood, p. li, believed the poet was a layman
because of the "decidedly unecclesiastical tone of his glorifi-
cation of marriage." Schofield (1909) 673-74 refuted Osgood's
viewpoint by citing a similar passage on love in marriage,
written by the monk Robert Mannyng. Concerning *Cl.*, Kelly &
Irwin (1973) 235 wrote: "The sexual drive, when properly chan-
neled in marriage, produces the family unit which, in its re-
lationship of a father to his children, symbolizes the rela-
tionship of God to man."

699  Gollancz' *doole* 'part, portion' is fitting here.
Morris defined 'gift', Anderson 'gift (of grace)', and other
editors tr. 'intercourse'. *Drwry* 'love' relates to sexual
intercourse in marriage. (Note *male and his make* 'male and
his spouse' 703.)

703  All editors followed Morris' suggestion to emend
*conne* to *come,* but MS *conne* 'be experienced' may be retained
as a pass. infin., from *MED cŏnnen* v. (OE *cunnan*), sense 7,
'to experience (an emotion)'.

708  Previous eds. read *sleke* 'quench, extinguish' instead
of *sheke* 'disturb', but there seems to be the small stroke of
an *h* in the MS squeezed against the *e.*

713  See 652n for retention of MS *chaunge.*

719  Morris defined þe *worre half* 'the weaker portion'.
Other editors also considered *worre* a variant of *wors:* "and
to weigh on the more wicked side those who never angered you"
(Andrew & Waldron). However, *worre* 'to protect' may be a
variant of *OED were* v., sense 2 (WFris. *warre*). For *half*
'group', see *MED half* n., 1c. (a), 'either of two groups of
persons distinguished by kind'.

735  Believing this line required another word beginning
with *t,* Gollancz suggested inserting *teueled in* after *haf.*
Andrew & Waldron inserted *towched* before *haf.* However, the
line may stand as it is with AB/BA alliteration on *haf--talke/
tatʒ--ille.*

745  Gollancz, believing the alliteration had to be on

the *b*'s, substituted þe *burne* for *Abraham* and *boȝsomly* 'meekly' for *loȝly*. Menner, following Fischer (1900) 47, emended *loȝly* to *hyȝly,* but, as Anderson noted, *him* may carry the alliteration in the second half of the line.

752 This line need not be emended. No previous editor took *what* as an interj., but it is used as such in lines 487, 846, 855, 1241, and 1583. For *schal* 'must', cf. 718. For the rendering of the first *if* as 'that', cf. 607. The words *if he* simply repeat *if my Lorde* and may be considered pleonastic. Morris' *leþe* 'destroy' seems closer to the mark than Menner's 'be merciful' and Gollancz' 'be softened', readings followed by subsequent editors. Abraham is concerned that God might do away with the worthy persons. The *MED* cited *Cl.* s.v. *lēþen* v., la, 'set free', but the meaning 'vanquish' may be derived from sense 3, 'of life: cease'. Cf. *leþe* 'is subdued' 648.

755 See 544n on reading þeweȝ 'ordinances' (Morris) instead of 'good nature' (Anderson). Menner defined 'gracious deed, courtesy', Gollancz and Andrew & Waldron 'noble qualities'. Anderson tr. *space* '(wide) extent, generosity', Menner, Gollancz, and the *OED* s.v. *space* sb.1, sense 12, 'course, custom', and Andrew & Waldron 'respite, delay'. For *in space* 'straightway', cf. the usage in 1606 and in *Ga.* 1199, 1418, and 1503.

766-76 In the Vulgate, after the number is reduced to ten, God leaves Abraham, and Gen. 18 ends abruptly at v. 33. The poet's addition here reaches a dramatic climax and makes clear the purpose of the preceding dialogue, Abraham's concern for Lot.

778 The repetition of *wepande* from the preceding line stresses Abraham's state of anguish. Emendation to a word beginning with *m* seems unnecessary since the alliteration may be ABB/A on *-warde--mere--Mambre/wepande.* (In the MS, the two syllables of the prep. *to warde* are divided.)
*Sorewe* was apparently written over another word by a later hand. Menner, Gollancz, and Andrew & Waldron favored *care* as the original; my own examination of the MS did not clarify the matter. *Sorewe* is clearly visible, and one cannot be sure that the second hand was not that of an authoritative corrector.

781 Gollancz and Andrew & Waldron emended *sondes* 'messengers' to *sonde* 'message' to have a sg. subject agreeing with *watȝ*, but a pl. subject conceived as a unit may take a sg. verb. (Cf. 385n on this point.)

*795* Morris' *autly* 'noble' (OE *ā̆htlīce*) does not suit the context. Gollancz and Moorman read MS *aucly*, but though the forms of *c* and *t* are similar, the long horizontal stroke here reveals a *t*. Other editors emended to *aucly*, and *MED auklī* 'amiss' cited *Cl.* However, *autly* 'lacking' may be interpreted as a variant of *MED authlī* adj. 'deprived of life'. For an example in *Cl.* of a stopped consonant varying with a fricative, cf. *Loot* 784--*Loth* 772. (See 504n for examples of the development of fricatives from stopped consonants.)

*796* For other examples of *and* 'when', see *MED and,* 6a, and cf. similar usage in 822 and 1597. Þat ... þat 'he who' refers to Lot. For ʒep 'agile angels' as a sb. adj. used coll., cf. ʒep 'agile nobles' in *Ga.* 284 and see the note. The v. *vnderʒede* 'caught sight of' follows its obj. ʒep. Cf. post. c. of the infin. in the next line, *ran hem to mete.* Other editors gave a different interpretation: "and the alert man [ʒep] who sits in the gate understood [*vnderʒede*] that" (Andrew & Waldron).

*805* Cf. *Ga.* 1836n on the use of *nay* 'refused'. TG-Davis and Anderson, comparing *lie/lay,* maintained that *nay* is the pt. of *nie,* unrecorded in the present, but from the stressed stem *ni-* of OF *neier.* However, in view of the several examples in this MS of omission of *-ed* before a word beginning with þ, *nay* is probably a variant of *nayed* 65. See *Pe.* 142n, Day (1919) 414, Gordon & Onions (1932) 133-35, and Luttrell (1956a) 291-92.

*812* *Arayed* may be tr. 'was arrayed'. For other examples of the use of a single v. for the pass. voice, cf. *dressed* 92, *demed* 110, and see *Ga.* 120n.

*819* Gollancz (1894) 646, comparing þ*erue* 'unleavened' 635, read þ*refte* as a variant of þ*erfte,* an example of metathesis. Eds. thus defined þ*refte* 'unleavened'. However, there is a reference to not having *sour* 'leavened bread' in line 820, and an important point in this passage is that the servants had to be þ*reftè* 'proper' in not putting any *salt in her sauce* (823). Þ*reftè* may be read as a variant of *OED thrifty.* Cf. þ*ryftyly* 635 to depict Abraham 'properly' serving þ*erue kakeʒ.* The first *e* and the *-è* that represents *-y* in þ*reftè* are substantiated by other *y(i)-e* variants in this MS. Cf., for example, *hym* 'them' instead of *hem* in line 820, *ferlylè* 1460, and *worthè* in *Ga.* 559.

*820* The order not to serve *sour* 'leavened bread' was apparently followed. Gen. 19.3 reads: "Ingressisque domum illius fecit convivium, et coxit azyma, et comederunt." ("And when they were come in to his house, he made them a feast, and

baked unleavened bread and they ate.") However, Lot's wife
was disobedient when she put salt in their stews (821-28); for
this and for looking back on Sodom, she is punished later (979-
1000). The Vulgate does not contain the incident of Lot's
wife sprinkling salt on the stews, but there is an account of
her other act of disobedience in Gen. 19.26: "Respiciensque
uxor eius post se versa est in statuam salis." ("And his
wife looking behind her, was turned into a statue of salt.")
Emerson (1915) suggested that the poet may have added to the
Biblical source from his knowledge of Jewish legends and
Hebrew commentaries on the Bible. (See also 1000n.)

    *821* As Menner pointed out, *wroth* 'sprinkled' may be taken
as a variant of *wroȝt* (OE *wrohte*). The *OED* s.v. *work* v., in
illustrating the forms of the pt., cited *Northern Passion*
(MS. Camb. Gg.): "Þei wrothin hit wit maistrie" (1367). An-
derson and Andrew & Waldron followed Gollancz who glossed
'turned' (OE *wrīþan*).

    *822* Previous eds. included the second half of this line
in the quotation, as if Lot's wife were talking about the
*hyne* (angels), but one may tr. *hyne* 'servant' (wife) and begin
the quotation at line 823. (Cf. the similar pattern of line
654.) For the elliptical [they] starting line 823, see 491n.
Eds. emended *vnfauere* to *vnsauere* 'disagreeable, unseasoned',
but the MS reading may be retained. *Vnfauere* 'ill-disposed',
a n. used attrib., is formed by the prefix *un* plus *MED fávŏur*
n. For other examples of nouns used attrib., see *Ga.* 683n.

    *827* Morris suggested *scelt* 'spread', which seems to be
the correct sense. (Cf. *skelt* 'spread' 1186, 1206.) Moorman
followed Menner who tr. 'served'. Anderson and Andrew & Wal-
dron agreed with Gollancz who glossed 'abused', but this pas-
sage gives no indication that Lot's wife was being openly
abusive to the angels. *Hem* may be taken as a variant of *hym*
'it'; the antecedent is *salt* 825. (Cf. *hem* 'him' 882, 915.)
For the meaning 'it', see *MED him* pron., 1a. (c), 'with refer-
ence to vegetable and inanimate things'. The phr. *scelt hem
in scorne* corresponds to *hit wroth to dyspyt* 'sprinkled it
for spite' 821.

    *831* For the separation to *Wela wynnely,* see *Ga.* 518n.

    *839* Gollancz, Anderson, and Andrew & Waldron emended
*clatȝ* to a form of *clateren,* but the *MED* recognizes *claten*
as a variant spelling. Anderson, taking the *-tȝ* of *clatȝ*
as equivalent to *s,* could make no sense of *clas,* but the *-ȝ*
of *clatȝ* may represent [z] as a northern pr. pl. ending.

    *840* Andrew & Waldron followed Gollancz in emending *worde*

to a pl. form; Anderson changed þyse to þys for sg. agreement.
However, worde 'words' may be rendered coll. Note the follow-
ing among many examples in this MS: mony blame 'many rebukes'
43, deȝter 'daughters' 939 (in reference to Lot's two daugh-
ters), and two ȝer 'two years' 1192.

846  Eds. adopted Menner's ȝestande sorȝe 'frothing filth',
but 'mounting disgust' also suits the context. (Cf. 75n on
the fig. use of sorȝe.) There may be word-play here involving
OED sorrow sb., sense 3, 'curse', which occurs in Ga. 1721.

856  Ne is pleonastic following wonded 855, the v. of fear.
(Cf. pleonastic ne 225, 1205 in subjunctive constructions.)
Eds. emended pil to peril, but pil may be retained as an un-
inflected gen., 'of (the) dwelling'. (Cf. pyle 'dwelling' in
Pe. 686.)  For abide 'confront', see MED abīden v., sense 12.

866-72  Cf. Gen. 19.8: "Habeo duas filias, quae necdum
cognoverunt virum, educam eas ad vos, et abutimini eis sicut
vobis placuerit, dummodo viris istis nihil mali faciatis, quia
ingressi sunt sub umbra culminis mei." ("I have two daughters
who as yet have not known man: I will bring them out to you,
and abuse you them as it shall please you, so that you do no
evil to these men, because they are come in under the shadow
of my roof.")  Lot's offer shocks the modern reader, but keep-
ing messengers of God from harm was of primary importance.

869  Eds. rendered ronk 'full-grown, adult', but 'impetu-
ous', as in Pa. 490, seems preferable. Anderson, following
Menner, glossed manne 'be manned' (OE mannian), commenting
that there is no parallel in the MS for manne as a variant
spelling of the n. 'man', but doubling of consonants is not
uncommon in the poet's language. Cf. talle 'story, word'
(Pe. 865, Cl. 48) alongside tale and walle 'choose' (Cl. 921)
instead of wale.

878  Morris and Menner rendered boy 'youth', but, as Gen.
13 reveals, Lot was evidently a wealthy man when he parted
from Abraham to go to Sodom. Other editors adopted Gollancz'
'low fellow'. MED boie n.1, 2a, 'a commoner', cites Cl.

882  Anderson rendered hem 'them' in reference to Lot and
the men who are harassing him, but hem as a variant of hi(y)m
'him' occurs elsewhere. (See 827n.)

883  Eds. glossed horyed 'hurried'. The MED s.v. horien
v.1 cites only Cl. but directs the reader to what may be the
correct derivation, herien v.2, 3b, 'to pull'. Cf. Gen.
19.10: et introduxerunt ad se Lot 'and drew in Lot unto them'.
Horyed, then, is a variant of herȝed, which alliterates with
hent in line 1179.

*885* Eds. interpreted differently: "They (the angels) struck a blow among that cursed people" (Andrew & Waldron). However, it seems that the poet is describing how the Sodomites act here, as they try to get into Lot's dwelling. Þay, referring to *banned peple,* is pleonastic.

*886* *Bayard,* originally a bay-colored horse, represented in proverbial sayings a type of blindness or blind recklessness. See Chapman (1951) 8 and *MED baiard* n.1.

*887* Eds. rendered *lest* 'lost, failed', but the v. may be a variant of *lyste* 'wished' 415. The *MED,* in line with the interpretation of eds., cited only *Cl.* s.v. *lessŏun* n., 4b, fig., 'knowledge, sight, view', but *lysoun* 'entertainment' may be from *OED lusion* 'game, pastime', adapted from L *lūsiōn-em,* n. of action, from *lūdēre* 'to play'. Anderson suggested 'opening', comparing the sense of OF *lumiere.*

*888* In agreement with editors' readings, *MED nitelen* 'to busy oneself ignorantly' cited only *Cl.,* interpreting the v. as a neg. form of *witen* 'to know' & *-el-* suf. (3). However, *nyteled* 'fretted' may be taken as a variant of *MED netlen* v. 'anger, irritate'.

*889* The usual reading for *ty3t hem* is 'took themselves off, went away' (Anderson). However, in this line and the next, the poet is apparently depicting the sinful actions of the Sodomites after they had failed to satisfy their lustful desire for the angels. *Ty3t* 'attracted' agrees with the original sense of OE *tyhtan* 'invite, attract, seduce'.

*890* Cf. 59n on *roþeled* 'brought together'. Most editors believed the poet was here describing the Sodomites' going to their rest (sleep). Menner, though he did not explain, glossed *roþeled* '? huddle' and *rest* 'remainder'.

*891* *Wrank* 'sinners (wrong-doers)' is interpreted here as a variant of *wrange* (76, 268) and a sb. adj. in apposition to *þay.* For unvoicing of the final stopped consonant, cf. þink 1359 instead of þing. Most editors interpreted the word as an adv. 'in the wrong way' (Gollancz). Anderson, thinking the *l* of *al* is "crossed out with vertical wavy line in original ink," read *awrank* 'awry, wretchedly', but, though that *l* is slightly marked, one cannot be sure the scribe intended to delete it.

*892* See *Ga.* 137n on syntax.

*893* Cf. the description in *Ga.* 1695.

*899  Wyȝeȝ,* the 'intended sons-in-law' of Lot's daughters, are mentioned in Gen. 19.12, 14.

*907*  Cf. *trayþly* 1137, and see Sundén (1929) 41-47 for discussion of this adv.

*912*  Cf. *Ga.* 1722.

*914*  Morris, Menner, and Andrew & Waldron rendered *fele* 'hide, conceal' (ON *fela*), but 'advance' from *MED fēlen* v.3, sense a (OE *fēolan*), seems preferable. Anderson tr. 'advance' and commented that Gollancz' 'entrust' cannot be supported by any known usage of *felen.*

*915*  See 827n and 882n on the use of *hem* as a variant for *hym.*

*917*  Cf. 54n and *Pe.* 1073n on the syntax of *to crepe* 'go'.

*924*  Abraham was Lot's uncle, but *broþer* is an appropriate reading. Note the use of *broþer* in line 772 to describe their relationship, and cf. similar terminology in Gen. 13.11 and 14.14, 16. Eds. followed Morris who read *þyn em,* noting "*broþer* is written over in a later hand," but it is difficult to determine if *þyn em* (or *eme*) was written first, and even if it was, the second hand may be that of an authoritative corrector. The alliteration is not lost by reading *broþer,* since there still remains excessive vowel (and *h* before vowel) alliteration in the line.

*926*  MS 'þen' may be retained by considering elliptical [there] in the Mod. E. tr. See *Pe.* 363n and *Ga.* 11n for several examples of ellipsis.

*935*  Emendation to *tayt* 'joke' seems unnecessary. The end of Gen. 19.14 reads: "Et visus est eis quasi ludens loqui." ("And he seemed to them to speak as it were in jest."), but the poet need not have given the exact equivalent of *ludens* 'jest'. (See 439n on altering of Biblical details.) Gollancz, adopting a suggestion given by Bateson (1918) 382-83, glossed *tyt* 'tittle-tattle', comparing ME *titereres* 'tattlers'.

*944*  Morris, Gollancz, and Andrew & Waldron tr. *bot* 'command', considering the n. a variant of *bode* 979. Menner's 'to advantage' seems preferable. For the meaning 'salvation', see *MED bōte* n.1, 3a. Anderson glossed *bi bot* 'quickly' from OF *a (de) bot, (tot) de bot.*

*951*  Cf. *Pe.* 875n on *torreȝ* 'peaks'. For *Cl.,* Menner glossed *torres* 'tower-shaped cumulus', Andrew & Waldron 'tower-

ing clouds'. Gollancz and Moorman tr. 'peak-like shapes',
Anderson 'tors, hill-like masses (of cloud)', readings which
pinpoint the simile better, for the poet is apparently saying
that the clouds *kesten vp torres* 'rose up like peaks'. For
other examples of the synthetic dat., see 32n.

*956 Swe* 'curled' may be taken as a strong pt. form and a
variant of *swey*. (Cf. pr. p. *sweande* 420, and see *Pa.* 429n
on *swey*.) Andrew & Waldron, following Gollancz, glossed *swe*
'soughed, moaned' (OE *swōgan*). Eds. rendered *hit* 'its', but
the form here may be interpreted as the v. that appears in all
four poems of the MS from ON *hitta*.

*958* Adama and Seboim are the two cities that were com-
pletely destroyed with Sodom and Gomorrah. Gollancz noted
that *fyue* cities were mentioned in line 940. Segor was in-
cluded, the place to which Lot fled. The poet, however, did
not say in 940 that all five cities were completely destroyed.
(See also 1015n.)

*959* Eds. interpreted *birolled* as a combination of the
prefix *bi* and *rolled* 'enveloped' (OF *roler*). *MED birolled*
cited only *Cl*. However, the form may be a variant of *brolled*
from OF *bru(s)ler* (*MED broilen* v.1). The intervening *i* ap-
parently emphasizes that the alliteration is on *r*. Cf. the
intervening *o* in *sower* 69 and *dowelle* 1674 where *w* alliterates.

*961* See *Pe.* 1085n on hunting images. *Helle* personified
may be rendered 'hellish fiend'. Emerson (1919) 509 noted
the *houndeȝ of heuen* are the *wyndeȝ* (948), *þunder-þrast* (952),
and *rayn* (953), all the elements that God the Hunter sends out
to afflict the evil ones. *MED hŏund* n., 3c, cites passages
which give the image of a hell-hound, but for 3d, '? a heavenly
power', only *Cl*. is cited. For application of the term 'hound'
to a heavenly power, Menner compared the *Veltro* of Dante's
*Inferno,* Canto I, line 101, observing that early commentators
considered Dante's 'Greyhound' a reference to Christ. Gol-
lancz compared the 'Gabriel-hounds', a "name popularly in
Lancashire and elsewhere in the North assigned to what is
supposed to be a spectral pack, whose yelping cries betokened
approaching death and disaster."

*979-1000* See 820n for discussion of the two faults com-
mitted by Lot's wife.

*980-84* Emerson (1919) 509 noted that looking over the
left shoulder indicated ill-fortune. See also Bateson (1923)
for discussion of evil portent and tracing of the lore from
the Egyptian era to more recent times.

*981*  *He* for 'her' is being retained, since a final *r* is
occasionally omitted in this MS.  Note *Balta3a* in *Cl.* 1746,
þervnde in *Pa.* 459, *he* for *her* 'their' in *Ga.* 1129, and *we*
for *wer* in *Ga.* 2171.  (See also *Ga.* 2171n.)

*987*  Eds. defined *loue3* 'hands, palms' (ON *lófi*), but
'praises' (OE *lof*) also suits the context.  There may be
double-entendre: Lot and his daughters lifted up 'praises'
with their 'palms' raised.

*989*  The *MED,* following Gollancz, cited only *Cl.* s.v.
*dampen* v., 'suffocate'.  (Andrew & Waldron agreed.)  Menner,
Anderson, and Moorman interpreted the v. as a variant of *MED*
*dampnen* 'condemn', which seems preferable.

*993*  Andrew & Waldron adopted the emendation of Gollancz
who placed a period after line 992 to end a quatrain, but had to
insert *lent* 'dwelt' after *lede3* to make line 993 begin a new
quatrain.  The emendation seems unnecessary, and the MS read-
ing presents evidence disproving the theory that the poet
intended to set his poem in quatrains.  Line 993 carries over
from the preceding one, makes good sense, and shows ABA/B
alliteration: þre *lede3* þerin/*Loth.*

*1000*  This incident does not appear in the Vulgate.  Emer-
son (1919) 509 cited Louis Ginsberg's *Legends of the Jews,* I
(1912), p. 255: "The pillar exists unto this day.  The cattle
lick it all day long, and in the evening it seems to have
disappeared, but when morning comes it stands there as large
as before."  Morris, p. 113, compared *Cursor Mundi* 2852-60.
(See also 820n.)
    Eds. read *alle* instead of *lalle,* but the MS has a long
stroke attached to the left of the *a*.  *Lalle,* then, may be
taken as a sb. adj. 'loyal creatures'.  *MED* *lēl* adj. & n.
lists *liale* as a variant spelling.  Even unreasoning animals
can be loyal, but Lot's wife was not.  The statue should re-
mind man to be *lalle* to God.

*1002*  Emendation of this line seems unnecessary.  Cf. Þat
'Because' to Þat 'Since' 992.  Elliptical [that] is one of
many examples in this MS.  (Cf. 926n and 1051n.)  Emerson
(1919) 509 joined *no mon,* equating it with the pp. *numen*
'taken'.  Menner and subsequent editors emended to *nomen.*

*1007*  *Aparaunt* 'heir apparent' may be rendered as a sb.
adj.  See *MED* *ap(p)araunt* (OF *aparant*) adj., sense c, where
*Cl.* is cited.  Most editors defined 'dependency'; Anderson
glossed 'comparable' (OF *aparier, s'aparer*).

*1009*  Morris glossed *roþun* 'rush', comparing *roþeled* 890.

Andrew & Waldron followed Gollancz who defined 'redness' (ON *roðna*). Moorman favored Menner's interpretation of *roþun* as a sb. adj., a variant of *OED rotten* a. (ON *rottin*). This reading seems fitting. (Cf. 504n on the spelling variant.) Anderson expanded MS *roþū* to *roþum* 'redness' (ON *roðmi*).

*1015-51* The poet drew much for his description of the Dead Sea from the French text of *Mandeville's Travels*; see C. Brown (1904) 149-53.

*1015* Menner anticipated the emendation of subsequent editors by suggesting *fyue* may have been written first in the MS, but *faure* suits the context. Þer *faure* may be written over other letters, but one cannot be sure what those letters are. In lines 956-58, mention is made of *Sodomas, Gomorra, Abdama,* and *Syboym, þise ceteis, alle faure.* In line 992, the poet says nothing was saved *bot Segor.* When he uses *fyue* in line 940, he is not talking about the destruction of the cities.

*1019* The *sm* alliteration is not maintained here, but it does not seem necessary to emend. Cf. the variable alliteration in 566: "Þat he schulde neuer, for no syt, smyte al at oneȝ."

*1031* Eds. glossed *losyng* 'perdition' (*MED lōsing(e)* ger. 1, sense b), but 'decay' from sense a, 'losing, waste', also suits the context.

*1037* Emerson (1919) 509-10 suggested *in waxlokes grete* 'in the shape of great curls of wax'. For *in* 'in the shape of', see *MED in* prep., 25a. *Waxlokes* combines *wax* and *lokes* from OE *locc* 'lock of hair, curl'.

*1038* The MS has five minims between *p* and *a,* and the fifth has a mark over it apparently signifying *i.* *Spuniande* is a variant of *spinnande.* The *u-i* variant in the stem may be compared to *dutande* 320 alongside *ditteȝ* 588 and *tylt* 832 alongside *tult* 1213. For the intervening *i,* cf. *vengiaunce* 247. For the meaning 'thriving', cf. *spun* 'flourishing' 1492 and see *OED spin* v., II. 7, 'to grow or rise rapidly'. Morris & Skeat (1872) suggested *spumande* 'foaming'; the *OED* and subsequent editors adopted the emendation.

*1040* Gollancz unnecessarily substituted *&* for *þe* between *fretes* and *flesch,* and tr. *fel* as the n. 'skin' instead of the adv. 'fiercely'. Emendation made by other editors of *festred* to *festres* also seems unnecessary, as Emerson (1919) 510 noted, since *festred* 'decayed' may be rendered as a part. adj.

*1043-48* Andrew & Waldron noted that the ultimate source

of the description of bitter fruit by the Dead Sea is Josephus (*Wars* IV. viii. 4), "but the idea had become a commonplace in medieval commentaries and encyclopedic writing." One is reminded of the apple that *enpoysened alle peple3* 242.

*1049-1148* Armstrong (1977), explicating this passage in relation to the theme of *Cleanness*, noted that the earthly source of Christ's purity is Mary, the "ark" of a new covenant. "Like Noah's ark, Mary is a 'kest,' a chest which encloses purity, i.e. Christ" (30). (See also 1070n.)

*1051* Anderson and Andrew & Waldron adopted Gollancz' emendation of *forferde* 'destroyed' to *forþerde* 'carried out'. Anderson commented that 'destroyed' does not suit the context, but rendering Þat 'When' and considering ellipsis of [the cities] after the v. provide good sense for the line. For Þat 'When', cf. the usage in 856, 1069, and 1169; for reference to other examples of ellipsis, see 926n.

*1056* Morris' retention of the MS forms here seems appropriate. Other editors, considering *counseyl counsayl* a dittograph, omitted a word that denotes the v., but *counseyl* 'counsel' n. and *counsayl* 'advise' v. suit the context.

*1057-64* Morris did not attempt to identify the precise part of *RR*, the poet's source. Menner and Gollancz cited lines 8021-38 but had difficulty reconciling Clopinel's bitter satire against women with the poet's favorable treatment of a lady to be loved. Other editors followed Menner and Gollancz, but it may be that Emerson (1919) 510 was right in identifying a part of the *Roman* written by Guillaume de Lorris, not by Jean Clopinel, de Meun-sur-Loire. In the beginning of *Cl.*, when he paraphrases the Parable of the Wedding Feast, the poet mentions only Matthew (line 51), not Luke from whom he also draws. (See also 1157-58n on the mentioning of Daniel, but not Jeremias.)
Lines 1057-64 appear to be a condensation of that part of the *Roman* in which the God of Love gives his commandments to the Lover (lines 2113-2354 of the ME tr. in John Fisher's edition of *Chaucer*). Note the following:

> And sette thy might and al thy will
> Women and ladyes for to plese,
> And to do thyng that may hem ese,
> That they ever speke good of the;
> For so thou mayste best praysed be.          (2234-38)

The God of Love advises: "Mayntayne thyselfe after thy rent,/Of robe and eke of garnement" (2255-56), and "Thyne hondes wasshe, thy tethe make white,/And lette no fylthe

upon the be" (2280-81). In reading these lines, one is re-
minded that he should not be like the unsightly man in the
Parable of the Wedding Feast, *vnþryuandely cloþed* 135.
The God of Love then exhorts the Lover to display any
talents he may possess:

> Do it goodly, I commaunde the.
> For men shulde, wheresoever they be,
> Do thynge that hem best syttyng is,
> For therof cometh good loos and pris.     (2307-10)

The poet of *Cl.* urges one to know what the lady loves best,
"And be ryȝt such in vch a borȝe, of body and of dedes."
Just as the God of Love says men should seek to please *whereso-
ever they be,* the poet of *Cl.* speaks of fulfilling the desires
of the lady *in vch a borȝe* 'in every place'.
In summarizing his commandments, the God of Love says:
"Whoso with Love wol gon or ryde,/He mote be curteyes and voyde
of pride" (2351-52). One need simply substitute the word *Kryst*
for *Love* and cf. lines 1065-68 to perceive the allegory in *Cl.*

*1063* Morris, Menner and Anderson glossed *wyk* 'wicked,
hostile', Gollancz 'aloof, unapproachable', Andrew & Waldron
'disagreeable, difficult'. 'Stern' seems fitting here.

*1067-68* Cf. 553-56 and 1116-32 in which the pure soul is
likened to a pearl, and see *Pe.* 730-35n for a discussion of
pearl symbolism.

*1070* The poet employed *kest* in an unusual way. Cf. *kyst*
346, denoting Noah's ark as the means of salvation for mankind
in the Old Testament. In the New Testament, Mary's womb is
the *kyst* (container) that through a *kest* 'miracle' bears *Kryst*
who brings salvation to mankind.

*1073-88* This nativity scene accords with the kind depicted
in medieval art. Menner, in his 1086n, compared Ch. 14 of the
*Pseudo-Matthew* in Cowper, *Apocryphal Gospels,* p. 53.

*1076* Emerson (1919) 510 recognized the compound *schroude-
hous* (Icel. *skrúð-hús* 'vestry'). Anderson compared OE
*scrūdelshūs.* . Moorman and Andrew & Waldron followed Menner who
glossed 'dwelling which affords shelter'. Gollancz defined
'tapestried hall'.

*1089* The poet applied courtly terms on a spiritual level.
*Cortays* 'refined' connotes 'full of divine grace'. Christ's
background is one of *nobleye* 'nobility' 1091. People call on
his *cortaysé* 'courtesy' (divine grace) 1097 and seek his *cort*
1109. Cf. the use of *cortaysye* in *Pa.* 417 and *Ga.* 653. (See
also *Pe.* 432n.)

*1091*  Cf. *Ga.* 919n on the use of *norture.*

*1093*  *Laȝares,* referring to the sick persons of 1094-96, derives from the proper name Lazarus, the beggar full of sores (Luke 16.20).

*1094-96*  See Matt. 8 and 9 for accounts of Christ's healing the sick and raising the daughter of Jairus to life, and Luke 7 for the story of Christ's bringing the widow's son back from the dead.

*1095*  Andrew & Waldron, after commenting that previous editors incorrectly glossed *fyres* 'fevers', noted that this word designates "diseases involving inflammation of the skin and putrefaction of the flesh."

*1097*  Anderson and Andrew & Waldron, apparently following Menner and Gollancz, did not accent the *e* of *cortaysé* and defined the word as a sb. adj., 'courteous one, gracious one'. (See *Pe.* 481n on Andrew & Waldron's similar usage there.) *Cortaysé* 'courtesy' (divine grace) is fitting here.

*1098*  Eds. did not recognize *ask* as a pt. with ending omitted before a vowel, but see *Pa.* 219n for other examples of such usage.

*1101*  Andrew & Waldron followed Gollancz who changed *clene* to *hende* 'gracious' to add to the alliterative pattern, but this emendation seems unnecessary since *his* may carry the alliteration in the first half of the line. Stressed syllables do not always alliterate in these poems, and unstressed syllables sometimes do.
   *Schouied* 'cast out' (OE *scūfan*) appears as *schowued* in line 44. Eds. read *schonied* (OE *scunian*), as if the *ordure* were shunning the touch, but apparently the poet is saying Christ's touch cast out disease and filth of all kinds.

*1102-8*  Menner, who noted that the basis for this passage is in Luke 24.30-35 where Christ appears to the apostles after his Resurrection, has supper with them in Emmaus, and is recognized by his clean breaking of the bread, cited Towneley Play (No. 28) *Thomas of India* 264-65: "Ihesu, goddis son of heuen at sopere satt betweyne;/Ther bred he brake as euen as it cutt had beyn."
   Kelly & Irwin (1973) 250, comparing the account of the Last Supper in Matt. 26.26, where Christ's breaking of bread points to the consecration of the Eucharist, commented that "just as on a literal level Christ's pure touch healed the corrupted body not by cutting away the diseased flesh but simply by curing it, so on a supernatural level the touch of

Christ's pure flesh in the bread of the Eucharist heals the
spiritual corruption of fleshly sin not by a violent excising
but by a redemptive process." For other references to the
Eucharist, see 11n and 1127n.

*1107* Gollancz' emendation of *pryuyly* 'carefully' to
*prystyly* 'readily' seems unnecessary. Anderson tr. 'delicately,
cleanly', Moorman favored Menner's 'skillfully', and Andrew &
Waldron rendered *displayed ... pryuyly* 'was exposed ... mysteri-
ously'.

*1108 Toulouse* in *Ga.* 77 denotes a fabric. Gollancz, pp.
xvii-xviii, because he could not "discover that Toulouse was
at all associated with the manufacture of cutlery," suggested
that the intended reference in *Cl.* was to Toledo in Spain, and
that the error was due to the poet or a scribe. However, Chap-
man (1951) 62 observed that Toulouse in France was celebrated
in the Middle Ages for the manufacture of cutlery and fine red
cloth.

*1109 Kyryous* 'perfect', a variant of *curious* 1353, 1452,
connotes other qualities of Christ, who was 'fastidious' in
despising filth and 'expert' in the breaking of the bread. As
Gollancz pointed out, the poet may have employed word-play on
the mass response *Kyrie eleison* 'Lord, have mercy'. (*Kyryous
and clene* approximates this sound.)

*1116-32* This passage praises the pearl as a symbol of
purity and concludes with mention of the beryl. (See 554-56n
and 1067-68n.)

*1118* Gollancz and Andrew & Waldron changed *hym* to *hit*,
Anderson used *ho,* but Menner avoided the emendation by suggest-
ing that *hym* may be rendered as a nom. here. Cf. expressions
like *hym byhoued* in *Cl.* 398 and *Ga.* 2040, where *hym* equals 'he'
and see *Ga.* 373n for examples of *hym* 'it' in the objective case

*1123* Gollancz and Anderson adopted Morris' suggestion to
insert *ho* into the line, but that subject has already appeared
twice, in lines 1121-22.

*1124* Morris' *in pyese* 'whole' seems to be the correct
sense. Bateson (1918) 383 proposed emending to *in pyere* '[in
use] among precious stones'. Anderson followed Gollancz who
interpreted the phr. as a variant of *o pece*, "used as a mere
emphasis of 'still, yet'." Andrew & Waldron adopted Menner's
suggestion to emend to *pryse* 'esteem'. However, *pyese* 'one
piece' suits the context well, especially since some kind of
physical damage is implied by the use of *payres*.

*1127* As Emerson (1919) 511 noted, washing pearls in alcohol to restore their luster is a practice of modern times, too. See Kunz & Stevenson, *The Book of the Pearl* (London, 1908), p. 396. The poet's allegory apparently involves the sacramental wine representing the blood of Christ in the Holy Eucharist, which people receive after confession to cleanse themselves of sin. See *Pe.* 648n and 766n on cleansing images dealing with the blood of Christ.

*1129-32* These lines dealing with the sacrament of penance echo 1113-16.

*1133* Cf. 165 and 545. All three instances of the poet's admonishing of his audience anticipate main episodes in *Cl.*

*1134* This simile relates to manuscript composition in the medieval period. Andrew & Waldron, citing R.A.B. Mynors, *Durham Cathedral Manuscripts* (Oxford, 1939) 9, noted that the comparison "is also found (in more extended form) in a 12th C. sermon designed to appeal to illuminators of manuscripts."

*1137* Cf. similar alliteration in line 1808; there, too, the poet describes provocation which makes the Lord punish.

*1141* Anderson and Andrew & Waldron rendered *likkes* 'tastes' (OE *liccian*) figuratively. Anderson argued that the ME v. *līken* 'to like' does not double the *k* in this MS; however, 'favors' suits the context, and there are other examples of unusual doubling of consonants. (See 869n.)
Most editors glossed *loses* 'loses'. Moorman followed Thomas (1922a) 66 who tr. 'praises'. Anderson rendered *loses hit ille* 'takes its loss badly'. For the sense 'banishes', cf. *losen* 'shall void' 909.

*1142* Most editors rendered *þewes* 'thieves', but 'virtues' (OE *þēawas*) suits this context. If man does wrong, his *sawele* (1139) would be robbed of its virtues by the sins. Moorman noted that Thomas (1922a) 66 tr. *wyth þewes* 'in respect of its qualities'.

*1145-47* Morse (1971) 205 noted the allegory: "The poet likens men to vessels in that both may be dedicated to God; he makes this analogy to point to the formal similarity of men and vessels as potential containers of God." (See also 11n.)

*1155* *Forloyne* 'sinful' is a part. adj. with loss of *-d* before a word beginning with þ. (See *Pe.* 142n for other examples.) *Forloyne* 1165 may be taken as a pt. form with loss of *-d* even though the next word does not begin with a dental. (See *Cl.* 1098n.)

*1157-58* Gollancz and Anderson supposed that *Dialoke͡ʒ* refers
to Daniel 1-6 and *Profecies* to Daniel 7-12. However, these two
words taken together may refer generally to the whole Book of
Daniel in which some dialogue appears after Ch. 6 and some
prophecies before Ch. 7. The poet did not mention Jeremias
from whom he also drew. In line 51, he named only Matthew
when he was about to employ verses from Luke also.

*1159* With his use of *Juise* 'Jewish people', the poet may
have been punning on *juise* 'doom'. The *Juise* met their *juise*.
Cf. in *Pa.*, "Bot Jonas into his juis jugge bylyue" (224).
Gollancz noted word-play in *Wars Alex.*, "I sall seche Iewes
(MS. Iewres) on the Iewes" (1191).

*1164* For elliptical [are], see 926n.

*1169* Anderson read *ʒedethyas,* commenting that "*t, th*
regularly alternate as spellings with *c, ch* in Latin and
French," but the scribe's *c* and *t* are so close in form that
one may read *ʒedechyas* here. In this instance, it is probably
part of the preceding *e*, touching the following letter, that
makes the *c* look like a *t*. Cf. the formation of *ec* in *profecie*
1308, read as MS *profetie* by Andrew & Waldron.

*1183* Emendation of *baytayled* to *batayled* seems unneces-
sary; there are many forms in the MS with intruding vowels.
For a discussion of the *a-ay* variant, see McLaughlin (1963)
80-82.

*1190* The *MED* cited *Cl.* s.v. *bretāȝe* n., sense a, 'a
defensive structure on a wall or tower, such as a parapet or
bastille'. Stone (1971) 127 noted: "In the Middle Ages tem-
porary wood breastwork was sometimes built on to battlements,
to accommodate soldiers who, from such a platform, could pre-
vent besiegers scaling or undermining the walls of a castle
or town." Anderson, in his 1383-84n, compared the *ouerþwert
palle* on the wall of Babylon, noting that hoarding or brat-
ticing was a usual feature of castle architecture from the
thirteenth century onwards. "It consisted of a wooden gal-
lery, roofed, floored, and faced, on the outside of the para-
pet. There were slits in the face and floor for directing
missiles, which allowed the defenders to command the foot of
the castle wall." (See also 1384n.)

*1200* Eds. read *goudes,* but there is a mark over the first
minim of the *u* that is similar to the contraction for *er*.
The reading may, therefore, be *gouerdes* from *MED gŏurd(e* n.
This plant bears melon fruit and squash, and the fruit con-
tains liquid with medicinal value. The poet may have been
referring to such a plant found in the fields beyond the
city walls.

*1231-32*  Menner changed the adj. *colde* to *C[a]lde* 'Chaldea',
the n. *Caldé* to a v., and tr., "All (Nebuchadnezzar's hosts)
would have been called away to Chaldea and the countries of
India--and they would have had little trouble in taking Turkey
by the way." However, *colde* 'powerless', the key word in this
passage, may be compared in sense to *MED cōld* adj., 5a, 'dimin-
ished zeal'. The MS has *Colde* ... *Calde,* but the scribe's
capitalization is often merely decorative. Note MS *ynde* and
*torkye* in lines 1231-32. In line 679, there is a majuscule
for *Cety* but a miniscule for *sodomas.* Fowler (1973) 334 would
read *to-calde* 'to-called' at the beginning of line 1231, but
his tr. of 1231-32 accords with the basic sense given by most
editors: "Though all Chaldea and the peoples of India were
assembled,/With Turkey thrown in for good measure, their wrath
would have been of little avail [against Jerusalem]."

*1234*  *Tuyred* 'stripped' may represent a variant spelling
and a shortened form of *tyrue* 630. Morris glossed 'destroyed'
without explanation. Other editors emended to *tyrued* 'over-
turned', but the MS form need not be changed. For the *uy-y*
variant, cf. *nuyeȝ* 578--*nyed* 1603 and *huyde* 915--*hyde* 682. For
the shortened form, see the *OED* s.v. *tirr* v., apparently a re-
duced form of *tirve* v.l.

*1239*  Eds. defined *burȝ* 'city', but the *bareres* are apparent-
ly the same as the *brutage of borde* (1190), and *burȝ* may mean
'bulwark', the towers on the walls (1189-90). See *MED burgh*
n.1, 3a, 'stronghold, small tower defending a strategic spot'.

*1243*  Eds. emended *fo* 'terribly' to *so,* but cf. the use
of *fo(o)* in *Ga.* 1304, 1344, and 2326.

*1247-53*  Cf. the Lamentations of Jeremias 2.21: "Iacuerunt
in terra puer et senex, virgines meae et iuvenes mei ceciderunt
in gladio, interfecisti in die furoris tui, percussisti nec
misertus es." ("The child and the old man lie without on the
ground : my virgins and my young men are fallen by the sword :
thou hast slain them in the day of thy wrath : thou hast killed,
and shewn them no pity.") The reference to children appears in
Jeremias and in *Cl.,* not in 2 Paralipomenon 36.17-20. Cf. also
Lamentations 5.11-13.

*1253*  As Anderson noted, citing Mustanoja (1960) 204-5, one
need not insert þat into this line, since a rel pron. is some-
times omitted in ME. Cf. *Pe.* 664 and 732.

*1259*  Anderson followed Gollancz in glossing *cayre at*
'drive', since this is the basic meaning of ON *keyra,* but the
sense 'pull at', given by other editors and the *MED,* seems suit-
able here. Cf. the use of *cayred* 'carried' in line 1478.

*1267  Ho kyllen,* like many other words in the MS, run to-
gether. For *ho* 'they', see 62n on *he* 'they'. Morris read
*hokyllen,* writing in his glossary, "Is this an error for
*hollkyen?* See *Holkke.*" However, *holkked* 1222 means to 'gouge'
out eyes. Menner substituted *he* for *ho,* but his glossary s.v.
*he* indicates that he tr. *he* 'they' here, as well as in 62 and
657. Gollancz called *hokyllen* 'cut down', accepted by Menner
(1922a) 361 and other editors, an "early and hitherto unnoticed
use of 'hockle', to cut up stubble, the earliest instance in
*NED* being 1746, from the *Complete Farmer.*" The *MED* cited only
*Cl.* s.v. *hŏkelen* v.2.

*1274  Sancta Sanctorum* 'Holy of Holies' is the innermost
chamber of the Jewish temple. Cf. 1491 and see Ezechiel 44.13.

*1275* Most editors glossed *crowne* 'crown' here and in 1444
where the spelling is *coroun,* but Andrew & Waldron's 'cincture'
pinpoints the meaning better, for the word "appears to desig-
nate a gold cincture or moulding, such as surrounded the ark
of the covenant and the incense altar made by Bezalel for the
tabernacle of Moses." The *MED* cited *Cl.* 1275 and 1444 s.v.
*corŏune* n., sense 8, 'a band of gold about the ark of the
covenant, the table of the shewbread, or the altar of incense'.

*1280  Vyoles* 'cups' is a variant of *fyoles* 1476, where the
alliteration is on *f.* Gollancz compared the Vulgate's *phialas*
'bowls' in 1 Paralipomenon 28.17.

*1283* Gollancz compared the Vulgate's *gazophylacium* 'trea-
sury' in Mark 12.41.

*1291  Nimmend* may be derived from MS 'nīmēd'. Morris read
'nummend', but he suggested the emendation to *nummen* adopted
by other editors. *OED nim* v. does not list any pp. with *-end,*
but there are many variant forms in the MS. Mustanoja (1960)
570, in identifying *aswagend* (*Pa.* 3) as an inflected infin.,
compared *Cl.* 1291. For *nimmend* as a pp. with *-end,* cf. pp.
*beholdyng* in Malory, noted by Mustanoja, p. 570. (See *Pa.* 3n.)

*1301* Ananias, Azarias, and Misael were Daniel's companions,
who came out of the burning furnace alive. (See Dan. 1.6-7
and 3.21-93.)

*1308* Morris gave no meaning for *profecie;* other editors
followed *OED prophecy,* sense 3, 'a company or body of prophets',
where only *Cl.* is cited. Rendering *profecie* 'prophecies' as a
n. coll. suits this context. Anderson read *profetie,* but the
MS apparently has the *ci* spelling, as in line 1158 also.

*1315* Anderson and Andrew & Waldron followed Gollancz who

substituted *gounes* 'robes' for *gomes*. Other editors tr. *gomes* 'men'. For the meaning 'prizes', see *MED gāme* n., 3c, 'the prize of victory' (OE *gamen, gomen*).

*1324-32* The poet plays on two meanings of *MED grāven* v.1 to stress the instability of earthly fortune, a dominant theme in the medieval period. (Cf. *Pa*. 473-88.) Nabucho had his name *grauen* 'engraved' as *god of þe grounde,* but he is eventually *grauen* 'buried' there.

*1326-28* That man is humble when he recognizes his dependence upon God is an essential theme in all four poems of this MS. (Cf. *Pe*. 401-8.)

*1333-38* Baltassar was apparently the grandson of Nabuchodonosor, but the poet, following the Vulgate (Dan. 5.2, 5.11), calls Nabucho the father, since Baltassar descended from him.

*1336* Eds., following Morris' suggestion, changed *no* before *erþe* to *on,* but the negatives are compounded in this line, and the MS reading may be retained by tr. *no* 'any' twice. For the meaning *erþe* 'land', see *MED ērthe* n.1, 4a.

*1341-48* As Menner noted, this passage describing Baltassar's idolatry anticipates 1522-28. (Cf. also 1717-20.) In 1165 and 1173, the reference is to the idolatry of the Hebrews and Sedecias.

*1358* Eds. changed *gorie* to *glorie,* but one may retain the MS form by reading *gorie* as a variant of *gore* 'filth' 306. Cf. *vanyté vnclene* 'filthy foolishness' 1713. For doubling of the final vowel, cf. *hardee* 543, *scheweed* 791, *swyþee* 1211, and *innoghee* 1303, all appearing at the end of a line.

*1381* See *Ga*. 2191n on *wruxled.* Morris glossed 'raised' for *Cl.*, but 'arrayed, adorned', given by most editors, seems preferable. Anderson glossed '? built up (with alternating courses of masonry)', referring to the discussion of McLaughlin (1963) 65-66. However, McLaughlin conjectured that "the form *wruxeled* refers to some kind of interlacing ornamentation, perhaps even a mosaic pattern of a sort" (66).

*1382* The *carneles* are openings in the battlements on a wall. Cf. *Ga*. 800-2, where pinnacles are dispersed among the *carnele3* so closely that Bercilak's castle seems *pared out of papure.* In *Cl.* 1408, the subtleties *Pared out of paper* decorate the platters of roasted meats. Other types of table subtleties were edible. See, for example, the citation from *Form Cury* s.v. *MED carnel* n.1, sense c, 'crenelated pastry', with *kerue ... keyntlich kyrnels* alliteration similar to *Cl.* 1382.

*1383* Cf. *Ga.* 795. Skeat (1901) 306-7 observed that *troched*, a hunting term originally applied to a stag's horn, meaning 'tufted at the tip with small tines', was later used figuratively for the architectural image.

*1384* See 1190n for reference to Anderson's discussion of *ouerþwert palle*, which he defined as "horizontal paling form-ing the face of the hoarding." Gollancz glossed *palle* 'brat-ticing', noting, "Here 'ouer-þwert palle' seems to be used for bratticing or board-work, galleries of wood with floors placed across the wall." However, *ouerþwert palle* apparently does not refer to the entire rampart.

*1385* Gollancz glossed *place* 'open space', Anderson 'area', readings which seem preferable to 'palace', given by most edi-tors. Menner glossed *pursaunt* 'space, enclosed ground', Gol-lancz and Andrew & Waldron 'precinct', Anderson 'surrounding wall'. The meaning 'boundary' is fitting here, for it is understood that the boundary is made by the surrounding wall. (Cf. *Pe.* 1035n on *poursent* 'compass'.)

*1389* Emerson (1921b) 239 defined *palayce* 'enclosure, royal compound', distinguishing it from the *palays pryncipal*(e) 1531, 1781, with which he equates *halle* 'palace' 1391. He appears to be correct. *OED palace* sb.1, sense 3, defines 'a dwelling-place of palatial splendour'. Eds. rendered *palayce* 'palace'.

*1390* For retention of MS *walle*, cf. 1098n and 1155n.

*1391* *Hit* 'them' refers to the *houses*, apparently living quarters joined to the main palace. (Cf. *hit* 'them' 1291, 1412, 1692.) *Med* 'connected' may be taken as the pp. of *mete* 'meet, join' from OE *mētan*. (Cf. *mette* 'met' 371.) For voicing of the final consonant, cf. *þad* instead of *þat* in *Ga.* 686. Menner emended to *mad*, pt. of *make*. Moorman and Andrew & Waldron followed Gollancz who equated *med* with *metteჳ* 'mea-sures' 625, noting, "To hit med = in proportion thereto, i.e. to the palace." Anderson tr. 'appropriate to it (the palace)', deriving *med* from OE *gemēde*.

*1392* *MED bai* n.2 cites *Cl.* s.v. sense a, 'section of a dwelling (set off by columns)'--(OF *bäee*). The outside is still being depicted; the poet begins to describe the inside of the banqueting hall in line 1394. Anderson rendered *in a bay* 'in the shape of a bay', deriving the word from *MED bai* n.3 (OF *baie*), but the first reading given by all other edi-tors seems suitable.

*1395* Menner and Gollancz defined *sete* 'throne', Anderson 'place (at table)', but *to sete* 'to sit' (*OED set* v., I. 5) seems preferable.

*1396* Menner, Anderson, and Moorman followed Morris who tr. *Stepe stayred stones* 'Bright shone the stones'. Andrew & Waldron followed Gollancz who tr., "He ascended the staired stones," defining *stepe* 'ascended' as a pt. form of OE *stæppan*. However, *stepe* may be tr. 'shiny'; for *stayred* 'raised', see *OED stair* v.1, sense 2, 'to make in the form of stairs', and Emerson (1919) 513. *Stones* 'above (the shiny, raised) stones' is a synthetic dat. (See 32n and *Ga.* 180n for other examples.)
    Gollancz, pp. xxvii-xxviii, compared descriptions of the raised thrones of the Great Khan and Prester John. See Ch. 23, p. 351, and Ch. 30, p. 386, in *Mandeville's Travels,* ed. Malcolm Letts, Vol. 2 (London: The Hakluyt Society, 1953). Part of the latter reads: "Et les degres a monter amont vers le throsne ou il siet, dont il en y a vii. de haut, lun est de onicle, lautre est de cristal, lautre de iaspre vert, de dyaspre, lautre de damatistes, lautre de sardines, lautre de gordehame, et le viii^e., sur quoy il met ses piez, si est de crisolite." For a Mod. E. tr., see *Mandeville's Travels,* ed. M.C. Seymour (Oxford UP, 1968), p. 213. (Cf. the gem imagery in 1467-72 and see the notes to those lines.)

*1397-1416* See *Ga.* 114-29n for discussion of the similar description of the start of the New Year's Day feast in the romance.

*1398* Reading *bounet* 'proceeded' as a pt. pl. agrees with Morris, Menner, Moorman, and the *MED* s.v. *bŏunen* v., 4a. Gollancz and Andrew & Waldron glossed pp. 'prepared'; Anderson also took the word as a pp. paralleling *hiled* 1397, but he tr. 'present, at hand' (*MED*, sense 3). For unvoicing of the final consonant in *bounet,* cf. *bluschet* 982 and *dresset* 1477.

*1402* Gollancz, Anderson, and Andrew & Waldron adopted the emendation of *Sturnen* to *Sturne,* proposed by Emerson (1919) 514 because *-en* is not the usual ending for an adj. in this MS. However, as Emerson also noted, *trumpen* is itself a rare pl. for a nom. case n. from OF. The poet may have been aiming for terminal repetition of *en* in *Sturnen trumpen ... steuen* to give the effect of ringing notes. Adjectives occasionally have a pl. ending in ME to agree with a n. Cf. *foles sages* (*P. Pl.* B xiii 423), noted by Mustanoja (1960) 277 in his discussion of French inflection of adjectives.
    *Strake* 'blow' may be taken as a pr. pl. v. Morris, Menner, and Gollancz interpreted it as a pt. Anderson rendered *strake* as a n. 'blast' and tr. 1402: "(There was) a loud blast of trumpets, clamour in the hall."

*1404* The banners hang from the *trumpen* (1402), as in *Ga.* 116-17.

*1406*  The platters are served with paper subtleties deco-
rating them, the *Lyfte logges* 'Raised arbors' described in
1407-12. Eds. believed the MS has *severed* because the abbr.
for *er* seems to be over the *v,* but the beginning of that abbr.
starts near the top of the first *e,* and one may read 'see*rved*'.
Anderson followed Gollancz who emended to *seve*[*s*] 'broths'.
Keeping þer *wyth* separate clarifies the meaning; *wyth* begins
a prep. phr., the obj. of the prep. being *logges* (1407). For
other examples of enjambement, cf. 157-58 and 365-66.

*1408*  Cf. *Ga*. 802n, and see Ackerman (1957) who observed
that while the table subtleties prominent in the fifteenth and
early sixteenth centuries were edible, "It is more likely that
the allusions in *Gawain* and *Purity* are to a quite different and
earlier sort of ornamental device, possibly a forerunner of the
subtlety proper" (p. 414). Ackerman cited Chaucer's *Parson's
Tale*: "Pride of the table appeereth eek ful ofte ... Also in
excesse of diverse metes and drinkes, and namely swich manere
bake-metes and dissh-metes, brennynge of wilde fir and peynted
and castelled with papir, and semblable wast, so that it is
abusioun for to thynke" (443-44).
    Moral significance in *Cl*. is developed through word-play
in lines 1409-10. The form of the n. in *Broþe baboynes* 'Gro-
tesque gargoyles' is close to *Babiloyne,* as the Babylonians
wallow in luxury. The *Foles* are 'Birds', but this n. may also
mean 'fools' or 'sinners'. *Besttes* may be applied to the
nobles who act like unreasoning 'beasts' in following their
fiendish king. The gargoyles themselves are devilish figures
above the beasts. Thus what appears to be a pleasant descrip-
tion is really a hellish one.

*1412*  This line concludes the description of the subtle-
ties, each apparently of a horse passing beneath an arbor.
*Blonkken bak* designates a part of the paper decorations. Cf.
the arrangement in the following citation in the *OED* s.v.
*subtlety,* sense 5, from *A Collection of Ordinances and Regula-
tions for the Government of the Royal Households, Edward III
to King William and Mary*: "A soteltee Seint-jorge on horseback,
and sleynge the dragun."
    Morris and Menner, though they gave no explanatory note,
apparently recognized that line 1412 is part of the descrip-
tion of the subtleties, but Gollancz placed a semicolon after
line 1411 and tr. 1412: "And all on horseback managed the
affair." Gollancz' interpretation has been widely accepted.
For example, Anderson tr., "And all (the servants) carried it
in their hands on horseback," and then he referred to Holin-
shead's account of the coronation feast in 1420 of Catherine,
queen of Henry V, in which the "Earl Marshal 'rode about the
hall upon a great courser ... to make and keep room' (W.E.
Mead, *The English Medieval Feast* [London, 1931], p. 187)."

However, an Earl Marshal is only one man on horseback in a hall, like the Green Knight in *Gawain*; it seems unlikely that the poet would be describing a whole group of servants in *Cl.* serving food on horseback.

*1413* Referring to Huntsman (1976) 278, who noted that *nakers* may denote either wind or percussion instruments, Anderson suggested that *nakeryn* here (and also in *Ga.* 118, 1016) "are probably horns of some kind, not drums." However, the meaning 'kettledrums' is fitting in all three contexts. (Huntsman's discussion refers to the use of *nakers* in Chaucer's *The Knight's Tale*, line 2511.)

*1416* See Brett (1915) 188-89 for discussion of the sense of *bougoun₃* 'drumsticks'.

*1419* Gollancz emended *loue* to *l[e]ue* 'dear ones', comparing *lef* 939, but *loue*, as Menner glossed it, is sg. coll. denoting the king's 'mistresses'. Cf. *luf* 'lover, beloved' 401.

*1421* *MED breithen* v., 'to rush', cites only *Cl.* All editors agree, except Andrew & Waldron who, with reference to *MED brēthen* v.1, 3a, 'rise as vapor', write, "It was believed that the effect of wine on the mind was caused by vapors rising from the stomach into the brain."

*1423* Eds. rendered *on wyde* 'round about, on every side', but defining *on* 'about' and *wyde* 'blankly' accords better with Baltassar's dulled state of mind. Cf. the meanings s.v. *OED wide* adv., senses 5 and 5b. As Emerson (1919) 514 observed, the king does not see clearly. "He looks at things near by and sees not the larger relations."

*1428* The *OED,* Menner, and Moorman, following Morris, read *lance* 'split open'. Luttrell (1956a) 294-95 showed that Gollancz' *lauce* is correct by pointing out that in line 1438 the chests are unlocked with keys. See *MED lōsen* v.3, 2b, 'open (a coffer)'.

*1432* Menner glossed *gentyle* 'heathen, pagan', which seems to be correct. Anderson and Andrew & Waldron followed Gollancz who tr. *in gentyle wyse* 'in noble manner', but though Nabucho cherished them afterwards, the vessels were not taken from the temple in a gentle way. (See lines 1261-80.) Cf. *gentyle* as an uninflected gen. to the usage in *Cl.* 76 and *Pa.* 62.

*1435* For þat 'this', see *Ga.* 645n.

*1436*  The irony is effectively presented.  Baltassar
thinks of his vices as virtues.  See also 1469-72n.

*1437*  Menner noted that Godefroy gave an instance of OF
*tresor* for *tresorer* in *Dictionnaire de l'Ancienne Langue
Française*.

*1444*  See 1275n for the rendering of *coroun* as 'band'.

*1445*  Menner compared line 1718.

*1459*  Cf. *Ga*. 790n, and see Gordon & Onions (1933) 184-
85.  Tolkien and Gordon, in their note to *Ga*. 790, pointed
out that *enbaned* means 'provided with *bantelles*', which are
"projecting horizontal courses of masonry set near the top
of the wall to render assault by means of scaling ladders
more difficult."  Andrew & Waldron tr. with this meaning,
given also by the *MED* s.v. *bantel* n., where only *Cl*. and *Pe*.
992, 1017 are cited.  In *Pe*. 992, *bantele3* designates the
twelve steps leading to the New Jerusalem.  (See *Pe*. 992n.)
    Moorman followed Menner who referred to the *Transactions
of the Philological Society* for 1903 (6.365), in which Skeat
concluded that "an *embanamen* was made with a kind of horn-
work, an outwork with angles, including a space like three
sides of a square beyond the main-wall; and such a horn-work
may well have been called a *bantel*."  Gollancz glossed *ban-
telles* 'corbel-tables'.  Anderson noted, "Probably 'machio-
lated [i.e., provided with an external gallery] under the
battlements, with skilfully-made stepped corbels.'"  (See
also Brett [1927] 456 for discussion of machiolation and
corbel-tables.)

*1460-63*  Cf. *Ga*. 796-800.  The image presented in 1463
corresponds to the *troched toures* (1383) set at intervals on
the wall around Babylon, to which *Ga*. 795 should be compared.
Bödtker (1911) discussed the use of *cauacles*.  Emendation to
*couacles* seems unnecessary.  See 41n and 72n for other exam-
ples of *a-o* spelling variants.  The spelling is *couacle3* in
line 1515.

*1464-68*  Cf. 1410-11 and 1481-85 for images of birds in
branches.  As Menner noted, the poet drew details from pas-
sages in *Mandeville's Travels* describing the magnificent
dwellings of the Great Khan and Prester John.  (Cf. 1396n.)
Kean (1967) 112-13, who compared *Pe*. 89-94, believed the poet
drew from *Mandeville* for *Cl*. and from *Cl*. for *Pe*.

*1469-72*  See *Pe*. 999-1016n on symbolic gem imagery.  Bal-
tassar, in desecrating the holy vessels, renounces the vir-
tues the gems represent.  The poet had mentioned the *vertuous*

*stones* on the vessels in line 1280. As Menner observed, though gem imagery is found frequently in medieval poetry, the correspondences between *Cl.* and *Pe.* are striking. Seven of the twelve stones appear in *Pe.*: sapphires, topaz, emeralds, amethystine stones, chalcedonies, chrysolites, and rubies. In *Pe.*, each gate is of a *margyrye* 'pearl' (1037). The *sardiners* of *Cl.* are named in Rev. 21.20 as *sardius,* and as *sardinis* in Rev. 4.3. Filling in for *Cl.* are three rare stones not listed in Rev. 21.19-20 or in *Pe.*, but they are mentioned in *Mandeville's Travels,* the first two in the description of the Great Khan's court, the third in Prester John's: *alabaundarynes* (OF *alabaundines*), *penitotes* (OF *peridoz*), and *pynkardines* (OF *corneline*). (Cf. *Cl.* 1396n.)

*1469* Bateson (1918) 385 and the *OED* suggested emending *sardiners* to *sardines,* but odd spellings of nouns occur frequently in this MS, as the following notes testify. The poet perhaps adapted spellings to sounds; the extra *r* in *sardiners* adds to the ring of *r*'s throughout this whole passage.

*1470* What Anderson took as an *ei* after the *d* may be an *a* with its top illegible in *Alabaundarynes*. MED *alaba*(u)*ndīne* defines 'a reddish or violet precious stone, probably some variety of garnet'. Note Trevisa's tr. of Bartholomew de Glanville's *De Proprietatibus Rerum* 197a/b: "Alabandina is a precious stoon and haþ þat name of a regioun of Asia þe which hatte alabandina." *Amar
aun3* 'emeralds' is a variant of *emerade* (*Pe.* 1005).
What looks like *amaffised* may be read as *amattised,* written with two flourishes on the tops of the *t*'s and the bar dissecting only the second *t*. *Amattised,* from MED *amatist*(*e,* is apparently a ppl. a. formed by adding *-ed*.

*1472* Holmes (1934) 199 discussed the *Chrysolithus* or 'peridot'. "In the time of Henry IV the royal treasury of England had 'un anell d'or ove i. peritot.'" Gollancz noted that MS *penitotes* is probably the form intended by the poet, since 'pen(n)y-' for 'perry-' is a characteristic English modification; cf., for example, pennywinkle for periwinkle.
Morris glossed *pynkardine* '? *perre carnadine,* carnelian stone', a variety of chalcedony. (See MED *cornelīne* and *corneōle.*) The poet, needing a word beginning with *p* for alliteration, formed a compound, using the first element *pyn* as a variant of *pyr* (OF *pierre* 'stone'), just as he used *pen* as a variant of *per* in *penitotes*. There are various forms to denote this gem in both ME and OF. Letts' note to *gordehame* in the citation from *Mandeville's Travels* given in 1396n reads 'corneline'.

*1474* Morris defined MS *bekyrande* 'bickering', as if the

description were of fighting men. Emerson (1919) 515-16, noting that such a reading was not appropriate to the context, proposed *bekyr ande.* (See *Ga.* 46n for similar disconnections.) Editors adopted Emerson's emendation of þe *bolde* to *bole* 'bowl', but *bolde* may stand (*MED bọ̄ld* n., sense a, 'an edifice, such as a castle or mansion'). The poet was apparently making a distinction between the *bekyr* and the *bolde,* the former being a reference to the goblet itself, the latter to the engraved design of a castle on it.

*1478* MS *biacost* needs to be disconnected. Anderson separated to *bi acost* 'alongside' (OF *par a coste*), believing *MED cost* n.1 (OE *cost*) gives a forced and unsupported reading. However, *cost* 'conveyance' relates to *MED* la, 'mode of procedure' and lb, 'contrivance, device'. Andrew & Waldron suggested that the *cost* is "evidently a kind of trolley."

*1483* For retention of the MS reading here and in 1485, see *Pe.* 26n. Menner adopted the emendations of Schumacher (1914) 183 who had followed the suggestions of K.D. Bülbring.

*1491* In view of the many examples of ellipsis in the poems of this MS, it does not seem necessary to insert [þer] before *soþefast Dryȝtyn.* (Cf. 926n.)

*1492* Eds. read *spiritually* from MS 'spūally'. For separation to *spun ally,* cf. 1474n. *Spun* 'flourishing' may be taken as a pp. tr. prog. (See *Pe.* 54n for other examples.) For meaning, cf. *spuniande* 'thriving' 1038 and *sponne* 'would spring' in *Pe.* 35. *Ally* 'to unite' (*MED allīen,* sense 1) suits this context.

*1494* Morris, Menner, and Moorman defined *plyt stronge* 'great sin', but the sense given by other editors seems preferable. (Andrew & Waldron tr. 'strange situation'.)

*1506* Anderson, noting as unlikely Gollancz' *stared* 'starred, adorned with star-like figures', interpreted the word as a pa. t. and tr., "and it [the *guere*] shone most brightly." Andrew & Waldron tr. similarly. However, *stared* 'shining' may be taken as a pp. tr. prog. (Cf. 1492n.)

*1507* Gollancz agreed with Emerson (1919) 516 who interpreted *vus* 'to make use' as a variant of the v. from OF *user.* Menner and Moorman, following a suggestion in Morris' glossary, emended to [b]*us* 'to drink' (MDu. *buizen*). Anderson and Andrew & Waldron considered *bede vus þerof* part of Baltassar's outburst; Anderson tr., "Serve us (drink) from it!"

*1514* Moorman and Andrew & Waldron followed Menner who

glossed *rok* 'palace', used fig. for *rok* 'rock' 446. The mean-
ing 'fortress, castle' was common in ML; see Du Cange's *Glos-*
*sarium* s.v. *rocca, roccha*. Anderson followed Morris and Gol-
lancz who defined 'crowd' (*OED ruck* sb.l).

*1515* Eds. defined *burdes* 'ladies', but it seems the refer-
ence is to the noblemen mentioned in 1510-12. Cf. *Ga.* 1954n
on *bordes* 'lords'.

*1517* Gollancz pointed to the ceremony of wassail-drinking,
one which requires that the drinker attempt to drain the cup
with one draft. Note *Wassayl!* 'Drink heartily!' (1508).

*1518* Menner glossed *dressed* '? portion out', Gollancz
'placed', Anderson and Andrew & Waldron 'served', and Moorman
'addressed'. Gardner (1965) 191 tr. 'offered toasts'; cf.
*MED dressen* v., 9a, 'address words to somebody'. The poet
creates the ironic image of all drinking to each other's
health, as they damn themselves.
  The line appears to be short on alliteration, but one may
work out an AB/BA pattern on *arn dressed/duke₃ and*. Schumacher
(1914) 184, on the suggestion of K.D. Bülbring, proposed the
emendation adopted by Menner. (Cf. 1483n.)

*1520* Morris glossed *in helde* 'in purpose, disposed';
Menner, Gollancz, Moorman, and Andrew & Waldron defined *helde*
'poured'. Anderson, taking *helde* as a variant of *elde* and
comparing Dan. 5.1, tr., "As each man was aged, (so) he drank
from the cup." For the reading given here, see *MED hẹld(e*
n.2, sense b, 'duty, allegiance'. As the guests drink, they
pledge their allegiance to Baltassar and false gods (1521-28).

*1522-28* Cf. 1340-45 and 1719-20.

*1524* *Astel* 'could be pledged' is from *MED astellen*, sense
b. Eds. agree with *MED astēlen* v., 'of speech: slip out',
where only *Cl.* is cited.

*1525* Eds. read *goude* 'good', but the MS reveals a mark
after the *d* that resembles the abbr. for another *e*. (Cf. the
abbr. for *e* after *r* in *were* 1551.) The poet is not saying
these false gods are 'good'; they are *goudee* 'yellowish', a
reference to the yellowish gold with which they are gilded.
See *MED gaudī* adj., and cf. 1460-63n on *a-o* spelling variants.

*1526* Chapman (1951) 8-9 noted that the names of these
false gods are not in the poet's main source, Dan. 5.4. Beel-
phegor appears in Numbers 25.3-5, Belial in Deuteronomy 13.13
and Judges 19.22, and Beelzebub in Matt. 12.24, where he is
called the prince of devils.

*1542*  MS *lers̄* may denote *lerms* 'anxieties'.  Morris, fol-
lowed by Menner and Moorman, read *lerns* and emended to *lers*
'features', Gollancz glossed *ler*[*u*]*s* 'features', and Anderson
and Andrew & Waldron read *leres* 'cheeks'.  However, *lerms* may
be taken as a variant of *larms,* an aphetic form of OF *alarm.*
Cf. the poet's source, Dan. 5.6: "cogitationes eius conturbab-
ant eum" ("his thoughts troubled him").  For the meaning, see
*MED alarm*(*e* interj. & n., sense c, 'state of alarm'.

*1545*  Cf. the alliteration in 1724, and see 96n for a dis-
cussion of *runisch* and related words.

*1559*  *Ede* 'proceeded' is from OE *ēode*.  As Emerson (1919)
517 observed, it is understood that the king had his servants
search throughout the city.  Most editors, following Morris'
suggestion, emended to *bede;* Gollancz emended to *eþede* 'ordered
with an oath'.

*1566*  Gollancz, Anderson, and Andrew & Waldron emended to
*makes,* but *make* 'causes' may stand as a v. in the subjunctive
mood.  (*Wysses* 1564 is also subj., proving that sometimes the
form of the subj. v. in this MS is not different from that of
the indicative.)  Moorman credited Thomas (1922a) 66 with this
interpretation.  For a full discussion, see Ohlander (1950).

*1576*  Eds. glossed *sage* as the adj. 'wise, learned', but the
word may be rendered as the sb. adj. 'sages'.  *Sathrapas* is then
gen. pl.  The word originally designated the Persian major gov-
ernors (OPer. *xshathrapāvan*).  Only Menner glossed 'governor',
which seems acceptable, based on *OED satrap*.  Other editors
favored the sense 'wise men', most of them feeling the precise
meaning was not known in ME.

*1577*  The usual definition given for *wyche*ʒ is 'wizards'
(OE *wicca* masc.), but derivation from OE *wicce* 'witch' seems
preferable.  (Morris tr. 'witches'.)  Cf. fem. *walkyries* 'sor-
ceresses' (OE *wæl-cyrie*), corresponding to ON *valkyrja* 'chooser
of the slain'.  Gollancz believed the term did not necessarily
refer to a particular sex, but it seems the poet was precisely
designating females in this line.

*1579*  Anderson and Andrew & Waldron followed Gollancz who
substituted *of* for MS *&* and tr. *sorsers of exorsismus* 'sorcer-
ers who work by means of exorcizations'.  However, *exorsismus*
'conjurers' may be rendered as nom. pl.  Other editors and the
*MED* s.v. *exorcisme* n.2 gave this interpretation.

*1584*  Morris, Menner, and Moorman tr. *heʒed* 'hastened';
Gollancz defined 'shouted', supposing that the v. was made from
the ME interj. *hei*.  Andrew & Waldron, crediting Fowler (1973)

334, interpreted *he3ed* 'vowed' as a variant of *hy3t* (*MED hōten* v.1). However, an appropriate reading is given by Anderson and the *MED* s.v. *hīen* v., 2b, 'desire strongly (to do sth.)'.

*1586  Chef quene* designates Baltassar's mother, not his wife. (See the note to Dan. 5.10 in the Douay Bible.) Anderson rendered *chambre* 'officers of the chamber, household', but as Andrew & Waldron, p. 376, noted, 'chamber' is more appropriate here, since the poet follows with a description of the queen coming down steps (line 1590), implying she had been in her own chamber.

*1595  Redles* may be rendered as a sb. adj. 'unwise ones', in relation to *ledes* 'persons' in the next line. Menner and Moorman compounded MS *for redles*; all eds. gave the sense 'for lack of counsel' (Anderson).

*1598* Andrew & Waldron adopted Gollancz' emendation of *gostes* to *gost* 'spirit', but the pl. form may be retained here. For the meaning 'revelations', see *MED gōst* n., sense 4, 'a spiritual force or insight', where *Cl.* is cited.

*1610* Cf. Dan. 5.12: "cui rex posuit nomen Baltassar" ("whom the king named Baltassar"). This Babylonian name was given to the prophet during Nabucho's reign. (See Dan. 1.7.)

*1614* Cf. 1300 and 1308. *Pryce* 'honored men' 1308 shows coll. usage of the sb. adj.

*1616* Eds. read *wayne,* but *wayued* appears in *Ga.* in a line with similar alliteration. (See *Ga.* 1032n.) The þe before *worchyp* is pleonastic in the tr.

*1618* Andrew & Waldron followed Gollancz who inserted [*cler*] into the line, but one may work out an AB/BA alliterative pattern on *schal -clar/clay stande.* MS *stande* may be retained as a subjunctive form after *also as* 'just as'; cf. the subjunctive mood in the preceding line, governed by þa3.

*1622* Andrew & Waldron needlessly followed Gollancz' emendation of *Leue* to [*B*]*eue* (a form of *beau* 'fine, handsome'). One may alliterate ABAB/B on *Balta3ar vmbe- brayde hym/he.* See Oakden II (1930-35) 191-92 for examples of some rare alliterative patterns in *Cl.*
    Most editors rendered *vmbebrayde* 'greeted, accosted', but Anderson's 'embraced', literally 'seized round', seems preferable, since the poet "readily uses the *umbe-* prefix with a verb of motion to give the general sense 'surround'."

*1632* Gollancz and Andrew & Waldron read *con quere* 'can

discover', but *conquere* may be rendered as subjunctive 'can
conquer', governed by *if*. (Other editors equated the v. with
*Conquerd* 1431.) It is difficult to tell, when viewing the MS,
if the scribe wrote *cō* apart from *quere,* but even if one sees
the syllables separated, there are numerous examples in this
MS of disconnected syllables that need joining. (Note *de
clar* 1618 and *vmbe brayde* 1622.)

*1634* Menner compared *Ga.* 35, where the reference is prob-
ably to the technique of alliterative verse. In *Cl.,* however,
*tede lettres* 'linked letters' refers to the unalliterating
writing on the wall: *MANE, TECHAL, PHARES* (1727), and may be
taken literally. Andrew & Waldron suggested the poet was
perhaps influenced by Vulgate *ligata* 'difficult (*lit.* bound)
things' (Dan. 5.16). Anderson glossed *tede* adj. 'divinely
ordained, fated', a unique survival of OE *getēod(e)*, because
he did not believe *tede* could be the pp. of *tie*. However,
the *OED* s.v. *tede* suggested association with *tied, tide* is
listed as pp. of *tie* v., and the *e-i* spelling variant occurs
quite frequently in this MS, as in *hem* for *hi(y)m*. (See 827n
for examples.)

*1635* Menner's *mode* 'thought' (OE *mōd*) was accepted by
most editors. Gollancz defined 'inscription cut', believing
the word represented *mote,* "not elsewhere found in English,
corresponding to ON. *mōt,* EFris. and Du. *moet,* meaning a
stamp or mark."

*1638* Anderson compared *P. Pl.* B-text Prol. 161 and C-
text I. 175. The C-text is closer to the line in *Cl.* because
of the addition of *golde* and the use of *þyn nekke* instead of
*here nekkes.*

*1648* For omission of *-d* in *deȝyre,* cf. 1155n.

*1655* Emendation seems unnecessary; one may alliterate
AAB/B on *whyle ... watȝ cleȝt/clos. Þat* refers to *hope* 'be-
lief' 1653; one may insert elliptical [belief] in the tr. of
1655. Schumacher (1914) 184, on the suggestion of K.D.
Bülbring, proposed the emendation adopted by Andrew & Waldron.

*1661-68* See E. Wilson (1976) 72-76 on the poet's pos-
sible indebtedness to religious drama. (Cf. *Ga.* 472n on the
dramatic element in that poem.) Davenport (1978) 71 also saw
echoes of the mystery plays in Nabucho's boasts. Nabucho's
speech echoes Lucifer's rebellious statement (211-12). How-
ever, Lucifer is eternally damned, whereas Nabucho repents
and is restored to his kingdom. Baltassar resembles Lucifer
more closely in that both are hard-hearted and beyond repen-
tance. (See 211-12n and 1757-58n.)

*1669* MS *one* 'alone' may be retained as an intensifier, pleonastic in a Mod. E. tr.

*1681-1700* The following note is given in the Douay Bible to Dan. 4.13: "It does not appear by scripture that Nabuchodonosor was changed from human shape; much less that he was changed into an ox; but only that he lost his reason, and became mad; and in this condition remained abroad in the company of beasts, eating grass like an ox, till his hair grew in such manner as to resemble the feathers of eagles, and his nails to be like birds' claws." The poet exaggerates the details, but his presentation accords generally with the Biblical interpretation. Doob (1974) 84-86 noted that the descriptions of Nabucho "seem to be derived at least as much from the traditional figure of the wild man as from Daniel or the commentaries."

*1684* Morris suggested *ay* 'hay'. Menner and Gollancz tr. *ay* 'ever', but the *MED* s.v. *hei* n., sense a, and other editors followed Morris. For omission of initial *h,* cf. *ayre* 'heir' 650, 1709 alongside *hayre* 666.

*1687* In the margin of his text, Morris tr., "His thighs grew thick." Moorman followed Menner who paraphrased, "Thick (tufts of hair) were growing about his flesh," glossing þik as a sb. adj., *thyȝe* as the v. 'grow' (OE þēon), and þryȝt as a ppl. a. '? crowded, thick'. Gollancz emended to *theȝe* 'thew, sinew' (OE þēaw), reading, "Many thick thews crowded around his flesh." Anderson, crediting Thomas (1922a) 66, tr., "many a thick thigh crowded." Andrew & Waldron, citing Dan. 4.30, emended *thyȝe* to *fytherez* and tr., "many thick feathers crowded." For the readings given in this edition, see *OED thigh* sb., sense 3, 'the stem of a plant', and *MED leir* n.1, sense c, 'lair'. Eds. equated *lyre* with *MED līre* n.2, 'flesh', but there are *i(y)-e* spelling variants in this MS. (See 1634n and *Pe.* 229n.)

Lines 1687-88 appear to be from Dan. 5.21: "et rore caeli corpus eius infectum est" ("and his body was wet with the dew of heaven"). However, the poet may have been recalling Dan. 4.20: "Succidite arborem et dissipate illam, attamen germen radicum eius in terra dimittite, et vinciatur ferro et aere in herbis foris et rore caeli conspergatur, et cum feris sit pabulum eius donec septem tempora mutentur super eum." ("Cut down the tree and destroy it, but leave the stump of the roots thereof in the earth, and let it be bound with iron and brass among the grass without, and let it be sprinkled with the dew of heaven, and let his feeding be with the wild beasts, till seven times pass over him.") Nabucho is like a great tree cut down, but the stump of the roots remains, indicating his kingdom will be restored to him.

The poet may have had this metaphor in mind; Nabucho in his 'lair' is the trunk surrounded by 'plant stems'.

*1689* Andrew & Waldron, crediting Fowler (1973) 335, emended *flosed* to *floȝed* 'flowed', but the *MED* s.v. *flōsen* v., sense b, '? to envelope; ? to droop about (someone)', cited *Cl.*, and 'circled' seems suitable here, especially with *vmbe* at the end of the line. Menner noted ON *flosna* 'to hang in threads' for etymology and glossed '? be shaggy'. Anderson tr. 'fell in strands'.

*1692* For *clyuy* 'interlocked', see *MED clēven* v.1, sense c, 'fit tightly together'. The final *y* represents *-e*, and *-d* is omitted. (See the notes to 1098, 1155, and 1390 for examples of the latter.) Morris, Menner, and Andrew & Waldron took *clyuy* as a v. Anderson, following Gollancz, glossed *clyuy* sb. 'burdock, bur', and tr., "Where many a bur stuck it together like a poultice." The *MED* s.v. *clyvy* n. gives this interpretation with *Cl.* as the only citation.

*1695* The poet is apparently describing hairs of the head, hanging down over Nabucho's eyes. Emerson (1919) 518-19 compared *kempe heeris* used by Chaucer in the *Knight's Tale* 2134, where the shaggy hairs of Lycurgus are depicted: "With kempe heeris on his browes stoute."

*1696* Anderson emended *clawres* to *clawes* (OE *clawu*), but the *MED* cited *Cl.* s.v. *clivres* n. (pl.) from OE pl. *clifras*, *clifra* (gen.).

*1697* *Pauue* 'feet' (OF *powe*) is rendered coll. here. Anderson emended to *paume* 'claw, talon' (OF *paume*), but as Gollancz noted, the MS form may be retained if one takes the four minims between *pa* and *e* as *uu*. Other editors read *paune* as a pl. form.

*1698* All editors, except Gollancz, compounded MS *ouer brawden* and tr. 'covered over'. Gollancz glossed *brawden* 'changed in appearance', but as Emerson (1919) 519 noted, 'bent' suits the context well, since it recalls, "He fares forth on alle faure" (1683). See *MED breiden* v.1, sense 2, and cf. the usage in *Ga.* 440.

*1707* Menner defined *hwe* 'form, aspect', Gollancz 'colour', and Anderson 'shape'. For the meaning 'crown', see *MED hŏuve* n. (OE *hūfe*) and *Ga.* 1738n on *hweȝ* 'coif'. Andrew & Waldron emended to *hwef* 'headdress'.

*1717* *Edé* 'splendid treasures' is a sb. adj. used coll. *MED ēdī* defines 'splendid' and shows the adj. used as a n.

Cf. þ'edé to the elision in þ'acces (Pa. 325). Most editors
read þede 'vessel'; Morris compared Provincial English thead
'a strainer used in brewing'. Gollancz, whose emendation was
accepted by Menner (1922a) 362, read þ'ydres 'bowls', deriving
the n. from L hydria (3 Kings 7.50). Andrew & Waldron's þ'edé
'the blessed vessels' is similar to the interpretation given
in this edition.

1718   Cf. 1445.

1720   Cf. 1343 and 1523.

1724   Cf. 1545 and see the note.

1725   Menner's werk 'ado' (OE we(o)rc) seems preferable to
Gollancz' 'pain, effort' (OE wærc, ON verkr).

1732   The antecedent of hit is kyndam. Lines 1730-32 ren-
der Dan. 5.26: "Mane, numeravit Deus regnum tuum et complevit
illud." ("Mane: God hath numbered thy kingdom, and hath fin-
ished it.") There may be word-play: after completing the
measurement (judgment), God will put an end to Baltassar's
realm.

1733   Since there is a n. teche denoting 'guilt' (Cl. 943)
and another denoting 'symbols (of evil)' in line 1049, teche
'tell' in relation to TECHAL may carry deeper connotations:
the 'symbols' on the wall 'tell' of the king's 'guilt'.

1734   Morris glossed walt 'rolled', the OED cited Cl. s.v.
walt v., sense 2, 'throw, cast', and other editors interpreted
the word as the pp. of walle 'choose' 921. However, walt 'com-
pelled' may be a pp. from OED wield v., 'command'. Cf. the pt.
form walt in Ga. 231 and 485.

1735   Cf. Dan. 5.27: "Et inventus es minus habens" ("And
art found wanting"). Gollancz, noting that fewe 'lacking' is
paralleled by ON sg. neut. of the adj. fār, especially with
numerals, compared vetri fātt ī fjōra tigu '40 years save one,
i.e. 39', and svefn-fātt 'lacking sleep'.

1736   Anderson tr. to frayst þe trawþe 'to seek the truth',
equivalent to Mod. E. 'to tell the truth'. However, 'to test
the truth', given by other editors, is suitable here in that
PHARES tests (proves) the truth of MANE and TECHAL.

1741-52   Cf. 1568-73 and 1637-40.

1746   Eds. added -r to Baltaȝa, but one may retain the MS
form, since there are other examples of the omission of -r.

Cf. ʒonde 721 alongside ʒender 1617, and see 981n.

1757-58 *Farand fest* 'excellent feast', which occurs also
in *Ga.* 101, is transposed from 1758 to 1757 in the tr.  Bal-
tassar does not change his ways.  Having rewarded Daniel, he
continues to revel, probably thinking he has time to prepare
for the invasion.  Contrast in *Pa.* 377-84 the reaction of the
King of Ninive, who repents immediately and is spared.  The
poet apparently did not have to explain to his audience the
concept in Dan. 4.24 which reveals that the sinner always has
a chance to attain salvation.  Daniel speaks to Nabucho: "Quam
ob rem, rex, consilium meum placeat tibi, et peccata tua
elemosynis redime et iniquitates tuas misericordiis pauperum;
forsitan ignoscet delictis tuis." ("Wherefore, O King, let
my counsel be acceptable to thee, and redeem thou thy sins
with alms, and thy iniquities with works of mercy to the poor :
perhaps he will forgive thy offences.")  The clause *tyl fayled
þe sunne* perhaps implies that Baltassar failed to reach for
God's light.

1761 Eds. defined *lyst* 'boundary, region, edge' (OE
līste) and *lyfte* 'sky, clear air' (OE *lyft*); Andrew & Waldron
tr. 'through the edge of the sky: i.e. along the horizon'.
However, it seems preferable to follow Emerson (1919) 520 who
rendered *þorʒ þe lyst of þe lyfte* 'through the pleasure of
the breeze', deriving *lyst* from ON.

1762 Anderson correctly observed that *Vche haþel* is not
a reference to Baltassar's guests, but to "ordinary people of
the town who hurry home to escape the worsening weather, and
whose simple pleasures contrast with the luxury of the palace."

1764 *Foundeʒ* 'forms' (*MED fōunden* v.2--OF *fonder* & L
fundāre) provides better sense in this context than *MED
fōunden* v.1 (OE *fundian*) 'to proceed'.  Eds. used the latter:
"Then later on in the night each party (of guests) departs"
(Anderson).  However, this line, like 1762-63, apparently
refers to the ordinary people of the town, not to Baltassar's
guests.  Fowler (1973) 335-36, though he did not discuss the
distinction between townsfolk and guests, tr. 1764: "Then
each seeks companionship for the rest of the night."

1771-72 Menner, noting that Porus of India does not
appear in the Bible but is associated with Darius through the
Alexander legend, compared *Wars Alex.* 3182-83: "How þat ser
Dary with his dukis eft drissis him to fiʒt,/Had prayd eftir
powere to Porrus of ynde."  Dan. 5.31 reads: "Et Darius medus
successit in regnum annos natus sexaginta duos." ("And
Darius the Mede succeeded to the kingdom, being threescore
and two years old.")  Modern Biblical scholars have pointed

out that it was Cyrus (c. 598-529 B.C.) who captured Babylon,
but the Vulgate named Darius the Mede, whose character was
probably modeled on Darius I (522-486 B.C.). Porus of India,
who was associated with Darius III, was defeated by Alexander
the Great at the Battle of the Hydaspes River in 326 B.C.

*1776* Emendation to *scaled* seems unnecessary. Morris
glossed *scaþed* 'to break, destroy', and Emerson (1919) 521
supported such a reading, for it may be understood that two
activities are taking place: some of the enemy are breaching
the walls; others are entering the city by means of ladders
(1777). According to Jeremias 51.58, the entire wall was
eventually destroyed: "Murus Babylonis ille latissimus suffos-
sione suffodietur." ("The broad wall of Babylon shall be
utterly broken down.")

*1779* Eds. separated MS *anoure* to *an oure* 'an hour', but
one may derive *anoure* from *MED anǒur* n., 1b, 'domain'. Some
editors read *myȝt* and changed the MS form to *nyȝt*, but the
first three minims may represent *ni* for *niyȝt*. A distinguish-
ing mark does not always appear over an *i*. See *Pe.* 630n on
the form *niyȝt*.

*1784* See 598n for discussion of *scarred*.

*1795* Anderson's *sounde* 'securely' seems preferable to
Gollancz' 'entirely'. Menner glossed 'safe' (quasi-adv.);
Andrew & Waldron interpreted the word as an adj., 'undamaged'.

*1803* Eds. read *of,* but the ultra-violet lamp revealed
what looks more like two minims of a *u* preceding the *f*. (Cf.
*Ga.* 2343.) Reading *uf* 'if' places 1803-4 in the subj. mood.
*MED lēten* v., 15a, defines 'to consider'. Eds. glossed 'hin-
dered, deprived' (*MED letten*).

*1804* The poet begins to complete his circular structure.
Cf. the similar alliteration but contrasting concept in line
28.

*1805* Means (1975) 168, rejecting the usual interpretation
of *þrynne wyses* as a reference to God's punishment in the nar-
ratives about The Flood, The Destruction of Sodom and Gomorrah,
and The Sacrilegious Feast of Baltassar, divided thusly: (1)
Lines 193-1048: *Fylþe of þe flesch* in the stories of Lucifer,
Adam, the Flood, and Sodom and Gomorrah; (2) Lines 1049-1148:
Exhortation to purity based on examples from the Life of Christ;
(3) Lines 1149-1804: God's vengeance for sacrilege. However,
Means' middle section has little to do with punishment, and
the *þrynne wyses* here all seem to refer to God's *wrake* (1808).
There may be word-play involving *þro* 'misfortune' (590)

and þro 'wrath' (754).  When the sinner raises God's 'wrath',
'misfortune' strikes.  The poet has þro 'earnestly' revealed
this.

*1805-12*  The Epilogue recalls passages at the start of the
poem.  Cf. lines 1805-8 to 5-6, and 1809-10 to 27-28.  In *Pe.*,
*Pa.*, and *Ga.*, the endings echo the beginnings.  (See *Pe.*
1212n.)

*1806  Tocleues* 'penetrates' agrees generally with the
sense given by most editors, 'cleaves asunder' (OE *tōclēofan*).
Anderson preferred 'sticks in' (like mud or filth), or, in
abstract terms, 'strongly affects' (OE *clēofian* 'adhere').
However, *tocleues in corage dere* 'penetrates within [the]
precious heart' not only reminds one that sin wounds the Lord
but also recalls the image of Christ on the cross in John
19.34: "Sed unus militum lancea latus eius aperuit et continuo
exivit sanguis et aqua."  ("But one of the soldiers with a
spear opened his side, and immediately there came out blood
and water.")  See *Pe.* 654n.  The Epilogue presents a triple
view: the New Testament Christ who gave his life for mankind,
the Old Testament Creator who punishes fiercely (*telled vp
his wrake* 1808), and the Holy Spirit who inspires man to lead
a good life (*þat grace he vus sende* 1811).

*1808  Telled* may be rendered as a pp. tr. prog.  (See *Pe.*
54n and *Ga.* 22n for other examples.)  Moorman and Andrew &
Waldron followed Menner who emended to *teldes* 'raises'.  Gol-
lancz recognized *telled* as a variant of *telded* 1342.  (See
the discussion s.v. *OED teld, tild* v.).  He tr. *telled vp
his wrake* 'his vengeance being raised up'.  Anderson noted,
"The construction is absolute: 'His hostility aroused'."

*1810*  Cf. 27-28 and see the note.  That the *seme* 'proper'
man is loyal to God when he is *swete* 'pure' recalls how the
poet has integrated the virtues of loyalty and purity through-
out the poem.  In contrast, the impure man is disloyal to God,
Baltassar, for example, who desecrated the holy vessels and
was *corsed* for his *vnclannes* (1800).  The poet's concept of
*clannesse* means freedom from sin of any kind, a freedom which
can be attained only through faith in God.  (See 1n.)

*1811*  Eds. rendered *gere* 'attire, apparel', which is
evidently the primary meaning, though there may be word-play
on *MED gēre* n., 5a, 'conduct'.  Tr. *gere* 'attire' reminds one
of the Parable of the Wedding Feast (51-160), in which the
*bryʒtest atyred* (114) represent the good people, and the man
in *wedeʒ so fowle* (140) symbolizes the sinner.

*1811-12* These lines convey a double concept: serving well
in the sight of God begins on earth and ends with the attain-
ment of the Beatific Vision, þer *solace neuer blynneȝ*.

APPENDICES

ABBREVIATIONS

BIBLIOGRAPHIES

APPENDICES


1. Miscellaneous Information
about the Manuscript


Printed on the spine of the bound MS is *The Pearl etc.*,
*Brit. Mus., Cotton MS. Nero A.X Art. 3.* Displayed on one of
the front pages is a piece of vellum; the notation reads: "The
patch of vellum on the facing page was removed from f. 86,
where it had been used to repair two natural holes, when the
MS. was rebound in November 1964."
Folio 43 of *Pearl* has what looks like a crescent moon at
the top, with a face in it, in the brown ink the scribe used.
It seems that part of this folio was trimmed at the top. It
may be that after the fire in Ashburnham House in 1731,
scorched edges had to be cut off. Occasionally a face appears
outside or inside an illuminated letter; note in *Pearl,* for
example, the *T* starting line 121 and the *G* starting line 661.
One may also note a hand, with finger pointing, in the upper
left margin of *Pe.* f. 53b, in the middle left margin of *Pe.*
f. 59b, and the middle left margin of *Cl.* f. 66b.
Brett (1927) 452 believed the *Hugo de* written at the head
of *Ga.* f. 95 is in a fifteenth-century hand; the hand appears
to be different from the scribe's, but the color of the ink is
the same brown the scribe used. Brett also pointed out in the
right-hand margin of f. 115b, opposite line 1535, "? *Romeson*
(a mere scribble)", and in the left-hand margin, opposite
lines 1544-45, "[?o] *ton,* in a contemporary or later hand."
The color of the ink is the same brown. The "HONY SOYT *QUI*
MAL PENCE" at the end of *Ga.* f. 128b seems to be by a hand
different from the scribe's, but so does the "AMEN" concluding
the poem, and all these words are in the same brown ink the
scribe used.
I have already noted, at the beginning of the section on
"The Poet and His Audience" in the Introduction, the appear-
ance of the name *J. Macy* in red ink among the ornamental de-
signs beneath the illuminated *N* on the verso of f. 62 in *Clean-*

*ness.* Note also the name *Macy* in red at the left-hand bottom of f. 114 of *Gawain.*

Brett (1927) 452 stated that the couplet above the illustration to *Ga.* on f. 129 is "in a hand contemporary with, and perhaps in the same hand as, that of the rest of the MS." The couplet reads: "Mi minde is mukul on on þat will me noȝt amende/ Sum time was trewe as ston & fro schame couþe hir defende." (*Miminde* runs together, and the second *on* is above the line.) These lines do not relate to the situation the illustration depicts (that of the lady visiting Gawain). The ink is the color of the darker brown found on many of the corrections in the MS.

Greg (1924) 226 noted that the twelve illustrations, described by Gollancz in his Introduction to the Facsimile Reproduction (*EETS* 162, 1923), pp. 9-11, are colored green, red, blue, yellow, brown, and white. They all precede the poems to which they relate, except for the three after *Gawain.* For a full description and discussion, relating the work of the artist to his milieu, see Lee (1977).

## 2. Common Authorship

That one poet wrote *Patience, Cleanness, Gawain,* and *Pearl* is generally accepted today by scholars. Because Middle English poets drew from a common stock of formulae, the best proof for common authorship is not in the similar alliterative combinations found among the four poems, though the large number of these does favor the theory. See Vantuono (1971) 58-63. For those seeking additional lists, especially in comparison to other Middle English poetry, see Fuhrmann (1886), Oakden II (1930-35) 263-363, Waldron (1957), and Benson (1965a) 281-82. Waldron's article on "Oral-Formulaic Technique and Middle English Alliterative Poetry" presents a study of phrases in relation to metrics.

Sounder proof for common authorship lies in similarity of themes and comparable verse techniques to be found among the four poems. (See the section on "Thematic Unity" in the Introduction and the next section on "Verse" in these Appendices.) John Clark, in four articles (*PQ* 1949, *JEGP* 1950, *MLN* 1950, and *MLQ* 1951), argued against it, but, as Loomis-HZ (1959) 5 noted, his reasons are "more ingenious than convincing." More recent attempts by Kjellmer (1975) and Tajima (1978) to disprove common authorship by comparing language and syntax are open to question. Kjellmer, for example, would remove *Pearl* from the group because of its shorter clauses and sentences, but the variation is obviously due to the fact that *Pearl* is the only poem in the MS that does not contain the alliterative long line. (Note the refutation of Kjellmer by Andrew & Waldron [1978] 16.)

In addition to the collected editions of Cawley & Anderson (1976), Moorman (1977), and Andrew & Waldron (1978), book-length critiques by Edward Wilson (1976) and Davenport (1978), there are articles that bring the four poems together, such as A. Kent Hieatt's "Symbolic and Narrative Patterns in *Pearl, Cleanness, Patience,* and *Gawain*" (1976) and Clark & Wasserman's "The *Pearl* Poet's City Imagery" (1978). Vantuono (1971) 37-38 lists earlier works that study the poems together.

The place of *St. Erkenwald* remains controversial. Savage, in the Introduction to his edition of that poem (1926) liii-lxv, upheld the theory that the legend was written by the *Pearl*-poet; Benson (1965b) questioned this attribution; McAlindon (1970) 475 stated, "For reasons which I hope to develop elsewhere, I cannot accept L.W. Benson's conclusion that the theory of common authorship is fallacious"; Peterson (1974a), in noting what he considered to be an anagram for *I. d. Masse* in *St. Erkenwald,* associated the legend with *Pearl*; Ruth Morse, in the Introduction to her edition of *St. Erkenwald* (1975) 45-48, spoke against grouping the legend with the *Pearl* poems; Peterson (1977b) 15-23, in his edition, favored the theory of one author for *Erkenwald* and *Patience, Cleanness, Gawain,* and *Pearl.*

## 3. Verse of *Patience, Cleanness, Gawain,* and *Pearl*

The following works, taken together, provide excellent studies of verse for the poems in the MS: Northup (1897); Saintsbury (1908) 100-111; Osgood (1906) xlii-xlvii; Menner (1920) liii-lviii; Gordon (1953) 87-91; Nakao (1961); Borroff (1962) 133-210; Benson (1965a); Gardner (1965) 85-90; Davis (1967) 147-52; Borroff (1967) 55-62; Schiller (1968); Stillings (1976); Joan Turville-Petre (1976); Borroff (1977) 32-39; Sapora (1977); Grant, Peterson & Ross (1978). For comprehensive coverage of Middle English poetry in general, including the *Pearl* poems, see "The Metrical Survey" in Oakden I (1930-35) 131-245. References to other works dealing with verse will be included at appropriate points in the following pages.

### The Question of Quatrains in *Patience* and *Cleanness*

Except for blank spaces after *Cleanness* 1156 and *Gawain* 490, 1125, and 1997, the lines of all four poems are set together in the MS. (What may be considered another exception to this statement is the fact that the short 'bob' line in *Gawain* is written alone to the right.) Stanzaic arrangements for *Gawain* and *Pearl* are easily determined because of the 'bob and wheel' rhyme that ends each stanza of *Gawain* and the rhyme scheme and concatenation in *Pearl*.

Since *Patience* and *Cleanness* were composed solely in the alliterative line, there are no similar clues. Gollancz printed both poems in quatrains, believing the marks that appear quite regularly every four lines along the left-hand side of the MS indicate the poet intended a quatrain arrangement. For a study favoring the view that these marks are due to the scribe rather than the poet, see Vantuono (1972a). What is said there of *Patience* applies just as well to *Cleanness*. (For a summary of various arguments relating to both poems and other Middle English alliterative poetry, see Duggan [1977] 224-26.)

A main argument is that there would be too many run-on quatrains if one were to believe that the poet composed in this form. For example, reading only the first 200 lines of *Patience* in four-line groupings reveals the following points at which one quatrain is integrally related to the next: 4-5, 32-33, 36-37, 40-41, 52-53, 68-69, 84-85, 104-5, 128-29, 140-41, 148-49, 180-81, 184-85, 196-97, 200-201. A similar survey of the first 200 lines of *Cleanness* shows the same high rate of run-on quatrains. Note the following points: 4-5, 12-13, 36-37, 40-41, 44-45, 52-53, 56-57, 104-5, 116-17, 120-21, 140-41, 144-45, 180-81, 184-85, 196-97, 200-201.


## The Alliterative Line

The following study will concentrate primarily on rhythmic patterns. The alliterative line of *Patience, Cleanness,* and *Gawain* descends from Old English; significant differences found in the Middle English line are due in large measure to changes that occurred in the language, with the synthetic forms of Old English giving way to analytic syntax. Oakden I (1930-35), in his Chapter 8 on "The Alliterative Revival," demonstrated that there was "no historical break between the Old English and Middle English alliterative poetry.... There is change, but continuity" (p. 180). Stobie (1940), after noting that French and Latin poetic forms enriched and stimulated English verse, studied "The Influence of Morphology on Middle English Alliterative Poetry" and concluded that the development of a rising or iambic rhythm "together with that of Old English poetry losing its temporal quality and becoming wholly accentual was not necessarily the result of the influence of foreign metres but was imminent through the changing nature of the English language" (336). Duggan (1977) 235-37 dealt briefly with the possible influence of Old Norse poetic techniques on English poets.

Pope (1966) 105-16, in discussing Old English versifica-
tion, reviewed the classification of syllabic patterns, based
on half-lines, made by Eduard Sievers (1885) and (1893): *Type
A*--lift, drop, lift, drop; *Type B*--drop, lift, drop, lift;
*Type C*--drop, lift, lift, drop; *Type D*--lift, lift, half-lift,
drop, or lift, lift, drop, half-lift; *Type E*--lift, half-lift,
drop, lift. A 'lift' is one syllable that receives primary
stress, a 'half-lift' is one syllable that receives secondary
stress, and a 'drop' is the one or more unstressed syllables
that come between those that have primary or secondary stress.
    The Middle English alliterative line may be scanned in dif-
ferent ways, depending upon the reader. There has been a vari-
ety of views on this subject, summarized by Borroff (1962) 264-
65. Rosenthal (1878) presented an eight-stress theory, counting
four in each half of the line. Trautmann (1896), noting that
the second half-line is shorter than the first, modified Rosen-
thal's theory and scanned the line with seven stresses. Among
the advocates of the seven-stress theory were Kuhnke (1900),
Fischer (1900), Kaluza (1909), and Leonard (1920). Among the
early scholars who favored the four-stress theory, based on
Sievers' analysis of the Old English line, were Luick (1889)
and J. Thomas (1908). Supporters of these different theories
allowed the presence of secondary stresses in their scansions.
Most modern scholars accept the four-stress theory, admitting
the addition of an extra stressed syllable in the extended
line; however, there have been differences of opinion on the
reading of these extended lines. Borroff (1962) scanned them
with four primary stresses and one secondary stress. Gardner
(1965) 347 criticized Borroff on this point. His own view is
that the lines are "simply pentameter, much like blank verse,
but rhythmically more flexible than normal iambic pentameter.
... Moreover, the tradition of alliterative poetry gives him
[the poet] the ability to shift, whenever he wishes to break
the pentameter effect, to a classical four-stress line" (87).
    C. Hieatt (1974), in reading extended lines with four pri-
mary stresses and one secondary, concluded that the Old Eng-
lish *D* and *E* verses "have not disappeared, but provide a more
satisfactory explanation of the lines with more than four prin-
cipal stresses than does the theory that they derive from the
hypermetric."
    Old English poets placed the metrical weight in the first
half of the line. This practice continued in Middle English.
The Middle English line is generally longer with more un-
stressed syllables, the number of which varies; the verse is
accentual. In Middle English, the caesura is not as pronounced
as in Old English, where there was more often a full stop in
the middle of the line with a new entity beginning at that
point and running into the next line. Thus in Old English en-
jambement was more frequent.
    The following analyses, in eight categories, based on the

Old English antecedents, will combine a scansion of lines with marking of alliteration, drawing examples only from the first 100 lines of *Patience, Cleanness,* and *Gawain.* (Choices for *Gawain* were drawn from lines 1-130 because six five-line 'bob and wheel' portions are included there.) For the use of alliterative symbols beneath the line, I am indebted to Borroff (1967) 55-62. Oakden, Pope, and C. Hieatt, previously cited, also provided essential information for the establishment of the working system found below.

The symbol ['] indicates primary stress and relates to the OE lift; ['] indicates secondary stress and relates to the OE half-lift. Unaccented syllables, which relate to the OE drop, will not be marked. A slanted line between words indicates the caesura. The small letters 'a', 'b', and 'x' beneath the line mark the alliterative pattern. An 'x' will go under any syllable of primary or secondary stress that does not alliterate. When an alliterating syllable does not carry primary or secondary stress, the (a) or (b) will be in parentheses.

The entire ME line will be cited in the following examples, but the choice in relation to the OE type is determined by either the on-verse, the first half line, or the off-verse, the second half line. The words 'on' and 'off' after the line number in parentheses will indicate the part that is being compared to the OE type. In a few instances, no such indication will appear because the rhythmic pattern is the same in both halves of the line. The comparison of the ME verse to the OE type is based only on rhythm. The first five categories deal with the normal verse that carries two main stresses; the last three categories cover extended lines in which an extra stressed or secondarily stressed syllable appears in the on-verse. Due to its greater variation, the on-verse is used more often as a basis for comparison.

Because of the technical aspect of the subject and controversy on many of its points, one may view some of the lines below in different ways and will undoubtedly find other lines that are exceptions to the rule in not fitting any of the eight categories. One example will illustrate:

When héuy hérttes ben húrt/wyth hépyng òþer élles.  (*Pa.* 2)
    a    a       a      a    a    a

This line, resembling iambic hexameter, was apparently influenced by OE hypermetric verses.


(I) *ME Falling Rhythm in Relation to OE Type A--Lift, Drop, Lift, Drop*

  (1) Súffraunce may aswágend hem/and þe swélme léþe.  (*Pa.* 3 on)
     a          a            a    x

  (2) Swýereʒ þat swýftly/swýed on blonkeʒ.  (*Cl.* 87)
     a       a    a      x

(3) Jústed ful jólilé,/þise géntyle kníȝtes.　　　(Ga. 42 on)
　a　　　　a　　　　　a　　　　　x

Patience, Cleanness, and Gawain, along with ME poetry in
general, reveal mostly a rising rhythm (iambic and anapestic),
with unstressed syllables at the beginning of the line, but the
poet frequently used initial stress for effective variation.
The falling rhythm extends through the whole line in 2; the
caesura is hardly noticeable there. Because of the large num-
ber of unstressed syllables, the falling rhythm patterns are
more dactylic than trochaic. Both 1 and 2 exceed the dactyl
with three unaccented syllables after the initial stress.

All three lines exhibit the classic aa/ax pattern found
most frequently in OE. The poet used this combination most of
the time, but he brought in other patterns often enough for
variation. For statistics, see Oakden I (1930-35) 168, 190-92.
The majority of stressed syllables in both OE and ME also al-
literate. In the lines under consideration in this study,
there is a predominance of 'a' alliteration, but the 'ab' pat-
tern, though in minor proportion, also appears.


(II) *ME Rising Rhythm in Relation to OE Type B--Drop, Lift,*
　　　*Drop, Lift*

(1) Wyth a róghlych rúrd,/równed in his ére.　　　(Pa. 64 on)
　　　　　　a　　　a　　　a　　　　　　x

(2) And thus schal he be schent/for his schrowde féble.
　　　x　　(a)　　　　　a　　　　　　a　　　x
　　　　　　　　　　　　　　　　　　　　　　　(Cl. 47 on)

(3) I schal télle hit as-tit/as I in tóun hérde.　　(Ga. 31 on)
　　　　　a　(b) (b)　a　(b)　　(b)　a　　b

The falling rhythm of the off-verse in 1 counterbalances
the first half of the line. The next two lines reveal a few
different ways in which the poet made use of less prominent
words. In 2, there is an example of a stressed syllable (*thus*)
that does not alliterate, and in contrast, an instance of an
alliterating syllable (*schal*) that does not bear stress. The
third line has the second element of a compound (*as-tit*) carry-
ing both stress and alliteration.
The 'ab' alliteration in 3 is excessive. Most, if not all,
of the 'b' pattern may be accidental, but I have marked it any-
way. See the notes on IV 3 below for a discussion of vocalic
alliteration.


(III) *ME Clashing Rhythm in Relation to OE Type C--Drop, Lift,*
　　　*Lift, Drop*

(1) Súnderlùpes, for hit dissért,/vpon a sér wýse. (Pa. 12 off)
　　　a　　x　　　　　　　　a　　　　a　　x

(2) As Maþew meleȝ in his masse/of þat man ryche.  (Cl. 51 of
        a              a          a    x

(3) Of sum mayn meruayle,/þat he myȝt trawe.  (Ga. 94)
        a    a              aȝt  x

In the first 100 lines of these poems, examples of this type
are found more often in the off-verses. It is assumed that
final e is sounded in each of the three examples. The third
line reveals an instance of clashing rhythm in the on-verse
also. (Cf. Ga. 51 on: "Þe most kýd knyȝteȝ"--noted by Davis
[1967] 148). Some examples of clashing rhythm in the on-verses
of extended lines are cited in Categories VI and VII below.

The different alliterative patterns in 1 and 2 are due to
the extended on-verses. See Categories VI, VII, and VIII for
more examples.


(IV) *ME Rising-Falling Rhythm--Type BA--Drop, Lift, Drop, Lift,
      Drop*

(1) For þeras póuert hir próferes,/ho nyl be pút vtter.
         a              a                  a   x
                                                    (Pa. 41 on
(2) Alle excused hem by þe skyly/he scape by moȝt.  (Cl. 62 on
         a                a          a        x

(3) Hit watȝ Ennias þe athel/and his highe kýnde.  (Ga. 5)
    (a)       a         a   (a) (a)         a   x

Tolkien & Gordon (1925) 119 called these *Type AB,* noting
this kind already existed in OE as *Type A* with an introductory
syllable (anacrusis). See Pope (1966) 109 for examples. Davis
(1967) 148 changed Tolkien & Gordon's designation to *BA.* Oakden
I (1930-35) 174-75 pointed out how the increased use of the
Auftakt (upbeat) with the falling rhythm produced the new
rising-falling rhythm, which passed from late OE verse into
ME and became very common.

In *excused* (*Cl.* 62), the sound of *sk* alliterates with *skyly*
and *scape.* (Menner [1920] lvii noted that the alliteration is
only on the second element of the word in *Cl.* 70: "Excuse ...
court./... com.") The third example exhibits a type of vocalic
alliteration the poet used, on unidentical vowels and with
initial *h* in the pattern. The (a) found three times may be
accidental. Alliterating on unidentical vowels follows the
OE practice; having initial *h* in the pattern is contrary to OE
practice, for OE *h* alliterates only with itself. Oakden I
(1930-35) 159-62 believed the tendency in ME to alliterate on
identical vowels shows the poetry was intended for the eye as
well as for the ear. Thus the high frequency of alliteration
on unidentical vowels in *Patience, Cleanness,* and *Gawain* per-
haps indicates the poet was more concerned with oral delivery.

(V) *ME Falling-Rising Rhythm—Type AB—Lift, Drop, Lift*

(1) Pácience is a póynt,/þaʒ hit displése ófte.  (*Pa.* 1 on)
    a        a           a   x

(2) And my fédde fóuleʒ/fátted wyth sclaʒt.  (*Cl.* 56 off)
        a     a      a       x

(3) ʒeʒed 'ʒéres-ʒiftes' on híʒ,/ʒélde hem bi hónd.  (*Ga.* 67 off)
    a    a     a      b    a  (b)     b

This type is found more often in the off-verse. Davis
(1967) 148-49, noting several examples in off-verses past line
130 of *Gawain,* argued in favor of their authenticity. Since
there is a preference for feminine endings in these poems, as
in ME alliterative poetry in general, some critics favored add-
ing final *e* to many verses of various types, attributing the
omission to the scribe's carelessness. See, for example, the
long lists of suggested metrical emendations made by Gollancz
for his editions of *Patience* (pp. 35-36) and *Cleanness* (pp.
77-80). However, masculine endings in *Patience, Cleanness,*
and *Gawain* are found often enough to justify retaining them
as the poet's.

The excessive 'ab' alliterative pattern of 3 is due in part
to the extended on-verse with a secondary stress in addition to
three primary ones. Lines with more than five stresses are the
exception rather than the rule. Discussion of extended lines
comes in the next three categories.


(VI) *ME Extended Line in Relation to OE Type D—Lift, Lift,*
     *Half-Lift, Drop, or Lift, Lift, Drop, Half-Lift*

(1) I hérde on a hálydày/at a hýʒe másse.  (*Pa.* 9 on)
    a      a    x     a    x

(2) Bróʒten báchlereʒ hem wýth,/þat þay by bónkeʒ métten.
    a      a        x      x  (a) a      x  (*Cl.* 86 on)

(3) Bischop Báwdewyn abóf/bigineʒ þe táble.  (*Ga.* 112 on)
    a      a       a  (a) x      x

    C. Hieatt (1974), adapting a system of scansion employed
by Borroff (1962), read several on-verses of extended lines in
*Gawain* with inclusion of secondary stress, showing that the OE
*Types D* and *E* did pass into ME. Scansion is often an arbitrary
matter, and Hieatt's study does contradict the general view of
most previous scholars who did not believe *Types D* and *E* influ-
enced ME verse; however, there does seem to be evidence in
*Patience* and *Cleanness,* as well as in *Gawain,* to advance this
new theory. The three on-verses above fit the *Lift, Lift, Drop,
Half-Lift* pattern, but with variations that were allowed in OE.
In 1, the unaccented *I* beginning the line is anacrusis. In
all three examples, there is an added drop between the two
lifts, making the type conform to OE expanded *D.* See Pope
(1966) 114-15 for examples, and cf. especially "onwéndeþ

wýrda g̀escèaft" in the on-verse of line 107 of *The Wanderer*.
   In 2, þay may be read with secondary stress. Off-verses
with more than two stresses are not found often.
   Example 1 shows triple alliteration on *h* before unidentical
vowels. This is not the rule in *Patience, Cleanness,* and
*Gawain,* where the patterns often combine words beginning with
*h* and words beginning with vowels, as in IV 3 above. (See
Oakden I [1930-35] 162 for statistics.) In 2, the alliteration
on *by* may be accidental. In 3, the alliteration on *bi* of
*bigine*ʒ is not accidental, since it provides the link to the
first half of the line. The practice in ME of alliterating on
an unstressed verbal prefix is "contrary to O.E. custom"
(Oakden, p. 159).


(VII)  *ME Extended Line in Relation to OE Type E--Lift, Half-
       Lift, Drop, Lift*

   (1) Múch, màugre his mún,/he mót nede súffer.        (*Pa.* 44 on)
       a      a           a     a         x
   (2) Krýst kỳdde hit hymsélf/in a cárp óneʒ.          (*Cl.* 23 on)
       a     a         x           a    x
   (3) Wýlde wèrbles and wýʒt/wákned lóte.              (*Ga.* 119 on
       a     a           a    a      x

   Concerning 1, the preceding line 43 when read together with
44 gives an example of enjambement, which is rarer in ME than
in OE. "And þereas pouert enpresses, þaʒ mon pyne þynk/Much,
maugre his mun, he mot nede suffer." One might argue for pri-
mary stress on *maugre,* because of the editorial comma after
*much,* but it seems justifiable to mark a less prominent word
like a preposition with secondary stress in this instance. In
3, if the final *e* of *Wylde* is pronounced, the type would fit
expanded *E* with an extra *Drop* between the *Lift* and *Half-Lift*.
See Pope (1966) 116 for examples in OE.
   There are extended on-verses with secondary stress that do
not fit the *D* or *E* types in OE. For example, it seems best
to read *Pa.* 98 with a *Lift, Drop, Half-Lift, Lift* pattern:
"Fýndes he a fàyr schýp/to þe fáre rédy." The type thus re-
sembles *AB* of the normal line (Category V) with a falling-
rising rhythm. Though *fayr* alliterates, it may carry secondary
stress as an adjective, since the more prominent word in the
clashing rhythm is the noun *schyp.*
   When there is clashing rhythm in the extended on-verse,
one of the two stresses is usually secondary. The syllable
carrying the secondary stress may be either the first one or
the second one, depending on factors such as natural rhythm,
the position of the clash, and the words involved. VII 1 and
2, for example, have a [´`] pattern in contrast to the [`´]
of *Pa.* 98 because the clashing rhythm is at the beginning of
*Pa.* 44 and *Cl.* 23, and the poet frequently placed heavy stress

on an opening syllable for variation.

(VIII) *ME Extended Line in Relation to OE Hypermetric Verses*

    (1) Góddes glám to hym glod,/þat hym vnglad máde.   (*Pa.* 63 on)
       a      a          a         a   x

    (2) Sáyde þe lórde to þo lédeӡ:/"Láyteӡ ӡet férre." (*Cl.* 97 on)
       x        a         a        a      x

    (3) Siþen þe sége and þe assáut/watӡ sésed at Tróye.
       a      a            a        a    x     (*Ga.* 1 on)

The term "Hypermetric Verses" is used here to distinguish the ME extended line with three primary stresses in the on-verse from the preceding examples that were apparently influenced by OE *Types D* and *E*. The triple primary-stress patterns still prevail in many instances, for it seems best to scan the lines in this way when prominent words are involved, usually bearing alliteration too, and when the stressed syllables are separated by unaccented syllables. The term "prominent words" is used here to distinguish vocabulary that carries the weight of meaning from "less prominent words" such as pronouns, auxiliary verbs, prepositions and conjunctions, and some adjectives and adverbs.

One will perhaps find some exceptions to these general rules, but it will be noted in the three on-verses above that all the words in the stress patterns, except *Siþen*, are prominent, that all the stresses are separated by unaccented syllables, and that all these stressed syllables, except *Sayde*, alliterate in their individual patterns. *Sayde* is in initial position, one in which the poet often used a heavy stress. *Siþen* is not a prominent word, but in its position at the start of *Gawain* it bears primary stress and alliteration. In fact, all the poems in the MS begin with a heavily stressed word that alliterates. In *Pacience, Clannesse,* and *Perle,* the opening words have become the titles of the poems.

Extended on-verses with three primary stresses may also be classified according to rhythmic types noted for normal verses. For example, 1 and 3 above show the falling-rising rhythm (*Type AB*) of Category V, and 2 above reveals the falling rhythm (*Type A*) of Category I. *Pa.* 7 has the rising rhythm (*Type B*) of Category II:

      Þen is bétter to abýde þe búr/vmbestóundes.
           a        a      a   x ⓐ x

*Ga.* 109 shows the rising-falling rhythm (*Type BA*) of Category IV:

      There góde Gáwan watӡ gráyþed/Gwenore bisýde.
          a    a        a       a    x

# Conclusion of the Alliterative Line

Swift movement and effective variation mark the metre of
*Patience, Cleanness,* and *Gawain.* The lines contain basic pat-
terns, but the poet avoids monotony by interrupting the flow
of rising rhythm with other types he had at his command. His
employment of initial stress, clashing rhythm, and the extended
line is especially significant in setting these poems apart as
the work of one man.

Oakden I (1930-35) 171 presented the following information:
(1) The percentage of extended lines in *Pa.* is 13.7, in *Ga.*
15.3, and in *Cl.* 15.8. Only the 17.5 percentage in *St. Erken-
wald* exceeds these figures. (2) Extended on-verses with the
first two syllables carrying stress is found in any consider-
able number only in *Pa., Cl.,* and *Ga.* (173). Oakden did not
read any syllable in the patterns with secondary stress, but
his findings still apply in favor of common authorship; "there
remains little doubt," he stated, since the "metrical test
corroborates the theory in a remarkable manner" (251). While
calling the theory for *Pa., Cl.,* and *Ga.* "unassailable," he
was more guarded in his statements about *St. Erkenwald.* Though
he would include this poem among the *Pearl*-poet's works, he
noted that it "is short, having only 352 lines; hence it is
more dangerous to argue from percentages" (253).

From my own survey of the first 100 alliterative lines of
each poem, the percentages of extended lines in *Pa., Cl.,* and
*Ga.* are even higher than Oakden's, and it is likely that higher
percentages appear in the poems as a whole, for Oakden did not
consider secondary stress along with primary stress.

The following figures are based only on the first 100 al-
literative on-verses, either with three primary stresses or
with two primary and one secondary. (The survey goes up to
line 130 for *Ga.* because of the 'bob and wheel' portions end-
ing the stanzas.) The percentage for *Pa.* is 21; note the fol-
lowing lines: 2, 7, 9, 10, (11), (12), 26, (44), (46), 48, 51,
(54), (62), (63), (65), (66), 82, (90), 93, 96, (98). The
numbers in parentheses indicate lines that begin with initial
stress. Of that group, those that have clashing rhythm at the
beginning, either with two primary stresses or one primary
and one secondary, are 11, 44, and 65. These statistics do
not include lines 31 and 32 in which there is initial stress
in four-stress on-verses. Among the first 100 lines, the fol-
lowing normal on-verses also have initial stress: 1, 3, 79,
80, 99.

The percentage for *Cl.* is 25; note lines (3), 5, 11, (16),
18, (23), 24, 25, 27, 40, (44), 50, 51, 52, 53, 57, 58, (60),
75, (80), 82, (86), (94), (97), (99). Parentheses indicate
initial stress. Among that group, initial clashing rhythm is
found in 23 and 94. In 3, 16, and 80, there would be initial
clashing rhythm if final *e* of the first word were not sounded.

The following normal on-verses have initial stress: 1, 10, 81, 87, 90, 98.

The high percentage of 36 in *Ga.*, apparently due to the short 'bob and wheel' portions ending the stanzas, shows the poet was seeking more variation with the extended line. Note the following: (1), 2, 8, 10, 13, (21), (25), (26), (39), 40, (47), 53, 61, (64), (65), (69), 73, (74), (75), (76), 77, 87, 89, 91, (98), (108), 109, 110, 111, (112), 113, 115, (118), (119), (121), 123. Parentheses indicate initial stress. Among that group, only 76 has initial clashing rhythm, but if the final *e* of the first word were not sounded, so would 21, 47, 64, 74, 98, 118, and 119 fit the pattern of initial clashing rhythm. Line 67 with initial stress in a four-stress on-verse is not included in these statistics. The following normal on-verses have initial stress: 7, 11, 12, 42, 122.

The artistic variation employed by this poet, witnessed in the alliterative lines of *Patience, Cleanness,* and *Gawain,* sets him above most of his contemporaries. As Gardner (1965) 90 stated, "Few poets in English, and for that matter few poets anywhere, can surpass the music of the *Gawain*-poet."

## The Rhymed Parts of *Gawain*

All 101 stanzas in *Gawain* end with a rhymed portion of five short lines. (Davis [1967] 147 noted that the number of un-rhymed alliterative lines in the stanzas varies from twelve, lines 20-31, to thirty-seven, lines 928-64.) The portion of end rhyme, patterned ABABA, usually contains alliteration also, and it has been called the 'bob and wheel'. The very short 'bob', containing one stressed syllable, is followed by the 'wheel' of four lines, each of which ordinarily contains three stresses. Note lines 15-19:

wyth wynne,
(a)

Where werre, and wrake, and wonder
(a)   a           a           a

Bi sýþeȝ hatȝ wont þerinne,
x   (a)   x           a

And oft boþe blysse and blunder
x   (a)   a           a

Ful skéte hatȝ skyfted synne.
a           a           a

The alliterative pattern I marked in line 17 may be acciden-tal, but if readers consider the five lines as a whole, they will note three links from 17 to what precedes and follows: *Bi* to the alliteration in the next line, *sýþeȝ* to the pattern in the last line, and *wont* to the patterns in the first two lines.

The stressed syllable in the 'bob' is usually preceded by only one unaccented syllable. This very short line in most instances relates to the unrhymed alliterative part that precedes, and, as Davis (1967) 152 noted, it "seldom adds anything essential to the meaning." The rhythm of the 'wheel' is usually rising, but other types found in the purely alliterative portion also occur. For example, there is clashing rhythm in, "Wyth lél létteres lóken" (35), and line 57 may be read with initial clashing rhythm if the second syllable is given secondary stress: "Kýng, hy ̀ʒest món of wýlle."

## The Verse of *Pearl*

Except for six stanzas in Group XV, the 101 twelve-line stanzas of *Pearl*, rhyming ABABABABBCBC, are in twenty groups of five. The poet combined native alliteration with foreign rhyme, and added to these the refrain and concatenation.

Considering only alliteration on stressed syllables, Northup (1897) 338 noted that the technique appears in almost 70% of the lines, usually on two stresses but often on three or even four. Types of alliteration found in *Pearl* are the same as those that appear in *Patience, Cleanness,* and the purely alliterative parts of *Gawain*. Gordon (1953) 91, believing the line in *Pearl* "is probably more truly understood as a modification of the alliterative line than as a basically French line partly assimilated to the alliterative tradition," noted that alliteration is heavier in the descriptive passages than in the discussions on theology.

Concatenation, the device of repeating the last word of one stanza in the opening line of the next, runs throughout entire stanza-groups. (The failing of this linking device at line 721 is probably intentional; see 721n in the Commentary.) The refrain that carries through the five stanzas is then marked by a similar C rhyme in the last line of each of the five.

Medary (1916) 270, after studying "Stanza-Linking in Middle English Verse," stated that the device, as it appears in other poems such as *The Avowynge of King Arther, The Awntyrs off Arthure, Sir Degrevant, Sir Tristrem, Thomas of Erceldoune,* and *Sir Perceval,* "may be differentiated from the linking of 'The Pearl', which involves a refrain and appears to be of a less popular origin." A. Brown (1916), in a follow-up to Medary's article, allowed for influence of some Romance model on *Pearl* (pp. 271-72) and admitted that not much should be made of the fact that the beginning and ending of *Gawain* is "with the same word in Celtic fashion" (p. 281), but he felt that models for *Gawain* may have included Celtic poetry, and he favored Celtic influence on Middle English alliterative poetry in general and on alliterative poems that include the devices of stanza-linking and beginning and ending with similar phrasing.

It is obvious that alliteration in *Pearl* associates the
verse of that poem with *Patience, Cleanness,* and *Gawain.* Be-
cause the lines are shorter and contain rhyme, it is less ob-
vious that the rhythmic patterns in *Pearl* are also the same as
those that appear in the other three poems.

The rhythm of *Pearl* is predominantly rising (iambic and
anapestic), almost always with four stresses to a line marked
by a caesura; the pause is frequently so slight it is hardly
noticeable. Sometimes more than two unaccented syllables come
between the stresses. The poet varied the flow of his lines
effectively, with employment of initial stress and clashing
rhythm at appropriate points.

The following survey, based on the first 100 lines of *Pearl,*
follows the preceding system used for the alliterative line in
*Patience, Cleanness,* and *Gawain;* but only the first five cate-
gories dealing with the normal line are covered, since the ex-
tended line is rarely found in *Pearl.* An example of an extended
on-verse, if one wishes to scan it in the following way, is in
line 75:

$$\text{Hóltewòde}\text{3 brý}\text{3t/abóute hem býde}\text{3.}$$
$$\text{x} \quad \text{x} \quad \text{a} \quad \text{a} \quad \text{a}$$

Considering that the *-e* of *Holte* is sounded, one notes here an
expanded OE *Type E;* cf. *Ga.* 119, example VII 3 in the preceding
survey.


(I) *ME Falling Rhythm in Relation to OE Type A--Lift, Drop,*
    *Lift, Drop*

      (1) Oúte of Oryent,/I hárdyly sáye.    (3 on)
         a      a      a    x

      (2) Fówle3 þer flówen/in frýth in fére.    (89 on)
         a      a      a    a

The poet used initial stress and a falling rhythm (trochaic
and dactylic) often enough to keep his verse patterns from be-
coming monotonous. Note how he switches to the usual rising
rhythm in the off-verse of both examples.


(II) *ME Rising Rhythm in Relation to OE Type B--Drop, Lift,*
     *Drop, Lift*

      (1) Þur3 grésse to gróunde/hit fró me yót.  (10)
         a      a      x    x

      (2) And héuen my háppe/and ál my héle.    (16)
         a      a      a    a

The common rising rhythm runs through the whole line in
both examples. Since the lines in *Pearl* are generally shorter
than the alliterative lines of *Patience, Cleanness,* and *Gawain,*

less prominent words carry stress fairly often. Note *fro* in 1
and *al* in 2. There is no alliterative pattern in the second
half of 1, but the poet did not strive for alliteration regu-
larly. Example 2 reveals an 'a' pattern found in the other
poems, on unidentical vowels and with initial *h* involved.

It should be noted that if *-e* were sounded in *grounde,*
*happe,* and *hele,* there would be no stressed syllable before
the caesura in 1 and 2, and no stressed syllable at the end
of 2. The question of the pronunciation of final *e* has been
controversial, but it seems safe to say that it is not sounded
before the caesura in these examples because the following
words begin with *h (hit)* and a vowel *(and).*

The *-e* in *hele* is another matter, since the word is in
rhyme position, matching other words with final *e.* Borroff
(1977) 34 presented evidence which implies that *-e* is "not pro-
nounced in rhyme-words in *Pearl,* even when it is present in all
the members of a rhyming group." Not sounding final *e* makes
the usage accord with what was taking place in the spoken lan-
guage of the poet's dialect.


(III) *ME Clashing Rhythm in Relation to OE Type C--Drop, Lift,*
    *Lift, Drop*

   (1) Where rých rókkeȝ/wér to dyscréuen.     (68 on)
     (a)    b     b      a       x

   (2) So fréch fláuoreȝ/of frýteȝ wére.     (87 on)
       a     a        a     x

Difficulty again arises because of the question of final *e.*
In this edition, no emendations have been made on metrical
grounds, but some previous scholars believed in emending freely
For example, Emerson (1921a), (1922), and (1927) suggested
numerous changes for *Pearl* involving final *e,* attributing what
he called errors to a careless scribe. As Gordon, p. 90, noted
Gollancz and Chase avoided clashing stress in their editions
by altering the text wherever possible. However, since the
poet was familiar with alliterative verse where clashing stress
occurs, there seems to be no reason to deny that he would use
it in *Pearl.*

Of the two examples above, Gollancz and Chase emended *rych*
to *ryche,* but they did not change *frech,* apparently because
*rych* (OE *rīce*) had *-e* at an earlier stage of the language but
*frech* (OE *fersc*) did not. Such matters cannot be settled with
certainty, but under the circumstances, it seems best to go by
what the MS contains, considering that the poet would have used
*-e* or not used it in accordance with what prosodic effects he
wanted at a certain point, not with the form of the early lan-
guage.

There are other lines in which emendation is seemingly jus-
tified. Consider the following:

(1) Þat dót₃ bot þrých/my hért þránge.        (17 off)
    (a) x       a      x    a

(2) Of hálf so dére/adúbménte.        (72 off)
    x        a    a  x

Gollancz and Chase emended *hert* (OE *heorte*) to *herte*.
Borroff (1977) 33-34 favored the change, comparing *herte*
*strayne₃* at the end of line 128. Several editors emended
*adubmente* (OF *adubement*) to *adubbemente*; the latter is the
spelling in the other refrains of the stanza-group. However,
in these instances it is possible that an *e* was sounded even
though not written. A similar circumstance seems to apply to
the rhymes *clot--spotte* (22-24) and *not--spotte* (34-36). In
oral delivery, the pronunciation of a *b* or a *t* at the end of
a syllable carries a faint sound of *-e*. A final point to be
made here is that sounding or unsounding of an unstressed
*e*, whether written or not written between two stressed syl-
lables, hardly changes the effect of clashing rhythm.


(IV) *ME Rising-Falling Rhythm--Type BA--Drop, Lift, Drop,*
     *Lift, Drop*

     (1) Ne próued I néuer/her précios pére.        (4 on)
         (a) b       a       b      b

     (2) So róunde, so réken/in vche aráye.        (5 on)
         a        a        x      a

     The alliteration of *Ne ... neuer* may be accidental.


(V) *ME Falling-Rising Rhythm--Type AB--Lift, Drop, Lift*

     (1) Sýþen in þat spóte/hit fró me spránge.        (13 on)
         a        a         x      a

     (2) Blóme₃, bláyke/and blwe and réde.        (27 on)
         a        a        a      x

     The falling-rising rhythm in these on-verses occurs be-
cause the *-e* of *spote* is elided before *hit*, as is the *-e* of
*blayke* before *and*.
     Though one must account for differences in *Pearl* because
of the shorter line that contains end rhyme throughout, the
rhythms are comparable to those found in *Patience, Cleanness,*
and *Gawain*. The statistics on initial stress in the first 100
lines compare favorably with those given for the other three
poems in the preceding survey. In *Pearl* there are 14 occur-
rences of initial stress, in lines 1, 3, 13, 14, 27, 29, 42,
43, 58, 67, 73, 75, 86, and 89. The numbers for the other
poems are 18 in *Patience*, 16 in *Cleanness*, and 24 in *Gawain*.
(Statistics on *Gawain* to line 130 discount the rhymed portions.)
     Definite instances of initial clashing rhythm are in *Pa.*
11, 44, 65; *Cl.* 23, 94; and *Ga.* 76. The problem of the sound-

ing or unsounding of final *e* then enters into the picture, but even if the unstressed *e* between the stresses were sounded in the following lines, the effect of initial clashing rhythm is almost the same: *Pa.* 31, 32; *Cl.* 3, 16, 80; *Ga.* 21, 47, 64, 74, 98, 118, 119. One would expect less initial clashing rhythm in *Pearl*, due to the almost complete absence of the extended alliterative line. The opening line, "Pérle plésaunte⁄ to prýnces páye," has the effect of initial clashing rhythm, as does the extended line 75: "Hóltewŏdeȝ brýȝt/abóute hem býdeȝ."

   *Patience, Cleanness, Gawain,* and *Pearl* reveal various verse techniques, but the similarities, especially in the areas of rhythm and alliteration, favor the view that one artist was at work in all four poems.


## 4. Dialect and Language


### Dialect

   For some information that relates to the Northwest Midland dialect of *Patience, Cleanness, Gawain,* and *Pearl*, see the section called "History of the Manuscript" in the Introduction to this edition. Lancashire, Cheshire, Derbyshire, and Stafford-shire are four counties to which the poems have been assigned, but it has not been possible to determine any one place within this Northwest Midland area. A non-dialectal piece of evidence that favors Cheshire is the naming of the *wyldrenesse of Wyrale* in *Gawain* 701. As Davis (1967) xxvi observed, the poet's mentioning of this region "surely implies that he was writing not far from it."

   Morris, *Early English Alliterative Poems* (1864; 2nd ed. 1869) xxi-xl, in examining details of dialect and grammar, leaned toward Lancashire as the place of composition. He also noted, "The uniformity and consistency of the grammatical forms is so entire, that there is indeed no internal evidence of subsequent transcription into any other dialect than that in which they were originally written" (p. viii). Osgood (1906), after referring to early studies by Schwahn (1884), Fick (1885), and Knigge (1885), pointed to the pitfalls of laying too great a stress on linguistic phenomena, for requirements of metre and the "poet's familiarity with the speech and literature of other regions than his own" make his literary language "not purely that of any spoken dialect" (p. xii).

   Osgood's statement accords with Davis' observation that the language is "not a simple and self-consistent local dialect" (p. xxvii); nevertheless, among twentieth-century scholars who have favored the naming of a specific place within the North-

west Midlands are: Bateson, *Patience* (1912; 2nd ed. 1918)
xxxii-xxxvii--Lancashire; Tolkien & Gordon (1925) xxii-xxiv--
Lancashire; Serjeantson (1927) 327-28--Derbyshire; Oakden I
(1930-35) 82-87--Lancashire; Gordon (1953) xliv-lii--"the area
stretching from the southern edge of the Peak district north-
west along the Pennine chain as far as Clitheroe and upper
Ribblesdale" (p. lii); McIntosh (1963)--"a very small area
either in SE Cheshire or just over the border in NE Stafford-
shire" (p. 5); and Jones (1972) 216--North Staffordshire.

Hulbert (1921) argued that one cannot tell if *Gawain* was
composed in the East or the West of the North Midlands, but
Menner (1922b), while not attempting to pinpoint any specific
county, refuted Hulbert's contention and established with
solid evidence the Northwest Midland dialect of the four poems
in the MS. (See also Menner [1926] for discussion of "Four
Notes on the West Midland Dialect.")

Among many features that favor the Northwest Midland
dialect are: *es/e₃* endings for some pr. pl. forms of verbs;
pr. p. ending in *ande*; dropping of inflectional endings; use
of the auxil. v. *con*; retention of *aw* from OE $\bar{a}w$ in a word
like *knawen* (*Ga.* 348); unvoicing of final plosives in a word
like *lont* (*Pa.* 322); rounding of *a* to *o* before nasal consonants
as in *hande* alongside *honde*; development of OE *éo* to *u* in a
word like *rurde* (*Ga.* 2337); and the representation of OE $\bar{y}$
as *u* in a word like *furst* (*Pa.* 150) alongside the usual *fyrst*.
For many more details concerning matters such as these, the
reader is directed to the bibliographical references given in
this study.


Language


In addition to references already noted, the following
provide material for a comprehensive study of language: Men-
ner (1920) lviii-lxii; Andrew (1929); Oakden I (1930-35) 72-
82; Serjeantson, pp. xli-lxvi, in Gollancz' ed. of *Gawain*
(*EETS, OS,* 210 [1940]); Gordon (1953) 91-116; McLaughlin (1963);
Kottler & Markman (1966); Davis (1967) 132-47; Anderson (1969)
73-78; and Anderson (1977) 108-12.

*Vocabulary:* Gordon (1953) 97-106 provides an excellent
study of the Scandinavian and French elements. A general
breakdown on a percentage basis for the four poems taken to-
gether follows: native words from 60 to 70%; Old French words
from 20 to 30%; Old Norse words about 10%. The statistics
prove true the often-repeated statements about the poet's
vocabulary being rich and varied. For those interested in
more precise figures, the following information is given.
(1) Oakden I (1930-35) 86 gave ON percentages for *Pa.* 9.4,
*Cl.* 7.6, *Ga.* 10.3, and *Pe.* 9.2. (2) Anderson (1969) 73, in
noting for *Pa.* ON 8%, OF 22%, OE 66-67%, and about 35 words

of other or uncertain origin, commented that the ON proportion is about the same as in *Cl.* and *Ga.*, but slightly higher than in *Pe.*, and the OF proportion is a bit less than in the other three poems "evidently because *Pat.* lacks the descriptions of ornate buildings, fine dress, jewels, and other trappings of 'high life'." Anderson's statistics do not agree precisely with Oakden's on the ON percentages, but there are many words in ME that seem to show either a Scandinavian or a native etymology, or the possibility of a blend, and a distinction in such instances is difficult to determine with certainty. (3) Davis (1967) 138 counted approximately 2650 different words in *Gawain*, most of them native, but about 250 Scandinavian and about 750 French. A rough estimate here on a percentage basis is ON 10%, OF 30%, and OE 60%.

*Spelling and Phonology:* (The following study is limited to forms that may present problems.) There are many variant spellings in the MS. Some involve sound changes, and some do not. In *Gawain*, for example, the *u* of *deuayed* (1493) is pronounced the same as the *v* in *devaye* (1497). The latter word is written *de vaye* in the MS, evidently because the second syllable alliterates with *vilanous* in the first half of the line. In line 1493, the alliteration is on *d*, and *deuayed* is joined. (One may also note here a confusion that often arose in spelling, for the scribe's two minims may represent *u* or *n*, and some editors read *denayed* in line 1493.)

On the other hand, the first letter of *gif* (*Ga.* 288) has the sound of Mod. E. *g* as in 'give', but ʒef (*Ga.* 1964) has an initial *y* sound, as the alliteration with *yow--youreʒ-- yowreself* proves. The reason for this is that *gif* is from ON *gifa* in which initial *g* remained a stop, and ʒef is from OE *ġiefan* in which initial *ġ* is pronounced like Mod. E. *y*. (In OE editions, one usually finds a dot over the *ġ*.)

While it is not always possible to determine if a variant spelling involves a sound change, one can be fairly certain about phonology in most instances. For example, the sounds of *e* and *o* would seem to be quite far apart, but in *coruen* (*Pe.* 40)--*coruon* (*Ga.* 797) the sound of *o* before *n* is probably the same as unstressed *e* before *n*.

The letters *i* (*y*) and *e* are sometimes interchangeable. Consider *him* (*hym*) 'him' and *hem* 'them'. These are the usual spellings for the sg. and pl. pronouns, but in several instances the forms are reversed. For example, *hym* (*him*) denotes '(to) them' in *Pa.* 213, *Cl.* 130, *Ga.* 49, and *Pe.* 635; *hem* denotes '(to) him' in *Cl.* 882, *Ga.* 862, and *Pe.* 1196. The *y* and *e* in final position sometimes vary, as in *skylly* (*Cl.* 529)--*scylle* (*Cl.* 151), and þretté (*Cl.* 317)--þretty (*Cl.* 751).

The letters *u*, *v*, and sometimes *w* are interchangeable phonologically. The scribe almost always wrote *v* initially even when the sound is *u*, as in words like *vnder*, *vpon*, and *vppe.* In words of French derivation, initial *v* represents its Mod. E. sound, as in *vengaunce* (*Pa.* 408), but occasionally initial *u* appears, as in *uengaunce* (*Cl.* 1013). The substitution of *w* is illustrated in the group *venged* (*Cl.* 199)--*uenged* (*Cl.* 559)--*wenged* (*Ga.* 1518). The sound is Mod. E. *v,* as the alliteration in *Gawain* proves: "And after wenged wyth her walour and voyded her care." (*Walour* denotes 'valor'.) Initial *v* may be used in place of *w,* as in *vyf* (*Pe.* 772)--*wyf* (*Pe.* 846). Again the alliteration proves the proper sound: "Þat þe wolde wedde vnto hys vyf." These variant spellings also occur in medial and final positions. Note *staued* (*Cl.* 357)--*stawed* (*Cl.* 360), *swete* 'matching' (*Ga.* 180)--*sute* (*Ga.* 191), and *bicnv* (*Cl.* 1327)--*beknew* (*Ga.* 903). Usually, within a word, the graph *u* represents either the vowel sound or consonantal *v,* as in *sunne* 'sun' (*Ga.* 520), *loue* 'to love' (*Pe.* 342).

A *qu* sometimes appears instead of *wh.* Note *quen* (*Ga.* 20) --*when* (*Ga.* 1727) from OE *hwanne.* Occasionally only *w* is used initially, as in *wen* (*Cl.* 343). Initial *wh* from OE *hw* alliterates with *w* even when it is spelled *qu*: "I wyst wel, when I hade worded quatsoeuer I cowþe" (*Pa.* 421). Davis (1967) 137 noted that in *Gawain* the convention is reversed in three places: in lines 74 and 2492, *whene* denotes 'queen' (OE *cwēn*), and in line 877, *whyssynes* denotes 'cushions' (OF *cuissin*). The alliteration confirms the initial *k* sound: "Whyssynes vpon queldepoyntes þa koynt wer boþe."

Of the two graphs that are not found in Mod. E., þ (ME thorn) causes no difficulty because it always represents *th,* but ʒ was used for a variety of sounds. (1) Mod. E. *y* occurs initially, as in *ʒoureʒ* (*Ga.* 1387)--*ycwreʒ* (*Ga.* 1037). After the vowels *e* or *i* (*y*), note *sweʒed* (*Pa.* 236)--*sweyed* (*Ga.* 1429) and words like *yʒe, yʒen, wyʒ(e),* and *hiʒe;* sometimes *gh* is substituted--*highe* (*Ga.* 5), *wyghe* (*Ga.* 1487). Davis (1967) 135-36 noted the sound of /i:/ at the end of *hyʒe* (*Ga.* 2087), rhyming with *by.*

(2) The *w* sound occurs in the following groups, with the spelling *gh* sometimes coming in: *folʒande* (*Ga.* 145)--*folewande* (*Pe.* 1040), *innoʒe* (*Cl.* 808)--*innowe* (*Ga.* 1401)--*innogh* (*Pe.* 661). In *Ga.* 1401, *innowe* rhymes with *lowe;* in *Pe.* 612, *inoghe* rhymes with *rescoghe,* spelled *rescowe* (*Ga.* 2308) in a rhyme with *browe,* spelled *broʒeʒ* (*Ga.* 305). See *Pe.* 613n on the echoing of the sound of *inoghe* in *now* for concatenation.

(3) Before *t* and after *e, i* (*y*), the graph ʒ has the voiceless fricative sound (front palatal) of German *ich,* as in words like *bryʒt* (OE *berht*), *myʒt* (OE *miht*), and *ryʒt* (OE *riht*). Before *t* and after the back vowels *a* and *o,* ʒ represents the voiceless fricative sound (back velar) of German *doch,* as in *aʒte* (*Cl.* 331) from OE *eahta, æhta* 'eight' and *soʒte* (*Pe.* 730) from OE *sōhte* 'sought'. The same sound occurs finally in a word like *þaʒ* from OE *þe(a)h, þah* 'though'.

(4) In all the categories noted above, ȝ is called medieval 'yogh'. (See the *OED* s.v. *Yogh*.). In this fourth category, the graph ȝ, from the letter *z*, has the sound of Mod. E. *z* in ȝ*eferus* 'Zephyrus' (*Pa*. 470, *Ga*. 517) from Latin *zephyrus*, and *ga*ȝ*afylace* 'treasury' (*Cl*. 1283) from OF *gazofilace* (from Latin *gazophylacium* 'treasury' in Mark 12.41). The sound is probably *z* in a ꞵword like *fynde*ȝ. It seems that the graphs ȝ and *s* in final position were sometimes used interchangeably for the voiced and voiceless spirants /z/ and /s/. In *fyndes* (*Pa*. 98, 107), final *s* is probably voiced; in the suffix of *berdle*ȝ (*Ga*. 280) from OE *beard-lēas*, the final ȝ is probably voiceless. (Cf. *berdles* in *Cl*. 789). The ending *t*ȝ, from OF *tz* (representing the sound /ts/ which was later simplified to /s/), appears in words like *dot*ȝ, *got*ȝ, and *wat*ȝ, the usual ending, but note the variants *dos* (*Cl*. 341; *Ga*. 1308, 1533), *gos* (*Cl*. 611, 1590; *Ga*. 935; *Pe*. 521), and *was* (*Cl*. 126, 257, 373, 1395; *Ga*. 169, 251, 573, 619, 726). The sound of final *t*ȝ in the poems of this MS is usually presumed to be /s/, but see McLaughlin (1963) 99-100 who argued that "the graphic sequence *t*ȝ is not used 'only for voiceless *s*,' ... and that the weight of the evidence seems to favor its interpretation as [z]."

*Grammar:* The following paragraphs will be limited to noting only some of the rarer aspects of nouns, verbs, verbals, adjectives, and adverbs. (Some comparisons to pronoun usage will be made.)

(1) *Nouns:* A type of *n. coll.* has no *-s*(ȝ) but is translated in the plural. *PA*: *wylle* 16, *gode* 20, *rop* 150; *CL*: *blame* 43, *schrowde* 170, *fende* 269; *GA*: *wonder* 16, *tyme* 22, *lorde* 38; *PE*: *spryg* 35, *lef* 77, *adubbemente* 85. In many instances, an adj. denoting a definite or an indefinite number modifies the noun: *two* ȝ*er* 'two years' (*Pe*. 483), *mony clustered clowde* 'many clustered clouds' (*Cl*. 367). In *Ga*. 16, *wonder* 'marvels' rhymes with *blunder* 18. The collective usage of nouns corresponds to that which is found among pronouns: *hit* 'them' (*Pa*. 47), *hit arn* 'they have been' (*Pe*. 895).

Examples of the *uninflected gen.* are in *PA*: *Jentyle* 62, *flode* 183, *wo* 317; *CL*: *gentyl* 76, *Noe* 425, ȝ*isterday* 463; *GA*: *Bretaygne* 25, *sister* 111, *Vryn* 113; *PE*: *water* 230, *wommon* 236, *helle* 643. Cf. the genitive usage without *-s*(ȝ) of the pronoun *hit* 'its' (*Cl*. 264, *Pe*. 108).

A grammatical feature usually noted only for pronouns in previous editions is the poet's use of the *synthetic dat.*, also known as *inflectional dat.*, but the dative case for nouns without preceding prep. occurs often enough, as the following examples show: *PA*: *folk* 'with (the) seamen' 251, *wynde* 'in (a) wind' 454; *CL*: *bor*ȝ*e* 'into (that) city' 45, *myrþe* 'with delight' 132, *hyue* 'into (the) hive' 223; *GA*: *here* 'with (the) hair' 180, *kynge* 'from (the) king' 393, *brydde*ȝ 'with birds'

610; *PE: perle* 'for (my) pearl' 53, *wele* 'in prosperity' 342,
*wo* 'in misfortune' 342, *coumforde* 'with (your) solace' 369.
The synthetic dative pronoun usage is more common. A few exam-
ples among many are *hym* 'to him' (*Cl.* 232) and þat 'to whom'
(*Pe.* 424).

(2) *Verbs:* There are many single verbs appearing in con-
texts that favor translating them into verb phrases. Six main
categories are *emphatic tense, progressive tense, future tense,
perfect tense, passive voice,* and *subjunctive mood.* The exam-
ples given below will follow that order for each poem: *PA:
fyndeჳ* 'does find' 278, *soჳte* 'was falling' 249, *aproche* 'will
approach' 85, *bihyჳt* 'had promised' 408, *dipped* 'was plunged'
243, *begynes* 'would begin' 76--(Note, in the last example,
that *-es,* the ending for the indicative mood, is used for the
subjunctive. This occurs quite often in the poems of the MS.
See *Cl.* 1566n.); *CL: hopeჳ* 'do think' 148, *fayled* 'was failing'
1194, *bytyde* 'shall come' 522, *herde* 'have heard' 197, *dressed*
'was arranged' 92, *helded* 'would proceed' 39; *GA: bisied* 'did
bestir' 89, *bycommes* 'is fitting' 471, *fayleჳ* 'will fail' 278,
*stowned* 'had stunned' 301, *dryuen* 'were served' 121, *help* 'may
help' 256; *PE: loueჳ* 'does like' 403, *deme* 'will direct' 324,
*forlete* 'had lost' 327, *vmbepyჳte* 'was surrounded' 204, *sponne*
'would spring' 35. (I have not noticed in *Pearl* any progres-
sive tense of the kind listed here.)

(3) *Verbals:* (See Mustanoja [1960] 511-82 for discussion of
"The Non-Finite Forms of the Verb," and the fact that there
are "striking functional points of contact," p. 511, involving
the infinitive, the participle, and the gerund.) The *plain
infinitive* occurs quite often, as in *neჳe* 'to approach' (*Cl.*
143). All editors, except Anderson, unnecessarily inserted
*to* before *neჳe.* Another form found frequently is the *passive
infinitive* without *be.* Note *PA: lyke* 'to be liked' 42, *CL:
to wyte* 'to be denounced' 76, *GA: to prayse* 'to be praised'
356, *PE: dyscreuen* 'to be seen' 68. For examples of the *in-
finitive translated progressively,* see *PA: bete* 'dashing' 302,
*CL: dysheriete and depryue* 'disinheriting and depriving' 185,
*GA: to bye* 'for purchasing' 79, *PE: for to deuyse* 'of depict-
ing' 99. This is a type of *gerundial infinitive.* Gollancz
noted the usage in his *Cl.* 185n. There are some rare occur-
rences of a *split infinitive,* as in *Ga.* 1863: *to lelly layne*
'to conceal faithfully'. Mustanoja (1960) 570 noted *aswagend*
in *Pa.* 3 as an *inflected infinitive.*

The participles also have varied usage and forms, some of
which are rare. The present participle usually ends in *and(e),*
but there is *guauende* 'throbbing' in *Cl.* 324 and an occasional
occurrence of an *en* ending, as in *cumen* 'approaching', *comen*
'coming' (*Ga.* 533, 1369) and *staren* 'gleaming', *runnen* 'run-
ning', *drawen* 'drawing' (*Pe.* 116, 874, 1193). The *yng* ending
is also rare. Note *GA: feჳtyng* 'fighting' 267, *sykyng* 'sigh-
ing' 753, *gruchyng* 'indignantly' 2126--(See 2126n for the *MED*

citation of this adverbial usage.); *PE: sykyng* 'sighing' 1175. (Hillmann, in her 1175n, cited Oakden I [1930-35] 81 to show that the *-yng* form was not dialectally impossible in the Northwest Midland area.)

The *past participle translated progressively* occurs in several instances. Note, for example, *CL: sweued* 'swirling' 222 and *hurled* 'whirling' 223; *GA: turned* 'passing' 22; *PE: fyrte* 'appalling' 54. (See 54n.)

Mustanoja (1960) 8, in the "Addenda and Corrigenda" after his Preface, noted the "use of the past participle in virtually the same sense as the present participle" in *Ga*. 1195: þe lede lay lurked 'the knight lay lurking'. Tolkien & Gordon, and Davis in his revision of their edition of *Gawain*, glossed *lurked* 'lurking'. There appear to be more examples of the *pp. tr. prog.* in the poems of this MS than the glossaries to previous editions show. One example of the situation in reverse, a form of the present participle being used as a past participle, apparently occurs in *Cl*. 1291: *nimmend* 'seized'. (See 1291n.)

*Herande,* a present participle in form, is translated as the perfect participle 'having heard' in *Ga*. 450. There are also past participial forms translated as perfect participles in *Gawain*. Note *cheued* 'having come' 63, *floten* 'having strayed' 714, *comen* 'having come' 907, and *sware* 'having sworn' 1108.

The gerund, as in Mod. E., functions as a noun, and it ends in *yng*. Note *amesyng* 'moderation' (*Pa*. 400); *marryng* 'marring' (*Cl*. 186); *laucyng* 'loosening' (*Ga*. 1334); *cnawyng* 'understanding' (*Pe*. 859).

(4) *Adjectives:* The *substantival adjective,* also called *adjective as noun,* occurs frequently in all four poems of the MS, occasionally in a collective sense. *PA: drye* 'dry land' 338, *schene* 'bright sun' 440; *CL: druye* 'dry land' 472, *bolde* 'noble man' 811, *hende* 'courteous people' 1083; *GA: bolde* 'bold warriors' 21, *hende* 'noble knight' 827, *schene* 'bright blade' 2268; *PE: schene* 'bright child' 166, *mylde* 'humble disciples' 721. The *sb. adj.* also occurs in the comparative and superlative forms. Note, for example, *PA: swetter* 'more favorable current' 236, *spakest* 'wisest (man)' 169; *GA: semloker* 'fairer queen' 83, *comlokest* 'most beautiful gem' 81.

(5) *Adverbs:* Adverbs often occur without *-ly*. Note the following alongside forms that end in *ly*. *PA: softe* 'gently' 469--*softly* 'gently' 529; *CL: reken* 'promptly' 10--*rekenly* 'courteously' 127; *GA: breme* 'firmly' 781--*bremely* 'fiercely' 1598; *PE: gracios* 'beautifully' 260--*GA: graciously* 'graciously' 970.

# 5. Sources and Analogues of
## Pearl and Cleanness

### Pearl

The following notes in the Commentary contain references to sources and influences in relation to Pearl: 1, 3, 9, 11, 19-22, 22, 25, 27-28, 29, 31-32, 39-40, 43, 52, 58-59, 67, 104-5, 107, 113, 137, 161-62, 163, 184, 197, 205, 221-28, 273-76, 277-78, 295-300, 307, 364-65, 417, 429-30, 432, 439, 445-48, 451, 457-66, 459, 462, 497-98, 501-72, 505, 529, 546, 555, 558, 565, 570-72, 581-82, 595-96, 603-4, 612, 648, 652, 654, 655, 675-76, 681, 690-92, 721, 730-35, 763-64, 766, 785-86, 797-804, 817-18, 830-34, 837, 859, 865-900, 869-70, 881-84, 885-88, 909, 952, 979-81, 992, 999-1016, 1001, 1007, 1012, 1029-30, 1041, 1052, 1064, 1093-96, 1110, 1111, 1124-27, 1126, 1135-37, 1185, 1186, 1204, 1209-10, 1211.

Scholars have pointed out that, besides the Vulgate, the poet knew and used many works, among them the writings of the Church Fathers, liturgical material, medieval lapidaries based on Marbodus' De Gemmis, Boethius' De Consolatio Philosophiae, Le Roman de la Rose, Dante's Divine Comedy, Boccaccio's Olympia, and Mandeville's Travels.

For those interested in studying Boccaccio's Olympia as a probable source for Pearl, see especially the Appendix, pp. 203-15, to Schofield (1904), the Latin text and Mod. E. translation of Boccaccio's eclogue at the end of Gollancz' 1921 edition of Pearl, and Billour (1933).

Wimsatt (1970) 117-33 studied Pearl in relation to several medieval authors, among them Boethius, Dante, Thomas Usk (Testament of Love), and the French scholar Jean Gerson (Consolation of Theology). Recognition of similarities between Pearl and the Divine Comedy led Wimsatt to comment, "It would indeed be wonderful if the Pearl Poet had not been familiar with Dante's work" (122). Niemann (1974) 218-25 related Pearl not only to the Divine Comedy but also to the twelfth-century Middle English Vision of Tundale.

For a study of Arabic influence on Pearl, through French and Latin translations, see Manzalaoui (1965). Lasater (1974) 69-95 also noted Islamic influence, especially (pp. 84-88) in the descriptions and ideas incorporated in the paradise and the meeting of the Pearl maiden.

Because alliterative poets used a common stock of formulae and many of their works cannot be dated precisely, it is not always possible to determine the influence of previous Middle English literature on the Pearl poet nor his influence on other writers. What appears to be a strong relationship between the Cotton MS. poems and the Wars of Alexander was noted by Bradley (1888) and studied extensively by Mabel Day in her Introduction to Gollancz' edition of *Gawain* (*EETS, OS,* 210, 1940), pp. xiii-xviii.

Tables such as the one presented below, showing the correspondences between lines in *Pearl* and verses in the Vulgate, are in the editions of Osgood (pp. 98-100) and Gordon (pp. 165-67). (Some passages include the poet's elaborations; lines 501-72, for example, add to Matt. 20.1-16.) Additions in this table are due primarily to previous researchers to whom I must express a general indebtedness. Parentheses around an entry mean the poet seems to have known and may have used that source, but the correspondence is not close enough to tell for sure.

| *Pearl* | Vulgate |
|---------|---------|
| (11) | (Song 2.5, 5.8) |
| (19-22) | (Song 2.14) |
| (25-28, 41-46) | (Song 4.12-16) |
| 31-32 | John 12.24-25; 1 Cor. 15.36-37 |
| (39-40) | (Rev. 14.13-16) |
| (57-60) | (Song 5.1-2) |
| (103-6) | (Gen. 2.9-14) |
| 107 | Rev. 22.1 |
| 163, 197 | Rev. 19.8 |
| (205-8) | (Ps. 20.4) |
| (285) | (Ps. 118.97, 118.163-65) |
| (301-12) | (John 20.29) |
| (304-5) | (Titus 1.2; Heb. 10.23) |
| (307) | (Ps. 88.35) |
| (362-63) | (Ps. 21.14) |
| (364-65) | (Ps. 21.15) |
| (401-4) | (1 Peter 5.5-6) |
| (413-14) | (Rev. 19.7) |
| (416) | (Ps. 22.6) |
| (417) | (Gal. 4.7; Rom. 8.16-17) |
| (439) | (1 Cor. 9.24-25) |
| (451) | (1 Cor. 9.25; James 1.12; 1 Peter 5.4) |
| 457-66 | 1 Cor. 12.12-27 |
| 501-72 | Matt. 20.1-16 |
| 595-96 | Ps. 61.12-13 |
| (612, 624, 636, 648, 660) | (2 Cor. 12.9) |
| (646-48) | (Rev. 7.14-17, 22.14-17) |
| 650, 654 | John 19.34 |
| (652) | (Rev. 2.11, 20.6, 20.14, 21.8) |
| (656-59) | (1 Cor. 15.22) |
| (675-76) | (Ps. 23.5-6; Matt. 5.8; 1 Cor. 13.12; Rev. 22.4) |
| 678-83 | Ps. 23.3-4, 14.1-2, 14.5 |
| (683) | (Ps. 120.3) |
| (685-86) | (Matt. 25.46) |

| Pearl | Vulgate |
|---|---|
| 687-88 | Ps. 23.4, 14.3 |
| 690-92 | Wisdom 10.10 |
| (692-94) | (Gen. 28.11-17) |
| 699-700 | Ps. 142.2 |
| 711-24 | Matt. 18.1-3, 19.13-15; Mark 10.13-16; Luke 18.15-17 |
| (721) | (Mark 9.34) |
| 727-28 | Luke 11.9-10 |
| 730-35 | Matt. 13.45-46 |
| 763-64 | Song 4.7-8 |
| 766 | Rev. 7.14, 22.14 |
| (767-68) | (Isaias 61.10) |
| 786-89 | Rev. 14.1, 14.3 |
| 785, 791-92 | Rev. 19.7 |
| 801-3 | Isaias 53.7 |
| 803 | Matt. 26.63, 27.12; Mark 14.61, 15.5 |
| 805-16 | Isaias 53.4-10; Matt. 26.67; Mark 14.65; Luke 22.63-64 |
| 817-18 | Matt. 3.13; Mark 1.4-5, 1.9; Luke 3.3; John 1.28 |
| 819 | Isaias 40.3; Matt. 3.3; Luke 3.4; John 1.23 |
| 820-24 | John 1.29 |
| 822-24 | Isaias 53.4-10 |
| 825 | Isaias 53.9 |
| 826 | Isaias 53.4-7, 53.10-12 |
| 827-28 | Isaias 53.8 |
| 835-40 | Rev. 5.1, 5.6-8, 5.13-14 |
| (841-44) | (Dan. 7.9; 1 Peter 1.19; Rev. 1.14) |
| (845-46) | (Rev. 14.5, 19.7) |
| (859) | (1 Cor. 13.11-12) |
| (860) | (Heb. 10.10, 10.12, 10.14) |
| 867-72 | Rev. 14.1 |
| 869-70 | Rev. 14.3-4 |
| 873-81 | Rev. 14.2 |
| 882-96 | Rev. 14.3-4 |
| 897-900 | Rev. 14.5 |
| (909) | (2 Cor. 11.3) |
| 943 | Rev. 21.2 |
| (952) | (Heb. 12.22; Rev. 3.12; Ezec. 13.16) |
| 966, 970, 972 | Rev. 21.27, 22.14 |
| 976, 979-81 | Rev. 21.10 |
| 982 | Rev. 21.11, 21.23 |
| 985-88 | Rev. 21.2, 21.10 |
| 989-94 | Rev. 21.14, 21.18-19 |
| 999-1016 | Rev. 21.19-20 |
| 1007 | Rev. 21.20; Exodus 28.17 |
| 1017-18 | Rev. 21.18 |
| 1023-24 | Rev. 21.16 |

| *Pearl* | Vulgate |
|---------|---------|
| 1025 | Rev. 21.21 |
| 1026 | Rev. 21.18 |
| 1029-32 | Rev. 21.15-16 |
| 1034-35 | Rev. 21.12-13 |
| 1036-38 | Rev. 21.21 |
| 1039-42 | Rev. 21.12; Exodus 28.9-11; Ezec. 48.31-34 |
| 1043-48 | Rev. 21.23, 22.5 |
| 1051-54 | Rev. 4.2-10, 7.9-11 |
| 1055-60 | Rev. 22.1 |
| 1061-63 | Rev. 21.22 |
| 1064 | Rev. 5.6, 5.9, 5.12 |
| 1065-66 | Rev. 21.25 |
| 1067-68 | Rev. 21.27 |
| 1069 | Rev. 21.23 |
| 1071 | Rev. 21.25, 22.5 |
| 1072-76 | Rev. 21.23, 22.5 |
| 1077-80 | Rev. 22.2 |
| (1093-96) | (Song 6.9) |
| 1099 | Rev. 14.4 |
| (1100-1) | (1 Cor. 9.25; James 1.12; 1 Peter 5.4) |
| (1102) | (Rev. 7.9, 7.14) |
| 1106 | Rev. 21.21 |
| (1107) | (Rev. 5.11) |
| 1110 | Rev. 14.1, 14.4 |
| 1111 | Rev. 5.6; (Song 5.11) |
| 1119-20 | Rev. 5.8, 5.14 |
| 1121 | Rev. 5.11; (Matt. 26.53) |
| 1122 | Rev. 5.8, 8.3-4 |
| 1123-27 | Rev. 5.11-13 |
| (1124) | (Song 5.11, 5.14-15) |
| (1126) | (1 Peter 3.22) |
| (1135-37) | (Rev. 5.6, 5.9) |
| (1146) | (Rev. 7.17, 22.14, 22.17) |
| (1183-85) | (Rev. 22.6) |
| (1204) | (Song 5.16; Wisdom 7.14; John 15.15) |
| (1211) | (Rev. 7.3, 22.3, 22.6) |

## Cleanness

The following notes in the Commentary contain references to sources and influences in relation to *Cleanness*: 27-28, 29-30, 51, 162, 208, 211-12, 216, 222-24, 231-32, 247, 269-72, 312, 427, 447, 448, 581-86, 592, 611, 620, 654, 655, 820, 866-72, 883, 924, 935, 961, 1000, 1015-51, 1057-64, 1073-88, 1094-96, 1102-8, 1157-58, 1247-53, 1274, 1283, 1301, 1333-38, 1396, 1464-68, 1469-72, 1526, 1576, 1681-1700, 1687, 1732, 1735, 1757-58, 1771-72, 1776, 1806.

Mabel Day's section of "Illustrative Texts" in Gollancz' edition of *Cleanness,* Vol. 9 of *Select Early English Poems* (1933), pp. 75-102, contains, besides the Vulgate sources, pertinent passages from *Cursor Mundi, Mandeville's Travels,* and the *Book of the Knight of La Tour Landry.* The poet used *Le Roman de la Rose* for lines 1057-64; see the note in the Commentary for discussion.

That he employed Latin works other than the Vulgate is quite certain, even though exact correspondences are not always determinable. Holthausen (1901) argued for the influence of Peter Comestor's *Historia Scholastica* (*PL* 198). Menner, in the note to lines 1317-20 of his edition, compared Jerome's *Commentariorum In Danielem Prophetam*: "Quamdiu vasa fuerunt in idolio Babylonis, non est iratus Dominus : videbantur enim rem Dei secundum pravam quidem opinionem, tamen divino cultui consecrasse : postquam autem humanis usibus divina contaminant, statim pœna sequitur post sacrilegium" (*PL* 25.519). Gardner (1965) 344 noted that "Tertullian's *pænitentia* and *pudicitia* (*Treatises on Penance: On Penitence and On Purity,* trans. William P. Le Saint, S.J., S.T.D. [Westminster, Md.: The Newman Press, 1959]) are curiously close in meaning to the *Gawain*-poet's *patience* and *purity*."

A comparison of the following two passages in *Incerti de Sodoma* and *Cleanness* with their common Vulgate sources seems to indicate that the Middle English poet knew the Latin poem. *Incerti de Sodoma* is printed along with *Eivsdem de Iona Propheta* in *CSEL* 23.

(1) Habeo duas filias, quae necdum cognoverunt
virum, educam eas ad vos, et abutimini eis
sicut vobis placuerit, dummodo viris istis
nihil mali faciatis, quia ingressi sunt sub
umbra culminis mei. (I have two daughters
who as yet have not known man : I will bring
them out to you, and abuse you them as it
shall please you, so that you do no evil to
these men, because they are come in under
the shadow of my roof.)                          (Gen. 19.8)


"Nunc, si fas iuuenale habet uastare pudorem,
sunt intus natae biiuges mihi, nubilis aetas;
uirginitas in flore tumet: iam dedita messi
digna cupido uiris; tulerit quam uestra uoluptas.
dedo pater proque hospitibus pensabo dolorem."
                                        (*Sodoma* 51-55)

                        ("Yet now,
If youthful vigour holds it right to waste
The flower of modesty, I have within
Two daughters of a nuptial age, in whom
Virginity is swelling in its bloom,

Already ripe for harvest--a desire
Worthy of men--which let your pleasure reap!
Myself their sire, I yield them; and will pay,
For my guests' sake, the forfeit of my grief!")

(Lines 70-78 in<br>
The Ante-Nicene<br>
Fathers trans.)

"I haf a tresor in my telde of tow my fayre deȝter,
Þat ar maydeneȝ vnmard for alle men ȝette.
In Sodomas, þaȝ I hit say, non semloker burdes.
Hit arn ronk, hit arn rype, and redy to manne.
To samen wyth þo semly, þe solace is better.
I schal biteche yow þo two þat tayt arn and quoynt,
And laykeȝ wyth hem as yow lyst, and leteȝ my
       gestes one."           (Cl. 866-72)

(2) Quia invenit servus tuus gratiam coram te, et
magnificasti misericordiam tuam, quam fecisti
mecum, ut salvares animam meam, nec possum in
monte salvari, ne forte apprehendat me malum
et moriar. (Because thy servant hath found
grace before thee, and thou hast magnified thy
mercy, which thou hast shewn to me, in saving
my life, and I cannot escape to the mountain,
lest some evil seize me, and I die.)     (Gen. 19.19)

               Timuit Loth ardua tardo
ereptare gradu. caelestes ne prius irae
opprimerent.                (Sodoma 91-93)
(Lot feared to creep the heights with tardy step,
Lest the celestial wrath-fires should o'ertake
And whelm him.)         (Lines 127-29 in
                           The Ante-Nicene
                           Fathers trans.)

"If I me fele vpon fote þat I fle moȝt,
Hov schulde I huyde me fro hem þat hatȝ his hate kynned
In þe brath of his breth þat brenneȝ alle þinkeȝ,
To crepe fro my Creatour and know not wheder,
Ne wheþer his fooschip me folȝeȝ bifore oþer bihynde?"
                                 (Cl. 914-18)

    In the first analogue, the Vulgate does not describe Lot's
two daughters as being in full bloom, ripe, and desirable to
man. The women are portrayed in this way only by the Latin
poet and the author of Cleanness. The Latin phrase, "iam
dedita messi," is especially close in meaning to, "Hit arn
ronk, hit arn rype." In the second analogue, the poet of
Cleanness has transformed the narrative verses of Incerti de

*Sodoma* into lines spoken by Lot. The Vulgate does not mention to move on foot, to creep, or to fear specifically heavenly wrath. Only the two poets include these details. Latin *ereptare* is especially close to Middle English *crepe*.

The table below follows the same system already explained for *Pearl*.

| *Cleanness* | Vulgate |
|---|---|
| 27-28 | Matt. 5.8 |
| (29-30) | (Matt. 5.20; Rev. 21.27) |
| 51-60 | Matt. 22.2-4; Luke 14.16-17 |
| 61-72 | Luke 14.18-20 |
| 73-108 | Luke 14.21-24; Matt. 22.8-9 |
| 109-64 | Matt. 22.10-14 |
| (177-92) | (Matt. 15.19; 1 Cor. 6.9-10; Gal. 5.19-21) |
| 205-34 | Isaias 14.12-14 |
| 235-48 | Gen. 3 |
| 249-92 | Gen. 6.1-7 |
| 293-308 | Gen. 6.8-13 |
| 309-32 | Gen. 6.14-18 |
| 333-42 | Gen. 6.19-22, 7.2-3 |
| 343-58 | Gen. 7.1-4 |
| 359-434 | Gen. 7.5-24 |
| 435-52 | Gen. 8.1-5 |
| 453-92 | Gen. 8.6-12 |
| 493-540 | Gen. 8.13-22 |
| 564-70 | Gen. 9.8-17 |
| 581-86 | Ps. 93.8-9 |
| 592 | Ps. 7.10; Wisdom 1.6; Jer. 17.10; Rev. 2.23 |
| 601-22 | Gen. 18.1-5 |
| 623-70 | Gen. 18.6-15 |
| 671-88 | Gen. 18.16-19 |
| 689-92 | Gen. 18.20-21 |
| (695-96) | (Rom. 1.27) |
| 713-80 | Gen. 18.22-33 |
| (748) | (Wisdom 12.18) |
| 781-832 | Gen. 19.1-3 |
| 833-80 | Gen. 19.4-9 |
| 881-945 | Gen. 19.10-22 |
| 946-1000 | Gen. 19.23-26 |
| 956-58 | Deut. 29.23 |
| 1001-14 | Gen. 19.27-28 |
| 1028 | Deut. 29.23 |
| (1102-8) | (Luke 24.30-35) |
| 1157-74 | 2 Para. 36.12-14; Dan. 3.28-33, 9.5-14 |
| 1175-1200 | Jer. 52.4-6 |
| 1201-24 | Jer. 52.7-11 |
| 1233-44 | Jer. 52.12-14 |

[For lines 1175-1244, see also Jer. 39.1-8 and 4 Kings 25.1-10.]

| _Cleanness_ | Vulgate |
|---|---|
| 1245-92 | Jer. 52.15-20; 2 Para. 36.17-20 |
| (1247-52) | (Lam. 2.21, 5.11-13) |
| (1262-68) | (Lam. 2.20-21) |
| [For lines 1245-92, see also 4 Kings 25.11-16.] | |
| (1341-44) | (Baruch 6.50) |
| (1345-48) | (Baruch 6.31, 6.40) |
| 1357-1424 | Dan. 5.1 |
| 1425-1528 | Dan. 5.2-4 |
| (1478-92) | (Exodus 25.31-37) |
| (1523-24) | (Baruch 6.7, 6.41) |
| 1529-85 | Dan. 5.5-9 |
| 1586-1618 | Dan. 5.10-12 |
| (1600) | (Dan. 2.22) |
| 1619-50 | Dan. 5.13-19 |
| 1651-1708 | Dan. 5.20-21, 4.27-33 |
| (1687-88) | (Dan. 4.20) |
| (1700) | (Dan. 2.21) |
| 1709-24 | Dan. 5.22-24 |
| 1725-40 | Dan. 5.25-28 |
| 1741-96 | Dan. 5.29-31 |
| (1776) | (Jer. 51.58) |
| (1785) | (Jer. 51.57) |

ABBREVIATIONS FOR PERIODICALS,
DICTIONARIES, AND SERIAL VOLUMES

(The abbreviation 'N.S.' designates 'New
Series'; 'UP' means 'University Press'.)

| | |
|---|---|
| ABR | American Benedictine Review |
| AN&Q | American Notes and Queries |
| AnM | Annuale Mediaevale |
| Archiv | Archiv für das Studium der Neueren Sprachen und Literaturen |
| BA | Beiblatt zur Anglia |
| BSUF | Ball State University Forum |
| ChauR | Chaucer Review: A Journal of Medieval Studies and Literary Criticism |
| CHEL | Cambridge History of English Literature |
| CSEL | Corpus Scriptorum Ecclesiasticorum Latinorum |
| E&S | Essays and Studies by Members of the English Association |
| EDD | The English Dialect Dictionary |
| EETS | Early English Text Society (This abbreviation alone indicates Original Series.) |
| EETS, ES | Early English Text Society, Extra Series |
| EETS, OS | Early English Text Society, Original Series |
| EGS | English and Germanic Studies |
| EIC | Essays in Criticism: A Quarterly Journal of Literary Criticism (Oxford, England) |
| ELH | Journal of English Literary History |
| ELN | English Language Notes (Boulder, Colorado) |
| EngR | The English Record |
| ES | English Studies |
| ESC | English Studies in Canada |
| EStn | Englische Studien |
| GHÅ | Göteborgs Högstolas Årsskrift |
| JEGP | Journal of English and Germanic Philology |
| JLDS | The Journal of the Lancashire Dialect Society |
| L&P | Literature and Psychology (Fairleigh Dickinson University) |
| L&S | Language and Style: An International Journal |
| LeedsSE | Leeds Studies in English |

| | |
|---|---|
| *LfGRP* | *Literaturblatt für Germanische und Romanische Philologie* |
| *LingS* | *Linguistic Science* (Kyushu University) |
| *LM* | *Les Langues Modernes* |
| *LQ* | *Language Quarterly* (University of South Florida) |
| *MÆ* | *Medium Ævum* |
| *M&H* | *Medievalia et Humanistica: Studies in Medieval and Renaissance Culture* |
| *MCR* | *The Melbourne Critical Review* |
| *MED* | *Middle English Dictionary* |
| *MichA* | *Michigan Academician: Papers of the Michigan Academy of Sciences, Arts, and Letters* |
| *MLN* | *Modern Language Notes* |
| *MLQ* | *Modern Language Quarterly* |
| *MLR* | *Modern Language Review* |
| *MP* | *Modern Philology* |
| *MS* | *Mediaeval Studies* |
| *MSE* | *Massachusetts Studies in English* |
| *N&Q* | *Notes and Queries* |
| *Neophil* | *Neophilologus* (Groningen, Netherlands) |
| *NM* | *Neuphilologische Mitteilungen* |
| *NMS* | *Nottingham Mediaeval Studies* |
| *OED* | *The Compact Edition of the Oxford English Dictionary* (This work is sometimes designated *NED.*) |
| *Parergon* | *Parergon: Bulletin of the Australian and New Zealand Association for Medieval and Renaissance Studies* |
| *PELL* | *Papers on English Language and Literature* (Continued as *PLL*) |
| *PG* | *Patrologia Graeca* |
| *PL* | *Patrologia Latina* |
| *PLL* | *Papers on Language and Literature: A Journal for Scholars and Critics of Language and Literature* (Continuation of *PELL*) |
| *PMLA* | *Publications of the Modern Language Association of America* |
| *PQ* | *Philological Quarterly* |
| *PRPSG* | *Proceedings of the Royal Philosophical Society of Glasgow* |
| *RES* | *The Review of English Studies* |
| *RPh* | *Romance Philology* |
| *RR* | *Romanic Review* |
| *SDAP* | *Studies in Descriptive and Applied Linguistics* (International Christian University, Tokyo) |
| *SELit* | *Studies in English Literature* (English Literary Society of Japan) |

| | |
|---|---|
| *SIcon* | *Studies in Iconography* (Northern Kentucky University) |
| *SMC* | *Studies in Medieval Culture* (Western Michigan University) |
| *SN* | *Studia Neophilologica* |
| *SoQ* | *The Southern Quarterly: A Journal of the Arts in the South* (University of Southern Mississippi) |
| *SP* | *Studies in Philology* |
| *SSF* | *Studies in Short Fiction* (Newberry, South Carolina) |
| *TGAS* | *Transactions of the Glasgow Archaeological Society* |
| *TLS* | *The Times Literary Supplement* (London) |
| *UpsalaE&S* | *English Institute in the University of Upsala: Essays and Studies in English Language and Literature* |
| *UTQ* | *University of Toronto Quarterly* |
| *Vivarium* | *Vivarium: An International Journal for the Philosophy and Intellectual Life of the Middle Ages and Renaissance* |
| *WSAS* | *William Salt Archæological Society* |
| *YWES* | *The Year's Work in English Studies* |

BIBLIOGRAPHY I

The editions cited at the end of the Preface to Text by
last name of editor and date are listed here. Most references
in this book are short: last name of author, date in paren-
theses, and page number(s), when needed. The reader is,
therefore, directed to the alphabetical listing of this Bib-
liography I for full information. An *a, b,* or *c* after a date
indicates more than one work in the same year by the same
author.

The symbols *B, C,* and *HZ* after names refer to the follow-
ing three volumes of collected articles: (1) Blanch (1966);
(2) Conley (1970); (3) Howard & Zacher (1968). References to
these volumes will add: *Blanch Collection, Conley Collection,*
or *Howard & Zacher Collection*; paginal listings are to the
reprint in the collection, not to the journal or book in which
the material first appeared.

Bibliography II, which comes after this Bibliography I,
contains references in the following categories: (1) Bibles;
(2) Condordance, Dictionaries, Grammars, and Index of Names;
(3) Texts and Translations (French, Greek, Italian, Latin
(Non-Religious), Latin (Religious), Old English and Middle
English); (4) Yearly Bibliographies and Other Bibliographical
Listings.

I have attempted to cover the essential scholarship on the
*Pearl* poems to 1980. Readers interested in expanding the
listings in this edition are directed to the section called
"Yearly Bibliographies and Other Bibliographical Listings"
at the end of Bibliography II.

---

ACKERMAN (1957), Robert W.  "'Pared out of Paper': *Gawain*
    802 and *Purity* 1408." *JEGP* 56, 410-17.

ACKERMAN-C (1964), R.W.  "The Pearl-Maiden and the Penny."
    *RPh* 17.  In *Conley Collection*, pp. 149-62.

ACKERMAN (1966), R.W.  "Middle English Literature to 1400."
    (Discusses research on *Pearl* and *Gawain*, pp. 91-93 and
    100.)  In *The Medieval Literature of Western Europe: A*

*Review of Research, Mainly 1930-1960.* Ed. John H. Fisher.
New York UP for the Modern Language Association of America.

ADAM (1976), Katherine L. *The Anomalous Stanza of Pearl: Does
It Disclose a Six-Hundred-Year-Old Secret?* Medieval Series
No. 1. Fayetteville, Arkansas: Monograph Publishers.

ALLEN (1971), Judson Boyce. *The Friar as Critic: Literary
Attitudes in the Later Middle Ages.* Nashville: Vanderbilt
UP.

ANDERSON (1969), J.J. Ed. *Patience.* Manchester: Manchester
UP; New York: Barnes & Noble.

ANDERSON (1977), J.J. Ed. *Cleanness.* Manchester: Manchester
UP; New York: Barnes & Noble.

ANDREW (1929), S.O. "The Preterite in North-Western Dialects."
*RES* 5, 431-36.

ANDREW & WALDRON (1978), Malcolm & Ronald. Ed. *The Poems of
the Pearl Manuscript.* York Medieval Texts, 2nd Series.
London: Arnold; Berkeley: California UP (1979).

ARMSTRONG (1977), Elizabeth. *"Purity."* *The Explicator* 36,
29-31.

BAIRD (1973), Joseph L. "Maskeleȝ, Makeleȝ: Poet and Dreamer
in the *Pearl.*" *AN&Q* 12, 27-28.

BARRON (1965), W.R.J. "Luf-daungere." In *Medieval Miscellany
Presented to Eugène Vinaver by Pupils, Colleagues and
Friends.* Ed. F. Whitehead, A.H. Diverres, and F.E. Sut-
cliffe. Manchester: Manchester UP, pp. 1-18.

BATESON (1912), Hartley. Ed. *Patience.* Manchester: Man-
chester UP. 2nd ed. (1918).

BATESON (1918), H. "The Text of *Cleanness.*" *MLR* 13, 377-86.

BATESON (1923), H. "Looking Over the Left Shoulder." *Folk-
Lore* 34, 241-42.

BATESON (1924), H. "Three Notes on the Middle-English *Clean-
ness.*" *MLR* 19, 95-101.

BENSON (1965a), Larry D. *Art and Tradition in Sir Gawain and
the Green Knight.* New Brunswick, New Jersey: Rutgers UP.

BENSON (1965b), L.D. "The Authorship of *St. Erkenwald*." *JEGP* 64, 393-405.

BILLOUR (1933), Elena. *La XIV Ecloga del Boccaccio Olimpia e La Perla, Poemetto Inglese del Secolo XIV*. Estratto dell'Annuario del R. Ginnasio Liceo "Piazzi" di Sondrio.

BINZ (1921), Gustav. Review of Menner's edition of *Purity*. *LfGRP* 42, 376-79.

BISHOP (1957), Ian. "The Significance of the 'Garlande Gay' in the Allegory of *Pearl*." *RES, N.S.*, 8, 12-21.

BISHOP (1968), I. *Pearl in Its Setting: A Critical Study of the Structure and Meaning of the Middle English Poem*. Oxford: Blackwell; New York: Barnes & Noble.

BLANCH-B (1965), Robert J. "Precious Metal and Gem Symbolism in *Pearl*." *The Lock Haven Review*, No. 7. In *Blanch Collection*, pp. 86-97.

BLANCH (1966), R.J. Ed. *Sir Gawain and Pearl: Critical Essays*. Bloomington: Indiana UP. (*Blanch Collection*.)

BLANCH (1973), R.J. "Color Symbolism and Mystical Contemplation in *Pearl*." *NMS* 17, 58-77.

BLANCH (1976), R.J. "Games Poets Play: The Ambiguous Use of Color Symbolism in *Sir Gawain and the Green Knight*." *NMS* 20, 64-85.

BLENKNER-C (1968), Louis, O.S.B. "The Theological Structure of *Pearl*." *Traditio* 24. In *Conley Collection*, pp. 220-71.

BLENKNER (1971), Louis, O.S.B. "The Pattern of Traditional Images in *Pearl*." *SP* 68, 26-49.

BLOOMFIELD-HZ (1961), Morton W. "*Sir Gawain and the Green Knight*: An Appraisal." *PMLA* 76. In *Howard & Zacher Collection*, pp. 24-55.

BLOOMFIELD (1969), M.W. "Some Notes on *Sir Gawain and the Green Knight* (Lines 374, 546, 752, 1236) and *Pearl* (Lines 1-12; 61, 775-776, 968)." In *Studies in Language, Literature, and Culture of the Middle Ages and Later: Studies in Honor of Rudolph Willard*. Ed. E. Bagby Atwood and Archibald A. Hill. Austin: Texas UP, pp. 300-2.

BÖDTKER (1911), A. Trampe. "*Covacle*, Not *Conacle*." *MLN* 26, 127.

BONE (1937), Gavin. "A Note on *Pearl* and *The Buke of the Howlat.*" *MÆ* 6, 169-70.

BORROFF (1962), Marie. *Sir Gawain and the Green Knight: A Stylistic and Metrical Study.* New Haven: Yale UP.

BORROFF (1967), M. *Sir Gawain and the Green Knight: A New Verse Translation.* New York: Norton.

BORROFF (1977), M. *Pearl: A New Verse Translation.* New York: Norton.

BRADLEY (1888), Henry. "The English *Gawain*-Poet and *The Wars of Alexander.*" *The Academy* 33, p. 27.

BRADLEY (1890a), H. "Middle English Notes." *The Academy* 37, p. 29. (Comments on *tramountayne* 211 & *olipraunce* 1349 in *Cleanness.*)

BRADLEY (1890b), H. "An Obscure Passage in *The Pearl.*" *The Academy* 38, pp. 201-2 and p. 249. (On lines 689-92 of *Pearl.*)

BRANDL & ZIPPEL (1917), A. & O. Ed. *Mittelenglische Sprach- und Literaturproben: Ersatz für Mätzners Altenglische Sprachproben.* Berlin: Weidmann; 2nd ed., (1927). Trans. as *Middle English Literature.* New York: Chelsea (1947). (Includes *Gawain* 491-535, 730-1125; and *Pearl* 1-360.)

BRETT (1915), Cyril. "Notes on *Cleanness* and *Sir Gawayne.*" *MLR* 10, 188-95.

BRETT (1927), C. Review of Tolkien & Gordon's edition of *Gawain.* *MLR* 22, 451-58.

BREWER (1966), Derek S. "Courtesy and the *Gawain*-Poet." In *Patterns of Love and Courtesy: Essays in Memory of C.S. Lewis.* London: Arnold, pp. 54-85.

BREWER (1967), D.S. "The *Gawain*-Poet; A General Appreciation of Four Poems." *EIC* 17, 130-42.

BREWER (1974), D.S. Trans. *Cleanness.* (With reprint of Gollancz' 1921 edition.) Cambridge: Brewer; Totowa, New Jersey: Rowman & Littlefield.

BRINK (1889), Bernhard ten. *Bis zu Wiclifs Auftreten. Geschichte der Englische Literatur,* I. Berlin: Oppenheim (1877). Trans. Horace M. Kennedy as *History of English Literature,* Vol. 1. New York: Holt (1889). (Discusses poet, pp. 336-51.)

BROOK (1967), Stella. *"Pearl."* *JLDS* 16, 11-17.

BROWN (1916), Arthur C.L. "On the Origin of Stanza-Linking in English Alliterative Verse." *RR* 7, 271-83.

BROWN (1904), Carleton F. "The Author of the *Pearl,* Considered in the Light of His Theological Opinions." *PMLA* 19, 115-53.

BROWN (1919), C.F. Review of Garrett (1918). *MLN* 34, 42-45.

BURROW (1971), John A. *Ricardian Poetry: Chaucer, Gower, Langland and the Gawain Poet.* New Haven: Yale UP.

BURROW (1977), J.A. Ed. *English Verse 1300-1500. Longman Annotated Anthologies of English Verse,* 1. London: Longman. (Includes *Pearl* 121-360, *Patience* 61-296, and *Gawain* 1998-2530.)

BUTTURFF (1972), Douglas R. "Laughter and Discovered Aggression in *Sir Gawain and the Green Knight.*" *L&P* 22, 139-49.

CARGILL & SCHLAUCH (1928), Oscar & Margaret. *"The Pearl* and Its Jeweler." *PMLA* 43, 105-23.

CARSON (1965), Mother Angela, O.S.U. "Aspects of Elegy in the Middle English *Pearl.*" *SP* 62, 17-27.

CASIERI (1970), Sabino. *"Pearl* e la Critica." *Acme* (Milan) 23, 283-315.

CASLING & SCATTERGOOD (1974), Dennis & V.J. "One Aspect of Stanza-Linking." *NM* 75, 79-91.

CAWLEY (1962), A.C. Ed. *Pearl and Sir Gawain and the Green Knight.* Everyman's Library. London: Dent; New York: Dutton.

CAWLEY & ANDERSON (1976), A.C. & J.J. Ed. *Pearl, Cleanness, Patience, Sir Gawain and the Green Knight.* Everyman's Library. London: Dent; New York: Dutton.

CHAPMAN (1931), Coolidge Otis. "The Musical Training of the *Pearl* Poet." *PMLA* 46, 177-81.

CHAPMAN (1932), C.O. "The Authorship of *The Pearl.*" *PMLA* 47, 346-53.

CHAPMAN (1939), C.O. "Numerical Symbolism in Dante and *The Pearl.*" *MLN* 54, 256-59.

CHAPMAN (1945), C.O.   "Virgil and the *Gawain*-Poet."   *PMLA* 60, 16-23.

CHAPMAN (1951), C.O.   *An Index of Names in Pearl, Purity, Patience, and Gawain.*   Ithaca, New York: Cornell UP.

CHASE (1932), Stanley P.   Trans. *The Pearl: The Fourteenth Century English Poem Rendered in Modern Verse.*   London: Oxford UP.

CHASE (1932), S.P.   Ed. *The Pearl: The Text of the Fourteenth Century English Poem.*   Boston: Humphries.   (Modernized text edited by members of the Chaucer course at Bowdoin College.)

CLARK (1949), John W.   "Observations on Certain Differences in Vocabulary between *Cleanness* and *Sir Gawain and the Green Knight*."   *PQ* 28, 261-73.

CLARK (1950a), J.W.   "'The *Gawain*-Poet' and the Substantival Adjective."   *JEGP* 49, 60-66.

CLARK (1950b), J.W.   "Paraphrases for 'God' in the Poems Attributed to 'The *Gawain*-Poet'."   *MLN* 65, 232-36.

CLARK (1951), J.W.   "On Certain 'Alliterative' and 'Poetic' Words in the Poems Attributed to 'The *Gawain*-Poet'."   *MLQ* 12, 387-98.

CLARK & WASSERMAN (1978a), Susan L. & Julian N.   "The *Pearl* Poet's City Imagery."   *SoQ* 16, 297-309.

CLARK & WASSERMAN (1978b), S.L. & J.N.   "*Purity*: The Cities of the Dove and the Raven."   *ABR* 29, 284-306.

CLARK & WASSERMAN (1979), S.L. & J.N.   "The Spatial Argument of *Pearl*: Perspectives on a Venerable Bead."   *Interpretations: Studies in Language and Literature* 11, 1-12.

COHEN (1976), Sandy.   "The Dynamics and Allegory of Music in the Concatenations of *Pearl*, a Poem in Two Movements."   *LQ* 14, iii-iv, 47-52.

CONLEY-C (1955), John.   "*Pearl* and a Lost Tradition."   *JEGP* 54.   In *Conley Collection*, pp. 50-72.

CONLEY (1970), J.   Ed. *The Middle English Pearl: Critical Essays.*   Notre Dame: Notre Dame UP.   (*Conley Collection.*)

COOK (1908), Albert S.   "*Pearl*, 212 ff."   *MP* 6, 197-200.

COULTON (1906a), G.G. "In Defence of *Pearl*." *MLR* 2, 39-43.
(Opposes allegorical interpretation of Schofield [1904].)

COULTON (1906b), G.G. Trans. *Pearl: A Fourteenth-Century
Poem, Rendered into Modern English*. London: Nutt; 2nd
ed. (1907); 3rd ed., Methuen's English Classics Series,
London: Methuen (1921). (A verse translation.)

COWEN (1978), J.M. "'In Krystes Dere Blessyng and Myn':
*Pearl* 1208." *N&Q*, *N.S.*, 25, 203.

CRAWFORD (1967), John F. *The Pearl*. San Francisco: Robert
Grabborn & Andrew Hoyem. (Unrhymed translation by Craw-
ford with Andrew Hoyem--includes Middle English text
printed interlinearly in red from Cotton MS--only 225
copies printed.)

CUFFE (1951), Edwin D., S.J. "An Interpretation of *Patience,
Cleanness,* and *The Pearl* from the Viewpoint of Imagery."
Diss., North Carolina.

CURTIUS (1948), Ernst R. *Europäische Literatur und Latein-
isches Mittelalter*. Bern: Francke. Trans. Willard R.
Trask as *Literature and the Latin Middle Ages*. Princeton:
Princeton UP (1953).

CUTLER (1952), John L. "The Versification of the '*Gawain*
Epigone' in Humfrey Newton's Poems." *JEGP* 51, 562-70.

DAVENPORT (1974), W.A. "Desolation, Not Consolation: *Pearl*
19-22." *ES* 55, 421-23.

DAVENPORT (1977), W.A. "The Word 'Norne' and the Temptation
of Sir Gawain." *NM* 78, 256-63.

DAVENPORT (1978), W.A. *The Art of the Gawain-Poet*. London:
Athlone.

DAVIS (1954), Norman. Review of Gordon's edition of *Pearl*.
*MÆ* 23, 96-100.

DAVIS-C (1966), N. "A Note on *Pearl*." *RES*, *N.S.*, 17. In
*Conley Collection,* pp. 325-29, with Appendix, pp. 329-34,
based on Davis' "Correspondence" in *RES*, *N.S.*, 18 (1967)
294.

DAVIS (1967), N. Ed. *Sir Gawain and the Green Knight* (Second
edition; revision of Tolkien & Gordon's *Gawain*). London:
Oxford UP.

DAY (1919), Mabel. "The Weak Verb in the Works of the *Gawain*-Poet." *MLR* 14, 413-15.

DAY (1923), M. "The Word 'Abloy' in *Sir Gawayne and the Green Knight*." *MLR* 18, 337.

DAY (1931), M. "Strophic Division in Middle English Alliterative Verse." *EStn* 66, 245-48.

DAY (1934), M. "Two Notes on *Pearl*." *MÆ* 3, 241-42.

DAY (1940), M. Introduction to Gollancz' edition of *Gawain*. *EETS* 210, pp. ix-xxxix.

DeFORD (1967), Sara. Ed. *The Pearl*. (Middle English text--includes verse translation by deFord and her former students: Dale Elliman Balfour, Donna Rosenbaum Blaustein, Myrna Davidov, Clarinda Harriss Lott, and Evelyn Dyke Schroedl.) New York: Appleton.

DOBSON (1940), E.J. "The Etymology and Meaning of *Boy*." *MÆ* 9, 121-54.

DONALDSON (1972), E. Talbot. "Oysters, Forsooth: Two Readings in *Pearl*." In *Studies Presented to Tauno F. Mustanoja on the Occasion of His Sixtieth Birthday*. *NM* 73, pp. 75-82.

DOOB (1974), Penelope B.R. *Nebuchadnezzar's Children: Conventions of Madness in Middle English Literature*. New Haven: Yale UP. (Pages 81-87 contain discussion of *Cleanness*.)

DUGGAN (1977), Hoyt N. "Strophic Patterns in Middle English Alliterative Poetry." *MP* 74, 223-47.

DUNLAP (1977), Louise. "Vegetation Puns in *Pearl*." *Mediaevalia: A Journal of Mediaeval Studies* 3, 173-88.

DUNN & BYRNES (1973), Charles W. & Edward T. Ed. *Middle English Literature*. New York: Harcourt. (Includes *Pearl* and *Gawain*, the texts partly modernized.)

EARL (1972), James W. "Saint Margaret and the Pearl Maiden." *MP* 70, 1-8.

EBBS (1958), John Dale. "Stylistic Mannerisms of the *Gawain*-Poet." *JEGP* 57, 522-25.

EINARSSON (1937), Stefan. "Old and Middle English Notes." *JEGP* 36, 183-87.

EKWALL (1912), Eilert. "Some Notes on the Text of the Alliterative Poem *Patience*." *EStn* 44, 165-73.

ELDREDGE (1975), Laurence. "The State of *Pearl* Studies since 1933." *Viator: Medieval and Renaissance Studies* 6, 171-94.

ELDREDGE (1978), L. "Imagery of Roundness in William Woodford's *De Sacramento Altaris* and Its Possible Relevance to the Middle English *Pearl*." *N&Q, N.S.*, 25, 3-5.

ELLIOTT (1951), Ralph W.V. "*Pearl* and the Medieval Garden: Convention or Originality?" *LM* 45, 85-98.

ELLIOTT (1961), R.W.V. "Landscape and Rhetoric in Middle English Alliterative Poetry." *MCR* 4, 65-76.

ELLIOTT (1974), R.W.V. "Some Northern Landscape Features in *Sir Gawain and the Green Knight*." In *Iceland and the Mediaeval World: Studies in Honour of Ian Maxwell*. Ed. Gabriel Turville-Petre and John S. Martin. Melbourne: Melbourne UP, pp. 132-43.

ELLIOTT (1978), R.W.V. "Hills and Valleys in the *Gawain* Country." *LeedsSE* 10, 18-41.

ELLIOTT (1979), R.W.V. "Woods and Forests in the *Gawain* Country." *NM* 80, 48-64.

EMERSON (1895), Oliver F. "A Parallel between the Middle English Poem *Patience* and an Early Latin Poem Attributed to Tertullian." *PMLA* 10, 242-48.

EMERSON (1906), O.F. "Legends of Cain, Especially in Old and Middle English." *PMLA* 21, 831-929. (Discusses *Cleanness* 269-92 on pp. 901-2.)

EMERSON (1915), O.F. "A Note on the M. E. *Cleanness*." *MLR* 10, 373-75.

EMERSON (1919), O.F. "Middle English *Clannesse*." *PMLA* 34, 494-522.

EMERSON (1921a), O.F. "Imperfect Lines in *Pearl* and the Rimed Parts of *Sir Gawain and the Green Knight*." *MP* 19, 131-41.

EMERSON (1921b), O.F. Review of Menner's edition of *Purity*. *JEGP* 20, 229-41.

EMERSON (1922), O.F. "Some Notes on *The Pearl*." *PMLA* 37, 52-93.

EMERSON (1927), O.F.  "More Notes on *Pearl*."  *PMLA* 42, 807-31.

EVANS (1967), W.O.  "'Cortaysye' in Middle English."  *MS* 29, 143-57.

EVERETT (1931), Dorothy.  "Middle English."  *YWES* 12, pp. 81-133.

EVERETT (1932), D.  "Middle English."  *YWES* 13, pp. 76-128.

EVERETT (1955), D.  *Essays on Middle English Literature.*  Ed. Patricia Kean.  London: Oxford UP.  (Discusses *Pearl* poems on pp. 68-96 of Ch. III, "The Alliterative Revival.")

EVERETT & HURNARD (1947), D. & Naomi D.  "Legal Phraseology in a Passage in *Pearl*."  *MÆ* 16, 9-15.

FAIRCHILD (1931), Hoxie N.  "Of Vyrgyn Flour."  *TLS*, March 5, p. 178.

FARLEY-HILLS (1971), David.  "The Authorship of *Pearl*: Two Notes."  (Appears with Barbara Nolan's Presentation in *RES, N.S.,* 22, 295-302.)

FARLEY-HILLS (1975), D.  "Correspondence."  (Answer to Thorlac Turville-Petre's argument against the identification of John Massy as the author of *Pearl* in *RES, N.S.,* 26 [1975] 129-33.)  *RES, N.S.,* 26, p. 451.

FICK (1885), Wilhelm.  *Zum Mittelenglischen Gedicht von der Perle: Eine Lautuntersuchung.*  Kiel: Lipsius und Tischer.

FINKELSTEIN (1973), Dorothee Metlitzski.  "The *Pearl*-Poet as Bezalel."  *MS* 35, 413-32.

FINLAYSON (1974), John.  "*Pearl*: Landscape and Vision."  *SP* 71, 314-43.

FISCHER (1900), Joseph.  *Die Stabende Langzeile in den Werken des Gawaindichters.*  Darmstadt: Otto.  Rpt. in *Bonner Beiträge zur Anglistik* 11 (1901) 1-64.

FISHER (1961), John H.  "Wyclif, Langland, Gower, and the *Pearl* Poet on the Subject of Aristocracy."  In *Studies in Medieval Literature in Honor of Professor Albert Croll Baugh.*  Ed. MacEdward Leach.  Philadelphia: Pennsylvania UP, pp. 139-57.

FISHER (1978), J.H.  Review of Moorman (1977).  *Speculum* 53, 833-35.

FLETCHER (1921), Jefferson B. "The Allegory of the *Pearl*." *JEGP* 20, 1-21.

FOWLER (1959), David C. "*Pearl* 558: 'Waning'." *MLN* 74, 581-84.

FOWLER (1960), D.C. "On the Meaning of *Pearl*, 139-40." *MLQ* 21, 27-29.

FOWLER (1973), D.C. "Cruxes in *Cleanness*." *MP* 70, 331-36.

FUHRMANN (1886), Johannes. *Die Alliterierenden Sprachformeln in Morris' Early English Alliterative Poems und in Sir Gawayne and the Green Knight*. Hamburg: Hintel.

GARDNER (1965), John. *The Complete Works of the Gawain-Poet*. Chicago: Chicago UP.

GARDNER (1977), J. *The Life and Times of Chaucer*. New York: Knopf.

GARRETT (1918), Robert M. *The Pearl: An Interpretation*. *University of Washington Publications in English* 4. Seattle, pp. 1-45.

GATTA (1974), John, Jr. "Transformation Symbolism and the Liturgy of the Mass in *Pearl*." *MP* 71, 243-56.

GEROULD (1929), Gordon Hall. Trans. *Beowulf and Sir Gawain and the Green Knight: Poems of Two Great Eras with Certain Contemporary Pieces*. New York: Ronald. (Prose translation of *Gawain*--Also contains verse translation of *Pearl*, lines 1-180.)

GEROULD (1936), G.H. "The *Gawain* Poet and Dante: A Conjecture." *PMLA* 51, 31-36.

GILSON (1908), Julius P. "The Library of Henry Savile, of Banke." *Transactions of the Bibliographical Society* 9. London: Blades, pp. 127-210.

GOLLANCZ (1890), Sir Israel. "An Obscure Passage in *The Pearl*." *The Academy* 38, 223-24. (On lines 689-92 of *Pearl*.)

GOLLANCZ (1891a), I. "Notes on the Review of *Pearl*." *The Academy* 40, 36-37. (In answer to Morris' Review in *Academy* 39, 602-3.)

GOLLANCZ (1891b), I. "*Pearl*." *The Academy* 40, 116-17. (In answer to Morris' observations in *Academy* 40, 76.)

GOLLANCZ (1891c), I.   Ed. *Pearl: An English Poem of the Four-
teenth Century*.   (With a Modern Rendering.)   London: Nutt.
(Revised and privately printed, 1897.)

GOLLANCZ (1894), I.   Report of paper read to the Philological
Society, "On Puzzling Words and Passages in Alliterative
Poems--*Patience, Cleanness,* and *Gawain and the Grene
Knyght*."   *The Athenæum* (November 10), p. 646.

GOLLANCZ (1898), I.   "Strode, Ralph."   In *The Dictionary of
National Biography*.   Ed. Leslie Stephen and Sidney Lee.
Vol. 55, pp. 57-59.   (Conjectures that Ralph Strode was
the author of *Pearl, Cleanness, Patience,* and *Gawain*.)

GOLLANCZ (1901), I.   Report of paper read to the Philological
Society, "Recent Theories concerning Huchoun and Others."
*The Athenæum* (November 23), p. 705.

GOLLANCZ (1907), I.   "*Pearl, Cleanness, Patience,* and *Sir
Gawain and the Green Knight*."   In *CHEL*, Vol. 1.   Ed.
A.W. Ward and A.R. Waller.   Cambridge: Cambridge UP,
Ch. XV, pp. 357-73.

GOLLANCZ (1913), I.   Ed. *Patience: An Alliterative Version
of Jonah by the Poet of Pearl*.   In *Select Early English
Poems*.   Vol. 1.   London: Oxford UP.   2nd ed. (1924).

GOLLANCZ (1918), I.   Trans. *Pearl: An English Poem of the
Fourteenth Century, Re-Set in Modern English*.   (British
Red Cross Edition.)   London: Jones.

GOLLANCZ (1919), I.   "The Text of *Cleanness*."   *MLR* 14, 152-62.

GOLLANCZ (1921), I.   Ed. *Cleanness: An Alliterative Tripartite
Poem*.   In *Select Early English Poems*.   Vol. 7.   London:
Oxford UP.   *Glossary and Illustrative Texts*.   Completed
by Mabel Day.   Vol. 9 (1933).   (A literal translation by
Derek Brewer is added to a reprint of Gollancz' edition.
Cambridge: Brewer; Totowa, New Jersey: Rowman & Little-
field, 1974.)

GOLLANCZ (1921), I.   Ed. *Pearl: An English Poem of the XIVth
Century*.   (With Modern Rendering, Together with Boccac-
cio's *Olympia*.)   London: Chatto and Windus.

GOLLANCZ (1922a), I.   "*Pearl* and *Purity*."   *TLS*, May 25, p.
343.   (In answer to an anonymous review of Gollancz'
1921 editions of *Pearl* and *Cleanness* in *TLS* [1922], May
18, p. 319.)

GOLLANCZ (1922b), I. "*Pearl* and *Purity*." *TLS*, June 1, p. 364.

GOLLANCZ (1923), I. Introduction to *Pearl, Cleanness, Patience, and Sir Gawain: Reproduced in Facsimile from the Unique MS. Cotton Nero A.x in the British Museum.* *EETS, OS,* 162. London: Oxford UP, pp. 7-44.

GOLLANCZ (1940), I. Ed. *Sir Gawain and the Green Knight.* (Introductory Essays by Mabel Day and Mary S. Serjeantson.) *EETS, OS,* 210. London: Oxford UP.

GORDON (1924), E.V. "Middle English." *YWES* 5, 83-84. (Comments on Bateson [1924] entry.)

GORDON (1953), E.V. Ed. *Pearl.* (Final revision by Ida L. Gordon.) London: Oxford UP.

GORDON & ONIONS (1932), E.V. & C.T. "Notes on *Pearl*." *ME* 1, 126-36.

GORDON & ONIONS (1933), E.V. & C.T. "Notes on the Text and Interpretation of *Pearl*." *ME* 2, 165-88. (Continued from preceding article.)

GOSSE (1923), Edmund. "*Pearl*." In *More Books on the Table.* London: Heinemann, pp. 181-86.

GRADON (1971), Pamela. *Form and Style in Early English Literature.* London: Methuen. (Discusses *Cleanness,* pp. 119-24; *Gawain,* pp. 131-39; *Pearl,* pp. 194-211.)

GRANT, PETERSON, & ROSS (1978), Judith, C., & Alan S.C. "Notes on the Rhymes of *Pearl*." *SN* 50, 175-78.

GREENE (1925), Walter Kirkland. "The *Pearl*--A New Interpretation." *PMLA* 40, 814-27.

GREENWOOD (1956), Ormerod. *Sir Gawain and the Green Knight: A Fourteenth Century Alliterative Poem Now Attributed to Hugh Mascy, Translated in Original Metre.* London: Lion and Unicorn Press.

GREG (1924), W.W. Review of Gollancz (1923) entry. *MLR* 19, 223-28.

GREG (1932a), W.W. "A Bibliographical Paradox." *The Library,* 4th Ser., 13, 188-91.

GREG (1932b), W.W. "The Continuity of Alliterative Tradition." *MLR* 27, 453-54.

GUEST (1838), Edwin. *A History of English Rhythms.* Two Volumes. London: Pickering. (A revised edition in one volume, ed. Walter W. Skeat. London: Bell, 1882.)

HAMILTON (1943), Marie P. "The Orthodoxy of *Pearl* 603-4." *MLN* 58, 370-72.

HAMILTON (1955), M.P. Review of Gordon's edition of *Pearl*. *JEGP* 54, 123-26.

HAMILTON-B (1955), M.P. "The Meaning of the Middle English *Pearl*." *PMLA* 70. In *Blanch Collection,* pp. 37-59.

HAMILTON (1958), M.P. "Notes on *Pearl*." *JEGP* 57, 177-91.

HAMMERLE (1936), K. "The Castel of Perseverance und *Pearl*." *Anglia* 60, 401-2.

HANNA (1974), Ralph, III. Ed. *The Awntyrs off Arthure at the Terne Wathelyn: An Edition Based on Bodleian Library MS. Douce 324.* Manchester: Manchester UP; New York: Barnes & Noble.

HART (1927), Elizabeth. "The Heaven of Virgins." *MLN* 42, 113-16.

HASKELL (1969), Ann S. *A Middle English Anthology.* New York: Doubleday. (Includes modernized texts of *Pearl* and *Gawain.*)

HEATHER (1931), P.J. "Precious Stones in the Middle-English Verse of the Fourteenth Century." *Folk-Lore* 42, 217-64 & 345-404.

HEISERMAN (1965), A.R. "The Plot of *Pearl*." *PMLA* 80, 164-71.

HIEATT (1976), A. Kent. "Symbolic and Narrative Patterns in *Pearl, Cleanness, Patience,* and *Gawain*." *ESC* 2, 125-43.

HIEATT (1965), Constance B. "*Pearl* and the Dream-Vision Tradition." *SN* 37, 139-45.

HIEATT (1974), C.B. "The Rhythm of the Alliterative Long Line." In *Chaucer and Middle English Studies in Honour of Rossell Hope Robbins.* Ed. Beryl Rowland. Kent, Ohio: Kent State UP, pp. 119-30.

HIGGS (1974), Elton D. "The Progress of the Dreamer in *Pearl*." *SMC* 4, 388-400.

HILL (1946), Laurita Lyttleton. "Madden's Divisions of *Sir Gawain* and the 'Large Initial Capitals' of Cotton Nero A.X." *Speculum* 21, 67-71.

HILL (1965), Ordelle Gerhard. "*Patience*: Style, Background, Meaning, and Relationship to *Cleanness*." Diss., Illinois.

HILL (1968), O.G. "The Audience of *Patience*." *MP* 66, 103-9.

HILLMANN (1941), Sister Mary Vincent. "*Pearl*: 'Inlyche' and 'Rewarde'." *MLN* 56, 457-58.

HILLMANN (1943), M.V. "*The Pearl*: 'west ernays' 307; 'Fasor' 432." *MLN* 58, 42-44. ('Fasor', misnumbered, is in line 431.)

HILLMANN (1944), M.V. "*Pearl*: 'Lere Leke,' 210." *MLN* 59, 417-18.

HILLMANN-C (1945), M.V. "Some Debatable Words in *Pearl* and Its Theme." *MLN* 60. In *Conley Collection*, pp. 9-17.

HILLMANN (1953), M.V. "*Pearl*, 382: 'mare reȝ mysse?'." *MLN* 68, 528-31.

HILLMANN (1961), M.V. Ed. *The Pearl: Mediaeval Text with a Literal Translation and Interpretation.* Convent Station, New Jersey: College of Saint Elizabeth. 2nd ed. with Introduction and additional Bibliography by Edward Vasta. Notre Dame: Notre Dame UP (1967).

HOFFMAN (1970), Donald L. "'Renischsche Renkes' and 'Runisch Saueȝ'." *N&Q, N.S.,* 17, 447-49.

HOFFMAN-C (1960), Stanton. "The *Pearl*: Notes for an Interpretation." *MP* 68. In *Conley Collection*, pp. 86-102.

HOLMAN (1951), C. Hugh. "'Marereȝ Mysse' in the *Pearl*." *MLN* 66, 33-36.

HOLMES (1934), Urban T. "Mediaeval Gem Stones." *Speculum* 9, 195-204.

HOLTHAUSEN (1893), F. "Zur Textkritik me. Dichtungen--*Pearl*." *Archiv* 90, 144-48.

HOLTHAUSEN (1901), F. "Zu dem Mittelenglischen Gedicht *Cleanness*." *Archiv* 106, p. 349.

HOLTHAUSEN (1909), F. "Zum me. Gedicht *The Pearl*." *Archiv*

123, 241-45.  (Review of Osgood's edition of *Pearl*.)

HOLTHAUSEN (1923), F.  Review of Menner's edition of *Purity*.
*BA* 34, 136-38.

HOPPER (1938), Vincent F.  *Medieval Number Symbolism: Its
Sources, Meaning, and Influence on Thought and Expression*.
*Columbia University Studies in English and Comparative
Literature* 132.  New York: Columbia UP.

HOWARD (1966), Donald R.  "Chivalry and the Pride of Life:
*Sir Gawain and the Green Knight*."  Chapter 5, pp. 217-54,
in *The Three Temptations: Medieval Man in Search of the
World*.  Princeton: Princeton UP.

HOWARD (1971), D.R.  "*Sir Gawain and the Green Knight*."  In
*Recent Middle English Scholarship and Criticism: Survey
and Desiderata*.  Ed. J. Burke Severs.  Pittsburgh: Du-
quesne UP, pp. 29-54.

HOWARD & ZACHER (1968), Donald R. & Christian.  *Critical
Studies of Sir Gawain and the Green Knight*.  Notre Dame:
Notre Dame UP.  (*Howard & Zacher Collection*.)

HULBERT (1921), James R.  "The 'West Midland' of the Romances."
*MP* 19, 1-16.

HULBERT (1927), J.R.  Review of Gollancz' 1921 edition of
*Pearl*.  *MP* 25, 118-19.

HULBERT (1931), J.R.  "A Hypothesis Concerning the Allitera-
tive Revival."  *MP* 28, 405-22.

HULBERT (1950), J.R.  "Quatrains in Middle English Allitera-
tive Poems."  *MP* 48, 73-81.

HUNTSMAN (1976), Jeffrey F.  "Caveat Editor: Chaucer and
Medieval English Dictionaries."  *MP* 73, 276-79.

JACOBS (1972), Nicolas.  "Alliterative Storms: A Topos in
Middle English."  *Speculum* 47, 695-719.

JEWETT (1908), Sophie.  Trans. *The Pearl: A Modern Version
in the Metre of the Original*.  New York: Crowell.  Rpt.
in *Medieval English Verse and Prose*.  Roger Sherman
Loomis and Rudolph Willard.  New York: Appleton (1948).

JOHNSON (1979), Lynn Stanley.  "The Motif of the *Noli Me
Tangere* and Its Relation to *Pearl*."  *ABR* 30, 93-106.

JOHNSON-C (1953), Wendell Stacy. "The Imagery and Diction of *The Pearl*: Toward an Interpretation." *ELH* 20. In *Conley Collection*, pp. 27-49.

JOHNSTON (1959), G.K.W. "Northern Idiom in *Pearl*." *N&Q, N.S.*, 6, 347-48.

JONES (1972), Charles. *An Introduction to Middle English*. New York: Holt.

KALMA (1938), D. Trans. *De Pearel: In Visioen ut it Middel-Ingelsk oerbrocht yn it Nij-Frysk*. Dokkum: Kamminga. (A Frisian version in original metre and rime, based on Gollancz' 1921 text.)

KALUZA (1892), Max. "Strophische Gliederung in der Mittelenglischen Rein Alliterirenden Dichtung." *EStn* 16, 169-80.

KALUZA (1909), M. *Englische Metrik in Historischer Entwicklung*. *Normannia* 1. Berlin: Felber. Trans. A.C. Dunstan as *A Short History of English Versification from the Earliest Times to the Present Day*. London: Allen (1911).

KASKE (1959), R.E. "Two Cruxes in *Pearl*: 596 and 609-10." *Traditio* 15, 418-28.

KEAN (1965), Patricia Margaret. "Numerical Composition in *Pearl*." *N&Q, N.S.*, 12, 49-51.

KEAN (1967), P.M. *The Pearl: An Interpretation*. London: Routledge.

KELLOGG-C (1956), Alfred L. "*Pearl* and the Augustinian Doctrine of Creation." *Traditio* 12. In *Conley Collection*, pp. 335-37.

KELLY & IRWIN (1973), T.D. & John T. "The Meaning of *Cleanness*: Parable as Effective Sign." *MS* 35, 232-60.

KIRK (1975), Elizabeth D. "Chaucer and His English Contemporaries." In *Chaucer: A Collection of Original Articles*. Ed. George D. Economou. New York: McGraw-Hill, pp. 111-27.

KIRK (1978), E.D. "'Who Suffreth More Than God?': Narrative Redefinition of Patience in *Patience* and *Piers Plowman*." In *The Triumph of Patience: Medieval and Renaissance Studies*. Ed. Gerald Schiffhorst. Orlando: University Presses of Florida, pp. 88-104.

KIRTLAN (1918), Ernest J.B. Trans. *Pearl: A Poem of Consolation: Rendered into Modern English Verse.* London: Kelly.

KITELEY-HZ (1962), J.F. "The Knight Who Cared for His Life." *Anglia* 79. In *Howard & Zacher Collection,* pp. 215-22.

KITTENDORF (1979), Doris E. "*Cleanness* and the Fourteenth Century *Artes Praedicandi.*" *MichA* 11, 319-30.

KJELLMER (1975), Göran. *Did the "Pearl Poet" Write Pearl? Gothenburg Studies in English* 30. Göteborg, Sweden: Acta Universitatis Gothoburgensis.

KNIGGE (1885), Friedrich. *Die Sprache des Dichters von Sir Gawain and the Green Knight, der Sogenannten Early English Alliterative Poems, und De Erkenwalde.* Diss., Marburg.

KNIGHTLEY (1961), William J. "*Pearl*: The 'hyȝ seysoun'." *MLN* 76, 97-102.

KOCK (1903), Ernt A. "Interpretations and Emendations of Early English Texts." *Anglia* 26, 364-76.

KÖLBING (1892), E. Review of Gollancz' 1891 edition of *Pearl*. *EStn* 16, 268-73.

KOLVE (1966), V.A. *The Play Called Corpus Christi.* Stanford: Stanford UP.

KOTTLER & MARKMAN (1966), Barnet & Alan M. *A Concordance to Five Middle English Poems: Cleanness, St. Erkenwald, Sir Gawain and the Green Knight, Patience, Pearl.* Pittsburgh: Pittsburgh UP.

KUHNKE (1900), Bruno. *Die Alliterierende Langzeile in der Mittelenglischen Romanze Sir Gawayn and the Green Knight. Studien zum Germanischen Alliterationsvers* 4. Berlin: Felber.

KUNZ & STEVENSON (1908), George F. & Charles H. *The Book of the Pearl: The History, Art, Science, and Industry of the Queen of Gems.* New York: Century.

LASATER (1974), Alice E. *Spain to England: A Comparative Study of Arabic, European, and English Literature of the Middle Ages.* Jackson: Mississippi UP. (Discusses *Pearl*, pp. 69-95; *Purity*, pp. 120-23; *Gawain*, pp. 168-96.)

LEE (1977), Jennifer A. "The Illuminating Critic: The Illustrator of Cotton Nero A.X." *SIcon* 3, 17-46.

LE GRELLE (1953), L. "*La Perle*: Essai d'Interprétation Nou-
velle." *Études Anglaises* 6, 315-31.

LEONARD (1920), William Ellery. "The Scansion of Middle Eng-
lish Alliterative Verse." *Studies by Members of the De-
partment of English*. *University of Wisconsin Studies in
Language and Literature* 2. Madison, pp. 58-104.

LETTS (1949), Malcolm. *Sir John Mandeville: The Man and His
Book*. London: Batchworth.

LETTS (1953), M. Ed. *Mandeville's Travels: Texts and Trans-
lations*. London: The Hakluyt Society. (Vol. 1, 2nd
Series, No. 101, contains a modernized version of the
Egerton text; Vol. 2, 2nd Series, No. 102, contains the
Paris text.)

LEVINE (1977), Robert. "The Pearl-child: Topos and Archetype
in the Middle English *Pearl*." *M&H*, *N.S.*, No. 8, pp.
243-51. (Review of Piehler [1971] *The Visionary Land-
scape*.)

LEYERLE (1975), John. "The Game and Play of Hero." In *Con-
cepts of the Hero in the Middle Ages and the Renaissance*.
Ed. Norman T. Burns and Christopher J. Reagan. Albany:
State Univ. of New York Press, pp. 49-82.

LOOMIS-HZ (1959), Laura Hibbard. "*Gawain and the Green Knight*."
From *Arthurian Literature in the Middle Ages: A Collabora-
tive History*. Ed. Roger Sherman Loomis. In *Howard &
Zacher Collection*, pp. 3-23.

LOOMIS & LOOMIS (1938), R.S. & L.H. *Arthurian Legends in
Medieval Art*. London: Oxford UP.

LUCAS (1977), Peter J. "Pearl's Free-Flowing Hair." *ELN*
15, 94-95.

LUICK (1889), Earl. "Die Englische Stabreimzeile im XIV.,
XV. und XVI. Jahrhundert." *Anglia* 11, 392-443 and 553-
618.

LUTTRELL (1952), C.A. "Baiting of Bulls and Boars in the
Middle English *Cleanness*." *N&Q* 197, 23-24.

LUTTRELL (1955), C.A. "The *Gawain* Group: Cruxes, Etymologies,
Interpretations." *Neophil* 39, 207-17.

LUTTRELL (1956a), C.A. "The *Gawain* Group: Cruxes, Etymologies,
    Interpretations.--II." *Neophil* 40, 290-301. (Continued
    from preceding entry.)

LUTTRELL (1956b), C.A. "The Baiting of Bulls and Boars."
    *N&Q, N.S.,* 3, 398-401.

LUTTRELL (1958), C.A. "Three North West-Midland Manuscripts."
    *Neophil* 42, 38-50.

LUTTRELL (1960), C.A. "*Cleanness* and the Knight of La Tour
    Landry." *MÆ* 29, 187-89.

LUTTRELL (1962a), C.A. "A *Gawain* Group Miscellany." *N&Q,*
    *N.S.,* 9, 447-50.

LUTTRELL (1962b), C.A. "The Mediæval Tradition of the Pearl
    Virginity." *MÆ* 31, 194-200.

LUTTRELL-B (1965), C.A. "*Pearl*: Symbolism in a Garden Set-
    ting." *Neophil* 49. In *Blanch Collection*, pp. 60-85.

LUTTRELL (1978), C.A. "The Introduction to the Dream in
    *Pearl*." *MÆ* 47, 274-91.

MacCRACKEN (1910), Henry Noble. "Concerning Huchown." *PMLA*
    25, 507-34.

MACDONALD (1953), A. Reviews of *An Index of Names in Pearl,*
    *Purity, Patience, and Gawain,* by C.O. Chapman; and *Middle*
    *English Sea Terms. I. The Ship's Hull,* by Bertil Sandahl.
    *RES, N.S.,* 4, 276-77.

MACKENZIE (1933), Agnes Mure. *An Historical Survey of Scot-*
    *tish Literature to 1714.* London: MacLehose.

MACRAE-GIBSON-C (1968), O.D. "*Pearl*: The Link-Words and the
    Thematic Structure." *Neophil* 52. In *Conley Collection,*
    pp. 203-19.

MADDEN (1839), Sir Frederic. Ed. *Syr Gawayne and the Grene*
    *Knyʒt.* In *Syr Gawayne: A Collection of Ancient Romance-*
    *Poems by Scottish and English Authors, Relating to That*
    *Celebrated Knight of the Round Table. The Bannatyne*
    *Club* 61. London: Taylor. Rpt. New York: AMS Press (1971).

MADELEVA (1925), Sister Mary. *Pearl: A Study in Spiritual*
    *Dryness.* New York: Appleton. Rpt. New York: Phaeton
    Press (1968).

MAHL (1966), Mary R. "The Pearl as the Church." *EngR* 17, i, pp. 27-29.

MANZALAUOI (1965), Mahmoud. "English Analogues to the *Liber Scalæ*." *MÆ* 34, 21-35.

MATHEW (1948), Gervase. "Ideals of Knighthood in Late-Fourteenth-Century England." In *Studies in Mediaeval History Presented to F.M. Powicke*. Ed. R.W. Hunt, W.A. Pantin, and R.W. Southern. London: Oxford UP, pp. 354-62. (Contains some of the same material in next entry.)

MATHEW (1968), G. *The Court of Richard II*. New York: Norton.

MATSUI (1971), Noriko. "Allegory of Courtesy in *Pearl* and *Sir Gawain and the Green Knight*." *SELit* 47, 123-40. (English synopsis in English No. for 1971, pp. 165-67.)

MATTHEWS (1960), William. *The Tragedy of Arthur: A Study of the Alliterative Morte Arthure*. Berkeley: California UP.

McALINDON (1970), T. "Hagiography into Art: A Study of *St. Erkenwald*." *SP* 67, 472-94.

McANDREW (1957), Bruno. "*The Pearl*: A Catholic Paradise Lost." *ABR* 8, 243-51.

McGALLIARD (1969), John C. "Links, Language, and Style in *The Pearl*." In *Studies in Language, Literature, and Culture of the Middle Ages and Later: Studies in Honor of Rudolph Willard*. Ed. E. Bagby Atwood and Archibald A. Hill. Austin: Texas UP, pp. 279-99.

McINTOSH (1963), Angus. "A New Approach to Middle English Dialectology." *ES* 44, 1-11.

McLAUGHLIN (1963), John C. *A Graphemic-Phonemic Study of a Middle English Manuscript*. The Hague: Mouton.

McNEIL (1888), George P. "Huchown of the Awle Ryale." *Scottish Review* (April), pp. 266-88.

MEAD (1908), Marian. Trans. *The Pearl: An English Vision-Poem of the Fourteenth Century Done into Modern Verse*. Portland, Maine: Mosher.

MEANS (1972), Michael H. "*Pearl*" in "The 'Pure' Consolatio," Ch. 4 of *The Consolatio Genre in Medieval English Literature*. Gainesville: Florida UP, pp. 49-59.

MEANS (1975), M.H.  "The Homiletic Structure of *Cleanness*."
     *SMC* 5, 165-72.

MEDARY (1916), Margaret.  "Stanza-Linking in Middle English
     Verse."  *RR* 7, 243-70.

MEDCALF (1973), Stephen.  "*Piers Plowman* and the Ricardian
     Age in Literature."  In *Literature and Western Civiliza-*
     *tion*, Vol. 2.  *The Mediaeval World*.  Ed. David Daiches
     & Anthony Thorlby.  London: Aldus, pp. 643-96.

MENNER (1920), Robert J.  Ed. *Purity*.  New Haven: Yale UP.
     Rpt. Hamden, Connecticut: Archon (1970).

MENNER (1922a), R.J.  Review of Gollancz' edition of *Clean-*
     *ness*.  *MLN* 37, 355-62.

MENNER (1922b), R.J.  "*Sir Gawain and the Green Knight* and the
     West Midland."  *PMLA* 37, 503-26.

MENNER (1926), R.J.  "Four Notes on the West Midland Dialect."
     *MLN* 41, 454-58.

MENNER (1935), R.J.  Review of *Cleanness: Glossary and Illus-*
     *trative Texts* (Mabel Day's completion of Gollancz' 1921
     edition).  *MLN* 50, 336-38.

MILROY (1971), James.  "*Pearl*: The Verbal Texture and the
     Linguistic Theme."  *Neophil* 55, 195-208.

MITCHELL (1964), Bruce.  "*Pearl*, Lines 609-610."  *N&Q, N.S.,*
     11, p. 47.

MOORMAN-C (1955), Charles.  "The Role of the Narrator in
     *Pearl*."  *MP* 53.  In *Conley Collection*, pp. 103-21.

MOORMAN (1965), C.  "Some Notes on *Patience* and *Pearl*."
     *SoQ* 4, 67-73.

MOORMAN (1968), C.  *The Pearl-Poet*.  New York: Twayne.

MOORMAN (1969), C.  "The *Pearl*-Poet Concordance."  *ChauR*
     3, 304-8.

MOORMAN (1977), C.  Ed. *The Works of the Gawain-Poet*.  Jack-
     son: Mississippi UP.

MOORMAN (1905), Frederic W.  "The *Gawayne*-Poet."  In *The*
     *Interpretation of Nature in English Poetry from Beowulf*
     *to Shakespeare*.  *Quellen und Forschungen zur Sprach- und*

*Culturgeschichte der Germanischen Völker* 95. Strassburg: Trübner, pp. 95-106.

MORGAN (1952), F.C. "Bull Baiting and Bear Baiting." *N&Q* 197, p. 107.

MORRIS (1864), Richard. Ed. *Early English Alliterative Poems in the West-Midland Dialect of the Fourteenth Century.* (*Pearl, Cleanness,* and *Patience.*) *EETS, OS,* 1, 2nd ed. (1869). Rpt. (1965). London: Oxford UP.

MORRIS (1867), R. Ed. *Specimens of Early English: Selected from the Chief English Authors.* London: Oxford UP. (Preceded Morris & Skeat [1872] entry.) (Contains lines 235-544, 947-972, 1009-1051 of *Cleanness,* and lines 1-490 of *Gawain.*)

MORRIS (1891a), R. Review of Gollancz' 1891 edition of *Pearl.* *The Academy* 39, 602-3.

MORRIS (1891b), R. "*Pearl.*" *The Academy* 40, 76.

MORRIS & SKEAT (1872), R. & Walter W. Ed. *From Robert of Gloucester to Gower, A.D. 1298--A.D. 1393. Specimens of Early English: A New and Revised Edition,* Part 2. London: Oxford UP. Rev. ed. (1894). (Contains same lines from *Cleanness* listed in Morris [1867] entry.)

MORSE (1971), Charlotte C. "The Image of the Vessel in *Cleanness.*" *UTQ* 40, 202-16.

MORSE (1978), C.C. *The Pattern of Judgment in the Queste and Cleanness.* Columbia: Missouri UP.

MORSE (1975), Ruth. Ed. *St Erkenwald.* Cambridge: Brewer; Totowa, New Jersey: Rowman & Littlefield.

MOSSÉ (1949), Fernand. Ed. *Manuel de l'Anglais du Moyen Age des Origines au XIVe Siècle.* Editions Montaigne. Paris: Aubier. Second part translated by James A. Walker as *A Handbook of Middle English.* Baltimore: Johns Hopkins (1952). (Contains *Pearl* 985-1092 and *Gawain* 713-762, 1126-1324, 1362-1401.)

MURTAUGH (1971), Daniel M. "*Pearl* 462: 'Þe Mayster of Myste'." *Neophil* 55, 191-94.

MUSCATINE (1972), Charles. "The *Pearl* Poet: Style as Defense." In *Poetry and Crisis in the Age of Chaucer.* Notre Dame: Notre Dame UP, pp. 37-69.

MUSTANOJA (1960), Tauno F. *A Middle English Syntax*, Part 1. Helsinki: Société Néophilologique.

NAKAO (1961), Toshio. "Alliterative Patterns in *Sir Gawain and the Green Knight*." *SDAP* 1, 58-66.

NEILSON (1900), George. "Huchown of the Awle Ryale." *TGAS* 4, 252-393.

NEILSON (1900-01), G. "Sir Hew of Eglintoun and Huchown off the Awle Ryale: A Biographical Calendar and Literary Estimate." *PRPSG* 32, 111-50.

NEILSON (1901), G. "Huchown of the Awle Reale." *Chambers's Cyclopaedia of English Literature*. Vol. I. London and Edinburgh: Chambers, pp. 171-75.

NEILSON (1902a), G. "Crosslinks between *Pearl* and *The Awntyrs of Arthure*." *The Scottish Antiquary* 16, 67-78.

NEILSON (1902b), G. *Huchown of the Awle Ryale, the Alliterative Poet: A Historical Criticism of Fourteenth Century Poems Ascribed to Sir Hew of Eglintoun*. Glasgow: MacLehose. (Revision of Neilson [1900] entry.)

NELSON (1973), Cary. "*Pearl*: The Circle as Figural Space." In *The Incarnate Word: Literature as Verbal Space*. Urbana: Illinois UP, pp. 25-49.

NEVANLINNA (1974), Saara. "Background and History of the Parenthetic *As Who Say/Saith* in Old English and Middle English Literature." *NM* 75, 568-601.

NEWSTEAD (1967), Helaine. "Arthurian Legends." In *A Manual of the Writings in Middle English: 1050-1500*. By Members of the Middle English Group of the Modern Language Association of America. J. Burke Severs, General Editor. Vol. 1. The Connecticut Academy of Arts and Sciences, pp. 38-79.

NIEMANN (1974), Thomas C. "*Pearl* and the Christian Other World." *Genre* 7, 213-32.

NOLAN (1977), Barbara. "*Pearl*: A Fourteenth-Century Vision in August." In *The Gothic Visionary Perspective*. Princeton: Princeton UP, pp. 156-204.

NOLAN & FARLEY-HILLS (1971), B. & David. "The Authorship of *Pearl*: Two Notes." *RES, N.S.*, 22, 295-302.

NORTHUP (1897), Clark S. "A Study of the Metrical Structure

of the Middle English Poem *The Pearl*." *PMLA* 12, 326-40.

NORTHUP (1907), C.S. "Recent Studies of *The Pearl*." *MLN* 22, pp. 21-22.

OAKDEN I (1930-35), James P. *Alliterative Poetry in Middle English: The Dialectal and Metrical Survey.* Manchester: Manchester UP. Rpt. Hamden, Connecticut: Archon (1968). (The reprints of this book and the next one are in one volume.)

OAKDEN II (1930-35), J.P. (With Assistance from Elizabeth R. Innes.) *Alliterative Poetry in Middle English: A Survey of the Traditions.* Manchester: Manchester UP. Rpt. Hamden, Connecticut: Archon (1968).

OAKDEN (1933a), J.P. "The Continuity of Alliterative Tradition." *MLR* 28, 233-34.

OAKDEN (1933b), J.P. "The Scribal Errors of the MS. Cotton Nero A.x." *The Library*, 4th Ser., 14, 353-58.

OAKDEN (1933c), J.P. "The Survival of a Stylistic Feature of Indo-European Poetry in Germanic, Especially in Middle-English." *RES* 9, 50-53.

OAKDEN (1968), J.P. "The Liturgical Influence in *Pearl*." In *Chaucer und Seine Zeit: Symposium für Walter F. Schirmir.* Ed. Arno Esch. *Buchreihe der Anglia, Zeitschrift für Englische Philologie* 14. Tübingen: Niemeyer, pp. 337-53.

OHLANDER (1950), Urban. "A Passage in *Cleanness*: A Note on Middle English Construction-Change." *GHÅ* 56, 311-23.

OIJI (1961), Takero. "The Middle English *Pearl* and Its Theology." *SELit*, English No. for 1961, pp. 39-57.

OLIVERO (1926), Federico. Trans. *La Perla, Poemetto Inglese del Secolo XIV: Traduzione, con Introduzione e Note.* Torino: Treves. (Italian verse translation from Osgood's [1906] text.)

OLIVERO (1936), F. Ed. *La Perla, Poemetto in Middle English: Introduzione, Testo, Traduzione, e Commento.* Bologna: Zanichelli. (Based on Osgood's [1906] text.)

OLSZEWSKA (1942), E.S. "Some English and Norse Alliterative Phrases." *Saga-Book of the Viking Club* 12, 238-45.

ORMEROD (1819), George. *The History of the County Palatine*

*and City of Chester,* 3 Volumes. 2nd ed. revised and en-
larged by Thomas Helsby. London: Routledge (1882).

OSGOOD (1906), Charles G. Ed. *The Pearl: A Middle English
Poem.* Boston: Heath.

OSGOOD (1907), C.G. Trans. *The Pearl: An Anonymous English
Poem of the Fourteenth Century, Rendered in Prose.* Prince-
ton, New Jersey. (Privately printed.)

OSGOOD (1935), C.G. "The *Gawain* Poet." In *The Voice of Eng-
land.* New York: Harper, pp. 93-99.

OTTEN (1971), Charlotte. "A Note on 'Gyltes Felle' in *Pearl.*"
*ES* 52, 209-11.

PARR (1970), Roger P. "Rhetoric and Symbol in *The Pearl.*"
*SMC* 3, 177-87.

PATCH (1950), Howard R. *The Other World: According to De-
scriptions in Medieval Literature.* Cambridge, Massachu-
setts: Harvard UP.

PEARSALL (1977), Derek A. *Old English and Middle English
Poetry: The Routledge History of English Poetry,* 1. Lon-
don: Routledge. (Contains section on "The *Gawain*-Poems,"
pp. 169-76.)

PEARSALL (1978), D.A. Review of Cawley & Anderson (1976).
*RES, N.S.,* 29, 69-70.

PEARSALL & SALTER (1973), D.A. & Elizabeth. *Landscapes and
Seasons of the Medieval World.* London: Elek; Toronto:
Toronto UP. (On *Pearl,* pp. 102-8 in Ch. 4, "The Enclosed
Garden"--On *Gawain,* pp. 147-53 in Ch. 5, "The Landscape
of the Seasons.")

PETERSON (1974a), Clifford J. "*Pearl* and *St. Erkenwald*: Some
Evidence for Authorship." *RES, N.S.,* 25, 49-53.

PETERSON (1974b), C.J. "The *Pearl*-Poet and John Massey of
Cotton, Cheshire." *RES, N.S.,* 25, 257-66.

PETERSON (1977a), C.J. "Hoccleve, the Old Hall Manuscript,
Cotton Nero A.X., and the *Pearl*-Poet." *RES, N.S.,* 28,
49-55.

PETERSON (1977b), C.J. Ed. *Saint Erkenwald.* Philadelphia:
Pennsylvania UP.

416

PIEHLER (1971), Paul. "*Pearl*: The 'Erber Grene'." In *The Visionary Landscape: A Study in Medieval Allegory*. Montreal: McGill-Queen's UP, pp. 144-62.

PIERLE (1968), Robert C. "*Sir Gawain and the Green Knight*: A Study in Moral Complexity." *SoQ* 6, 203-11.

PILCH-C (1964), Herbert. "The Middle English *Pearl*: Its Relation to *The Roman de la Rose*." *NM* 65, where it appeared on pp. 427-46 under the title "Das Mittelenglische Perlengedicht: Sein Verhältnis zum Rosenroman." Trans. Heide Hyprath in *Conley Collection*, pp. 163-84.

POPE (1966), John C. Ed. *Seven Old English Poems*. Indianapolis: Bobbs-Merrill.

RATHBORNE (1963), Isabel E. "New Light on *Pearl* 690." *Traditio* 19, 467-69.

REISNER (1973), Thomas A. "*Pearl*, 44." *Explicator* 31, Item 55.

REISNER (1975), T.A. "The 'Cortaysye' Sequence in *Pearl*: A Legal Interpretation." *MP* 72, 400-3.

REVARD (1962), Carter. "A Note on 'stonden' [in] *Pearl* 113." *N&Q, N.S.*, 9, pp. 9-10.

REVARD (1964), C. "A Note on 'at the fyrst fyne' (*Pearl* 635)." *ELN* 1, 164-66.

REVIEW (1891). Anonymous rev. of Gollancz' 1891 edition of *Pearl*. *The Athenæum* (August 8), pp. 184-85.

RICHARDSON (1962), F.E. "The *Pearl*: A Poem and Its Audience." *Neophil* 46, 308-16.

ROBBINS (1943), Rossell Hope. "A *Gawain* Epigone." *MLN* 58, 361-66.

ROBBINS (1950), R.H. "The Poems of Humfrey Newton, Esquire, 1466-1536." *PMLA* 65, 249-81.

ROBERTSON-C (1950a), D.W., Jr. "The 'Heresy' of *The Pearl*." *MLN* 45. In *Conley Collection*, pp. 291-96.

ROBERTSON-C (1950b), D.W., Jr. "*The Pearl* as a Symbol." *MLN* 45. In *Conley Collection*, pp. 18-26.

ROBINSON (1977), Ian. "*Pearl* and Ontology." In *In Geardagum*

*II: Essays on Old and Middle English Language and Litera-
ture.* Ed. Loren C. Gruber and Dean Loganbill. Denver:
Society for New Language Study, pp. 1-8. (Corrected re-
print, 1978.)

RØNBERG (1976), Gert. "A Note on 'Endorde' in *Pearl* (368)."
*ES* 57, 198-99.

ROSENTHAL (1878), F. "Die Alliterierende Englische Langzeile
im 14. Jahrhundert." *Anglia* 1, 414-59.

RØSTVIG (1967), Maren-Sofie. "Numerical Composition in *Pearl*:
A Theory." *ES* 48, 326-32.

RUPP (1955), Henry R. "Word-play in *Pearl*, 277-278." *MLN*
70, 558-59.

SAINTSBURY (1908), George. *A History of English Prosody:
From the Twelfth Century to the Present Day.* Vol. I,
*From the Origins to Spenser.* New York: Macmillan. 2nd
ed. (1923). Rpt. New York: Russell & Russell (1961).

SALTER (1963), Elizabeth. *Piers Plowman: An Introduction.*
Cambridge, Massachusetts: Harvard UP.

SALTER (1966), E. "The Alliterative Revival. I." *MP* 64,
146-50.

SALTER (1967), E. "The Alliterative Revival. II." *MP* 64,
233-37.

SALTER (1968), E. "Medieval Poetry and the Figural View of
Reality." Sir Israel Gollancz Memorial Lecture. *Pro-
ceedings of the British Academy* 54, pp. 73-92.

SANDAHL (1951), Bertil. *The Ship's Hull: Middle English Sea
Terms,* 1. *UpsalaE&S* 8. Upsala: Lundequistska Bokhandeln;
Cambridge, Massachusetts: Harvard UP.

SANDAHL (1958), B. *Masts, Spars, and Sails: Middle English
Sea Terms,* 2. *UpsalaE&S* 20. Upsala: Lundequistska Bok-
handeln; Cambridge, Massachusetts: Harvard UP.

SAPORA (1977), Robert William, Jr. *A Theory of Middle Eng-
lish Alliterative Meter: With Critical Applications.*
Speculum Anniversary Monographs, One. Cambridge, Massa-
chusetts: The Mediaeval Academy of America. (Studies
*Purity, Patience, Gawain, St. Erkenwald,* and 1,000-line
portions of *Morte Arthure, The Destruction of Troy,* and
the A-text of *Piers Plowman.*)

SAVAGE (1926), Henry L. Ed. *St. Erkenwald*. New Haven: Yale UP. Rpt. Hamden, Connecticut: Archon (1972).

SAVAGE (1931), H.L. "A Note on *Sir Gawain and the Green Knight* 700-2." *MLN* 46, 455-57.

SAVAGE (1938), H.L. "*Sir Gawain* and the Order of the Garter." *ELH* 5, 146-49.

SAVAGE (1956a), H.L. *The Gawain-Poet: Studies in His Personality and Background*. Chapel Hill: North Carolina UP.

SAVAGE (1956b), H.L. Review of Gordon's edition of *Pearl*. *MLN* 71, 124-29.

SCHILLER (1968), Andrew. "The *Gawain* Rhythm." *L&S* 1, 268-94.

SCHNYDER (1959), Hans. "Aspects of Kingship in *Sir Gawain and the Green Knight*." *ES* 40, 289-94.

SCHOFIELD (1904), William Henry. "The Nature and Fabric of *The Pearl*." *PMLA* 19, 154-203. (On pp. 203-15 is an Appendix in which Schofield argues that Boccaccio's *Olympia* is the source of *Pearl*.)

SCHOFIELD (1909), W.H. "Symbolism, Allegory, and Autobiography in *The Pearl*." *PMLA* 24, 585-675.

SCHOTTER (1979), Anne Howland. "The Poetic Function of Alliterative Formulas of Clothing in the Portrait of the Pearl Maiden." *SN* 51, 189-95.

SCHUMACHER (1914), Karl. *Studien über den Stabreim in der Mittelenglischen Alliterationsdichtung*. *Bonner Studien zur Englischen Philologie* 11. Bonn: Hanstein. (Herausgegeben von K.D. Bülbring.)

SCHWAHN (1884), F. *Die Konjugation in Sir Gawayn and the Green Knight und den Sogenannten Early English Alliterative Poems: Ein Beitrag zur Mittelenglischen Grammatik*. Strassburg: Heitz.

SERJEANTSON (1927), Mary S. "The Dialects of the West Midlands in Middle English." (In Three Parts.) *RES* 3, pp. 54-67, 186-203, and 319-31.

SIEVERS (1885), Eduard. "Zur Rhythmik des Germanischen Alliterationsverses: Erster Abschnitt, Die Metrik des *Beowulf*." *Beiträge zur Geschichte der Deutschen Sprache und Literatur* 10, 209-314.

SIEVERS (1893), E. *Altgermanische Metrik*. Halle: Niemeyer.

SISAM (1921), Kenneth. Ed. *Fourteenth Century Verse and Prose*. London: Oxford UP. Corrected editions (1937), (1955). (Includes *Pearl* 361-612 and *Gawain* 2069-2428-- Glossary by J.R.R. Tolkien.)

SKEAT (1901), Walter W. *Notes on English Etymology*. (Chiefly reprinted from the Transactions of the Philological Society.) London: Oxford UP.

SKLUTE (1973), Larry M. "Expectation and Fulfillment in *Pearl*." *PQ* 52, 663-79.

SLEDD (1940), James. "Three Textual Notes on Fourteenth-Century Poetry." *MLN* 55, 379-82.

SMITHERS (1948-49), G.V. "Four Cruces in Middle English Texts." *EGS* 2, 59-67.

SPEARING-B (1962), A.C. "Symbolic and Dramatic Development in *Pearl*." *MP* 60. In *Blanch Collection*, pp. 98-119.

SPEARING (1966), A.C. "*Patience* and the *Gawain*-Poet." *Anglia* 84, 305-29.

SPEARING (1970), A.C. *The Gawain-Poet: A Critical Study*. Cambridge: Cambridge UP.

SPEARING (1976), A.C. "The Alliterative Tradition: *Pearl*." In *Medieval Dream-Poetry*. Cambridge: Cambridge UP, pp. 111-29.

SPENDAL (1976), R.J. "The Manuscript Capitals in *Cleanness*." *N&Q, N.S.*, 23, 340-41.

STERN-C (1955), Milton R. "An Approach to *The Pearl*." *JEGP* 54. In *Conley Collection*, pp. 73-85.

STILLINGS (1976), Justine T. "A Generative Metrical Analysis of *Sir Gawain and the Green Knight*." *L&S* 9, 219-46.

STOBIE (1940), Margaret M. Roseborough. "The Influence of Morphology on Middle English Alliterative Poetry." *JEGP* 39, 319-36.

STONE (1964), Brian. Trans. *Patience* and *Pearl*. In *Medieval English Verse*. Baltimore: Penguin.

STONE (1971), B. Trans. *Cleanness* (along with *The Owl and* the *Nightingale* and *St Erkenwald*). Baltimore: Penguin.

SUNDÉN (1929), K.F. "The Etymology of ME. *Trayþ(e)ly* and *Runisch, Renisch.*" *SN* 2, 41-55.

SUNDÉN (1930), K.F. "The Etymology of the ME. Verbs *Roþe, Roþele,* and *Ruþe.*" In *A Grammatical Miscellany Offered to Otto Jesperson on His Seventieth Birthday.* Ed. N. Bøgholm, Aage Brusendorff, and C.A. Bodelsen. Copenhagen: Levin & Munksgaard, pp. 109-22.

SUTTON (1970), Robert F. "Characterization and Structure as Adjuncts to Theme in *Pearl.*" *MSE* 2, 88-94.

TAJIMA (1975), Matsuji. "The *Gawain*-Poet's Use of 'Con' as a Periphrastic Auxiliary." *NM* 76, 429-38.

TAJIMA (1976), M. "The Neuter Pronoun *Hit* in the Works of the *Gawain*-Poet." *LingS* 11-12, pp. 23-36. English Summary, pp. 89-90.

TAJIMA (1978), M. "Additional Syntactical Evidence against the Common Authorship of MS. Cotton Nero A.X." *ES* 59, 193-98.

THIÉBAUX (1970), Marcelle. "*Sir Gawain,* the Fox Hunt, and Henry of Lancaster." *NM* 71, 469-79.

THOMAS (1908), Julius. *Die Alliterierende Langzeile des Gawayn-Dichters.* Coburg: Rossteutscher.

THOMAS (1883), Martha Carey. *Sir Gawain and the Green Knight: A Comparison with the French Perceval, Preceded by an Investigation of the Author's Other Works and Followed by a Characterization of Gawain in English Poems.* Zurich: Füssli.

THOMAS (1922a), Percy Goronwy. "Notes on *Cleanness.*" *MLR* 17, 64-66.

THOMAS (1922b), P.G. Review of Gollancz' edition of *Cleanness.* *YWES* 3, p. 40.

THOMAS (1929), P.G. "Notes on *Cleanness.*" *MLR* 24, 323-24. (Presents W.P. Ker's notes, received in correspondence.)

THOMAS (1938), P.G. "Notes on *The Pearl.*" In *London Medieval Studies.* Vol. I, Part 2. Ed. R.W. Chambers, F. Norman, and A.H. Smith, pp. 221-24.

TOLKIEN (1975), J.R.R.  Trans. *Sir Gawain and the Green Knight, Pearl, and Sir Orfeo*.  London: Allen.

TOLKIEN & GORDON (1925), J.R.R. & E.V.  Ed. *Sir Gawain and the Green Knight*.  London: Oxford UP.  (Reprinted with corrections, 1930.)

TRAUTMANN (1876), Moritz.  "*Cleanness, Patience* und *Sir Gawayn*."  In *Über die Verfasser und Entstehungzeit Eineger Alliterierender Gedichte des Altenglischen*.  Halle: Niemeyer, pp. 25-33.

TRAUTMANN (1878), M.  "Der Dichter Huchown und Seine Werke."  *Anglia* 1, 109-49.

TRAUTMANN (1896), M.  "Zur Kenntnis und Geschichte der Mittelenglischen Stabzeile."  *Anglia* 18, 83-100.

TRISTMAN-C (1970), Richard.  "Some Consolatory Strategies in *Pearl*."  In *Conley Collection*, pp. 272-87.

TRISTRAM (1976), Philippa.  *Figures of Life and Death in Medieval English Literature*.  New York: New York UP.  (Discusses *Gawain* on pp. 28-34 of Ch. II, "Youth and Its Mentors"--Discusses *Pearl* on pp. 205-12 of Ch. VI, "Christ and the Triumph of Eternal Life.")

TURVILLE-PETRE (1976), Joan.  "The Metre of *Sir Gawain and the Green Knight*."  *ES* 57, 310-28.

TURVILLE-PETRE (1975), Thorlac.  "Hoccleve, 'Maister Massy' and the *Pearl* Poet: Two Notes."  (Appears with Edward Wilson's Presentation in *RES, N.S.,* 26, 129-43.)

TURVILLE-PETRE (1977), T.  *The Alliterative Revival*.  Cambridge: Brewer; Totowa, New Jersey: Rowman & Littlefield.

TUTTLE (1920), Edwin H.  "Notes on *The Pearl*."  *MLR* 15, 298-300.

VANTUONO (1971), William.  "*Patience, Cleanness, Pearl,* and *Gawain*: The Case for Common Authorship."  *AnM* 12, 37-69.

VANTUONO (1972a), W.  "The Question of Quatrains in *Patience*."  *Manuscripta* 16, 24-30.

VANTUONO (1972b), W.  "The Structure and Sources of *Patience*."  *MS* 34, 401-21.

VANTUONO (1975), W. "A Name in the Cotton MS. Nero A.X. Article 3." *MS* 37, 537-42.

VANTUONO (1979), W. Review of Charlotte C. Morse's *The Pattern of Judgment in the Queste and Cleanness*. In *Studies in the Age of Chaucer*. Vol. 1. Ed. Roy J. Pearcy. The New Chaucer Society, The University of Oklahoma. Norman: Pilgrim Books, pp. 177-83.

VANTUONO (1981), W. "John de Mascy of Sale and the *Pearl* Poems." *Manuscripta* 25, 77-88.

VASTA (1965), Edward. *Middle English Survey: Critical Essays*. Notre Dame: Notre Dame UP.

VASTA-C (1967), E. "*Pearl*: Immortal Flowers and the Pearl's Decay." *JEGP* 66. In *Conley Collection*, pp. 185-202.

VISSER-C (1958), F.T. "*Pearl* 609-611." *ES* 39. In *Conley Collection*, pp. 338-43.

WALDRON (1957), Ronald A. "Oral-Formulaic Technique and Middle English Alliterative Poetry." *Speculum* 32, 792-804.

WARTON (1774-1790), Thomas. *The History of English Poetry, from the Close of the Eleventh to the Commencement of the Eighteenth Century*. Four Volumes. Rpt. New York: Johnson (1968). (Citations from *Pearl* and *Cleanness* are in Vol. 3, pp. 107-8.)

WATTS (1963), V.E. "*Pearl* as a *Consolatio*." *MÆ* 32, 34-36.

WELLEK-B (1933), René. "The *Pearl*: An Interpretation of the Middle English Poem." *Studies in English by Members of the English Seminar of Charles University*, 4. In *Blanch Collection*, pp. 3-36.

WESTON (1912), Jessie L. Trans. *Romance, Vision, and Satire: English Alliterative Poems of the Fourteenth Century*. Boston: Houghton Mifflin. (Includes verse translations of *Cleanness* 1357-1812, *Patience* 61-344, and all of *Pearl* and *Gawain*.)

WHITELEY (1931), M. "Of Vyrgyn Flour." *TLS*, January 15, p. 44.

WHITING & WHITING (1968), B.J. & H.W. *Proverbs, Sentences, and Proverbial Phrases from English Writings Mainly before 1500*. Cambridge, Massachusetts: Harvard UP.

WILLCOCK (1947), Gladys D. "Middle English II--Before and After Chaucer." *YWES* 26, 61-76.

WILLIAMS (1970a), David J. "The *Gawain* Group: *Cleanness* (or *Purity*), *Patience, Sir Gawain,* and *Pearl*." In *History of Literature in the English Language.* Vol. 1, *The Middle Ages.* Ed. W.F. Bolton. London: Barrie & Jenkins, pp. 143-56.

WILLIAMS (1970b), D.J. "The Point of *Patience*." *MP* 68, 127-36.

WILLIAMS (1949), Margaret, R.S.C.J. Trans. "*Pearl*-Poetry." In *Glee-Wood: Passages from Middle English Literature from the Eleventh Century to the Fifteenth.* New York: Sheed and Ward.

WILLIAMS (1967), M. Trans. *The Pearl-Poet: His Complete Works.* New York: Random House.

WILLIAMS (1970), M. "Oriental Backgrounds & the *Pearl*-Poet." *Tamkang Review* 1, 93-107.

WILSON (1976), Anne. "*Sir Gawain and the Green Knight*." In *Traditional Romance and Tale: How Stories Mean.* Cambridge: Brewer; Totowa, New Jersey: Rowman & Littlefield, pp. 96-108.

WILSON (1968), Edward. "The 'Gostly Drem' in *Pearl*." *NM* 69, 90-101.

WILSON (1971a), E. "'Gromylyoun' (Gromwell) in *Pearl*." *N&Q*, *N.S.*, 18, 42-44.

WILSON (1971b), E. "Word Play and the Interpretation of *Pearl*." *MÆ* 40, 116-34.

WILSON (1975), E. "Hoccleve, 'Maister Massy' and the *Pearl* Poet: Two Notes." (Appears with Thorlac Turville-Petre's Presentation in *RES*, *N.S.*, 26, 129-43.)

WILSON (1976), E. *The Gawain-Poet.* Medieval and Renaissance Authors. Leiden: Brill.

WILSON (1977), E. Note added to Peterson (1977) article. *RES*, *N.S.*, 28, 55-56.

WIMSATT (1970), James I. *Allegory and Mirror: Tradition and Structure in Middle English Literature.* New York: Pegasus. (Discusses *Pearl* in Ch. V, "The Allegory of Revelation"--Discusses *Gawain* in Ch. VIII, "The Ideal of Chivalry: Gawain and Lancelot.")

WINTERMUTE (1949), Edwin. "The *Pearl's* Author as Herbalist." *MLN* 64, 83-84.

WOOD (1973), Ann Douglas. "The Pearl-Dreamer and the 'Hyne' in the Vineyard Parable." *PQ* 52, 9-19.

WRENN (1943), C.L. "On Re-Reading Spenser's *The Shepheardes Calender*." *E&S* 29, 30-49.

WRIGHT (1960), Cyril Ernest. *English Vernacular Hands from the Twelfth to the Fifteenth Centuries*. London: Oxford UP.

WRIGHT (1939), Elizabeth M. "Notes on *The Pearl*." (Wrongly entitled, "Additional Notes on *Sir Gawain and the Green Knight*.") *JEGP* 38, 1-22.

WRIGHT (1940), E.M. "Additional Notes on *The Pearl*." *JEGP* 39, 315-18.

WRIGHT (1977), M.J. "Comic Perspective in Two Middle English Poems." *Parergon* 18, 3-15. (On *Pearl* and Chaucer's *Knight's Tale*.)

WYLD (1913), Henry C. "The Treatment of OE. $\breve{Y}$ in the Dialects of the Midland, and SE. Counties, in Middle English." *EStn* 47, 1-58.

ZAVADIL (1962), Joseph Benedict. "A Study of Meaning in *Patience* and *Cleanness*." Diss., Stanford.

BIBLIOGRAPHY II

## Bibles

*(Biblical citations in this edition
are to the first two entries.)*

*Biblia Sacra*: Vulgatae Editionis Sixti V Pontificis Maximi
Iussu Recognita et Clementis VIII Auctoritate Edita.
Editiones Paulinae. Rome, 1957.

*The Holy Bible.* Translated from the Latin Vulgate. Re-Edited
by the Reverend James A. Carey. Turnhout, Belgium: Brepols,
1935. (The Old Testament was first published by the Eng-
lish College at Douay, 1609. The New Testament was first
published by the English College at Rheims, 1582.)

*The Septuagint Bible.* Trans. Charles Thomson. Ed. C.A. Muses.
Indian Hills, Colorado: Falcon's Wing Press, 1954.

*Wyclif Bible.* Ed. J. Forshall and F. Madden. 4 Vols. London:
Oxford UP, 1850.

## Concordance, Dictionaries, Grammars,
## and Index of Names

*An Anglo-Saxon Dictionary.* Ed. J. Bosworth. Supplement by
T.N. Toller. London: Oxford UP, 1882-1920.

*The Compact Edition of the Oxford English Dictionary.* 2 Vols.
London: Oxford UP, 1971. (Complete text reproduced micro-
graphically from *A New English Dictionary on Historical
Principles.* Ed. J. Murray, H. Bradley, W. Craigie, and
C.T. Onions. 10 Vols. Oxford UP, 1888-1928.)

"A Computer Concordance to Middle English Texts." Alan M. Markman. *Studies in Bibliography* 17 (1964) 55-75.

*Concise Dictionary of Old Icelandic*. Ed. G.T. Zoëga. London: Oxford UP, 1910.

*A Concordance to Five Middle English Poems: Cleanness, St. Erkenwald, Sir Gawain and the Green Knight, Patience, Pearl*. Barnet Kottler & Alan M. Markman. Pittsburgh: Pittsburgh UP, 1966.

*A Dictionary of the Old English Language: Compiled from Writings of the XIII, XIV, and XV Centuries*. Ed. Francis H. Stratmann. Krefeld: Kramer and Baum, 1864-1867. Revised by Henry Bradley. London: Oxford UP, 1891. (Also known as *A Middle-English Dictionary*.)

*Dictionnaire de l'Ancienne Langue Française et de Tous ses Dialectes du IX$^e$ au XV$^e$ Siècle*. Ed. Frédéric Godefroy. 10 Vols. Paris: Vieweg, 1881-1902. Rpt. New York: Kraus, 1961.

*An Elementary Middle English Grammar*. Joseph Wright & Elizabeth Mary Wright. London: Oxford UP, 1923. 2nd ed., 1928.

*The English Dialect Dictionary*. Ed. Joseph Wright. 6 Vols. London: Oxford UP, 1898-1905.

*Glossarium ad Scriptores Mediæ et Infimæ Latinitatis*. Charles Dufresne Du Cange. Rev. ed., G.A.L. Henschel. 10 Vols. Graz, Austria: Akademische Druck-U. Verlagsanstalt, 1954.

*An Index of Names in Pearl, Purity, Patience, and Gawain*. Coolidge Otis Chapman. Ithaca: Cornell UP, 1951.

*Middle English Dictionary*. Ed. Sherman M. Kuhn *et al.* (Completed through *P.2* at the time this Bibliography was compiled.) Ann Arbor: Michigan UP, 1954-.

*A Middle English Syntax*, Part 1. Tauno F. Mustanoja. Helsinki: Société Néophilologique, 1960.

*Promptorium Parvulorum*. By Galfridus Anglicus. (The first English-Latin Dictionary.) Ed. A.L. Mayhew. *EETS, ES,* 102. London: Trübner, 1908.

## Texts and Translations

### French

*The Bodley Version of Mandeville's Travels.* Ed. M.C. Seymour.
   *EETS* 253. London: Oxford UP, 1963.

*The Book of the Knight of La Tour-Landry.* Ed. Thomas Wright.
   *EETS* 33. London: Trübner, 1868.

*The Buke of John Maundeuill.* Ed. Sir George F. Warner.
   (Printed for the Roxburghe Club.) Westminster: Nichols,
   1889. (Contains English version in unique Egerton MS.
   1982 and a French text.)

*Le Livre du Chevalier de la Tour Landry.* Ed. Anatole de
   Montaiglon. Bibliothèque Elzévirienne. Paris: Jannet,
   1854.

*Mandeville's Travels.* (Modernized English Text.) Ed. M.C.
   Seymour. London: Oxford UP, 1968.

*Mandeville's Travels: Texts and Translations.* Ed. Malcolm
   Letts. London: The Hakluyt Society, 1953. (Vol. 1, 2nd
   Series, No. 101, contains a modernized version of the
   Egerton text; Vol. 2, 2nd Series, No. 102, contains the
   Paris text.)

*Le Roman de la Rose.* Par Guillaume de Lorris et Jean de Meun.
   Ed. Ernest Langlois. 5 Vols. Paris: Société des Anciens
   Textes Français, 1914-1924.

*The Romance of the Rose.* By Guillaume de Lorris and Jean de
   Meun. Trans. Harry W. Robbins. Ed., and with Introduc-
   tion, by Charles W. Dunn. New York: Dutton, 1962.

*Romaunt of the Rose.* In *The Complete Poetry and Prose of
   Geoffrey Chaucer.* Ed. John H. Fisher. New York: Holt,
   1977.

### Greek

Origen. "Commentary on Matthew." *The Ante-Nicene Fathers.*
   Trans. of the Writings of the Fathers down to A.D. 325.
   Ed. Allan Menzies. Vol. 9. New York: Scribner's, 1912.

*Patrologia Graeca.* In *Patrologiae Cursus Completus.* Ed.
   Jacques Paul Migne. 161 Vols. Paris: Seu Petit-Mont-

rouge, 1857-1866.  (Contains Greek texts and Latin translations.)

## Italian

*The Divine Comedy*.  By Dante Alighieri.  Text with Translation in the Metre of the Original.  By Geoffrey L. Bickersteth. Cambridge, Massachusetts: Harvard UP, 1965.

## Latin (Non-Religious)

*(The works of Boccaccio and Boethius, though they contain much Christian thought, are placed in this section rather than in the following one which lists literature that is primarily patristic in nature.)*

Boccaccio, Giovanni.  *The Fourteenth Eclogue, Entitled Olympia*.  Ed. Sir Israel Gollancz.  (Latin text and English translation.)  In the Appendix to his edition of *Pearl*.  London, 1921.

Boethius, Anicius Manlius Severinus.  *De Consolatio Philosophiae*.  With the English translation of "I. T." (1609). Revised by Hugh F. Stewart.  (Volume also contains *The Theological Tractates*, with an English translation by Stewart and Edward K. Rand.)  The Loeb Classical Library. London: Heinemann, 1918.  (Chaucer's translation of this work is in *The Complete Poetry and Prose of Geoffrey Chaucer*.  Ed. John H. Fisher.  New York: Holt, 1977, pp. 816-903.)

Geoffrey of Vinsauf.  *Documentum de Modo et Arte Dictandi et Versificandi, Poetria Nova,* and *Summa de Coloribus Rhetoricis*.  In *Les Arts Poétiques du XII$^e$ et du XIII$^e$ Siècle*. Ed. Edmond Faral.  Paris: Champion, 1924.  (*Poetria Nova* has been translated by Margaret F. Nims, Toronto: Pontifical Institute of Mediaeval Studies, 1967.)

Matthew of Vendôme.  *Ars Versificatoria*.  In *Les Arts Poétiques du XII$^e$ et du XIII$^e$ Siècle*.  Ed. Edmond Faral. Paris: Champion, 1924.

Latin (Religious)

Albertus Magnus. *De Laudibus Beatae Mariae Virginis.* In
Volume 36 of his *Complete Works.* Ed. Augusti Borgnet.
38 Vols. Paris: Lodovicum Vivès, 1890-1899. (From the
earlier edition by Petri Iammy, 21 Vols., 1651.)

*The Apocrypha and Pseudepigrapha of the Old Testament in Eng-
lish.* Ed. R.H. Charles. 2 Vols. London: Oxford UP,
1913.

Augustine. *De Civitate Dei.* Ed. Bernard Dombart & Alphonse
Kalb. *Corpus Christianorum (Series Latina).* Volumes
47-48. Turnhout, Belgium: Brepols, 1955. (Trans. John
Healey as *The City of God.* Ed. R.V.G. Tasker. 2 Vols.
Everyman's Library. London: Dent; New York: Dutton,
1945.)

Augustine. Commentary on "De Sermone Domine in Monte" (Sec-
tion on Eight Beatitudes.) In *PL* 34.1229-1236. (Trans.
D.J. Kavanaugh, O.S.A. In *The Fathers of the Church.*
Vol. 11. New York: Fathers of the Church, 1951, pp.
19-32.)

Augustine. "Sermo XC" on the Parable of the Wedding Feast in
Matthew 22.1-14. In *PL* 38.559-566. (Trans. in *A Select
Library of the Nicene and Post-Nicene Fathers of the
Christian Church.* Ed. Philip Schaff. Vol. 6. Rpt.
Grand Rapids, Michigan: Eerdmans, 1956, pp. 392-97.)

Comestor, Peter. *Historia Scholastica.* In *PL* 198.

*Incerti de Sodoma.* In *CSEL* 23. Ed. R. Peiper. Vienna:
Akademie der Wissenschaften, 1891, pp. 212-20. (Trans.
S. Thelwall. In *The Ante-Nicene Fathers.* Trans. of the
Writings of the Fathers down to A.D. 325. Ed. Alexander
Roberts and James Donaldson. Vol. 4. Buffalo: The
Christian Literature Publications Company, 1887, pp.
129-32.)

Jacobus de Voragine. *Legenda Aurea Vulgo Historia Lombardica
Dicta.* Ed. Johann Georg Theodor Grässe. Leipsig: Arnold-
ianae, 1850.

Jerome. "Commentariorum in Danielem Prophetam." (Caput V.)
In *PL* 25.518-522.

Marbodus, Bishop of Rennes. *De Gemmis.* In *PL* 171.1735-1780.
(Trans. Charles W. King as *Antique Gems.* London: Murray,
1860. 2nd ed., 1866, pp. 391-417.)

*Patrologia Latina.* In *Patrologiae Cursus Completus.* Ed.
Jacques Paul Migne. 221 Vols. Paris: Garnier, 1844-1905.

Tertullian. Latin Texts of *Apologeticus* and *De Spectaculis.*
Trans. T.R. Glover--and *Minucius Felix.* Trans. Gerald H.
Rendall. The Loeb Classical Library. London: Heinemann,
1931.

Tertullian. *Liber de Patientia.* In *PL* 1.1249-1274. (Trans.
Sister Emily Joseph Daly, C.S.J. In *The Fathers of the
Church.* Vol. 40. New York: Fathers of the Church, 1959,
pp. 193-222.)

## Old English and Middle English

*Ancrene Wisse.* Ed. J.R.R. Tolkien. *EETS* 249. London: Oxford
UP, 1962.

*Cædmon's Hymn.* In *Seven Old English Poems.* Ed. John C. Pope.
Indianapolis: Bobbs-Merrill, 1966. (Includes also *The
Battle of Brunanburh, The Dream of the Rood, The Battle of
Maldon, The Wanderer, The Seafarer,* and *Deor.*)

*The Complete Poetry and Prose of Geoffrey Chaucer.* Ed. John
H. Fisher. New York: Holt, 1977. (See also entry under
*The Works of Geoffrey Chaucer.*)

*The Complete Works of John Gower.* Ed. G.C. Macaulay. 4 Vols.
London: Oxford UP, 1899-1902. (Besides the Middle English
poem *Confessio Amantis,* Gower's principal works include
French and Latin poetry: *Mirour de l'Omme* and *Vox Claman-
tis.*)

*Cursor Mundi.* Ed. Richard Morris. 6 Parts. *EETS* 57, 59, 62,
66, 68, 99. London: Trübner, 1874-1892. Part 7 by H.
Hupe. *EETS* 101, 1893. (This series prints the four manu-
scripts of the poem in parallel texts: Cotton, Fairfax,
Göttingen, and Trinity.)

*Death and Life.* In *Bishop Percy's Folio Manuscript.* Ed. John
W. Hales and Frederick J. Furnivall. Vol. 3. London:
Trübner, 1867-1868. (Ed. also by Sir Israel Gollancz in
*Select Early English Poems.* Vol. 5. London: Oxford UP,
1930.)

*An Early English Psalter.* (Also known as *Northern Verse
Psalter* and *Surtees Psalter.*) In *Yorkshire Writers:
Richard Rolle of Hampole and His Followers.* Vol. 2. Ed.
C. Horstmann. London: Swan, 1896, upper pp. 129-273.

*English Mediaeval Lapidaries.* Ed. Joan Evans and Mary S. Serjeantson. *EETS* 190. London: Oxford UP, 1932. Rpt. 1960.

*The Fall and Passion.* In *Early English Poems and Lives of Saints.* Ed. Frederick J. Furnivall. Berlin: Asher, 1862, pp. 12-15. (Published for the Philological Society of London.)

*The Gest Hystoriale of the Destruction of Troy.* Ed. G.A. Panton and D. Donaldson. *EETS* 39 and 56. London: Trübner, 1869 and 1874. Rpt. New York: Greenwood, 1969.

*Hymns to the Virgin & Christ, The Parliament of Devils, and other Religious Poems.* Ed. Frederick J. Furnivall. *EETS* 24. London: Trübner, 1868. Rpt. New York: Greenwood, 1969.

*Ipomedon* (Three Versions). Ed. Eugen Kölbing. Breslau: Koebner, 1889.

*Joseph of Arimathie.* Ed. Walter W. Skeat. *EETS* 44. London: Trübner, 1871. Rpt. New York: Greenwood, 1969.

*The Parlement of the Thre Ages.* Ed. M.Y. Offord. *EETS* 246. London: Oxford UP, 1959.

*The Peterborough Chronicle.* In *Two of the Saxon Chronicles Parallel.* Revised text, ed. Charles Plummer, on the basis of an edition by John Earle. London: Oxford UP, 1892-1899.

*Piers the Plowman* (in Three Parallel Texts) and *Richard the Redeless.* By William Langland. Ed. Walter W. Skeat. 2 Vols. London: Oxford UP, 1886. Rpt. with addition of Bibliography, 1954.

*Saint Erkenwald.* Ed. Clifford J. Peterson. Philadelphia: Pennsylvania UP, 1977.

*St Erkenwald.* Ed. Ruth Morse. Cambridge: Brewer; Totowa, New Jersey: Rowman & Littlefield, 1975.

*St. Erkenwald.* Ed. Henry L. Savage. New Haven: Yale UP, 1926. Rpt. Hamden, Connecticut: Archon, 1972.

*Sir Ferumbras.* (From Ashmole MS 33.) In *The Charlemagne Romances: 1.* Ed. S.J. Herrtage. *EETS, ES,* 34. London: Trübner, 1879. (Also edited by Mary O'Sullivan. *Firumbras and Otuel and Roland. EETS* 198. London: Oxford UP, 1934.)

433

*The Wars of Alexander.* Ed. Walter W. Skeat. *EETS, ES,* 47. London: Trübner, 1886.

*William of Palerne or William and the Werwolf.* Ed. Walter W. Skeat. *EETS, ES,* 1. London: Trübner, 1867.

*The Works of Geoffrey Chaucer.* Ed. F.N. Robinson. Boston: Houghton Mifflin, 1933. 2nd ed., 1957. (See also entry under *The Complete Poetry and Prose of Geoffrey Chaucer.*)

*Wynnere and Wastoure.* Ed. Sir Israel Gollancz. (With Modernized Version.) In *Select Early English Poems.* Vol. 3. London: Oxford UP, 1920. Revised by Mabel Day, 1931. Rpt. Cambridge: Brewer; Totowa, New Jersey: Rowman & Littlefield (1974).


Yearly Bibliographies
and Other Bibliographical Listings

*Annual Bibliography of English Language and Literature.* "Middle English." Modern Humanities Research Association of Great Britain, 1920-.

*Bibliography of English Translations from Medieval Sources.* Clarissa P. Farrar and Austin P. Evans. New York: Columbia UP, 1946.

"A Bibliography of *Purity* (*Cleanness*), 1864-1972." Michael Foley. *ChauR* 8 (1974) 324-34.

*The Gawain-Poet: An Annotated Bibliography, 1839-1977.* Malcolm Andrew. New York: Garland, 1979.

*A Manual of the Writings in Middle English: 1050-1500.* By Members of the Middle English Group of the Modern Language Association of America. J. Burke Severs, General Editor. Bibliography on *Gawain* in Vol. 1, pp. 238-43. Bibliography on *Pearl, Patience,* and *Cleanness* in Vol. 2, pp. 503-16. New Haven: The Connecticut Academy of Arts and Sciences, 1967 and 1970.

"A Middle English Bibliographical Guide." Compiled by Stanley B. Greenfield. In *Guide to English Literature from Beowulf through Chaucer and Medieval Drama.* David M. Zesmer. New York: Barnes and Noble, 1961. (Section X, "The Alliterative Revival," pp. 342-51, includes annotated references to *Pearl* and *Gawain.*)

434

*MLA International Bibliography.* "Middle English." Modern Language Association of America, 1921-.

*The New Cambridge Bibliography of English Literature.* Ed. George Watson. Vol. 1, 600-1660. Cambridge: Cambridge UP, 1974. (Listings for *Gawain,* col. 401-6; for *Pearl, Cleanness,* and *Patience,* col. 547-54.)

"The *Pearl*-Poet (Fourteenth Century): *Patience, Pearl, Purity, St. Erkenwald, Sir Gawain and the Green Knight.*" Compiled by Walter H. Beale. In *Old and Middle English Poetry to 1500: A Guide to Information Sources.* Detroit: Gale, 1976.

"*Sir Gawain and the Green Knight*: An Annotated Bibliography, 1950-1972." Roger A. Hambridge. *Comitatus* 4 (1973; published 1974) 49-84.

"Supplement to a Bibliography of *Purity* (*Cleanness*), 1864-1972." Allan A. Metcalf. *ChauR* 10 (1976) 367-72.

*The Year's Work in English Studies.* English Association. Vol. 1, 1919/1920-. London: Oxford UP.